The
Economist
Guide

SOUTH EAST
ASIA

The
Economist
Guide

SOUTH EAST
ASIA

The
Economist
Books

Hutchinson

Published in Great Britain by
Hutchinson Business Books Limited
An imprint of Century Hutchinson
Limited
20 Vauxhall Bridge Road, London
SW1V 2SA

The publishers welcome corrections
and suggestions from business
travellers; please write to
The Editor,
The Economist Guides,
Axe and Bottle Court,
70 Newcomen Street,
LONDON SE1 1YT

Series Editor Stephen Brough
Assistant Series Editor Brigid Avison
Editors Jane Carroll (*first edition
overview*); Joanna Evans, Tim Locke
(*first edition travel*); Jane Carroll and
Anthony Goldstone (*second edition
overview*); Andrew Shaw (*second
edition travel*)
Designer Alistair Plumb (*first edition*);
Alison Donovan (*second edition*)
Editorial Assistants Mary Pickles,
Bettina Whilems
Production Controller Shona Burns
Indexer Fiona Barr

Contributors *Overview* Garth
Alexander, Paddy Bowie
Nick Cumming-Bruce, Vaudine
England, Anthony Goldstone,
Alison Hahn, Simon Long, Jo
McBride, Gerald Roberts,
Susan Ware, Michael Williams, Dick
Wilson; *travel* Christopher Catling

Consultants Anne Crawford, Ken
Davies, Gillian Desborough, Derek
Elley, Sam Hobohm, Edith
Hodgkinson, Christopher Lowsley,
Stewart McRorie, Bob Taylor

First edition published in Great
Britain 1988
Second edition published in Great
Britain 1990

Copyright © 1988 and © 1990 The
Economist Publications Limited and
Webster's Business Traveller's Guides
Limited
Maps and diagrams copyright © 1988
and © 1990 The Economist
Publications Limited and Webster's
Business Traveller's Guides Limited

**British Library Cataloguing in
Publication Data**

S.E. Asia.- (The Economist guides)
1. South-east Asia - Visitors' guides
915.9'0453

ISBN 0-09-174341-9

Maps and diagrams by Oxford
Illustrators, Oxford, England
Typeset by SB Datagraphics,
Colchester, England
Printed in Italy by Arnoldo
Mondadori, Verona

Contents

Glossary	6
Using the guide	7
Introduction	8

Hong Kong — 18
The political scene — 19
The economic scene — 21
The business climate — 26
The business framework — 30
Market entry — 32
The financial scene — 34
Who can help — 38
Business and cultural awareness — 39
Hong Kong — 41
Planning and reference — 60

Indonesia — 62
The political scene — 63
The economic scene — 64
The business climate — 68
The business framework — 71
Market entry — 73
The financial scene — 75
Who can help — 76
Business and cultural awareness — 77
Jakarta — 81
Planning and reference — 96

Malaysia — 98
The political scene — 99
The economic scene — 100
The business climate — 104
The business framework — 107
Market entry — 110
The financial scene — 112
Who can help — 113
Business and cultural awareness — 114
Kuala Lumpur — 119
Planning and reference — 133

Philippines — 135
The political scene — 136
The economic scene — 137
The business climate — 140
The business framework — 143
Market entry — 145
The financial scene — 147
Who can help — 148
Business and cultural awareness — 149
Manila — 153
Planning and reference — 168

Singapore — 170
The political scene — 171
The economic scene — 172
The business climate — 175
The business framework — 179
Market entry — 181
The financial scene — 184
Who can help — 186
Business and cultural awareness — 187
Singapore — 192
Planning and reference — 209

South Korea — 211
The political scene — 212
The economic scene — 213
The business climate — 216
The business framework — 218
Market entry — 220
The financial scene — 223
Who can help — 225
Business and cultural awareness — 226
Seoul — 230
Planning and reference — 244

Taiwan — 246
The political scene — 247
The economic scene — 248
The business climate — 252
The business framework — 255
Market entry — 258
The financial scene — 259
Who can help — 261
Business and cultural awareness — 262
Taipei — 265
Planning and reference — 277

Thailand — 279
The political scene — 280
The economic scene — 281
The business climate — 285
The business framework — 287
Market entry — 289
The financial scene — 291
Who can help — 292
Business and cultural awareness — 293
Bangkok — 297
Planning and reference — 311

International dialling codes — 313
Conversion charts — 313
Index — 314

Glossary

ADB Asian Development Bank. Founded in 1966, it has 32 regional and 15 non-regional members.

ASEAN Association of South East Asian Nations, founded in 1967. Members are Brunei, Indonesia, Malaysia, Philippines, Singapore and Thailand.

Berne Convention One of the major international agreements on the protection of copyright. It dates back to 1886 but has been revised several times, most recently in 1971.

Bhd Berhad: public limited company (Malaysia).

"Big Eight" The leading international accountancy firms: Arthur Andersen and Co; Coopers & Lybrand; Deloitte, Haskins & Sells; Ernst & Whinney; Peat, Marwick, Mitchell and McClintock; Price Waterhouse; Touche Ross and Co; and Arthur Young.

BNP Banque Nationale de Paris.

c&f Carriage and freight.

CD Certificate of Deposit.

cif Carriage, insurance and freight.

COMECON Council for Mutual Economic Assistance (the Communist bloc economic and trade cooperation organization).

EC European Community.

EPZ Export Processing Zone.

fob Free on board.

G5 Plaza accord Agreement signed in Japan in 1985 by finance ministers of the Group of Five (G5) countries: Britain, France, Japan, the USA and West Germany. It had the effect of revaluing the Japanese yen against major world currencies.

GATT General Agreement on Tariffs and Trade, which came into force in 1948. It is the world's major forum for negotiating the reduction of tariffs and other barriers to trade.

GDP Gross Domestic Product. The best measure of a country's economic performance, GDP is the total value of a country's annual output of goods and services. Normally valued at market prices, it can be calculated at factor cost, by subtracting indirect taxes and adding subsidies.

GSP Generalized System of Preferences. A system agreed under the auspices of UNCTAD (UN Conference on Trade and Development) which gives developing countries certain tariff advantages for their exports of manufactured and processed goods to the developed countries.

GNP Gross National Product. A country's GDP plus residents' income from investments abroad minus income accruing to nonresidents from investments in the country.

grt Gross registered tons.

Hang Seng Index The main share index in Hong Kong.

Hong A historical Chinese term for a

IBRD International Bank for Reconstruction and Development (World Bank).

IDA International Development Association (the "soft" loan arm of the World Bank).

IMF International Monetary Fund.

KMT Kuomintang: Nationalist Party (Taiwan).

MFA Multi-fibre Arrangement. An international agreement under the auspices of GATT allowing developed countries to re-organize their textile and clothing industries in the face of competition from low-cost production in developing countries. It came into force in 1974 and has been renewed several times.

OBU Offshore Banking Unit.

OECD Organisation for Economic Cooperation and Development.

OPEC Organization of Petroleum Exporting Countries.

Paris Convention The main international agreement on the protection of industrial copyright. It was first signed in 1883.

ROC Republic of China (Taiwan).

SAR Special Administrative Region. The status of Hong Kong after it reverts to Chinese sovereignty in 1997, agreed under the terms of the Sino-British Joint Declaration of December 1984.

Taipan "Boss." Historical Chinese term.

Towkay Business magnate (Chinese).

Using the guide
The Economist Guide to South-East Asia is an encyclopedia of business and travel information. If in doubt about where to look for specific information, consult either the Contents list or the Index.

City guides
Each city guide follows a standard format: information and advice on arriving, getting around, city areas, hotels, restaurants, bars, entertainment, shopping, sightseeing, sports and fitness, a directory of local business and other facilities such as secretarial and translation agencies, couriers and hospitals. There is also a map of the city centre locating recommended hotels, restaurants and other important addresses.

Abbreviations
Credit and charge cards AE American Express; DC Diners Club; MC MasterCard (Access); V Visa.
Figures Millions are abbreviated to m; billions (meaning one thousand million) to bn.

Publisher's note
The Economist Guides have been prepared for the international market place. This particular volume provides first and foremost practical information for any business person travelling in the region. The general background information and analysis will also be helpful to anyone doing business in the eight countries featured in the guide, wherever and however that business may be conducted.

Price bands
Price bands are denoted by symbols (see below). These correspond to the following actual prices at the time of going to press. (Although the actual prices will inevitably go up, the relative price category is likely to remain the same.)

Hotels
(one person occupying a standard room, including tax and service)

$	up to US$60
$$	US$60 to $90
$$$	US$90 to $120
$$$$	US$120 to $150
$$$$$	over US$150

Restaurants
(three-course meal with half a bottle of house wine, coffee, tax and service)

$	up to US$15
$$	US$15 to $30
$$$	US$30 to $50
$$$$	over US$50

Based on exchange rates US$1 =

HK$	7.80 (Hong Kong)	S$	2.07 (Singapore)
Rupiah	1600.00 (Indonesia)	Won	790.00 (South Korea)
M$	2.46 (Malaysia)	NT$	31.00 (Taiwan)
Peso	20.00 (Philippines)	Baht	25.85 (Thailand)

INTRODUCTION

Economic success is the one theme common to the otherwise very diverse countries surveyed in this guide. The progress registered by all eight over the past 20 years has been astonishing. Four are newly industrializing countries (NICs): Hong Kong, Singapore, South Korea and Taiwan. These are known as Asia's "Four Little Dragons," having each achieved an economic miracle that has brought them almost into the ranks of the world's advanced economies. The other four – Indonesia, Malaysia, the Philippines and Thailand – are all more dependent on exports of primary commodities and have therefore been more vulnerable to the vagaries of the world economy, but are nevertheless at the forefront of development in the Third World.

The region encompasses a rich variety of people and tradition. With the exception of Thailand, all the countries have been colonized by Britain, Japan, the Netherlands, Spain or the USA, and all these former imperial powers have left an imprint on the countries they once ruled.

Jostling for influence

Buddhism and Christianity, Confucianism and Islam jostle for influence among the people of the region. The vast majority of Indonesians, most Malaysians and a significant minority of Filipinos are Muslim. The only overwhelmingly Christian country in South-East Asia is the Philippines, where almost 90 per cent of the people are Roman Catholic. Elsewhere there are important Christian minorities, most notably in South Korea. Hinduism is the majority religion of the Indian community of Malaysia and Singapore, and, in indigenous form, of most of the inhabitants of Bali. Religion is of more than demographic significance. The Confucian emphasis on authority, discipline and practical learning may well have something to do with the economic success of the four NICs, all of which embrace this tradition. The Thai disdain for ideology is often linked to the pre-eminence in that country of Theravada Buddhism, with its tolerance of diversity.

This religious diversity coincides in several of the countries with a racial mix that in some cases has been a cause of underlying social tension. The Malaysian government, for example, has to induce three communities to live together in harmony: the indigenous Malays, or Bumiputra (57%), Chinese (33%) and Indians (10%). Singapore, with more than 75% Chinese, also has substantial Malay and Indian minorities. In Thailand, Indonesia and the Philippines there are considerable Chinese minorities. Chinese mainlanders came across to Taiwan after the Communist takeover in 1949 to join the native Taiwanese, themselves mostly descendants of earlier migrants from China. The vast majority of Hong Kong's population are newcomers to the territory, they too having fled from the mainland since 1949. South Korea's population is by far the most racially homogeneous in the region, but includes many people who fled from the North during the

Korean War of the early 1950s.

The settlement of Chinese traders in South-East Asia long predates Western colonialism, but the main influx started in the mid-19th century stimulated by local demand for ''coolie'' labour and the breakdown of order in China. The overseas Chinese mostly stand on the

Hong Kong	p 41
Jakarta	p 81
Kuala Lumpur	p 119
Manila	p 153
Singapore	p 192
Seoul	p 230
Taipei	p 265
Bangkok	p 297

periphery of politics but at the core of business life. There have been exceptions to this rule, however, particularly in the Philippines and Thailand where assimilation has been greatest.

The Communist spectre retreats

Much of the region's economic success can be ascribed to the long stretches of uninterrupted political stability it has enjoyed since the mid-1960s. The spectre of Communism had retreated from previously threatened countries, notably Indonesia and Malaysia, well before its now decidedly tarnished triumph in Indochina.

Economic progress, in its turn, has helped to maintain that political stability. Great strides have been made throughout the region in improving literacy, education and health care. There has been welcome progress towards liberalization and democratic government, particularly in the Philippines, South Korea and Thailand – though the Philippines has still to find stability in the face of opposition from both Communist insurgents and a right wing with military backing. And Lee Kuan Yew's Singapore, used to slapping down opponents who bridle at his tight rein, seems unwilling to break old habits despite the promptings of the new middle class. Meanwhile the Malaysian system of government, based on ethnic coalitions whose cohesion has required the liberal distribution of largesse among the racial communities, looks precarious at times of economic downturn.

A key contributor to peace and social stability in the region is the Association of SouthEast Asian Nations (ASEAN), which groups Brunei, Indonesia, Malaysia, the Philippines, Singapore and Thailand. Founded in 1967, it has proved to be one of the most successful regional associations in the developing world; although little progress has been made on economic cooperation within the group. ASEAN has been able to act as a forum, giving members a collective say in world affairs which otherwise they would not have been able to aspire to. It now maintains regular dialogue with the EC, the USA and Japan.

China's decision in the late 1970s to launch its "open door" policy and to embrace a considerable degree of internal liberalization has had a highly beneficial political and economic effect throughout the region, an effect further strengthened by the agreement signed in 1984 between China and the UK, granting Hong Kong the status of a special administrative region within China and safeguarding its capitalist way of life for at least 50 years after the transfer of sovereignty to China in 1997. China's new pragmatism is evident in its readiness to come to the rescue of the Hong Kong stock market and, even more heretical, in its growing (if indirect) trade with South Korea and Taiwan.

Joining the big league

The achievements of the "Four Little Dragons" rest above all on the successful pursuit by their respective governments of export-led growth based on the rapid development of their manufacturing and service sectors. The results are impressive.

Singapore is the world's second busiest port and the third largest oil refining centre; Hong Kong is the world's fourth most important financial centre, after London, New York and Tokyo; South Korea hopes to join the Organisation for Economic Cooperation and Development (OECD) within a few years, when it should have caught up with the world's most advanced economies. Taiwan's vast trade surpluses have enabled it to amass holdings of foreign exchange reserves which in late 1987 were second only to Japan's. However, as the NICs enter the big league, they are finding – as Japan did – that an export-led strategy places a high premium on flexibility and social consensus, the prices of staying ahead of would-be rivals in skills, productivity, technology and quality.

As aspiring NICs, Indonesia, Malaysia, the Philippines and Thailand are not in the same league as the region's four NICs in terms of economic and specifically of industrial growth. Nevertheless, they have advanced at a remarkable pace, and all have made substantial inroads into the world's markets for textiles, garments and electronic goods. Manufactured goods represent about one-third of the group's total exports against an insignificant proportion 20 years ago.

All four are however still heavily dependent on the export of raw materials and are therefore vulnerable to fluctuating world commodity prices. In addition, although the economic contraction of the later Marcos years has already been reversed, the Philippines is burdened with a huge foreign debt as well as with the legacy of the previous regime's economic mismanagement and large-scale corruption. Indonesia's economy remains alarmingly dependent on the export of oil and gas, and has been hard hit by the successive downturns in petroleum prices. Even though its resources are now available, political and bureaucratic obstacles threaten the development of the infrastructure Thailand needs for more evenly spread growth. And, in the absence of private-sector confidence in its political stability, Malaysia has had to resort increasingly to public investment and budget deficits to promote the industrial growth necessary to lessen its overdependence on commodity exports.

At the same time, all have altered the pattern of their commodity exports: Indonesia now exports timber and bauxite as well as rubber, coffee and oil; Malaysian palm oil is overtaking rubber as an export earner; Thailand's tapioca already earns more than its rubber and is poised to overtake rice, traditionally the leading export; and the fruit-canning industry in the Philippines is gaining, as the traditional products of coconuts and sugar lose ground.

Stiff competition

It will be difficult for these four countries to catch up with the "Four Little Dragons," yet they ought to be able to compete on price in the world's markets for the manufactured goods which they export. All four, however, plus Singapore would benefit from increased economic cooperation within ASEAN. At present only 20% of total ASEAN trade is between its members – a proportion unchanged since 1980 – but efforts to expand intra-regional trade by reducing tariff and other barriers have constantly been frustrated by the reluctance of individual governments, particularly that of Indonesia, to abandon their protectionist stance.

All the countries in this guide face the threat of protectionism in their main markets, particularly the USA. They also have to cope with sharply increasing competition from each other and, as standards of living at home push up wages, the NICs have to struggle to produce at competitive prices. The domestic market in most cases is too small to absorb more than a small proportion of output, either because the population is tiny, as in the case of Singapore, or because of the limited purchasing power of most of the population, as in Indonesia and the Philippines.

A convivial milieu – and exceptional opportunities

South-East Asia presents, in general, a convivial work milieu for the foreign business person. On the whole, the countries have well-educated, hard-working and skilled workforces. English is the first language of commerce in Hong Kong, Singapore and the Philippines and is widely spoken elsewhere in the region. Doing business here does require great patience, recognition of the importance of personal relationships and sensitivity towards cultural attitudes which are difficult for a Westerner to interpret. However, the governments of all eight countries favour private enterprise and foreign investment to a greater or lesser degree and all are eager to import technology.

The four NICs, and Taiwan and South Korea in particular, will be rapidly increasing their imports over the next few years. They are under pressure from the USA to reduce import barriers and appreciate their currencies. They are also about to enter a phase where domestic demand is allowed its head and where high technology becomes the key to continued export competitiveness. There are, it is true, serious problems regarding piracy and counterfeiting of foreign imported goods, but most governments are beginning to take measures to protect copyright and patents.

The readiness to respond to market needs, and the ingenuity, hard work and skilfulness of the region's inhabitants have transformed their economies in a couple of decades, and today make it an area of exceptional business opportunities.

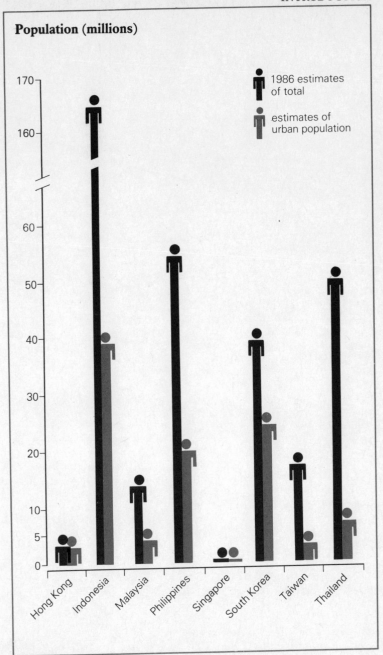

Population (millions)

170 —

160 —

60 —

50 —

40 —

30 —

20 —

10 —

5 —

0 —

1986 estimates
of total

estimates of
urban population

Hong Kong   Indonesia   Malaysia   Philippines   Singapore   South Korea   Taiwan   Thailand

Total merchandise trade (including re-exports)

Source: International Economic Appraisal Service   The Economist Publications

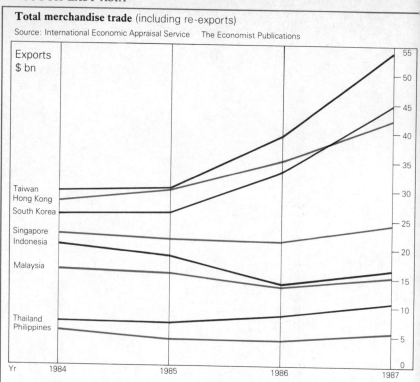

Exports
$ bn

Taiwan
Hong Kong
South Korea

Singapore
Indonesia

Malaysia

Thailand
Philippines

Yr   1984   1985   1986   1987

Commodity   [Exports]   [Imports]   1986 (*1985)

Source: International Economic Appraisal Service   The Economist Publications

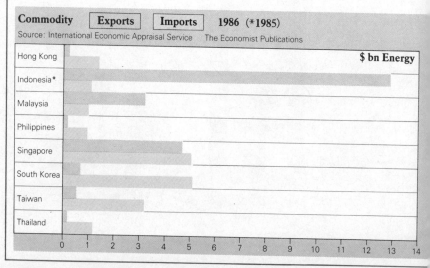

$ bn Energy

Hong Kong
Indonesia*
Malaysia
Philippines
Singapore
South Korea
Taiwan
Thailand

0 1 2 3 4 5 6 7 8 9 10 11 12 13 14

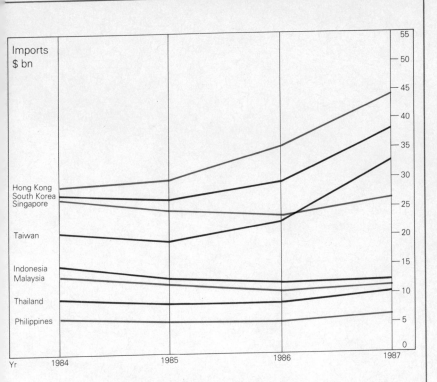

Imports
$ bn

Hong Kong
South Korea
Singapore

Taiwan

Indonesia
Malaysia

Thailand

Philippines

Yr   1984   1985   1986   1987

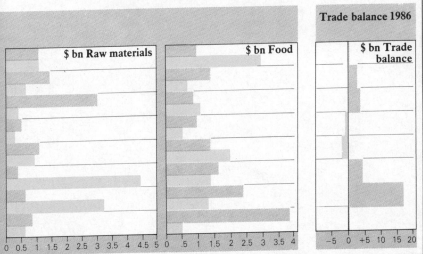

$ bn Raw materials

$ bn Food

Trade balance 1986

$ bn Trade balance

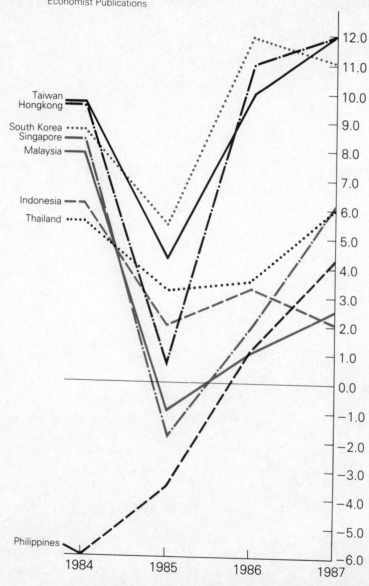

Real GDP Growth %

Source: International Economic Appraisal Service, The
Economist Publications

Taiwan
Hongkong
South Korea
Singapore
Malaysia

Indonesia
Thailand

Philippines

1984　　1985　　1986　　1987

GDP

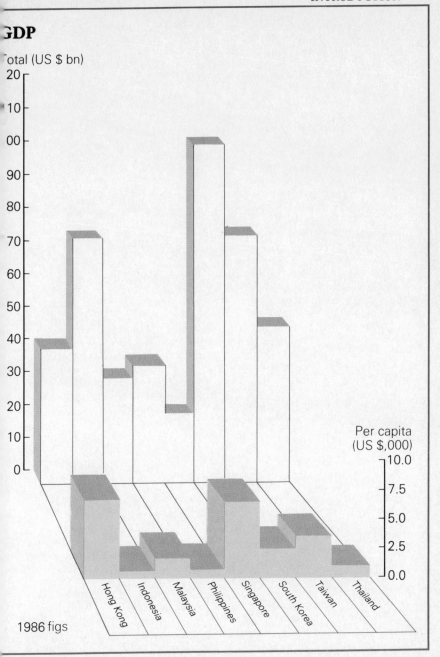

Total (US $ bn)

Per capita
(US $,000)

1986 figs

Hong Kong

A century and a half ago Lord Palmerston ridiculed Hong Kong, which his government had just acquired from China, as a "barren island" sheltering only a few fishermen and farmers. In those 150 years it has vaulted to become the second busiest container port in the world, the largest exporter of garments in the world, and a model of successful unregulated free-trade capitalism with a trade as large as China's itself. It is home to 5.5m Chinese and has the highest standard of living anywhere on the Asian mainland. In 1997 Hong Kong will graduate from British colonialism to become a Special Administrative Region of China, free, it is promised, to carry on for at least 50 years the capitalism and free trade which have fuelled its success.

Hong Kong's population is 98% Chinese, mainly from neighbouring Guangdong province, though with an energetic minority from the Shanghai region, and its citizens are mostly people (or their descendants) who fled from China when the Communist government took over in 1949. The government is British at the very top, but Chinese at the middle and lower levels.

The entrepôt trade was the making of Hong Kong until 1949. The "fragrant harbour" (as its name means) is the best deep-water port on the Chinese coast, and an ideal staging post for Western consumer goods and machinery entering China, as well as for Chinese products – tea, silk, lacquer – destined for America or Europe. That entrepôt function was eroded after 1949 when China became a centrally-planned economy, and manufacturing was begun on a large scale in Hong Kong to provide an alternative livelihood. Textiles led to garments and then to toys and electronics, all made with minimal regulation under free competition. Wages were low in the 1950s, but over the years they have reached Italian levels and the current thrust is towards capital-intensive high technology. Many factory owners have moved their primary production over the border to China where labour is 70–80% cheaper.

Currently manufacturing is somewhat static, while the entrepôt trade is having a renaissance now that China is committed to getting Hong Kong back again and using its facilities to the full. The service industries are also expanding, partly to serve the regional market in East and South-East Asia, partly to serve China's new "open door" policy and partly to cater to the demands of a growing affluent population.

In Hong Kong the entrepreneurial skills of the Chinese and their "Confucian" work ethic truly flourish. But there has always been a certain volatility, especially on the stock market, and a bandwagon mentality that gives too much credence to rumour. It was this that made many uneasy about the prospect of Chinese sovereignty after 1997. But because of the long transition period, the Hong Kong business community was not unduly worried about the future – until the events in Tiananmen Square.

The political scene

Hong Kong is a British colony, although that word is now avoided: "territory" is preferred. It is ruled in unfashionably autocratic style by a governor with almost unlimited powers answerable to the foreign secretary of the British government. Some kind of representative government is to be put in place before July 1997, when the sovereignty reverts to China. It is not yet clear how democratic that new structure will be, but it will consist of local Chinese with a degree of autonomy ultimately accountable to the Beijing government.

A semi-independent colony

The governor, who is appointed by the British monarch, heads the government and presides over the two major consultative bodies, the Executive Council (EXCO) and the Legislative Council (LEGCO). Sir David Wilson took office in 1987, having previously served as a diplomat. A Mandarin-speaker, he played a leading part in negotiating the agreement with China in 1984 for the return of Hong Kong.

The governor's councils EXCO comprises 16 appointed members, of whom six are senior government officials (including the commander of the British forces) and the rest leading private citizens from the professions and commerce. Its theoretical role is to advise the governor on policy matters, but in practice it acts as a corporate decision-maker. It meets every week. LEGCO is much larger, with over 50 members, of whom 10 are government department heads and the rest private citizens. Roughly half of these are appointed by the governor, another half elected indirectly through nine functional constituencies (commerce, industry, finance, labour, social services, law, medicine, teaching and engineering) and 12 electoral colleges representing geographical district boards, the Urban Council and the Regional Council. Elections are normally triennial. LEGCO also meets weekly to enact bills and put questions to the government. Its meetings are televised. The non-government members of the two councils form the Office of the Members of the Executive and Legislative Councils (OMELCO), which monitors government actions and considers public complaints against it.

Efficient civil service The vital ingredient in this type of colonial administration is the civil service, deservedly recognized as probably more efficient, less corrupt and less tempted into unnecessary interventions than any in Asia. Including the police, health, public works, education and fire services, it numbered almost 175,000 in 1987. Only 2% were expatriate (mostly British). It is headed by the chief secretary, who deputizes for the governor in his absence and is the senior defender of government policy in EXCO and LEGCO. An Independent Commission Against Corruption (ICAC) was set up in 1974, responsible directly to the governor. Initiated to probe complaints against the police, it now investigates problems in all sectors, public and private, and in 1986 its inquiries led to over 250 prosecutions for corruption offences.

The helmsman of the Hong Kong economy is the financial secretary, who ranks third in the administration and oversees the work of the Finance, Monetary Affairs, Trade and Industry and Economic Services branches of the government. He presents and defends the budget every February–March.

The reins of power

Sir David Wilson, David Ford (chief secretary), Piers Jacobs (financial secretary) and Jeremy Matthews (attorney-general) are the key government figures. Business leaders are equally powerful in Hong Kong, politically as well as commercially. Sir Y.K. Pao (worldwide shipping), Lord Kadoorie (China Light and Power) and Li Ka-shing (Hutchison Whampoa) are the outstanding veterans of the business scene, while Sir Sze-yuen Chung and Miss Lydia Dunn lead the private sector on EXCO and LEGCO respectively.

An end to apathy Local government affairs centre on the Urban Council, which provides municipal services to some 4m city dwellers, and the Regional Council, which has similar responsibility for the rural areas. Some of the members are elected by district constituencies, and there is a lower level of district boards elected by those same constituencies, by adult voters with seven years' residence in Hong Kong. There was a reluctance to take advantage of such democratic machinery: election turn-out has usually been between a quarter and a third of those registered (or only 10–15% of those qualified). After the June 1989 massacre in Beijing calls for greater participation grew much louder.

International relations

As a dependent territory, Hong Kong has limited direct relations with other countries, but in practice has been granted by Britain considerable freedom of international action; China has agreed to act similarly after 1997. In 1986, for example, Hong Kong became a contracting party to the General Agreement on Tariffs and Trade (GATT) in its own right, and China endorsed this move. After 1997 Hong Kong, as a Special Administrative Region (SAR) of China, will become a separate customs territory qualified for contracting party status using the name "Hong Kong, China."

Representative offices The Hong Kong government maintains representative offices in London, Geneva, Brussels, Washington, New York and San Francisco, primarily to safeguard its economic and trading interests abroad. These offices lobby during the negotiation and implementation of successive GATT multi-fibre arrangements, which significantly affect Hong Kong, and multilateral trade rounds.

The political adviser The person who serves in effect as foreign minister in the government is the political adviser, traditionally a sinologist seconded from the British foreign service. His office advises on, and coordinates, cross-border dealings with Guangdong province authorities (on transport, pollution, customs, immigration and communications issues, for example) as well as negotiations with Beijing. He is a key figure, along with the general duties secretary, in implementing the Joint Declaration of 1984 wherein the British and Chinese governments agreed on the reversion of sovereignty in 1997. These two officers monitor Hong Kong interests in the Joint Liaison Group of the two governments which is to meet frequently until just after 1997 to iron out final details of the reversion.

Transition to "1997"

The Joint Declaration (signed December 1984) provides that the Hong Kong SAR will have its own government and legislature composed of local inhabitants, enjoying a high degree of autonomy under the official Beijing principle of "one country, two systems." Chinese leaders have pledged that Hong Kong will be allowed to carry on its capitalist economic and social system for 50 years after 1997, or even longer. Hong Kong expects to continue after 1997 as an international financial centre, with all that that involves, including its British-style legal system. Chinese socialism, it is hoped, will not be imported.

The Joint Liaison Group has already agreed on numerous

transitional measures between now and 1997, including the use of identity cards and travel documents for Hong Kong citizens, establishment of a separate Hong Kong shipping register, the negotiation of separate air service agreements previously signed by the UK (the first such new agreement was made with the Netherlands in 1986), and Hong Kong's membership of the Asian Development Bank.

Drafting a new Basic Law China has appointed a Basic Law Drafting Committee and Consultative Committee to draw up the "constitution" of the future SAR, with prominent Hong Kong citizens represented. Its work was not due to be completed until 1990, but it was clearly opting for a strong chief executive appointed by Beijing, backed by a weak legislature rather similar to the old colonial one. Hong Kong "democrats" were disappointed, since China had earlier pledged an elected legislature. The British government slowed down its own plans for introducing direct elections for a minority of seats in 1988. Some in Hong Kong fear a stealthy build-up of Chinese Communist Party presence via the official New China News Agency, which represents the Beijing government in Hong Kong.

Against communism Most of today's Hong Kong Chinese (or their fathers) had "voted with their feet" against communism by fleeing to Hong Kong in 1948–49, and they are not inclined to trust Beijing's promises. Probably 150,000 had left for North America or Australia by the end of 1987, and more will certainly follow before 1997, leaving gaps in entrepreneurship and professional expertise – though some of those who left were expected to return after qualifying for foreign citizenship, resuming work in Hong Kong under the protection of a foreign passport.

Mounting unease Apprehension among the people of Hong Kong about China's attitude was mounting even before the killings in Tiananmen Square. One issue was China's refusal to entertain or answer environmental protests about a proposed nuclear power station at Daya Bay, close to the Hong Kong border. Another was a Hong Kong government film censorship bill introduced to bar films hostile to China. And a third issue was the conviction in Guangzhou of a Hong Kong computer salesman for being a "counter-revolutionary."

British legal system

The law broadly follows that of England, though American and Commonwealth cases are cited and considered with respect in the courts. There is appeal from the Supreme Court to the Privy Council in London. Laws are being codified to some degree, and translated into Chinese, preparatory to "1997." China has fully accepted the independence of the judiciary from the executive.

The economic scene

Hong Kong is dependent on imports for most of its requirements, while exports provide the main impetus to growth. Real GDP growth fell in 1985 to almost nil, but in 1986 it reached 11% and in 1987 was even higher at nearly 14%.

Human resources

Hong Kong's population of 5.6m (as of the end of 1986) lives in a mountainous area of 1,070 sq km/669 sq miles (one-third the size of Rhode Island, a half of Surrey). The density is 5,192 persons per sq km, one of the highest in the world. In the ten years to 1986 the population grew on average by 2% a year, but that rate fluctuates with immigration from China, legal or illegal, and the inflow of refugees from Vietnam, direct or via China. The natural increase is only 0.8% a year. The population was young in the 1970s, but in 1986 fewer than 25% were under 15, and the over-65s constituted 7.7%. Life expectancy is 76 years. The working population (those aged 15–64) has risen in recent years to almost 70% of the total.

Many immigrants Only 60% of the population were born in Hong Kong, the vast majority of the rest having crossed from neighbouring Guangdong province. Several thousands immigrate annually from China, while several thousands each year emigrate to Australia, Canada, the USA and the UK.

Education The Chinese value education highly, and 97% of children attend school to the age of 14 and 77% to the age of 16. There were 34,000 full-time students in higher education in 1986 (and another estimated 20,000 in overseas universities were expected to join the Hong Kong labour force on graduation).

Natural resources

Hong Kong's only natural resources are its deep-water port and the ingenuity of its population. All raw materials are imported. Agriculture occupies only 9% of the land area and 2% of the labour force. Most of the rice, vegetables, meat and even water consumed is imported from China, and only in fish is there a high rate of self-sufficiency. Some US$2.9bn was spent on food imports in 1986.

Infrastructure

The infrastructure, by contrast, is impressive. The port was used by 14,000 ocean-going ships in 1986, discharging 34m tonnes/37.5 US tons of goods, 44% containerized. The average turn-around time is 60 hours at mooring buoys or 13 hours at the Kwai Chung container terminals.

Railways and ferries There is an electrified rail link to Guangzhou which carried 311,000 passengers daily in 1986. A Mass Transit Railway links urban centres on both sides of the harbour, carrying 1.6m passengers each weekday, and a new Light Rail Transit system began operating in September 1988 to serve the rural areas off the main rail and subway systems. A complex network of ferries connects the urban centres with outlying places, including Macao.

Airport The single-runway airport at Kai Tak handled 10.6m passengers and 536,000 tonnes/590,000 US tons of cargo in 1986. About a quarter of all imports and exports by value are air-borne. Some 30 scheduled airlines use the airport, with an average of over 150 flights a day to or from 70 cities. Cathay Pacific Airways and Hong Kong Dragon Airlines are the two local carriers.

External trade

Hong Kong lives by trade. Its two-way foreign trade in 1986 was US$71bn, or US$1,280 per head. It ranks 13th among the trading nations, and its commerce overseas represents 180% of its gross domestic product – or more than double the GDP if trade in services is included. It is a traditional entrepôt port and a free port, with no import duties as such and no impediments placed on the free movement of goods.

Exports reached HK$276bn in 1986. Most were domestically produced goods from local factories, but 44% (HK$123bn) were re-exports. Clothing was the biggest component of local exports, accounting for one-third of the total, but textile fabrics, plastic toys, electrical and electronic goods, watches, cameras and printed matter were also important. The re-export trade falls into two distinct categories: Chinese products re-shipped to the West, Japan or South-East Asia, on the one hand, and

Western-made and Japanese machinery and raw materials delivered to China on the other. As a re-export intermediary, Hong Kong makes possible some trade that would be frowned upon if done directly – trade between China and Taiwan or South Korea, for example. Some industrial components are increasingly exported to China for assembly into products which are then re-exported back to Hong Kong for shipment to third markets – and vice versa. The customs figures are not easy to interpret.

Imports Hong Kong's imports spread across the board. In 1986 HK$26bn went on food, beverages and tobacco. Purchases also included HK$40bn of raw materials (especially textile fibres and fur or hide), fuels (mainly oil) and chemicals (especially dyeing and tanning). But the bulk of the import bill was HK$207bn for manufactures including textile yarn and fabrics (21%), clothing (10%), telecoms and recording equipment (7%), office and data-processing machinery (3%), other electrical machinery (11.3%), industrial and power equipment (7%), watches and clocks (6%), and steel, road vehicles and aircraft, and paper and board (each about 3%).

Trading partners are worldwide. Hong Kong products are in demand chiefly in North America and Europe, though Japan has recently assumed more importance as a market. The re-exports mostly go either to China or to Western countries. Import sources vary according to competitiveness. In 1987 30% of imports came from China, 19% from Japan, 9% each from Taiwan and the USA, 5% from South Korea, 4% from Singapore and 3% from the UK.

China's open-door policy Trade with China has grown because of its open-door policy and the imminent reversion of Hong Kong to China. Although China's foreign trade always fluctuates with foreign-exchange availability and political factors, the long term favours Hong Kong–China commerce.

Other trends Japan's role as supplier appears to have peaked, with the yen appreciation and the growth of rival industries in East Asia. The USA and the UK are also losing ground, both as suppliers and markets for Hong Kong products, while leading continental EC and East Asian countries are improving their share.

Balance of payments
There is no exchange control, and figures for invisible trade are not available. It is known, however, that there is a surplus on invisible accounts from such things as tourism

Leading trade partners (1986)

Exports	HK$bn	Re-exports	HK$bn	Imports	HK$bn
USA	64.2	China	40.9	China	81.6
China	18.0	USA	22.4	Japan	56.4
West Germany	11.0	Japan	6.7	Taiwan	24.0
UK	9.9	Taiwan	5.9	USA	23.2
Japan	6.2	South Korea	5.9	South Korea	11.0
Canada	4.9	Singapore	5.3	Singapore	10.9
Australia	3.4	West Germany	2.7	UK	9.3
Netherlands	2.8	Macao	2.6	West Germany	8.0
Singapore	2.8	UK	2.5	Switzerland	5.5
France	2.6	Indonesia	2.4	Italy	4.4
Switzerland	2.1	Philippines	2.0	Australia	3.7
Italy	1.8	Australia	1.8	France	4.0

and the considerable export of financial services, enough to offset the occasional small visible trade deficit. Aid inflows are very modest, coming mainly for social service schemes from international charitable or religious institutions, or development agencies. Investment flows in and out freely as befits a financial centre of Hong Kong's standing. The government does not normally borrow; its outstanding borrowings at the end of 1986 were only HK$1.4bn.

Currency

The Hong Kong dollar exchange rate is linked to the US$ at around HK$7.8 to US$1, so that it has depreciated until recently against the yen and European currencies, while appreciating against the Chinese renminbi. Interest rates also tend to follow US rates. There is no central bank, and two leading commercial banks – the Hongkong and Shanghai Banking Corporation and the Standard Chartered Bank – issue local currency notes. The government's financial assets are chiefly held in the Exchange Fund, in the form of foreign currency and Hong Kong dollar bank deposits and interest-bearing instruments in foreign currencies.

The budget

The government's consolidated revenue and expenditure in 1986 were HK$48bn and HK$44bn respectively. Direct taxes provided HK$17bn, indirect taxes HK$12bn and other sources of revenue HK$19bn. There are small duties on certain liquors, tobacco, spirit fuel and cosmetics, whether imported or locally produced.

Tax-revenue sources Taxes or duties on betting, cinemas, horse-racing, estates, hotel accommodation and the airport, as well as property rates and profits on salaries tax, are the main tax-revenue sources.

Budget expenditure in 1986 was HK$7bn on general services,

HK$6bn on security, HK$1.5bn on economic and HK$29.5bn on community or social services. Fiscal reserves at the end of the year were HK$17bn.

Inflation The money supply (M1) totalled HK$56bn at the end of 1986, up 24% on the previous year. The best available index showed a 5% rise in consumer prices in 1987, while 7–8% was expected for 1988.

Free enterprise or organized opportunism

The free-enterprise approach which has characterized the Hong Kong government throughout its history means that there is no attempt to plan the economy. The field is left firmly open to the entrepreneurs, who in the case of manufacturing are not protected, for example, by import duties. The most that the financial secretary will own to is a rolling five-year forecast of revenue and expenditure of the kind that any prudent corporate treasurer would undertake. Otherwise, the principle of the Hong Kong economy could be described as well organized and often enlightened opportunism. It is not all laissez-faire, however. There are schemes of control whereby the government franchises a corporation to provide such services as electricity, gas or telephones on condition that it follows official guidelines on prices and profits.

Growth The GDP registered average annual growth of around 6% over the period 1981–86, though in 1987 it came close to reaching 14%. The World Bank puts Hong Kong's GDP per head in 1985 at US$6,200, reflecting a 6.3% average growth in the preceding three years. This ranked Hong Kong 24th in the world league for GDP per head, ahead of Spain, Ireland and several other European countries, as well as Israel, Argentina and South Korea. But such comparisons are unjust because Hong Kong is virtually fully urban, and a more meaningful comparison would be with other cities.

Industry

Manufacturing was of little importance until 1949 when a number of Shanghai textile industrialists fled from the Communist take-over in China. They brought their skilled technicians and some funds with them, and even diverted new machinery on order from Europe to the United States to be delivered to Hong Kong. Thus was the famous Hong Kong textile industry, soon to develop into garment manufacture, born.

Manufacturing proved the salvation of Hong Kong when trade alone could not have employed the postwar population. Today manufacturing accounts for 22% of the GDP and 36% of employment. There is a gradual decline in those shares in favour of service industries, but manufacturing is still regarded as the bedrock of the economy. Nine-tenths of the production is for export.

The rag trade Textiles and clothing account for over 40% of both domestic exports and industrial employment. Some HK$63bn-worth was exported in 1986. Output in that year was 195m kilograms of yarn, 781m square metres of fabrics and 42m kilograms of knitted fabrics – all mostly cotton. The clothing factories now dominate the industry, with exports of HK$52bn and employing one-third of all industrial workers.

Import quotas Hong Kong manufactures were put on import quotas in the UK and the USA more than 25 years ago, but the measure was by volume, not value. They were thus given a direct incentive to upgrade their products and increase their profits within the (guaranteed) quotas. Over the years their operations have been mechanized and automated and the goods produced have progressively crept upmarket. The latest trend is for labour-intensive work to be done in China where wages are low, except for the US market where certificate-of-origin requirements are stiff.

Electronics, the second biggest industry, exported HK$33bn-worth of goods in 1986 from 1,090 factories employing 75,000 workers. The industry's strength is adaptability to fast-changing shifts in consumer demand. Production ranges from radios and recorders to hi-fi and TVs, from telephones, calculators and photocopiers to micro-computers and computer-aided design and testing equipment, as well as multilayer printed circuit boards, liquid crystal displays and integrated circuit wafers. The other industries are smaller.

Other goods Plastic toys, watches, jewellery, cameras and travel goods all achieve healthy sales in world markets. Many of these industries have begun to manufacture in China as well as Hong Kong.

No heavy industry Heavy industry is not appropriate for Hong Kong's market size and environment. There are some large shipbuilding and repair yards on Tsing Yi Island which service oil rigs, and an aircraft engineering industry with a good maintenance and repair reputation. Machine-building industries are also active, and Hong Kong boasts a number of modern power stations.

No planning criteria The government does not submit these industries to planning criteria, but it does provide industrial support and technical back-up services, tries to promote investment from overseas, sells industrial land, develops and manages industrial estates, and guides technical training in the polytechnics.

Labour shortage The chief problem of Hong Kong industry is labour shortage. The average daily wage was HK$108 (US$14) in 1986, no statutory minimum being laid down. Labour unions are not strong. There is a Productivity Council with a staff of 280, and upgrading of production is continuous. Manufacturers are shifting labour-intensive operations to Mauritius, Sri Lanka, Thailand, Macao, China and elsewhere, while developing higher technology operations in Hong Kong.

The business climate

To many, Hong Kong is the epitome of successful capitalism – a cosmopolitan, bustling enclave of money-making where free-market principles rule, if not benignly, at least efficiently. Not infrequently, fortunes are made and, if they are lost, can be made again. Tiny Hong Kong was the first of the newly industrialized Asian countries to prosper and export in large amounts to the West, long before Singapore and South Korea. Hong Kong can be understood only in the context of trade and business with the outside world – without that, Hong Kong has very few resources apart from its people. It not only encourages business, it lives and breathes business.

The pro-business environment
Hong Kong can boast a long list of attractions. Its free port and free trade have been important to Hong Kong's development – unprotected, it has had to adapt quickly to changing economic forces and learn how to use its resources most efficiently and productively. The absence of import duties, and simple import and export procedures naturally make Hong Kong an attractive market to foreign firms, especially given its dependence on imports, and domestic producers are more competitive in return.
Freedom from exchange controls complements free trade; trade and capital movements are unrestricted. The Hong Kong dollar is fully convertible, and profits and other funds can be fully repatriated.
Stable government As a colony, Hong Kong has a stable government, and after the Sino-British Joint Declaration in December 1984, with its guarantee that the present system can continue unimpeded for 50 years after 1997, local jitters subsided in the face of Hong Kong's normal optimism and desire to make the best of what is available. Most investment in Hong Kong is recovered within three to five years, making a short-term view feasible. Free enterprise has always characterized Hong Kong; local people – and outsiders – are free to make money, and to lose it. Hard work and entrepreneurship can reap their own rewards.

Superb location Hong Kong's location and communications are superlative. At the hub of international trade for the Far East and the Pacific Basin, Hong Kong has the finest container port in the world outside Rotterdam and New York, and is on all the major air and sea routes in the area.
Long experience Commercial and financial experience have been accumulated over a longer period than in any other city in the region, and as this experience has mainly been culled from the presence of foreigners, the environment is still more suitable for foreign companies than elsewhere. The banking and service sectors in particular are highly sophisticated.
Industrial sites are widely available and there is a good range of supporting industries, especially as new towns are being developed in the New Territories.
The flexibility of the labour market is another prime factor, reflected in almost nil unemployment rates, although recently labour shortages have become apparent.

The laissez-faire economy?
No excessive regulations are imposed by government on private business, although there is a sound body of commercial law in existence. The government has traditionally operated balanced-budget fiscal policies, which have in fact led to the accumulation of large fiscal reserves

and almost a total lack of public debt, despite a very low – and simple – taxation system.

The public sector is normally defined as the government plus the Housing Authority, the Urban Council and the Regional Council. Expenditure by institutions in the private or quasi-private sector is included to the extent that it is met by government subventions, but expenditure by organizations in which the government has only an equity position, such as the Kowloon-Canton Railway Corporation (KCRC) and the Mass Transit Railway Company (MTRC), is not included.

Government's role in both the economy and in society, partly funded by its reserves, is in fact larger than many outsiders imagine. Spending over HK$40bn per year, the government or public-funded organizations provide free or subsidized education at all levels, medical, health and hospital services, social welfare, and public housing for nearly half of the population, proportionately more than anywhere else in the world.

Public works There are extensive programmes of public works, including the water supply, highways, railways and the new towns in the New Territories – for an eventual population of 2–5m – the airport, harbour and so on. Public utilities such as electricity and telephones, both largely privately owned, are regulated, as is the financial sector. Industry is controlled only in such areas as safety and welfare, but is actively encouraged through bodies such as the Hong Kong Trade Development Council, the Export Credits Insurance Corporation and the Productivity Council, and is provided with facilities such as a standards and calibration laboratory.

Industrial training is also organized by a central body, with subsidiaries for various industrial sectors, and two new industrial estates are being built in the Tai Po and Yuen Long areas. Add to all this the organization of considerable cultural and sports facilities and activities, often on an international scale, traffic and environmental management, and the extensive role of government becomes clearer.

Privatization is however under discussion, with proposed candidates including the port of Hong Kong, the second airport, Lion Rock and Aberdeen Tunnels, the collection and disposal of rubbish (including the controversial chemical waste treatment plants), the water supplies, hospitals and the government vehicle fleets. No assets would be sold, only management contracts, a system which has been tried successfully before with the government-owned parking areas and abattoirs. This involves a type of "corporatization," whereby the administration makes statutory provision for the setting up of bodies that operate off the government's financial books, as happened with the Kowloon-Canton Railway Corporation (KCRC) in 1983; operating its own budget, the financially independent KCRC has proved enormously profitable.

The foreign presence

Hong Kong industry is 90% Hong Kong-owned; of the remaining 10%, over 50% is US-owned, 21% Japanese and 7% UK. These figures do not, however, anywhere near reflect the extent of foreign influence in the economy, much of which is channelled into the service sector.

The USA in 1983 accounted for 46.2% of total foreign investment in manufacturing industry, with the UK at 5.8%. By September 1986 the figures were 53.4% and 6.7% respectively, and in early 1986 Americans outnumbered British expatriates in the colony by 16,000 to 14,000. Given the US preponderance in trade – accounting for 42% of Hong Kong's domestic exports and 18% of its re-exports in 1986 – this is not surprising. It is, however, in banking, law, accountancy and other services that the Americans are strongest.

Japan has been gearing up strongly in Hong Kong recently, and when figures are available that show the full effects of the yen revaluation, the extent of the Japanese presence may be startling. Japanese now form 20% of the expatriate population. At the end of 1985, 550 Japanese companies were in Hong Kong, 80% of these in commerce, finance, transport and services. Unlike other foreign investors, Japanese manufacturers have tended to supply the local market, rather than using Hong Kong as a base for re-exports to the USA or Europe.

China is the third largest investor, with February 1987 statistics showing an 18.4% share in Hong Kong manufacturing worth HK$2.85bn. Chinese interests are involved in 30–40 manufacturing establishments with 50,000 workers, the bulk in electronics. The Chinese prefer to buy existing companies, gaining the established expertise, rather than set up new enterprises. There are also significant investments in banking, shipping and aviation.

Foreign investment

Foreign investment is welcome in Hong Kong. All but 3% of Hong Kong's 48,000 factories (which provide 40% of total employment) employ fewer than 100 workers, mainly in garments, electronics, toys, plastic products, watches and clocks production. Although manufacturers are quick to respond to external changes, investment has tended to be devoted to expanding capacity rather than to automation, quality improvement or research and development. In recent years the threat of protectionism and increased competition from other Asian countries has forced some companies to move up-market and invest in R&D, but the authorities have been concerned that investment has not been growing as fast as GDP; private

investment in plant and machinery has been growing at under 1% per annum, while GDP has been growing at about 6% per annum. Hong Kong has been losing its share of the US electronics market, while its neighbours are increasing their investment in high technology. Hence foreign investment is welcome not only for the capital injection, but also for the technology transfer. Half of overseas investment has been in the form of joint ventures.

Property has been a particular favourite of foreign investors, especially as the property sector has recovered since the Joint Declaration. In 1986 HK$5bn went into property from abroad. Commercial factors too played their part; commercial property yields reached 11% in 1986, and with financing costs at about 7%, the return was immediate. Economic recovery brought a rising demand for office space, spurring developments such as the Bond Centre and new buildings for the big three banks, the Hongkong and Shanghai Banking Corporation, Standard Chartered and the Bank of China. Australians, such as Alan Bond, have proved enthusiastic in this sector and the upswing has helped those hit badly by the depression in 1981–84, such as Hongkong Land, to recover. The hotel sector is particularly important, as Hong Kong's hotels are generally full and yield gross operating profits of up to 50%. Twenty-four new projects on the board in late 1986 will increase capacity by 52% to 32,000 rooms by 1990. Again the Japanese have been conspicuous.

Power in business

The four "hongs" until recently dominated Hong Kong's business – Swire's, Jardine Matheson, Hutchison Whampoa and Wheelock Marden, huge empires ruled by British born-and-bred Taipan families and administered by a Western-dominated elite. They covered commodity trading, property, shipping, aviation, and to a

lesser extent industry, retailing and financial services. Similarly the three most powerful men in Hong Kong were said to be the governor, the chairman of the Jockey Club and the chairman of the Hongkong and Shanghai Bank, with sometimes one man occupying both the latter posts.
The scene is changing Challenged now from both outside and inside, the scene is changing and becoming more complex. Swire's is still very bullish about Hong Kong, although Jardine Matheson moved its corporate headquarters to Bermuda in 1983 and has recently floated off the Dairy Farm and Mandarin Oriental (hotels) interests. Chinese tycoon Li Ka-shing acquired effective control of Hutchison Whampoa in 1979 and has since increased his stake, and the troubled shipping-based Wheelock Marden was rescued by Sir Y.K. Pao in 1985.
Local interests are now predominant The names of billionaires Sir Y.K. Pao and Li Ka-shing are famous worldwide. The latter heads the Cheung Kong group, which has been very acquisitive in recent years. Sir Y.K. Pao's family owns 70% of the World International Group, which covers such companies as Wharf Holdings, Hong Kong Realty, Wheelock International and Lane Crawford. He also has a 15% stake in Standard Chartered Bank and was a founding sponsor of Dragonair, the aspirant rival to Cathay Pacific. Other famous names include Joseph Lau of Chinese Estates and Gordon Wu, chairman of Hopewell Holdings and famous for the scale of his ambitions; it is Wu who has sponsored the Kowloon-Canton superhighway and is behind the Lantau Island second airport scheme. The Hang Seng Index (see *The Financial Scene*) is a useful guide to Hong Kong's powerhouses.
Foreign interests Australian, Singaporean and Japanese property and commercial interests are increasing their stake and power in Hong Kong. Between them, Japanese retailers such as Matsuzakaya and Isetan account for one-third of Hong Kong's retail sector, and the Japanese construction companies dominate all new projects, from the new Bank of China building to the second cross-harbour tunnel.
China is also extremely influential, partly for political and partly for economic reasons. The head of the New China News Agency (*Xinhua*) is widely regarded as China's "governor" in Hong Kong, while financial, industrial, trading and property groups such as the Bank of China, China Resources (Holdings) Inc and China Merchants Steam Navigation Co have been in the colony for decades and are pretty muscular. The China International Trust and Investment Corporation (CITIC) recently acquired 12.5% of the shares of Cathay Pacific from Swire's and the Hongkong and Shanghai Bank. China's influence will no doubt increase in future, aided by the influx of Chinese corporations into Hong Kong branches and offices.

Employment
The workforce in Hong Kong amounted to 2.64m in mid-1986, 64% of which was male. In the manufacturing sector, textiles, electronics and plastics were the greatest employers, with centres in the urban areas of Hong Kong and Kowloon, and 35% of manufacturing employment now in the new towns of the New Territories.
Shift to China A labour shortage and rising wages, in part due to the emigration of skilled labour and in part to competition from the services sector and an increased demand for manufactures, has been causing a shift of production facilities to China, especially into neighbouring Guangdong province, where, in theory at least, there is a large pool of cheap labour. By June 1987 there were 2,000 production outlets in Guangdong partly or wholly Hong Kong-owned, plus 60,000

agreements involving the subcontracting of work on textiles, toys, watches, plastics and electronics.
Wages and salaries No minimum wage is statutory and average daily rates in September 1986 were HK$128 for men and HK$99 for women. There is little profit sharing or participation in management. Social security benefits are funded by government. For local salaried staff, office managers earned on average HK$85,800–156,000 per annum, qualified accountants HK$55,000–86,000, executive secretaries HK$47,000–86,000 and junior clerks HK$25,000–40,000. Expatriate salaries are extremely high, with often a wide range of fringe benefits including housing, schooling and home-leave flights.
Unions The unionized workforce comprises only 20% of the total, and there were only three work stoppages in 1985. All workers have the right to belong, but there are no closed shops. At the end of 1986 there were 448 unions including three employers' associations and 15 mixed employer/employee organizations. Most of the industrial unions are grouped under either the pro-China Hong Kong Federation of Trade Unions or the pro-Taiwan Hong Kong and Kowloon Trade Union Council.
The Labour Department covers labour matters for the government, and has been active in getting legislation passed on matters such as hours and conditions, holiday pay, redundancy pay, child labour and injury compensation. The Labour Relations Ordinance provides conciliation and arbitration machinery, and also provides an Employment Service for both employers and those out of work. The government has also been active in industrial and technical training.

The business framework

Company law in Hong Kong is relatively simple. The Hong Kong Companies Ordinance is based on the UK Companies Act of 1929 and incorporates some of the amendments of later UK companies acts. Hong Kong law on the form and content of accounts is generally the same as that in the UK. Here again, the government traditionally does not interfere, although recently business opinion is forcing it to regulate more, especially in the financial sector. There are no special incentives for foreign investment.

Corporate structure

Establishing a business in Hong Kong can be by sole proprietorship or partnership, by private limited company, by public limited company, or by establishing a branch of a company incorporated outside Hong Kong. Given the tax structure, most foreign companies prefer to incorporate (usually privately) within the colony, perhaps involving a joint venture. No prior permission is needed to form a company, and there are no restrictions on foreigners or residency requirements for directors and shareholders. The only industries closed to private enterprise (to date) are those directly controlled by the government – the postal system, the harbour and airport, the water supply, KCRC and Radio Television Hong Kong, for example. There is no price control except among utilities and public transport.
Forming a company Once the proposed name is approved by the Companies Registry, it is filed with the company's memorandum and articles of association and a statutory declaration of compliance with Chapter 32 of the Companies Ordinance. There must be at least two shareholders for a private company and seven for a public one,

and shares are usually denominated in HK$1 or HK$10; shares of no par value are not permitted. There are no restrictions on initial authorized share capital, and no minimum capital requirements, except for banks, deposit-taking companies, securities and trust companies. Normal restrictions apply to the liability of shareholders, and there are legal restrictions on the reduction of capital.

A private limited company must have two directors, two shareholders and a secretary. Law firms and other organizations are usually willing, for a fee, to provide nominee directors and shareholders. A private limited company is one whose articles restrict the right to transfer the company's shares, limit the number of members (excluding employees) to 50, and prohibit any invitation to the public to subscribe for shares. It must maintain a registered office in Hong Kong with records and a cash book, and appoint auditors who are certified public accountants with the Hong Kong Society of Accountants. Such a company can be incorporated in six to eight weeks, and costs of legal and other fees and expenses are roughly HK$7,000–10,000.

Shell companies purchased ready-made, and with wide-reaching clauses in their memoranda of association, are an alternative preferred by some investors who need a legal entity to, say, sign a lease.

A public company wanting to issue shares must provide a prospectus giving full details of the proposed share issue, its own activities and so on, supported by certificates from its promoters, directors and reporting accountants. There are particular listing requirements, but otherwise company law is similar in this area to that in the UK.

Branch offices of companies incorporated outside Hong Kong must be registered with the Registrar of Companies, who requires a certified copy of the company's documents of incorporation, particulars of directors, registered addresses abroad and in Hong Kong, and other information, including a power of attorney appointing the person authorized to accept notices in Hong Kong. Normally the company will also have to file an annual copy of its balance sheet.

Registration Every business in Hong Kong must register within one month of incorporation under the Business Registration Ordinance and obtain a Business Registration Certificate for an annual fee of HK$500, plus a HK$100 contribution to a "protection of wages on insolvency" fund. Since 1984 branches of foreign companies have also needed a certificate, for an annual fee of HK$15. This applies even where the "branch" is a representative office not transacting business.

Land is government (Crown) owned but leases are sold at auction, and can be resold freely or leases renewed. Since the signing of the Joint Declaration, until June 30 1997 new leases can be granted (or leases expiring after 1997 renewed) only for terms up to June 30 2047.

Acquisitions The Hong Kong Code on Takeovers and Mergers does not have the force of law, but in practice is upheld by the securities industry. It requires that any person acquiring shares carrying 35% or more of the voting rights in a company must make a general offer to the other shareholders, and once over this threshold, but below 50%, annual acquisitions are limited to 5% if a general offer is to be avoided.

Taxation

Taxation is levied under the Inland Revenue Ordinance and charged only on income or profits arising in or derived from Hong Kong each fiscal year ending March 31st, although occasionally some foreign-source income is deemed to have a Hong Kong source. Because only Hong Kong is considered, there are no tax conventions with other countries, although there is limited double taxation relief available for income chargeable to Hong Kong taxation that has already borne tax in another Commonwealth country, excepting the UK, Canada and Australia.

Personal taxation can be no higher than 15.5%, but in practice, given the allowances available, the effective rate is even lower.

Profits tax is levied on local and foreign companies and their branches alike, at a maximum rate of 17%. Profits arising from the sale of capital assets and dividend income, wherever arising, are not taxable.

Property tax is levied on the owner of land or property other than his residence, although when this property is for business purposes the tax may be exempted or set against taxable profits. Rates are also payable on property, up to a maximum of 5.5% per annum on rateable value.

Stamp duty is levied on sales of immovable property and leases, and on share transfers. Interest tax, a withholding tax, is nil rate on Hong Kong dollar and foreign exchange deposits with financial institutions; on all other Hong Kong-source interest it is 17%. Interest received is liable to profits tax.

Market entry

Hong Kong is one of the easiest places in which to do business in East Asia and more and more companies are using it as the route through which to establish a foothold in China.

Importing and exporting

Import and export regulations are minimal and licensing formalities simple. Licences are required only to fulfil international obligations and for health, safety and security reasons. Exports of certain textiles are subject to bilateral restraint agreements negotiated under the Multi-fibre Arrangement. These are administered by the Trade Department by means of export licences and quotas.

Certificates of origin may be required for Hong Kong exports. These are issued by the Trade Department and other approved organizations, and are of two types. "Certificates of Hong Kong Origin" are issued for goods that qualify as Hong Kong products by virtue of the production process. "Certificates of Origin Form A" are issued for Hong Kong exports eligible for tariff preference under various Generalized System of Preference schemes.

A declaration charge is payable on all imports and exports, at HK$5 for the first HK$10,000 worth of goods, plus 50 cents for each additional HK$1,000. Gifts, personal baggage

and items with a through bill of lading are exempted.

Excise duties are levied on tobacco, alcoholic liquor, soft drinks, cosmetics, methyl alcohol and some hydrocarbon oils, whether imported or manufactured locally, at varying rates according to origin.

Samples Goods carried as baggage and regarded by the authorities as samples or advertising matter of no commercial value and not for resale are exempt from duty.

Documentation for customs is standard, the main items being two copies of a commercial invoice showing exact details of shipment and one negotiable bill of lading with the importer to effect clearance.

Packing needs to withstand heat, humidity and heavy rain. Shipping marks in English are easily recognized by Hong Kong warehousing firms. Many such firms have their own marks which they ask exporters to use on cases.

The Export Credits Insurance Corporation is Hong Kong's equivalent of the British Export Credits Guarantee Department. It insures Hong Kong exporters against both political and commercial risk for short, medium and long-term trade and capital goods exports, generally providing 90% indemnity against non-payment. South Seas Centre Tower 1, 2nd Fl, 75 Mody Road, Kowloon ☎ 3-7233883.

Excellent port and warehouse (godown) facilities The container terminal at Kwai Chung has one of the fastest throughput times in the world, and is being expanded. Storage is relatively cheap, and distribution is normally handled without problems by the Hong Kong agent/importer. Much high-value cargo is airfreighted into Kai Tak.

Agents
Agents are common in Hong Kong. On the trading side they operate on both a commission and on a sole importing basis. The indent system, whereby the agent takes the orders, the goods are shipped direct to the customer and the agent draws his commission direct, is widely used. Alternatively, many firms purchase on their own account and resell to wholesalers or retailers.

A different type of agent has emerged in recent years, one who acts on behalf of a foreign principal in China. Many commercially-minded Hong Kong Chinese speak Mandarin and/or one of the other Chinese languages, and many have good family, business and political connections. Such agents run from the small sole operator to large firms of consultants employing qualified staff who can negotiate the technical as well as the commercial aspects of contracts.

Insurance
There are many companies with offices in Hong Kong dealing in insurance, reinsurance and broking. Of the 286 registered for underwriting business in December 1986, 127 were local. British firms were the most numerous among the remainder. Business is restricted to authorized companies and there are minimum paid-up capital and net asset requirements, which vary according to whether the company is a life, general or composite insurer.

Advertising and PR
The full range of facilities is available among the media – black and white or colour advertising using the latest techniques in newspapers and magazines, on radio and TV, in the cinema and on billboards. The major international advertising companies mostly have Hong Kong offices, sometimes in conjunction with a local partner – for example, McCann Erickson has teamed up with Jardine Matheson. Public relations companies, too, have multiplied in recent years, and no exporter should suffer any problems finding a reputable firm.

Trademarks, patents and copyrights
The Hong Kong laws governing trademarks, patents, copyrights and designs are based on UK laws, and in October 1977 Hong Kong became a member of the Paris Convention, thereby obtaining reciprocity with other members.

Applications for trademarks are made to the Trade Marks Registry of the Registrar General's Department, and policing is the responsibility of the trademark owner. Registration lasts seven years and can be renewed for periods of 14 years. Trademarks can be cancelled if there has been no bona fide use for five years.

Patents No original patents are granted by Hong Kong; local applicants for confirmation need a patent from the UK authorities or a European patent designating the UK before registering it at the Patent Office.

Copyright protection is extended by provisions of the UK Copyright and Registered Designs acts and the Hong Kong Copyright Ordinance 1975. Protection covers all literary, musical, dramatic and artistic works.

The financial scene

Asia's premier financial market and lagging behind only London and New York, Hong Kong is a curious mixture of sophistication and relative backwardness. It is much more than merely an offshore banking centre, and Hong Kong's superb communications facilities, prime geographical position, minimal government interference, major corporate presence and low tax rates have attracted foreign financial institutions like bees to a honeypot. Following them have gone back-up services – insurance, accountants, lawyers and consultants. With domestic savings averaging two years' income, the banking sector is also critical to Hong Kong's social and economic health. It has suffered in recent years both with Hong Kong's general economy and on its own account, and is now undergoing a series of government-inspired improvements. It will, however, have to keep on its toes if it is not in future to be overshadowed by Tokyo, especially as 1997 approaches, and if Tokyo sets up an offshore market.

Central banking

No central bank as such exists, the Hong Kong dollar being issued mostly by the Hongkong and Shanghai Banking Corporation (HSBC) but also by Standard Chartered. The supply of these notes is regulated by the Exchange Fund, whose reserves are held in both Hong Kong dollars and foreign exchange. There is no lender of last resort; the banks are allowed to transfer undisclosed amounts to "hidden reserves" – contingency funds – and are required to keep a minimum of 25% of their assets in liquid form to meet calls.

Other central bank functions such as the prudential supervision of financial institutions, managing official foreign exchange reserves and conducting open-market operations are exercised by government offices including the Commissioner of Banking and the Monetary Affairs Branch of the Government Secretariat. The HSBC manages the interbank clearing house, while interest rates are set by a committee of the Hong Kong Association of Banks (HKAB). This "cartel," which sets maximum retail and short-term deposit rates, has been profitable to the banks, but has recently come under criticism as the Hong Kong

dollar–US dollar link, in force since 1983, has pushed the strain of Hong Kong/US interest-rate differentials onto money market rates.

Commercial banks

The traditional dominance of the commercial banking sector is being eroded by merchant banks, brokers and others as the range of markets operating in Hong Kong expands. Banks and Deposit-Taking Companies (DTCs) are licensed under the 1986 Banking Ordinance. All licensed banks must be members of the HKAB, which was formed in 1981 to supervise banking activities and to regulate charges and deposit rates. The major domestic banks include HSBC, Standard Chartered, Hang Seng Bank (an HSBC subsidiary) and Bank of East Asia. A three-tier system covers deposit-taking:

Licensed banks can take deposits of any amount and maturity in the course of their banking business. Only licensed banks can operate checking and savings accounts.

Licensed DTCs can take deposits of not less than HK$500,000 and of any maturity.

Registered DTCs can take deposits of not less than HK$100,000 and three months' maturity. These are a major source of deposits, whereas licensed DTCs have been increasingly moving into merchant banking activities.

Hong Kong is overbanked relative to population. In December 1986 the 151 licensed banks had 1,393 banking offices, and only 35 of these banks were incorporated in Hong Kong. Of these, 15 were foreign-owned or controlled. Others had foreign equity participation. Another 136 foreign banks had representative offices in Hong Kong. Banks incorporated in Hong Kong had 952 local branches and 179 overseas branches. There were 254 registered and 38 licensed DTCs, all but 67 of the former being related to Hong Kong or foreign banks.

The moratorium on granting banking licences was lifted in May 1981. Prior to this many foreign banks had entered the market via DTCs, but the expansion of both sectors has not halted: total bank and DTC assets rose by 41.5% and 7.5% respectively between September 1985 and September 1986. Both international and domestic banks are subject to various conditions concerning minimum paid-up share capital, assets and regulation.

New rules on capital adequacy were introduced by the Banking Ordinance of August 1986, establishing a general 5% risk-asset ratio, strengthening capital requirements for DTCs and stipulating minimum 50% bank ownership for registered DTCs.

The banking environment
Turbulent conditions characterize the market. A cut in 1985 margins resulted from overbanking and increased competition from the Bank of China (BOC) group, the Japanese and others, plus the high liquidity (50.7% on average for banks in 1985), and added to weak credit demand stemming from the economic and trade slowdown. There were also serious problems due to imprudent lending and corruption at the smaller banks. During 1983–85 the

government had to step in and rescue several banks which failed. All this was exacerbated by problems in the shipping sector and slowdown in the traditional markets in the Middle East and South-East Asia.

1986 saw improvements as the Hong Kong economy picked up and the new regulatory environment took effect. Main areas of loan demand include project finance, property mortgages, visible trade finance, consumer finance and the China market; the last, while politically important and of medium-term potential, accounts for no more than 5% of major banks' portfolios.

Evolutionary changes Hong Kong, like other financial markets, is now, however, seeing a blurring of barriers between markets, increasing securitization and globalization – and the associated increased competition and risk.

Reduced foreign presence
Foreign banks, an overwhelming majority of the banks in Hong Kong, have recently been reducing their presence as competition has reduced margins. Barclays and Bank of America have more or less pulled out of retail banking, while BNP, the Royal Bank of Canada, Citibank and others have either downgraded their activities or shifted to Tokyo.

The foreign contingent includes 25 Japanese, 15 Chinese, 5 Singaporean, 4 Australian, 8 West German, 8 French, 7 UK, 22 US, 6 Canadian and 2 Middle Eastern banks, plus 134 foreign representative offices. The Japanese also won five of the ten new banking licences granted in 1986 (although these five are limited to one branch each). They are mainly involved in the wholesale market.

The foreign exchange market has been strengthened by the absence of foreign exchange control and the shortage of money market instruments denominated in Hong Kong dollars, due to the lack of marketable government debt (Hong Kong being very much a balanced budget economy). This has meant that bank and DTC reserves tend to be held in foreign exchange. The government has been little involved in the markets, except in linking the Hong Kong dollar to the US dollar in October 1983.

The Bank of China group, better known as the "sister banks," comprises 13 banks overseen by the BOC's Hong Kong and Macao Regional Office. Four of these are incorporated in Hong Kong – Nanyang Commercial Bank, Po Sang Bank, Hua Chiao Commercial Bank and Chiyu Banking Corporation. The remainder are the Bank of Communications, Kwangtung Provincial Bank, China and South Sea Bank, China State Bank, Kincheng Banking Corporation, National Commercial Bank, Sin Hua Trust, Savings and Commercial Bank and Yien Yeh Commercial Bank.

These all expanded their capital bases in 1985, and by December 1986 accounted for 18% of all Hong Kong bank deposits (HK$102bn), a rise of 50% over the year. This was mainly at the expense of smaller Hong Kong banks, although even HSBC's market share has fallen slightly. The group operates 256 branches and a wide ATM network, and has aggressively concentrated on the lower end of the loan market, especially mortgages. Other Chinese interests have also been involved in bank rescues – Ka Wah Bank was taken over by the China International Trust and Investment Corporation, while China Merchants Steam Navigation Company has acquired Union Bank.

Banking reform is still a high priority for the Hong Kong government. The 1986 Banking Ordinance improved the legislative framework, but is considered still inadequate to meet the risks arising from new market practices such as the securitization of debts and the shift of many DTCs into investment banking activities. Five papers were published in 1987 by the government, including the introduction of a limited service banking licence (allowing the bank to enter the regional and interbank markets but not retail deposit-taking), the grouping of all DTCs under one umbrella, and stricter requirements on the minimum capital of DTCs.

These proposals and the closer supervision of debt securities – commercial paper, CDs, bonds and notes, which form 75% of all securities dealing – became the basis of a new banking bill which took effect in September 1988. A more regulated environment will no doubt strengthen confidence and allow foreign financiers to feel more at home in the market.

Merchant banks and the capital markets

Capital markets, the stock market and other non-commercial banking activities are developing apace as Hong Kong's traditional focus on visible international trade is diluted by trading within the financial markets.

Merchant banks without banking licences engage mainly in the management of syndicated bank credit, foreign exchange services, lease financing, investment management and underwriting securities, functions which they have successfully assumed from the commercial banks. Although still the major base for the Asian leasing market, leveraged leasing and sale and lease-back have been hurt by 1986 legislation designed to strengthen the tax net on these and other activities.

Capital markets Hong Kong's capital market transactions grew from HK$4.58bn in 1984 to HK$26.37bn in 1986, aided by declining interest rates during the period, excessive bank liquidity and the move by merchant banks away from a shrinking syndicated loans market into CDs, floating-rate notes (FRNs), corporate bonds and other debt instruments.

The development of a secondary market has been hampered by the dominance of the commercial banking sector as a source of external corporate finance and the absence of a market for government debt. Many capital market issues are tied to Hong Kong dollar interest and/or currency swaps, and 60% of paper is held by the institutions rather than the retail sector.

The capital markets are likely to continue growing, but possible hindrances are the lack of opportunity to hedge risks – the financial futures market is underdeveloped – the reluctance of the Hong Kong government to see over-reliance on Hong Kong dollar funding, and the difficulty of arranging large volumes of swaps requiring demand for fixed-interest Hong Kong dollar funding.

The securities market

The Hong Kong Stock Exchange Ltd was formed in April 1986 by the merger of the four existing exchanges, and in trading volume now lags behind only London, New York and Tokyo. By mid-June 1987 daily turnover averaged HK$1bn, a rise of four times on 1984. Hong Kong now contributes 0.9% of the world's stock market capitalization, and trading, especially by small investors, is encouraged by the low brokerage rates.

Although the actual size of the market is very small – there are only around 250 publicly listed firms – many of those listed are sizable, well-established corporations, and an increasing number of foreign firms are seeking a listing. Of the domestic firms, 70% are involved in property and construction, which renders the market somewhat vulnerable to the health of those sectors.

The Hang Seng Index, Hong Kong's best known, is based on the daily market value of 33 leading stocks selected on the basis of their capitalization and market stature. In line with other world stock markets, the Hang Seng hit record levels in 1986–87. In April 1986 the Hong Kong Index, comprising 45 stocks, was introduced, but the Hang Seng remains predominant.

Over 1,000 brokerage houses trade on the exchange, and major investors include 200 unit trusts/mutual funds, which are governed by the Code on Unit Trusts and Mutual Funds under the Securities Commission. By 1986 those funds run by banks, DTCs, etc had US$12bn under management.

Volatile reputation The Hong Kong Market's reputation for being somewhat volatile and speculative was only strengthened by its performance during the October 1987 crash. Losses were very heavy and the exchange closed for four days. The government stepped in with a HK$4bn rescue package and a Securities Review Committee was established to report on the industry.

Supervision No specific stock exchange legislation exists, although the Commissioner for Securities provides prudential supervision by enforcing the Securities Ordinance and other ordinances. Listing rules stipulate that the minimum value of shares for listing must be HK$50m, although in practice it is generally HK$100m. One-quarter of new issues must be made available to the public.

Commodities markets

The Hong Kong Commodities Exchange Ltd is the only company licensed under the Commodities Trading Ordinance to operate a commodity exchange in futures contracts. There are four three-month markets – gold, cotton, sugar and soya beans. The exchange was given a new lease of life by the introduction of a Hang Seng Index contract in May 1986.

Gold trading is important, and is mainly conducted through the Chinese Gold and Silver Exchange Society.

Who can help

Government organizations

The Trade Department is responsible for Hong Kong's commercial relations with foreign governments. It has five divisions, three responsible for bilateral relations, divided geographically, one for the multilateral aspects of external commercial relations, and another concerned with the more mundane aspects of trade such as certificates of origin and import/export licensing. 13–15 Fl, Ocean Centre, 5 Canton Rd, Kowloon ☎ 3-7222333.

The Industry Department comprises an Industrial Development Division, an Environment and Resources Division, a Promotion Consultancy Division, a Technical Support Division and a Science and Technology Division. These are responsible for assisting Hong Kong industry in its relations with government departments, advising on policy formation, land use and planning, and in promoting foreign investment in Hong Kong. 14 Fl, Ocean Centre, 5 Canton Rd, Kowloon ☎ 3-7222333.

The Customs and Excise Department comprises a uniformed Customs and Excise Service that performs policing functions, and an Administration and Trade Controls Division, which mainly covers intellectual property matters. 8 Fl, Harbour Bldg, 38 Pier Rd, Central ☎ 5-8523324.

The Hong Kong Trade Development Council is a vast organization with large resources. It has 25 offices overseas and organizes over 80 international projects every year, including trade fairs and exhibitions. Suite 2904, 30–32 Fl, Great Eagle Centre, 23 Harbour Rd ☎ 5-8334333.

The Productivity Council and Centre gives technical assistance, industrial consultancy and computer and economic research services to Hong Kong industry, and implements a wide range of training programmes. 12 Fl, World Commerce Bldg, Harbour Centre, 11 Canton Rd, Tsimshatsui ☎ 3-7235656.

The Hong Kong General Chamber of Commerce has 2,800 members. It engages in trade promotion activities and is also authorized to issue certificates of origin and commercial carnets. It can act as an arbitrator in commercial disputes. 22 Fl, United Centre, 95 Queensway, Wanchai ☎ 5-299229.

The Federation of Hong Kong Industries acts as a bridge between government and industry, and is another government-approved certificate-issuing organization. It also oversees the Hong Kong Industrial Design Council and the Hong Kong Packaging Council. Room 407, Hankow Centre, 5–15 Hankow Rd, Kowloon ☎ 3-7230818.

Other sources of help

Lawyers are legion – there are several major local firms, but the foreign business person is less likely to use their services, as all the leading international firms have offices in Hong Kong, many of which act as a base for their activities in China.

Accountants too are in abundance, again available to the China market. All the Big Eight have offices. There are also many local companies.

The banks can also offer a wide range of services, both for Hong Kong and the China trade. The Hongkong and Shanghai Banking Corporation and Standard Chartered are the best known.

Media Hong Kong has a thriving press. The main English language daily newspapers are the *South China Morning Post*, the *Hong Kong Standard*, the *Asian Wall Street Journal* and the *International Herald Tribune*. Cantonese papers include the *Oriental Daily News*, the *Sing Pao Daily News* and the *Ming Pao Daily News*. The authoritative *Far Eastern Economic Review* is printed in Hong Kong and specialist trade and technical publications abound.

Business and cultural awareness

Situated as it is in the middle of the Pacific trade routes and heavily populated by foreigners and foreign companies, Hong Kong is exposed to a multitude of international influences and is permeated through and through by the same type of international business culture that one finds in London and New York. Nearly all Western business people would feel at home in downtown Hong Kong, although if they wander into Wanchai or Kowloon, they will be in another, very Chinese, world.

Hong Kong society

Hong Kong society embraces many racial and ethnic groups. It is also a recent society; even the predominant Cantonese Chinese have been on the island only for the past 150 years or so, and their numbers have been steadily added to over the decades by further immigration from many different provinces of China. Around the core population exist other races and ethnic communities, of which perhaps the Indian is the most noticeable indigenous group. All have been attracted to Hong Kong by its relatively free business environment. Business is also the *raison d'être* of the more sophisticated floating expatriate population, which tends to keep apart socially even though it mixes in the office and on the tennis court.

Change is also a salient feature of Hong Kong society. It has had to keep pace with the worldwide technological revolution, especially in the financial and information technology areas. Demand for business and residential space and the consequent property boom of recent years have kept the skyline ever-changing and have transformed once tranquil agricultural plots in the New Territories into bustling new towns.

Religion There are over 360 Buddhist and Taoist temples and monasteries, plus both Roman Catholic and Anglican churches and the well-known St John's Anglican Cathedral. There are also synagogues, mosques, Hindu and Sikh temples and yet more exotic places of worship. Missionaries are also active. Many business and professional people are active Christians and Christian schools are generally preferred even by non-Christian parents.

Education The government provides nine years of free and compulsory education for local children, and also subsidizes senior secondary schools. Of the 2,600 schools, only 100 are government-run; 1,550 are privately funded and the rest private, but government aided, and therefore subject to a degree of control by the Education Department. Chinese children work hard at school, driven by a strong desire to achieve. There are also British, American, French, German and Japanese schools, and the Hong Kong International School run by the Lutheran Church-Missouri Synod.

There are two major universities, one English and one Chinese-speaking, with roughly 14,350 students between them, and several polytechnics with roughly 27,550 students in total. There are also technical and other specialist colleges.

Foreigners (mostly) welcome For the most part Hong Kong welcomes foreigners with open arms – they are, after all, the mainstay of the business and tourist communities and the media, and Hong Kong as a trading and entrepôt community is utterly dependent on contact with foreigners. In some ways the concept "foreigner" is inaccurate; many senior government officials are British. English is the main business language, and there are many people of different nationalities who have been born and bred in Hong Kong. Yet there are divisions between the ethnic Cantonese and other communities. The family-centred Chinese do not mix much socially with other nationalities, even among the higher, more sophisticated levels of the business community, and occasionally there are signs of resentment at the comfortable lives that foreigners lead.

The business method

Business attitudes are mixed, like Hong Kong society itself. These days many local Hong Kong people are employed by large corporations, but the entrepreneurial spirit is still strong. People work hard and often long hours, and are quick and efficient. The Chinese community is traditionally one of brokers and traders, but a growing body of professionals is emerging to complement the Western lawyers, accountants and so on.

Working hours for the banks are weekdays 9–4.30 and Saturday 9–12.30. Most businesses work weekdays 9–5.30 and half of Saturday.

After hours There is a strict division between work and play. Central District feels deserted on a Sunday, and most business people would not welcome being telephoned to discuss work after they have reached the sanctuary of their homes.

Business dress is formal: suits and ties for men, even in summer, as most offices are air-conditioned. Dress for women is much the same as in the City of London or Wall Street; trousers are rarely worn.

Business cards are essential. They should be printed in your own language on one side and in Chinese on the other. The old-style "complicated" Chinese characters should be used, as opposed to the simplified characters used in mainland China.

Women in business Women are found in career positions more frequently now, which is largely because of the influence of the Americans on Hong Kong business.

Hong Kong women themselves can be formidable in business, the professions and politics, as the examples of Lydia Dunn and Maria Tam show. Secretaries are still always female and, because they need to be bilingual, are usually local. Foreign businesswomen should experience no unusual problems.

Hospitality Business entertaining is a great feature of the Hong Kong scene, with restaurants rather than homes as the venue. Hospitality should be returned. The restaurants in the top hotels are the safest choice.

Gifts Gift-giving is not taken so seriously in this cosmopolitan place as it would be in Japan or Korea or even China itself. Nobody will be upset if you do not produce a gift at an appropriate moment, but on the other hand gifts to juniors – not equals or seniors – are acceptable if handed over discreetly so as not to embarrass others. Good quality liquors and scarce or out-of-season food always go down well.

Etiquette The Hong Kong Chinese with whom the foreign business visitor is likely to be dealing will generally be Westernized in both language and manners and there are no formalities peculiar to Hong Kong. Many Hong Kong Chinese have Westernized their names, but if this is not the case, then the surname comes first in a name of two or three syllables. As in many countries in the region, age is revered and should be treated with respect. Dignity and "face" are similarly valued, although not to the same very high degree as in some other Asian countries. The foreign business traveller should nonetheless always be polite; losing one's temper is completely unproductive. Superstition is similarly muted among the Hong Kong business community and unlikely to be encountered, although the traditional laws of *feng-shui* (wind-water) still govern the siting of new buildings and other structures which must be reconciled with the water currents and winds.

HONG KONG

Area codes: Hong Kong Island ☎ 5, Kowloon ☎ 3, New Territories ☎ 0

Even after many visits Hong Kong's visual appeal never stales. The green peaks of Hong Kong Island and the hills of Kowloon provide a dramatic backdrop to the Territory's crowded skyscrapers and tenements, while vessels of every size criss-cross the harbour. At night, after a brief but vivid sunset, Hong Kong is illuminated by neon signs and the lights of waterside office buildings. No wonder an office with a harbour view is a much envied senior management perk.

Huge variations of character make Hong Kong seem much larger than it really is. The total land area is only 410 sq miles/1,060 sq km which includes scores of islands and large areas of unpopulated national park. The majority of the 5.6m population live in the 45 sq miles/115 sq km which make up Hong Kong Island and Kowloon.

Anywhere else Hong Kong's combination of population density and high-rise living could be a recipe for social disaster. Not so here: it may be claustrophobic, but its spirit is irresistible – a patchwork of Chinese and Western culture where colourful street markets live cheek by jowl with sophisticated department stores, and squatter huts co-exist on the same hillside with luxurious condominiums.

Hong Kong is largely peopled by immigrants and refugees from the postwar upheavals that ultimately led to the triumph of Communism in China. Whether out of necessity or choice, everyone is interested in seizing every legitimate opportunity for improving his fortunes – hence the vibrant, ever-busy atmosphere of the place. Factories work around the clock; 60-floor buildings are erected in less than 18 months; shops remain open as long as there are customers to buy; office workers think nothing of working a 12-hour day if it means a bigger year-end bonus; and Hong Kong has yet to discover the five-day week. Nothing stops Hong Kong from working except the Chinese New Year Holiday and the occasional very severe typhoon.

Arriving

Nearly all visitors arrive by air. Kai Tak airport serves about 30 airlines; many flights from Europe and the USA are daily. Plans to build a second airport have been discussed for years.

Kai Tak International Airport
Kai Tak is in Kowloon 3½ miles/6km northeast of Central district (on Hong Kong Island). The single terminal is fairly drab. Bottlenecks often occur at immigration, although Western visitors are rarely subjected to more than a swift random baggage check; allow 60min to clear the airport. Departing passengers have to pay HK$100 airport tax. Until the system is computerized be prepared for long lines at emigration. Jardine Airways operates an early check-in desk for British Airways passengers. Armed with your passport, ticket and bags, a messenger can obtain a boarding pass in advance and cut out some of the waiting.
Facilities Coffee shops open at 7am, restaurants later; they remain open until the last flights (11pm landside, midnight airside). They are very basic and passengers with time to

spare should take the elevator to the Regal Meridien Airport hotel three floors above. Foreign exchange desks, charging a hefty commission, are in the corridor beyond customs, between exits 6 and 7, and 1 and 2. The Hong Kong Hotels Association has an efficient reservation desk between exits 2 and 3. Airport shops open at 7am. Buying liquor, tobacco and perfume will save the minimal duty Hong Kong imposes. All other goods are cheaper downtown. There are VIP lounges both landside and airside. They have no business services although Cathay Pacific can provide basic secretarial support. IDD calls can be made airside (7am–11pm) and landside (8am–12pm). There are mail facilities both sides.

Airlines tend to charge for all excess baggage, but *Unaccompanied Baggage* ☎ 3-7698275 can usually arrange for your baggage to be on the following flight. Couriers at the airport include *Air Couriers* ☎ 3-822026, DPE ☎ 3-835028. Inquiries ☎ 3-7697531.

City link You may have to wait for a taxi, so if time is tight, take the precaution of arranging hotel transport in advance. Take exit 1 for taxis and buses, exits 2 or 3 for hotel transport. Hong Kong's roads are always congested, especially the Cross Harbour Tunnel and its approach roads. Allow 30min to Causeway Bay, 40min to Central and 15min to Tsim Sha Tsui, plus an extra 20min in rush hours (8–9.30am and 4.30–6pm).

Hotel transport is comfortable and avoids the occasional long lines for taxis and buses. Transport should be arranged in advance with the hotel and ranges from Rolls Royce to minibus.

Taxi Cabs are favoured by most visitors, though you may have to wait for 15–30min. Typical fares are HK\$30 to Tsim Sha Tsui, HK\$55 to Causeway Bay and HK\$60 to Central, plus HK\$2 per item of baggage. The latter two fares include the HK\$20 tunnel toll (you pay for

the driver's return toll fee).

Bus Buses are reasonably convenient if you do not have too much baggage. Route A1 serves Tsim Sha Tsui hotels (HK\$6); route A2 serves Central (HK\$8); and route A3 Causeway Bay (HK\$8). Pay the exact fare on entry. Departures are every 15min, 7am–11pm.

Getting around

Taxis are plentiful and cheap and the subway system is a model of cleanliness and efficiency. Roads are congested during the 8–9.30 and 4.30–6 rush hours. The Cross Harbour Tunnel approach roads are particularly slow-moving at these times.

Hotel transport All the main hotels have limousines with English and Japanese speaking drivers at around HK\$150 an hour.

Taxi Taxis are often scarce between 5.30–6.00pm, at Saturday lunch time and during heavy rain. Waiting arrangements are usually chaotic, so walk to the nearest hotel where doormen ensure that the lines are orderly. Alternatively, call one of the many cabs listed in the *Yellow Pages*. All taxis are air-conditioned.

At all other times it is easy to get a taxi and they operate day and night all over the Territory. Hail them anywhere except in streets marked with yellow lines. A vertical red flag on the passenger side of the windscreen indicates the taxi is for hire: at night a lit sign on the roof indicates the same thing. Some drivers cover their flag with a red card with Chinese characters; if you are Hong Kong-side this means they are going to Kowloon (and vice versa). Only hail them if you are going their way.

Apart from major hotels and office buildings, taxi drivers do not always know their way around and this is exacerbated by language differences. Ask hotel staff to write down the Chinese characters for your destination. Fares are cheap; Causeway Bay to Central costs about

HK$13; Kowloon is about HK$50. If you cross between Hong Kong Island and Kowloon you usually have to pay the cost of the tunnel toll both ways.
Driving Traffic drives on the left, drivers are often unpredictable, parking is difficult and roads are congested. Car rental is available from *Avis* ☎ 5-8906988 and *National* ☎ 3-7399162, but is expensive. *Avis* also has Mercedes limousines.
Walking Walking can be delightful in winter. Maps are plentiful, and distances within (though not between) districts are short. The police are becoming stricter about jay walking: never cross main roads at points other than designated crossings. In summer, no one walks far because of the heat and humidity.
Bus and tram Cheap, hot, crowded, prone to break down but worth trying once for fun.
Ferry The Star Ferry, with its two-decker green and white craft, operates between the southern end of Kowloon and Central, and is a spectacular way to cross the harbour. First-class seats on the upper deck cost only HK$1; the journey takes 10min. Departures every 3min, 6.30am–11.30pm.
Subway For short journeys between Causeway Bay and Central, and across the harbour, the Mass Transit Railway (MTR) is faster and cheaper than taxi. Trains are clean and frequent, operating 6am–midnight. Services to Kowloon go from Admiralty or Central.

Area by area

Hong Kong consists of three distinct areas. The two most important are *Hong Kong Island*, the business hub of the Territory, and *Kowloon*, a densely developed area of light industry and housing estates. The harbour separates the two; locals talk of "going Hong Kong-side" or "Kowloon-side." Hong Kong-side is affluent, service-oriented and cosmopolitan – most expatriates live here. Kowloon-side is predominantly Chinese, has most of the poverty, and

is the manufacturing centre. Not all of the Territory is built up; partly because of the steepness of the hills, large areas of the island and mainland are undeveloped and designated as national parks. Hong Kong Island is abruptly hilly in the middle; nearly all development is around the edge.

The remaining area is known collectively as the *New Territories*: it includes the rural mainland north of Kowloon up to the Chinese border as well as the outlying islands, some of which are arid and unpopulated while others serve a variety of purposes, including prisons, drug rehabilitation centres, and weekend hiking and water sports resorts.

All addresses in this guide which are not specified as being in Kowloon are for locations on Hong Kong Island.

Hong Kong Island

Central Hong Kong's prime business area is tightly concentrated into the Central district, bounded by Exchange Square to the west and Murray Road to the east. Many of the skyscrapers are huge – some are over 60 floors high – yet parts of Central feel airy and open.

Key landmarks surrounding Statue Square are the Hong Kong Club and the headquarters of the Hongkong and Shanghai Banking Corporation, the controversial but undoubtedly impressive design (likened by critics to a land-locked oil rig) of Norman Foster.

In front of these is the former Supreme Court, one of the very few remaining colonial-style buildings in Hong Kong; it is now used for meeting of the Legislative Council, Hong Kong's ruling body. West of Statue Square is The Landmark, which has several floors of high-class shops built around an atrium. It is also the headquarters of the Hong Kong Land Company, owner of much of the prestige commercial property in Hong Kong. The company also owns the Exchange Square development on the water

HONG KONG

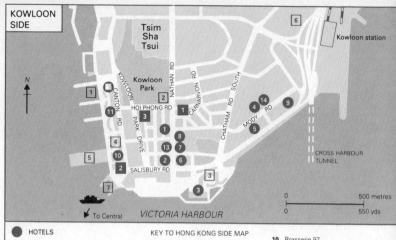

Tsim Sha Tsui

Kowloon station

N

Kowloon Park

HOI PHONG RD

SALISBURY RD

CROSS HARBOUR TUNNEL

To Central

VICTORIA HARBOUR

| 0 | | 500 metres |
| 0 | | 550 yds |

KEY TO HONG KONG SIDE MAP

HOTELS

1. Excelsior
2. Furama Inter-Continental
3. Hilton
4. Mandarin
5. Park Lane
6. Lee Gardens
7. Victoria

RESTAURANTS

Benkay's (building 25)
Bentley's (building 30)
Eagle's Nest (hotel 3)
Hilton Grill (hotel 3)
1. Landau's

Mandarin Grill (hotel 4)
Man Wah (hotel 4)
Pierrot (hotel 4)
Jade Garden (building 33)
2. Fook Lam Moon
3. Luk Yu Tea House
   Peking Garden (building 2 & hotel 1)
4. New American
5. Cleveland
6. Sze Chuan Lau
7. Pep'n Chilli
8. Red Pepper
   Rainbow (hotel 6)
   Maxim's Palace (building 34)
9. Camargue

10. Brasserie 97
11. California
12. Casa Mexicana
13. Jimmy's Kitchen
14. Rigoletto
    Brown's Wine Bar (building 12)

BUILDINGS AND SIGHTS

1. Admiralty Centre
2. Alexandra House
3. Arts Centre
5. Bank of America
6. Bank of China
7. Beaconsfield House
8. Central Government Offices

VICTORIA HARBOUR

CENTRAL

7 330 metres/ 360 yds

CONNAUGHT RD

DES VOEUX RD

QUEEN'S RD

STANLEY ST

PEDDER ST

CHATER RD

D'AGUILAR ST

WYNDHAM ST

N 1

To Kowloon

Statue Sq

Chater Garden

GARDEN RD

COTTON TREE DRIVE

Zoological and Botanical Gardens

| 0 | | 200 metres |
| 0 | | 220 yds |

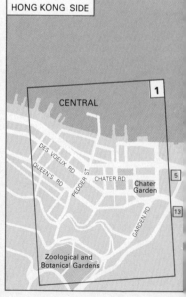

HONG KONG SIDE

CENTRAL

1

DES VOEUX RD

QUEEN'S RD

PEDDER ST

CHATER RD

Chater Garden

GARDEN RD

5

13

Zoological and Botanical Gardens

KEY TO KOWLOON SIDE MAP

HOTELS

1 Hyatt Regency
2 Peninsula
3 Regent
4 Royal Garden
5 Shangri-La
6 Sheraton
7 Ambassador
8 Holiday Inn
  Golden Mile
9 Holiday Inn
  Harbour View
10 Hong Kong
11 Kowloon
12 Marco Polo
13 Prince
14 Regal Meridien

RESTAURANTS

1 Au Trou Normand
  Belvedere (hotel 9)
  Chesa (hotel 2)
  Gaddi's (hotel 2)
  Hugo's (hotel 1)
  Lalique (hotel 4)
  Margaux (hotel 5)
  Plume (hotel 3)
  Verandah Grill (hotel 2)
2 Jade Garden
  Spring Moon (hotel 2)
3 Jimmy's Kitchen
  Baron's Table (hotel 8)

BUILDINGS AND SIGHTS

1 Ocean Galleries
2 Kowloon Mosque
3 New World Centre
4 Ocean Centre
5 Ocean Terminal
6 Polytechnic
7 Star Ferry Terminal

9 City Hall
10 Jardine House
11 Edinburgh Tower
12 Exchange Square
13 Flagstaff House Museum
14 Gloucester Building
15 Government House
16 Great Eagle Centre
17 Happy Valley Racecourse
18 Harbour Centre
19 Hennessy Centre
20 Hong Kong Academy for Performing Arts
21 Hong Kong Exhibition Centre

22 Hong Kong & Shanghai Banking Corporation
23 Hopewell Centre
24 Hutchison House
25 Landmark
26 Legislative Council Building
27 Outlying Islands Ferry Terminal
28 Peak Tram Terminal
29 Post Office
30 Prince's Building
31 Queensway Plaza
32 Star Ferry Terminal
33 Swire House
34 World Trade Centre

front. The Square has attracted major multinationals and houses the Hong Kong Stock Exchange.

Adjacent is Jardine House, headquarters of the oldest of the foreign trading firms and virtual founder of modern Hong Kong – Jardine Matheson. Below it is the Star Ferry Terminal and, farther west, the City Hall, a venue for orchestral concerts.

Hong Kong's tallest building is the new headquarters of the Bank of China on Cotton Tree Drive, to the east of Central. This massive structure, designed by I M Pei, is seen by many as symbolic of China's intention to dominate the territory after 1997. Another recent (and controversial) addition to the Hong Kong skyline is the Bond Centre which lies between Central and Wanchai.

The Mid-levels and the Peak
Immediately above Central, on the Mid-levels and the Peak (the hill which rises immediately south of Central), are to be found the houses of many of Hong Kong's expatriates and senior civil servants. As a general rule, the top people (including the chief executive of the Hongkong and Shanghai Banking Corporation) live on the Peak in houses set in their own well-tended gardens, while those who do not yet have a seat on the company board live in Mid-levels condominiums. However, the governor's residence is in Upper Albert Road, in the Mid-levels.

Wanchai East of Central is the district of Wanchai. By day it is an area of small thriving businesses; at night neon lights and girlie bars come into their own.

Causeway Bay Farther east still is Causeway Bay and the entrance to the Cross Harbour Tunnel. The opening of the tunnel in 1973 did much to stimulate the development of this area, which now has the most prestigious office accommodation outside Central. The waterfront is dominated by the World Trade Centre and the Excelsior hotel.

Behind is an area of shopping arcades and several of the island's best department stores. The area is very crowded at weekends when thousands of Chinese cross the harbour by subway to window-shop. Inland is the district of Happy Valley, best known for its racecourse.

Victoria Park and Quarry Bay
East of Causeway Bay is Victoria Park, a favourite early morning exercise and recreation area for the local population where the young jog and practise aerobics, while the older generation practise *Tai Chi.*

Continuing east is the Quarry Bay district, where many of Hong Kong's leading publishers and printers are based. The newly-built Tai Koo Shing housing development, much favoured by young affluent Chinese families, is here. Quarry Bay is linked to Central by a spectacular elevated highway.

The Western District A colourful concentration of Chinese stalls and shops lines a network of steep streets leading off Queen's Road West. Farther west are the busy ferry terminals serving Macau and the outlying islands. After dark the terminal car park is transformed into the "poor man's nightclub," a large number of stalls specializing in fresh seafood.

At the westernmost part of the island lie the wharfs and warehouses where much of Hong Kong's imported foodstuffs are unloaded from lighters which shuttle to and from ships berthed in the harbour.

A little way inland are the red-brick buildings of Hong Kong University and another Western enclave called Pok Fu Lam, home to mostly British university lecturers.

The south Before the opening of the Aberdeen Tunnel, the south of the Island was accessible only to those who could afford a car and were prepared to drive an hour or more to work. Long-term residents speak of the area's former tranquillity. Today it is the Island's weekend playground; beaches are very crowded, the air is tainted by the smell of hundreds of beach barbecues.

Visitor attractions include Aberdeen Harbour with its hundreds of fishing junks and floating restaurants and Stanley Market, in which factory seconds can be purchased at rock-bottom prices.

Kowloon

Tsim Sha Tsui, at the southern tip of the Kowloon peninsula, is the area most shoppers aim for, and it is the site of most of the tourist hotels. At its southernmost point are both the Star Ferry Terminal, carrying passengers across the harbour, and the Ocean Terminal where cruise liners berth.

The vast Harbour City shopping plaza holds well over 6,000 shops. At weekends it is noisy and crowded because the locals enjoy its air-conditioned malls as an escape from the heat and claustrophobia of their own tiny homes.

Nathan Road, running parallel to Harbour City, is lined with even more shops, malls and plazas. Nicknamed "The Golden Mile," this area is at its best after dark when you can stand and enjoy the dazzling display of neon signs.

Kowloon suburbs The rest of Kowloon is a flat area of high-density housing and factories in which most of the Chinese population of Hong Kong live and work.

Hotels

Hong Kong attracts over 5.6m visitors a year and the better hotels are nearly always full in October and November. It is essential to reserve, preferably at least one month in advance.

Despite this, hotel managers are not complacent and standards are very high. Most business travellers favour a hotel on the Island in order to be close to the business district. The Mandarin receives the most plaudits but the best Kowloon-side hotels, such as the Regent, Peninsula and Shangri-La are not, by any measure, less good. The major Kowloon-side hotels are all in the Tsim Sha Tsui district of Kowloon and within a short walk of the MTR station and the Star Ferry terminal, so it is no more than a 20min journey from Central.

All rooms have air conditioning, 24hr room service, IDD telephone, TV, radio and minibar. Standard business facilities in almost every case include photocopying, typing, telex, fax and translation. All hotels have limousines for hire. A service charge of 10% and 5% tax are additional to quoted rates.

Excelsior $$$$$
281 Gloucester Rd, Causeway Bay
☎ *8948888* ™ *74550 Fax 5-8956459*
• *Mandarin Oriental Group* • AE DC
MC V • *923 rooms, 30 suites,*
4 restaurants, 3 bars
Though not the most luxurious hotel in Hong Kong, the Excelsior has a loyal clientele among business travellers and has recently been refurbished. It is a favoured lunch and after-hours resort for the surrounding offices and is also used by upmarket Japanese and US tour operators. Although not in the same class as other hotels in the Mandarin Oriental group rooms are spacious and used by many visitors as an operational base, and there is a fully equipped business centre where service is excellent. The restaurants make the best of the harbour view. Shops, florist, hairdresser, disco • tennis courts • typewriter rental, 4 meeting rooms (capacity up to 450).

Furama Inter-Continental $$$$$
1 Connaught Rd, Central ☎ *5-255111*
TX *73081 Fax 5-8459339* • *AE DC MC*
V • *468 rooms, 55 suites, 5 restaurants,*
3 bars

The Furama used to be considered an also-ran among Hong Kong's top hotels. Its external design is undoubtedly somewhat dated, but internally it is much improved following refurbishment and hosts major events such as the All Asia Antique Fair. It is five minutes' walk from the heart of Central and overlooks the tropical greenery of Chater Gardens. Most rooms have uninterrupted views of the harbour or the Peak. La Ronda restaurant has panoramic night views and is much used for working lunches by local companies. Shops, florist, hairdresser, nightclub • sauna, jacuzzi, massage • typewriter rental, library, 14 meeting rooms.

Hilton $$$$$
2 Queen's Rd, Central ☎ *5-233111*
TX *73355 Fax 5-8452590* • *AE DC MC*
V • *663 rooms, 87 suites, 8 restaurants,*
3 bars

Thanks to its central position, the Hilton can be very busy during the day as its function rooms are much in demand for press conferences, fashion shows and meetings of the local chambers of commerce. Nevertheless its opulence and genuinely helpful staff make it popular with affluent tourists as well as business travellers. Rooms on any of the five executive floors are more gracious and enjoy better views, staff on call to make appointments and reservations, use of the executive lounges, and proximity to the business centre. The Eagle's Nest (Chinese) and Hilton Grill (see *Restaurants*) are two of Hong Kong's best restaurants, and the poolside restaurant is ideal for informal rendezvous with colleagues. Shops, florist, nightclub • pool, sauna, jacuzzi, massage, gym, tennis • personal computer and typewriter rental, library, 11 meeting rooms.

Hyatt Regency $$$$$
67 Nathan Rd, Kowloon ☎ *3-662321*
TX *43127 Fax 3-7398701* • *AE DC MC*
V • *706 rooms, 17 suites, 4 restaurants,*
2 bars

The Hyatt Regency is one of the few good hotels in Kowloon not situated on the waterfront, although it is not too far from the MTR station or the Star Ferry terminal. It compensates for the absence of harbour views by focusing the eye inward, on the interiors reminiscent of Japanese country inns – screens, panels and well-chosen furniture. Shops, nightclub • 3 meeting rooms.

Mandarin Oriental $$$$$
5 Connaught Rd, Central ☎ *5220111*
TX *HX 73653 Fax 5-297978* • *AE DC*
MC V • *489 rooms, 58 suites,*
5 restaurants, 4 bars

Year in, year out, business travellers elect the Mandarin as one of the world's top three hotels. It is an unassuming building, at the heart of, and a part of, Hong Kong's financial centre. The main reason the hotel earns its praise is for its VIP-style service towards all its guests. Those who have stayed once are never forgotten and always greeted by name, and likes and dislikes are recorded for future reference. The best rooms are very comfortable, with original works of art and individual furnishings. Lunching at the Mandarin Grill (see *Restaurants*) on any weekday will be several of Hong Kong's leading chief executives; its coffee shop is much used for business breakfasts. The rooftop pool used to be a water storage tank and is now a superb colonnaded Roman-style bath. Shops, florist, hairdresser, nightclub • pool, sauna, jacuzzi, massage, gym • typewriter rental, library, 11 meeting rooms.

Park Lane Radisson $$$$
310 Gloucester Rd, Causeway Bay
☎ *5-8903355* TX *75343 Fax 5-767853*
• *AE DC MC V* • *825 rooms, 25 suites,*
3 restaurants, 3 bars

A busy hotel, popular with tourists, and working hard to attract more business travellers. Its decor is predominantly golden and rose-coloured and marble, and its rooms are well furnished. The lounge bar opens directly onto the noisy public areas but the Gallery Bar is more relaxing and the rooftop Park 27 restaurant overlooks Victoria Park. Shops, florist, hairdresser, disco • sauna, gym • computer and typewriter rental, 7 meeting rooms.

Peninsula $$$$$
Salisbury Rd, Kowloon ☎ *3-666251*
TX *43821 Fax 3-7224170* • *AE DC MC V* • *188 rooms, 22 suites, 7 restaurants, 2 bars*
Hong Kong's oldest hotel, built in the late 1920s, is one of the few colonial-style buildings left in Hong Kong, redolent of an age of ocean transport and gracious living. Service is excellent and the hotel has fewer rooms by far than any other major hotel in the Territory. Tourists visit just to admire the magnificently gilded ceiling. Past failings of the hotel have been remedied at great cost, and the refurbished rooms have rich European-style furnishings and US-style walk-in showers. Although the Peninsula is less well-equipped in terms of facilities than its newer competitors, (there is no health club and business services are handled through the concierge), the hotel has three of Hong Kong's best restaurants (Gaddi's, Chesa and the Veranda – see *Restaurants*) as well as Japanese and Chinese restaurants much frequented by local TV and film personalities. Shops, florist, hairdresser • massage • 2 meeting rooms (capacity up to 30).

Regent $$$$$
18-24 Salisbury Rd, Kowloon ☎ *3-7211211* TX *37134 Fax 3-7394546* • *AE DC MC V* • *521 rooms, 81 suites, 4 restaurants, 2 bars*
The courtyard fountain, rich red granite and huge glass walls providing an uninterrupted view of the harbour, where junks sail almost right past the windows, all contribute to the Regent's atmosphere of opulence and tranquillity. It does not have the cachet of the Mandarin, but many, including the sporting and show-business personalities who stay here, rate it as good if not better. Rooms on the harbour side have sweeping views and balconies. Shops, nightclub • pool, sauna, jacuzzi, massage, gym • computer rental, 9 meeting rooms.

Royal Garden $$$$
69 Mody Rd, Kowloon ☎ *3-7215215* TX *39539 Fax 3-699976* • *AE DC MC V* • *389 rooms, 44 suites, 4 restaurants, 1 bar*
The Royal Garden is built around a spacious atrium dominated by a flowering plum tree, a Chinese symbol of health and fortune. This one flowers perpetually, but all the other greenery in the hanging gardens is real and there are plants and flowers in every room to continue the garden theme. A relaxing place to stay, popular with European tourists but with a wide range of business services. Shops, hairdresser, florist, shuttle service • gym, sauna, massage, jacuzzi • office equipment rental, 3 meeting rooms (capacity up to 180).

Kowloon Shangri-La $$$$$
64 Mody Rd, Kowloon ☎ *3-7212111* TX *36718 Fax 3-7238686* • *Westin Hotels* • *AE DC MC V* • *689 rooms, 30 suites, 5 restaurants, 3 bars*
A hotel which is spacious and elegant, big enough to exclude all sense of the busy shopping plazas which surround it. The Shangri-La has a fountain in the lobby, coffered ceilings and chandeliers, Italianate marble floors, wide staircases and large rooms with picture windows looking onto the harbour. Yet it is not impersonal and the staff are friendly and competent. Shops, florist • pool, sauna, jacuzzi, massage, gym • computer rental, 11 meeting rooms (capacity up to 750).

Sheraton $$$$$
20 Nathan Rd, Kowloon ☎ *3-691111*
℡ *45813 Fax 3-7398707 • AE DC MC
V • 874 rooms, 48 suites, 10 restaurants,
3 bars*

A busy, typical tourist hotel until you reach the 16th floor where there is a 122-room hotel within a hotel, the Sheraton Towers, reserved for business travellers, with its own separate check-in desk. Facilities include an executive lounge, with free refreshments available during the day. The business centre is open half-day on Sundays and public holidays, unlike those of most other hotels. For meals it is necessary to join the throng below but both the Grandstand Grill and Pink Giraffe restaurants, with touring cabaret stars, are priced to be exclusive. Shops, florist, hairdresser, nightclub • pool, sauna, massage, gym • typewriter rental, library, 6 meeting rooms (capacity up to 150) and ballroom (1,000).

OTHER HOTELS
Ambassador ($$$$) *26 Nathan
Rd/Middle Rd, Kowloon* ☎ *3-666321*
℡ *43840 Fax 3-690663 • AE DC MC V.*
Grand Hyatt ($$$$$)
1 Harbour Rd, Wanchai ☎ *5-8611234*
℡ *68434 Fax 5-8611677. AE DC MC V.*
Holiday Inn, Golden Mile ($$$)
49-52 Nathan Rd, Kowloon
☎ *3-693111* ℡ *56332 Fax 3-698016
• AE DC MC V.*
**Holiday Inn, Harbour View
($$$$$)** *70 Mody Rd, Kowloon*
☎ *3-7215161* ℡ *38670 Fax 3-695672
AE DC MC V.*
Hong Kong Marriott ($$$$$)
Pacific Place, 88 Queensway, Wanchai
☎ *5-8108366* ℡ *66899
Fax 5-8450737 • AE DC MC V.*
Omni Hong Kong ($$) *3 Canton
Rd, Kowloon* ☎ *3-676011* ℡ *43838
Fax 3-7234850 • AE DC MC V.*
Omni Marco Polo ($$$) *Harbour
City, Canton Rd, Kowloon*
☎ *3-7215111* ℡ *40077
Fax 3-7217049 • AE DC MC V.*
Omni Prince ($$) *Harbour City,
Canton Rd, Kowloon* ☎ *3-7237788*

℡ *50950 Fax 3-7215545 • AE DC MC V.*
Kowloon ($$) *19 Nathan Rd,
Kowloon* ☎ *3-698698* ℡ *47604 Fax
3-698698 • AE DC MC V.*
Lee Gardens ($$$$) *Hysan Ave,
Causeway Bay,* ☎ *5-8953311*
℡ *75601 Fax 5-769775 • AE DC MC V.*
New World Harbour View ($$$$)
1 Harbour Rd, Wanchai ☎ *5-8662288*
℡ *68967 Fax 5-8663388 • AE DC MC
V.*
Nikko Hong Kong ($$$$$) *72
Mody Rd, Kowloon* ☎ *3-7391111*
℡ *31302 Fax 3-3113122 • AE DC MC
V.*
Regal Meridien ($$$$) *71 Mody
Rd, Kowloon* ☎ *3-7221818* ℡ *40955
Fax 3-7236413 • AE DC MC V.*
Victoria ($$$$$) *Shun Tak Centre,
200 Connaught Rd, Central*
☎ *5-407228* ℡ *86608 Fax 5-8583398
• AE DC MC V.*

Clubs

Clubs are a significant part of expatriate life in Hong Kong, and visitors are almost certain to be invited to one.

Foreign Correspondents' Club, 2 Lower Albert Rd, North Block, Central ☎ 5-211511. This is the same club (though not in the same building) that features in John Le Carré's novel, *The Honourable Schoolboy*. It was a famous meeting place for journalists and photographers during the Vietnam War and some of their haunting pictures are hung around the bar walls. This is the liveliest, least formal club in Hong Kong.

Hong Kong Club ☎ 5-258251. Overlooking Statue Square in Central this is the oldest and most exclusive club in town. The modernity of the new club building, with its huge floor-to-ceiling windows and spectacular views, belies the strong conservatism of its members, who include many of Hong Kong's ruling businessmen and administrators. Men and single women only may apply for membership. Dress code is formal.

Royal Hong Kong Jockey Club ☎ 5-8378111. With premises at the

Happy Valley Racecourse, this club has the most Chinese members and two of the best club restaurants in Hong Kong, the Derby Room (Continental cuisine) and the Fortune Room (Chinese). Dress code is formal.
Royal Hong Kong Yacht Club ☎ 5-8322817. Opposite the Excelsior Hotel in Causeway Bay. Most members are boat owners and the atmosphere is lively and informal.

Other clubs The *American Club* at the top of Exchange Square ☎ 5-8427400 is relaxed and commands aerial views of the harbour. The *Ladies Recreation Club*, Old Peak Rd ☎ 5-220151, the *Tennis Club*, in the Excelsior Hotel ☎ 5-767365 ext 401, and the *Football Club* in Happy Valley ☎ 5-762808 are all friendly and easy-going. Popular at weekends with family groups.

Restaurants
Chinese and expatriates are very hospitable, and discussing business over a meal is one of Hong Kong's most civilized practices. Working lunches are usual and dining out in the evening is looked upon by many as an extension of business – a reward for a hard day's work, or a means of getting to know better the people with whom you work.

Most ethnic restaurants are considered too noisy and informal for serious business entertaining. The expatriate community prefers the more tranquil atmosphere of hotel dining rooms – the Mandarin and Hilton grills at lunch time and Gaddi's at the Peninsula in the evening. Chinese executives tend to choose a top-class Chinese restaurant, but will just as happily eat Western food.

Many hotels now serve fixed-price lunches, thus competing with those independent restaurants which used to fill the gap between the luxury end of the market and the ethnic.

Reservations are advisable for all the restaurants listed.

Au Trou Normand $$$
6 Carnavon Rd, Kowloon ☎ *3-668754*
• *AE DC MC V*
Tucked away in a side street off the Nathan Road, this is a popular business restaurant with true French provincial character. Tables are arranged around a large farmhouse-style fireplace, and the food is authentic *cuisine bourgeoise*. Excellent cheeseboard and an extensive French wine list.

Belvedere $$$
Holiday Inn Harbour View
☎ *3-7215161* • *AE DC MC V*
Not the finest harbour view in Hong Kong, but the culinary standards are extremely high. The menu frequently features the work of a visiting chef.

In addition there is an extensive buffet of smoked salmon, oysters, lobster and king prawns, and champagne by the glass.

Benkay's $$$
1st Basement, Gloucester Tower, The Landmark, Des Voeux Rd, Central
☎ *5-213344* • *AE DC MC V*
The older generation of businessmen and the Japanese themselves come here for Japanese food in a traditional environment. Waitresses in kimonos provide impeccable service, and if you want to discuss business secluded booths are available as an alternative to the more public tables. The food is prepared in style by Japanese chefs from ingredients flown in fresh every day; the set menu is excellent value.

Bentley's $$$
B4, Basement, Prince's Bldg, Central
☎ *5-8680881* • *closed Sun* • *AE DC
MC V*
Bentley's is a branch of the London
oyster bar and differs little from its
British counterpart; the mahogany
and marble dining room with high-
backed booths would not be out of
place in London, nor would the
clientele. Fish is cooked according to
the menu suggestions or to your own
choice. The Oyster Bar serves
shellfish and other seafood.

Chesa $$$
Peninsula Hotel ☎ *3-666251* • *AE DC
MC V* • *jacket and tie*
A rustic Swiss inn, complete with
antique clocks, pewter and painted
chests. There are no windows, which
makes the passage of time difficult to
detect, and executives are often seen
still deep in conversation well into
the afternoon. The Swiss menu
includes a selection of regional dishes
that is changed monthly.

Eagle's Nest $$$
Hilton Hotel ☎ *5-233111* • *AE DC
MC V*
A good choice for entertaining guests
who enjoy top-flight Chinese food.
The restaurant is on the rooftop of
the hotel with views on three sides
and has not long been refurbished in
unostentatious lavender and grey
with white marble walls. The food is
classic Cantonese and northern
Chinese, imaginatively presented.
There is plenty of space between
tables and two private rooms each of
which seats 12.

Gaddi's $$$$
Peninsula Hotel ☎ *3-666251* • *AE DC
MC V* • *jacket and tie*
Gaddi's, considered alongside the
Mandarin Grill and the Plume as one
of Hong Kong's top three
restaurants, has the decorative
elegance of a 19thC salon, with huge
Parisian chandeliers and silverware
which was rescued from the
company's hotel in Shanghai. The

impeccable *maître d'hôtel*, Rolf
Heiniger, knows a great deal about
Hong Kong and its top people, many
of whom dine here frequently. The
menu changes seasonally, but
regulars expect and find their old
favourites, which include liver terrine
with elderberry jelly, oyster soup,
and quail breasts on spinach and wild
rice. All but the host are given
unpriced menus. Gaddi's also serves
an excellent value three-course lunch.
The wine list includes some *premiers
crus* Bordeaux.

Hilton Grill $$$
Hilton Hotel ☎ *5-233111* • *closed Sun
L* • *AE DC MC V* • *jacket and tie*
The decor is unexceptional but the
waiters treat regulars with special
deference and there is plenty of space
for private conversation. The Grill is
at its best when, as frequently
happens, the hotel flies in a well-
known Continental chef to add
variety to an otherwise standard
menu of international fare. Well-
chosen wine list, mainly French and
Californian.

Lalique $$$$$
Royal Garden Hotel ☎ *3-7215215* •
AE DC MC V • *closed Sun L*
The most distinctive decor of any
Hong Kong hotel restaurant: a series
of etched and cut-glass Art Deco
panels of female nudes. They were
designed by René Lalique, after
whom the restaurant is named. The
surroundings provide privacy and
interest, and attract a predominantly
young business clientele. The menu
concentrates on French food and the
plate of *hors d'oeuvres* is almost a meal
in itself. Good value fixed-price lunch.

Landau's $$$
*2/7 Sun Hung Kai Centre, 30 Harbour
Rd, Wanchai* ☎ *5-8912901* • *AE DC
MC V*
Part of the Jimmy's Kitchen chain,
the restaurant was established in 1928
and although it did not move to this
site until 1976, the dark wood
interior and photographs of old Hong

Kong are a reminder of the prewar era. Landau's is very popular with executives from nearby offices and has the widest, most eclectic menu of any in Hong Kong with daily specials as well. The main courses range from light seafood salads to substantial middle European dishes.

Mandarin Grill $$$$
Mandarin Hotel ☎ *5-220111* • *AE DC MC V* • *jacket and tie*
The only place in Hong Kong for top-level talks with the scions of Hong Kong's business world who make it their daily retreat. The service is unobtrusive and the menu represents the best obtainable ingredients from around the world. Specials of the day are wheeled to the table and cooked to your choice. *Flambé* dishes are a speciality. Extensive wine list.

Man Wah $$$
Mandarin Hotel ☎ *5-220111* • *AE DC MC V* • *jacket and tie*
The Chinese equivalent of the hotel's grill, with penthouse views. The seasonal menu often features dishes from the court of the Chinese emperors. A good choice for entertaining senior Chinese businessmen.

Margaux $$$
Shangri-La Hotel ☎ *3-7212111* • *AE DC MC V* • *jacket and tie*
The decor is sparse apart for the reproductions of French impressionist paintings with a culinary theme, but the cooking is far from plain; it combines French technique with Asian ingredients to produce dishes like birds nest and pigeon soup or local fish with spinach and oysters in filo pastry. The style of cuisine makes it popular with both Chinese and expatriate executives.

Pierrot $$$$
Mandarin Hotel ☎ *5-220111* • *AE DC MC V* • *jacket and tie*
Pierrot has large well-spaced tables

and a luxurious red and gold decor as the setting for a meal of classical French cuisine. The comprehensive menu includes unusual and rich soups and soufflés, and the freshest top quality meat and fish. Pierrot also has the best visiting chefs of any Hong Kong restaurant, bringing their own individual or regional contributions to the menu.

Plume $$$$
Regent Hotel ☎ *3-7211211* • *AE DC MC V* • *smart dress*
The Plume vies with the Mandarin and Gaddi's for the position of Hong Kong's most exclusive restaurant. The decor is plain but diners have an uninterrupted view of Hong Kong Island, and the food, described as original creations based on French cuisine, is skilfully prepared and attractively presented.

Verandah Grill $$$
Peninsula Hotel ☎ *3-666251* • *AE DC MC V*
The dome of the space museum has destroyed what was once a fine view, but the bevelled glass panels which separate the tables are a guarantee of privacy and beautiful at night when they reflect candlelight. Among the restaurant's many strengths are the lamb and the seafood, the latter piled in abundance on a bed of ice. Very good value set lunch, and an extensive international wine list.

Good but casual
Chinese Visitors can virtually pick any Cantonese restaurant at random and be assured of good cooking at reasonable prices. The *Jade Garden* chain with branches in Swire House, Central ☎ 5-263031 and Star House, Kowloon ☎ 3-7306888 are always reliable; *Fook Lam Moon,* 35 Johnston Rd, Wanchai ☎ 5-8660663 is an expatriate favourite, and the *Luk Yu Tea House,* 24 Stanley St, Central ☎ 5-235464 is an oasis of old-world charm and manners.

For Beijing duck, the best restaurants in the *Peking Garden* chain are in the basement of Alexandra House, Central ☎ 5-266456; and the Excelsior hotel shopping centre; or try the confusingly named but excellent *New American Restaurant*, 179 Wanchai Rd, Wanchai ☎ 5-750458.

Szechuen food is best at the *Cleveland*, 6 Cleveland St, Causeway Bay ☎ 5-763876 or *Sze Chuen Lau*, 466 Lockhart Rd, Causeway Bay ☎ 5-8919027, but expatriates also like the more Westernized ambience of *Pep'n Chilli*, 12-22 Blue Pool Rd, Happy Valley ☎ 5-738251, and the *Red Pepper*, 7 Lan Fong Rd, Causeway Bay ☎ 5-768046.

The best and the greatest variety of *dim sum* in Hong Kong is served at the *Rainbow*, Lee Gardens Hotel ☎ 5-8953311, and the *Spring Moon*, Peninsula Hotel ☎ 3-666251. For the authentic bustling atmosphere of a 2,000-seater *dim sum* hall try *Maxim's Palace* in the World Trade Centre, Causeway Bay ☎ 5-760288.

Western Three restaurants in the Lan Kwai Fong area of Central are popular with a younger set. *Camargue*, 24/7 Regent Centre, 88 Queen's Rd, Central ☎ 5-257997 must be Hong Kong's smallest restaurant and has a French café ambience; its food is good and simple, and wines are reasonably priced. A HK$300 membership fee is charged. *Brasserie 97*, 9 Lan Kwai Fong, Central ☎ 5-8109333 is another small restaurant with unpretentious food; service is friendly but can be slow. There are non-stop pop videos at the *California*, 30–32 D'Aguilar St, Central 5-211345, an excellent US West-coast style restaurant. Steer well clear of the cocktail bar and disco if you want to talk in the evening.

Handily located close to Citibank, *Casa Mexicana*, Ground Floor, Victoria Centre, 15 Watson Rd, Causeway Bay East ☎ 5-665560, has an extensive Mexican menu. *Jimmy's Kitchen*, 1–3 Wyndham St, Central ☎ 5-265293 and 1st Fl, Kowloon Centre, 23–39 Ashley Rd, Kowloon

☎ 3-684027, is run by the same family who opened the first of the restaurants in 1928 to provide "wholesome, home-style cooking" for the Royal Navy. The menu has something for most tastes; the restaurant in Central is home from home for British expatriates with its mock-Tudor beams, while the Kowloon branch has a lighter, colonial style. For a good choice of German regional dishes, try the *Baron's Table*, Holiday Inn Golden Mile ☎ 3-693111. *Rigoletto*, 16 Fenwick St, Wanchai ☎ 5-277144 attracts most of its custom from nearby offices, plus a few devotees of authentic Italian food from farther away; the wine list includes some good Italian wines. The Verdi opera after which the restaurant is named provides the theme for the decor.

All these *Good but casual* restaurants fit into the $$ or $$$ categories, and most accept credit cards.

Floating restaurants Many visitors regard a visit to the floating restaurants of Aberdeen as a must. Locals tolerate, rather than enjoy, a visit because of the tourist gimmickry, the high prices and food that is not always as fresh as downtown. There is not much to differentiate the *Jumbo Floating Restaurant* ☎ 5-539111 from the *Tai Pak Seafood Restaurant* ☎ 5-525112.

Breakfast Breakfast-time meetings are on the increase. The best venues are the *Coffee Shop* at the Mandarin and *Brown's Wine Bar*, 104–206 Exchange Sq, Tower 2, Central, ☎ 5-237003.

Out of town

Stanley's, 86 Stanley Main St ☎ 5-8138873 is a 30min drive on the south of the island and popular for its Mediterranean ambience. The top floor has a balcony overlooking the beach, and tables must be reserved well in advance.

The *Verandah* at the Repulse Bay hotel ☎ 5-8122722 is again on the south side of the island. The original hotel, built in 1920, was demolished in 1982, much to the dismay of expatriates for whom Pimms and cucumber sandwiches on the veranda was the perfect way to finish the weekend. Now it has been rebuilt in all its former glory including the Art Deco lamps and stained glass. *J.K's Restaurant on the Peak*, 2E Dairy Farm Shopping Centre, 100 Peak Rd ☎ 5-8497788 is a recent addition to the Jimmy's Kitchen group.

Bars

There are plenty of bars, but few with any real character. Many expatriates prefer to rendezvous at their club but hotel bars provide a degree of privacy, particularly the *Captain's Bar* at the Mandarin and the *Noon Gun Bar* at the Excelsior. *La Ronda* at the Furama Inter-Continental and *Revolving 66*, 62nd Fl, Hopewell Centre, 183 Queen's Rd East, Wanchai, both have commanding views. *Brown's*, 104-206, Exchange Sq, Tower 2, Central and *Le Tire Bouchon*, 9 Old Bailey St, Central, are wine bars that attract young professionals.

British-style pubs with imported beer are often crowded. The *Bull and Bear*, Hutchison House, 10 Harcourt Rd, Central, is a long-established expatriate watering-hole with plenty of oak beams (closed Sun); *Mad Dogs*, 33 Wyndham St, Central, is decorated with colonial memorabilia and has regular live folk music. *The Galley*, in the Connaught Centre, is a spit-and-sawdust pastiche with good bar food, and the *Dickens Bar* in the Excelsior hotel is a good place for relaxed drinking in Causeway Bay.

Schnurrbart, 13 Wing Wah Lane, Central and 6 Hart Ave, Kowloon, is popular for its German draught beers and wholesome bar food. Topless bars are seedy and rundown since their Vietnam War heyday. *Bottoms Up* (14-16 Hankow Road, Kowloon) is classier than most and featured in "The Man with the Golden Gun." *Red Lips*, Lock Rd, Kowloon, is Hong Kong's oldest girlie bar.

Expatriates take visitors there to show them how harmless the nightlife really is and how old some of the "hostesses" are.

Entertainment

Both the *South China Morning Post* and the *Hong Kong Standard* contain comprehensive daily listings of events, including dinner concerts organized by the major hotels, which cater to all tastes from opera to cabaret and are of international standard. The weekly *TV and Entertainment Times* contains both listings and reviews.

Theatre, dance, music The *City Hall*, Edinburgh Place, Central, is the main venue for Western and Chinese classical music. The resident Hong Kong Philharmonic Orchestra is competent but sometimes under-rehearsed because of its heavy programme. Concerts by visiting performers are quickly sold out. The box office ☎ 3-7349009 is open 10–8 and accepts credit card reservations. The *Arts Centre*, 2 Harbour Rd, Wanchai ☎ 5-8230230, is the main venue for modern and experimental dance, drama and art. The *Hong Kong Academy for Performing Arts*, 1 Gloucester Rd, Wanchai ☎ 5-8231500, mounts music, dance and drama productions as a showcase for home-grown talent, and performances by visiting artists.

Cinema Hong Kong's cinemas are clean, comfortable and air-conditioned. Those specializing in the latest general release English-language films are the *Palace Theatre* 280 Gloucester Rd (next to the Excelsior hotel) ☎ 5-8951500 and *Columbia Classics*, Great Eagle Centre, 23 Harbour Rd, Wanchai ☎ 5-738291. The *Arts Centre* (see above) has excellent film seasons showing the best of world cinema, with English and Chinese subtitles. The major events of the cultural year are the International Film Festival in April, and the Asian Arts Festival and the Arts Festival, both in October. These are often full weeks in advance but try *City Hall* box office ☎ 5-229928 (☎ 3-7349009 for telephone booking).

Discos usually attract a very young crowd. *Nineteen 97*, 9 Lang Kwai Fong, Central ☎ 5-260303 and *Disco Disco*, 38 D'Aguilar St, Central ☎ 5-248809 have the latest UK and US record and video releases.

Nightclubs proliferate both inside and outside hotels. *Talk of the Town* at the Excelsior hotel is popular. Reasonably priced Japanese-style hostess clubs with multilingual staff, good dance bands and spectacular decor include *China City*, Peninsula Centre, 67 Mody Rd, Kowloon ☎ 3-7230388; and *Club Deluxe*, New World Centre, Salisbury Rd, Kowloon ☎ 3-7210277.

Shopping

With no import duty, no sales tax and low shipment costs from manufacturing centres in Asia, shopping in Hong Kong is cheap. Remember that the best prices are reserved for cash buyers; credit-card purchasers will pay a premium of up to 8%. The Hong Kong Tourist Association's free booklet *The Official Guide to Shopping, Eating Out and Services in Hong Kong*, available in hotels, contains wise advice on bargaining, avoiding rip-offs, fakes and pirated goods, and gives the telephone numbers of all the official importers of cameras and electrical goods, so you can check out the official list price and the compatibility with systems back home. Bargaining is a practice which some tourists seem to enjoy, but it nearly always works in favour of the retailer. Very few shopkeepers are prepared to offer prices below the manufacturer's recommended retail price, and the first price offered is usually much higher. The best approach is to telephone the importer (see the above Tourist Association guide for telephone numbers), obtain the list price and use this as your guide. It probably won't be necessary to spend much time shopping around

for the best price, but make sure the price includes standard accessories if applicable.

Shop opening hours are 10–9 (10–6 in Central) but some shops stay open later. Busy travellers will probably not step outside of the hotel shopping arcades, where the prices are higher but the advice and help are reliable.

Harbour City, Canton Rd, Kowloon houses 600 shops. Here you will find *Charlotte Horstmann's* antique shop which dominates the Ocean Terminal entrance by the Star Ferry and has the best antique stock in Hong Kong. *Banyan Tree*, 304, Ocean Galleries, Harbour City, Canton Rd, Kowloon and 214–217 Prince's Bldg, Chater Rd, Central, is an Aladdin's cave of furnishings, fabrics arts and crafts from all over Asia. In between are scores of smaller antique shops whose stock consists largely of carved and painted snuff bottles, ivory, porcelain and jewellery. On Hong Kong Island, Hollywood Road has a dozen or more good antique shops. Leading off Hollywood Road, north and south, are steep, granite-paved streets known as The Ladders; they are lined with stalls selling a huge range of goods. At the western end of Hollywood Road, by the Man Mo Temple, is Cat Street, filled with bric-à-brac stalls selling genuine and fake antiques.

The best bet for inexpensive gifts are the mainland Chinese emporia which offer a vast range of goods at the same prices as in China. Silk, cashmere and table linen, jade, porcelain, cloisonné and carpets are all good buys.

The stores with the most upmarket stock are the *Chinese Merchandise Emporium*, 92–104 Queen's Rd, Central, *Chinese Arts and Crafts*, Star House, Kowloon (by the Star Ferry terminal) and *China Resources Artland Centre*, China Resources Bldg, 26 Harbour Rd, Wanchai.
Cameras and electronic goods
The greatest choice and concentration of shops are in Nathan

Rd, especially around the Silvercord Building, and behind the World Trade Centre in Causeway Bay. Reliable stores include *Wood's Photo Supplies*, 131A Ocean Centre, Harbour City, Kowloon and *Excel Hi Fi*, 269 Harbour City, Nathan Rd, Kowloon.

Clothes Hotel shopping arcades are best for Hong Kong's famous 24hr suits, though generally tailors like longer to do a proper job. The most exclusive, expensive and stylish shops are all to be found in the Prince's Building, Swire House and The Landmark in Central, all connected to each other by covered walkways. Apart from the many international designer names, *Jenny Lewis* in Swire House has distinctive evening wear based on antique Chinese designs. The newly opened *Marks and Spencer* store, Ocean Centre, Kowloon, has a wide range of clothes. The clothes market at Stanley is good for bargain price factory rejects.

Jewellery Of the many shops in the tourist areas selling gold, jade and pearls, knowledgeable and helpful service is found at *King Fook Gold and Jewellery*, 30–32 Des Voeux Rd, Central and *Trio Pearl* in the Peninsula hotel.

Sightseeing

Hong Kong is a sight in itself; the combination of mountains, buildings and water is remarkable, and the panoramas are constantly changing.

The Peak Hong Kong's most famous hill gives fine views and is easily accessible. If you have time, leave an hour before sunset, walk some of the way round to the Peak on the level Lugard Road and then enjoy the sight of Hong Kong lighting up, over a drink in the Peak Tower Restaurant. The Peak Tram runs from Garden Road to the top, daily every 10min, 7am–midnight.

Flagstaff House Museum of Teaware Housed in Hong Kong's only remaining mid-19thC Western-style building, this museum gives a fair idea of colonial life at that time,

and provides an insight into the Chinese character through an explanation of the rituals surrounding the tea ceremony. *Open daily exc Wed and public hols. Off Cotton Tree Drive.*

Outlying islands Several of the islands surrounding Hong Kong are easily accessible by ferry from the Outlying Islands Ferry Pier, Connaught Rd, Central (for information contact the *Hong Kong Tourist Association* ☎ 3-7225555 or the *Hong Kong Ferry Co.* ☎ 5-423081). Ferries depart at roughly hourly intervals and are very cheap; sailing time to both Lantau and Lamma is 35–40min.

Lantau is actually bigger than Hong Kong Island and has the cleanest beaches as well as a bus service to all parts of the island. *Lamma* has no public transport but has many meandering paths among tiny intensively farmed fields and terraces, as well as a number of village temples to explore. By the ferry piers on both islands are open-air restaurants serving freshly-caught fish at very reasonable prices.

Guided tours

The Hong Kong Tourist Association's *Sightseeing* guide describes tours that can easily be reserved at any hotel travel desk, either travelling with a group or an individual guide. The best standard trips are the half-day New Territories tour which leaves the 20th century firmly behind to visit farms, old walled villages and rural markets; the Aberdeen Harbour tour where fishing boats cram the typhoon shelter and traditional junks are still made; and the cruise to Lantau Island and the Po Lin Monastery. Hotel travel desks can usually arrange for the charter of a motorized junk with crew for up to 20 passengers, and the *Hilton*'s luxury brigantine is available for private charter. *Seaview Harbour Tours* ☎ 5-416026, *Watertours* ☎ 5-254808 and the *Hilton* organize inexpensive cruises.

Out of town

China Your hotel will be able to make a reservation on a day trip for around HK$450 which includes the journey by hovercraft or jetfoil to Macau, and then coach across the border. The itinerary usually includes a visit to the birthplace of Dr Sun Yat Sen (whose anti-imperialist movement toppled the Ching Dynasty and led to the birth of the Republic of China in 1911) as well as a "typical" farm, village and school. The tone of the tour is didactic, but most people find their first glimpse of the Chinese way of life unforgettable. Two-, three- and four-day tours taking in Guangzhou and the Pearl river delta or Guilin can also be arranged through hotels. Alternatively contact the *China Travel Service*, 77 Queens Rd, Central ☎ 5-8533888.

Macau For an escape from the bustle of Hong Kong spend a day, or better still a weekend, in Macau, 50 miles/80km away on the opposite side of the very wide Pearl river estuary. Lacking a deep-water harbour, Macau – the Portuguese equivalent of Hong Kong – never developed to the same degree and today is a fascinating mixture of pretty Baroque buildings and modern casinos which attract the gambling-mad Chinese in their thousands. If you plan to go at a weekend, be sure to reserve your jetfoil ticket by Wednesday afternoon.

Spectator sports

Golf, rugby, tennis attract international standard players and are used by companies as an opportunity to entertain important clients. Events include the Open Golf Championship (late Feb), the Seven-a-Side Rugby Invitation Sevens (late Mar), and the Super Tennis Classic (late Oct).

Horse-racing is Hong Kong's passion – the Chinese are inveterate gamblers and this is the only form of gambling legally allowed. Races are organized by the *Royal Hong Kong Jockey Club* and held alternately at

Shatin in the New Territories and *Happy Valley* on Hong Kong Island Sep–May, Wed evenings and Sat afternoons. Most companies have boxes at both courses and regularly use them for business entertainment. Visitors who have been in Hong Kong for less than 21 days gain admission to the members' enclosure by taking their passport to the Badge Inquiry Office at the entrance to the enclosure, or through a Hong Kong Tourist Association tour package which includes a meal and transport. Inquiries ☎ 5-8378111 (club) ☎ 3-7225555 (tourist office).

Keeping fit

The choice is effectively limited to the well-equipped health centres of your own hotel, as most other facilities are for members only. Business associates in Hong Kong may be willing to help; some expatriates live in apartment blocks with tennis or squash courts, and keen sailors often welcome an extra crew member for an evening or weekend sail.

Golf, squash, swimming, tennis The best golf courses are some way out from Central. Visitors can use the 9-hole course at Deepwater Bay on Hong Kong Island (30min by car) or the three 18-hole courses at Fanling in the New Territories (1hr by car; Mon–Fri only). Inquiries ☎ 0-6701211.

Visitors can use the *Clearwater Bay Golf and Country Club* with tennis, squash, golf, swimming (Tue and Fri) by joining one of the Hong Kong Tourist Association's Sports and Recreation Tours. Tour members are collected from their hotel around 8am and returned around 5.30pm (Tue and Fri only). Inquiries ☎ 5-244191.

Jogging Despite the heat and humidity, many people jog in Hong Kong. Hotels have jogging maps of favoured routes around Victoria Park in Causeway Bay, or along the paths surrounding Government House in Central; most spectacular of all, take the Peak Tram and jog the 2-mile/3.7km contour path (Lugard Road) around the Peak.

Local resources
Business services
Hotels in Hong Kong are the best in Asia for business support and visitors will rarely need to seek outside help. The *American Chamber of Commerce* 10th Fl, Swire House, Central ☎ 5-260165 has office space for short-term rental and its business services include a very extensive reference library.

Photocopying and printing
Copykat Printing Centre ☎ 5-226191.
Secretarial *Margaret Sullivan Secretarial Services* ☎ 5-265946; *Lindy Williams Typing and WP Services* ☎ 5-8456777.

Translation and interpretation
Interlingua Language Services ☎ 5-430188; *Polyglot Translations* ☎ 5-215689; *Translanguage Center* ☎ 5-732728.

Communications
Local delivery *Document Express* ☎ 5-782341; *Evergreen* ☎ 3-903307.
Long-distance delivery *DHL* 24hr hotline ☎ 3-7644888.
Post offices Main offices: Connaught Pl, Central (by Star Ferry) ☎ 5-231071; 405 Nathan Rd, Kowloon ☎ 3-7808598; Beaconsfield House, Queens Rd, Central ☎ 5-230226.
Telephones There are relatively few public phone boxes, but all hotels, restaurants and shops have phones for public use. All hotels offer IDD, usually with a 20% surcharge, and the quality of lines is excellent. Note that the area codes (5, 3 and 0) are not required when phoning from within the territory.
Telex and fax *Cable and Wireless* 102A, Tower 1, Exchange Sq, Central (open 24hr) ☎ 5-8439439.
Conference/exhibition centres
The *Hong Kong Exhibition Centre*, China Resources Bldg, Gloucester Rd, Wanchai ☎ 5-8318831; *Hong Kong Convention and Exhibition*

Centre, 1 Harbour Rd, Wanchai ☎ 5-864888.

Embassies and consulates
Australia 23rd Fl, Harbour Centre, 25 Harbour Rd, Wanchai ☎ 5-731881.
Austria Room 2201, Wangkee Bldg, 34–37 Connaught Rd, Central ☎ 5-228086.
Belgium 9th Fl, St John's Bldg, 33 Garden Rd, Central ☎ 5-243111.
Canada 11th–14th Fl, 1 Exchange Sq, Central ☎ 5-8104321.
China 5th floor, Lower Block, 26 Harbour Rd ☎ 5-8939569.
Denmark Suite 2101-2, Great Eagle Centre, 23 Harbour Rd, Wanchai ☎ 5-8936265.
Finland Room 1818, Hutchison House, 10 Harcourt Rd, Central ☎ 5-255385.
France Admiralty Centre, Tower II, 26th Fl, 18 Harcourt Rd, Wanchai ☎ 5-294351.
Greece Room 914, Tower B, Hung Hom Commercial Centre, 37-39 Ma Tau Wai Rd, Kowloon ☎ 3-7741682.
Indonesia 6–8 Keswick St, Causeway Bay ☎ 5-8904421.
Italy Room 805, Hutchison House, 10 Harcourt Rd, Central ☎ 5-220033.
Japan 25th Fl, Bank of America Tower, 12 Harcourt Rd, Central ☎ 5-221184.
Malaysia 24th Fl, Malaysia Bldg, 47–50 Gloucester Rd, Wanchai ☎ 5-270921.
Netherlands Room 301, 3rd Fl, China Bldg, 29 Queen's Rd, Central ☎ 5-225120.
New Zealand Room 3414, Connaught Centre, Connaught Rd, Central ☎ 5-255044.
Norway Room 1401, AIA Bldg, 1 Stubbs Rd, Happy Valley ☎ 5-749253.
Philippines 21-22 Fl, Regent Centre, 88 Queen's Rd, Central ☎ 5-8100183.
Portugal Room 1001-1002, 2 Exchange Sq, 8 Connaught Pl, Central ☎ 5-225488.
Singapore 901-902, Tower 1,

Admiralty Centre, 18 Harcourt Rd, Central ☎ 5-272212.
South Korea 5-6 Fl, Far East Finance Centre, 16 Harcourt Rd, Central ☎ 5-294141.
Spain 8 Fl, Printing House, 18 Ice House St, Central ☎ 5-253041.
Sweden 8th Fl, Hong Kong Club Bldg, 3A Chater Rd, Central ☎ 5-211212.
Switzerland Room 3703, Gloucester Tower, The Landmark, 11 Pedder St, Central ☎ 5-227147.
Thailand 8th Fl, 8 Cotton Tree Bldg, Fairmont House, Central 5-216481.
UK No embassy as Hong Kong is a British Dependent Territory. Trade inquiries to the Trade Commissioner, 9th Fl, Bank of America Tower, 12 Harcourt Rd, Central ☎ 5-230176.
USA 26 Garden Rd, Central ☎ 5-239011.
West Germany 21st Fl, United Centre, 95 Queensway, Central ☎ 5-298855.

Emergencies
Hospitals All major hotels have clinics and resident nurses. *Allied Medical Practices Guild* ☎ 5-8108101 and *Anderson & Partners* ☎ 5-238166 have 24hr emergency services. Hospitals with 24hr casualty services include *Queen Mary*, Pokfulam Rd, Pokfulam ☎ 5-8192111; *Adventist*, 40 Stubbs Rd, Happy Valley ☎ 5-746211; *Queen Elizabeth*, Wylie Rd, Kowloon ☎ 3-7102111. For dental treatment, *Bayley and Jackson* Shop 208, Exchange Sq 2 ☎ 5-247116.
Pharmacies *Watson's* and *Manning's* chains are all over Hong Kong and open until 9pm. *7-Eleven* stocks basic pharmaceuticals and is open 24hr.
Police Pickpocketing is the major crime visitors suffer in Hong Kong. English-speaking policemen have red shoulder tabs. Crime Hotline ☎ 5-277177. Emergencies ☎ 999. General inquiries ☎ 5-284284 ext. 484.

Government offices
The *Information Services Department*,

Beaconsfield House, Queen's Rd, Central ☎ 5-8428777 provides statistics. The *Hong Kong Trade Development Council*, 31st Fl, Great Eagle Centre, 23 Harbour Rd, Wanchai ☎ 5-8334333 is a useful starting point for most inquiries.

Information sources
Local media The *South China Morning Post* has the best local and business coverage; the *Hong Kong Standard* mainly carries wire service stories. The *Asian Wall Street Journal* and *International Herald Tribune* are authoritative. The *Financial Times* is widely available and may be planning an Asian edition. The *Far Eastern Economic Review* is packed with sound political and economic analysis. *Radio 3* (567kHz) carries news and current affairs.
Tourist information Hong Kong *Tourist Association*, Shop 8, Basement, Jardine House, Central ☎ 3-7225555. *China Travel Service*, 77 Queen's Rd, Central ☎ 5-8533888 and 27 Nathan Rd, Kowloon ☎ 3-7211331.

Thank-yous
Julie Florist, World Trade Centre Foyer, Causeway Bay ☎ 5-777715. *Furama Inter-Continental Hotel Gift Service* ☎ 5-255111 ext 416 for flowers; ext 346 for gateaux, hampers and chocolates. *Oliver's Delicatessen* Prince's Bldg ☎ 5-8107710, and in the Ocean Centre, Kowloon ☎ 3-7309233 sells chocolates, gourmet food, wines and champagnes.

Planning and reference
Entry details
Documentation All visitors must possess a valid passport. British citizens can enter for six months without a visa, EC and Commonwealth members for three months, US citizens one month. Extensions from the Immigration Department, 61 Mody Rd, Kowloon ☎ 3-7333111. Visitors are officially

advised to carry their passport at all times.

Health precautions Inoculation against typhoid and polio is advisable.

Driving licence Visitors intending to drive must hold an international driving licence, or an overseas licence.

Customs regulations The duty-free allowances are 1 litre of wine or spirits, 200 cigarettes or 50 cigars or 250gm tobacco, 60ml of perfume and 250ml of toilet water. Everything else is duty free. Firearms, explosives and pornography are prohibited.

Climate

The climate is sub-tropical. December to February is dry with temperatures of 59–68°F/15–20°C but with unpredictable hot and cold extremes. Spring is humid and foggy with occasional rain storms, May to September is very hot, (82–93°F/28–34°C) and very humid (83%); rainstorms can last several days. There can however be abrupt local variations in weather. Typhoons from July to September rarely bring more than strong winds and rain, but everyone goes home if signal number 8 or higher is raised. Autumn is pleasantly sunny and dry, temperatures range from 77–82°F/25–28°C.

Everyone dresses smartly for business in Hong Kong and men generally arrive at meetings in a jacket, even if it is soon removed. On Saturdays, open-necked shirts and slacks are the office norm. Most smart restaurants expect men to wear jacket and tie; women usually carry a shawl as protection against the fierce air conditioning.

Holidays

It can be difficult to arrange business meetings at Christmas, Chinese New Year, Easter and during the school summer holidays when expatriates take home leave. All businesses close on public holidays, though many shops remain open.

Jan 1 New Year's Day

Mid Feb Chinese New Year (3 days)
Mar/Apr Good Fri, Easter Sat, Easter Sun
Early Apr Ching Ming
Early Jun Dragon Boat Festival
Jun 15 Queen's birthday
Last Mon in Aug Liberation Day
Early Oct Mid-Autumn Festival
Late Dec Chung Yeung Festival
Dec 25 Christmas Day
Dec 26 Boxing Day

Money

Local currency The Hong Kong dollar is officially pegged to the US dollar but local rates can vary. Notes are issued in denominations of HK$1,000, 500, 100, 50, 20 and 10. Coin denominations are HK$5, 2 and 1, and 50, 20 and 10 cents. There are no exchange control restrictions.

Changing money Banks offer the best rates, followed by the major hotels. Some money-changers give a fair rate without commission, others give poor rates or charge up to 5% commission. Money-changers are required to detail all charges before the transaction is completed. Traveller's cheques are widely accepted in all currencies. It is easy to open a bank account but there are no cheque guarantee cards in Hong Kong and shopkeepers dislike personal cheques. Standard bank opening hours are 9–3, though some banks maintain exchange services up to 5pm, weekdays only. All the major foreign banks are represented.

Credit and charge cards All credit cards are accepted throughout Hong Kong. Shops often add 2–7% surcharge if you pay by card.

Tipping Restaurants invariably add a 10% service charge and staff expect a small additional personal tip; usually the loose change will do. Taxi drivers expect HK$1 for short trips and 10% of the fare on longer journeys. In hotels tip doormen, porters and room service staff up to HK$10. Give cloakroom attendants a dollar or two; hairdressers, masseurs and beauticians expect 10%.

Indonesia

Until it won independence in 1949 after four years of hard struggle, Indonesia was the Netherlands East Indies, Holland's only significant colony. For 350 years, Dutch interest in the archipelago was chiefly economic, and military and political control was imposed piecemeal as economic considerations dictated. The Dutch presence did no more to efface the diversity of the world's largest archipelago than had that other major outside influence, Islam. The greatest of the Javanese empires, Majapahit, succumbed to the spreading influence of Islam in the 16th century and Islam is now nominally the religion of 80% of Indonesians. This history explains certain aspects of modern Indonesia: a suspicion of the outside world's motives, a preoccupation with unity – "unity in diversity" is the national motto – and an uneasy relationship between the dominant Javanese culture and orthodox religious tastes.

Under one president, Suharto, Indonesia has now enjoyed over 20 years of political stability combined until recently with rapid economic growth. In 1965, after the violent attempted coup – allegedly masterminded by the Communist Party – the "New Order" established itself in power and abandoned the strident nationalism of the Sukarno years, opening Indonesia to the Western world and its investors. Yet, while acknowledging that on grounds of sheer size, economic potential and strategic location Indonesia is an "important country," the world seems unable to bring it into focus.

One reason is that the regime's anti-communism has not translated into an uncomplicated pro-Westernism. A prickliness suffuses Indonesia's relations with its natural friends, the USA, Australia and Japan. The three key terms in the country's political lexicon are *Pancasila* (the state philosophy based on belief in God, national unity, democracy, justice and humanitarianism) whose acceptance has become the chief test of ideological conformity; the 1945 Constitution (*UUD '45*), which sets out the generous limits of executive power; and *dwifungsi*, the doctrine of the "double function" of the armed forces by which their non-military activities are justified.

The military-technocratic government can claim some success in achieving its principal goals of "depoliticization" and "development." The lesson it drew from the horror of 1965 was that politics was a curse and stability the key to development. Oil revenues transformed Indonesia's industrial base and enabled it to become self-sufficient in rice. The crash of the state oil company Pertamina in 1975 nudged the regime into a slightly more austere attitude to corruption, or *korupsi* as it is known, although nepotism still deforms the policy-making process.

A transfer of power is under way from Suharto and his peers to a younger group. Debate about economic policy, revolving around the crucial issues of vested interest and nationalism, will be one of the main ways in which the chief contenders stake out their positions.

The political scene

At the apex of Indonesia's political system for more than 20 years has been the inscrutable figure of President Suharto. Whereas his flamboyant predecessor, Sukarno, liked to be known as the "Great Leader of the Revolution," the withdrawn Suharto prefers the more mundane *Bapak Pembangunan*, "Father of Development." Most of the time he acts as arbiter between the contending camps within his administration, leaning one way or another but only rarely seeking a definitive resolution of these antagonisms.

Political parties

In addition to Golkar, the government-backed coalition of "functional groups" which prefers not to be known as a party and consistently wins the elections, only two parties are permitted. These are the United Development Party (PPP), an uncomfortable amalgam of Muslim parties, and the Indonesian Democratic Party (PDI), an alliance of the non-Muslim (nationalist and Christian) parties. In the April 1987 elections, Golkar easily met its target of winning 70% of the vote.

Parliament

The powers of parliament (the DPR) are limited and its elective element is leavened by a bloc of 100 appointed military men. The 500 members of the DPR also sit – together with 500 appointees – in the People's Consultative Assembly (MPR) to elect the president. Suharto was their unopposed choice for the May 1988 election, his fourth and probably last term of office.

Tight central control The president has created an extremely centralized system of government, with regional officials frequently having to travel distances equal to that between Rome and London even for quite minor decisions. Virtually all of the decision-making power of the vast bureaucracy, which employs about 2m civil servants, is concentrated in government offices in Jakarta.

The military

The military jealously protects its pre-eminence. It rejects suggestions that it return to the barracks. In 1988, fearing that Golkar was slipping out of its control, the military establishment eased out the party's chairman. The "Generation of '45," formed in the independence struggle, is now handing over to a younger, more professional group, from which Suharto's successor is expected to come. To be a presidential candidate, it is necessary to combine the correct religious (Muslim), ethnic (Javanese) and military service background. The current top contender with the right credentials is the commander in chief, General Try Sutrisno.

Business involvement The military are also heavily involved in business and run many of the state enterprises. Large military conglomerates, often relying on local Chinese capital and entrepreneurial skills, have grown out of the armed forces' historic and now perennial need for "off-budget" funds.

External relations

Indonesia's foreign policy is non-aligned with a distinct pro-Western tilt. Nevertheless, among its partners in the Association of Southeast Asian Nations (ASEAN), Indonesia has been the most conciliatory towards socialist Vietnam, seeing it as a buffer against the far more threatening China. Despite suspicions of China relations, "frozen" in 1967, were normalized in 1989 and trade links are becoming more vigorous. Trading contacts are also being renewed with COMECON countries.

The economic scene

Indonesia's GDP in 1970 was US$11bn; by 1985 it was nearly US$87bn. Per capita income rose during that period from US$80 to US$530. This conveys something of the speed of Indonesia's recent economic development. The key to growth has been oil. In the oil boom years 1972–81 annual growth averaged 7%. Since the weakening of oil prices the rate has halved. However, the oil boom enabled other sectors to make great strides and to gain a degree of resilience in the face of the fall in oil prices. Even so, oil, and increasingly gas, remain crucial to Indonesia's prospects.

Human resources

Indonesia's population, at around 170m, is the world's fifth largest. Despite a vigorous family-planning programme, the national birth rate is just over 2% a year – in some provinces it is more like 4% – and there will be at least 220m Indonesians by the year 2000.

Overall population density at 77 per square km gives a misleading picture because 65% of the population live on the "inner" islands of Java, Madura and Bali, which together comprise only 7% of the land area. An official "transmigration" policy has for the past 40 years tried to disperse the population by opening up new lands in the outer islands and by providing infrastructure there. However, fewer than 1% have transmigrated in recent years, while spontaneous migration to overcrowded Java from the outer islands continues.

Ethnic origin The indigenous people of Indonesia's major islands – Sumatra, Java, Bali, Kalimantan, Sulawesi and West Nusa Tenggara – which together contain about 96% of the total population, are mainly of Malay stock. The remaining indigenous people are largely of Melanesian origin. There are sizable concentrations of ethnic Chinese in the urban areas of most of the major islands, and smaller numbers of Indians, Arabs and Europeans also hold Indonesian citizenship.

Urbanization Indonesia's population is predominantly rural, less than a quarter of the people living in urban centres, but migration to the cities is a continuing feature of population trends.

Natural resources

For centuries its rich volcanic soils have made Java a centre of wet-rice cultivation. About two-fifths of the 18m ha/44.5m acres of land under permanent cultivation is on Java, with only a fifth of potentially arable land on the outer islands actually under cultivation. Some 60% of Indonesia's surface area is forested, though only about 16m ha/39.5m acres are exploitable. The country is the world's second-largest producer of palm oil, and is a leading producer of robusta coffee, tea, distinctive local varieties of tobacco, as well as rubber, sugar, cloves and pepper.

Minerals Surveys have shown Indonesia to be rich in tin, bauxite, copper, nickel and iron sands, and there are also small quantities of manganese, phosphate rock, sulphur and silver. Gold output has increased steadily in recent years.

Fisheries The great potential of this sector remains unrealized because most of the country's sea-fishing industry relies on traditional methods and equipment and only about a third of the vessels are motorized. Shrimp accounts for about 75% of export revenue from fishing. Tuna and skipjack are the other main products, exported mainly to Japan.

Energy

The National Energy Coordinating Board (Bakoren) monitors and plans utilization of the nation's energy resources. The share of oil as a source of domestic energy is to be reduced from its current level of around 80% to 60% by 1990 as other sources of energy – especially gas, coal, hydroelectric power and geothermal power – are developed.

Oil Indonesia, a member of OPEC, is a major oil producer and has an estimated production capacity of 1.5m barrels a day. Reserves are unofficially put at between 8.5bn barrels (proven) to 50bn barrels (unproven).

Gas Indonesia has natural gas reserves estimated at more than 80 trillion cubic feet. Large-scale exploitation began in the late 1970s and liquefied natural gas (LNG) is now Indonesia's second largest earner of foreign exchange. Agreements for the sale of LNG have been signed with Japan, South Korea, and Taiwan. A programme has also been launched to expand output of liquefied petroleum gas (LPG) following the signing of an export contract with Japan.

Coal production and exports have risen rapidly in recent years and steps have been taken to increase exploration for, and output of, coal.

Hydroelectricity Indonesia has several hydropower plants, the largest of which is at Saguling on the Citarum river, with an installed capacity of 700MW that can be doubled to 1,400MW.

Geothermal power Because of its position on the cross-point of two volcanic belts, Indonesia has substantial geothermal reserves. So far proven capacity of about 900MW has been found in Java and Sulawesi.

Agriculture

Agriculture is the most important sector of the economy, both in terms of GDP and employment. Although its relative share in both has been declining, 45% of non-oil/gas exports are still agricultural.

Food crops The food-crop subsector is the most important component of Indonesian agriculture and is almost entirely in the hands of smallholders. Government efforts to boost the productivity of this sector have involved provision of chemical inputs, irrigation and credit as well as a variety of price incentives. The world's largest importer of rice in the late 1970s and early 1980s, Indonesia became self-sufficient in 1984.

Cash crops Only after the oil bonanza began to peter out did priority begin to go to the development of non-oil exports, which include rubber, palm oil, coffee, tea and tobacco. Output of these crops has risen, but at a time of worldwide overproduction and weak prices.

Infrastructure

Indonesia's far-flung geography and the regime's preoccupation with development and security are the reasons why infrastructure has been the only sector to escape budgetary cuts. Although Jakarta, the capital, has been the chief beneficiary of spending on transport and communications, the inter-island air and telecommunications services have improved greatly.

Airports Cenkareng International Airport is 20km/12 miles from Jakarta and Ngurah Rai is 13km/8 miles from Denpasar on Bali. Distances within the country are great and, except to Bandung, most visitors travel by air outside Jakarta. The national airline Garuda and its subsidiary Merpati operate extensive domestic services.

Seaports The main port is Jakarta's Tanjung Priok which has container facilities. Other important ports are Tanjung Perak at Surabaya, on Java, and Belawan on Sumatra.

Roads There is a 204,000km/128,000-mile road network, 25% of which is surfaced. Secondary roads are frequently impassable in the rainy season.

Railways The rail network is limited to Java, Sumatra and Madura and consists of 8,600 km/5,300 miles of track, mostly on Java. Services can be slow, with many stops.

External trade

Oil and gas still account for the surplus Indonesia enjoys in its external trade, even though their overall share in total exports has fallen sharply. Oil/gas export revenues fell by 44.5% from US$12.44bn in 1985/86 to US$6.91bn in 1986/87, according to Bank Indonesia data. During the same period the value of non-oil/gas exports rose from US$5.87bn to US$6.52bn.

Other commodities traded are rubber, plywood, coffee, ready-made garments, sawn wood, tin and tin products, aluminium and bauxite, textiles, shrimp and tuna, palm oil, tea and logs.

Main imports are machinery and equipment, chemicals, mineral products, base metals, transport equipment and prepared food and drinks.

Main trading partners are Japan, the USA and Singapore (the regional entrepôt), but in order to increase exports an effort is under way to improve trade links with the COMECON countries. Trade with China received a major boost in 1985 when an Indonesian delegation, the first in 20 years, went to China and signed valuable sales contracts. Trade agreements have also been signed with Chile and Iran.

Reforms Indonesia's non-oil export drive in the face of weakened oil prices includes reforms aimed at reducing production costs. In addition, devaluation of the rupiah in September 1986 reduced the dollar price of exports by more than 31%.

Balance of payments

Chronic deficits on invisibles (due to transport costs and the remittance of investment income) make sure that the current account is usually in the red. A 1987 USAID report suggests a 1986/87 deficit of US$3.9bn. These deficits have been financed by capital inflows, mainly in the form of aid.

Tourism The prospect of declining export revenues from oil, plus the need to provide jobs for Indonesia's rapidly rising population, has given rise to a new appreciation of the value of tourism as a non-oil earner of foreign exchange and as a labour-intensive service industry. Numerous measures have therefore been introduced to promote the industry, including the lifting of visa requirements for tourists from Australia, the EC, Japan, the USA, Canada, and a large number of other countries. After an inevitable time lag during which the growth in tourist arrivals failed to keep pace with hotel construction and so resulted in very low occupancy rates, the industry is now booming.

Foreign exchange reserves Indonesia's holdings of foreign exchange rose steadily from US$2.6bn at the end of 1982 to US$4.8bn at the end of 1985. They fell to US$3.9bn a year later but government measures helped to boost the level to a record US$5.3bn in July 1987.

Currency

The Indonesian rupiah is freely convertible, but free convertibilitiy and fears of devaluation periodically prompt flights of capital. The government has therefore maintained a sizable cushion of reserves. The rupiah has been aligned with the dollar since 1970. This poses problems: with most of its exports denominated in dollars and most of its debts in non-dollar currencies, Indonesia loses out when the dollar is weak.

External debt

With a public external debt by the end of 1987 estimated at US$43bn, Indonesia has climbed to sixth place among the world's developing-country borrowers. Most aid since 1966 has been channelled through a consortium of Western aid donors and multilateral agencies collectively known as the Inter-Governmental Group on Indonesia (IGGI). The share of foreign-aid receipts in

development expenditure has recently shot up to around 70% from about a quarter during the oil-boom years.
Roll-over looks inevitable With substantial repayments now coming due and the demand for its exports weak, for the next few years the debt service payments will hover around 40% of export earnings. The government has consistently ruled out rescheduling, but some form of roll-over looks inevitable.

The budget
Falling oil revenues have been largely to blame for substantial cutbacks in development expenditure in recent years. Petroleum earnings' share of total domestic revenues fell from 70% in 1981/82 to 40% in 1987/88.
Broadening the tax base Efforts to broaden the tax base through improved collection and the introduction of value-added tax have proved surprisingly successful.
Debt-service burden The squeeze on capital spending also came from the growing claims of current expenditure and, in particular, of debt service. Debt service's share of routine expenditure increased between 1983/84 and 1987/88 from 25% to 45%.
Inflation The hyper-inflation of the Sukarno years has stuck firmly in the minds of the New Order's economic policymakers. Control of inflation has been achieved through balanced budgets, price controls and a tight rein on money supply. Following the September 1986 devaluation, prices started rising sharply and continued upwards throughout 1987, but budgetary austerity and maintenance of a tight ceiling on monetary growth kept the inflation rate below 10% in 1987.

Development planning
Since they began in 1969, a series of five-year plans (*Repelita*), have set sectoral growth targets aimed at raising the economy to ever-higher levels of value-added and technological sophistication. By the fourth plan, the focus had shifted to building on the established industrial base. The economy's sensitivity to outside forces has meant that the plan targets have been a fallible guide to reality. The fourth plan set a relatively modest target of 5% growth, but average GDP growth of about 3% is probably the best that can be hoped for.

Industry and investment
Heavy investment in manufacturing – which has absorbed 70% of total investment and 70% of foreign investment outside oil and gas since 1967 – has paid off in rapid growth since the early 1970s, Manufacturing has continued to outperform the economy as a whole and its share of GDP had risen to 13% by 1985, compared with 8% in 1970.
Wide range of goods Indonesia produces a vast range of manufactured goods, from textiles, paper products and fertilizer to cement, car tyres, vegetable oil, TVs and helicopters. There is also a wide range in the scale of its producing units, from cottage industries to steel and chemical plants.
Import-substitution The growth in manufacturing has been devoted largely to import-substitution and the creation of job opportunties. With little attention being given to export promotion, the process has taken place at the expense of quality.
Protective measures have fostered the inward orientation of domestic industry, in the form of tariffs and quantity restrictions. This has resulted in significant inefficiencies in the manufacturing sector which render particular industries less competitive than they might be. Major policy efforts are now needed to improve efficiency and competitiveness and to reorient the sector towards export growth. Numerous reforms introduced in recent years indicate that the government recognizes the urgent need for such change.

The business climate

Indonesia's economic base consists of a vast mass of smallholders working in simple and primarily agricultural rural-based ventures. Superimposed on this are pockets of industries and some large-scale mining and forestry operations. National statistics often conceal the dispersed nature of the country's business.

The public sector

Ever since independence in 1949 when the Indonesians nationalized all Dutch enterprises, the country's state sector has been vast, cumbersome and often obstructive. There are 214 state-administered firms along with 200 others in which the state has substantial shareholdings. State firms reach into virtually every business sector.

State-owned enterprises The government controls shipping, railways, communications, production of oil and gas and the other major commodities, most trade, all mining, electricity and water, a chain of hotels, printing works and insurance firms. The state also has significant shareholdings in industries such as steelworks, logging, highways construction, pharmaceuticals, fertilizers and cement.

A feudal approach to administration is still applied to the economy. In practice, this restricts private opportunities to the less attractive areas or to firms well connected to the state apparatus. There is a far greater awareness of this now and reforms instituted in the mid-1980s lay the basis for hope that a strenuous restructuring of the economy is under way.

The private sector

Since oil revenues became less certain in the early 1980s, a series of reforms has placed the private sector on a slightly stronger footing. The financial sector was partially deregulated in 1983, taxes were overhauled in 1981–85 and deregulation packages on trade and investment were notable features of 1986–87.

Disincentive The impact of these measures has been significant in terms of the trend of government thinking, but the government's unwillingness to tackle more entrenched seats of power is a serious disincentive to further private-sector participation in the economy.

Non-economic goals Part of the unwillingness stems from the fact that the government has goals other than purely economic ones. Policy directives stress the need to provide employment, spread the distribution of development to far-flung parts of the archipelago and support weaker economic groups.

Elite relationship Much of the interventionist rhetoric serves, however, to mask power relationships in business which do more to promote the Indonesian-Chinese elite and their government or military patrons than they do to promote growth. Public debate has in recent years become bolder on the subject of these oligopolies, many of which can be traced directly to the president's family. Suharto's wife, sons and daughters are all deeply involved in a wide range of basic industries, through their own companies or through influence in existing state firms.

This phenomenon is the most serious and sensitive in the economy. It explains the government's ambivalence towards the private sector, obvious in the often contradictory policy requirements. Until the business community sees brave steps taken by Suharto to change the system and open it to more equitable competition, Indonesia's private sector is likely to remain frustrated and underutilized.

Selling state firms President

Suharto made his most aggressive statements on privatization in early 1987, suggesting that many state firms should be sold, but only those deemed to be non-strategic. The process of sorting out which companies can be sold, who will buy them and how, is expected to stretch out into 1989.

Foreign investment

It was only in 1967 that Indonesia opened its doors to foreign investors and even since then the official attitude to outsiders in the economy has fluctuated. Indonesia remains sensitive to domestic lobbies which fear the intrusion of foreign money. In 1974, violent riots, called the Malari Riots, rocked the capital city of Jakarta. The issue was Japanese control of the economy. That level of protest has not been seen since but it is in the foreign visitor's interest to be aware of the depth of feeling that foreign capital can arouse in a newly independent country. The only way to invest in Indonesia is through joint venture and although rules governing foreign investment are gradually being simplified, the Indonesian administration remains keen to control almost every step a foreign investor takes.

The investors These warnings notwithstanding, the last twenty years have seen a total of almost US$16bn in foreign investment. The biggest investor is Japan. Advertising signs in the capital, which had been pulled down in the 1974 riots, are again announcing the presence of Daihatsu, Toyota, Nissan and others. Hong Kong appears on statistics sheets as the next largest investor, but its share is widely assumed to include investments by Indonesians domiciled overseas. The USA follows, with major companies including IBM, Bechtel and the large oil firms. European investment is most obvious in communications, with Siemens and Philips being long-term presences in Indonesia.

Investment sectors Following the guidelines laboriously compiled each year by the government, investment has been concentrated in secondary industries, especially basic metal and metal goods industries. Chemicals, cement and mining are other areas with a large foreign investment component.

The outlook for foreign investors is as bright as ever, with Indonesian companies eager for foreign money and expertise. Both the government and individual firms will stress to the foreigner the importance of the transfer of technology. Frustration exists among Indonesians with what is seen as the slow progress made on this so far, and the local press sometimes reports calls for Indonesians to steal technology if it is not going to be given.

Power in business

Without the right connections, it is not worth doing business in Indonesia. As a rule of thumb, such connections start at the top with the president's family and associates and filter down through a range of mainly Chinese-Indonesian business groups.

Historical bonds Much of the explanation for Indonesia's business structure is found in history. When the Indonesians fought the Dutch for independence, the finance and supplies necessary were provided by Chinese traders. Close relationships between military leaders and the Chinese merchant class were cemented at that time and have lasted to the present day. But in the late 1980s there has been a gradual disengagement of the old military-trader alliances as a result of the growing confidence of indigenous Indonesian business people, who can do without the sometimes politically expensive Chinese middlemen.

The First Pacific Group The best known of the long-established groups is the multinational empire of Liem Sioe Liong. Known in Indonesia as the First Pacific Group, and domiciled in Hong Kong, it has interests in finance, international trade and real estate, together with extensive power over flour (the Bogasari Mills), cement (through Indocement), steel (through Giwang Selogam and the state firm Krakatau Steel), clove production (for *kretek* cigarettes), palm oil (through Sinar Mas Inti Perkasa and the Bimoli group of Mrs Eka Tjipta Wijaya), among others. First Pacific also owns or has interests in various banks and trading outlets around the world, including the Hibernia Bank of California and Sears World Trade.

Mochtar Riady Closely affiliated with Liem is Mochtar Riady, head of Indonesia's largest private bank, Bank Central Asia, and of a range of other finance, trading and estate companies. It is no secret that most of Liem's empire has flourished through the support of Suharto himself, whom Liem used to supply when Suharto was a commander in central Java.

Bob Hasan is another old Chinese-Indonesian friend (and golfing partner) who now heads an efficient domestic plywood production cartel, and has interests in sports promotion and commodity estates. Through Nusamba, Hasan is involved in tea, timber, oil, insurance, the import and sale of Nissan cars, tinplate production and steel. Many of these companies are in partnership with Sigit Harjojudanto, a son of President Suharto. The contract for the next major expansion of the telecommunications network can be expected to go to one of these companies.

Bakrie and Brothers An exception to the military-Chinese link-up is the prominence of this Indonesian firm. Achmad Bakrie and his son Nirwan are in partnership with the Suharto family in a range of businesses, especially commodity trading, the manufacture of steel pipes and oil trading.

The Tosiba group These people, among others, are all linked into the "Tosiba" group – a Jakartan joke,

since the name is a contraction of Tommy, Sigit and Bambang, the names of Suharto's sons in business. Each has his own investment group.

Bambang Trihatmodjo (Suharto), with his Bimantara Group, is the most visible. The group includes over 60 companies, covering hotels, shopping centres, liquefied natural gas, tanker shipping and oil marketing, oil and gas services, construction, telecommunications, trading, insurance, sport and recreation, milk powder manufacture, pharmaceuticals, airport services, shipping and more.

Hutama "Tommy" Mandala Putra (Suharto) works through his Humpuss Group, with interests in aviation electronics, toll roads, real estate and forest concessions.

Other Suharto family members Suharto's oldest daughter, Toetoet, with her more active husband, Indra Rukmana, has a group called Citra Lamtoro Gung Persada. This has interests in plantations, general trade, animal husbandry, industry and toll roads. Indra is in partnership with Liem, Hasan and with his brothers-in-law as well.

Influence peddling Although some of the companies are professionally run by top-class managers, others are venues for influence peddling, a process which often adds large percentages on to the costs of doing business for any other firms both upstream and downstream.

Joint-venture partners The Investment Coordinating Board produces a booklet listing potential joint-venture partners and specifies groups and their fields of business.

Labour unions Union membership is voluntary and all unions must be affiliated to the official labour federation. Strikes, which are rare, are recognized only if they "do not obstruct national development." Negotiations between unions and management are allowed and collective agreements can be entered into, but these need government approval to be valid.

The business framework

The rules governing foreign involvement in business in Indonesia are strict and heavily weighted in favour of Indonesians. Foreign investment is permitted only through joint ventures and only in certain sectors.

Private companies

A company in Indonesia, identified by the letters PT (Perseroan Terbatas), requires at least two founders. It is managed by a board of directors, with a fixed capital divided into shares with limited liability of shareholders. Although it is not mandatory, many companies also have a board of supervisors, known as Dewan Komisaris, to oversee the activities of the directors. The founders of a PT are legally required to subscribe at least 20% of the authorized capital and to pay up at least 10% of the issued capital before a PT can come into existence.

Foreign ownership rules

Foreign direct equity investment in Indonesia is officially promoted in a restricted number of sectors through the form of joint ventures, known by the initials PMA. All matters relating to non-oil/gas investment are administered by the Investment Coordinating Board (BKPM), including initial investment approval, granting of licences, fiscal facilities and work permits for expatriates.

Areas open to investors In May 1989 the Investment Priority List (DSP), an annually updated listing of areas open to foreign investors, was abolished. It was replaced by a much shorter "negative list" of 75 areas closed to foreign investment, though even applications to operate in many of these may be approved if, for example, output is primarily for export.

Joint-venture shareholding
Foreigners can hold up to 80% of a PMA's shares, but this must be reduced to less than 50% within 15 years. A PMA company is not allowed to act in consumer or retail trade, but requires an Indonesian agent or distributor to do so. Equity up to 95% may be held by a foreigner for five years, however, if export capabilities are increased through the investment, if the project is located in a remote area, or if it involves high-risk or high-technology. Postponement of divestment, liberal interpretation of the US$1m minimum investment rule and extension of the standard 30-year operating permit may also be granted.

Fully Indonesian-owned If a foreign company either sells 75% of its equity to an Indonesian firm, or floats 51% of its shares on the stock market, or sells a 51% stake to an Indonesian including a 20% equity flotation on the stock market, then it will be treated as a fully owned Indonesian firm. This allows it access to local currency credit from state banks and the right to distribute its product directly. Foreign investors may also buy shares in existing Indonesian companies with export potential.

Little protection for foreigners
Investors should note that there is little protection in law or in practice if the local partner wants to oust or reduce the influence of the foreigner. Wise choice of a local partner is therefore vital and the BKPM provides little help in this, other than publishing a list of potential partners.

Fully Indonesian-owned investment companies, known as PMDNs, must also have approval from BKPM at every step of the way, but are free of most restrictions facing foreigners. Both PMA and PMDN firms must report twice yearly to the BKPM and to the central bank, Bank Indonesia. Reports to the Bank must be signed by a registered public accountant and include details of any foreign currency loans.

Land problems Significant hitches still facing foreign investors concern primarily the acquisition of land. Foreigners cannot buy land and may lease land only for restricted amounts of time. Investors in plantation projects must adhere to the Nucleus Estate and Smallholder Scheme (NES), in which 60% of an investor's land and capital must go to smallholder development, increasing to 80% after ten years.

Other ways to operate

Foreigners can operate outside a PMA arrangement in a variety of ways. But attention must be given to the quality of the relationship with the Indonesian partner – all other factors are secondary.

Appointing an agent Foreigners wanting to sell products domestically and surmount other restrictions can appoint an agent or distributor. The personal relationship established is crucial as agreements on paper probably would not help in event of a dispute.

Representative office Establishing a representative office allows a foreigner to act as an intermediary, handle promotion and collect information for a head office abroad. It cannot trade, accept orders, bid for tenders, sign contracts, import, export or distribute. In most cases it requires an application to the Department of Trade. A three-month provisional licence is followed up to eight weeks later by a two-year permanent licence. No branch licences have been issued in recent years.

As a contractor Participation of a foreign company as a contractor, in a construction or foreign aid project for example, usually requires some kind of operational registration with a government department.

"Cooperation" agreements to provide technical assistance from abroad, indirect equity investment through an Indonesian nominee, or participating convertible debentures in an Indonesian organization are other options, but professional advice should be sought.

Expatriate employment

Expatriates may be employed in Indonesia only where there is no Indonesian national qualified for the post, but the complicated work visa process requires an Indonesian sponsor. The sponsor is responsible for the employment of the expatriate during his or her time in Indonesia. Work permits are granted usually for one year and are extendable. Shorter-term permits still require a sponsor and visa processes must be started in the Indonesian embassy in the foreigner's country of origin. Many business travellers do not apply for visas, however, taking advantage of the visa-free two-month stay provision intended for tourists.

Firing problems Local labour law, wherein union membership is voluntary and strikes are not recognized unless they follow strict guidelines, provides problems for the employer who wants to dispose of staff. This requires approval from the Ministry of Manpower, issuance of three warnings over 27 months and substantial termination payoffs. An offence such as theft allows the employer to fire the offender instantly, but incompetence is not regarded as a valid reason for dismissal. The lack of a state social security system means most employers provide worker insurance, income tax payments, medical and travel expenses and one month's bonus pay at *Lebaran*, the annual Muslim celebration.

Taxation

Resident organizations and individuals must pay income tax on a scale up to 35% of taxable income in excess of Rp50m. Nonresidents are subject to tax at 20% of gross income earned in Indonesia, subject to reciprocal tax agreements with the foreigner's country of origin.

Repatriation of funds Repatriation of profits and dividends is guaranteed in Indonesia and there are no reporting requirements for foreign exchange transfers, regardless of size. The law also provides for compensation in case of nationalization and repatriation of remaining invested capital in case of liquidation.

Market entry

Finding an Indonesian partner is undoubtedly the biggest hurdle facing a foreign investor. The only ways to surmount this are to act on a trusted recommendation, spend weeks or months researching the market and interviewing, or seek help from consultancies in Jakarta. Questions should be asked regarding active – not merely letterhead – experience in business, accounting records and family/military connections.

Importing and exporting

Unless an importing agent is used, anyone wishing to import certain categories of goods must have a licence to do so. Some goods cannot be imported, such as fully assembled cars or pharmaceutical products and printed matter in Indonesian or Chinese. Other items such as rice, lubricants, electrical goods, newsprint, and various items of machinery, chemical products, textiles and dairy products are imported under exclusive licensing arrangements with state trading firms. In addition, special rules apply to goods due for display at exhibitions, imports financed by foreign aid, or by expatriates employed by the government or by diplomatic missions.

Documentation Necessary documentation includes a pro forma invoice, commercial invoice, certificate of origin, bill of lading, insurance certificate, packing list, supplier's certificate (if importing under an aid scheme).

Customs inspection The system (hitherto, amazingly corrupt) of customs and import inspection and duties was revolutionized in 1985 with the appointment for three years of the Swiss firm SGS (Société Générale de Surveillance). SGS inspects goods at the port of origin, issues an inspection exactness report (LKP), determines the duties applicable and, after payment is cleared through a bank, releases the goods. However, a new system is being devised in which customs staff will again take part, possibly with SGS training and assistance. The new system may also include a fast-release mechanism whereby recognized importers take possession of goods before procedures are completed. Imports destined to contribute directly to the manufacture of non-oil exports are duty-free.

Export licences are needed to export from Indonesia and exports are prohibited to Angola, Israel and South Africa. Items such as precious metals, raw rattan and antiques are restricted. Exports are subject to customs checks at the export destination only and can be paid for in any currency. If a company is exporting its own produce directly to the consuming country, forward sales contracts of up to six months are permitted.

Counter-purchase agreements are required for imports worth over Rp500m and are tied to exports of Indonesian non-oil and gas products. Exempted from this policy are those purchases financed by aid or multilateral agencies and those required by the government.

Bonded warehouse areas are being developed where customs privileges and special trade rules assist export-oriented and labour-intensive industries. There are already in Jakarta such free trade zone and industrial estate facilities. On Batam Island, 20km/12 miles south of Singapore, a 400-sq km/154-sq mile bonded area allows imports without an LKP from SGS and an attractive package of investment incentives.

Copyright and patents

Indonesia has attained worldwide prominence for the efficiency of its piracy industries. It excels in producing good copies of music cassettes within two weeks of their release in the USA and foreign investors have long been frustrated by the lack of effective protection against piracy of films, books and software. Late in 1987, however, a new law was signed by the president which, if it is implemented rigorously, increases protection. The new law extends protection to computer software and videos, as well as to books published outside Indonesia.

Patents Despite the progress made on copyright legislation, work on patent protection is expected to continue for a few years. There is minimal protection of patents at present.

Distribution

Outside the largest cities, the consumer market is small and accessible only to Indonesian firms. Distribution networks within Indonesia comprise extensive air, sea and land links. But, apart from land routes, there are problems with limited cargo capacity, constant delays, local cartels and corruption.

Transportation is complex, given the size of the country, and administration becomes more discretionary the farther away from Jakarta the transport office is. International transport firms such as Global and Crown Pacific are represented in Jakarta, while the largest domestic company is PT Cardig Air, which has IATA approval for cargo and customs clearance, warehouse operation and international freight forwarding.

Marine links are most important and Indonesia has licensed many foreign shipping firms to operate in Indonesian waters because of the weakness of the domestic shipping industry. But delays are not unusual, sometimes dragging over months. Ports are being upgraded and those in the major cities of Jakarta, Surabaya, Medan, Menado and Ujang Pandang are increasing their container capabilities. Large rivers are used to transport everything from people to logs and televisions in provinces such as Kalimantan and Sumatra.

Difficult terrain Trucks provide extensive freight possibilities, although the roads, traffic, floods or just plain breakdowns give no guarantee of punctuality. Trains cover Java and will take some freight. Garuda, the national airline, with its subsidiary Merpati, has a monopoly over jet aircraft and flies regularly to all major domestic destinations. But farther-flung sites, such as those in Kalimantan, are covered by the private airline Bouraq. Private helicopter and air services, some of them run by missionary groups, are available at great expense, and for supplies to a gold mine, for example, the terrain leaves no alternative.

Advertising and PR

Jakarta's advertising industry is still young in terms of originality, design and techniques. There is only one TV channel, run by the government, and it does not take advertising. However, hundreds of private radio stations across the country do. Placing advertisements in the print media is expensive, especially in newspapers.

Billboards are a popular means of advertising. There are even a couple of large electronically run digital boards in the capital for advertising and announcements.

Top advertising agencies in Jakarta include Grafik, Matari, Fortune, Citra Lintas and Nu-Age. **Public relations facilities** are more limited, although many so-called advertising agencies incorporate this function.

The financial scene

Indonesia's financial system is the least developed in South-East Asia and is very largely limited to the products and services offered by the banking sector, since the country's tiny stock market and even smaller bond market are at present able to contribute very little to it.

Banks and other financial institutions

Bank Indonesia today fulfils the classic functions of a central bank, including supervision of the nation's financial institutions, but this role has taken time to evolve. In the 1960s Bank Indonesia also acted as a commercial bank. When earnings from the country's gas and oil exports shot up in the 1970s, the bank was still the major provider of funds (drawn from the nation's foreign reserves) to a banking system which had been slow to attract the savings of ordinary Indonesians.

By 1983, however, Bank Indonesia had acted to introduce more up-to-date mechanisms designed to push the banks into managing their own liquidity. Chief among these was the introduction of a market in government debt (represented by central bank certificates on indebtedness). This is a move which has also armed Bank Indonesia with a tool for controlling money supply.

Commercial banks

The commercial banking segment alone comprises 86 entities, of which 5 are state-owned, 70 are private-sector concerns controlled by Indonesians, 10 are foreign bank branches and one is a joint venture. *Other banks* To these must be added 29 development banks, 3 savings banks and 5,810 rural banks, mostly one-branch affairs. *The dominant five* This apparent diversity is, however, misleading as 70% of all lending is done by the government-owned Bank Bumi Daya, Bank Negara Indonesia 1946, Bank Dagang Negara, Bank Rakyat Indonesia and Bank Ekspor and Impor Indonesia. Their large pools of deposits owe much to inflows from the state corporations.

Foreign banks In the battle for the bits of the action left over by these giants, foreign banks are further hampered by restrictions which limit their branches to Jakarta and six provincial cities, confine their lending to companies outside Jakarta, and oblige them to obtain the permission of Bank Indonesia for loans of over one year's duration. But they may establish joint ventures with local banks in which they are allowed to hold 85% of the equity. They are also able to pass Indonesian business on to their Singapore branches, which are free to make foreign-currency loans to such customers since Jakarta imposes no foreign-exchange controls.

The markets

The problem for the bond market is that if issuers attract investors to their paper, they need to pay on it rates even higher than those available on bank deposits. In consequence only three such issues have been made and the market has gone into hibernation.

A similar difficulty faces Indonesia's stock market. Closed to foreign investors, the Jakarta Stock Exchange offers the shares of only 24 companies. Almost all these have taken to paying dividends at a guaranteed level competitive with bank interest rates, with the result that some are paying cash dividends which total more than their net after-tax profits. In 1989 an over-the-counter market was established in Jakarta and the first privately operated stock market in a provincial city (Surabaya) was opened.

A commodity exchange trades actively in rubber and coffee.

Who can help

Lawyers

Legal help in Jakarta is limited, at least partly because the legal system is undeveloped and highly discretionary. Following early Dutch conventions, most contracts must be processed by a notary. *Kartini Mulyadi and Associates*, Bina Mulia Building, Jalan Rasuna Said Kav 10, Jakarta ☎ 516968 ✆ 44998, the largest notary firm, will help with finding local partners and the practice covers all corporate and financial legal needs.

Gani Djemat and Partners Jalan Imam Bonjol 7, Jakarta ☎ 332461 caters to a range of large foreign clients. MKK or *Mochtar, Karuwin & Komar*, 14th Fl, Wisma Metropolitan II, Jalan Sudirman Kav 31, Jakarta ☎ 5781130, is similarly respected.

Many international firms such as *Coudert Brothers* are based in Singapore and have staff who regularly fly to Jakarta for their Indonesian clients.

Accountants

Accountancy firms provide advice and a wide range of business assistance, and most international firms are represented locally. Foremost among them are *Kantor Akuntan Sudjendro*, 11th Fl, Prince Centre, 3–4 Jalan Jenderal Sudirman, Jakarta ☎ 588051 ✆ 44344. Correspondent for Peat, Marwick, Mitchell & Co, specializing in taxation, audit, investigation, administration and accounting. It also offers help with recruitment, advice on business practice, liaison with legal advisers and assistance with registrations and licensing.

Drs Hadi Sutanto, Ficorinvest Building, Jalan Rasuna Said Kav C-18, Kuningan, Jakarta ☎ 513516 ✆ 62300. Represents Price Waterhouse and offers services matching those of Kantor Akuntan Sudjendro.

Drs Utomo & Co, Chase Plaza, Jalan Sudirman Kav 21, Jakarta ☎ 584030 ✆ 44168. Represents SGV

Consultants and specializes in tax and accounting assistance.

Malonda, Johan and Co, Jalan Pluit Raya 200 ☎ 669 0170. Represents Ernst & Whinney International and provides tax, accounting and management assistance as well as computer consultancy.

Business consultancies

Two experienced business consultancies which will help find local partners and investment opportunities are *Business Advisory Indonesia*, Kuningan Plaza Suite 304, Jalan Rasuna Said Kav C-11-14, Jakarta ☎ 517696 ✆ 62151, which is staffed by expatriates and has subsidiaries around the region; and the smaller firm, *Summa International*, 2nd Fl, Menara Duta, Jalan Rasuna Said Kav B-9, Jakarta ☎ 517839 ✆ 45504.

Chamber of commerce

The *Indonesian Chamber of Commerce and Industry* (KADIN), Gedung Chandra, 4th Fl, Jalan M.H. Thamrin 20, Jakarta ☎ 324000 or 324064, is a source for a local partner. Foreigners cannot join KADIN, but can meet and learn from its members.

Other sources of information

Information in English about business in Jakarta is hard to find. *Business Advisory Indonesia* publishes a monthly newsletter, and the Hong Kong-based *Business Asia* (a subsidiary of *The Economist*) publishes regional newsletters with relevant Indonesia coverage. *Pusat Data Business Indonesia*, Jalan Kartini 54-i, Jakarta ☎ 6391998, provides unparalleled databanks on business groups and individuals in Indonesia as well as regular reports on specific sectors. *Business News*, Jalan Abdul Muis 70, Jakarta ☎ 361399, publishes a newsletter in English including latest government regulations concerning business and economic matters.

Business and cultural awareness

Two passions are pre-eminent among the Indonesians. Foremost is the interwoven net of family, village and ethnic group, a necessary pillar of identity in a country spread across 13,677 islands. Following closely is the sense of nationhood, and an intense pride in a typically Indonesian spirit and way of doing things despite centuries of foreign influence.

Unity in diversity

A simplistic but popular anecdote attempts a summation of the diversity between Indonesia's 27 provinces and countless ethnic groups. A man has his toe trodden on. If he were Balinese, he would pray. If he were Buginese or Madurese, he would immediately beat up the offender. If he were Padang he would offer some money to alleviate shame all round. If he were Batak, he would scowl and rant and rave and do nothing. If he were Javanese, he would clear his throat politely, gesture vaguely at his sore toe, call a large crowd around him to discuss the subject and arrive at a decision by consensus possibly to do something about it sometime. An Indonesian-Chinese would probably ignore the whole thing as he has business to do.

The Chinese (2% of the population) are often resented by other Indonesians for their commercial acumen. A distinction is made, however, between *peranakan* Chinese, those who have been settled for generations, with Indonesian names, language and aspirations, and the *totok* Chinese, the late arrivals who are trusted less.

A blend of pragmatism Given that all these communities come from a village environment, living off the land and relating to feudal power structures as a matter of course while maintaining their own religious and mystical practices, it is little wonder that the country's motto is "Unity in diversity." Although more than 80% of Indonesia's 170m people are nominally Muslim (the others are Christian, Hindu and animist), daily life is informed with a syncretic blend of mystic pragmatism.

Pancasila

In an attempt to bolster the ideal of unity in diversity – and consolidate their own control – both of the presidents have added the so-called state ideology, *Pancasila*, to the pantheon of national values. Pancasila comprises five basic principles: faith in one God, in a just and civilized humanity, the unity of Indonesia, democracy guided by consensus, and social justice for all. Most Indonesians must take a course in Pancasila to signify conformity.

Phrase of approval Pancasila can also be a catch-all phrase applied to anything the government approves of. If something is deemed non-Pancasila – for example, direct criticism of the first family or a confrontational attitude to religion or politics – one is advised to change it fast or at least describe it differently. Pancasila thus becomes an imperative to stick to the middle of the road.

Consensus

Fundamental to business as well as personal relationships is the notion of consensus. Closely tied in to the general Asian emphasis on "face" and the importance of appearances, decisions should be arrived at through *musyawarah mufakat*, or agreement through consensus. Herein is found harmony and the avoidance of shame in the broadest sense (*malu*). Consensus, rather than confrontation, is essential in any negotiations.

Mutual assistance The other concept to understand is that of *gotong royong*, the long-established pattern of mutual assistance. It is more than the Western concept of "you scratch my back and I'll scratch yours." It involves helping another for no immediate reward, a far more subtle obligation.

Religion

Indonesia is the largest Muslim country in the world, but Westerners should be wary of assuming this means the country is awash with veiled women and fanatic preachers. Small pockets of fundamentalist Muslims do exist (especially in Aceh, on the western tip of the archipelago), but they have no political clout and little impact on the vast majority of Indonesians who pray regularly and observe Muslim festivals but eschew the radicalism found in some other Muslim countries.

Christians are the largest religious minority, and Roman Catholic Indonesians are found in key positions. The minister of defence General Benny Murdani is the most obvious example, and the respected daily paper *Kompas* is owned by a Roman Catholic. Hindus are found primarily in Bali, where Balinese versions of Hindu rites are fervently performed.

However, traditional animist beliefs and mystical practices hold perhaps greater sway than any of these world religions in the daily life of most Indonesians.

Language

Visitors can almost manage to get around in Jakarta simply by speaking English, but anyone wishing to go beyond city limits will have severe language problems. Apart from learning a few basic words in Indonesian, the only other language that might be useful – and then only with older, well-educated Indonesians – is Dutch. The well-prepared visitor should therefore learn a few Indonesian words to help his or her own mobility.

Education

The government's schooling system covers primary to tertiary levels. Almost all children between the ages

of 7 and 12 attend primary school and thousands of new schools – from one-room huts to vast urban complexes – are being built. Junior high school attendance is about a quarter of that at primary level, while senior high schools take half of that again. There are vocational colleges in most large towns.

Higher education About 5% of all those in the 19 to 24 age bracket attain higher education. There are about 50 state universities and 637 private institutions. The leading universites are the University of Indonesia in Jakarta, the Institute of Technology in Bandung (the "Oxford of Indonesia"), the Institute of Agriculture in Bogor, Jogjakarta's Gajah Mada University, and the Airlangga University in Surabaya. Of the elite students who study abroad, about 99% choose to return to Indonesia.

Attitudes to foreigners

Foreigners are regarded as guests, treated politely and are often invited into Indonesian homes, especially outside Jakarta. But only if a foreigner patiently and genuinely makes an effort to learn the language and understand the culture will he or she make lasting friendships. The most common attitude to foreigners is friendly non-comprehension.

Boorish and blunt Foreigners are often regarded as boorish and blunt, as well as foolish for being so open about everything. An Indonesian announcing the death of his wife is more likely to laugh than show how devastated he really is. Although there is a surface identification with Western trends, such as in music, fashion, movies and junk food, it does not take a sensitive foreigner long to realize that Indonesians still do things their way.

Business attitudes

Indonesians have a more relaxed attitude to business and a more elastic concept of time than do many Westerners. Most Indonesian business will take far longer than hoped or planned for. Officially, working hours are from 8 to 4, with an hour for lunch taken sometime between 12 and 2. On Fridays, the Muslim day of prayer, government offices close at 11am. Saturday mornings are usually working mornings, at least for low-level staff.

Getting to work Nearly all the roads in Jakarta will be clogged for at least two hours every morning from 7.30am, and for another two hours between 4pm and dusk. In between those times, traffic is frustrating and often incomprehensibly complex.

The telephones are the other main bugbear. Monday mornings are particularly bad as most city exchanges are overloaded and getting a line is difficult. Experience has shown that certain numbers are hardest to get, such as those beginning with 51, 578, 67 and 33. Calling Indonesians at home should be done only in emergencies or if the recipient is a good friend. However, there is a good chance of contacting an Indonesian early in the morning.

Women in business

There is a growing number of Indonesian women in business and the professions, but they make headway by staying within traditionally defined expectations of women. The foreign businesswoman will find the most common question asked is "are you married?" Tradition would have it that a single women should answer "*belum*," meaning "not yet." You are regarded as a freak otherwise.

Old concepts Conversation will often rely on old concepts of "ladies first" and a "good girls/bad girls" mentality. That a woman can be bits of both is something that is only gradually being accepted. Morality is conservative, too, though nothing like that found in strict Muslim countries.

Courteous respect Despite these social inhibitions, women are treated with courteous respect by Indonesian businessmen. Women business travellers are regarded as foreigners first and foremost. In general, they must prove themselves, as men must, and should accept that they are a rarity, and that they will be stared at more – staring back won't help, neither will irritation. And save the revealing outfits for your homecoming.

Business meetings

These are organized through intermediaries – either secretaries or a local agent for a foreign firm. There is a strong habit of delegation so that even if initial contacts are made directly, the venue, confirmation and transport required will be dealt with by others. First meetings with an Indonesian will rarely happen over a drink, unless the Indonesian suggests it. Courtesy calls at the Indonesian's office are more common. At all stages, business cards are invaluable.

Punctuality Although Indonesians are not renowned for their punctuality, foreigners are expected to be on time. There may well be delays or simply no-shows in the initial stages of a difficult relationship. This is to test foreigners' patience, not necessarily to send them away for good. If weeks have gone by with no answer to an inquiring phone call, it is probably a message that the inquiry will not be answered. The Indonesian would just rather not say "no" directly.

Breaking the ice Once in the meeting, a lot of handshaking takes place and some ice-breaking chat about how long the foreigner has been in town. Sweet tea is often served but it is best not to start drinking until after the host has done so. The same goes for smoking. Indonesians are avid smokers, and if the visitor has foreign cigarettes to offer, they may be rejected in favour of the local *kretek* or clove cigarettes.

Hospitality

Invitations for dinners or cocktails are first sent in writing and confirmed later by phone. Guests normally arrive half an hour after the appointed time, expecting to have a drink – soft or alcohol – for another half-hour before eating. Buffet dinners are very popular and practical, with the most senior or honoured guest being asked to begin. Servants will sometimes serve at the table directly, and no effort should be made by a guest to help clear up. Walking into the kitchen in search of a drink is trespassing on the servants' domain. By the time coffee is served, Indonesian guests may well start leaving, murmuring *"Permisi,"* meaning "excuse me."

Gifts Anyone returning from a holiday, from Bali or New York, is expected to bring back small gifts or souvenirs for friends and staff. These can range from earrings to T-shirts to foreign candles, but should not be too lavish. Indonesians will usually not open presents in front of the giver, but will always remember the gift. Small offerings of flowers, chocolates or candy are welcomed by Indonesian hostesses at dinners as a matter of course.

Etiquette

Politeness is crucial in Indonesia. Foreigners need to be formal until the lead is given by the Indonesians to be more relaxed. Familiarity with one's host, and with his staff, is not advisable. Nor is talking loudly, complaining, or initiating physical contact (like backslapping) other than handshakes.

Unequal status The foreigner must learn that although everybody has status of some kind, that status must be recognized. As a guest, a foreigner should keep to a traditional hierarchy, greeting or honouring the boss/host first, giving special deference to the aged.

Deference to one's boss can be taken to extremes in Indonesia. If you are boss you may be told only what you are expected to want to hear. In this case, don't confront the information-giver directly, but find out what you

want to know in another way and thank everybody for their help.

Introductions can become complicated with titles and long names, but Indonesians will happily explain a pronunciation. The most formal introduction would include the following information, in roughly this order: *Bapak* or *Ibu* (meaning Sir or Madam, and universally applicable), an academic or professional title if applicable, the noble title if the person uses it, and the person's given and family names.

Academic titles will confuse those unfamiliar with Dutch. *Drs* means *Doktorandus,* a male graduate of any field but engineering or law. *Dra* is the female equivalent. *Ir* stands for *Insinjur,* the title for any graduate of engineering, while *S Econ, SH* and *SS* stand for *Sarjuna Economics, Hukum* and *Sastra* respectively. These are graduates in economics, law and letters.

Start with small talk

Conversations begin with the predictable subjects, particularly with questions about origin, what part of Indonesia a person is from, how many children they have, and the like. Subjects such as age, a foreigner's extravagance, intimate problems, or specific personal inquiries should be avoided.

Avoid blunt talk If there are grievances to be discussed, talk around the subject, politely persistent, and the Indonesian will see your point. Direct talk will only embarrass him. Unpleasant news should be delivered only in private, if at all.

Favourite subjects include a foreigner's efforts to learn the language, Indonesian food and art, the beauty of the country and how much the foreigner likes Indonesia.

JAKARTA

Jakarta is the capital of a country that straddles the world's largest archipelago – 13,677 islands in total, including the whole of Sumatra and large parts of Borneo and New Guinea, three of the world's five largest islands. Indonesia's population is estimated at over 170m, making it South-East Asia's most populous nation and the fifth most populous in the world. Of these people, 100m live on the island of Java, where Jakarta is located. Conservative estimates put the city's population at 7m – others make it as high as 10m – all living in an area of 650 sq km/250 sq miles, just larger than Singapore. Most of Jakarta's inhabitants were not born there, but drifted to the city from all parts of the archipelago.

Although officially Muslim, many Javanese still cling to older Hindu and animistic beliefs. Among these is the desire to live upon the ground and maintain contact with the earth, which means that high-rise living is an alien concept. This has had a profound influence on the nature and appearance of the city. From the upper floors of the few tall office blocks the observer looks over a sea of single-floor dwellings with warm, orange-brown roofs. Jakarta's inhabitants have brought with them to Jakarta an essentially rural way of life, creating urban versions of the *kampong*, numerous sprawling but basically self-contained villages. To the Western visitor, much of the city will seem very unsophisticated indeed; at the edge of modern Jakarta it takes courage to penetrate the beaten earth tracks bordered by open drains and high walls which lead off every highway.

With a spiralling birthrate – 40% of Jakarta's population was born since 1970, and forecasts put the city's population at 25m by 2005 – family planning, transmigration and infrastructural improvements all command a high priority in government thinking. To discourage the continuing drift towards the city, volunteers are sought who are willing to start new lives in Indonesia's vast areas of virgin territory. With World Bank and EC funding, willing migrants are provided with land, housing, tools and livestock as an incentive to begin a new life and so far more than 4m have taken up the challenge. Even so, Jakarta's city planners have already framed a huge development programme that will engulf the surrounding cities of Bogor (already a suburb), Tangerang and Bekasi, resulting in a 12,000 sq km/4,600 sq mile 21stC city to be known by the acronym Jabotabek. Work on the infrastructure has already begun, with the construction of a new airport, roads, residential areas and industrial parks underway. Historical buildings are being restored and *kampongs* provided with hospitals, schools, community centres and fresh water supplies, resulting in a gradual improvement that retains the city's essential character and avoids wholesale clearance. Jakarta is one of the most foreign, the least modern and, for the business visitor, the most challenging of big cities in South-East Asia. But it is now cleaner and greener than it has been since World War II and improving all the time.

Arriving

You can get to Jakarta by ship but most people fly. There are daily flights from Singapore and services from Europe, North America and Australasia. Garuda, the national airline, is not held in high regard by either seasoned business travellers or the international travel trade though its service and image is said to be improving.

Soekarno-Hatta International Airport

All scheduled international and domestic flights arrive at the Soekarno-Hatta International Airport, 20km/13 miles west of Jakarta on the coastal plain near Cengkareng. The three adjacent terminals, two international and one domestic, are built in a style based on ancient Indonesian village architecture: clusters of red-roofed pavilions surround courtyards with well-kept gardens. The doors from the customs exit lead directly to the airport service road and the pick-up points for taxis and other transport. It should not take more than 30min to clear the airport. Departing passengers pay a tax of Rp3850 on domestic flights and Rp9900 on international flights.

Facilities The Visitor Information Service Office is immediately to the left of the exit. Staff also help with hotel reservations and transport; always bargain over prices. There are banks, restaurants, VIP lounges, a duty-free shop, newsstands and souvenir shops in the departure lounge beyond passport control, and the same range of facilities, minus the duty-free shops, in the domestic terminal; there are also exchange facilities in the baggage claim area. The lost and found counter is for baggage lost in the baggage reclaim area; for articles mislaid elsewhere, contact the security duty officer. Most services open 8–8; banks stay open until 11pm, and the coffee shop opens early. Airport inquiries ☎ 550 5179.

City link Tighter control means that passengers are no longer mobbed on arrival by porters and taxi drivers. Go for Bluebird, Steady Safe or Kosti Jaya taxis (all painted blue) if possible, or use hotel transport. The journey into Jakarta takes about 45min.

Hotel transport Some hotels operate a complimentary transfer service to and from the airport or a bus shuttle service at around Rp4,000; others provide an air-conditioned car at Rp24,000. It is best to arrange hotel transport in advance.

Taxi The taxi rank is to the right of the airport exit. Taxi drivers will approach before you reach the rank and you can negotiate a competitive fare if you wish. However, the chances are that the cab will be in poor condition and lack air conditioning. It is better to join the line and take a blue-coloured air-conditioned taxi. Make sure that the taxi meter is operating; the cost will be around Rp17,000 including tolls and airport surcharge.

Car rental Avis ☎ 5507088 and Hertz ☎ 5507125 will provide a limousine to meet you at the airport. Avis will also rent out self-drive cars, but prefers not to do so.

Bus The airport bus service operates at 30min intervals to five destinations in Jakarta; the most central for the hotels is Gambir Railway Station, where you can pick up a cab. The fare is Rp2,000. The buses are air-conditioned and clean, but this is not a service for anyone with a lot of bags or a tight schedule.

Getting around

Taxis are the best way of travelling around the city.

Hotel transport Few hotels run their own limousine service. Most use Avis or Hertz, or one of the reliable taxi firms.

Taxi You seldom wait long for a taxi in Jakarta. Indeed, kerb-crawling drivers will immediately approach any foreigner on foot in the city and firmness is required to shake them off. However, you face three problems when picking up a cab in the street. First, the taxi may not have air conditioning and a long journey will not be very comfortable. Second, the driver will attempt to haggle over the fare and if he refuses to use the meter it is best to alight and find another cab. Check too that the fare is set at Rp500 (Rp600 for air-conditioned vehicles) and not ten times that amount; many meters have been tampered with to favour the driver in this way. Finally, the driver may not understand you, and a map is useful to show him where you want to go.

To avoid all these difficulties, stick to the blue taxis: *Blue Bird* ☎ 325607; *Kosti Jaya* ☎ 581022; *Steady Safe* ☎ 333333. These are clean, well-maintained and air-conditioned, with drivers who are used to dealing with visitors and know their way around the city. Fares are relatively low; a typical journey across the city costs Rp7,000–19,000.

Driving Car rental firms are reluctant to allow visitors to drive themselves, particularly in Jakarta itself. Drivers are no more aggressive than they are in many big cities in the region but the traffic laws are complex, signs difficult to read, and the police only too ready to leap on anyone unfamiliar with the city. *Avis* ☎ 3329000 will rent you a self-drive car if you insist. They, along with *Hertz* ☎ 336942, will provide limousines for a minimum eight-hour day.

Walking As far as possible you should avoid walking around Jakarta; the heat is intense and the humidity debilitating. In addition you have to contend not only with a lack of sidewalks, piles of rubbish and open sewers, but with unwanted attention from every beggar, schoolboy, hawker and taxi driver you encounter along the route.

Public transport Buses are stifling, recklessly driven and not to be recommended.

Outside Jakarta
Air Domestic carriers, principally *Garuda*, operate an extensive internal network and provide the only realistic way to travel around this vast country. Flights are often full and it is essential to make reservations at least two weeks ahead and reconfirm every time. Garuda has many offices and agents in Jakarta; reservations ☎ 333408 ext. 2116. Of the other main domestic carriers, *Merpati Nusantara* ☎ 417404 operates in Eastern Indonesia and serves the many small islands between Sulawesi and Irian Jaya; *Bouraq Indonesia* ☎ 655170 operates throughout the archipelago.
Driving Drivers are unpredictable and roads are poor and full of primitive vehicles. *Avis*, *Hertz* and *Blue Bird* will all quote rates for a chauffeur-driven car for long-distance travel.
Trains in Indonesia are slow and often late. Most inter-city trains leave Jakarta in the early evening and reach their destination the following morning. The first-class Bima express service with air conditioning, sleeping cars and a dining car departs from Kota Station daily at 4pm for Yogyakarta, Solo and Surabaya. From Surabaya an air-conditioned boat train takes a further 11hr to reach Bali where the rail system ends. Tickets can be bought up to a day in advance from the station ☎ 278515 or from *Carnation Travel* ☎ 344027.

Area by area
More than 300 years of Dutch colonial rule followed by rapid postwar expansion have left a distinctive mark upon modern Jakarta. Business visitors are likely to be based around Medan Merdeka or the long, congested north-south highway (Jalan M.H. Thamrin, which becomes Jalan Jenderal Sudirman going south), bisecting the centre of the city.
Old Dutch quarter The Portuguese were the first Western explorers to reach Indonesia, but it was the

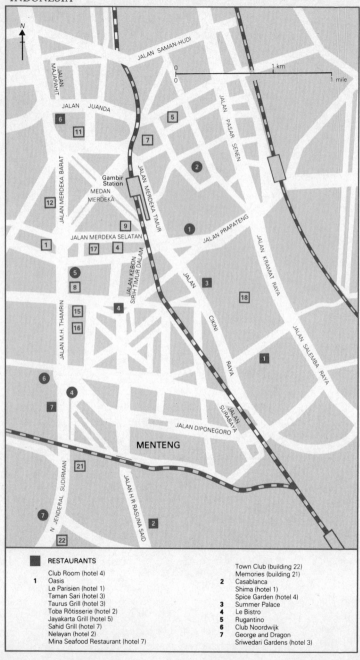

RESTAURANTS

Club Room (hotel 4)

1 Oasis
Le Parisien (hotel 1)
Taman Sari (hotel 3)
Taurus Grill (hotel 3)
Toba Rôtisserie (hotel 2)
Jayakarta Grill (hotel 5)
Sahid Grill (hotel 7)
Nelayan (hotel 2)
Mina Seafood Restaurant (hotel 7)

Town Club (building 22)
Memories (building 21)

2 Casablanca
Shima (hotel 1)
Spice Garden (hotel 4)

3 Summer Palace

4 Le Bistro

5 Rugantino

6 Club Noordwijk

7 George and Dragon
Sriwedari Gardens (hotel 3)

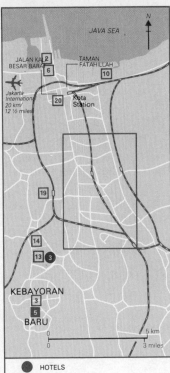

● **HOTELS**

1 Aryaduta
2 Borobudur
3 Hilton
4 Mandarin
5 Sari Pacific
6 Indonesia
7 Sahid Jaya

□ **BUILDINGS AND SIGHTS**

1 Bank of Indonesia
2 Bahari (Maritime) Museum
3 Blok M
4 City Hall
5 General Post Office
6 Harbour Master Tower
7 Istiqlal Mosque
8 Jakarta Theatre Building
9 Jakarta Trade Fair Complex
10 Jaya Ancol Dreamland
11 Merdeka Palace
12 National Museum
13 National Stadium
14 Parliament Building
15 Sarinah Department Store
16 Skyline Building
17 Stock Exchange
18 Taman Ismail Marzuki Arts Centre
19 Textile Museum
20 Wayang Museum
21 Wisma Indocement
22 Wisma Metropolitan II

Dutch who, lured by the lucrative spice trade, settled and built the city. Named Batavia after the Germanic tribe from which the Dutch trace their origins, the city was renamed Jakarta (city of victory) by the Japanese in 1942. The harbour and the restored Dutch buildings grouped around the Taman Fatahillah (the old town square) are charming to look at now, but in the 18th century malaria and cholera were rife and the canals, modelled on those of Amsterdam, were full of stinking refuse.

Medan Merdeka In the 19th century the old city was largely demolished and replaced by a new and improved city to the south. The focus was Koningsplein, or King's Square, the modern Medan Merdeka (Freedom Square). Here the present and past of Jakarta overlap and the graceful classical buildings which surround it house all the main ministries of the Indonesian government. On the north side is the Merdeka Palace, built in 1879 for the Dutch governors-general and now the official residence of the president. Parades celebrating independence are held annually in the square in commemoration. At the centre is the 137-metre Monumen Nasional, topped with a bronze flame, which is visible from many parts of the city.

Jalan M.H. Thamrin/Jalan Jenderal Sudirman Most of Jakarta's development has taken place in the post-Sukarno period when foreign investment has begun to return to Indonesia. Almost all the high-rise buildings which are scattered along the main artery, Jalan M.H. Thamrin/Jalan Jenderal Sudirman, were built during the last two decades. Long stretches of vacant land separate one building from the next, but slowly the areas in between are being filled to house the foreign banks and the trading, computer and petrochemical companies which have established offices in Jakarta, plus the hotels to support Indonesia's important tourist industry.

Southern suburbs Farther south still is the modern parliament building, next to the enormous Senayan (National) Stadium, built for the 1962 Asian Games. Across the road is the beginning of Blok M, one of Jakarta's new housing areas, and the main shopping district for the more affluent citizens who live in large mansions in the neighbouring district of Kemang. New industrial areas are developing in the hinterland between here and the southern city of Bogor, once the summer retreat of the Dutch merchants.

The modern port of Tanjung Priok is about 10km/6 miles northeast of the city.

Hotels

There are many hotels in Jakarta, but few of a very high standard. Hotels which appear to be inexpensive usually charge inflated prices in the bar and for telephone calls. Sound-proofing often tends to be poor, which means the amplified prayers from Jakarta's many mosques and the sound of television sets in neighbouring rooms are often intrusive.

Among the few first-class hotels, long-stay visitors may prefer those with large grounds and sports facilities; there is little to do in the city after work, and the working day usually finishes in the middle of the afternoon. The Hilton and the Borobudur have the best sports facilities, but the Mandarin, Aryaduta and Sari Pacific are all central and perfectly acceptable choices for a brief visit.

All rooms have 24hr room service, air conditioning, IDD telephone, minibar, radio and TV. All hotels have a travel desk, and standard business facilities include photocopying, typing, translation, telex and fax. Several hotels have licensed money-changers on the premises who give better rates than the hotel exchange desk. Quoted rates are subject to 15.5% service charge and tax.

Aryaduta $$$
44–46 Jalan Prapatan, 10110
☎ *376008* ⊤⊠ *46220 Fax 349896* • *AE DC MC V* • *Hyatt International* • *304 rooms, 36 suites, 4 restaurants, 2 bars*
The Aryaduta is in the city centre, close to the Presidential Palace, government offices and major embassies. After total renovation in 1987, it has moved up a notch into the first league of Jakarta hotels and is now one of the most pleasantly furnished. The predominant colour scheme is soft grey, with vividly painted indigenous carvings in the public rooms. Bedrooms are large, light and airy, with rattan furniture upholstered in the locally woven material known as *ikat*, and free-standing desks. Those staying in the Regency Club rooms have the use of a private lounge. Le Parisien (French) and Shima (Japanese) are both excellent (see *Restaurants*). Shops, florist, hairdresser • pool, gym, sauna, squash • computer rental, 4 meeting rooms (capacity up to 600).

Borobudur $$$$
Jalan Lapangan Banteng Selatan, 10710 ☎ *370108* ⊤⊠ *44156 Fax 359741* • *AE DC MC V* • *Inter-Continental* • *977 rooms, 195 suites, 4 restaurants, 2 bars*
Standing in extensive lush tropical gardens which contain a range of excellent sports facilities, the Borobudur has the added advantage of being very close to the city centre, just off the northeast corner of Medan Merdeka. The lobby is grand with marble columns and rows of Buddhist statues, inspired by the great carved temple at Borobudur

from which the hotel derives its name. The room decorations make liberal use of local crafts: *wayang* shadow puppets and carved statues of the island deity, Garuda, and woven *ikat* upholstery. Desks provide ample working space and private offices can be rented through the business centre. The Toba Rôtisserie is brassy but formal (see *Restaurants*) and the coffee lounge is a popular spot for informal meetings. Shops, hairdresser, florist • pool, gym, jogging track, tennis, squash, badminton, racquetball, mini-golf, roller-skating track • 13 meeting rooms including ballroom (capacity up to 2,400).

Hilton $$$$
Jalan Jenderal Gatot Subroto, 10002 ☎ 583051 ⊤⨉ 46673 Fax 583091 • *AE DC MC V* • *603 rooms, 61 suites, 6 restaurants, 3 bars*
The Hilton is on the southern fringe of the business district, only 15 minutes from Medan Merdeka. Yet the short distance is enough to make a difference in the atmosphere; the air is fresher, the temperature a degree or so cooler, and cool breezes blow through the large gardens. The hotel is a favourite retreat; the dining rooms are full of business people at lunch time and the function rooms are in constant use. The main lobby with its magnificent crimson and gold lacquered ceiling is a replica of the palace of the Sultan of Jogyakarta in Central Java. The rooms have all been redecorated in pastel colours with local rattan furniture and batik upholstery. Rooms in the Garden Tower are considerably larger than average with big free-standing desks. There are 15 garden suites overlooking the large pool and an elegant penthouse with private pool, fitness centre and helipad. There are two nonsmoking floors and 20 rooms reserved for female executives. As well as the excellent Taman Sari (see *Restaurants*), two attractive outdoor restaurants under thatched pavilions are popular in the evenings when,

released from the usual formality of hotel dining rooms, guests tend to mingle more easily. In the grounds are an executive club with its own sports centre, bar, grill room and ballroom, and an Indonesian-style bazaar, selling local crafts, set around a lake. The business centre is open 24hr. Shops, florist, hairdresser • 2 pools, 2 gyms, sauna, tennis, squash • UPI news service, meeting rooms (capacity up to 800), 2 ballrooms (350 and 900).

Mandarin $$$$
Jalan M.H. Thamrin, PO Box 3392, Jakarta ☎ 321307 ⊤⨉ 61755 *Fax 324669* • *AE DC MC V* • *Mandarin Oriental* • *436 rooms, 19 suites, 3 restaurants, 2 bars*
At the Mandarin the emphasis is on outstanding service and top-class food. Messages are delivered to rooms as soon as they arrive, requests are promptly carried out and staff are efficient and discreet. The Club Room (see *Restaurants*) and Spice Garden both serve food of the highest quality. Opinions are mixed about the room decor and working space is limited. The handmade bedspreads were designed by the famous batik artist Iwan Tirta (who has made clothes for Queen Elizabeth II and the Reagans). The executive centre has willing and capable staff, although sending a telex late at night can be painful. Shops, florist, hairdresser • pool, gym, sauna, squash • city-wide paging system, Reuter's news service, 5 meeting rooms (capacity up to 200) plus ballroom (capacity 800).

Sari Pacific $$$$
6 Jalan M.H. Thamrin, 10340 ☎ 323707 ⊤⨉ 44514 Fax 323650 • *AE DC MC V* • *Pan Pacific* • *480 rooms, 20 suites, 3 restaurants, 2 bars*
The mainly European guests, a mixture of tourists and business travellers, enjoy the relaxed style and friendly service of the Sari Pacific, and find its central location extremely convenient. Many of the

catering staff are European too, which may explain the popularity of the restaurants, and the excellent pastry shop-cum-delicatessen is reputed to be the best in town. The rooms are comfortable, if not spectacular, with adequate working space. The hotel has a business centre, and the Pitstop discotheque attracts the local expatriate community at weekends. Shops, florist, hairdresser • pool, gym, sauna • Reuter's news service, 3 meeting rooms (capacity up to 400).

OTHER HOTELS

Indonesia ($$$) *Jalan M.H. Thamrin, PO Box 54* ☎ *320008* ⊤⊠ *61347 Fax 321508* • *AE DC MC V.* Reasonably priced, central hotel with pool, tennis courts and business centre.

Sahid Jaya ($$$) *86 Jalan Jenderal Sudirman, PO Box 41* ☎ *587031* ⊤⊠ *46331 Fax 583768* • *AE DC MC V.* On the central highway and popular with European tourists and executives prepared to accept no-frills service. Comfortable rooms, pool and business centre.

Restaurants

High-spending executives are in a minority in Jakarta. Certainly there are not enough of them to sustain more than a handful of first-class restaurants, and these few are mainly in the hotels. Even smart establishments like the Club Room at the Mandarin find it necessary to mount special promotions and put on entertainment at weekends just to pull in enough customers. On their own, Indonesian business people tend towards the steak and chicken chains that have begun to spring up in the city, filling the gap between inexpensive local and pricier Western-style restaurants. For entertaining, a buffet lunch at one of the major hotels is the usual choice.

With the honourable exceptions of the Taman Sari and the aptly named Oasis, restaurants serving Indonesian food have been slow to improve their appeal to Westerners by stepping up standards of food preparation, service and atmosphere. Most are still canteen-like, though several hotels are leading the way in presenting the varied local cuisine more attractively. Reservations are advisable, though not usually necessary. Restaurants charge 21% service and tax on top of menu prices.

Club Room $$
Mandarin Hotel ☎ *321307* • *AE DC MC V*
The Club Room is one of Jakarta's few restaurants with class and so appeals to those who want to discuss business seriously in an atmosphere of calm. Only quiet piano music is played on weekday evenings but a traditional jazz band takes over on Saturdays when guests are encouraged to dress in 1920s style. The predominantly white dining room is decorated with English sporting and humorous prints, and

smart waiters provide polished service. The menu is brief but supplemented by seasonal local dishes. Fine French wines, not outrageously priced.

Oasis $$$
47 Jalan Raden Saleh ☎ *327818* • *closed Sun* • *AE DC MC V*
The Oasis is one of the most celebrated restaurants in Asia, famed as much for its setting as for its food, and is much used by Jakarta's top business executives and government ministers. Reservations are essential.

It is housed in a Dutch colonial mansion, furnished with an intriguing collection of antiques and indigenous art from the far-flung reaches of the archipelago. A Continental menu is offered but the Oasis is best known for its local cooking, in particular *rijsttafel*, a vast selection of the best of Indonesian cuisine which, to be appreciated, needs a party of at least four. A troupe of Indonesian singers entertains from 9pm.

Le Parisien $$
Aryaduta Hotel ☎ *376008* • *D only* • *AE DC MC V*

A light and airy restaurant decorated in the *belle époque* style and a popular venue with local executives. The atmosphere is comfortably formal and the service friendly but unobtrusive. The food is French in style and attractively presented, with a strong emphasis on a huge range of delicious seafood.

Taman Sari $$
Hilton Hotel ☎ *587981* • *AE DC MC V* • *closed Sun* •

Considered by many to be the best restaurant in town, the Taman Sari is styled after the old water-palace of the same name, built by royalty in Jogjakarta as a playground for royal mistresses. It is very suitable for top-level entertaining. There are private dining rooms attached, and a subdued quartet to entertain in the evening. It is the home of Indonesian *nouvelle cuisine*, which is served in the evenings only while lunches are European.

Taurus Grill $$
Hilton Hotel ☎ *583051* • *AE DC MC V*

The Taurus Grill is reserved for members of the Hilton's executive club and hotel guests, but anyone who expects to do a lot of formal entertaining might well choose to stay at the Hilton for access to the Grill. A lunch-time haunt of locals and expatriates, its formal atmosphere is softened by large floral displays of multicoloured orchids. The food is standard grill-room fare with a popular beef trolley, served with flair. Extensive wine list.

Toba Rôtisserie $$
Borobudur Hotel ☎ *370108* • *AE DC MC V*

A safe and central choice for business entertaining with top-quality imported beef and *flambé* dishes. The restaurant has a somewhat dark and over-decorated feel but is comfortable and private.

Good but casual

Jakarta has several other restaurants which, although smart enough to attract a business clientele, are essentially variations on a limited theme. Reliable grill rooms include the comfortable and friendly *Jayakarta Grill* in the Sari Pacific hotel ☎ 323707, and the *Sahid Grill* in the Sahid Jaya hotel ☎ 587031, which is on the roof with good views, although the music can obtrude in the evening. Two good seafood restaurants are the *Nelayan* in the Borobudur hotel ☎ 370108, and the *Mina Seafood Restaurant* in the Sahid Jaya hotel ☎ 587031.

All commercial office blocks have at least one restaurant, most of them geared to the swift one-hour lunch break. A few rise above this level. One of the best and busiest is the *Town Club*, 16th Fl, Wisma Metropolitan II, 31 Jalan Jenderal Sudirman ☎ 5781659. Specializing in lobster, it is elegant but rather small and with little room between tables. Nearby, *Memories*, Ground Fl, Wisma Indocement, Jalan Jenderal Sudirman ☎ 5781008, is more private and has a large collection of Dutch colonial antiquities. *Casablanca*, Kununigan Plaza, Jalan Rasuna Said ☎ 514800, a supper club with dancing and entertainment in the evenings, is popular with the local young professionals. The Bedouin-style decor is stunning and the food is excellent.

Of the many Japanese restaurants, the *Shima* in the Aryaduta hotel ☎ 376008 has the most pleasant atmosphere and cosmopolitan clientele. Chinese restaurants are generally disappointing with the exception of the Mandarin hotel's *Spice Garden* ☎ 321307, whose short menu manages to include all the best-known Sichuan dishes; and the *Summer Palace*, 7th Fl, Tedja Buana Bldg, 29 Jalan Menteng Raya ☎ 332969, staffed by Hong Kong chefs who turn out authentic Cantonese and Sichuan cuisine. Restaurants serving European food and which are popular with expatriates include *Le Bistro*, 75 Jalan K.H. Wahid Hasyim ☎ 347475, offering a limited but typically French menu in an intimate setting where the atmosphere frequently becomes lively in the evenings; *Rugantino*, 28 Jalan Melawai Raya ☎ 714727, staffed by Italian chefs; and *Club Noordwijk*, 5 Jalan Ir. H. Juanda ☎ 353909, decorated with memorabilia of old Jakarta and serving both Continental and Europeanized Indonesian food.

When they have only themselves to please, expatriates go to the *George and Dragon*, 32 Jalan Telukbetung ☎ 325625, for grilled marlin and various curries and a British pub atmosphere. The *Sriwedari Gardens* in the Hilton hotel ☎ 583051 is best for open-air eating around the pool.

Bars

The distinction between bars and restaurants is not always clear; in most places that call themselves pubs and bars, drinking and conversation seem incidental to the main business of serving food. It is also difficult in Indonesia to find somewhere to enjoy a drink without the infliction of vocal groups singing bland versions of the latest pop songs. Even the Mandarin's *Captain's Bar*, an otherwise relaxing meeting place, has a pianist alternating with country-and-western groups and sports videos, and is a popular late-night

spot. Because it is music-free, the *Kudus Bar* at the Hilton has become Jakarta's favourite meeting place for social or business discussions, but be prepared for the freezing air conditioning. *The Tavern* at the Aryaduta hotel is pleasant enough and the *Pendopo Bar* at the Borobudur hotel has a lively atmosphere, helped by the highly professional jazz band which performs on Sunday evenings. Three bars have a more authentic after-work, tie-loosening atmosphere: the *George and Dragon*, 32 Jalan Telukbetung, is frequented by the local rugby team and attracts a cosmopolitan crowd of traders and financiers (see *Restaurants*); *Vic's Viking*, round the corner at 31 Jalan M.H. Thamrin, is less lively but provides a wide selection of open sandwiches; and the *Green Pub*, Jakarta Theatre Bldg, M.H. Jalan Thamrin ☎ 359332, has Mexican decor and food and a lively jazz band. The aptly named *Hotmen Bar*, Hotel Menteng, 28 Jalan Gondangdia Lama, is the haunt of unattached oilmen in search of local female company.

Entertainment

The daily *Jakarta Post* has a comprehensive "where to go" section listing popular and more serious entertainment with reviews. Jakarta is not particularly strong on culture and few performances by visiting artists are ever sold out.

Theatre, music, dance Western artists rarely appear but any who do usually perform at the *Taman Ismail Marzuki Arts Centre*, 73 Jalan Cikini Raya ☎ 337357. This cultural complex is also the home of the Jakarta Symphony Orchestra and has nightly performances of Javanese dance-drama (*wayang orang*), and shadow puppet plays (*wayang kulit*) as well as modern Indonesian drama. Polished performances of Indonesia's intricate *gamelan* music, which has inspired many contemporary Western composers, can be heard every Sunday 9.30–10.30am at the *National Museum*, Jalan Merdeka Barat.

The *Hilton* often stages performances of opera, cabaret and plays, notably those put on by the British Airways Playhouse company, a group of professional actors.
Cinema The Indonesian Board of Censors wields a clumsy pair of scissors so, rather than allow films to be butchered, distributors tend to avoid Indonesia. Most films on show are second-rate local productions, but you might catch an old classic if you are lucky. Well worth seeing, however, is the cinerama film *Beautiful Indonesia*, designed as propaganda but still a spectacular quick guide to the country. It is shown on gigantic screens at the *Keong Emas Imax Theatre* ☎ 8401021, part of the "Indonesia in Miniature" complex off the Jagorawi Toll Road.
Nightlife In most Jakarta discos up to half the clientele is for sale, but the *Pitstop* at the Sari Pacific hotel and the long-established *Tanamur Disco*, 14 Jalan Tanah Abang Timur ☎ 535947, are both sociable rendezvous for relaxed drinks and dancing, and the Tanamur is a comfortable place for women to visit. More up-to-the-minute is the Borobudur hotel's *Music Room* with its lighting and effects. Local taste is for the vast and crowded *Stardust Disco* at the Jayakarta Tower Hotel, Jalan Hayam Wuruk ☎ 6294408, or the expensive and more exclusive *Ebony Videotheque*, Kuningan Plaza, Jalan H.R. Rasuna Said ☎ 513700, the first in Jakarta with laser and video systems. *Pete's Club*, 57 Jalan Jenderal Sudirman ☎ 587401, has live rock bands but look twice before befriending any of the beautifully dressed and made-up young ladies: the club is a haunt of the city's many *bancis* or transvestites.

Among the city's nightclubs, the *Oriental* at the Hilton attracts a lively crowd. The cabaret at the *Nirwana Supper Club* at the Hotel Indonesia,

Jalan M.H. Thamrin ☎ 320008, attracts many local businessmen and their wives; and the *Blue Ocean*, 5 Jalan Hayam Wuruk ☎ 361134, has a large and lavish ballroom for dancing with the resident hostesses.

Shopping
Jakarta can in no way compete with Singapore and Hong Kong for shopping. Imports are heavily taxed and so the best buys are local crafts and antiques, sold by a large number of shops. Many of these have sprung up recently in the new hotel shopping arcades or in the vast Blok M development in Kebayoran Baru. Most shops here are open 9–6, and a few accept major credit cards. A good place to start is the *Sarinah Department Store*, Jalan M.H. Thamrin (also at Blok M) which stocks a vast range of inexpensive batik and handicrafts including silver and leatherware, cane furniture, masks, woodcarvings and wood or leather puppets. Or try the arts and crafts mart in the Jaya Ancol Dreamland complex on the bay in north Jakarta, where you can watch the craftsmen at work.
Antiques It takes an experienced eye to tell the difference between the genuine and the imitation in Jakarta's main flea-market, Jalan Surabaya. More reliable are the three shops dating from colonial times in Jalan Majapahit: *Garuda Antiques* (12), *Arjuna* (16A) and *Lee Cheong* (32). Near to the Aryaduta hotel is another street of shops, Jalan Kebon Sirih Timur Dalam, selling everything from genuine Chinese porcelain to primitive carved wooden figures; *Djody's* at 22 is where many professional dealers find their stock, and new objects are continually being brought in. Especially fine are the ancient Suvanese *ikat* textiles and terracottas and Balinese costume jewellery. Another concentration of antique shops is in Jalan Palatehan, part of the Blok M shopping plaza, Kebayoran Baru, where the stock includes furniture, jewellery,

puppets, paintings and dance masks. **Batik** in Java is of unsurpassed quality. For some of the finest prints, visit the boutique of leading designer *Iwan Tirta*, 25 Jalan Panarukan ☎ 337244. His designs, based on Wotan styles and traditional native patterns, have influenced others whose products may be cheaper: try *Batik Dana Hadi*, 1A Jalan Raden Saleh, and the batik cooperative *GKBI*, 39 Jalan H.A. Salim.

Jewellery Native art has also inspired Indonesian jewellers to create striking contemporary pieces in silver and opal. *Jay's Jewelry* in the Mandarin hotel shopping arcade is a long-established outlet for leading designers, whereas the shops in the Borobudur and Sari Pacific hotels specialize in the work of the artist Joyce Spiro. *Iwan Holmes*, another accomplished craftsman, has a shop at 12 Kebayoran Baru, Blok M, and other fine work can be bought at the *Opal Centre* in the Indonesian Bazaar in the grounds of the Hilton.

Sightseeing

The old harbour of Sunda Kelpa and the restored Dutch buildings to the south make an attractive and photogenic walk. The old town square area, which has been renamed *Taman Fatahillah*, is an attractive cobbled square with a fountain. To sit astride the cannon – known as Si Jagur – on the north side of the square is said to be a cure for infertility. Several of the buildings contain excellent museums, though most close by 2pm at the latest (3pm on Sun). Beyond Jakarta, Bogor may be visited on a day-trip but Yogyakarta needs at least three days to be appreciated fully.

Sunda Kelapa One of the delights of the old harbour, at the northernmost point of Jakarta, is the fleet of Buginese *pinisi* moored along the dock. These colourful hand-built schooners with their graceful curved prows are some of the world's last remaining commercial sailing ships and play an important role in inter-island trade. To see them you must pay a nominal fee at the port's entrance. Alternatively, climb the 19thC watchtower (Uitkijk) for a superb view of the harbour.

Bahari Museum Opposite the Uitkijk, this building was originally a Dutch East India Company godown, or warehouse, built in 1652 to store coffee and spices. It now houses old city maps and models of traditional Indonesian sailing craft. Behind the museum is the Pasar Ikan fishmarket. *Open Tue–Thu, 9–2; Fri, Sat, 9–1; Sun, 9–3; closed Mon.*

Wayang Museum A comprehensive collection of puppets from all over Indonesia, as well as Cambodia and China. Shadow puppet plays are performed every Sunday morning. *Taman Fatahilla. Open Tue–Thu, Sun, 9–2; Fri, 9–11; Sat, 9–1.*

Jakarta History Museum In the former City Hall, modelled on that in Amsterdam and the city's administrative centre from 1642 to World War II, is a rich collection of antique furniture, maps, European porcelain, portraits and domestic utensils illustrating colonial life in old Batavia. *Taman Fatahilla. Open Tue–Thu, 9–2; Fri, Sat, 9–1; Sun, 9–3; closed Mon.*

Museum of Fine Arts and Ceramics The neoclassical building on the east side of the old town square was formerly the Hall of Justice, completed in 1870. It exhibits works by 19thC and 20thC Indonesian painters, and the rare porcelain collection of the late vice president Adam Malik. *Taman Fatahilla. Open Tue–Thu, 9–2; Fri, 9–11; Sat, 9–1; Sun, 9–3; closed Mon.*

National Museum In front of its columned portico stands a brown statue of an elephant, a gift from Prince Chulalongkorn of Thailand, given in 1871, three years after the building was completed. This is one of the finest museums in South-East Asia, with a superb collection of objects illustrating the prehistory, history and culture of the various ethnic peoples of Indonesia. Its most famous exhibit is the 500,000-year-old skull of *Pithecanthropus erectus* (Java man) discovered in 1892, and until recently the oldest known relic of *homo sapiens*. *Medan Merdeka Barat. Open Tue–Thu, 8.30–2; Fri, 8.30–11; Sat, 8.30–1; Sun, 8.30–3; closed Mon. Tours in English Tue–Thu, 9.30; in French Wed, 9; in Japanese Tue, 9.*

Textile Museum A fascinating display of several hundred examples of Indonesian *batik* and *ikat*. *4 Jalan Satsuit Tubun. Open Tue–Thu, Sun, 9–2; Fri, Sat 9–1.*

Guided tours

Setia Tours ☎ 6390008, part of the Gray Line organization, and *Pacto Ltd*, at the Borobudur hotel ☎ 370108, offer both individual tours and group packages.

Outside Jakarta

Taman Mini Indonesia Indah, 10km/6 miles southeast of Jakarta off the toll road to Bogor, is a large park where you can see "Beautiful Indonesia in Miniature." Pavilions devoted to each of the 27 provinces in Indonesia display handicrafts, clothing and agricultural products. Many of the pavilions put on performances of dance and drama at weekends. Also within the complex is a scenic orchid garden and the *Museum Indonesia*, packed with traditional handicrafts. *Open 9–5; museum 9–3.*

Ragunan Zoo, 16km/10 miles south of Jakarta in Pasar Minggu district, concentrates on Indonesian wildlife. The giant lizard, the Komodo dragon, found only on Indonesia's Komodo Island, is a popular attraction. *Open 9–6.*

Bogor, 60km/38 miles south of Jakarta on the foothills of Mount Salak – and so appreciably cooler – is reached by a fast toll road (30min). The chief attraction is the world-famous *Botanical Gardens*, opened in 1817. Near the gardens is the graceful summer palace of the governors-general of the Dutch East Indies,

now used by the president. This trip can be extended by a visit to the Botanical Gardens extension at *Cibodas*, 40km/25 miles southeast of Bogor, where plants requiring a temperate climate are grown. Here you can view the tea plantations and the 3,000-metre peaks of several active but dormant volcanoes in the *Puncak Hill Resort*.

Yogyakarta and neighbouring *Solo* are the cultural heart of Java. The palace is still lived in by the royal family and may be visited. Javanese dance, drama, painting and puppetry are all best experienced in Yogyakarta. The best way to reach it is by air (30min). Once there, it is about an hour's drive to *Borobudur*, the most amazing of the many beautiful ancient monuments in the area. Here the largest Buddhist monument in the world, covered with carvings, rises on nine massive terraces. It was built in the 9th century and discovered in 1814 under centuries of jungle growth and volcanic ash. Restoration was completed in 1983 although further repairs were required a year later following a terrorist bombing.

The other magnificent temple complex in the region is at *Prambanan*, where the reliefs depict stories from the Hindu *Ramayana* epic. The floodlit temples provide an unforgettable backdrop to the Ramayana Ballet Festivals held over four nights every full moon between May and October.

Spectator sports

Most sporting events of significance take place in the *National Stadium and Sports Complex* ☎ 582820, including badminton (at which Indonesian players excel), soccer and athletics. Ask hotel staff to find out what is going on and to obtain tickets.

Keeping fit

There are few public sports facilities in Jakarta. Most of the best hotels have fitness facilities, and both the

Hilton and the Borobudur hotels have extensive sports complexes. Joggers can choose between the Medan Merdeka (closed to traffic on Sundays), or the paths in and around the National Stadium by the side of the Hilton hotel where the only major hazard is the early morning flower market.

Golf The British introduced the sport and many wealthy Indonesians, including the president, are devotees. There is a fair choice of courses and hotels are used to requests for help in arranging use of the local facilities. The *Jakarta Golf Club*'s Rawamangun Course ☎ (4) 891208 is the oldest, laid out in 1872 and with plenty of shade, stately palms and old bridges crossing the numerous water courses. It is supposedly free of snakes since the club's president ordered a renowned snake-charmer to clear the course. The *Pondok Indah Golf and Country Club* ☎ 764906, just outside Jakarta, is a championship course created on the undulating hills of a former rice paddy. Club facilities include a pool, tennis courts and bowling greens. *Kebayoran* ☎ 582508 is a small course in the city centre.

Local resources
Business services
Companies offering business services are largely based in the hotels. The following handle word processing, arrange translation and provide secretaries and interpreters: *Business Centre*, Borobudur hotel ☎ 370108; *Business Services*, Indonesia hotel ☎ 322008; *Carlos Secretarial Services*, Sari Pacific hotel ☎ 323707; *Jakarta Executive Service Centre*, Menara Duta Bldg, Jalan H.R. Rasuna Said ☎ 516202; *The Executive Business Centre*, Hilton hotel ☎ 587981; and the *World Trade Centre Club*, 16th Fl, Wisma Metropolitan II, Jalan Jenderal Sudirman ☎ 5781945.

Communications
Local delivery Most hotel business centres will arrange this service.

International delivery DHL (head office), 8th Fl, Wisma Metropolitan II, 31 Jalan Jenderal Sudirman ☎ 5781616; *TNT Skypak*, 20th Fl, Summitmas Tower, Jalan Jenderal Sudirman ☎ 5781157.

Post offices The General Post Office is on Jalan Pos Utara 2 (open Mon–Thu, 8–3; Fri, 8–11am; Sat, 8–2). Most hotels offer mailing services.

Telex and fax Public services require some mastery of the Indonesian language, so it is wiser to stick to the facilities provided by hotels; the Borobudur hotel fax and telex centre is open 24hr Mon–Sat, 7am–10pm on Sun and national holidays.

Telephone Local calls made from public telephones cost Rp50 for three minutes. Most hotels have IDD telephones but add enormous surcharges (50% plus is not uncommon). If you want to avoid this, you can make international calls from the *Kantor Telepon*, Skyline Bldg, 9 Jalan M.H. Thamrin. To make collect calls ☎ 101 for the international operator. Collect calls cannot be made to most Asian cities.

Conference/exhibition centres
The *Jakarta Trade Fair* complex in Medan Merdeka ☎ 359223 is the main centre with exhibitions mainly geared to exports; the fair itself takes place annually between June 20 and July 18. The *Hilton* ☎ 583051 and *Indonesian* ☎ 320008 are the hotels most used for conventions and commercial exhibitions.

Emergencies
Hospitals All the top hotels have in-house medical staff. For routine medical and dental treatment, expatriates use the *Metropolitan Clinic*, Cipto Mangunkusumo, 71 Jalan Diponegoro ☎ 343021, open Mon–Sat, 9–7. SOS *Medica* operates a 24hr emergency service, as does the newer *Medikaloka Clinic*, Kuningan Plaza, Jalan Rasuna Said, Kuningan ☎ 520 0387. A doctor will visit your

hotel room and, if necessary, act as interpreter and accompany patients to the *Pertamina Hospital*, Jalan Kyai Maja, which has a 24hr emergency department ☎ 775890. Patients are expected to pay cash for all services, which are generally much cheaper than private medical treatment in the West.

Pharmacies Hotel newsstands stock painkillers and patent medicines. Most shopping centres have a pharmacy (called "Apotik" in Indonesian). Two of the best stocked are *Apotik Melawai*, 191 Jalan Melawai Raya ☎ 716109, and *Apotik Senayan*, Jalan Pakubuwono ☎ 735021, both open daily, 8–5.

Police Jakarta is not a violent city and women can move about freely without harassment, but petty crime, especially pickpocketing and jewellery snatching, are common enough to make it necessary to take sensible precautions.

To contact the police ☎ 587771 (24hr), but you are strongly advised to seek the help of hotel staff first, since few members of the police speak English.

Embassies
Australia 15 Jalan M.H. Thamrin ☎ 323109
Austria 44 Jalan Diponegoro ☎ 338090
Belgium 4 Jalan Cicurug ☎ 348719
Canada 5th Fl, Wisma Metropolitan 1, 29 Jalan Jederal Surdiman ☎ 510709
Denmark 4th Fl, Bina Mulia Bldg, Jalan H.R. Rasuna Said ☎ 518350
Finland 10th Fl, Bina Mulia Bldg, Jalan H.R. Rasuna Said ☎ 516980
France 20 Jalan M.H. Thamrin ☎ 332807
Greece 16 Jalan Kebon Sirih ☎ 247422
Italy 45 Jalan Diponegoro ☎ 348339
Japan 24 Jalan M.H. Thamrin ☎ 324308
Malaysia 17 Jalan Imam Bonjol ☎ 336438

Netherlands 5-3 Jalan H.R. Rasuna Said, ☎ 511515
New Zealand 41 Jalan Diponegoro ☎ 330620
Norway 4th Fl, Bina Mulia Bldg, Jalan H.R. Rasuna Said ☎ 511990
Philippines 6–8 Jalan Imam Bonjol ☎ 348917
Singapore 23 Jalan Proklamasi ☎ 348761
South Korea 57-8 Jalan Jenderal Gatot Subroto ☎ 512309
Spain 12th Fl, Wisma Kosgoro, 53 Jalan M.H. Thamrin ☎ 325996
Sweden 12 Jalan Taman Cutmutiah ☎ 333061
Switzerland Jalan H.R. Rasuna Said, Blok X, 3–2 Kuningan ☎ 516061
Thailand 74 Jalan Imam Bonjol ☎ 343762
UK 75 Jalan M.H. Thamrin ☎ 330904
USA 5 Jalan Medan Merdeka Selatan ☎ 360360
West Germany 1 Jalan M.H. Thamrin ☎ 323908

Government offices
English is not widely spoken even at senior government level, so you will need the help of a local expert to contact and communicate with government departments. *Department of Foreign Affairs* ☎ 371508; *Department of Information* ☎ 360113; *Central Bureau of Statistics* ☎ 372808; *Bank Indonesia* ☎ 372408; *Department of Immigration* ☎ 322108; *National Investment Coordination Board* (BKPM) ☎ 512008; *National Development Information Office* ☎ 517193.

Information sources
Local media The *Jakarta Post*, *Indonesian Observer* and *Indonesian Times* are the three English language newspapers in Jakarta and all carry business and political news. The *Asian Wall Street Journal*, *International Herald Tribune* and other major dailies are available in most hotels.

Tourist information There are visitor information centres in the Jakarta Theatre Bldg, 9 Jalan M.H. Thamrin ☎ 354094 and Oriental Bldg, 51 Jalan M.H. Thamrin ☎ 332067 (open Mon–Thu, 8–3; Fri, 8–11.30am; Sat, 8–2). The Department of Tourism *Guide to Jakarta* is available free in most hotels.

Thank-yous

Alcohol would not be an appropriate present to give to a Muslim host. *Sari Delices*, Sari Pacific hotel ☎ 323707 has the best range of chocolates, French pâtisserie and wines (open daily, 9–8), while the *Borobudur Delicatessen*, Borobudur hotel ☎ 370108 runs a close second. *Puntjak Florists*, 11 Jalan Pasar Baru Selatan ☎ 341987, takes credit card orders and delivers, as does *Lesmana International* in the Hilton shopping arcade ☎ 587981, and the *Flower Shop* in the Borobudur hotel ☎ 370108.

Planning and reference
Entry details

Documentation All visitors' passports must be valid for at least six months from the day of arrival. Entry without a visa is permitted only when arriving or leaving Indonesia via Jakarta, Ambon, Bali, Batam, Biak, Manado, Medan or Pekanbaru. Visas are mandatory at all other ports of entry or exit. Nationals of the USA, Canada, New Zealand, Australia, non-Communist European and ASEAN member countries are admitted without a visa for a period of up to two months. Anyone who wishes to stay longer must apply for a 30-day tourist or business visa from an Indonesian embassy or consulate and applications must be accompanied by evidence of onward passage reservations. This visa is extendable up to a maximum of three months on application to the Department of Immigration in Jakarta ☎ 322108.

Driving licence An international driving licence is required to rent a car.
Health precautions An international certificate of inoculation against yellow fever may be required if a traveller has visited an infected area during the previous six days. Visitors are advised to be inoculated against cholera, typhoid and polio, and to take both maloprim and nivaquine (anti-malarial tablets).
Customs regulations Visitors complete a baggage declaration form on arrival. Those whose total baggage is less than US$250 in value can opt for the green, "nothing to declare" channel and are subject only to random checks. Fines may be imposed on anyone using this channel who is found carrying dutiable items. Everyone else has to go through a baggage check, which is usually cursory. Personal possessions such as watches and jewellery can be brought in duty free. Cameras, cassettes, recorders and business equipment must be declared and re-exported. Television sets, radios, radio/cassette recorders, pornography, printed matter in Chinese characters and Chinese medicines are prohibited. Films and video cassettes have to be submitted to the Office of the Public Prosecutor for censorship. Anyone carrying promotional videos should use a local agent to clear the material in advance. All commercial goods are subject to import formalities and are dutiable. There are no limits on the import and export of foreign currency but not more than Rp50,000 may be taken in or out of the country. The duty-free allowances are two litres/2 quarts of alcohol, and 200 cigarettes or 50 cigars or 100gms/4oz of tobacco.

Climate

Jakarta lies just south of the equator and remains hot and humid all the year round. Daytime temperatures of 28°–34°C/82–93°F with 80% humidity are the norm, with nighttime temperatures a cooler 25°C/77°F. The rainy season is from October to April, characterized by torrential downpours every afternoon which temporarily refresh the atmosphere. Outside Jakarta the temperatures are generally a few degrees lower, with balmy evenings.

Light clothing in natural materials is the most comfortable for the heat and humidity. A suit and tie are necessary only for formal meetings and the smarter restaurants. Otherwise, open-necked shirts, even safari suits, are well accepted business attire for men. Women may wear whatever is comfortable provided it is modest. Indonesian businessmen often wear long-sleeved, open-necked batik shirts, even on formal occasions.

Holidays
There are hundreds of holidays related to a particular region or religious or cultural group. These rarely affect business in the capital, but it is important to check whether a holiday is imminent before travelling beyond Jakarta.
Jan 1 New Year
Mar/Apr Mohammed's Ascension
Late Mar Nyepi
Late Mar/early Apr Good Friday
Mid-May Waisak
Mid/late May Ascension Day
Late May End of Ramadan fast (2 days)
Early Aug Idul Adha
Aug 17 Independence Day
Late Aug Muslim New Year
Nov Birth of Mohammed
Dec 25 Christmas Day

Money
Local currency Indonesia rupiahs (Rp) are issued in denominations of 10,000, 5,000, 1,000, 500 and 100 bank notes; and 100, 50, 25, 10, 5 and 1 coins. The largest note is worth a mere US$6, so you need to carry a lot of notes, especially as taxi drivers never seem to have change.

Prices in tourist haunts and hotels are usually quoted in US dollars but payable in local currency. The US dollar is the best currency to take; and travellers with most other currencies get a poor rate. Some banks in Jakarta, and most outside the capital, will not change other currencies at all, though hotels and licensed money-changers usually will.
Traveller's cheques are the safest way to carry money around, since theft from hotel rooms and pickpocketing are on the increase. Licensed money-changers and some hotels will accept most issuers' cheques in most denominations. Banks are idiosyncratic as to what they will accept.
Credit and charge cards are accepted by hotels, better restaurants and department stores, tourist gift shops and airlines in Jakarta. Elsewhere they are almost unusable, except in major hotels.
Changing money Licensed money-changers give the best rates for US dollars and do not charge commission; banks are marginally better for other currencies but the slight difference does not justify the trouble it takes to find one willing to change a particular currency. Hotels give the worst deal. Banks are open Mon–Fri, 8 or 8.30–noon, Sat, 8–11. Some foreign banks open Mon–Thu, 8.30–3. The American Express Bank, Hongkong and Shanghai Banking Corporation and Standard Chartered Bank all have offices along Jakarta's main north–south highway. The bank at the Borobudur hotel is open daily, 8–noon, 1–5. Hotel exchange desks generally operate 7–7. The licensed money-changer Sahid Artha Sari, at the Sahid Jaya hotel ☎ 587031 ext. 1133, is open Mon–Sat, 8–9, Sun, 9–4.

Tipping
A 10% service charge is automatically levied on all hotel and restaurant bills and further tipping is unnecessary. Porters expect Rp500 per bag, hairdressers 10% of the bill, and taxis around Rp200 for short journeys, 10% for longer ones.

Malaysia

Malaysia is a country richly endowed with natural resources. It is the world's largest producer of rubber and palm oil, produces large quantities of tin, pepper, coconut and cocoa, has enormous supplies of timber, vast reserves of coal, oil and gas and its hydropower potential has yet to be quantified. Based on buoyant commodity exports which contributed to growth rates of 6–8% until the 1985–86 collapse of world prices, its economy has been transformed since independence from Britain in 1957 to the point where manufacturing now contributes over 20% of GDP.

Potentially one of the richest countries in the world, Malaysia is also extremely complex in racial, religious, social and, therefore, political terms. Ethnic Malays make up over half of the 16m population; traditionally farm workers, they have held very little of the country's economic power. This tends to be in the hands of the Chinese, who comprise about a third of the population and are mainly city dwellers involved in finance and commerce. Indians account for 10%, and the census lists another 53 ethnic groups.

The country is also divided physically. Peninsular Malaysia, stretching south from Thailand to Singapore and bounded by the Straits of Malacca to the west and the South China Sea to the east, is some 640km/400 miles across the sea from the two states of Sabah and Sarawak in East Malaysia.

The status and class tensions underlying Malaysia's racial composition erupted into bloody riots in 1969 and were directly responsible for the formulation by the Malays, who have political power, of the New Economic Policy (NEP) guiding the country's development since 1971. The NEP has sought to eradicate poverty and remove the association of race with economic function, and in that sense it has been the embodiment of the country's aspirations and also the framework of its policy decisions.

British colonial interests in the region in the 19th century brought the Chinese and Indians to the peninsula, the former to work as labourers in the tin mines, the latter from Madras to work on the rubber estates. A communist guerilla movement which fought with the British against the Japanese during World War II resisted continuing British rule after the war. The ensuing communist "emergency" (1948–60) was only slowly brought to an end. In 1963 the Malay areas of the island of Borneo (Sabah and Sarawak) were brought into a new Malaysian Federation to counterbalance the influence of the Chinese in Singapore and the peninsula, but in 1965 Singapore left to become an independent country.

As Malaysia climbed out of the recession, it acknowledged in very practical ways that the main engine of growth was to be the private sector. In the drive to industrialize, conditions for foreign investors were made increasingly attractive.

The political scene

The Federation of Malaysia comprises the 11 states of Peninsular Malaysia and the states of Sabah and Sarawak across the sea on the island of Borneo. It is a constitutional monarchy and its political system is a unique blending of its own feudal heritage with the Westminster traditions of its former colonial administrators.

Legislature

The king – the Yang di-Pertuan Agong – is elected every five years by a conference of nine royal state rulers. He appoints a council of ministers from the members of the federal parliament. This consists of a 177-member house of representatives, the *Dewan Rakyat*, elected every five years, and a senate, the *Dewan Negara*, which has two elected members from each state and 32 appointed by the king.

State autonomy Each state has its own constitution and legislative assembly and most have rulers who are hereditary sultans. Malacca, Penang, Sabah and Sarawak are each headed by a governor appointed to a four-year term by the king. The capital, Kuala Lumpur, was designated a federal territory in 1974.

Tense relations Relations between state governments and the central authorities have frequently been tense, with the tendency towards autonomy at its strongest in the non-peninsular states of Sabah and Sarawak.

Dominant Bumiputra Since independence in 1957 political power has continuously been in the hands of the Bumiputra, the "sons of the soil" or ethnic Malays. Their main party, the United Malays National Organization (UMNO), dominates the *Barisan Nasional*, a "national front" coalition of 13 political parties that governs the country. As UMNO is by far the largest party, its president automatically becomes the country's prime minister who, since 1981, has been Datuk Seri Dr Mahathir Mohamad.

Split Malays Despite the government's landslide victory in the August 1986 general election, Mahathir was challenged as leader of UMNO in April 1987 because of his autocratic style, his handling of the economy and his alleged toleration of corrupt goverment officials. He narrowly beat his rival, Tengku Razaleigh Hamzah, but moves to challenge the poll split the party. UMNO itself is also being challenged by Malay Islamic groups who have given their backing to the Parti Islam Sa-Malaysia (PAS), whose long-term objective is to make the country an Islamic republic.

Chinese also split The main Chinese party, the Malaysian Chinese Association (MCA), has lost its traditional dominant position among the Chinese community. Other Chinese parties are prospering, largely because the MCA has internal problems and is seen not to have delivered the goods. Many Chinese, particularly professionals, complain that life in Malaysia has become harder for them because the NEP favours the Malays in the job market even when Chinese applicants are far more highly qualified.

The main Indian party, the Malaysian Indian Congress, has been making greater efforts to improve the conditions of its members, who comprise the country's poorest community.

Foreign relations

Malaysia is genuinely non-aligned but has good relations with both superpowers. As a member of ASEAN it has sought to end Vietnam's occupation of Kampuchea. It is still a member of the Commonwealth and helped to found the Organization of the Islamic Conference.

The economic scene

With its abundant natural resources, Malaysia has enjoyed one of the highest growth rates in the world over the past 20 years, averaging 7–8% a year. It is the world's largest producer of tin, rubber, palm oil, pepper and tropical hardwoods, but the economy has been diversifying away from the primary sector. The sudden drop in prices of all the country's commodities in the mid-1980s dealt a heavy blow to the nation's solvency and real GDP fell by 1% in 1985. But all major sectors of the economy except construction and services registered higher production levels in 1986 and GDP grew by almost 5% in 1987 and by just over 8% in 1988.

The New Economic Policy

The cornerstone of the government's attempt to raise the economic level of the Bumiputra and end the association between race and status in society is the New Economic Policy (NEP). This was adopted in 1971 in response to the situation which had led to race rioting in 1969. At that time the Malays owned only 2.4% of registered share capital, compared with 34.3% in non-Malay Malaysian (mainly Chinese) hands and 63.3% owned by foreigners.

Missing the target The target was to have Bumiputra owning 30% of the corporate sector by 1990, with other Malaysians owning 40% and foreigners' holdings reduced to 30%. By mid-1987 Bumiputra owned only 18%. The target was clearly not going to be met and Prime Minister Mahathir said: "We are holding NEP in abeyance for the time being."

Human resources

Malaysia's population at the end of 1986 was about 16m. Of these, just under 13m lived on the peninsula, which accounts for only 40% of total land area. The remaining 3m inhabitants were in Sabah and Sarawak on the island of Borneo. The population is young, about 60% being under the age of 25. It is growing at 2.6% a year and is expected to reach 18m by the end of 1990. Life expectancy at birth is high: 68 years for men, 73 for women.

Under-populated Government policy assumes that Malaysia is under-populated, that it has the natural resources to sustain fast population growth and that, accordingly, everything should be done to increase the birth rate, especially of the ethnic Malays. It believes that Malaysia's economy suffers from having too small a market for local manufactures. The expressed aim is for a total population of 70m by 2100, which would mean a nearly fivefold increase within 100 years.

Educational standards The literacy rate for adults in 1980 was 71% and thousands of Malay students graduate from university each year, either at home or abroad.

Urbanization Peninsular Malaysia has at least 10 cities of over 100,000 inhabitants, including Kuala Lumpur, the national capital, with about 1m people. In East Malaysia, Kuching, the capital of Sarawak, has about 150,000 people and the population of Kota Kinabalu, Sabah's capital, is put at 120,000.

Unemployment was on a rising curve to 9% in 1986. Graduates who traditionally would have been employed in the public sector are now finding themselves without jobs. There have been calls to lower the retirement age for civil servants from 55 to 50 to help ease the problem.

Natural resources

As well as being the world's largest producer of rubber, palm oil, pepper and tropical hardwoods, Malaysia also produces rice, cocoa, coconut oil, copra and pineapples. Its minerals include tin, iron ore, bauxite, and copper has been discovered in the central belt of Peninsular Malaysia and in Sabah. It is particularly well endowed with sources of energy.

Tin problems The world tin market collapsed in 1985 under the weight of ever-growing buffer stocks held by the producer/consumer price stabilization body, the International Tin Council (ITC). Some of the mines which closed as a result of the crisis have now reopened but tin is no longer of any great significance in exports. Malaysia has admitted its own ill-judged and expensive attempt to corner the tin market in 1982. With the ITC effectively in liquidation, tin is now traded on Kuala Lumpur's own commodities exchange.

Diversifying In mid-1987 Malaysia Mining Corporation (MMC), one of the world's biggest tin mining companies, announced plans to expand beyond Malaysia and to invest in the search for diamonds, gold and other precious minerals.

Rubber prices firmer Malaysia has 2m ha/4.9m acres of rubber trees, of which 60,000 ha/148,260 acres are replanted each year. After the traumatic fall in 1985, the price of rubber has become firmer, helped by the increased demand for condoms and surgical gloves in the wake of the AIDS epidemic, and rubber producers have honed their costs. There have been moves by the estate sector out of rubber into palm oil.

Palm oil Malaysia accounts for 60% of world palm oil production. The sector started from a low base in the 1960s but is now more important than rubber.

Energy prospects bright
Malaysia's oil and gas sector earned M$7.3bn in 1986, accounting for 15% of total exports, the second largest earner after electrical

components. Foreign oil companies have reacted favourably to the government's new production-sharing contract which will give producers increased allowances for cost recovery.

Cutting back output Although not a member of OPEC, Malaysia has generally observed recent production quotas, and was expected to cut back output by 10% in 1987 to 450,000 barrels a day. In 1988, however, output rose to 540,000 barrels a day. Substantial reserves – estimated at 3bn barrels – have an expectancy of 15 years, according to Petronas, the state oil and gas company.

More gas Malaysia's production of liquefied natural gas increased by 17.8% in 1986 to 5.3bn tonnes, all of which was shipped to Japan. The Peninsular Gas Utilization pipeline project is expected to be completed by mid-1991, when natural gas will be supplied from offshore Terengganu to power stations at Paka, Port Dickson, Port Kelang, Connaught Bridge and Pasir Gudang. Singapore will also be supplied. The Japanese government is expected to lend M$1bn for the project.

Agriculture
Although agriculture's share of GDP has declined in recent years – to 21.2% in 1986 – as other sectors have grown, it still plays an important part in the economy through its contribution to employment and foreign exchange earnings. Commodities such as rubber, rice, palm oil, pepper and cocoa grow easily in the tropical climate.

Policy to alleviate poverty A National Agriculture Policy was formulated in 1983 to reduce poverty and improve productivity, especially in the non-estate sector, where smallholdings tend to use traditional methods and be uneconomically small. The government aims to support agriculture through new land developments and by providing support services and incentives.

Infrastructure

Road and rail communications are more highly developed in Peninsular Malaysia than in Sabah and Sarawak. As the third Malaysia Plan drew to a close in 1980, it became clear that the country's infrastructure was inadequate to meet the rate of economic expansion envisaged for the decade. Plans are underway to expand and modernize airports and to develop roads and seaports.

Roads Most of the roads in the peninsula run north-south, but there are plans to build an east-west highway from Kota Bahru to Penang. About 70% of the 26,000km/16,250 miles of road in Peninsular Malaysia is paved. Monsoon driving can be difficult. Sabah and Sarawak have a small road network centred on Kuching and Sibu.

Railways The 2,090km/1,305 miles of single-gauge track is due for modernization. Sabah's railway links Kota Kinabalu and Tenom. There is no railway in Sarawak.

Airports There are nine domestic airports and MAS operates an extensive network of services to main centres and, particularly in Sabah and Sarawak, to smaller towns.

Seaports The major seaports of Peninsular Malaysia are those at Penang and Port Kelang, recently extensively expanded. Labuan is the main port of Sabah. Sarawak's ports are at Kuching, Sabu and Miri.

External trade

The Malaysian economy is heavily export-oriented (56.9% of GNP in 1986), hence the government's policy to increase the birth rate so as to expand the domestic market.

Vulnerable export markets The country's vulnerability to fluctuations in foreign markets was devastatingly demonstrated during the 1984–86 collapse in world trade in commodities. In 1985 sales of petroleum products accounted for 23% of export earnings, timber 10%, palm oil 10%, rubber 8% and tin 4%. In 1986 the figures were petroleum

products 15%, timber 12%, rubber 9%, palm oil 8% and tin 2%, with electronics and electrical goods (18%) overtaking petroleum products for the first time.

Imports are dominated by machinery and manufactures which made up 58% of the total in 1986. Other significant imports are food, mineral fuels and chemicals.

Trading partners Japan, the most important buyer of oil and gas and supplier of capital goods, is Malaysia's biggest trading partner, followed by Singapore and the USA. Together they accounted for over 56% of exports in 1986 and 54% of imports. Prime Minister Mahathir's quarrel with Britain resulted for several years in a "Buy British Last" policy which was dropped in 1985. In 1986 the UK accounted for 4.5% of Malaysia's imports, the same amount as West Germany.

South-South Having burned its fingers in the tin market, Malaysia is a leading advocate of South-South cooperation on trade matters. It was Dr Mahathir who instigated the South-South Commission that was launched at the 1986 non-aligned summit.

Balance of payments

Despite hiccups in the early 1980s, austerity measures have reduced imports so that Malaysia was in surplus in 1985 and 1986 on its merchandise account (by about US$3.5bn). Exports also fell as a result of the problems in the various commodity markets.

Manufactures up Following the 1983–85 slump in demand for electrical goods, manufactures exports entered an upward trend in 1986–87. The trade surplus rose from US$432m in 1983 to an estimated US$4.1bn in 1987, while the current account deficit fell from US$3.6bn in 1982 to US$723m in 1985.

Invisibles deficit The substantial invisibles deficit is made up of repatriated profit, interest and dividends, as well as freight and insurance charges, with Singapore the major beneficiary.

Currency

The local currency is the Malaysian dollar or ringgit, which is pegged to a trade-weighted basket of currencies and has been subject to devaluation rumours. But rather than once-and-for-all realignments, Bank Negara, the central bank, has preferred a creeping depreciation against the US dollar.

External debt and aid

Encouraged by years of high growth rates, Malaysia went on a borrowing spree in the late 1970s and early 1980s to finance ambitious development plans. Although the amount of public external debt – about US$16bn in 1986 – is not a serious worry to Malaysia or its creditors, the bunching of maturities could be a problem.

Good terms Malaysia still attracts good terms, however, in both the floating rate loan market and the capital markets. Foreign exchange reserves excluding gold stood at US$5.6bn at the end of November 1986.

Debt-service ratio The national debt-service ratio peaked at 19% of export earnings in 1986 but pre-payments and buoyant exports brought it down to 13% in 1988. The government's aim is to keep it below 20%. Although now too well off to qualify for the cheapest finance from multilateral aid donors, Malaysia is a recipient of long-term World Bank and Asian Development Bank project financing. It also receives significant aid for trade from Japan's Overseas Economic Cooperation Fund.

Government finances

As times have become harder for Malaysia, the current account deficit has been dwarfed by the public sector's fiscal deficit. Since 1982, government budgets have aimed to reduce both shortfalls. The most serious drains on government funds are the debt service and civil service salaries and benefits.

Narrow tax base The tax base is narrow and collection is hampered by inefficiencies and corruption. Direct taxes in 1986 accounted for about 46% of government revenue. Indirect taxes, including export and import duties and sales tax, made up about 36%. The balance of 18% non-tax revenue included hefty dividends from Petronas.

Industry

Industrial strategy has been characterized by the drive to develop value-added processing industries for Malaysia's abundant raw materials, and by a push into heavy industry. The latter has been the special preserve of the government's Heavy Industries Corporation of Malaysia (HICOM) but in 1988 the government announced plans to restructure HICOM's loss-making companies with a view to selling some off.

Malaysian car Prime Minister Mahathir has been associated with some of HICOM's prestige projects, most notably the Malaysian car, the Proton Saga, the product of a joint venture with Mitsubishi of Japan.

The Industrial Master Plan aims to transform Malaysia into an industrial economy by 1995. It sets out a strategy for promoting resource-based industries, for example, in rubber, wood and food processing. It also targets further electronics and electrical manufacturing and assembly, and engineering products. Manufacturing and assembly industries are mainly located on the west coast of the peninsula and in the free trade zone of Penang.

The business climate

Malaysia, in earnest pursuit of foreign investment and technology, today looks north, south, east and west. No longer able to rely exclusively on its natural resources, it is diversifying into export-led, resource-based manufacturing. Foreign expertise and investment are welcomed, with one overriding qualification (though this is not as much of a constraint as it used to be): conformity with the goals laid down by the National Economic Policy (NEP). At the forefront of these is the commitment to correct economic imbalances identified with race, primarily by uplifting the Bumiputra.

A big public sector

In the past the main impetus for growth has come from massive public investment. In 1986 there were over 160 state-owned enterprises, accounting for 57% of total investment. The government is active in oil, utilities, plantations, mining, banking, and public services such as transport. It has promoted industrialization through HICOM, the Heavy Industries Corporation of Malaysia, and through state economic development corporations.

Strategic considerations Often, state intervention was prompted by the NEP requirement for greater Bumiputra participation in commerce, through trust agencies like PNB (Permodolan Nasional Berhad), the leading Bumiputra investment and unit trust, and Pernas, the Malay Trading Corporation. The government has also sought to return key resources to Malaysian hands, by taking over foreign-owned plantations and tin-mining operations. Similar national strategic considerations have led to the setting up of Petronas, the National Petroleum Corporation.

Takeover terms All government acquisitions of companies have been by purely commercial means via purchases in the open stock market. Malaysia has signed Investment Guarantee Agreements with 12 countries as a protection against expropriation or nationalization.

Emphasis on private sector

The Fifth Malaysia Plan (1986–90) shifted the growth emphasis to the private sector, so reversing the long trend of state participation in industry.

Privatization of selected public enterprises was introduced, first in the transport sector – involving partial divestment of the national airline MAS, the national shipping line MISC, and the container terminal. The services sector comes next. Telecommunications and the National Electricity Board should be fully privatized by 1990.

Deregulation During the 1970s and early 1980s sustained prosperity (averaging 6–7% GNP growth) encouraged overregulation. Recession in the mid-1980s encouraged the reverse. Deregulation began as far back as 1983. Even the sacrosanct NEP requirements have in part been relaxed. Measures to create a climate conducive to business have streamlined bureacratic procedures, cut operating costs by reducing utility and service charges, and boosted incentives.

Foreign investment

The foreign investor is the main beneficiary of the new Malaysian deal. Recent years have seen a dramatic shift in policy to relax constraints on specifically foreign equity, always a critical issue. Under the new pragmatism, the NEP target to reduce foreign holdings to 30% has been put on the back burner and it is now possible, given certain conditions, for companies to be 100% foreign-owned.

Power in business

Malaysia's commercial traditions go back to when trade followed the interests of its British colonial administrators, attracting Chinese and Indian immigration in its wake. These, and later foreign influences, are still important but in today's public sector-dominated and NEP-directed economy, a great deal of business clout is in different hands.

Foreign investment this century has brought in a heterogeneous crop of multinationals including Shell, Esso, ICI, Nestlé, Blue Circle, East Asiatic Motorola, IBM, Unilever, Colgate Palmolive, Dow Chemicals and BAT. All the leading European and US banks are present. Standard Chartered and the Hongkong and Shanghai Banking Corporation once dominated and still have the strongest profile in the foreign banking community, but the giants today are the government-controlled Malayan Banking and Bank Bumiputra – the storm centre of financial scandal in the early 1980s but now rehabilitated within the Petronas stable.

The supremacy of the state The parastatal organizations have a high profile. Examples are Malaysian Mining Corporation (MMC), Pernas and PNB. The latter, headed by the redoubtable Tun Ismail Ali, former central bank governor and *enfant terrible* among the management community, is Malaysia's largest holding company. These are convenient vehicles for taking over British interests – as when plantation giants Guthrie and Harrison and Crosfield were absorbed by PNB and London Tin by MMC. Sime Darby, also largely taken over by PNB, and now headed by Tunku (Prince) Ahmad Yahaya, a successful businessman, is Malaysia's largest homegrown multinational.

The Bumiputra factor These organizations are all largely Bumiputra-dominated. Typically, they are run by ex-civil servants (except Sime Darby) and are characterized by public service

principles and a bureaucratic mentality. The average Bumiputra entrepreneur, even with discretionary funding, rarely graduates beyond the small to medium-sized business. Paradoxically, the bankruptcy rate is highest in this most protected sector. The Datuk Syed Kechik Group and Rahim & Co are among the few prominent successes. Promet, with a respectable Malay front but strong Chinese management from Singapore, had a spectacular rise and an equally spectacular fall in 1986 from which it has, however, partly resurrected itself.

The Bumiputra private sector is spearheaded by a few commercially minded royal houses whose influence and privilege make them attractive to foreign joint venturers. The Antah Group is the model, headed by brothers Tunku Naquiddin and Tunku Imran of Negri Sembilan – or "Bill" and "Pete" respectively, as they are known to Westerners. Antah is involved among others with the Biwater rural water scheme, the largest single project in Malaysia in 1986, and has a 20% holding in the Arab Malaysia Bank.

Chinese energy The immigrant sector is lower profile but aggressive. Economic opportunities first drew the Chinese and continue to sustain a high level of commercial energy, but it is narrowly based. The Chinese tend to stick to their original interests such as tin mining and retail distribution, which they dominate. Yong Poh Kong of Selangor Pewler, and the Tan family of Langkawi Marble are examples. Any diversification is likely to be into construction, where Lim Goh Tong and Tan Chin Nam lead the field.

Old boys In Malaysia's small and socially ingrown community, a group of prominent individuals are permutated through a multiplicity of official appointments. Among the privileged and sought-after Bumiputra it is not unknown for an individual to hold 40 directorships. The most influential Malays are top civil servants who, by way of reward, later tend to be politically appointed to head large state enterprises. Raja Tan Sri Mohar and Tan Sri Abdullah Salleh, former chief secretary of government, became president and CEO respectively of Petronas after their government service. They typify the elite of the older generation, among whom royal and civil titles abound. Educated to a man in Britain, their bias in favour of the former colonial power in part inspired the so-called Anti-British Directive. These are the people who succeeded at independence and have stayed in power a disproportionate length of time.

New boys are from the meritocracy – technocratic and more inclined to the US system of education, with Harvard MBAs providing the elite. Among the Chinese, where the success ethic reigns, the most influential are the *towkays* or business magnates. Robert Kwok tops the league. He is one of the few who have been able to transform the original family enterprise into a diversified conglomerate of international scope. Kwok operates on the world stage and is arguably South-East Asia's most successful businessman.

Special influence Other Chinese exercise a unique type of influence: a high degree of acceptability with the politically dominant Malays. Men like Geh Ik Cheong are found, as the rare exception, on otherwise exclusively Bumiputra boards such as Bank Negara, PNB and Petronas.

Malay influence is felt most where personal connections with politicians and civil servants are critical. The establishment is Bumiputra-controlled. Private-sector Malays are correspondingly in demand as joint-venture partners to front for licences or government contract bids. This prompts an outflow of bureaucrats into business at increasingly earlier retirement.

Smoothing the way Numerous approvals are required from the various ministries where former colleagues can smooth the path. The ex-civil servant can chart the way through the intricate workings of the government machine, understand its strategic decision-making processes, and know how to identify the best contact point. Former bureaucrats and retired politicians used to be resurrected as non-executive directors. The criteria have, however, changed in favour of the younger professional, less well known but able to contribute substance, not just political clout.

Easy access Malaysia has the advantage over most countries for relative ease of access to the highest political and executive levels. It is advisable, however, to use the opportunity not just as a courtesy call, but rather to discuss matters of suitable importance and mutual interest.

The concept of "Malaysia Inc," which led to some concrete initiatives by government to consult the private sector, has helped to strengthen organizations like the chambers of commerce.

Who you know Business still relies to a degree on who you know. Here contemporaries from the same school or college tend to have the same special rapport as the Western old-boy network.

Gossip and rumour The Bumiputra community is very cohesive. Malay bureaucrats have their lines into the private sector through their contemporaries in business. Leakage of information can be a problem, among all races. Business is rumour prone.

The union movement is disciplined but limited; less than 20% of the corporate sector comes within its scope. The workforce is, however, very amenable – reasonably skilled and eminently trainable. Overseas graduates are still preferred in the corporate sector. Non-Malays who have difficulty in breaking into the corporate sector's preferential system find refuge in the professions and easily become critics of the system.

The business framework

The regulations that govern corporate organization are set out in the Malaysian Companies Act which follows the UK pattern. Much official policy is expressed in guidelines rather than hard and fast rules. The rationale is the desire for flexibility, leaving room to treat each case on its merits. In practice this leads to inconsistency irritating to the foreigner conditioned to one law for all. Guidelines, moreover, are less precise and are open to varied interpretation within the bureaucracy. The onus on the investor is to negotiate his case. It is a mistake to ignore the guidelines – they may not be strictly binding in any legal sense, but they are mandatory. Trying to "get round" the system is not wise. The recommendation is to frame your proposals in conformity with Malaysian policy and, as always, to get to know the system thoroughly.

Company structure

The main types of structure are limited companies (public and private), branches of foreign incorporated companies, partnerships (2–20 persons) or sole proprietorships.

Limited company This is the vehicle most favoured by the foreign investor. It can be set up by two founders without restriction as to their nationality or residence. But at least two directors must be "normally resident." Expatriates with approved residence permits qualify.

Manufacturing companies are subject to separate legislation embodied in the Industrial Coordination Act (ICA). This requires them, in addition to registering with the Registrar of Companies, to obtain a licence from the Ministry of Trade and Industry. In the past the ICA was used to coerce compliance with the NEP. This is now considerably relaxed and the level of exemption raised; companies with shareholder funds below M$2.5m or fewer than 75 full-time employees need not apply for a licence.

Public companies The public company wishing to have its shares quoted on the Kuala Lumpur Stock Exchange requires the prior approval of the Capital Issues Committee (CIC). A prospectus has to be submitted. Details of the governing regulations are easily obtainable.

Branches of a foreign company can be established by the simple process of listing them with the Registrar of Companies within one month of start-up; but they are not encouraged and there is no particular tax advantage. The government is reluctant to approve branch registration except where a foreign-based company has been specifically invited to participate in a government project.

Foreign ownership rules

The recommended vehicle for foreign investment is the joint venture combining local capital with imported technical and managerial skills. The standard NEP formula for the division of equity is 30% Bumiputra, 40% other Malaysian, 30% foreign. However, certain categories of joint ventures in the priority areas of manufacture for export can now qualify for a much higher level of foreign equity, provided they come in during a limited period of grace from October 1986 to December 1990.

The export factor A distinction is made between export-oriented companies and those producing mainly for the domestic market. Companies exporting 80% or more of output are allowed up to 100% foreign control. Exports of 51–79% qualify for at least 51% foreign equity. For the domestically oriented where exports will be lower, 20–50% exports qualifies for 30–51% foreign equity; below 20% exports, the maximum equity obtainable is 30%. There are nine successful free-trade zones designed to facilitate export-oriented industries.

High-technology companies come in another distinct category and are automatically eligible for up to 51% foreign ownership.

Non-renewable resources Projects involving non-renewable resources such as petroleum are allowed 100% foreign equity, but companies then work as contractors to Petronas which oversees and controls their operation.

MIDA The Malaysian Industrial Development Authority (MIDA) makes all decisions on the level of foreign equity that will be allowed. Proper presentation and subsequent skill in negotiating can make all the difference to how much foreign equity will be allowed.

Priorities It is essential to appreciate the MIDA priorities. With some exceptions a minimum 30% Bumiputra share is paramount. Many companies give much more in the hope this will gain greater approval. The "other Malaysians'" share easily gets overlooked. Use of local materials and components for value-added weighs significantly. Location too can be important. Where investors are willing to go to a designated priority area, concessions will be made in return.

The most common constraint is the difficulty of finding suitable local partners. MIDA is always ready to help identify candidates, but most companies wish to retain their management prerogative in this regard. The share allocated to local equity can be held in reserve pending a thorough partner search.

Government contractors

Those whose business prospects lie mainly with the government must be aware of certain special conditions.

Registration The first step is to become a "registered" government contractor for which the company will need to demonstrate a 30% level of Bumiputra participation.

"Bumiputra status" is awarded to companies with a minimum of 51% Bumiputra equity and merits a degree of preferential treatment for the award of public-sector contracts, provided all the other specifications for the tender are met. If it can do the job, a Bumiputra status company may be given the contract even when its price is 5% (or even more) above that of its nearest competitor.

Incentives

Companies starting up as one of the promoted activities have a range of incentives offered, in some cases as alternatives. The choice will most often depend on the lead time required for a specific industry to come onstream.

Promoted activities encompass manufacturing, agriculture, integrated agriculture and tourism.

Pioneer status projects attract a tax-free holiday for a flat five years from production date. This is renewable for up to five more years only in exceptional cases.

Investment tax allowances (ITAs) give exemption on up to 100% of qualifying capital expenditure during the first five years after the project is approved.

Other taxes are spelt out clearly in the MIDA booklet obtainable from the MIDA office in Kuala Lumpur, 6th Floor, Wisma Damansara, or MIDA offices abroad.

Setting up

A foreign company must obtain a licence to do business. But the regulations (printed in English as well as Malay and based on English practice) are clear-cut and there are numerous services on hand from accountants, lawyers, and others less reputable, offering to "facilitate" and speed up the process. It is in fact eminently possible and often better to deal directly. Government officials if they find you sympathetic can be very helpful and the state economic development corporations, to be found in all states, usually create and manage industrial estates with highly developed infrastructures and widely available, inexpensive factory accommodation. In addition MIDA will always give you assistance.

A slow process The foreign visitor's main frustration is having to adjust to the extended time-scale it takes to push things through and the lack of urgency with which business is conducted. Impatience is counterproductive. Malaysians, especially the bureaucrats, cannot be hurried. Nor is it wise to try to "fix" matters. The best way to shorten the process is to prepare your application thoroughly; to know and to state clearly and precisely what you seek in terms of equity, management control, the number of expatriate posts and so on; and to be unwilling to negotiate too far beyond this.

Expatriate employment

A progressive Malaysianization policy has been in force since independence, but foreign personnel are granted employment passes where there is a shortage of trained nationals to do the job.

Expatriate posts As a special concession, foreign companies are also allowed designated "key posts" which may be permanently filled by expatriates to safeguard shareholders' interests and technical know-how. The quota was recently raised to as many as five such posts in priority industries.

Renewable work permits Standard work permits range from one to three years, and these are renewable. Applications must be accompanied by realistic projections for the company's phased Malaysianization programme, including training schemes. It is also advisable where possible to name the intended Malaysian successor for each expatriate post. It is better to emphasize the thorough preparation

of Malaysians for management succession than the quick replacement of foreigners.

Permits procedure The procedure for obtaining individual work permits is through the Controller of Immigration, but preliminary negotiations may be held with MIDA. Permits relating to the oil industry must have the prior recommendation of Petronas.

Normally applications are considered by the Interministerial Standing Committee on Malaysianization. Industries in the priority category have an easier ride than those from trading or service companies. The process was once protracted, but now MIDA facilitates a package deal by sending a common submission along with other applications for manufacturing licences and incentives, and a time limit is laid down for bureaucracy to reach a decision. A full package deal may take from one to six months. If it is operationally necessary to bring an employee in before his or her employment pass is approved, a temporary business pass can usually be obtained.

Directors Expatriates may serve as directors without restriction, but at the non-executive level companies find it more diplomatic and effective, to have Malaysians on their board.

Taxation

Corporate taxes in the mid-1980s were the highest in the region, with a total tax rate of 48% made up of a 40% basic rate plus a 5% development tax and a 3% excess profits tax. In 1987 the government abolished the excess profits tax and in 1989 began the phased abolition of the development tax.

Repatriation of funds

Malaysia permits free repatriation of funds. It has a liberal and non-discriminatory system of control regulations administered with minimal hassle by the central bank.

Market entry

Malaysia with only 16m people is a relatively small market although the per capita purchasing power exceeds that of its neighbours, Singapore excepted. The concept of ASEAN becoming a larger "common market" is a pleasant theory about which little has been done.

Importing and exporting

Most goods may be imported freely, although quotas may be imposed to protect new industries. There are no import restrictions on capital for new projects.

Segmented market The peculiarities of a multiracial society segment the market far more than is usual in other countries. Imported goods would seem outrageously over-priced compared with cheaper local options were it not such an elitist society. For luxury and semi-luxury items, the overseas product is more prestigious. The well-known names are eagerly sought. There is also a strong government drive to promote "Made in Malaysia" products.

Import duties Companies manufacturing directly for the export market, and companies supplying their feed stock, are given full exemption from import duty and surtax (if applicable) on raw materials/components not obtainable locally. This concession does not apply to companies producing for the domestic market. Note also that the level of exemption is decided arbitrarily. Import tariffs are now standardized at a 20% rate for almost all raw materials and components.

Labelling Guidelines stress the obligatory use of Malay, the national language, and the inclusion of guarantees in the instructions that food (or leather) products are halal (permitted by Islam).

Choosing your partner

Whatever your entry option – joint venture, incorporation, or agency arrangements – in all likelihood you will require a partner. Because of the NEP, a Bumiputra is almost mandatory, although you can have Chinese partners as well. Some firms "front" with a Bumiputra agent when bidding for public-sector contracts to disguise a strongly foreign equity. While this is expedient, it is still essential to make the right choice of associates.

Partner search can slow things up. If newcomers are at a loss as to where to start looking, MIDA is able to nominate candidates. There will in fact be no lack of recommendations from different sources, this being another prime opportunity for nepotism. It is always prudent to check these recommendations. You can always place equity on hold until you find your way around and have a better feel for who's who.

Ethnic considerations The choice will be dictated very largely by ethnic considerations matched to the geographic location – Chinese mostly in the towns, with an occasional Indian for the Tamil areas, but increasingly Bumiputra to penetrate the rural districts. Nepotism is perhaps most rife in the appointment of agents or contractors.

Distribution

The smallness of the market does not warrant a highly developed distribution network. Linking up with an established local company is often the way, with the added advantage that a local firm will know the problems, demands and idiosyncracies of the market place.

Chinese dominate Retail and distribution channels have traditionally been dominated by the Chinese. In many a Malay village the one shopkeeper will be Chinese. Retail and transport are the province of the small family business with a complicated support structure of suppliers, contractors and subcontractors who are part of the clan. The only concession to official policy is the "Ali Baba" device, the Chinese *towkay* who "fronts" with a Malay without relinquishing control. This system is frowned on by the authorities who wish to create a genuine Malay entrepreneurial class and who will press you to appoint Bumiputra agents wherever possible. Language barriers often make it impossible, however.

Chinese commerce has its own modus operandi, unrepentantly following business practices that seem curious to Western eyes and with scant regard for modern management or marketing theory, but which work for them. It is difficult for the outsider to break in, since success depends on inside knowledge, personal connections and knowing the language. What may be involved is not just proficiency in Malay, Tamil or Chinese, but specific dialects such as Hokkien, Cantonese, Teochew or Hakka.

Local trucking operations can be a closed shop, and companies can thus get away with minimal maintenance of their vehicles. Nevertheless, even the most decrepit specimens usually prove reliable.

Port facilities Port Kelang, not far from the capital, is the main container terminal, and international forwarders are available. Neighbouring Singapore, however, now the largest port in the world in terms of shipping tonnage, attracts much of Malaysia's freight still, by road and rail to its southern neighbour for transshipment. Malaysia's ports are not nearly so efficient, although actual stoppages or strikes are rare. The problems tend to be of a bureaucratic nature and, with patience, get sorted out. Again, a good agent is invaluable; he can oil the wheels considerably.

Other services such as insurance are readily available and up to international standards. Telex and fax facilities and international telecommunications are in place, but strains on the system can lead to delays and the very occasional breakdown. The infrastructure of roads, warehousing facilities and transport is reasonably good.

Advertising and PR

Advertising is quite sophisticated. Madison Avenue, Dentsu of Japan, and leading European agencies are well represented, many still headed by expatriates, although the profession is otherwise thoroughly Malaysianized. Foreign concerns have the option to use the same agency that handles their business worldwide. The use of international campaigns is now restricted, however. Advertisements not only must be carried in all the three main languages, but must be appropriate in content and style. The Ministry of Information, which controls the electronic media, imposes a partial ban on advertisments which feature explicit sex themes or immodest dress, cigarettes or alcohol, or contravene other Islamic taboos. Radio, TV and the print media are the main outlets.

Public relations is less developed, but is a maturing profession, and is now accepted as a part of business. Many companies engage an officer in-house or an outside consultant, most of them ex-journalists. PR agencies are modest in scale. Well-known names such as Saatchi & Saatchi and Burson-Marsteller feature. The rest tend to be Bumiputra, operating on contacts and influence-peddling. It is an open, unregulated profession and therefore lets in a dubious fringe of self-styled, mainly small-time and short-lived consultants.

Protection from pirating

A secondary industry has come into being, blatantly pirating famous brand names. Even ordinary consumer goods such as household wares and food products find themselves up against cheap imitations. The new Patents Act does, however, now offer better safeguards.

The financial scene

Like many other South-East Asian nations, Malaysia has a very stratified banking system, highly regulated by the central bank and loaded against foreign banks. Its stock market, however, is unusual in that it is virtually twinned with that of Singapore.

Banks and other financial institutions

Central bank The rather school-masterly supervisory approach which Bank Negara Malaysia (the central bank) adopts to financial institutions has not stopped a few of them getting into well-publicized trouble – though it has prevented them going bankrupt. Bank Negara's weapons of choice in controlling money supply and interest rates are altering the level of reserves it requires banks to keep, or open-market operations in government debt.

Commercial banks There are 23 domestic and 16 foreign commercial banks. Three domestic institutions – Bank Bumiputra Malaysia, Malayan Banking and United Malayan Banking – account for almost half the sector's loans, while two foreign banks – Hongkong and Shanghai Banking Corporation and Standard Chartered Bank – make up another quarter. Bank Bumiputra is a wholly-owned subsidiary of the state oil company Petronas, while United Malayan is over 50% owned by the state trading company Pernas. Malayan Banking is a publicly quoted company in which the government has an equity share. The Hongkong and Shanghai Banking Corporation and Standard Chartered, Singapore's Chung Khiaw Bank and Oversea-Chinese Banking Corporation have branch networks bigger than most local banks.

Merchant banks are required by law to draw a minimum of 30% of their earnings from fee (rather than interest) income, which they draw from services such as mergers and acquisitions, corporate advisory work and underwriting securities issues. Almost all the 12 merchant banks have foreign bank shareholders.

Finance companies Of relatively minor importance are the 43 finance companies which typically provide consumer credit and housing loans. Deposit-taking cooperatives – many of which became virtually bankrupt in 1986 because of fraud and mismanagement – have attracted private investors away from the banks.

Development finance institutions Aside from the Malaysian Industrial Development Fund, which operates nationally, the economic development boards of the 10 states of Malaysia offer finance to individuals and groups.

The markets

The stock market Of the 226 companies listed on the Kuala Lumpur Stock Exchange (KLSE), 183 are also listed in Singapore. One third of new share issues is supposedly reserved for Bumiputra entities, the biggest of which is the Permodalan Nasional Berhad (PNB), an investment trust which is the largest single shareholder in companies listed on the KLSE. US, Swiss and UK institutions are also active players.

The exchange is self-regulating though its activities are monitored by the Ministry of Finance and Bank Negara. The Capital Issues Committee operates a wait-in-line system for new flotations as well as fixing their issue price.

The only agency licensed to act as an issuing house (sponsor) of issues coming to the KLSE is MIDF Consultancy & Corporate Services, a subsidiary of the Malaysian Industrial Development Fund.

The commodities market The Kuala Lumpur Commodity Exchange offers the world's only contract in palm oil futures as well as dealing in rubber and tin.

Who can help

Law firms

Almost all the law firms in Malaysia are now run by Malaysians. Many of the firms, however, retain the European names of their founders and most of the large firms have a correspondent relationship with leading law practices in Europe. The legal system is based on English law.

Leading firms in Kuala Lumpur include *Skrine & Co* ☎ 298 5111, *Shearn & Delamore* ☎ 230 0644, *Allen & Gledhill* ☎ 291 4366, *Arifin & Partners* ☎ 293 6184, *Ng Ek Teong & Partners* ☎ 238 0344, *Shook, Lin & Bok* ☎ 248 0088.

Accountants

Many of the well-known international firms have branches in Kuala Lumpur. Local firms include *Hanafiah Raslan & Mohammed* ☎ 255 7000 and *Kassim Chan & Co* ☎ 230 6822. Most of the senior practitioners qualified as chartered accountants in Britain or Australia. Standards of practice are strict and audit standards rigorous. Malaysians do not hesitate to qualify accounts that fall short. Many firms have developed a specialized service preparing submissions to government on tax incentives. Many accountants go on to become bankers. The present governor of Bank Negara was formerly with Price Waterhouse.

Other sources of help

MIDA The first stop for any prospective investor is the Malaysian Industrial Development Authority (MIDA), located in Wisma Damansara, Kuala Lumpur ☎ 254 3633, but with offices in London, New York and other major cities overseas.

Headhunters Internationally known headhunters such as Korn Ferry will assist in Bumiputra search.

Chambers of commerce The Malaysian International Chamber of Commerce and Industry (MICCI), which is located in Wisma Damansara, is the organized voice of the foreign investment community in consultations with government. It also liaises with the Chinese, Malay and Indian chambers and belongs with them to the umbrella body of the National Joint Chambers of Commerce. This carries a degree of political clout with the government. The chamber has a full-time secretariat with Peter Jenkins as its executive director. It has built up a respectable reference library and a data bank and is a most useful source of information on government legislation and corporate case histories. Practical help in the way of introductions will also be forthcoming.

Foreign associations The British Malaya Trade Association (BMTA), affiliated to the Confederation of British Industry, is headed by Henry Barlow. The US equivalent is the American Business Council headed by Don Jerone. The French, German, Italian, Japanese and others have their own smaller groupings.

Other associations Rotary clubs or the Malaysian Institute of Management (MIM) or associations such as the Malaysian British Friendship Association are a good way to meet Malaysian and foreign business people.

Embassies The commercial section of the various embassies and high commissions are much more active than they used to be in promoting and supporting business interests.

Media All the dailies carry a business section, but the best source of economic/commercial journalism is probably the English-language *Business Times. Malaysian Business* is the only really reputable local journal, but many business people prefer to subscribe to the regional press, notably the *Far Eastern Economic Review. Business International*, part of the Economist group, has a *Malaysia Country Programme* for multinationals and other overseas clients, publishing a monthly political and economic *ALERT*, and organizing regular forums.

Business and cultural awareness

Malaysia is a multiracial society divided between the indigenous Malays (the Bumiputra) and the Chinese and Indians of immigrant stock. Each community jealously guards its cultural identity. The visitor must assimilate several different cultures at once; and negotiate the nuances and sensitivities that pervade all aspects of life. There is always a racial dimension to business and the potential for interracial tension cannot be ignored.

The racial factor at work

The visitor's experience of Malaysia can vary enormously, because of racial divisions. The Malays dominate the political establishment, the Chinese commerce. The Malays will be encountered overwhelmingly in politics, the bureaucracy and the armed forces. Bidding for public-sector contracts or dealing with the authorities means negotiating almost exclusively with the Bumiputra. Private-sector business, conversely, soon comes up against the Chinese, and the ethos is radically different. Malays are imbued with the purposes of government, the Chinese with profit. Middle-level civil servants often come across as over-zealous nationalists. Political criteria outweigh economic ones; and at times they can be inflexible "in the national interest." The commercially minded Chinese are more pragmatic, but self-interest makes them aggressive and shrewd operators. They are rated as more efficient than the bureaucrats, who are slowed down by red tape. There is, in fact, no generic "Malaysian" and one needs to adapt to the differing styles and values of the two camps. A perception gap separates the two groups. The Malays see themselves as the true patriots and the Chinese as self-seeking opportunists. The Chinese can appear chauvinistic and arrogant – conscious of superiority over the "barbarians," including the "red-haired foreign devil" variety. The Malays, constantly exposed to Chinese achievement, are easily made to feel inferior. Both sides can close ranks – behind a Chinese mafia in business and a Malay closed shop for government opportunities. The cultural gap is wide. No one could have dreamed up two races as disparate as the urban, materialistic, pork-loving, hard-working Chinese and the poorer, rural, conservative, religious and easy-going Malays.

Race relations While there is a tendency to mix with one's own kind, friendships do cross communal lines. Social gatherings are fully mixed; intermarriage takes place, but is restricted by religious barriers. Racial integration has been achieved at ground level.

Racial tension Race relations can be marred by residual antipathies, dramatically exemplified in the 1969 race riots. These were a sobering lesson in the need for tolerance, but their legacy of mistrust is a kind of national albatross. Racial tensions can be the hidden agenda in Malaysian affairs – and the NEP's racially discriminating policies have rekindled the resentments. The Chinese, who see themselves as second-class citizens, are increasingly vocal in their grievances. The Malays, rejecting the stereotype of "nature's gentleman," in other words nice but exploitable, are out to assert themselves.

Interference (even comment) by the foreigner is unacceptable. In extreme cases it has prompted the removal of work permits. Foreigners must be careful not to take sides or favour one group over the other, beyond the dictates of official policy.

Social structure

The Malays The basic social unit of

the Malays is the rural village, a close-knit, traditional community ruled by the palace and the mosque. From the village headman through the territorial chief to the sultan, it is almost feudal in structure and ethic. Loyalty, the cement in the system, is the prime value. Malays are the most status-conscious of the country's races, favouring big houses and cars and the perks of office over high salaries. Nowadays, 25% are urbanized – the new professional middle class. But despite their modern education they are often insecure when uprooted from their community and need time to adapt to urban pace and pressure. Many retreat from the private sector or seek the company of their own kind, promoting a degree of social inwardness.

The Chinese are more able to fend for themselves, but are very clannish. The family is central; the Confucian extended family is often synonymous with the family business, run by relatives and built up on kinship trust, including even an elaborate network of overseas Chinese. Family hierarchy is patriarchal. The individual has his or her fixed place, subservient to the group. Trust is what matters and is the most important ingredient in any business arrangement. Western partners who win the trust of the Chinese are made honorary family members, expected to attend all family occasions. A complicated web of loyalties and "godfathers" creates a kind of freemasonry very powerful in business.

The minority Indian community are disadvantaged, the butt of good-natured humour. They are forced into clannishness, and upward mobility through the professions – a disproportionate number of doctors and lawyers are Indian. The most articulate of the races, they tend to be litigious, adopt causes and lead trade unions. As a result, they have earned a reputation as potential troublemakers.

Hierarchy and patronage

The hierarchical social structure encourages authoritarian styles. It is a protective syndrome: the sultan will take care of his subjects, the Chinese patriarch his family, in return for unquestioning loyalty. Malaysians are reluctant to question or argue with anyone in authority.

Patronage is part and parcel of the system, as is nepotism, at least unofficially. The employment of relatives (never-ending in the extended family system) and favours requested for "cousin brothers" is common practice; at the political level it is seen as entirely justified given the overwhelming importance of family.

The group ethic In all the cultures, the individual is subordinate to the group and there is a corresponding reluctance to accept individual responsibility. The Malays especially love committees and collective decision-making that harks back to the village practices of *gotong royong* (mutual cooperation) and *meshuarat* (problem-solving by consensus).

Religion

Islam is the state religion, but other creeds are guaranteed freedom of worship. All the great religions of the world are here – Islam, Buddhism, Christianity, Hinduism, Sikhism, even animist cults among the tribal peoples – resulting in more temples, religious festivals and public holidays than probably anywhere in the world.

Islam pervades the Malays' whole way of life, but is not too intrusive. Signs of growing fundamentalism are probably over-estimated because of their visibility (the veil for women; whipping for drinking alcohol). Friday lunch hour is prolonged for prayers at the mosque and the obvious taboos like dietary restrictions are observed. Pork is not served before Muslims; the Hindus eschew beef, and many are vegetarians. State functions are dry and the "safe" chicken is the ubiquitous menu choice. The fasting month of Ramadan is fairly scrupulously observed. By and large Malaysia is relaxed and tolerant about religion, and all religious persuasions are practised quietly and undisturbed.

Courtesy

The onus in communal living is to achieve harmony. Politeness expressed in elaborate rules of etiquette is the mechanism for avoiding conflict and reducing anxiety. The aggressive modes of the West are found too abrasive: coming on too strongly can be counter-productive. Ideal behaviour is *halus*, low key, deferential and self-effacing. Humility is prized and should not be taken for weakness. Malaysians, especially Malays, are often suspected of being timid when in fact they are being courteous. Compromise is preferred in business to confrontation, and the Malays are skilled in the art.

Face

The compulsion to stand well in one's community and the intense humiliation of being shamed before others is all-pervasive. Loss of face can have disastrous consequences, including the breakdown of business negotiations. Westerners should be careful not to argue with those in authority (who thereby would lose face) or criticize anyone in public. Overt displays of anger are rare; to lose control is to lose face yourself. It is hard to know when offence has been given. The fractional raising of the voice can amount to the equivalent of a Western outburst of temper. Any form of rejection brings shame. People are often reluctant to say "no" to your face, and resort to hints and insinuations the visitor must decode. Intermediaries may be used to avoid embarrassment and find convenient face-saving formulas. Litigation should be avoided.

Language

Bahasa Malay is the national language but the other languages are designated "official." There has been some resistance to the extension of Malay for official purposes. Most Malaysians are bilingual, if not trilingual, and are most comfortable with English. The switch to Malay in schools has meant a deterioration in the standard of English, but it is spoken in all but the most remote areas and is workable for international commerce. The vernacular languages and dialects are used for trading at grassroots level. All official communication with government has to be in Malay, but English translations may accompany. Advertising and the media are conducted in three languages. Where it was once an advantage to belong to the English-educated elite, proficiency in Malay now matters. Foreigners are not pressed to learn it but gain Brownie points if they do.

Education

Malaysia's education system, a legacy of the missionaries, follows the UK's. The social elite among the Malays (beneficiaries of government scholarships) and the monied elite among the rest send their children abroad for schooling. Malaysia sends more students to Britain than any other country (12,000 a year) but US education is the current vogue (25,000 annually) with the emphasis on MBAs. Australia attracts because of its proximity. Academic excellence is the goal, resulting in a paper chase for qualifications. Malaysian institutions suffer from over-emphasis on exam results.

The business method

The Chinese are workaholics. Construction sites work round the clock. Holidays are rare except the sacrosanct New Year. Leisure hours are devoted to more money-making – gambling, conducting business at nightclubs, making contacts on the golf course. The Chinese are driven by both the work ethic and the success ethic. The Malays by contrast are easy-going hedonists and in business prefer to rely on contacts and influence. Contemporaries from school or college have a special rapport.

Office hours Malaysia is a fairly hardworking environment where the pace is set by the Chinese. Office hours are generally 8 to 5, but many executives work late. Office staff leave on the dot because of shared transport. Western-style working lunches and American-style breakfast meetings prolong the working day. Government offices work on Saturdays, and so do the Chinese, but international firms have adopted a five-day week. If a public holiday falls near a weekend, longer absences are usual.

After-hours meetings are often held in clubs, a legacy of colonial days. It is not usual to invade the privacy of the home with phone calls out of hours, but private-sector executives are more likely to be tolerant of this than government servants.

Dress The dress code is conservative, but with concessions to the climate – long-sleeved shirts and ties for the office, but formal appointments dictate a full suit. Government officials compromise on a bush jacket-type suit. Up-country and for outdoor sites shorts are worn. The younger executives, especially more fashion-conscious Malays, sport designer clothes.

Rumours are prevalent, sometimes malicious; 90% of the grapevine can be discounted. Because of the informal network of kinship loyalties, no secrets are kept and leakages of information pose a problem. The foreign media are not always reliably informed, but do influence overseas headquarters.

Business meetings

Malaysians feel no sense of urgency. Meetings can take a long time to set up and are frequently postponed. Inaccessibility of key players is a related problem and is not necessarily strategic. Top officials are very busy

people. Attempts to chase or force the pace do not work. The conduct of business meetings also calls for patience. These can be very pleasant but inconclusive. The first encounter rarely deals with hard business; its purpose is to set the tone. Social conversation and mere exchange of information can seem agonizingly slow, but are necessary business rituals. In the end people sell people; Malaysians prefer to do business with those whom they know and like.

Negotiations Malaysians dislike the Western legalistic approach to business in which the watertight contract is the key objective. They rely more on trust and are out to develop a relationship. They are reluctant to do combat. As Westerners seek to score points, Malaysians look for compromise. They will avoid contentious issues, hoping they will "melt away." Direct confrontation can offend. Too smart an approach or blinding with science is seen as arrogance.

Trust Malaysians are usually faithful to their bargains and intensely loyal to their partners. The Westerner's obsession with black letter law is regarded as a lack of trust. The Malaysian has little concern for legal niceties and fine print. He is looking for sincerity and flexibility.

Misunderstandings may be a problem. It is well to use clear simple English for any critical discussion and to take minutes. Cultural signals are also misread. A Malaysian "yes" means "I hear you," not necessarily "I agree." Silence does not mean consent, merely time taken to reflect. Nor are Malaysians uncomfortable or disconcerted by silence. True discussion and debate are hard to achieve because of the tendency to go along with the views of the most senior person present or conform to the consensus view.

Status is behind the formal ritual of exchanging business cards. It is necessary to know an individual's precise rank to accord him or her the correct level of courtesy. One also needs to know relative rank to meet the tacit rules of correct distance. You do not send a junior colleague to a senior official or the latter will lose face. Business cards need to be as precise as possible and often declare a wealth of information on qualifications. Corporate designations matter. "Chairman" may imply a figurehead. VIPs given a sinecure on retirement may have the courtesy title "Adviser." American titles like president and vice-president are the latest vogue. Both royal and civil titles abound. Honorifics and protocol surround them; this is a society fond of ceremonial. One needs to learn the proper form of address. Business status is most often expressed through plush offices and chauffeur-driven cars.

Good joss The old-style Chinese *towkay*, however, will continue to occupy the decrepit shop house where he started because it brings good joss. The *fung-shui* or atmosphere must be right before going into new premises. Astrologers will be consulted on all important decisions including business ones.

Women in business

There is equal opportunity for women but business is still a male preserve. More female executives will be found in government. Resistance comes from the diehards – the Chinese *towkays*, for example – but is reserved more for their own women, who are expected to adhere to outmoded ideas of modesty almost as inhibiting as the bound feet of their predecessors. Malaysian women are traditionally sheltered, without the freedom to travel alone or be out late on business. The Western visitor is not under such constraints and by and large will be accepted, provided she conforms in public to the dress codes and the decorum imposed by the Islamic culture.

Hospitality

Malaysians lead an intense social life. Business relationships are cemented through entertaining. The visitor is fêted in a round of partying. The cocktail party circuit is small and incestuous. You must be prepared to eat at roadside stalls as well as first-class hotels, and to be venturesome about food. Guests will be proffered the "delicacies," invariably the most alien to Western palates. The Chinese will prefer a prestigious restaurant – the importance of the occasion will be judged by the number of tables and of courses (anything up to twelve). Malays and Indians receive in their homes. Male business visitors may be offered a visit to a massage parlour or a female companion.

Malaysians are casual in their response to invitations. They rarely reply and can turn up and stay away at will, making catering difficult. They can seem very personal, at times capable of asking what the visitor considers the most intimate questions from the cost of a watch to one's earnings. Malaysia being a Muslim country, alcohol must be served with discretion.

The open house One triumph of racial co-existence is the charming and very Malaysian custom of the open house. At festivals homes are open to all comers irrespective of class, race or status. The humblest citizen may call on the prime minister – and thousands do. So can the foreign visitor. Hari Raya is the main Muslim festival. The Chinese reciprocate at their New Year, the Hindus at Deepavali. No special invitation is needed. Visitors should understand that they are free, and at times expected, to call on business contacts "to give face." Shoes are removed at the door and food proffered must be taken or offence will be caused.

Gifts

Bribery is offically condemned, but giving and receiving of favours is a way of cementing business relationships. Malaysians rarely go visiting empty-handed. Malaysia works by contacts and influence.

KUALA LUMPUR   Area code ☎ 03

Regular visitors to Kuala Lumpur have witnessed something of a transformation. Stung by criticisms of garbage-strewn streets and polluted rivers, the city fathers set the wheels in motion for a city-wide clean-up in time for the important Pacific Area Travel Agents Association Conference in 1986 – a chance to prove that Malaysia had been maligned and deserved to be Asia's number one holiday destination. Sceptics said the gloss would not outlast the conference. Newly planted verges would be denuded and the expensive shrubs find their way into private gardens; streets would soon be piled with rubbish, once again. They were wrong. Taxi drivers ask whether Kuala Lumpur is not now like Singapore – the comparison, though, is unrealistic. Proud new office blocks, some with a distinct Islamic design, stand gleaming in the sunshine. But behind the façades many offices are unoccupied. New shopping centres packed with imported goods attract throngs of people, but most are window-shopping; few have the means to buy. Attempts have been made to clean the river but it remains an eyesore. Kuala Lumpur is still the capital of a third-world nation; outwardly prosperous and undoubtedly one of the most developed, but still seeking a breakthrough into the league of affluent nations.

The city was built on tin and rubber, the latter controlled by a tough breed of British plantation managers. Many estates later turned to palm oil production. Today, however, it is petroleum that is the main cause of Kuala Lumpur's prosperity.

The city has large Chinese and Indian populations, the descendants of immigrants who came to work the plantations and mines, and who now occupy powerful positions in trade, industry and finance. Each strongly asserts its own separate identity, with the result that – on the surface at least – the city appears to be an exotic blend of Muslim, Chinese and Hindu cultures.

Arriving

Kuala Lumpur is served by about 20 international airlines providing direct flights from Europe, North America and Australasia. The most heavily used routes are those from Singapore (40min), Bangkok (1¾hr), Jakarta (2hr) and Hong Kong (1¾hr).

The 400km/250-mile drive from Singapore is slowest at the weekend, since long lines build up at the customs and immigration checkpoints north of the Johor Straits from noon on Friday. There are seven trains from Singapore daily; the journey takes 7hr. From Thailand the train takes 34hr.

Subang International airport

Subang airport handles international and domestic flights with relative efficiency, even at peak periods. Immigration and customs are usually handled swiftly. It rarely takes more than 25min to clear the airport. There is an airport tax of M$15 on international flights, M$5 to Singapore and M$3 on internal flights.

Facilities There are banks in the baggage reclaim hall and in the departure hall upstairs. Immediately beyond customs there is a well-stocked duty-free shop. The tourist information desk is in the arrivals hall, but the hotel reservations and car rental office is just outside the building, on the left. This is staffed by hotel reps who compete with each other for custom – not all hotels are represented. For first-class passengers without baggage there is a telephone check-in facility ☎ 746 2806, and an express check-in desk. Other facilities include a telegram, telex and international telephone office, VIP lounges, first aid and lost property desks, limited catering (bars serving hot snacks) and souvenir shops. Most are open 8.30am–11.30pm. Airport inquiries ☎ 746 1235.

City link The airport is 20km/12 miles southwest of Kuala Lumpur; the journey to the city centre takes around 30min but allow 45min during the rush hours (7.30–9.30, 4.30–6). It is best to take a taxi, or pay a little more for hotel transport.

Hotel transport This can be arranged in advance, or at the office just outside the terminal exit on the left. Most hotel cars cost around M$20 for the single journey, though the Regent and Shangri-La have luxury limousines at higher rates.

Taxi Outrageous overcharging has been stopped by the introduction of a voucher system. Vouchers can be bought from the desk to the right of the terminal exit and are given to the driver at the end of the journey. The cost varies according to the destination but is usually M$15 to centrally situated hotels.

Car rental The major car rental firms are in the same office as the hotel bureau (open 6am–9pm; Sun and hols, 6–5). For advance reservations: Avis ☎ 242 3500, Hertz ☎ 243 3014 or Sintat ☎ 274 3028.

Bus The no. 47 bus runs between the airport and the Jalan Sultan Mohammed terminal, from where taxis can be hailed, at any time between 6am and 11pm.

Getting around

Taxis in Kuala Lumpur are plentiful and adequate for short trips, but if you have a busy schedule it is worth paying extra for a limousine.

Hotel transport Most hotels use the car rental firms. You might as well cut out the commission and service charge and contact them direct. Some hotels have their own limousines which cost from M$25 per hour.

Taxi All of Kuala Lumpur's taxis have a yellow top, and it is difficult to distinguish between those with and those without air conditioning – though those that carry an advertising sign on their roof are generally the newer, better and air-conditioned ones. A lamp lit on top indicates a taxi is available for hire. All hotels and all shopping malls have a rank. Watch that the meter is switched on, though cheating is far less common than it used to be. The dishonest drivers try to take advantage over the airconditioning supplement; this should be 20% of the metered fare. A typical journey from the centre of the city to the hotel and business district costs M$6. Between midnight and 6am there is a 50% surcharge. Generally, taxi drivers understand English and know their way about, but because of the loss of face involved most will be reluctant to admit that they do not know a particular place. It is advisable not to board a vehicle if you feel that the driver does not know your destination. Radio taxis calculate the fare from their departure point. Central taxi firms are *Aswan* ☎ 298 8073, *Silvertop* ☎ 423 1267 and *Sri Kuning Transport* ☎ 456 2239.

Driving.Traffic drives on the left. Seat belts are compulsory for drivers and front-seat passengers, and there are on the spot fines for failure to comply. Anyone new to Kuala Lumpur should use limousines rather than rent a self-drive car, because Kuala Lumpur's system of inner ring roads takes time to master. However, good maps are published by all of the major fuel companies and Kuala Lumpur's roads are well-signposted in English. For car rental

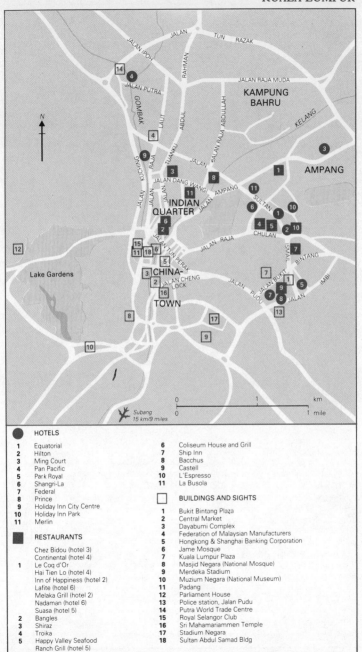

HOTELS

1	Equatorial
2	Hilton
3	Ming Court
4	Pan Pacific
5	Park Royal
6	Shangri-La
7	Federal
8	Prince
9	Holiday Inn City Centre
10	Holiday Inn Park
11	Merlin

RESTAURANTS

	Chez Bidou (hotel 3)
	Continental (hotel 4)
1	Le Coq d'Or
	Hai Tien Lo (hotel 4)
	Inn of Happiness (hotel 2)
	Lafite (hotel 6)
	Melaka Grill (hotel 2)
	Nadaman (hotel 6)
	Suasa (hotel 5)
2	Bangles
3	Shiraz
4	Troika
5	Happy Valley Seafood
	Ranch Grill (hotel 5)

6	Coliseum House and Grill
7	Ship Inn
8	Bacchus
9	Castell
10	L'Espresso
11	La Busola

BUILDINGS AND SIGHTS

1	Bukit Bintang Plaza
2	Central Market
3	Dayabumi Complex
4	Federation of Malaysian Manufacturers
5	Hongkong & Shanghai Banking Corporation
6	Jame Mosque
7	Kuala Lumpur Plaza
8	Masjid Negara (National Mosque)
9	Merdeka Stadium
10	Muzium Negara (National Museum)
11	Padang
12	Parliament House
13	Police station, Jalan Pudu
14	Putra World Trade Centre
15	Royal Selangor Club
16	Sri Mahamariammen Temple
17	Stadium Negara
18	Sultan Abdul Samad Bldg

and limousine reservations see *Arriving*.

Walking Kuala Lumpur's ring roads keep traffic away from the centre, the sidewalks are safe, newly paved and clean, and the only real disincentive to walking is the heat. Major commercial buildings in the city centre, bounded by the ring roads, are mostly within easy walking distance. Local people are usually helpful with directions.

Bus Buses are clean by Asian standards, and cheap. Drivers are generally helpful to anyone who does not understand the system. Many visitors use buses for sightseeing. The Visitors' Centre provides details of the main routes (see *Information sources*).

Outside Kuala Lumpur

Air *Malaysian Airlines System* (MAS) operates an extensive network of domestic routes covering the tourist destinations of Langkawi, Penang and Malacca. Most destinations, with the exception of the two east Malaysian states on the island of Borneo, are very close. Some airlines (particularly MAS) insist on check-in 90min before departure. If you are unavoidably delayed, call the airline: *MAS* ☎ 774 7000, *Singapore* ☎ 292 3122 and *Thai* ☎ 293 7100.

Driving This can be pleasurable, and is a good way of exploring the countryside independently. Filling stations and service facilities for most makes of car are plentiful. The West Coast highway, part of a system linking Singapore, Malaysia and Thailand, rarely presents problems, nor does the new East/West highway linking Penang, Butterworth and Kota Bahru. But the less developed roads of the east coast can be hazardous, particularly during the Oct–Feb monsoon season. Car rental is cheap for use outside the capital and it is possible to leave a car at a different city from where you rented it (for reservations, see *Arriving*).

Train The railway station is located on the south side of the city centre.

The main rail route runs from Singapore to Bangkok via principal towns in west Malaysia. A second line runs from Gemas up the centre of the peninsula, via Kuala Lipis, to Tumpat near Kota Bahru on the east coast. Most cities on the main line can be reached within a day, and it is one of the few lines in Asia which runs according to the timetable; the minor services are much less convenient. For seat reservations ☎ 238 7197.

Area by area

Kuala Lumpur is one of the smallest South-East Asian capital cities. It has grown organically within the arms of the Y-shaped junction of the rivers Kelang and Gombak, and the lack of an ordered street plan only adds to the city's charm, although visitors may initially find the maze of narrow streets confusing. The network of ring roads which surrounds the city is reasonably successful in maintaining traffic flow and keeping the old city centre relatively free of vehicles.

The city had its origins in a trading post established to carry tin down the River Kelang to the estuary town of Kelang, 27km/17 miles southwest. In the 1850s, rich deposits of tin ore were found in what is now the commercial and hotel district of Ampang. The invention of canning as a means of preserving food led to strong world demand for the commodity, and the strategic importance of Kuala Lumpur was soon recognized.

City centre Most of the area to the west of the station is devoted to major public buildings. Nearby, the Lake Gardens contain the monument to Malaysia's national heroes and the former residence of Malaysia's revered second prime minister, the late Tun Abdul Razak, popularly known as the "Father of Development." Parliament House is on the western fringe of the gardens. The building contains the House of Representatives and Senate, while the 18-floor office tower which dominates the complex contains the offices of the main government ministries. Formerly, many of the administrative arms of government were housed in the Sultan Abdul Samad Building, a splendid pink-brick building of spiralling staircases and Islamic archways; it now contains the Judicial Department and High Court. The building provides a suitably dramatic backdrop for the National Day celebrations which take place on the Padang opposite. For this and other important occasions, the very British Tudor-style pavilions of the Royal Selangor Club are used by the prime minister to review parades. Towering above is the Hongkong & Shanghai Bank Building – one of the few high-rise blocks in the heart of the city. Just east of the Jame Mosque the borders of Chinatown and the Indian quarter merge, and it is a few minutes stroll to the Hindu Sri Mahamariamman and the Chinese Chan See Shu Yuen Temples.

East of the centre the atmosphere changes abruptly. High-rise development came late to Kuala Lumpur but has rapidly gained a foothold; the city's offices, hotels and new shopping complexes are mostly concentrated here. Jalan Bukit Bintang was the first area to be covered in hotels and shopping complexes. More recently, Jalan Ampang and Jalan Sultan Ismail have been transformed from rural suburbs into a commercial centre of gleaming skyscrapers. These house Malaysia's most prestigious companies, though many floors still remain vacant behind impressive façades.

The suburbs
The thriving industrial and middle-class residential suburb of Petaling Jaya, 12km/7 miles south of the city, is the centre of the country's electronics, automobile, food processing and rubber industries. Petaling Jaya is linked by the Federal highway to Kelang, 27km/17 miles southwest of Kuala Lumpur. Kelang is now an important service centre for the rubber and palm oil plantations which surround the town and home for many of the people who work in nearby Port Kelang, where an international container terminal has been built. The area north of the centre is expected to expand rapidly now that the Putra World Trade Centre is completed.

Hotels

The Shangri-La is by a long way the best hotel in Kuala Lumpur, but there are many other perfectly acceptable hotels in the city. All rooms in the ones listed here have air conditioning, TV, radio, IDD telephone, minibar and 24hr room service. Standard business facilities include typing, photocopying, telex and fax. Quoted rates are subject to 15% service and tax. Discounts are often available because of excess capacity due to a recent surge in hotel building.

Equatorial $$
Jalan Sultan Ismail, 50250
℡ *261 2022* ℡ *30263 Fax 261 7920*
• *AE DC MC V* • *284 rooms, 16 suites,*
4 restaurants, 2 bars
One of Kuala Lumpur's oldest hotels, once a favourite with seasoned travellers, the Equatorial is still a place in which the guests seem at ease and ready to chat with fellow executives, particularly in the popular Equatorial Bar. Regular fashion shows, with buffet dinner in the ballroom, are part of the Kuala Lumpur entertainment calendar and attract the local affluent journalists and would-be models. Altogether it is a lively hotel where the service is friendly and the restaurants are informal but perfectly adequate for all but top-level entertaining. Rooms are not large and have fixed desks

but you could opt for a more spacious studio suite on the upper floors. Shopping arcade, hairdresser, florist, limousine hire • pool • 6 meeting rooms (capacity up to 450), all with audiovisual equipment.

Hilton $$
Jalan Sultan Ismail, 50750
℡ 242 2222 ™ 30495 Fax 243 8069 •
AE DC MC V • 537 rooms, 44 suites,
3 restaurants, 3 bars

The Hilton's somewhat harsh copper and lacquered wood interior is softened by exuberant displays of tropical plants and flowers and comfortable modern furnishings. If you ask for a room at the back you will have superb views of the leafy Kuala Lumpur suburbs, the race course and the highlands beyond. Otherwise, you see nothing but the surrounding city tower blocks. All rooms have bay windows and light furnishings with a small, movable desk. Executive floor suites are much more like a well-designed living room with glass-top tables, sofas and ample armchairs. The Inn of Happiness and Melaka Grill (see *Restaurants*), a pub with snooker table, a bar with a lively jazz band and a disco provide fully for entertainment needs. The sports facilities are comprehensive.
Shopping mall, hairdresser, florist • pool, sauna, jacuzzi, massage, gym, tennis and squash, use of nearby golf and riding facilities • 22 meeting rooms and ballroom.

Ming Court $$
Jalan Ampang, 50740 ℡ 261 9066
™ 32621 Fax 261 2393 • *AE DC MC V*
• *410 rooms, 36 suites, 5 restaurants, 1 bar*

A little farther out of the centre of Kuala Lumpur than most hotels, Ming Court is ringed by embassies and newly built office blocks. These are creating a new commercial focus in an area which was a quiet suburb until recently but which still retains some stylish colonial bungalows and giant umbrella-like trees. The Ming Court is a new, crescent-shaped

ziggurat, designed so that most rooms have balconies with views. It has yet to establish itself, but has the ingredients to attract a diverse clientele. Chez Bidou (see *Restaurants*) is popular with staff from the surrounding offices. Taipan Club suites are well equipped and include extras such as kimonos. Other rooms are on the small side. Service is alert and helpful. Shops, florist, hairdresser • pool, sauna, gym, tennis • 11 meeting rooms.

Pan Pacific $$
Jalan Putra, 50746 ℡ 442 5555
™ 33706 Fax 291 7226 • *AE DC MC V*
• *556 rooms, 15 suites, 4 restaurants, 2 bars*

Although only a 10min drive from the centre of Kuala Lumpur, the Pan Pacific is considered by many to be too out of town. However, the Putra World Centre is next door, and The Mall, an upmarket shopping galleria is opposite. The public areas of the hotel are in the high-tech mould: bare girders, ventilation ducting and highly polished surfaces. Guest rooms are large, with spacious, well-finished bathrooms and all have an office desk and multiple telephone points. Staff are cheerful and go out of their way to be helpful; messages are delivered instantly. The hotel deserves, and will probably earn, a loyal and appreciative clientele. Shopping arcade, florist, delicatessen • pool, sauna, gym, tennis, squash • 8 meeting rooms.

Park Royal $$
Jalan Sultan Ismail, 50250
℡ 242 5588 ™ 30486 Fax 241 5524 •
AE DC MC V • 315 rooms, 25 suites,
3 restaurants, 2 bars

As many tourists as business travellers now stay at the Park Royal (formerly the Regent), but it remains a hotel which has an established niche in local expatriate life. Its versatile chefs are called upon to produce appropriate menus for Bavarian, French, British and American high days and holidays (see

Restaurants). The hotel also has a tradition of sponsoring the arts, with exhibitions on its mezzanine floor and touring-theatre productions in the ballroom. Thus the Park Royal maintains its position as an entertaining hotel in which to stay, with something always on the go. Its decor is the most consciously Malaysian of all Kuala Lumpur's hotels; warm, richly carved wood panelling echoes the style of artistocratic Malay palaces. Guest rooms have been refurbished recently and many have original paintings and antiques. Bathrooms are luxurious with huge, tiled tubs and separate showers. The business centre is open 24hr. Extensive shopping arcade, florist, hairdresser • pool, sauna, jacuzzi, gym, tennis, squash • library, 9 meeting rooms (capacity up to 700).

Shangri-La $$
11 Jalan Sultan Ismail, 50250 ☎ *232 2388* Ⓣ *30021 Fax 230 1514* • *AE DC MC V* • *686 rooms, 36 suites, 7 restaurants, 2 bars*
Opened in 1986, the Shangri-La quickly established itself as *the* place to stay in Kuala Lumpur. It is central, spacious and stylish, and standards of service are in the best South-East Asian traditions. Guest-rooms are very large and many have bay windows forming a full semicircle, antique furniture, full-sized desks and bathrooms with separate showers. The very stylish Lafite (see *Restaurants*) is ideally suited to high-powered business entertaining. The gardens have yet to reach full maturity but, in time, will be a haven for relaxation. The business centre is open 24hr. Shops, florist, hairdresser • pool, sauna, jacuzzi, massage, gym, tennis,

squash • 12 meeting rooms (capacity up to 2,000) including convention centre with 8 simultaneous translation channels, video, film, slide and overhead projectors, and electronic voting panels.

OTHER HOTELS
Federal ($) *35 Jalan Bakit Bintang, 55100* ☎ *248 8144* Ⓣ *30429 Fax 243 8381* • *AE DC MC V*. Run by Nikko hotels with excellent views from its 18th floor revolving restaurant.
Prince ($$) *Jalan Imbi, 55100* ☎ *243 8388* Ⓣ *21117 Fax 243 8381* • *AE DC MC V*. A modern and well equipped hotel with good service.
Holiday Inn on the Park ($) *Jalan Pinang, 50732* ☎ *248 1066* Ⓣ *30239 Fax 243 5930* • *AE DC MC V* and the **Holiday Inn City Centre ($)** *Jalan Raja Laut, 50350* ☎ *293 9233* Ⓣ *28130 Fax 293 9634* • *AE DC MC V*, are both reliable hotels, comfortable and well-run.
Merlin ($) *2 Jalan Sultan Ismail, 50250* ☎ *248 0033* Ⓣ *30487 Fax 242 6917* • *AE DC MC V*. Central, popular and cheerful.

Clubs
The *Royal Selangor Club* ☎ 298 8106, is one of Asia's oldest and most venerable. Its striking Tudor-style clubhouse is a central Kuala Lumpur landmark; cricket is played on the adjacent sports field. Membership is multiracial but exclusive. Considered by many to be more upmarket these days, however, and much favoured by senior civil servants, is the *Lake Club* ☎ 298 5133. Also prestigious is the recently opened *Bankers Club* ☎ 242 4166, with a membership list that reads like a Kuala Lumpur *Who's Who?*

Restaurants
To a businessman or woman in Kuala Lumpur, ambience is far less important than the quality of the food. Really trusted colleagues, those who are prepared to accept the most basic surroundings without demur, will be taken to some unpretentious establishments where the food,

often Chinese, is superb. To find such restaurants requires considerable local knowledge; the visitor is best advised to stick to the better hotel dining rooms. Outside of hotels, Kuala Lumpur restaurants are slowly becoming more sophisticated, but many still shun fancy pretensions for fear of alienating the local trade upon which they depend. Restaurants charge 15% service and tax on top of menu prices.

Chez Bidou $$
Ming Court Hotel ☎ *261 9066 •*
closed Sat, Sun • AE DC MC V
Chez Bidou is a lively restaurant which attracts a lot of lunch-time trade from nearby offices. It seems all the busier because the dining room is compact, and the sense of intimacy is increased by the low, rustic-beamed ceiling, antique dressers and coral-coloured furnishings. The lunch-time buffet is good value. In the evenings, which are quieter and better for private conversation, the standard grill menu is supplemented by well-prepared French provincial dishes.

Continental $$$
Pan Pacific Hotel ☎ *442 5555 •* AE DC MC V
The Continental is all glass and dramatic lighting under a greenhouse-like canopy, and tables are almost completely enclosed in octagonal banquettes around the restaurant perimeter. Serving excellent appetizers and good fish dishes, it is well suited to working or more social meals.

Le Coq d'Or $$
121 Jalan Ampang ☎ *242 9732 •*
AE DC MC V
Although no longer quite the exclusive and elegant restaurant it once was, Le Coq d'Or is nevertheless a good choice for entertaining. The restaurant is in a fine old house surrounded on all four sides by a sweeping veranda giving deep shade and a perfect setting for cocktails before lunch or dinner. Behind the bulging pillars of the portico and the diamond-paned windows shaded with bamboo blinds is a dining room filled with marble statues and Victorian oil paintings

where elderly and respectful waiters provide courtly service. Its popularity with a cross-section of citizens from chief executives to secretaries, particularly at lunch time, means that the atmosphere can be frenetic at times, and the dog-eared menus have seen better days. The choice of dishes is extensive, an eclectic compilation of European and Malay. Not to be missed, despite a few shortcomings.

Hai Tien Lo $$
Pan Pacific Hotel ☎ *442 5555 •* AE DC MC V
An uncluttered, airy and spacious dining room, predominantly green and gold, is the setting for one of Kuala Lumpur's best Cantonese restaurants, specializing in crisp, light seafood dishes, steamed *dim sum* and winter melon delicacies.

Inn of Happiness $$
Hilton Hotel ☎ *242 2222 •* AE DC MC V
Visitors to the Hilton's large and grandiose Chinese dining room are greeted by the tanks of live fish in which the restaurant specializes. Senior business people eat here. Ask for a table overlooking the colourful Chinese garden.

Lafite $$$
Shangri-La Hotel ☎ *232 2388 •*
AE DC MC V
Lafite is Kuala Lumpur's premier restaurant, the correct choice for top-level entertaining. It has all the touches that impress: a beautiful wood-lined interior, etched Art Deco mirrors, colourful and original works of art, immaculate table settings and crisp service, a varied Continental menu and an extensive wine list. The buffet is the best value in town.

Melaka Grill $$$
Hilton Hotel ☏ *242 2222* •
AE DC MC V

The Melaka Grill is decorated in ornate 19thC Portuguese style, with intricately carved wooden panelling and antique chandeliers. At lunch there is a fixed-price menu or a short list of daily specials. In the evening there is a full grill room *à la carte* menu plus mild versions of usually spicy classic Malay dishes.

Nadaman $$
Shangri-La Hotel ☏ *232 2388* • *AE DC MC V*

The Shangri-La's Japanese restaurant is somewhat functional – tables are on the small side and lined in regimented rows – but the food is authentic and presented with artistic flair. A popular venue for informal business lunches.

Suasa $$$
Park Royal Hotel ☏ *242 5588* • *AE DC MC V*

There is nothing sham about the Suasa's turn-of-the-century elegance. All the antiques, including the dining-chairs and tables, are genuine; the perfect setting for a leisurely lunch or a candlelit dinner. The menu is soundly international.

Good but casual
Kuala Lumpur has several restaurants, serving Northern Indian or Moghul cuisine. The food tends to be drier and spicier than is served in similar restaurants in the West. Both *Bangles*, 60 Jalan Tuanku Abdul Rahman ☏ 298 3780, and *Shiraz*, at the Shiraz Hotel, Jalan Medan Tuanka ☏ 291 0035, serve tandoori dishes, including lobster, prawn and local fish. *Troika*, Komplek Kewangan, Jalan Raja Chulan ☏ 261 6734, is a local favourite specializing in borscht and shashlik. *Happy Valley Seafood*, Menara Promet Bldg, Jalan Sultan Ismail ☏ 241 1264, is like Chinese restaurants throughout Asia; large, and full of noisy, good-natured

diners who all rate highly the seafood dishes and shark's fin soup, the Beijing duck and suckling pig.

Expatriates go to the *Ranch Grill* at the Park Royal Hotel ☏ 242 5588 for authentic American-style food – large grilled steaks, deep-pan pizza, Mexican burritos, good home-made bread and an extensive salad selection. Steak, cottage pie, beer and expatriate atmosphere make the *Coliseum* (see *Bars*), 98 Jalan Tuanku Abdul Rahman ☏ 292 6270, and the *Ship* (see *Bars*), 40 Jalan Sultan Ismail ☏ 241 8805, popular for casual, shirtsleeves lunch and dinner. *Bacchus*, basement of Bangunan Safuan, Jalan Raja Abdullah ☏ 291 5898, serves commendable French provincial and Mexican. Bistro-style restaurants include *The Castell*, 81 Jalan Bukit Bintang ☏ 242 8328 and one which is popular with young executives, *L'Espresso*, Wisma Stephens, Jalan Raja Chulan ☏ 241 4669. For Italian food *La Bussola*, Wilayah shopping Complex, Jalan Dang Wangi ☏ 291 5832 is considered one of the best.

All of these restaurants fall within the $ or $$ categories and accept major credit cards.

Street food
After dusk, many of the streets in central Kuala Lumpur are closed to traffic and the sidewalks fill with hawker stalls selling inexpensive *satay*, Malay curry and rice dishes, and skewers of deep-fried fishballs or squid. The eating arrangements are as basic as it is possible to get, but the open-air stalls are heavily patronized by locals and visitors alike. The best places for food and atmosphere are the markets in Jalan Munshi Abdullah, Jalan Melayu, Jalan Masjid India, the Old Klang Road, the Campbell stalls in Jalan Dang Wangi and, on Saturday nights, the market at Kampung Bahru.

Bars

Kuala Lumpur's hotels have plenty of smart bars, many of which are modelled on the British pub. The *Pub* at the Shangri-La and the *Club Bar* at the Hilton are two of the best, while the *Library Bar* at the Regent is plush and clubby but may be too small for private conversation. The *Aviary Bar* at the Hilton has a cage of exotic and occasionally very noisy birds, but they are no competition for the excellent jazz band which performs there at night. The *Coliseum*, 98 Jalan Tuanku Abdul Rahman is the place to go to sample an atmosphere evocative of the planter-pioneer days. By contrast, the *Ship*, 40 Jalan Sultan Ismail is a tamer affair, full of nautical trappings, but with good music, including folk and jazz.

Entertainment

Theatre, dance, music Western-style cultural entertainment is rare in Kuala Lumpur. Organizations such as the British Council ☏ 298 7555 host touring dance and musical performances, and classic British comedies are occasionally on offer at the Regent. For indigenous culture – everything from Chinese opera to Malay and Indian dance – the *Yazmin Theatre Restaurant*, 6 Jalan Kia Peng ☏ 241 5655, is one of the pleasantest venues. The nightly show, which starts at 8.30, includes a high-quality Malay buffet and barbecue.

Cinemas in Kuala Lumpur show fast-action Western movies; James Bond is a perennial favourite. Screenings are listed in the *Straits Times*, *Star* or *Malay Mail*.

Discos are an important part of the social scene and on a Friday or Saturday night, everyone who still considers themselves young at heart heads for one of the city's many nightspots. *Tin Mine* at the Hilton is one of the classiest and local bands consider they have made it once they get to play there. *Club Oz* at the Shangri-La is more restrained. Of the

town discos, most of which are crowded with young Chinese and Malays showing off the latest fashions, *Hot Gossip* at the Kuala Lumpur Plaza ☏ 243 6775 can be pretty frenzied. Others, which have the latest sound, light and video effects include *The Cave*, 145 Jalan Ampang ☏ 261 1589; the *Pyramid Club* in Wilayah Shopping Complex, Jalan Munshi Abdullah ☏ 292 3092; *Sapphire*, Plaza Yow Chuan, Jalan Tun Abdul Razak ☏ 243 0043; and *High Voltage*, Sungei Wang Plaza ☏ 242 1220. The *Federal Club*, at the Federal hotel, which started the disco craze in Malaysia, still has its faithful supporters.

Nightclubs The *Paddock* on the roof-top of the Hilton offers Malay and Continental food with dancing to international bands. Town clubs are neither as expensive nor as meretricious as similar establishments elsewhere in Asia. Music is provided by live dance bands and entertainment by way of GROs (guest relations officers). They are mostly patronized by Japanese and Korean businessmen. Among the top clubs is *Toppan*, Wisma Stephens, Jalan Raja Chulan ☏ 248 9304.

Shopping

Shops in Kuala Lumpur open daily, 10–10. The two products most representative of Malaysia are pewter and batik. Although shops in every hotel arcade and every shopping plaza stock both in abundant variety, it is more fun to buy direct from producers. At local stores and bazaars, you are expected to bargain over prices; it is often possible to agree on 50% of the stated price.

Pewter The art of pewter-making was introduced from China in the mid-19th century, and the fineness of the surface derives from the very high proportion of tin (97%) used in its manufacture. Jugs, bowls, plates, ashtrays, mugs and jewellery from the factory are sold throughout the country. The *Selangor Pewter Factory* at Jalan Usahawan off Jalan Pahang in the Setapak district, northeast of the city, has pewter-making demonstrations throughout the day Mon–Fri, 8–5. The main showroom is on Jalan Genting Kelang and is open 9–4.30 (Sun, 9–4).

Batik Vividly coloured cloth with exuberant patterns created by successive applications of wax and dye, is sold by the length or made up into shirts, blouses, bed-linen and tableware. The best place for demonstrations of both hand-drawn and block-printed batik-making is at the factory in Selayang, along Jalan Ipoh, 15km/9 miles north of the city; open Mon–Fri, 9–5; Sat, 9–1. *Wisma Batik*, on Jalan Tun Perak, always has a comprehensive stock of the best batik, or try the *Karyaneka Handicraft Centre*, Jalan Raja Chulan.

Handicrafts The *Karyaneka Handicraft Centre* is a government-run complex of 14 craft houses representing the products of all the states of Malaysia, including silverware, gold and silver woven cloth, pottery and primitive baskets open Mon, 9.30–5; Tue–Sun, 9.30–6.

Shopping complexes In the city's modern shopping complexes it is possible to buy anything from jewellery to designer-label clothes but most of the goods are imported and are as expensive as anywhere else in the world. One of the latest shopping centres is *The Mall* opposite the Pan Pacific hotel. Another upmarket complex is *Yow Chuen Plaza* at the corner of Jalan Tun Abdul Razak and Jalan Ampang. Many smaller retailers are to be found in Bukit Bintang Plaza and the Sungai Wang Plaza, all on the intersection formed by Jalan Sultan Ismail and Jalan Bukit Bintang.

Markets For browsing among the inexpensive market stalls, stocking a wide range of local products, try the Central Market on Jalan Cheng Lock or the "Sunday" market in Kampung Bahru, which operates after dusk every Saturday.

Sightseeing

Kuala Lumpur has much fine 19th and 20thC architecture concentrated in its centre, though visitors must be content to admire the exteriors since most buildings are closed to the public. In 1886, the new and energetic British resident, Frank Swettenham, decided to move the British headquarters to the city from Kelang. During his long residency, Swettenham set about rebuilding the town. His public buildings, of distinctive salmon-pink brick, were mostly designed by the architect A.C. Norman, who looked to the Moghul architecture of northern India for the inspiration to create a city that would reflect the Islamic faith of the indigenous population.

Among the finest buildings are the *Railway Station* (1911), with its spectacular minarets and Moorish arches outside and cast-iron pillars inside; the *Sultan Abdul Samad Building* (1897); and the *Royal Selangor Club* (1884).

Jame Mosque A striking late 19thC building with striped domes and minarets which stands in a coconut grove at a point where the city's two rivers meet and is surrounded by Moorish-style constructions. *Closed Fri during prayers.*

Muzium Negara The National Museum contains a traditional aristocratic Malay house, totem poles, coffins and primitive statues from east Malaya in its grounds, and galleries devoted to Malay culture, industry and natural history. *Jalan Damansara. Open 9–6, closed Fri.*

Masjid Negara Built in 1965, the huge National Mosque, which can accommodate 8,000, is now the centre of the Islamic activities of Malaysia. The umbrella-shaped dome of its Great Hall forms an 18-pointed star representing the 13 states of Malaysia and the 5 pillars of Islam. *Closed Fri during prayers.*

Guided tours

A guide is scarcely necessary for the major landmarks in the city, which are close together in the centre. *Mayflower Acme* ☎ 626 7011 is Malaysia's leading tour operator and will tailor individual tours led by trained guides in a limousine, in addition to its scheduled group tours. It offers 3hr city tours of Kuala Lumpur taking in the main buildings of the historic centre plus batik and pewter workshops.

Out of town
National Zoo 13km/8 miles northeast of the city centre, set in 26 ha/64 acres of shaded forest around a lake and containing a representative collection of Malaysian species, including orang-utans, tigers, tapirs and dwarf crocodiles. *Open 9–6*.
Batu Caves 13km/8 miles north of the city centre, high up on an outcrop of limestone cliffs and reached by a steep flight of 272 steps. The main cave, 113 metres/370ft high, serves as a Hindu shrine; there are many Hindu sculptures as well as colourful rock formations. During the festival of Thaipusam (Jan/Feb) devotees work themselves into a trance during which they walk through fire or pierce their cheeks, tongue and torso with sharp, steel spikes.
Templer Park A huge park, 16km/10 miles beyond the caves, laced with a network of paths following streams past waterfalls and pools set under giant tropical trees. The adjacent 350-metre high Bukit Takun limestone column harbours rare flora, and the nearby Anak Takum has many caves. The area is rich in animal, bird and insect life.
The Highlands Three mountain resorts lie to the north and east of Kuala Lumpur, formerly British hill stations. The closest, and least tranquil, is the luxury resort of the *Genting Highlands*, which contains casinos, hotels, a golf course and a modern convention centre. At *Fraser's Hill*, 10km/6 miles from Kuala Lumpur and 1,500 metres/5,000ft above sea level, neat bungalows with English rose gardens

cling to seven hills crisscrossed by jungle paths with nature trails and panoramic views. The *Cameron Highlands*, 225km/140 miles from Kuala Lumpur, is the most remote and least spoilt of the three but has several good hotels, a golf course and other sports facilities. Its central plateau is entirely surrounded by mountains, whose slopes support tea plantations, flower nurseries, terraced fruit and vegetable gardens, and extensive strawberry beds. Visitors can explore the jungle paths, abundant with large and colourful butterflies, swim in the streams and lakes, and enjoy the highland air.
Penang This island, 388km/241 miles northwest of Kuala Lumpur, is easily accessible by road or air. Varied, with much of interest, including the bustling Chinatown at Georgetown (the island's "capital") and the Snake Temple, but it is big enough to escape the crowds completely. Ringed by coves with good sandy beaches, it is ideal for swimming, diving and water sports. The beach at Batu Ferringhi is particularly fine, and has many international hotels and motels.
Malacca (Melaka), 153km/95 miles southeast of Kuala Lumpur, can be comfortably visited in a day. For centuries, it has been an important trading port, and the city is rich in Dutch, Portuguese and British architecture as well as the culture of the Nonya, or Straits' Chinese. You can obtain panoramic views by climbing the hill on which stand the ruins of the old Portuguese fortress. The fine Dutch Stadthuys (the massive town hall) houses the Malacca Museum. The city's narrow streets also contain many antique and curio shops. The interesting, older parts of Malacca are found close by the waterfront, and cruises can be taken round the harbour.
East coast Terengganu and Kelantan are the most traditional and unspoilt Malay provinces, and have the best beaches and some luxury-class hotels.

Spectator sports

Cricket, rugby and hockey are played on the Padang most weekends during the season; entry to the *Royal Selangor Clubhouse* ☏ 298 8106 is restricted to members and their guests; spectators can watch from the sidelines.

Horse-racing Meetings are held at the *Selangor Turf Club Race Course* ☏ 261 5181 at weekends and public holidays.

Soccer and badminton are Malaysia's most popular sports. International events are either held in the *Stadium Merdeka* ☏ 230 4112 or the *Stadium Negara* ☏ 232 1422.

Keeping fit

The Hilton, Shangri-La and Pan Pacific hotels all have comprehensive sports facilities.

Golf The *Royal Selangor Golf Club*, Jalan Kampong Pandan ☏ 242 8433, is the most central course in Kuala Lumpur, located at the junction of Jalan Bukit Bintang and Jalan Tun Razak, 15min east of the city centre. The oldest course in Malaysia, it hosts the annual Malaysian Golf Tournament and has one 9-hole and two 18-hole courses, plus swimming pool, tennis and squash courts. The *Saujana Golf and Country Resort* ☏ 746 1466, is at Subang, 20min from the city centre and has two 18-hole courses maintained to international standards. The *Awana Golf and Country Club* ☏ 211 3015 is a 45min drive from the city in the cool Genting Highlands. The complex includes a swimming pool, tennis and squash courts, and sauna complex, in addition to the 18-hole course.

Horse-riding The *Selangor Polo and Riding Club* ☏ 456 4531, open Mon–Sat, 7–9.30 and 3.15–6.30.

Jogging is best in the *Lake Gardens* west of the city centre.

Local resources

Business services

Hotel business centres provide the most convenient source of secretarial, photocopying, fax and telex services but in some cases it may be marginally less expensive to go direct to one of the following sources.

Worldwide Business Services, 8th Fl, UMBC Bank, Annexe Tower, Jalan Sultan Sulaiman ☏ 274 7533, rents offices and provides a comprehensive range of services including secretarial, interpretation, personnel recruitment and government liaison.

Photocopying and printing For small jobs to tight deadlines, try *Stenoprint* ☏ 248 7989 or *Tanin* ☏ 243 3242; for large-scale quality jobs, *Sally Printing Services* ☏ 441 4829.

Secretarial *Worldwide Business Services* ☏ 274 7533 and *Business Girl* ☏ 230 0688 will supply temporary and permanent staff. *Mascaya Business Centre* ☏ 241 2650 and *Tele Secretarial Service Centre* ☏ 782 2144 handle typing and word processing.

Translation *Worldwide Business Centre* ☏ 274 7533, *O&M Management Consultants* ☏ 232 9988.

Communications

Local delivery *Office Boy Service* ☏ 238 3311, *Nationwide Express* ☏ 755 8566.

Long-distance delivery DHL head office ☏ 291 2188, *Express Centre* ☏ 243 5075, *TNT Skypak* ☏ 755 7744.

Post offices General post office, Dayabumi Complex ☏ 274 1122, open 8–6, handles all types of mail and *Poslaju* (Speedpost) services. All of the hotels sell postage stamps. Mail services are generally quite efficient.

Telephone Malaysia's telephone service is modern and reliable. Public telephones accept 10 sen coins and are for local calls only; you need to press the release button when the person called responds. Direct-dial local, long distance and international calls can be made from all hotel telephones; calls made between 6pm Sat and 6am Mon, and at off-peak hours during the week, are 30% cheaper, but not all hotels pass this economy on to guests. Operator ☏ 101 for internal long distance and

108 for international services.
Telex and fax Public telex and fax
(Intelpost) services are available at all
Kedai Telekom and Telegraph offices.
The office at Bukit Bintang Plaza,
Jalan Bukit Bintang is in the middle
of the hotel district.

Conference/exhibition centres
The *Putra World Trade Centre*
293 3888 is used for the city's
trade fairs and can accommodate up
to 6,500 convention delegates. The
Shangri-La, Regent and *Hilton* hotels
are all used to host smaller-scale
events.

Embassies and consulates
Australia 6 Jalan Yap Kwan Seng
242 3122
Austria 7th Fl, MUI Plaza, Jalan P.
Ramlee 248 4277
Belgium 4th Fl, Bangunan Sateras,
152 Jalan Ampang 248 5733
Canada 7th Fl, MBF Plaza, Jalan
Ampang 261 2000
China 209 Jalan Ampang 242 8495
Denmark 22nd Fl, Wisma Angkasa
Raya, 123 Jalan Ampang 241 6088
Finland 6th Fl, Wisma MCA, Jalan
Ampang 261 1088
France 218C-F, Jalan Ampang
248 4122
Indonesia 233 Jalan Tun Razak
242 1011
Ireland 3rd Fl, Straits Trading Bldg,
4 Leboh Pasar Besar 203 7555
Italy 99 Jalan U Thant 456 5122
Japan 11 Jalan Persiaran Stonor
243 8044
Netherlands 4 Jalan Mesra, Jalan
Damai, off Jalan Ampang
248 5151
New Zealand 193 Jalan Tun Razak
248 6422
Norway 11th Fl, Wisma Ankasa
Raya, 123 Jalan Ampang 243 0144
Philippines 1 Changkat Kia Peng
248 4233
Singapore 209 Jalan Tun Razak
261 6404
South Korea 422 Jalan Tun Razak
248 2177
Spain 15th Fl, Wisma Lim Foo
Yong, Jalan Raja Chulan 241 4582

Sweden 6th Fl, Wisma Angkasa Raya,
Jalan Ampang 248 5931
Switzerland 16 Persiaran Madge
248 0622
Thailand 206 Jalan Ampang
248 8222
UK 13th Fl, Wisma Damansara,
Jalan Semantan 254 1533
USA 376 Jalan Tun Razak
248 9011
West Germany 3 Jalan U Thant
242 9666

Emergencies
Hospitals Standards of treatment
are reliable and costs compare
favourably with medical services in
the West. American Express is an
accepted method of payment. All
major hotels have doctors on call.
The private hospital, *Subang Jaya
Medical Centre*, 1 Jalan subsection 12,
1A Subang Jaya, Selangor, has a
casualty and 24hr emergency service
734 1212. The *University Hospital*,
Petaling Jaya, Selangor 756 4422
also has a good emergency
department. For routine medical
problems, many expatriates use the
practices of Drs *Catterall, Khoo and
Partners*, AIA Bldg, Jalan Ampang
238 3200 or Drs Young and
Newton, Chartered Bank Bldg,
4 Jalan Ampang 238 2967; and for
dental treatment, the *Thurai Dental
Surgery*, Wisma Damansara, Jalan
Semantan 254 2131.
Pharmacies Most open normal
shop hours, daily 10am–10pm.
Several small chains exist, including
City Chemist and *Guardian Pharmacy*;
these shops are usually found in the
big shopping complexes such as City
Plaza, Sungai Wang Plaza, Kuala
Lumpur Complex and Printemps
Complex. Most hotel drugstores-
cum-newsstands stock a range of
non-prescription drugs.
Police Crime against visitors is rare,
though carelessness with wallets and
handbags is never wise anywhere. In
a major attempt to clear up the city,
police are alert for litterbugs, who
face a M$500 fine. The police are
friendly and will provide assistance to

anyone who asks for it at the numerous police posts scattered around the city. In emergency ☎ 999. The *Jalan Pudu Police Station* ☎ 985 0222, is the closest to the hotel district.

Government offices

Sources of general information include the *Ministry of Finance* ☎ 254 6066; *Ministry of Information* ☎ 274 5333; and the *Ministry of Trade and Industry* ☎ 254 8044. For visa extensions contact the *Immigration Department* ☎ 757 8155, and for taxation, including customs and excise, the *Inland Revenue Department* ☎ 254 7055.

Information sources

Local media The *Business Times* provides the most comprehensive in-depth coverage of economic and trade news; the *New Straits Times* covers general news with some financial highlights.

Tourist information The *Kuala Lumpur Visitors' Centre* is at 3 Jalan Sultan Hishanuddin (opposite the railway station) ☎ 230 1369, open Mon–Fri, 8.30–4.45; Sat, 8.30–1. There is also a tourist information counter in the *Putra World Trade Centre*. It provides free maps and guides to each of Malaysia's 13 states and is generally helpful with information about tours, transport and costs.

Thank-yous

Florists Most florists in Kuala Lumpur are open daily, do free deliveries and will make up fruit baskets as well as bouquets. Telephone orders are accepted by SEA *Park Florist* ☎ 719 5469; *Wangi Florist* ☎ 248 7795; *Sayang* ☎ 291 7653 and *Karen Florist* ☎ 719 8915.

Chocolates and wine *Gourmet Corner* and *Riche Monde Wine Corner*, both in the Shangri-La hotel shopping mall, have the best range of hand-made chocolates and quality wines (open daily 8–8).

Planning and reference

Entry details

Documentation Visitors must be in possession of a passport valid for at least six months beyond the period of stay allowed in Malaysia, or an internationally recognized certificate of identity. In general, Malaysia allows visa-free entry to most nationals visiting for business or pleasure for a stay of up to 14 days. Citizens of Commonwealth countries (except Indian nationals who must have a visa for all visits), Pakistan, Ireland, Lichtenstein, the Netherlands, San Marino, Switzerland and the USA can stay indefinitely without a visa provided they do not take up local employment. Citizens of Austria, Belgium, Denmark, Finland, Iceland, Italy, Japan, Luxembourg, Norway, South Korea, Sweden, Tunisia and West Germany can stay up to three months visa free. Citizens of ASEAN member states can stay up to one month without a visa. Nationals of South Africa and Israel are not allowed to enter Malaysia. In addition, anyone of particularly scruffy appearance is likely to be turned away, regardless of nationality. Visa extensions are granted as a matter of course, provided applicants have evidence of the means to travel onwards, by the Immigration Department in Kuala Lumpur, Jalan Pantai Baharu ☎ 757 8155.

Driving licence Visitors who are intending to drive must have an international driving licence. UK licences can be used for the first month of a stay.

Health requirements Visitors who have stayed in a yellow fever infected country less than six days before their arrival must have a certificate of inoculation. Vaccination against cholera, typhoid and polio, and use of both maloprim and nevaquine (anti-malaria pills) are advisable.

Customs regulations Visitors are rarely charged duty on "reasonable quantities" of personal effects. If there is any dispute, Malaysian customs officials will usually accept a deposit for temporary importation, refundable on departure on production of an official receipt. You should also retain any receipts for antiques you take into Malaysia, as proof that they were purchased outside the country, since Malaysia is very strict in prohibiting the export of its own antiques. It is wise, as a double precaution, to declare imported antiques on arrival and ask for written permission to re-export.

Duty-free allowances are 200 cigarettes or 200gm of cigars or tobacco and 1 litre of wine or spirits. There are no currency restrictions. Drug smugglers are put to death.

Climate

Malaysia is sunny, hot and humid all the year round, with temperatures ranging between 21°C–32°C (70°F–90°F). The rainy seasons are Sep–Dec on the west coast and Oct–Feb on the east, though rain generally falls in short, heavy outbursts in the mid-afternoon. It scarcely disrupts life in the capital, but frequently makes travelling difficult in the countryside, particularly on the east coast which is prone to flooding.

A jacket and tie is considered proper dress for non-Malays at business meetings and for dining out, though long-sleeved, open-necked batik shirts are also often acceptable. Women should dress modestly, but otherwise virtually anything goes.

Holidays

The 13 states of Malaysia all have their own holidays, though most only last a day. Many of the holidays are Muslim and their date can vary widely from one year to the next. The public holidays for the whole country are:

Jan 1 New Year's Day
Late Jan/Feb Chinese New Year
May 1 Labour Day
Mid/late May Wesak Day
May, Jun or Jul Hari Raya Puasa
Jun 3 King's birthday

Aug, Sep or Oct Hari Raya Haji
Aug Muslim New Year
Aug 31 National Day
Oct/Nov Deepavali
Nov/Dec Muhammad's birthday
Dec 25 Christmas Day

Money

Local currency The basic unit of currency is the Ringgit – almost always referred to as the dollar in conversation – which is divided into 100 sen. The note denominations are M$1,000, 500, 100, 50, 20, 10, 5 and 1. Coins are sen 50, 20, 10, 5 and 1. Obtaining change is rarely a problem, although taxi drivers will sometimes claim not to have any so as to increase the size of their tip. There are no exchange control restrictions and Malay dollars are easily purchased on demand in nearby countries, though you may find that notice is required elsewhere.

Changing money Traveller's cheques in all major currencies can be freely exchanged in Kuala Lumpur and tourist centres. There is a fixed handling charge per cheque. Banks give the best rate, followed by licensed money changers. Hotels give the worst rate. Banks open Mon–Fri, 10–3, and Sat 9.30–11.30am. Banks with extensive networks in Kuala Lumpur and Malaysia as a whole are the Bank Bumipatra, Malayan Banking Berhad, and the United Malayan Banking Corporation. Most major foreign banks have an office in Kuala Lumpur, while Standard Chartered and the Hongkong and Shanghai Banking Corporation both have country-wide branches.

Credit and charge cards All major credit cards are accepted (AE DC MC V) in most hotels, restaurants and department stores, and by filling stations and airlines. Many hotels prefer credit card payment and will ask cash payers to put down a large deposit.

Tipping Tipping is officially discouraged, but in the capital a few people seem to expect it.

Philippines

Sixteenth-century Spanish conquistadors gave the Philippines its name and its unity, hammering the 7,100 islands of the archipelago into a single feudal territory. But it was forceful Roman Catholic friars who imposed a common culture and religion on the Malay and aboriginal inhabitants. Towards the end of the 19th century, anti-clerical revolts became increasingly frequent. The rebels received powerful American support after the US naval victory at Manila Bay in 1898, during the Spanish-American war; but their new friends soon became their enemies. Having wrested the Philippines from Spain (with Filipino help), the US was not inclined to let it go. After two more years of fighting, the Filipinos surrendered to their new colonial masters. Nevertheless, the Americans, who liberated the Philippines from Japanese occupation during World War II, are today remembered with devotion. American tutelage gave Filipinos a passion for education, the law and politics. It also gave them the form, though not the substance, of democracy. After independence in 1946, powerful landowners retained control of the two-party political system, and disparities of wealth and privilege have remained enormous ever since. Social uprisings, such as the agrarian and communist-inspired Hukbalahap rebellion (1948–53), were skilfully suppressed by the landed elite, who manipulated local politics and the law, and played on the influential Catholic church's dread of Communism to keep genuine reformers out of power. Similar tactics were used in 1972 by Ferdinand Marcos to win popular support for the imposition of martial law and to extend his presidential term beyond the eight-year legal limit, which was due to expire in 1973. But discontent with the government's increasing brutality and corruption, and with growing poverty and unemployment, finally provoked a split in the army and a popular, bloodless uprising which toppled Marcos in 1986.

The succession of Malay, Chinese, Arab, Spanish and American influences that have swept across the Philippines has left a rich and varied culture. But it has also left unresolved conflicts and a crisis of purpose. The Philippines is still looking for an economic success formula. The rise of Marcos's corrupt "crony monopolies," combined with a world recession and falling world prices for the country's major exports, led to serious economic decline. Liberal economic reforms and various reflationary measures introduced by the government of President Corazon "Cory" Aquino, started to revive the economy in late 1987. Communist insurgency and factious infighting in the army persuaded Cory Aquino to seek an accomodation with the right which involved the departure of most of the liberals in her cabinet and disappointed those who had hoped she would use her enormous popularity to undertake unprecedented economic and social reforms including major land reform.

The political scene

The 1986 change of government brought about fundamental changes in political representation and power sharing. Almost all the senior members of government came to office without experience and it will be some time before it is possible to say whether they and the "cause-oriented" groups which brought them to power are genuinely nationalistic, radical and reformist, as they claim to be.

Legislature

In 1987 the Philippines returned to a bicameral, quasi-American political system (abolished in 1973) with the ratification of a new constitution and the holding of congressional elections. Two hundred members of the House of Representatives are elected every three years and the other 50 are appointed by the president and the leading parties. The Senate has 24 members, who – like the president – are elected every six years by the country at large. The president cannot be re-elected.

The president's men

The strongly centralized powers of the president have been retained in the new constitution. But Aquino's lack of political experience means that she may find it difficult to control Congress, even though her political supporters, the PDP-Laban and Unido parties and the Salonga wing of the Liberal party, dominate both houses. Aquino depends on a small cabal of advisers. The most intimate of these are Joker Arroyo, René Saguisag and Teodoro Locsin. All are former cabinet ministers who during Aquino's first two years in power provoked strong criticism – Arroyo and Saguisag from the right, Locsin from the left – forcing her to call for the resignation of the entire cabinet in September 1987. Although not reappointed to the cabinet, the three men remain influential. On economic matters Aquino used to defer to her former finance secretary, Jaime Ongpin, who died in December 1987, apparently having committed suicide. Like his replacement, Vincente Jayme, Ongpin belonged to a group dubbed"the Council of Trent," composed of businessmen and technocrats who studied at the Jesuit university, the Ateneo de Manila. On political strategy Aquino is most influenced by the allies of her late husband, Benigno Aquino, whose assassination in 1983 sparked the demonstrations that finally led to Marcos's downfall; of these, her brother, Congressman José Cojuangco, and Senator Aquilino Pimentel are the most important.

The opposition

Marcos's party, New Society Movement (KBL), has splintered since he went into exile and most of its old members have been discredited. A "loyal but critical" opposition, the Philippine Nationalist Party, has evolved out of one wing, led by Marcos's old labour minister, Blas Ople. Another wing, the Nacionalista Party, is led by former defence minister Juan Ponce Enrile. **Battling reds** The communist insurgency, which began in 1969, has claimed more than 40,000 lives; government troops are fighting against the New People's Army on every major island in the archipelago.

Uncle Sam

Foreign policy remains firmly anti-communist, but strong nationalist sentiment in the new Congress means that it will not be so pro-American as it once was. The continuing existence of the USA's two largest overseas military bases has been placed in doubt by a clause in the new constitution banning, in principle, nuclear weapons and by increasingly strident student demonstrations against the bases.

The economic scene

Aquino inherited a mismanaged and deteriorating economy, in which per capita GNP was only US$550 in 1986. Total GNP had fallen by 10% between 1983 and 1985. The trend was reversed in 1986, when the growth rate was 1.5%. The new development plan involves fundamental economic reforms and aims at a real annual growth rate of 6.5% for the six years starting in 1987. The annual rate of inflation was brought down from 50.3% in 1984 to about 5% in 1987.

Human resources

The Philippines' population in 1987 was almost 57m, and its labour force (23m) is expanding by nearly a million a year. Attempts to reduce population growth (2.7% a year) and provide more jobs in industry have largely failed; in 1986 half the work force were totally or partially unemployed. In 1985 over 70% of the population were considered to live below the poverty line (compared with 28% in 1965).

Educational standards are high (88% of the population are literate), but university graduates sometimes end up serving in cocktail bars. Wages are now among the lowest in Asia.

Drift to the city Many areas of the country are disproportionately underdeveloped, particularly the Muslim areas of Mindanao and Sulu and those of the ethnic minorities in the Luzon Cordillera. There has been a ceaseless stream of job-seekers to the big city; approximately a third of Manila's population of 8m live in squatter settlements around the capital.

Emigration During the past decade more than a million Filipinos have left the country to seek employment, mostly as labourers in the Middle East or as domestic servants in Europe, the USA and Hong Kong.

Natural riches

The Philippines is abundantly endowed with minerals, forests, tropical crops, marine life and various sources of energy.

Energy Volcanic geysers have become an important new power source, and the country is the second largest producer of geothermal energy in the world. Hydroelectric and coal-fired plants account for about 33% and 30% respectively of total generating capacity. Two small oil fields were discovered and developed in the Sulu Sea in the 1970s. Exploratory oil drilling resumed in 1987.

Minerals The Philippines is among the world's 10 biggest producers of copper and gold. Other major mineral exports include silver, chromium and nickel.

Timber For years timber has been unofficially the largest export earner, but rampant smuggling and illegal logging have denuded much of the 14m ha/38m acres of forest, leading to extensive soil erosion, flooding and droughts. Log exports have now been banned but the export of plywood and other processed timber is permitted.

Fish is the major source of protein for Filipinos and an important export; half is exported fresh, and much of that goes to Japan.

Improved infrastructure

Marcos left his country a much improved system of roads, harbours and airports, but not a good railway system. Only two relatively short lines exist on Luzon and Panay, but the new Light Rail Transit System has proved a boon to congested Manila and is being extended.

Telex and satellite communications are up to international standards, though mail and telephone services are poor, particularly when disrupted by seasonal monsoons.

Agriculture

Nearly 30% of GDP is contributed by agriculture, which employs half the labour force (compared with 9% in manufacturing, 12% in trade and 16% in services). Although the country is more or less self-sufficient in rice and corn (maize), and although exported crops provide one-third of all export earnings, productivity is low and most farms are uneconomically small.

Export crops Coconuts (two-thirds of the world's total exports) and sugar (once the dominant crop) traditionally have been the two largest exports. Both were controlled by pernicious trading monopolies in Marcos's time and have lost much of their market share. Earnings from sugar are now being overtaken by those from bananas. Many of the sugar estates have been abandoned or converted to domestic crops. Coconuts are grown mainly by smallholders whose ageing trees produce diminishing crops, but cooperative trading arrangements should alleviate their plight.

In the last two decades large joint-venture plantations producing bananas and palm oil have been successfully developed alongside prewar and foreign-owned abaca (Manila hemp), pineapple and rubber estates in Mindanao.

External trade

Between 1975 and 1985 the market share of exports going to the USA, Japan and the EC fell from 83% to 74%, as a result of the government's policy to diversify export markets. Agricultural exports are still the major concern of the government's economic programme but emphasis is now also being given to seven industries: electronics, garments, furniture (mostly rattan), processed food, gifts and housewares, footwear and leather goods, and construction services.

Recession and chronic payments crises led to a fall in imports between 1980 and 1985 from US$9bn to US$5.1bn. Emergency foreign exchange controls have been eased, but imports are still restricted by the selective issuing of import licences.

The USA was by far the largest trading partner in 1985 (39% of exports and 25% of imports), followed by Japan (20% exports and 14% imports), the EC (15% and 8%) and the growing ASEAN market (12% and 15%).

Principal exports in 1985 were electronics, garments, coconut, copper, sugar, bananas, gold, iron, lumber and canned pineapple.

Main imports in 1985 were oil, materials for electronics manufacture, materials for garment manufacture, non-electrical machinery, electrical machinery and appliances, cereals, chemicals, base metals, fertilizers, resins, and plastics.

Balance of payments

Persistent trade and payments deficits have dogged the Philippines since 1970, but the fall in oil prices and the development of alternative domestic energy sources helped turn around the trade figures in the second half of 1986. Trade shortfalls (offset to some extent by transfers from overseas workers – worth about US$1bn a year – and tourism) have tended to produce negative current accounts, but these have been mitigated by regular capital account surpluses in the form of long- and short-term foreign loans.

Reserves, including gold, stood at US$2.4bn (equivalent to nearly six months' merchandise imports) at the end of 1986.

Currency

The peso was officially devalued three times between 1983 and 1985, from 8.20 pesos to 18 pesos to the US dollar; black market rates went as high as 30 pesos to the dollar in 1985. Freely floating (slowly downwards) since 1986, the official and black market rates by 1987 were more or less the same, at about 20 pesos to the dollar.

External debt
Debt rescheduling has become a regular part of the Philippines' financial life since the suspension in 1983 of interest payments on US$26.2bn of public debt (74% of GNP). After prolonged negotiations, in 1985 a rescheduling package, backed by an IMF-approved austerity programme, was agreed with creditors. These terms were rejected by the new government in 1986 (50–60% of export earnings were still marked for debt servicing), and a new programme that allowed for some economic expansion was agreed in 1987.

Although the government now renounces borrowing as a means for balancing external accounts, debt is expected to rise to US$36bn by 1992. A new US$220m standby facility was arranged with the IMF in 1986, and a US$300m structural adjustment loan was approved by the World Bank in 1987. Development plans are predicated on loans of US$2bn a year being provided by commercial banks and US$2bn a year by multilateral and bilateral lenders until 1992.

The big lenders The USA and Japan top the list of bilateral donors and lenders. US banks (Citibank, US$1.5bn) are the biggest commercial creditors; the World Bank (US$4.5bn) is the largest institutional lender.

Government budget
Increased public investment and maintenance spending were the main features of Aquino's first and second budgets and will remain so, according to the IMF-backed programme, in the years ahead. Heavy allocations will be necessary for some years to service the foreign debt and support state corporations. Budgetary deficits will be reduced but not immediately eliminated (3% of GNP in 1987 and 2.6% in 1988).

Revenue Extra revenue is being sought in tax reforms (including the introduction of a value-added tax) and reduced corruption.

Spending Debt servicing took 39% of the 1987 budget. The largest sectoral allocations were for social services (22%), infrastructure (18%) and defence (6.6%).

Development plan
Fundamental economic reforms are contained in Aquino's radical six-year development plan (1987–92).

Boost for private sector A more market-oriented economy is to be created, returning US$5bn-worth of state enterprises to the private sector, dismantling all monopolies and monopsonies and liberalizing imports. Emphasis is on developing small-scale rural infrastructure and community projects.

Industry and investment
The industrial sector, which accounts for 31% of GDP, contracted sharply in 1984 and 1985 but began growing again at the end of 1986 (with textiles, electrical machinery, footwear and paper products leading the way). Direct investments declined 21% in 1984, 36% in 1985 and 15% in 1986.

Policy changes Most of the ambitious major industrial projects of the Marcos era have been cancelled or modified. In future the emphasis will be on smaller schemes and on agro-industrial projects that will increase the processing of local raw materials.

Behind the times The manufacturing sector has generally remained primitive, with little technology transfer, fabrication or integration. Most operations concentrate on assembling imported parts and kits, and there is little value added to the two major exports, electronics and garments, which contain a very high proportion of imported inputs.

Manila dominates More than 90% of all investment is concentrated in the capital region. It is the policy of the Aquino government to encourage investment in the depressed outer regions.

The business climate

A distinguished team of former businessmen has replaced Marcos's technocrats at the head of the government's major economic departments. They now shape economic policy. The result is a dramatic shift away from government involvement in business and a return to reliance on free market forces.

The public sector

In 1987 state corporations still dominated almost every field of business activity from commercial banking, insurance, construction and aviation to hotels, shipping, plantations and fertilizer production. When the country defaulted on its loans in 1983, 67% of the outstanding debt was owed by government corporations, much of which had been assumed from Marcos's bankrupt cronies during the first half of the decade. After Aquino came to power in 1986 the public sector expanded still further as the remaining crony empires – or large parts of them – were sequestered by the government.

The private sector

The private sector is identified as the "motor of economic recovery" in the 1987–92 development plan.

Ambitious privatization plans A crash programme to privatize 206 government corporations, convert part of the public debt into equity, and encourage foreign investment (with the promulgation of new incentives) was launched in 1987. Foreign aid will be used to hasten these reforms and "create the environment for investment," instead of financing capital-intensive projects as in the past.

Lame ducks Selling off so many corporations will take time. For several years to come, these lame ducks will continue to gobble up government funds and domestic credit and will compete with private business for scarce domestic and foreign markets.

A strong starting base Despite Marcos's friends' insatiable appetite for acquisitions, and the government's subsequent appropriation of their fiefs, the private business sector remains large and vibrant, although badly under-funded. The most successful survivors of the transition appear to have been the perennially resourceful and resilient Chinese Filipinos whose economic power and influence, particularly in banking, grew steadily under Marcos.

Dependence on foreign investment

Gross domestic investment rose rapidly from 1972 (19.3% of GDP) to 1981 (30.6% of GDP) before slumping to 15.8% in 1985. Capital formation has always been a problem, and without the boost of foreign loans would not have grown during the 1970s. The two stock markets, in Manila and neighbouring Makati, have snapped back to life since Marcos's downfall. But they are still narrow and speculative and need to expand much more before they can serve as a real source of investment capital.

The USA leads the field As the last colonial rulers, Americans, not surprisingly, hold the largest share of registered foreign investments. Their assets exceeded US$5bn in 1985 and contributed about US$1.5bn a year to the economy. Castle and Cooke, United Fruit, Citibank and Procter and Gamble are some of the well-established names. But equally famous ones, such as GM, Ford and Goodyear, have pulled out in recent years because of the depressed domestic market and the unfair advantages enjoyed by favoured competitors under the Marcos regime.

New US investment between 1968

and 1984 continued to outstrip all others, accounting for 40.3% of all foreign investment. Japan provided 14.22%, Britain and the Netherlands 6% each. Total EC investment inflows accounted for 22.4%.

New investment needed Foreign investment inflows slowed to a trickle in 1985 (US$124m) and 1986 (US$79m). The government is now actively trying to drum up new foreign investment, particularly from overseas Filipinos who withdrew large sums during the Marcos era.

Power in business

Traditionally, politics and business in the Philippines have always gone hand in hand. Cronyism has flourished in the past and is likely to do so in the future, even though Aquino – whose personal integrity is beyond question – has set up a permanent body to stamp out favouritism and corruption. The centre of economic power has shifted inexorably from the Spanish mestizo (Spanish-Malay) elite to the Filipino Chinese, who, although accounting for only 3% of the population, control as much as 60% of the country's banking and commerce. The local Chinese are more racially exclusive than the Spanish. Their names are often unknown to other Filipino business people, and most of their foreign business is conducted with relatives and clansmen in other countries.

The Aquino clan Cory Aquino is from a wealthy Chinese mestizo family, the Cojuangcos. Her cousin, Eduardo Cojuangco, was Marcos's richest friend and now lives in exile. His vast corporate empire, built out of the coconut trading monopoly, has been sequestered by the government, but some of his businesses are still being run by more favoured relatives. Another cousin of Aquino controls the lucrative and private telephone monopoly, Philippine Long Distance Telephone (which the government does not intend to dismantle). The prosperous trading operations of the president's brother and brother-in-law, José Cojuangco and Ricardo "Baby" Lopa, seem bound to expand rapidly. Other members of the large Cojuangco clan have begun enthusiastically moving into business, giving rise to fears of a new generation of favourites.

Other Aquino beneficiaries are likely to be the families and business partners of several members of the new government (who have officially severed all ties with their former businesses): José Concepcion, secretary of trade and investment (RFM Corporation, flour trading); Dante Santos, head of Philippine Airlines; José Fernandez, head of the central bank and founder of Far East Bank; Vincente Jayme, founder of PDCP investment bank, former head of Philippine National Bank and now finance secretary; Ramon del Rosario, a former banker, now treasurer of the San Miguel brewing conglomerate; and Chito Ayala, monetary board member and plantation owner.

Old faces The spectacular rise of the Marcos cronies (at the expense of the old oligarchs), followed by their sudden eclipse after Aquino came to power, has thrown the business scene into some confusion but has also opened up big opportunities for smaller businessmen. Inevitably some of the new faces belong to the old elite, to whom Aquino's courts have returned businesses and estates seized by Marcos and his friends. An early example is the Lopez family, once the most powerful in the Philippines: Eugenio Lopez Jr returned from exile in 1986 to repossess his father's television stations and several other businesses.

Mestizo muscle weakened Although much diminished in power and resources the small, tightly-knit Spanish mestizo community remains the most respected and influential. The largest manufacturing corporation (San Miguel), the largest mining company (Atlas), one of the largest private commercial banks

(Bank of the Philippine Islands) and the second largest private insurance company (Insular Life) are all run by members of an extended family which includes the Sorianos, Zobels and Roxases. The most influential at present is the head of the bank and of Ayala Corporation, Jaime Zobel de Ayala. A former ambassador to the UK (and one of his country's best photographers), Zobel replaced his cousin, the polo-playing Enrique Zobel, as the head of the family business after a series of disastrous corporate decisions led to a Marcos nominee gaining majority control of San Miguel in 1983. One notable mestizo who survived the Marcos era – despite his bitter opposition to the ex-president, the incarceration of a brother and the seizure of his printing presses – is the octogenarian press baron, Ramon Roces.

Old Chinese Among the older families the important alliances are those headed by Peter Dee (China Banking) and his father-in-law, Alfonso Yuchengco (Malayan Insurance, Rizal Commercial Development Bank), José Yao Campos (United Drug) and his brother, Yao Shiong-Shio (Oriental Petroleum), Ching Tan (La Suerte cigarettes) and his cousin, Alfred Ching (Philippine Blooming Mills), Carlos Palanca (La Tondena distillery) and Patricio Lim (synthetic fibre monopoly). The Chinese mestizo relatives of Aquino, such as the Lopas, have become a powerful new force.

New Chinese groups include those headed by the Marcos crony Lucio Tan (Fortune Tobacco, Allied Bank), Henry Sy (Shoemart department stores), Emilio Yap (President Lines, Philtrust Bank, *Manila Bulletin*), John Gokongwei (Robinson department stores, Robina food and drink products), Wellington Ty (Metro Bank), Domingo Lee (molasses) and Lu Do Luym (copra).

Americanized Chinese A third group of more Americanized Chinese

is well represented in the professions and government. Washington Sycip (Sycip, Gorres, Velayo, accountants), the doyen of the discredited old technocracy, is still influential. His brother David, a banker, is in charge of the government's privatization programme. Ramon Sy, formerly head of Bank of America's local branch, has been appointed by the government to head the United Coconut Planters Bank. But his near-namesake, Ramon Siy (Consolidated Mills and Security Bank), is more powerful and a second cousin of Aquino.

Union power

The militancy of unions, which grew in proportion to the increasing repression of Marcos's twilight years, now appears to be on the wane. But communist control of the most militant union, the Kilusang Mayo Uno (KMU), continues to create problems. In some sectors the unions are powerful, dictating high wages and safety standards (particularly at the US military bases and the free-trade zones), and some newspapers have had to close as a result of labour strikes, but most are divided and small. Membership represents a small fraction of the total workforce, and average wages are among the lowest in Asia. Labour skills are well developed and rapidly learned in those regions where there are industries.

Strike restrictions The Employers' Confederation of the Philippines and the unions agreed to a "code of industrial harmony" in 1987 which should limit strike action and give Aquino's government the chance to get the economy moving. Some of Marcos's more restrictive labour laws have been repealed, but the government retains the right to impose compulsory arbitration in certain industries and to place under arrest any workers who forcibly attempt to halt company operations.

The business framework

Most Philippine businesses take the form of corporations or, in the case of professional firms, partnerships. Both have to be registered with the Securities and Exchange Commission (SEC). Foreign investment is restricted in some sectors but encouraged through incentives in many others.

Foreign ownership rules

The restrictions placed on foreign investments by former constitutions have been retained in the 1987 constitution. A new omnibus investment code introduced in 1987 consolidated existing rules and made some small improvements to incentives. Companies established before Philippine independence are not necessarily bound by the restrictions, and the government may – in special circumstances – permit a higher level of foreign ownership in new companies.

Absolute prohibitions No foreign company is allowed to engage in retail trade or own rural banks or mass media operations.

The 40% rule Only companies that are at least 60% owned by Filipinos may own land, exploit natural resources or operate public utilities, inter-island shipping or commercial banks.

Getting approval Foreigners may invest in most business activities without seeking the approval of the Board of Investments (BOI) so long as their investment does not exceed 40% of the enterprise's capital.

Delays in the issuing of initial business licences can be cut to a minimum by forming, at the outset, a company that has less than 40% foreign ownership – BOI approval of subsequent increases in foreign investment is relatively easy to obtain. Otherwise expect some roadblocks in the areas of nationality limitations, "overcrowded" industries, and the submission of adequate supporting documents and project studies. The BOI also requires the publication of licence applications and conducts hearings if objections to the application are received.

Pioneer status Full foreign ownership is permitted in so-called pioneer areas. An investment enjoys pioneer status if it
• involves the manufacture or processing (not merely assembly or packaging) of goods or raw materials that have not been produced in the Philippines before
• uses a method of production or transformation of any substance or raw material into another or into finished goods that are new and untried in the Philippines
• engages in agricultural activities or services which help the country attain self-sufficiency in designated commodities
• produces non-conventional fuels or manufactures equipment which utilizes non-conventional sources of energy
• involves a training programme that constitutes a considerable investment in its own right and benefits the country
• is made in one of the country's 37 designated depressed areas; these include Sulu, Mindanao, Palawan, Samar, the Cordillera of Luzon and smaller islands.

The export factor Companies exporting 100% of production can be wholly owned by foreigners, and majority foreign ownership is permitted in non-pioneer projects if more than 70% of production is exported. But firms established in any of the eight export-processing zones can remain 100% foreign-owned indefinitely; fully-owned foreign firms outside the Export Processing Zone Authority (EPZA) areas, on the other hand, have to divest within 30–40 years.

Setting up

Setting up business is relatively straightforward, since it follows basic Western business practices and all laws and regulations are printed in English. Consultancy services are offered by leading accountants and lawyers (see *Who can help*). Government officials are also quite helpful and will point out omissions or obvious mistakes in licence applications before passing judgment on them.

Licences A foreign corporation must obtain a licence to do business before it can open an office in the Philippines. Licences are issued by the BOI, EPZA, SEC (in the case of multinational corporations) and the Central Bank (for offshore banks). Before filing the appropriate application the prospective foreign investor should appoint a resident agent in the Philippines for the purpose of answering summonses and securing a legal presence.

Paperchase Once a licence has been issued the bureaucratic paperchase begins in earnest. Registration must be made with the Bureau of Internal Revenue. The company's name must be registered with the Bureau of Domestic Trade. Its employees must be registered with the Social Security System, Medicare, the State Insurance Fund, the Home Mutual Development Fund and the Ministry of Labor and Employment. Further applications must be made for clearance of any intended construction with the Human Settlements Regulatory Commission (a zoning authority) and the National Pollution Control Commission. An operational permit must be obtained from the local municipality. And, of course, the company must be registered with the Central Bank for the purposes of monitoring inward and outward remittances.

Feed the workers One special demand is made of companies employing more than 500 workers. They must provide, either through farming or importation, sufficient rice and corn to feed their employees.

Incentives

The rules governing incentives are based on much the same criteria as those which allow higher-than-usual levels of foreign investment. To qualify for incentives the investment must be in one of the preferred areas listed in the Investment Priority Plan (IPP).

Perks for pioneers As a general rule a tax holiday is granted for the first eight years to all preferred pioneer projects (as opposed to six years for companies in preferred non-pioneer areas). They are also exempt from all tariff duties and compensating taxes on imported capital equipment in the first five years. Any taxes charged on the interest on foreign loans may be reclaimed.

Manufacturing Almost all manufacturers or producers, whether pioneer or non-pioneer, are entitled to exemption from tariff duties and compensating taxes on imported capital equipment in the first five years; carry-over of net operating losses incurred in any of the first 10 years of operation, inclusive of financial charges, into the following six years; deduction of research and development expenses and management training expenses; deduction of organizational and pre-operating expenses; deduction of expansion reinvestment; accelerated depreciation; the right to employ foreigners in supervisory, technical or advisory positions.

Export bonus Any business exporting more than 50% of production is automatically entitled to incentives and inclusion in the IPP. They are also exempt from export taxes, duties and fees, and from sales taxes. Those exporting at least 70% of output are exempt from taxes and duties on spare parts imports. Businesses located in one of the export processing zones are exempt from most regulations although subject to certain taxes and costs.

Key sectors Additional incentives are granted to, among others, semiconductor electronics industries, tourism enterprises, agricultural producers, offshore banking units and regional headquarters located in the Philippines.

Expatriate employment

Treaty trader visas are granted to those engaged in substantial trade or in managing an enterprise in which they are investing, or have invested, a large amount of capital. In practice this usually means that only one foreign "general manager" is permitted, but "foreign technicians" may be admitted if the skills they possess are not available in the country.

Members of the board In all joint ventures the majority of the executive board must be residents of the Philippines, and the secretary must be a Filipino citizen. In the case of banks and banking institutions and domestic air carriers, however, at least two-thirds of the members of the board must be Filipino citizens. All the executive and managing officers of public utility firms have to be Filipinos.

Multinationals Special concessions are granted to employees of multinational corporations establishing regional headquarters in the Philippines. Foreigners may be employed in supervisory positions for the first five years and a foreign president, general manager and treasurer may remain indefinitely.

Repatriating profits

There are no restrictions on the repatriation of profits, capital gains, dividends or capital of nonresidents, provided that they are not based on local borrowings and that the original foreign investment (and reinvestment, if any) was registered with the Central Bank.

Royalties can be charged and repatriated, provided that they have been approved and registered with the Technology Transfer Board and the Central Bank. They are taxable in the Philippines (35% when remitted to a nonresident foreign corporation and 20% when paid to a resident foreign company).

Market entry

The creation in 1985 of a one-stop agency to handle the complicated procedures of importing, coupled with the abolition and reduction of many tariffs, has made getting a foothold in the Philippines market much easier than it used to be. However, distribution remains a problem and a good local agent is a necessity.

Importing and exporting

Under the import liberalization programme agreed with the IMF some 1,300 items previously subject to strict controls were deregulated between April 1986 and April 1987 and tariffs were fixed at a maximum of 50%.

BOI-registered firms can avoid the remaining restrictions and import raw materials and supplies free of tax and duty by obtaining a custom-bonded warehouse. There are no trade restrictions in the export processing zones.

Export permits are issued by the Central Bank without restriction, except in the case of certain export products where there are requirements designed to prevent overshipping, to maintain standards of quality and to control quota allocations. The export duties on all export products except logs were abolished in mid-1986.

Official procedures The processing of import and export licences is still cumbersome but, thanks to the one-stop Export Documentation Center, no longer involves journeys to several different government departments and the signatures of dozens of different officials. Tariff reform and the transfer of some quality checks to foreign ports and assessors have helped to speed up the process.

Unofficial procedures For those wanting to expedite things further the answer is invariably to distribute generous "tips" all along the line (a practice best left to a trusted local agent who knows the rules of the game).

Distribution

Distribution of products is a problem. The domestic market is small, and there is little demand for well-developed distribution networks. The big exception is the huge fleet of trucks and agents developed to market San Miguel beer (and the wide range of soft drinks, including Coca Cola, which San Miguel also produces).

The formidable problems and costs of distributing in an archipelago favour the rise of oligopolies or the confinement of distribution to limited areas (such as urban Manila and Cebu). This is one good reason to link up with a local corporation that already has an established network and knows the market problems. Several large foreign and local businesses have tried in recent decades to establish a distribution network to distribute beer and break San Miguel's monopoly. All failed and were eventually forced to sell their breweries and trucks to San Miguel.

Delays Although there are numerous shipping and trucking companies, many are less than reliable. Poor servicing and the shortage of spare parts mean that vehicles often break down and shipments are delayed – the only compensation is that Filipinos are accustomed to this and do not fret about late deliveries.

Containerization Most freight arrives and leaves the country in containers. These are transferred directly between ship and company premises. Several of the international freight movers operating in Manila are run by foreigners.

Copyright and patents

Anyone who introduces a good product can expect to see counterfeits propagating like mushrooms. Lax local policing means that hundreds of patented products are copied – most perniciously in the field of pharmaceuticals. Almost every famous brand of Western clothing and accessory, from Gucci bags to Levi jeans, is imitated. So are popular drinks, like Johnny Walker whisky. Books are usually reprinted and music discs copied without permission. Foreign companies can patent their products and trademarks and can take their counterfeiters to court if they can catch them. But the procedures of artful Filipino lawyers can prove as tedious and costly as the original piracy. Far better to leave the settling of such matters to a skilled local agent.

Insurance

Insurance is readily available from a number of well-established companies, many of which are subsidiaries of Western firms or have Western affiliates. Large insurance risks are reinsured with foreign firms. Most types of insurance are available.

Advertising and PR

Advertising is a well-developed art in the Philippines, with several Madison Avenue agencies represented in Manila. Television (five channels in Manila) and radio (more than 30,000 station licences issued in 1982) are the principal outlets, with newspapers (total Manila circulation over 1m) and billboards (on major highways) attracting far less.

Public relations are an important part of business, and all large companies have their own PR officers or retain private PR consultants (mostly ex-newspapermen).

The financial scene

Judged by the number and diversity of its institutions, the Philippines' financial system is on a par with that of many developed nations, but a study commissioned by the Asian Development Bank in 1983 suggested that what the system needed was less innovation and more consolidation.

Banks and other financial institutions

At the heart of the activity is the Central Bank of the Philippines, which exercises wide regulatory power over more than 1,500 bank and non-bank financial institutions. Its governor also chairs the country's Monetary Board.

Commercial banks Heading the financial institutions are the 34 commercial banks which together account for almost 60% of the system's assets. By far the largest of the commercial banks is the state-owned Philippine National Bank, which was so mismanaged during the Marcos era that in 1983 it was found to have almost as many bad loans as good ones on its books. It is now being rehabilitated and may eventually be privatized. Other leading local institutions include Metropolitan Bank and Trust, Far East Bank and Trust Company and Bank of the Philippine Islands.

Reprivatization plans The Aquino government took control of six formerly private banks which had been taken over by the Marcos regime but hopes to have them all returned to the private sector by the end of 1988 were not realised.

Foreign and offshore banks Although the Bank of America, Standard Chartered Bank, Citibank and Hongkong and Shanghai Banking Corporation are the only overseas banks licensed to conduct local currency business, a further 28 have opened offshore banking units.

Development bank The state-owned Philippines Development Bank, crippled with bad debts of over US$2.5bn incurred during the Marcos years, has been restructured and now operates on a smaller scale.

Thrift and rural banks A plethora of institutions operate mostly at the community level. These are the thrift (savings) banks (of which there are 136) and rural banks (about 950, mostly one-branch affairs).

Non-bank financial institutions There are 14 investment houses, some of which are subsidiaries of commercial banks. They play an important part in making a market for corporate commercial paper and other money market instruments such as Treasury bills and Central Bank certificates of indebtedness.

Finance companies cater largely to consumer instalment-buying needs. There are over 330 of them. Several investment houses and finance companies have leasing company subsidiaries, as do some thrift banks.

The markets

Stock market The two Philippine stock exchanges (Manila and Makati, in the capital's business district) are small by world standards. At the end of 1986 their 127 listed companies had a market capitalization of less than US$2bn. The market is regulated by the Securities and Exchange Commission.

Bond market The Philippines once had the beginnings of a corporate bond market, but it was little understood by local investors and the last issue made on it was in 1977.

Commercial paper Asia's money market was pioneered in Manila in the late 1960s. The market expanded rapidly until, in 1981, it almost collapsed as a result of lax controls and a lot of bogus paper. Now, under tighter controls, it has again become an important source of investment funds.

Who can help

Lawyers

Accustomed to sharp business practices and shady operators, Filipinos accept the need for watertight contracts and expert legal advice. They are also remarkably litigious.

Almost a closed shop All law firms are run by Filipinos. Foreign professionals are not permitted to practise, although the American lawyer William Quasha, and the Filipino-Chinese accountant Washington Sycip (who holds US citizenship papers) were both given permission to practise by special Acts of Congress.

Prominent law firms The following are well versed in both international and corporate law.

William H. Quasha and Associates, 6th Fl, Don Pablo Bldg, 114 Amorsolo St, Makati, Metro Manila ☎ 863011; specializes in various fields, including corporate, foreign investment, patents, trademarks, taxation, labour and banking law.

Sycip, Salazar, Feliciano, Hernandez Associates, 4th Fl, PAIC Bldg, 105 Paseo de Roxas, Legaspi Village, Makati, Metro Manila ☎ 8179811; specializes in labour, commercial, estate and taxation law.

Syquia Law Offices, Cattleya Bldg, Makati, Metro Manila ☎ 8171096; specializes in international law.

Bengzon, Zarraga, Narciso and Associates, 6th Fl, Sol Condominium Bldg, Amorsolo St, Legaspi Village, Makati, Metro Manila ☎ 866636; specializes in corporate, patents, trademarks, taxation, insurance, mining, utility and labour law.

Bito, Misa and Lozada, 140 Alfaro St, Salcedo Village, Makati, Metro Manila ☎ 8182321; specializes in corporate, shipping, patent, trademarks, mining, utility, banking and labour law.

Accountants

Accounting firms handle a wide range of advisory and auditing functions and constitute an important part of the business scene. Practices conform to US accounting principles, except in the case of revaluing property, plant and equipment, and the capitalization or deferral of foreign exchange fluctuations.

The top two *Sycip, Gorres, Velayo*, 6070 Ayala Ave, Makati, Metro Manila ☎ 8190301; affiliated with Arthur Andersen and by far the largest and most influential company, with branches all over South-East Asia. *Joaquin Cunanan*, 8th Fl, BA-Lepanto Bldg, 8747 Paseo de Roxas, Makati, Metro Manila ☎ 8187622; affiliated with Price Waterhouse.

Other help

The Philippine Chamber of Commerce ☎ 403082 has both local and foreign firms as members and provides an active forum for the exchange of market information and business introductions. There are also active and helpful US, European and Chinese chambers of commerce. Other good sources of information for potential investors are the trade sections of embassies in Manila and the four foreign commercial banks – Citibank, Bank of America, Hongkong and Shanghai Banking Corporation and Standard Chartered. The Philippine Trade and Industry Center, affiliated with the Board of Investments, provides information and guidance on preferred fields of investment and entitlement to incentives.

The media All major dailies carry business sections, the most comprehensive appearing in the *Manila Bulletin*.

Join the Rotarians The best place to be introduced to leading businessmen (but not necessarily to talk business) is at the weekly luncheons of the prestigious Manila Rotary Club, membership of which was once considered a *sine qua non* to business success. Not so any more, but it is still worth joining just to sit close to the high and mighty.

Business and cultural awareness

The continuing presence of American "Coca-Colonization," vast US military bases and the official "American" language (the Philippines is the third largest English-speaking nation in the world) have helped to create a curiously ambivalent nation of 57m people who are neither Occidental nor Oriental, capitalist nor socialist, democratic nor feudal. In business personal connections are all important and personal "face" should always be respected.

Family honour

The family is the centre of Philippine life. Third and even fourth cousins are a closely knit part of the extended family, which also includes a large number of honorary kinships (usually referred to as *compadres*, or godfathers). In accordance with the family-based sense of values which prevails over all others (social and Christian), any member of the extended family is entitled to help from his more fortunate kinsmen; nepotism, although outwardly condemned, is widely practised. Intensely partisan feelings are expressed in support of the family and its interests.

Face and shame

Appearances are everything. Nothing is more important than a Filipino's sense of "face" or dignity in his community. To be shamed or embarrassed (*hiya*) in front of others can provoke violent, even fatal, consequences. Filipinos are particularly sensitive to anything that may be construed as a personal rejection or insult.

This peculiar sensitivity and propensity for violence has produced elaborate social conventions and controls. Intermediaries are called in to negotiate between two people in any potentially embarrassing situation, from applying for a job or a pay increase to proposing a marriage.

The fear of rejection is so acute that Filipinos will go to enormous lengths to avoid a direct request and a direct reply. Blunt and emphatic words are carefully avoided, and often a meaning or intent has to be divined from a person's hints and insinuations. Three-quarters of all civil cases are settled out of court on the urging of judges, who know that any ruling by them would make somebody lose face and could lead to violence.

Foreigners are not expected to appreciate these nuances. They are traditionally perceived to be "heavy-handed" and "thick-faced," and can get away with fairly direct language. But it is important to realize that a Filipino will mask his emotions and, if pushed beyond a certain point, can suddenly change from a total charmer to a raging bull.

Religion

Filipinos are said to be the most church-going Christians in the world and crowds of worshippers on Sundays often overflow into the streets. But social conformity may be a more important factor than devotion. Eighty-four per cent of the population are Roman Catholic, 10% belong to other Christian sects (mostly Protestant), and 5% are Muslim (in the southern islands of Mindanao and Sulu where a Muslim secessionist movement, mercilessly crushed in the 1970s, has shown sporadic signs of revival). Animist beliefs are practised by the small aboriginal tribes scattered through the highlands and remoter islands.

All Filipinos are superstitious and will never do business in a house with steps in multiples of three; all tall business buildings deny the existence of a 13th floor.

Education

The educational system is derived from the American public school system, in many cases using the same textbooks and grading system. Elitist attitudes influence students in selecting courses, regardless of the overcrowding of professions such as law. Low social status attaches to being an engineer, and there are few good technical schools. The best private schools and universities are run by Roman Catholic religious orders.

Language

Pilipino, derived from Tagalog, is the national language but all government announcements and laws, as well as major newspapers, are printed in English. All educated Filipinos are bilingual and the old mestizo landed elite still speaks Spanish at home. There are also 13 major dialects, spoken in rural areas.

Friendly to foreigners

The exposure to foreign influences (through American colonization and, more recently, through the great amount of overseas travelling that Filipinos have had to do in search of jobs) has made Filipinos, despite their natural diffidence and conservatism, remarkably open-minded and adaptable. No other South-East Asian country is as open and friendly towards foreigners, although a residual antipathy exists towards the Japanese, whose atrocities during the wartime occupation have not been completely forgotten.

The US connection A strongly pro-American bias is evident in everything from the structure of government and the courts to the adversarial role of the press. Filipinos comprise the largest Asian community in the USA (officially close to 1m; unofficially nearer to 2m) and personal contacts between the two countries are as frequent as those between some American states.

But the extent of US influence is deceptive. Beneath the surface Filipinos remain passionate Malays with a rich tradition of Spanish and pre-Spanish mystical beliefs.

The business method

Filipinos have eagerly adopted Western business and financial management methods (Asia's best Harvard-style business school is in Manila). Nevertheless, the Protestant work ethic has never taken hold. Even the most industrious Filipino businessman frowns on the idea of a job that dirties his hands. He cherishes his siesta and his long weekend. And he prefers to conduct business on the golf course or over leisurely lunches and evenings in nightclubs. Most Filipinos firmly believe that financial success comes from lucky connections or foxy deals and not from hard work – although this attitude is slowly changing.

Office hours vary but usually begin between 8.30 and 9.30 and end between 4.30 and 5.30. Most government offices open from 9 to 5 and close for lunch between 12 and 1. Retail banks open from 9.30 to 4; a few open some branches on Saturday morning. Senior government officials usually work late and accept telephone calls after office hours, but not when they are at home. Private businessmen usually may be reached at home.

Business cards Filipinos are not so fussy about business cards as some Orientals, but the ceremonious exchange of cards is still a part of the business introduction, with the visitor proffering his first. Do not be offended if your host forgets to reciprocate; but if he does, consider his handwritten addition of a home telephone number as a generous invitation to call.

Dress Filipinos are fastidious dressers and tend to dress rather formally in the office (suit or barong, the embroidered native shirt made from finely-spun banana or pineapple fibre). After-office wear tends to be expensively casual.

Knowing who's who A few
hundred families control all business
and wealth, most of it inherited. The
few thousand members of this elite
all know one another and deal with
each other on first-name terms,
which often presents the outsider
with the baffling image of a vast
mafia-type syndicate. Knowing
people's precise relationship to one
another (through honorary as well as
blood ties) is essential to
understanding how corporate battles,
and even political events, will unfold.
No foreigner can hope to do big
business without one of the elite as a
partner.

Etiquette

The quickest way to alienate a
Filipino is to treat him merely as a
business partner. All his
relationships, including his business
dealings, are highly personalized.
Long-standing business partners
invariably become "godfathers" to
each other's children, and they
frequently share social and sports
activities; golf and tennis are the top
businessmen's sports. Never refuse a
Filipino's invitation to dine at his
home: he may take it as a sign that
you think you are too good for him.

Like many Orientals, Filipinos
tend to act in the way and say the
things that they hope will please their
listeners. This gives a false
impression of their candour and
makes it extremely difficult to know
what they think. Advocating new
ideas requires an elliptical approach
which avoids implying any criticism
of previous practices or of anyone
present; remember that an offended
Filipino will willingly sacrifice a big
business opportunity if he feels he
has been slighted.

Women

Foreigners often fall into the trap of
believing that their tough-talking,
worldly-wise Filipino friends are as
cynical as they are. This can be a
dangerous mistake. In many ways
they are still old-fashioned and

prudish. Although every successful
businessman has his *querida*
(mistress) and, as a matter of
customary politeness, offers to
procure his guest a "companion,"
the sanctity of womanhood is
inviolable. The statutory punishment
for rape is death. Asking an
accompanied woman for a dance at a
nightclub, without first being
formally introduced and obtaining
her escort's consent, has resulted in
at least one fatal shooting (of a Hong
Kong visitor) in recent years. For all
their macho bravado, however,
Filipino men are dominated by their
women. In many households it is the
woman who handles the finances,
deciding how much of her husband's
pay to give him to spend on gambling
(a national obsession) and drink.

Women in business The natural
male chauvinism and cliquishness of
Filipino businessmen presents
enormous barriers to businesswomen,
whose successes are few and far
between. Women visiting the
Philippines are obliged to be quite
forceful in their approach if they are
to avoid being taken for weak-
minded dilettantes or pleasure-
seeking holiday-makers. But once
they have made their point they are
quickly and graciously accepted by
their male counterparts – accustomed
as they are to deferring to a woman's
judgment on the domestic front.

Women should, however, accept
the old world politeness that is
extravagantly extended to them by
this macho society and not try to be
"one of the boys." Success comes
from reflecting, as closely as possible,
the sentiments and values of the
Filipino's own revered mother.

Gifts and hospitality

Gift-giving is a strong Filipino
custom, not only at Christmas
(which is lavishly celebrated) and
birthdays (important), but also on
various other occasions. Resident
expatriates returning from a trip
abroad are expected to bring some
token of affection, even if it's only a

bottle of spirits for their colleagues and a box of chocolates for the secretaries. The greatest gift that a Filipino can give or receive is that of generous hospitality. Partying is every Filipino's delight. An executive newly posted to the Philippines is invariably fêted with several parties, and must return the compliment when he leaves with just as many *despedidas*.

A friendly manner and a tasteful but relatively insignificant gift can win important friends and protection in the grindingly slow bureaucracy. Numerous petty payoffs are obligatory if you expect to receive prompt attention and service.

Titles and nicknames
Almost every Filipino is given a nickname as a child and keeps it for the rest of his life. The Central Bank governor, José Fernandez, really does answer to the name "Jobo." President Aquino's 60-year-old millionaire brother-in-law, Ricardo Lopa, answers only to "Baby." Her right-hand-man, former executive secretary Arroyo, was, however, christened with the name Joker and is called just that.

The head of a clan is given the honorific title, "Don," which is used either before his whole name or, when addressing him personally, before his first name alone.

Filipinos are particularly fastidious about titles, however modest they may sound. An engineer is addressed as "Engineer So-and-so." Holders of PhDs are always addressed as "Doctor" or "Doctora" (for women).

The Filipino instinctively prefers to address a foreigner by his or her nickname, if any, which helps to establish a friendly, and therefore more binding, relationship.

Debt of honour
No custom is more important, or more mysterious to the foreigner, than that of *utang na loob* or lifelong debt of gratitude. Much of Philippine

business and politics is meaningless without appreciating this element. A very small favour on the part of a foreigner (such as helping to arrange an immigration visa for someone's nephew) can reap enormous benefits in return. Theoretically help given to someone in need is never forgotten and can never be adequately repaid. The complex network of loyalties that this builds up throughout society is the invisible web that influences all business and political decisions and that also makes minority groups remarkably resilient when under attack.

Consensus
The other extremely important cultural trait is *pakikisama*, which basically means cooperating with the majority view of your particular group or team. Filipinos find strength in group identification and expect foreigners to do the same. They retain close ties with old school fraternities and gangs and invariably seek the advice and approval of their *bakadas* (buddies) before making any important decision (including the choice of a wife or a business partner). Often the quickest way to bring a Filipino around to your way of thinking is to convert his *bakadas* first. But at all times it is important to appear to defer to the group sentiment and not to rock the boat.

Scuttlebutt
Manila is a city of coffee shops, where influential Filipinos gather to swap the latest rumours and scandals, usually before going to work; during the day they will base many business decisions on what they have heard over breakfast. But foreigners beware! Ninety percent of the stories peddled at these lively and convivial gatherings are malicious lies. Filipinos tend to take everything they hear with a pinch of salt. But it is equally true that no Filipino can keep a good secret. For the discerning listener the rumour-mill offers many valuable grains of information.

MANILA

Area code ☏ 02

Manila is a likeable city despite its many shortcomings which tend to dominate the visitor's first impressions. The streets are filthy and visitors are constantly harassed by beggars. Equally frustrating, from the business point of view, is the prevailing Latin philosophy of never doing today what can be put off until tomorrow – a sharp contrast to the renowned industry and resilience of Filipino migrant workers. Manila itself works to a different rhythm. Energy is reserved for animated discussions of the latest political developments, or for practising the latest disco dance steps. Pop music blares from every hotel, bar, shop and vehicle and everybody croons along. All this is irritating at first, but the Manileños' essential good nature and their warm sense of humour (rare in Asia) eventually win one over.

As the jumping-off point for remoter islands Manila does a brisk trade, and it sometimes seems that every Manileño is a travel agent or is in the pay of one. The tourist trade also has its seamy side; no unaccompanied male can walk more than a few paces in Manila's tourist belt without being asked if he wants to meet "beautiful girls." It is one of the ironies of the city that churches and brothels co-exist side by side, frequently with a VD clinic nearby. Religious groups preach against city vice generally but do little to halt it, while "hotel" owners argue publicly in the columns of the local newspapers that they contribute to the national economy, promote tourism and provide employment.

Manila is a service-dependent city, the centre of the nation's financial sector and the central marketplace for the agricultural products which constitute the bulk of the country's exports. The wealth earned by these products is now being used to finance industrialization, so that the country can process its own value-added products; and the discovery of substantial gold, copper and iron deposits in recent years guarantees that the country will not lack wealth-generating commodities if it can learn to use them. Trade in Manila has been notoriously corrupt in the past, and the rot has not entirely been stemmed, but since President Aquino took over, Manileños talk of future economic development with confidence.

Arriving

There are daily scheduled flights to the Philippines from more than 50 cities worldwide, all landing at Manila's international airport. The domestic airport, from which flights fan out to other cities north and south, is 5min away by taxi.

Ninoy Aquino International
Whatever the time, Ninoy Aquino International only just manages to stay on the right side of chaos.

Migrant Filipino workers returning to visit their families contribute to the melee, jostling for advantage in disordered lines. Immigration procedures are usually handled with efficiency, but in the baggage reclaim area 20min delays are normal. Trolleys cost P22 or US$1 to rent. A porter is included in the price, and it is best to let him steer a way through the crowd. Only those with goods to declare will need much time to clear customs, but the exit doors lead straight into a crowded arrivals hall where anyone who looks vaguely lost will be constantly harassed by touts of various kinds. Despite the confusion, however, it should not take more than 30min to clear the airport.

Facilities There is a tourist information and hotel desk, but it operates like a marketplace, with hotel reps vigorously competing for trade. If arriving without a reservation you should know which hotel you want to stay at so that you can home directly in on the appropriate rep. You can change money at a bank desk between customs and the arrivals hall. On the departures side there is a duty-free shop, a restaurant, bars, buffet, telephones, banks and mail services; some airlines have private lounges. Passengers arriving for flights before 9am may find all but the buffet closed. Airport information ☎ 8338135.

City link Hotel transport is the quickest and easiest way to get into the city, with cabs a poor alternative. The journey takes 20–40min depending on the time of day. The airport bus is not recommended.
Hotel transport The better hotels will send a limousine if ordered in advance. Otherwise the hotel reservations desk will arrange transport from a pool of cars which are generally better maintained than public taxis. The standard fare for this is P153 or US$7, nearly four times the taxi fare. The driver and hotel rep at the airport will probably try to find out what your sightseeing plans are. In order to avoid persistent phone calls to your room from the hotel travel agent it is best to say that you have already made arrangements through your host.
Taxi Manila taxis are small, usually decrepit and uncomfortable. A ride to the hotels in Ermita or Makati will cost around P60 including tip. The rank is to the left of the exit, and there is rarely a long wait.

Car rental Avis and Hertz have offices at the airport, open Mon–Sat, 7–7; Sun, 7–9.

Getting around
Using taxis in Manila will not do much for personal dignity or company image. Status-conscious visitors with a lot of travelling to do are strongly recommended to use a hotel limousine or chauffeur-driven rental car. Drivers are not unwilling to enter into private arrangements at lower-than-standard rates.

Hotel transport Hotels in Ermita and Malate run a shuttle bus service throughout the day to the Makati business district. Some hotels also run their own fleets of clean, air-conditioned taxis; these charge a 50% premium on the normal taxi rate. All hotels operate ten-seater minibuses and limousines. The rates tend to be the same for both: around P350 per hour with a 3hr minimum period.

Taxi Although uncomfortable, dirty and dilapidated, Manila's taxis are easily hailed in the street, day and night, and the English-speaking drivers can be relied upon to know their way around the city – usually at speeds some passengers will find exciting, others simply terrifying. Fares are low: from Ermita to Makati costs about P40. *Golden Taxi Cabs* ☎ 596701 is one of the largest and most reliable taxi firms.

Driving Avis ☎ 586228 and *Hertz* ☎ 8172761 have several offices, with representatives in many hotels. Package deals are often available for weekly or weekend rental. Cars with drivers cost about 30% more than the standard rate.

Walking For short distances in the Makati business district it is practical to walk. Elsewhere you will encounter foul streets (many without sidewalks) and beggars, pimps and hawkers at every corner. The pestering increases at night, when it is risky, particularly for unaccompanied women, to be out on the streets.

Public transport Jeepneys –
colourfully decorated jeeps – are an
attractive feature of Manila's streets,
but passengers must expect to cling
precariously to a hard bench amid
assorted shopping parcels which may
include a live hen or two. The
Metrorail elevated light railway was
designed to bring commuters in from
the suburbs. None of its stations is
close to Ermita or Makati.

Outside Manila

For travel within the Philippines, air
is the only practical option. Buses,
trains and ferries are for those with
time to spare.

Air *Philippine Air Lines* (*PAL*)
☎ 832279 runs extensive domestic
services with discounts available to
those who fly PAL to Manila and
make reservations for domestic and
international flights at the same time.
Night-time (*Bulilit*) services are up
to 30% cheaper than peak-time
flights. For reservations ☎ 8323166
(24hr), or go to one of PAL's many
hotel ticket offices or agents. There is
usually only one class and most of the
short-haul aircraft are 50-seater
turbo-props. There are 11 flights
daily from Manila to Cebu (journey
time about 1hr) and less frequent
services to other destinations. Several
charter companies work out of
Manila Domestic airport. These
include *Aerolift* ☎ 8172369, which
operates 20-seater Twin Otter and BN
Islander aircraft to any point within
the archipelago, and *Delta Airlines*
☎ 8322706, which operates propeller
and jet aircraft and helicopters. The
facilities at Manila's domestic airport
are rudimentary: a buffet, telephones
and crowded waiting rooms. Airport
information ☎ 8338135.

Driving For all but the most
adventurous (and with ample time) it
is best to rent a car only after
reaching your destination by air.
Driving is on the right in the
Philippines and is easy enough on the
highways, since they are all well
signposted in English; elsewhere,
both a good map and willingness to
ask directions are essential. Roads
in the mountainous north of Luzon
Island are frequently blocked by
landslides during the rainy season
(Jun–Nov) for up to three days, and
it is sensible to find out first if
country roads are passable. In major
tourist resorts, taxis and hotel rental
cars are cheap and plentiful. *Avis*
☎ 586228 (Manila) has offices in
Angeles ☎ 4552267, Baguio
☎ 4424018, Cebu ☎ 3299823 and
Olangapo ☎ 2223873. *Hertz*
☎ 8172761 (Manila) is also in
Angeles ☎ 4556111, Baguio
☎ 4425626 and Olongapo
☎ 2225415. Both companies allow
one-way rental.

Bus Luxury air-conditioned buses
operate over the entire archipelago.
Most travel agents have timetables
and will handle ticketing.

Ferry Inexpensive inter-island
ferries with first-class, air-
conditioned cabins operate from the
domestic shipping terminal at the
North Harbor in Manila.

Area by area

In an attempt to impose a degree of
planning on the capital's sprawling
growth, the government joined 13
suburban cities to Manila proper in
1976 to create Metro Manila. For
most business visitors only two of
these cities are relevant: Manila (for
hotels) and Makati (the business and
shopping centre). Manila itself is
divided into several districts: the old
city (Intramuros), the hotel strip
(Ermita and adjoining Malate), and
the market areas north of the Pasig
River (Santa Cruz and Quiapo).

Intramuros Now of interest only as
a tourist attraction, Intramuros was
the first settlement laid out with
heavy defences by the Spanish
conquistadors in the late 16th
century. The privileged lived within
the walls, while separate communities
of Spanish and Chinese – later Dutch
and American – traders settled the
adjacent banks of the Pasig River.

Ermita and Malate The architect Daniel Burnham laid down the rectangular grid system of the Ermita and Malate districts with their long north-south avenues, which now form the heart of Manila. Ermita subsequently became the fashionable residential district until it was largely razed by heavy bombing during the liberation of the Philippines from Japanese occupation in 1944. It enjoyed a renaissance in the 1970s with the construction of several big hotels; with them came a proliferation of bars, restaurants, gift shops and nightclubs. Yet Ermita's parks, squares and undeveloped bomb sites are home to some of the

city's poorest inhabitants who live in the streets or in slums and survive on the pesos they can beg from tourists.

Malate is the location of the Cultural Center Complex, a pet project of Imelda Marcos which, if it ever sees completion, may shift the whole commercial and financial community back to the waterside. On a long strip of reclaimed land areas have been zoned for a new stock exchange, business park and high-tech village. All that has been completed so far is the Cultural Center itself, convention and exhibition halls, a design centre, folk art and film theatres, and the city's best hotel for sports facilities, the

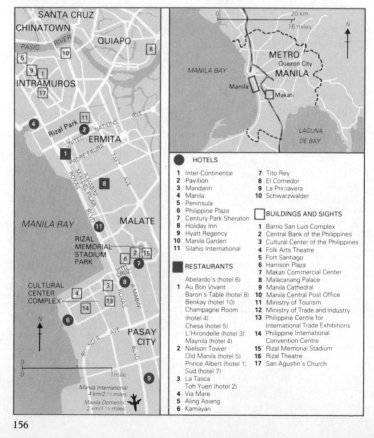

HOTELS

1 Inter-Continental
2 Pavilion
3 Mandarin
4 Manila
5 Peninsula
6 Philippine Plaza
7 Century Park Sheraton
8 Holiday Inn
9 Hyatt Regency
10 Manila Garden
11 Silahis International

7 Tito Rey
8 El Comedor
9 La Primavera
10 Schwarzwalder

BUILDINGS AND SIGHTS

1 Barrio San Luis Complex
2 Central Bank of the Philippines
3 Cultural Center of the Philippines
4 Folk Arts Theatre
5 Fort Santiago
6 Harrison Plaza
7 Makati Commercial Center
8 Malacanang Palace
9 Manila Cathedral
10 Manila Central Post Office
11 Ministry of Tourism
12 Ministry of Trade and Industry
13 Philippine Centre for International Trade Exhibitions
14 Philippine International Convention Centre
15 Rizal Memorial Stadium
16 Rizal Theatre
17 San Agustin's Church

RESTAURANTS

Abelardo's (hotel 6)
1 Au Bon Vivant
   Baron's Table (hotel 8)
   Benkay (hotel 10)
   Champagne Room (hotel 4)
   Chesa (hotel 5)
   L'Hirondelle (hotel 3)
   Maynila (hotel 4)
2 Nielson Tower
   Old Manila (hotel 5)
   Prince Albert (hotel 1)
   Sud (hotel 7)
3 La Tasca
   Toh Yuen (hotel 2)
4 Via Mare
5 Aling Asiang
6 Kamayan

Philippine Plaza (see *Hotels*).

Santa Cruz and Quiapo North of the Pasig River is the main port facility and the two districts of Santa Cruz and Quiapo, areas of crowded narrow streets and vast open markets, populated mainly by Chinese and Muslims. The streets to the east, which lead to the Malacañang Palace, former home of Ferdinand and Imelda Marcos, were once heavily guarded. Now they are festive with weekend visitors to the palace, which is now open to the public since President Aquino has chosen to make her home in another part of the city.

Makati Affluent Manileños have long since decamped from Ermita to the southwestern Forbes Park district of Makati. Adjoining this area is the business and commercial district, where most of the capital's offices and banks, upmarket restaurants and department stores are to be found. Until the 1950s this area of high-rise buildings was an uninhabited swamp.

Outlying districts Two important business/administration districts lie out in the suburbs of northern Metro Manila: light industry and food processing are concentrated in Caloocan City, while most government offices and the campus of the University of the Philippines are in Quezon City.

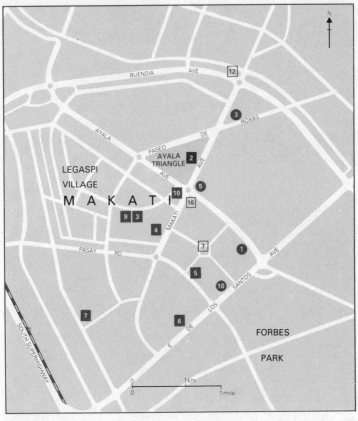

Hotels

There are top-class hotels both in Makati and along the harbour front in the Ermita/Malate tourist belt. Makati is most convenient for the business district, but prices tend to be lower in Ermita and Malate. The city's best hotels are the Mandarin and the Manila.

Rooms in all the hotels listed have air conditioning, TV, radio, minibars, IDD telephones and 24hr room service. Standard business facilities include typing and/or word processing, photocopying and telex. All listed hotels have a travel desk and limousine service. Fruit, flowers and free international newspapers are often included as part of the competition for customer loyalty. Room rates are usually quoted exclusive of 10% service charge and 13.7% government tax. It is always worthwhile trying to negotiate a discount or an upgrade.

Pavilion *$$*
United Nations Ave, Ermita ☎ *573711*
🆃 *63387 Fax 5223531* • *AE DC MC V*
• *376 rooms, 17 suites, 5 restaurants, 1 bar*
The Pavilion overcomes the disadvantage of being neither in Makati nor on the waterfront by concentrating on high standards of comfort and service. It is decorated throughout in native Filipino style, with rattan furniture, mahogany panelling inlaid with mother-of-pearl arabesques, and flowers at every turn. The rooms are spacious, with picture windows and balconies; the best overlook the quiet hotel garden and pool. There is an efficient business centre and messages are delivered promptly. Shopping arcade, hairdresser, florist, casino • pool, gym • 13 meeting rooms (capacity up to 1,200).

Inter-Continental *$$$*
Ayala Ave, Makati Commercial Center, Makati ☎ *8159711* 🆃 *23314 Fax 8171330* • *AE DC M V* • *371 rooms, 26 suites, 4 restaurants, 2 bars*
This was once Manila's leading business hotel, but others have caught up with it. It is in the heart of the commercial centre, with upmarket department stores, cinemas, restaurants and offices a short stroll away. The standard rooms are narrow, and most of the floor space is taken up by a large bed

and sofa, so it is worthwhile asking for a superior room. The Prince Albert Rôtisserie is a good choice for entertaining (see *Restaurants*), but apart from the poolside snack bar the hotel lacks a relaxing place for casual meals; breakfast and buffet lunch are served in an impersonal section off the busy lobby, and there is a gimmicky coffee shop where guests can, if they like, sit inside converted jeepneys. There is, however, a quiet bar which is useful for confidential meetings, and the business centre is excellent. Shopping arcade, hairdresser, florist, disco • pool, sauna, solarium, massage, gym • reference library, news teleprinter, 7 meeting rooms (capacity up to 800).

Mandarin *$$$$*
Makati Ave, Makati ☎ *8163601* 🆃 *63756 Fax 8172472* • *AE DC MC V* • *442 rooms, 28 suites, 4 restaurants, 1 bar*
Unmistakably in the same mould as its namesake in Hong Kong, the Mandarin ranks among the world's finest hotels. About half of the guests are holidaymakers, but the business traveller can count on efficiency as well as a congenial atmosphere. The black and white marble lobby is certainly more stylish than any other Makati hotel, having deep leather armchairs and sympathetic lighting. The fixed-price buffet at the Clipper

Lounge attracts the local business community for lunch, and L'Hirondelle (see *Restaurants*) is good for more serious entertaining. Service is of a very high standard. The guest rooms are comfortable and large, with full-size desks, and the business centre is one of the few in Manila with fax. Shopping arcade, florist • outdoor pool, gym, sauna • 5 meeting rooms.

Manila $$$$
Rizal Park, Ermita ☎ 470011 ⊠ 40537 Fax 471124 • AE DC MC V • 514 rooms, 56 suites, 7 restaurants, 3 bars
The Manila is an elegant hotel, opened in 1912 and built in the grand tropical style of Singapore's Raffles, or Hong Kong's Peninsula. Ernest Hemingway once said it was as inspiring as a good story. Painstaking restoration in 1977, which endowed the building with a cascade of green tiled roofs, fanciful wrought-iron work balconies and a glorious Doric-arched lobby, earned the hotel the Pacific area Landmark Preservation Award, as well as several interior design accolades. The rooms, suggestive of the Spanish colonial period, have four-poster beds, cane furniture and marble-topped tables. The standard suites are vast, with large balconies and sweeping views of either the harbour or the ruins of the walled city of Intramuros. In addition there is the richly panelled MacArthur Suite, home for seven years to General Douglas MacArthur, the "hero of the Pacific." Even at a rate of over US$1,200 a night, this suite and the Penthouse suite, with its private roof-top pool, have no shortage of takers. The Maynila and Champagne Room are both highly suitable for entertaining. The hotel also offers the most pleasurable outdoor dining in Manila at the Roma Italian restaurant and Sea Breeze Grill, both set in the manicured hotel gardens. Shopping arcade, hairdresser, disco • access to Bay Club's pool, sauna,

gym, squash, tennis, putting green • reference library, personal computer rental, 15 meeting rooms (capacity up to 100).

Peninsula $$$$
Corner of Makati and Ayala Aves, Makati ☎ 8193456 ⊠ 22507 Fax 8154825 • AE DC MC V • 514 rooms, 21 suites, 3 restaurants, 2 bars
Character is not a strong point of the Peninsula, for despite its attractive setting of hanging gardens and cascading water, the interior is bland and anonymous, with textured concrete walls, relieved here and there by wood panelling. It is, however, a much more tranquil place than most of Manila's hotels. The giant lobby is hushed, and the poolside gardens are free from exuberant adolescents. The rooms are plain but large, with a proper desk. The Old Manila is widely considered Manila's best restaurant for entertaining, though the Chesa is also much favoured (see *Restaurants*). Shopping arcade, hairdresser, florist • pool • 6 meeting rooms (capacity up to 50), ballroom (850) with cinema and slide projection facilities.

Philippine Plaza $$$
Cultural Center Complex, Roxas Blvd, Malate ☎ 8320701 ⊠ 40443 Fax 8323485 • AE DC MC V • Westin Hotels • 625 rooms, 50 suites, 7 restaurants, 1 bar
The Philippine Plaza was conceived as an integral part of an ambitious new cultural and high-technology city to be built on reclaimed land along the southern fringes of Roxas Boulevard, close to Ninoy Aquino International Airport. The cultural complex has been completed, but it looks like being many years before the rest of the plan reaches fruition. In the meantime the hotel remains somewhat remote, but it has three points in its favour. It is opposite the Philippines International Convention and Trade Exhibition Centers and so is a natural choice for exhibitors and delegates. It is separated from the sea

only by a retaining wall and thus enjoys uninterrupted views of the ever-changing sky and the distant island of Corregidor. All the spacious rooms have good-sized desks, armchairs and furnished balconies. To maintain its occupancy levels, the hotel does a lot of discounted tour group trade, but there is a professionally run business centre. Shopping arcade, florist, hairdresser, shuttle bus, disco • pool, gym, tennis, putting green, jogging trail • news teleprinter, 13 meeting rooms (capacity up to 150), ballroom (capacity 2,000) with simultaneous translation and audiovisual equipment.

OTHER HOTELS

Century Park Sheraton (*$$$*) *Corner of Vito Cruz and M. Adriatico, Malate* ☎ *5211011* ⊤⊠ *40489 Fax 5213413* • *AE DC MC V*. Part of the Harrison Plaza shopping complex, but surrounded by seedy

streets. Very busy, and staff can be offhand. The Sud restaurant serves excellent Mediterranean food (see *Restaurants*).

Holiday Inn (*$$$*) *3001 Roxas Blvd, Pasay City* ☎ *597961* ⊤⊠ *63487 Fax 5223985* • *AE DC MC V*. Spacious rooms and a good business centre make this a popular hotel.

Hyatt Regency (*$$$*) *2702 Roxas Blvd, Pasay City* ☎ *8312611* ⊤⊠ *63344 Fax 8187372* • *AE DC MC V*. Modern and well-equipped, but inconveniently located with no rapid access to the business district.

Manila Garden (*$*) *Fourth Quadrant, Makati Commercial Center, Makati* ☎ *857911* ⊤⊠ *45883 Fax 8171862* • *AE DC MC V*. Owned by the Japanese Nikko group and offering much the same standards as the Hyatt Regency.

Silahis International (*$$*) *1990 Roxas Blvd, Malate* ☎ *573811* ⊤⊠ *63163 Fax 2502526* • *AE DC MC V*. Home to the city's Playboy Club.

Restaurants

Eating out commands a high priority in the daily life of the Filipino business community. Offices virtually close down between noon and 2pm as everyone from the chairman to the filing clerks set off for restaurants. No visitors will ever be left to fend for themselves; indeed, an invitation to lunch is almost as automatic as shaking hands, and an invitation to dinner is a sure sign that the relationship is growing warmer. Even Manila's finest restaurants are inexpensive and casual by Western standards, though the cost begins to mount if one chooses imported beef, lamb, lobster or game. Seafood, pork and poultry, the basic ingredients of the local cuisine, are cheap. Perhaps because of the Spanish influence, wine is more commonly ordered, and is more reasonably priced, than is usual in Asia, although the local San Miguel beer or freshly pressed fruit juices make acceptable alternatives. Menu prices do not include service (usually 10%) or sales taxes of 4.2% on food and 8.7% on alcohol. Filipinos like to dress up for evening entertaining, generally opting for expensively casual clothes. Dinner usually begins at 8 with final orders at around 10.30.

Abelardo's *$$$ Philippine Plaza Hotel* ☎ *8320701* • *D only* • *AE DC V* Women are presented with roses at this restaurant, which takes its name from a Filipino composer of

traditional love songs, Nicanor Abelardo. The cuisine is quasi-*nouvelle* – grilled seafood with herbs, light soufflés of local smoked fish – and there is an extensive wine list. Not a place for serious business discussions, but a good choice for returning hospitality.

Au Bon Vivant $$
1133 L. Guerrero, Ermita ☏ *898874* • *closed Sat, Sun* • *AE DC MC V*
Manila's first French restaurant is now a local institution. Chefs trained in France by masters of *cuisine bourgeoise* place great emphasis on using ingredients fresh from the market, and the menu changes daily. The tables are too close for confidential discussion, although this doesn't prevent it from being popular with expatriate business people. Service is respectful. The wine list is short but sound.

Baron's Table $$
Holiday Inn ☏ *597961* • *closed Sat, Sun* • *AE DC MC V*
Mock medieval beams and panelling seem incongruous in Asia, but this is the Holiday Inn group's chosen theme for its restaurants throughout the region, and there is a hint of the Middle European in the Continental dishes on the menu. Good for a working lunch but nothing more special; choose the corner tables if you want privacy.

Benkay $$
Manila Garden Hotel ☏ *857911* • *AE DC MC V*
This Nikko group's hotel restaurant is in a pavilion surrounded by lush gardens, and the beautifully prepared and presented Japanese cuisine attracts a cosmopolitan business clientele, especially at lunch time. The alternative set menus make choosing easier.

Champagne Room $$$$
Manila Hotel ☏ *470011* • *AE DC MC V*
The Champagne Room shares the colonial atmosphere that sets the Manila hotel apart from all its competitors: severe white walls, glass Art Deco palm trees inside and real trees outside, framing the view of Manila Bay through the graceful semi-circular windows. The menu is

French *haute cuisine*, with liberal use of caviar, *foie gras* and truffles. The restaurant specializes in veal medallions with morel sauce and flambé prawns or duckling. Some very fine wines.

Chesa $$
Peninsula Hotel ☏ *8193456* • *AE DC MC V*
This is a favourite among local business people, serving traditional Swiss air-dried and smoked meats, sausages, raclette and veal, and cheese fondues. (A local fondue variation includes mango and prawns.) The decor suggests a mountainside chalet but the wrought-iron work is distinctively Spanish. Vintage French wines at a price, but also a good selection of Swiss and German.

L'Hirondelle $$
Mandarin Hotel ☏ *8163601 ext. 2310* • *AE DC MC V*
A lot of business is discussed in the understated and relaxed surroundings of this restaurant. Grilled beef and lamb are the staples, but seafood and lighter dishes are also on the menu. Service is attentive, and the list of French vintage wines is unmatched in the city.

Maynila $$$
Manila Hotel ☏ *470011* • *closed Sun* • *AE DC MC V*
If you do not know your guests very well, the Maynila is a good ice-breaker, full of conversation pieces that will encourage them to talk about Philippines history, culture and food. The decor resembles that of an old mansion in Intramuros, with wrought-iron balconies, stained glass and wooden panelling. The cooking is equally traditional, including such dishes as *sinabawang lamang ng dagat*, a local version of bouillabaisse laced with rum, and *lomo basilan*, tenderloin stuffed with lobster, mushrooms and local cheese. A band plays nightly. Long and varied wine list.

Nielson Tower $$
Makati Ave, Makati ☏ *8171180*
• *closed Sun L* • *AE DC MC V*
The former control tower of Manila's
prewar airport is now an atmospheric
restaurant/club patronized by the
most influential of the city's business
leaders. It serves only members at
lunch but is open to the public in the
evening, when reservations are
essential. Cocktails are served in the
small circular bar upstairs, from
which there are views of the
surrounding park. The restaurant is
1930s in style, and specializes in
sorpresa de balu – baked duck eggs
with a pastry lid. Great fun, but not
the place to entertain someone who is
already a member.

Old Manila $$$
Peninsula Hotel ☏ *8193456* •
AE DC MC V
Many rate this Manila's top
restaurant for its polished service,
fine cuisine and period atmosphere.
From the raw concrete of the hotel's
lobby, visitors step into a spacious
room lined with ornate panelling,
hung with prints of prewar Manila
and furnished with antiques. The
restaurant prides itself on prime,
aged beef imported from Chicago,
but there is also a short selection of
native dishes, including stuffed squid
and grilled prawns. The wine list has
selections from most wine-producing
countries.

Prince Albert $$$
Inter-Continental Hotel ☏ *8159711*
• *closed Sun L and Sat* • *AE DC*
MC V
First and foremost a rôtisserie,
with an established reputation for
grilled meats and seafood, the Prince
Albert is a safe if unadventurous
choice for entertaining business
colleagues. It is centrally located and
has the merit of being within walking
distance of most offices. The dining
room is decorated with plush red
velvet and gleaming copper pans.
Service is attentive, but also
unobtrusive.

Sud $$$
Century Park Sheraton Hotel
☏ *506041* • *closed Sun* • *AE DC MC V*
The prettiest dining room in Manila
overflows with plants and serves
some delightfully light and inventive
dishes, which owe something to the
Mediterranean but also borrow from
Japan. This is a restaurant to choose
if you know your guests take a real
interest in good food. There is a wide
selection of reasonably priced wines.

La Tasca $$
Legaspi Street, Makati ☏ *868541*
• *closed Sun* • *AE DC MC V*
This is one of Manila's most popular
business restaurants, combining a
central position with reasonable
prices, polished service and an
extensive menu specializing in
Spanish dishes but with several
native Filipino offerings as well.

Toh Yuen $$
Pavilion Hotel ☏ *5733711* • *dim sum
only Sun L; closed Sun D* • *AE DC*
MC V
Toh Yuen is held to be one of the
city's top Chinese restaurants and has
a loyal business clientele, which is not
restricted to the Chinese Filipino
community. Simply decorated with a
few fans and screens, it is staffed by
Hong Kong chefs who have mastered
all culinary styles, so it is possible to
include Cantonese suckling pig,
Peking duck and Sichuan spicy
prawns in a meal which might also
include steamed local lapu-lapu fish,
sharksfin soup and scallops with
"deep-fried milk." All wine-
producing countries, including
China, are represented on the wine
list.

Via Mare $$
Paseo de Roxas, Makati ☏ *852306*
• *closed Sun L* • *AE DC MC V*
This is a smart seafood restaurant,
much liked by young Manileños. It is
decorated in cool greens and blues,
and a guitarist plays gently in the
background. The menu changes
regularly, but usually there are fresh

oysters and a choice of cheese, spinach, crab or lobster soufflé.

Good but casual

Restaurants highly regarded for their local cooking include *Aling Asiang*, Plaza Bldg, Greenbelt Center, Makati ☎ 8190006, and *Kamayan*, 47 Pasay Rd, Makati ☎ 883604, which offers a more exotic menu. Another local restaurant is *Tito Rey*, Sunvar Plaza, Amorsolo, Pasay Rd, Makati ☎ 8164461, where diners eat with their hands from wooden plates lined with banana leaves (conventional service is provided in the lounge). For Spanish cooking and wine try *El Comedor*, 1555 M. Adriatico, Ermita ☎ 502838; for Italian food, *La Primavera*, Exedra Bldg, Legaspi St, Makati ☎ 8181942; and for German cuisine, there is *Schwarzwalder*, Makati Ave, Makati ☎ 865179, which serves goulash, pork hock, sour herring and sausages or cosmopolitan steaks and grilled fish. Also offering steaks and grilled fish along with cajun and creole fare is *New Orleans*, Legazpi St, Makati ☎ 8172956.

Bars

Most of Manila's bars are noisy, rough-and-ready places. Signs proclaim "ice cold beer," but it rarely is; and only a token beam or two distinguishes so-called English pubs from other bars. The cleanest and most enjoyable bars are: *Kangaroo Club*, 476 United Nations Ave; *Old English Pub*, corner of Padre Faura and M. Adriatico; *San Mig* in Legaspi St; *Prince of Wales* and *Greenbelt* in Padre Faura; *Blackout*, 475 Padre Faura also occasionally shows US sports videos. Much more suitable for meeting clients are the *Clipper Lounge* in the Mandarin hotel, the *Tap Room Bar* at the Manila and the *Lobby Bar* at the Peninsula. But even in hotel bars it's difficult to escape from live or piped music.

Entertainment

Popular music and "girlie" bars dominate Manila's entertainment scene, but the city has a cultured side, and concerts by leading international musicians are well attended by the city's affluent classes. *What's On In Manila*, distributed free at the airport and in hotels, is the best guide to the main events.

Theatre, dance and music
Touring productions and performances by the Philippine Ballet, Manila Chamber Orchestra and Philippine Philharmonic are all held at the *Cultural Center of the Philippines* ☎ 8321125 (inquiries), 8323704 (ticket office). Lively performances of native music and dance are regularly staged at the nearby *Folk Arts Theater* ☎ 8323706. The *Rizal Theater*, Makati Commercial Center ☎ 862020, is the main venue for repertory theatre and comedy shows. Credit card reservations are accepted for all performances; tickets can also be purchased at the *Goodwill Bookstore*, Makati Commercial Center ☎ 857209.

Cinema The *Quad Theater*, Makati ☎ 874255, *Makati Cinema Square* ☎ 874081 and the *Greenbelt Cinema Complex* ☎ 876767, are all modern cinemas but don't be surprised if you have never heard of the films on show; most of them are mawkish B movies or local films with a strong religious theme.

Nightclubs and discos Most hotel lounges, bars and restaurants in Manila have a resident band, so look no further if all you want by way of entertainment is to listen to renditions of chart hits. Perhaps the most popular nightclub, particularly with young visitors, is *Après* at the Manila hotel, although *Tipanan* at the Inter-Continental also has a lively atmosphere. Discos include the popular *Rumors*, South Drive, Makati Commercial Center ☎ 861196, the *Stargazer Lounge* at the Silahis International hotel and *Lost Horizon* at the Philippine Plaza hotel. Bars offering sex shows, striptease and the company of so-called "hostitutes" abound in

Ermita, particularly along M.H. del Pilar. Some are classier than others, with imported rock videos and disco music; among these are *Superstar*, *Pitstop*, *The New Bangkok Club*, *Domino's* and *Firehouse*.

Shopping

The Philippines produces wonderful furniture, basketry, shellwork and cigars. It is also possible to buy a wide range of Spanish antiques. The furniture industry began to expand after the completion of the Suez Canal (1869) opened up a European market for bentwood chairs and wicker furniture. The tradition continues with fine rattan beds, sofas, dining chairs, tables and armchairs. They are light but durable and though bulky can be shipped inexpensively by all the leading department stores. The Ifugao tribespeople of the northern Philippines make fine functional and decorative basketry of bamboo, rattan and palm. Cebu province in the south specializes in shellcraft objects, such as ashtrays, wind-chimes, coasters and Tiffany-style lampshades. The best place to shop for all these crafts is at *Tesoro's* on South Drive, Makati Commercial Center; other selections can be found at both *Anson's Emporium* and *Rustan's Department Store* in the same centre.

The *Nayong Pilipino Museum* of traditional Philippine culture has a comprehensive choice of crafts, including primitive Ifugao wood carvings, colourful handwoven fabrics and brassware from the Muslim south. It also has the most trustworthy antique outlets, selling a wide range of items from ornate Dutch oil lamps and four-poster beds to 18thC and 19thC figurines of saints and religious paintings. Most antique shops are clustered in Mabini and M.H. del Pilar streets in Ermita. The supply of genuine antiques has dwindled over the years and prices are steep; look for the stamp of the National Museum for authenticity.

All hotel arcades and department stores sell the world-famous Tabacalera and Alhambra cigars, but the best bargains are at the *Tabacalera* showroom, 936 Romualdez St. Boxes of 50 cigars in a handsome narra-wood humidor can be personalized with a name or logo, either carved on the box or printed on the ring bands at a minimal charge.

Sightseeing

Manila's principal sights can be seen in the odd hours snatched from a busy schedule and without a guide, but the two recommended trips out of town both take a day and are best done during the week to avoid crowds.

Intramuros The original massive walls of this area once enclosed numerous pretty Baroque churches, grand houses and the governor's palace. Much was destroyed during the liberation of Manila in 1944, and for decades Intramuros festered as a slum. Belatedly it has been recognized as a potential money-earner, and work has begun to restore the few remaining Spanish courtyard houses and build new ones in the old style re-using the masonry which remained after the air raids. *San Agustin*, built in 1599, is the only church to have survived the war. It contains the tombs of two famous Spanish explorers: Legaspi, who founded modern Manila, and Salcedo, who fought many courageous battles against Chinese pirates. Nearby is the Plaza Roma and *Manila Cathedral*, originally built in 1571 and subsequently rebuilt six times. The fine bronze west doors illustrate the cathedral's calamitous history. Inside are contemporary stained-glass windows, Italian mosaic work and a bronze crucifix donated by General Franco. The main attraction of Intramuros is the *Casa Manila* within the restored buildings of the Barrio San Luis Complex opposite San Agustin. Formerly the house of an affluent Filipino merchant, it is now a museum (*open*

9–6; closed Mon). In the same complex are craft and antique shops, and a tearoom in the delightful setting of a bougainvillea-filled courtyard. At the northernmost tip of Intramuros is *Fort Santiago*, built to defend the harbour and Pasig River over a period of 150 years beginning in 1590. It has since served various functions: first as the seat of Spanish and then American colonial government, later as a prison camp and torture chamber under Japanese occupation; and most recently as the setting for many an extravagant party during the Marcos era.

Malacañang Palace Museum The former presidential palace is known locally as the "Shoe Mart," a reference to Manila's biggest department store chain and to the notorious collection of thousands of pairs of shoes discovered in Imelda Marcos's wardrobe. The early 19thC palace has been kept exactly as it was on the night the family fled the country: the rooms cluttered with garish bric-à-brac, the vast lace-canopied bed, the oxygen cylinders as a reminder of the former president's ill health and the many idealized portraits of Imelda and Marcos. *Open 10–5; closed Wed and Sun.*

Nayong Pilipino Another pet project of Imelda Marcos, the Nayong Pilipino (Philippine Village) is a 54-acre/22-ha park alongside the Manila Domestic airport runway featuring reconstructions of the architecture of the islands and regions of the Philippines archipelago. It is a serious, professionally run enterprise, a cross between an anthropological theme park and trade promotion centre for native crafts, with a large store and showroom in the National Cottage Industries Administration Building.

Guided tours

Manila has hundreds of none-too-reliable tour agents. Stick to the hotel travel firm, or go to the *Bureau of Tourism Services* ☎ 501703, Agrifina Circle, Rizal Park (open daily),

where you can sign up for the same tours at lower prices.

Out of town

Tagaytay This tour takes visitors to the awe-inspiring Taal volcano, 33 miles/53km south of Manila, past scenic villages and farmhouses. The volcano last erupted in 1976 and is still active. It consists of a lake-filled crater, within which is an island containing another lake-filled crater. This lake has, in turn, another crater within it which occasionally emits sulphuric steam.

Pagsanjan falls A spectacular and exciting river journey through deep gorges and over rapids in a dugout canoe. (Francis Ford Coppola shot the final half hour of *Apocalypse Now* in this valley.) At the second of the two powerful waterfalls, visitors have the option of transferring to a raft which is pulled by rope through the icy waters into the small cave behind. Even those who do not opt for this invigorating soaking should bring waterproof clothing and plastic bags to protect cameras. Pagsanjan is a 2hr drive south of Manila; the tour usually lasts 8hr and is very popular.

Spectator sports

Basketball, baseball and soccer are played at the *Rizal Memorial Stadium* in Malate ☎ 582136.

Horse-racing Manila has two horse-racing tracks, the *Philippine Racing Club* at Santa Ana Race Track and the *Manila Jockey Club* at San Lazaro Hippodrome. Information ☎ 879951.

Polo is played at the *Manila Polo Club* during the winter months; inquiries ☎ 8176956.

Keeping fit

The facilities at the Philippine Plaza and Manila hotels are open to non-residents. The Reed Fitness Center at the Century Park Sheraton has a resident trainer and dance and aerobics classes.

Golf Details of all courses are given in *Play Golf in the Philippines*, published by the Ministry of Tourism, which also runs the *Muni* course within the former moat around the walls of Intramuros ☎ 501703. The *Wack Wack Golf and Country Club* ☎ 784021, in the eastern suburbs at Mandaluyong, hosts the annual Philippine open tournament. The *Fort Bonifacio Golf Club* ☎ 858464 is close to the business centre of Makati. Some 45min from Manila is the *Puerto Azul Beach and Country Club* ☎ 8153993, with a championship course carved out of the craggy cliffs bordering the sea.

Jogging Early in the morning and in the cool early evening, groups of avid joggers flock to the *Cultural Center Complex* and *Rizal Park*, both on Roxas Blvd, to the *Rizal Memorial Stadium* (admission P2) on Adriatico St and the *Ayala Triangle* park in Makati.

Riding The *Lostamaraos Polo and Equestrian Center*, Las Piñas ☎ 8271011, is open to the public from 8 to 5 daily and offers riding on imported thoroughbreds.

Local resources

Business services

All the big hotels offer an extensive range of in-house business services.

Photocopying and printing Photocopy shops abound throughout Manila, and usually double as photo-processing outlets; just look for *Ricoh* or *Canon* shop signs. For printing, *Capitol Publishing House*, 54 Don Alejandro Roces Ave, Quezon City ☎ 999628 handles everything from business cards to catalogues and has its own design studio.

Secretarial and translation *Manpower* ☎ 887888 has temporary secretarial staff who will also act as translators. (Companies advertising "social secretarial services" are call-girl agencies.)

Communications

Local delivery BM *Express Messenger* ☎ 859560.
Long-distance delivery IRS

Express ☎ 875776, for next-day deliveries to most points in the Philippines. International couriers: DHL ☎ 888511; TNT *Skypak* ☎ 8172871.

Post offices All the main hotels sell stamps. For international express services go to *Manila Central Post Office*, Liwasang Bonifacio, Intramuros (by MacArthur Bridge) or *Makati Central Post Office*, Buendia Ave (or Gil J. Puyat Ave), open Mon–Fri, 8–5.

Telephones Local call boxes are plentiful and accept P25 coins. All the better hotels have IDD telephones. Otherwise ☎ 109 for domestic long-distance calls and ☎ 108 for international calls. For directory inquiries ☎ 114. Rates for international calls are 25% cheaper on Sundays. Operators are efficient and speak English. Line quality, though, can be poor.

Telex and fax *Philippine Telegraph and Telephone Corporation* head office, Spirit of Communications Center, 106 Alvarado St, Makati ☎ 8180511.

Conference/exhibition centres

The *Philippine International Convention Center* ☎ 8320309 is run by the Philippine Convention Bureau ☎ 575031 and accommodates 5,000 delegates. The *Philippine Center for International Trade Exhibitions* (Philcite) ☎ 8320304 is on the same harbour site, along with the Cultural Center; the whole district is to be developed as a business park.

Embassies and consulates

Australia 3rd Fl, China Banking Bldg, Paseo de Roxas, Makati ☎ 874961
Austria 4th Fl, Prince Bldg, 117 Rada St, Legaspi Village, Makati ☎ 8179191
Belgium 6th Fl, Don Jacinto Bldg, corner of De la Rosa and Salcedo sts, Legaspi Village, Makati ☎ 876571
Canada 9th Fl, Allied Bank Center, Ayala Avenue, Makati ☎ 8159536
China 4896 Pasay Rd, Dasmarinas

Village, Makati ☎ 572585
Denmark 10th Fl, Citibank Center,
8741 Paseo de Roxas, Makati
☎ 856756
Finland 14th Fl, Bank of the
Philippine Islands Bldg, corner of
Ayala Ave and Paseo de Roxas,
Makati ☎ 8162105
France 3rd Fl, Filipinas Life Bldg,
Ayala Ave, Makati ☎ 876561
Greece 10th Fl, Doña Narcisa Bldg,
Paseo de Roxas, Makati ☎ 8162309
Indonesia Indonesian Embassy Bldg,
185 Salcedo St, Legaspi Village,
Makati ☎ 880301
Ireland 2nd Fl, 1123 Maria Orosa St,
Ermita ☎ 501816
Italy 6th Fl, ZETA II Bldg, 191
Salcedo St, Legaspi Village, Makati
☎ 874531
Japan 375 Senator Gil J. Puyat Ave,
Makati ☎ 8189011
Malaysia 107 Tordesillas St, Salcedo
Village, Makati ☎ 8174581
Netherlands 9th Fl, King's Court
Bldg, 2129 Pasong Tamo, Makati
☎ 887753
New Zealand Gammon Center, 3rd
Fl, 126 Alfaro St, Salcedo Village,
Makati ☎ 8180916
Norway 6th Fl, Atlantica Bldg,
corner of Herrera and Salcedo sts,
Legaspi Village, Makati ☎ 881111
Singapore 6th Fl, ODC International
Plaza, 217–219 Salcedo St, Legaspi
Village, Makati ☎ 8161764
South Korea 3rd Fl, ALPAP I Bldg,
140 Alfaro St, Salcedo Village,
Makati ☎ 8175705
Spain 5th Fl, ACT Towers, 135
Senator Gil J. Puyat Ave, Salcedo
Village, Makati ☎ 8183561
Sweden 15th Fl, Citibank Center
Bldg, 8741 Paseo de Roxas, Makati
☎ 858746
Switzerland 5th Fl, V. Esguerra Bldg,
140 Amorsolo St, Legaspi Village,
Makati ☎ 8190202
Thailand Thai Embassy Bldg, 107
Rada St, Legaspi Village, Makati
☎ 8154219
UK Electra House, 115–117 Esteban
St, Legaspi Village, Makati
☎ 891058
USA 1201 Roxas Blvd, Ermita

☎ 5217116
West Germany 5th Fl, Citibank
Center, 8741 Paseo de Roxas, Makati
☎ 864906

Emergencies
Hospitals The major hotels all have
medical and dental clinics. Despite
horror stories (sometimes true) of
counterfeit drugs and non-existent
hospital supplies, medical standards
in Manila are good, particularly in
hospitals run by religious orders,
which have Western-trained doctors.
Charges are reasonable by US
standards, and American Express is
generally accepted in payment. The
Makati Medical Center, 2 Amorsolo
St, Makati ☎ 8159911, is the best
equipped and has 24hr emergency
services. Private general practitioners
include *Dr Heinz R. Varwig*, Cibeles
Bldg, Avala Ave, Makati ☎ 8172632
and, for dental treatment, *Dr
Adoracion Torres-Chu*, Jardine Davies
Bldg, 222 Senator Gil J. Puyat Ave,
Makati ☎ 856011.
Pharmacies Hotel newsagents sell
some non-prescription drugs.
Mercury Drug, North Drive, Makati
Commercial Center and at Harrison
Plaza, Malate, is open daily 10–9 and
stocks most Western drug brands.
Police Police patrol the streets of
Manila on foot and can be found just
about anywhere. They can be
stopped and asked for assistance and
are generally friendly. The two
commonest crimes affecting visitors
to Manila are jewellery snatching and
pickpocketing, so take sensible
precautions at all times and never
leave valuables in your room – always
deposit them in the hotel safe.
Emergencies ☎ 599011 or the Public
Information Desk ☎ 702593. The
Department of Tourism has a hotline
for visitors lost or in distress:
☎ 501728 and ask for the Tourist
Assistance Unit.

Government offices
Department of Trade and Industry, 361
Senator Gil J. Puyat Ave, Makati
☎ 8185701; *Bureau of Customs*, Port

Area ☎ 484161; *Commission on Immigration and Deportation*, Magallenes Dr, Intramuros ☎ 407651.

Information sources
Local media It is possible to glean useful economic and political information from *Bulletin Today*, but more reliable are the *Asian Wall Street Journal* and international weekly magazines, available in all bookshops.
Tourist information The *Department of Tourism*, Agrifina Circle, Rizal Park ☎ 501703, provides information and tour reservations and publishes *What's On In Manila*, a weekly events listing, as well as an excellent free map of Manila.

Thank-yous
For one-stop shopping, *Rustan's Bon Appétit and Floral Shop* in Ayala Ave, Makati (open 10–9) has the most comprehensive stock of flowers, chocolates, wines, spirits and gift items in Manila. The *Cake Shop* at the Mandarin hotel, Makati Ave (open 10–7), is the best for hand-made, gift-wrapped chocolates and vintage wines. The hotel also has an excellent florist.

Planning and reference
Entry details
Documentation Only those who wish to stay longer than 21 days or who are residents of Hong Kong or Taiwan, or citizens of communist countries, need a visa.
Health precautions Anyone arriving from a yellow fever infected area must have a certificate of inoculation against that disease. All visitors are advised to be inoculated against cholera, typhoid and polio, and to take both maloprim and nivaquine (anti-malaria pills).
Driving licence An international driving licence and passport are required to rent a car, and drivers must be over 25 years of age.
Customs regulations All incoming passengers are asked to complete a baggage and currency declaration form, though you will not usually have to pay duty on personal effects in reasonable quantities, and visitors with normal amounts of baggage rarely have the contents examined. Anyone carrying more than US$3,000 or its equivalent must declare the amount on a separate form obtainable at the customs desk. The duty-free allowances are 400 cigarettes or 50 cigars or 8oz/250gm tobacco, plus 2 quarts/2 litres of wine or spirits.

Climate
The Philippines has only two seasons, distinguished from each other by the quantity of rain. The monsoon period is June to November, and visitors who do not intend to travel outside Manila can virtually disregard it. Monsoons bring heavy storms of several hours' duration, usually in the afternoons, accompanied by strong winds. Outside the capital the rains frequently result in landslides and flooding which make roads impassable, and flights are often delayed. Otherwise the temperature is a fairly consistent 85°F (30°C) by day and 72°F (22°C) by night with pleasant sea breezes in Manila and the south. In the mountainous north, the temperature is cold enough to make heating welcome even in summer and a warm sweater is a must.

A suit is only necessary for the best restaurants and top-level meetings. Normal business wear is practical; an open-necked shirt and smart lightweight trousers, and simple but modest dresses or shirt and blouse. Filipino men wear *barong tagalog*, embroidered shirts worn outside the trousers, even for formal occasions.

Holidays
Expatriates usually take extended leave in July and August so it may be difficult to make appointments with foreign firms during those months. Nov 1 (All Saints' Day) and Dec 31 have been declared "special"

holidays in the past but official national holidays are:

Jan 1   New Year
Late Mar/early Apr   Maundy Thursday and Good Friday
May 1   Labor Day
May 6   Araw Ng Kagitangan
Jun 12   Independence Day
Aug 30   National Heroes Day
Nov 30   Bonifacio Day
Dec 25   Christmas Day
Dec 30   Rizal Day

Money

Local currency In Filipino currency, one peso equals 100 centavos. Notes are issued in denominations of P100, 50, 20, 10, 5 and 2, and coins of P5, 2 and 1, plus 50, 25, 10, 5 and 1 centavos. This means there are no high-value notes, since the highest, P100, is equivalent to around US$5. So small change is not a problem but a bulging wallet may be. In Manila, US dollars are so widely accepted that it is scarcely worth changing more than a small amount into Filipino currency, and prices are often quoted in dollars rather than pesos. Outside Manila, dollars are accepted in tourist haunts only. Pesos are not supposed to be purchased outside the Philippines. Visitors may bring into the country any amount of foreign currency.

Credit and charge cards are accepted in all large hotels, stores and most restaurants in Manila and in tourist resorts. Beware the prevalence of credit-card fraud in the Philippines.

Changing money Banks, hotels and leading department stores all give virtually the same rate as do the official exchange brokers to be found in tourist districts such as Ermita. When changing traveller's cheques you may have to produce the original purchase agreement. Do not use any dealer not authorized by the Central Bank of the Philippines, however good the rate offered seems. Pickpockets and bag-snatchers congregate where these dealers operate.

Bank opening hours are Mon–Fri, 9–4. Nearly all banks exchange US dollars but for other currencies the bigger banks are best, including the United Coconut Planters Bank (Cocobank), the Savings Bank of Manila, the Manila Banking Corporation and the Philippines Commercial International Bank. Many overseas banks have offices in Manila, including Citibank, Bank of America, Standard Chartered and the Hongkong and Shanghai Banking Corporation. Outside Manila most banks will only change US dollars.

The leading hotels all have exchange desks which open from early to late and at weekends. Leading stores, such as Shoe Mart and Rustan's, all have exchange desks open during shop hours (10–8 daily).

Tipping Everyone in Manila expects a tip. For waiters, taxi drivers, hairdressers and in cocktail lounges, 10% is normal. Others who expect a tip of P10 are porters, parking valets, pool and cloakroom attendants and even hotel staff when delivering drinks or meals to your room.

Singapore

Singapore is a vigorous city-state at the maritime crossroads of Asia, the natural business centre of the South-East Asian archipelago. Important in the Middle Ages but abandoned in the 14th century, it had been called Temasek (sea town) by the Malays and Singapura (lion city) by Sumatran conquerors. When that far-sighted British empire-builder Sir Stamford Raffles first annexed it in 1819, its only inhabitants were a few Malay fishing families. Raffles recognized the worth of the sheltered, deep-water harbour, and Chinese and Indian workers were later brought in to hack the jungle back and develop a thriving free port.

Their descendants jumped at the opportunity to do business in the region's abundance of commodities – tin, rubber, spices and copper, to name only the leaders. Singapore's GDP per head is now the highest in Asia after Japan and tiny, oil-rich Brunei. This achievement, rare in tropical climes, stems largely from Chinese energies. The Singaporean Chinese are mostly third or fourth generation immigrants from China's southern coastal regions. They no longer feel political loyalty to China but confidently act out many features of the old South Chinese social tradition – the tightly knit family, a drive to achieve, a nose for business. Although people of Chinese origin are prominent in all South-East Asian countries, mainly in business and the professions, only in Singapore do they form a majority – 76% of the republic's population. They operate the modern Western institutions bequeathed by British colonialism on the basis of Confucian paternalism.

One man stands out. After almost 30 consecutive years as prime minister, Lee Kuan Yew is probably Asia's best-known statesman, renowned for plain speaking, tough administration and a keen common-sense perception of the national interests of the republic whose independence he proclaimed in 1965. He claims to be a socialist. But socialism has little scope in an entrepôt port so dependent on external transactions that the value of foreign trade is three times the GDP. The government has deliberately and efficiently encouraged private enterprise, both local and foreign, while retaining a firm hand – often to the irritation of business people – on overall economic strategy.

Under Lee and his shrewd former colleague, Goh Keng Swee (one-time finance minister and architect of the Jurong industrial township), Singapore has industrialized and maintained average economic growth of 9% a year in the two decades 1968–85, one of the best performances in the world. Singapore's fortunes still hang, however, on those of its region. When world commodity prices slump, demand for the republic's manufactures and services falls away. The authorities had not anticipated the mid-1980s' recession and were shocked by a reverse to economic growth in 1985. Their reaction was to liberalize further and develop the financial markets, restrain wages and extend privatization – all of which augur well for the future business climate.

The political scene

Singapore's parliamentary democracy and legal system are based on the British model, though voting is compulsory. The People's Action Party (PAP) has ruled unchallenged and openly resents opposition members (only one of whom was elected in the September 1988 elections). In the 1984 election the PAP's share of the popular vote fell from 76% to 63%, but stayed steady at 62% in the 1988 elections.

One-party stability

The country benefits from the advantages of one-party continuity and stability, while also enjoying considerable civil freedom. Interference with the media is, however, a part of life.

No extreme left The PAP came to power in the late 1950s on the backs of the Communists, whom Lee then successfully fought off and banned. The extreme left is thus hardly represented in Singapore politics.

One man dominates Lee Kuan Yew is a Cambridge double-first of uncanny ability who has been prime minister since 1959. He used to say he would retire at 65, which would have been in September 1988, but the economic recession of the mid 1980's prompted second thoughts. He now plans to go by the end of 1990 but will retain some influence, staying in the cabinet as a senior minister. Reluctance to relinquish power may get the better of him, however, and his departure may be postponed once again.

Successors Goh Chok Tong, the first deputy prime minister, born in 1941, is the most likely immediate successor, but a relative newcomer who is a strong contender for the top eventually is Lee's own son, Brigadier-General Lee Hsien Loong. The "BG," born in 1952, is another brilliant academic with a distinguished military career behind him and is Minister of Trade and Industry.

The civil service Many leaders came to politics from the civil service, and there is a close collaboration between the two sets of power-wielders. The Finance Ministry is the senior government department and supplies executives to all kinds of enterprises in the public sector. The judiciary is independent, but generally supportive of the government (there is still a final appeal to the Privy Council in London). It is in the civil service and judiciary that Singaporean Indians shine, though they constitute only 6% of the population.

Defence and foreign relations

The armed forces – comprising some 55,000 personnel (two-thirds conscript) – have been built up since the 1960s to an impressive level of training and equipment. Under the Five-Power Defence Arrangement, Britain, Australia and New Zealand, as well as Malaysia, are involved in the republic's defence preparedness. Lee Kuan Yew repeatedly lobbies for a stronger Western (especially US) military presence in the region as a discouragement to Communist influence.

Singapore's major international alignment is with ASEAN, of which it was a founder member. The Singapore government tries to push ASEAN collaboration into constructive economic channels, especially by lowering tariffs, but the other countries, realizing they are uncompetitive, are less keen.

After 20 years Singapore is sufficiently confident to take foreign policy initiatives. It has vigorously opposed the Vietnamese intervention in Kampuchea, for example, and even risked hosting an official visit by a president of Israel (to which it is quite close), despite angry protests from its two Muslim neighbours.

The economic scene

In parallel with its authoritarian management of the political system, and despite its laissez-faire image, the government is highly interventionist in the running of the economy. At the macro and micro levels, policies for industrial development have been imposed, with the support of some 80 statutory bodies, while the state is involved in more than 450 companies.

Human resources

At just over 2.6m, Singapore's population is comparable with Jamaica's and only half of Hong Kong's. It is an overwhelmingly urban body of people enjoying a relatively good standard of living. Population growth is about 1% a year.

A young citizenry It is also a young population, with 33% under 20 years old, and only 26% over 40 years of age. Average life expectancy is 71 years. The crude death rate and birth rate per 1,000 population in 1986 were 5 and 15.2 respectively.

Educated workforce The literacy rate is 85%, and the average level of education high, particularly among the young. Of the 2.6m population at mid-1986, some 1.1m were in employment. The labour force is expanding faster than the population itself, and more women, in particular, are taking jobs. The unemployment rate went over 6% during 1986, but began 1987 at 4.5%. Over 30% of the workforce have secondary school qualifications and 17% higher qualifications.

Wages Average earnings maintained growth of 10% or more in the early 1980s, but only 3% in 1985 and less than 1% in 1986. Unit labour costs in manufacturing fell by 17% in 1986 (resuming their 1982 level) but were still in 1986 higher than in Taiwan, South Korea and Hong Kong.

Almost strike free There had been no strikes for eight years until one at a US oil equipment plant in 1986.

No natural resources

Singapore has virtually no agriculture. Food, like everything else, is imported. The only important exceptions are eggs and pork (though pig farming is soon to cease), plus a small quantity of vegetables and fish. Singapore also lacks all energy resources, minerals and forests. Even marine resources are restricted by the contiguity with Malaysia and Indonesia. Singapore's only resources, as its leaders never tire of reiterating, are the wit, industry and invention of its people.

Strong infrastructure

The port, airport, roads, housing, hotels, telecommunications and services are the best in the region.

Large seaport Singapore is one of the largest seaports in the world, clearing vessels with a total net registered tonnage of 200m tonnes/220.5m US tons in 1986. The seaborne cargo handled was 113m freight tonnes, a large proportion of it being mineral oil in bulk.

Transport Neptune Orient Lines, the Singapore flag-carrier, runs containerized liner services to Europe, America and Australia, and Singapore Airlines, also the national carrier, flies worldwide. The glossy international airport at Changi opened in 1981 and will be able to handle 17m passengers a year when its second phase is completed in 1989. Aircraft landing totalled 36,500 in 1986, and tourist arrivals were 3.2m in that year.

External trade is the key

Singapore's foreign trade totalled US$45bn in 1986, almost as big as that of China, South Korea or Hong Kong, level with Taiwan's, and considerably larger than that of any other Asian country, including India and Indonesia. Of the US$21.3bn exports, roughly two-thirds was domestic and one-third re-export following the old entrepôt pattern envisaged by Raffles. Singapore remains an ideal place to offload bulk cargo from ocean ships and to break it into smaller lots, to be delivered by coastal or inland transport throughout South-East Asia.

Main exports The largest domestic export used to be petroleum products, but in 1986 oil was overtaken by machinery and transport equipment, including radios and TV sets. Overseas sales of Singapore-made garments are increasing, while another traditional export industry, veneer and plywood, is suffering from the competition of the countries where the trees grow.

Re-exports are a mixed bag of regional goods to Europe and Western equipment to neighbouring countries.

Best export markets The USA, Malaysia and Japan take some 58% of Singapore's total exports. The USA is the biggest market, taking 23% in 1986. Second came Malaysia, and third the EC. TV sets and garments are the major attractions for the USA and EC. Exports to Japan declined in value in 1986 because of lower oil prices and of petroleum products.

Sources of imports The same areas constitute the major suppliers of Singapore's imports: Japan held a 20% market share in 1986, the USA 15%, Malaysia 13%, the EC 12% and China 6%.

Main imports are food, mineral fuels, machinery and equipment, and manufactured goods.

Balance of payments

The overall balance of payments weakened in 1985 and 1986 with the outflow of funds through the banking system reflecting excess domestic liquidity. The current account had steadily improved during the 1980s, crossing into surplus in 1986, and official foreign reserves at the end of

1986 totalled S$28bn (almost US$13bn), enough to finance nine months' retained imports. Foreign indebtedness at US$176m represents less than 1% of GNP.

Services surplus The merchandise trade deficit of S$5.1bn in 1986 was more than offset by a services surplus of S$6.5bn to make a current account surplus, after a small net outflow of transfer payments, of S$1bn. But the capital account showed a S$2.7bn deficit.

A strong currency

The Singapore dollar, fully backed by gold and foreign assets, has floated freely since 1973. It lost ground to the US dollar and yen in the second half of the 1980s, while appreciating over the Malaysian and Indonesian currencies. Consumer price inflation was -1.4% in 1986.

The budget

Public sector spending in 1986 totalled S$17bn, revenue S$18.8bn. Just over a quarter of government revenues came from income tax, and just over a third from excise and import duties, property and motor vehicle taxes and stamp duty. Of the S$12.6bn spent by government in 1986, half went on current items, including government salaries. Another quarter went on development expenditure. The budget for the fiscal year 1987–88 was a tight one, anticipating a drop in tax revenue.

Savings and GDP Savings exceed S$60bn a year, over 40% of GDP, a proportion surpassed only by Japan. Trade used to be the largest contributor to the GDP in the 1950s, accounting for more than one-third, but that has now been cut in half. The contributions of manufacturing and of financial and business services have each doubled to take up the strain. In 1985 the shares were 22% for manufacturing, 21% financial and business services, 18% trade, 14% transport and communications, and 25% from other sources.

No formal planning

Singapore's leaders think far into the future, but knowing how little they can control the external environment on which the republic depends, they place flexibility and quickness of response above rigid and doctrinaire planning. There is nevertheless a strong overriding ambition to become a centre of economic, industrial and intellectual excellence, the "brain centre" of South-East Asia.

Incentives and pressures Planning takes the shape of incentives and pressures on entrepreneurs. Singapore has the best of both worlds, enjoying an intrinsic freedom of enterprise while having some risks underwritten by the government.

Industrial expansion

Singapore now boasts about 3,500 factories employing 265,000 men and women to produce S$40bn worth of goods (60% of them for export), and with value-added estimated at more than S$10bn.

Changing structure The composition of Singapore's key manufacturing industry has changed rapidly since 1980 with government-initiated economic restructuring. Labour-intensive enterprises have been phased out, with a corresponding flow of new investments into electronics and other high-tech industries.

Electronics is the largest single employer, with more than 60,000 workers in 230 companies producing microchips and complex printed computer circuit boards, etc. More than 160 foreign manufacturers have invested in the electrical and electronics industry in Singapore.

Oil centre The republic is the third largest oil-refining centre in the world after Rotterdam and Houston. Crude oil throughput declined in the early 1980s but picked up in 1986 to an average of 0.74m barrels a day (77% of refinery capacity). Some 44m tonnes/48.5m US tons of oil were imported in 1986, of which only 10% was for domestic consumption.

The petroleum industry is still of enormous international importance but faces a thinner future as traditional overseas customers install more of their own refining capacity and Middle-East competition rises.

Chemicals have begun to take off, though they still account for only 5% of total industrial output. After protracted efforts by the government, a new petrochemical complex has started to supply the smaller pharmaceutical and specialized chemical plants in which well over 60 well-known brand names from Europe, the USA and Japan have invested.

Transport equipment With four large shipyards, Singapore ranks among the major transport equipment makers in East Asia, but with fewer orders these have had to cut dry-dock utilization and concentrate on smaller specialized craft. The aircraft-components industry is worth S$765m a year. There is also a fledgling car-parts industry.

Garments and printing The garment industry is prospering, especially in the European and US markets, and local designs are now being promoted aggressively. Another industry of which high hopes are held is printing and publishing. Books can be printed and published in Singapore faster than almost anywhere in the world, and with high standards of both English language and technical production. More and more international journals and newspapers are printing, publishing and distributing in Singapore for the East Asian region.

Tourism Singapore has enjoyed a tourist boom in recent years and tourism represents some 6% of GDP. The number of hotel rooms was expected to have increased from 14,500 in 1983 to 27,000 by 1988.

Consumer products The food, beverage and tobacco industry is another stalwart, though cigarette manufacturers are threatened by the vigorous anti-smoking campaign.

The business climate

Singapore is one of the most open free market economies in the world and is run like a successful business corporation. Many multinationals have set up their regional headquarters in the republic, serviced by over 130 banks. The government's open door policy has attracted leading manufacturers from around the world. It remains the most favoured investment location in ASEAN.

Stability and spark

With the same government and the same man (Lee Kuan Yew) in power since independence, Singapore is a regional oasis of political, economic and social stability. Lee's administration has created an environment in which business can grow. Clear-sighted, no-nonsense policies based on a comprehensive package of incentives have kept the industrial base expanding and maturing. The government intends to retain Singapore's position as a key service centre for its immediate neighbours, while competing with the other newly industrialized economies in Asia for world markets.

Survival of the fittest Singapore's migrant population is only a generation away from that first challenge of survival. So is the republic, which came out of Malaysia empty handed – separated like Siamese twins by political surgery. Allegedly the weaker twin, Singapore made a virtue of necessity. This bred a government responsive to change, willing and quick to adapt to new realities. Always quick off the mark, it was, for instance, the first port in ASEAN to use containerization. It has similarly favoured a liberal, unfettered business climate.

The confidence factor Among foreign investors, Singapore carries the legend which sustains a high level of investor confidence. Its strategic location and access to the US market (aided until January 1989 by its General System of Preference status) has attracted increasing numbers of Japanese companies, refugees from the heady ascent of the yen.

The public sector

The state sector is very active in the economy, but eschews monopolies. Only public utilities and telecommunications, because of their strategic importance, have been totally reserved for the state (and they are now potential candidates for privatization). Seven major utilities account for 46% of GDP and exert a strong influence on government and business.

Standards of excellence The Public Utilities Board (PUB), the Port of Singapore Authority (PSA) and the telecommunications authority are models of efficiency. Brown-outs are rare and Singapore has some of the most sophisticated (and cheap) telecommunications facilities in the world. It is also an acknowledged leader in the field of information technology. Singapore Airlines became a byword for excellence in the aviation business, and has now been part-privatized.

The state as pace-setter The government prefers the pace-setting role in economic development. In order to promote strategic areas such as shipbuilding and repair, electronics and petrochemicals, it casts its lot with the multinationals, via joint ventures in which it is content with a minority shareholding in exchange for technology and know-how.

Jurong has been developed as a new heavy and light industry town on reclaimed land, and is now the island's industrial heart. The port is directly involved in the petroleum industry through the Singapore Petroleum Corporation (SPC) and has a 40% share in the Singapore Refining Company (SRC), a joint venture with Caltex and BP. A joint venture with the Japanese introduced petrochemicals to complement the island's huge refining capability.

Certain high technology ventures come under the Singapore Technology Corporation. These are wholly owned government operations, but they enlist foreign help by means of technical service agreements.

Selling Singapore The government runs its own international promotion agencies and is aggressive in backing its trade and industry. Intraco is the government body for promoting international trade.

The private sector

Singapore is historically a commercial community where British-style agency houses and Chinese mercantile ventures grew up with the entrepôt trade; Chinese family businesses were built up via a network of kinship and clan connections. The ones that flourished best grew into the great merchant dynasties. Lee Rubber was once the single largest fortune in Asia. This healthy trading activity still thrives, although submerged somewhat today with the onset of modern developments. The local Chinese sector in particular pursues its business in its own self-contained way outside the mainstream of the republic's industrial progress, but drawing ancillary benefits from it and burgeoning with Singapore's growing prosperity.

Increasingly upmarket The new direction is towards more and more sophistication. Investors have recently poured money into pharmaceuticals manufacture, petroleum processing and the making of computer peripherals. The labour-intensive, low-technology, cheap-labour sweatshop approach of Thailand or Indonesia has been abandoned. Many of Singapore's low-tech factories are relocating to

the other side of the causeway (in Malaysia), in favour of high-tech knowledge-based industries.

Privatization The next phase of Singpapore's development will be a robust privatization policy to help create more of an enterprise society. Government is keen to invest in high-technology ventures, and wishes to divest in other sectors.

A Private Sector Divestment Committee was set up in February 1986 which, with typical thoroughness, will mastermind the orderly disposal over a 10-year period of government interests in private companies. A total of 99 were looked at and it was recommended that 41 enterprises should be fully privatized. Partial privatization is also planned for Telecoms, the Public Utilities Board, the Port of Singapore Authority and the Civil Aviation Authority. This programme is expected to generate S$380m annually. The process of privatization began successfully with the partial disposal of Singapore Airlines (SIA).

The missing dimension is that, so far, Singapore has failed to create its own multinationals. Few of its companies are truly international, with the qualified exception of the banks, which have to have overseas operations in any case, and the very successful SIA. However, Singapore Press Holdings, which is the second biggest industrial company and owns all the major newspapers – English-language, Chinese and Malay – together with the British publishing subsidiary Marshall Cavendish, is striving to use its press and satellite printing operations as a springboard to international prominence in information technology.

Foreign investment

Foreign investment plays a crucial role in Singapore's manufacturing industry, with S$12bn cumulative gross fixed assets by the end of 1984 and an average of S$1bn more in 1985 and 1986. A third of this came from Europe, and another third from the USA. Among the European countries the UK and the Netherlands lead.

The largest recipient of this investment has been the oil refineries, which account for about 30% of the total. Next in importance is the electric and electronic industry, with a cumulative total of S$2.7bn, followed by chemicals and plastics with S$1.6bn. According to Singapore's Economic Development Board, outstanding investment commitments at mid-1986 were for S$1.1bn in 215 projects. Just over 20% of this amount came from local investors, the remaining 80% from overseas, with the Americans and Japanese taking a larger share than before – more than the Europeans.

Regional centre

International firms continue to find Singapore an attractive regional market centre and distribution base. Support industries supplying precision tools, component parts and assembly have prompted multinationals to set up their international procurement operations in Singapore to obtain competitive parts and materials for manufacturing plants around the world. The government is very keen to encourage multinational corporations to set up their regional headquarters in the republic. The right attributes are all there – political stability, industrial peace, good workers, superb air and sea transport, cheap and efficient telecommunications. The logic is also there for Singapore: it is harder to close down an HQ than subsidiaries.

Power in business

Foreign presence Of the long-established businesses, the doyen is Shell, the largest single manufacturer. Other oil companies include Esso, BP, Caltex and Mobil. The longer the company has been established, the more likely it is to be British. The legacy of empire, besides Anglo-Dutch Shell, includes ICI,

Metal Box, Beecham, Singapore Tobacco Co (BAT), Rothmans, Dunlop, Guinness and Glaxo. Later arrivals show a global spread: Nestlé, Siemens, Electrolux, Diethelm, Sperry, Berger Paints, Yardley, Du Pont, Bayer, Liptons, Reckitt & Colman, John Lysacht, Tetrapak, Brown Boveri, Olivetti, Philips, Nixdorf and Union Carbide. The offshore oil business attracts all the big names, as does the electronics sector. The Japanese are there in force, including Mitsubishi, Mitsui, Sumitomo, Matsushita, Sanyo, Hitachi, Fujitsu, NEC, Toshiba and Yamaha. Printing is represented by Heinemann, Longmans, McGraw Hill, Time Inc. and Dow Jones Publishers.

Banking was historically dominated by Standard Chartered Bank and the Hongkong and Shanghai Banking Corporation, but now there are dozens of banks including all the leading US ones.

Old Chinese families The archetypal Chinese *towkay* is a dying breed – Tan Chin Tuan, former head of Overseas Chinese Banking Corporation (OCBC), typifies the genre. Old money in Singapore belongs to the old Chinese families, especially the merchant dynasties. In today's economy, they are being replaced by the new breed of technocrat. Yong Pung How, lawyer turned businessman, who replaced Tan Chin Tuan at OCBC, is a case in point. The largest trading company is Straits Trading, now owned by OCBC.

Political connections In Singapore's tightly controlled regime, the most influential individuals are usually those who have political connections. Because of the small recruitment base, talented individuals appear and reappear as heads of the various private sector bastions of the economy. J.Y. Pillai is one example – chairman of Singapore Airlines (SIA), managing director of the Monetary Authority of Singapore (central bank), and permanent secretary at the Ministry of Trade and Industry. Michael Fam, chairman of Fraser & Neave (the leading brewer) and of the Mass Rapid Transit System, and on the board of Singapore Press Holdings, is another.

Private sector talent is quickly identified and mopped up by the government. Dr Richard Hu, ex-chairman of Shell, is now Minister of Finance. Other Shell alumni include Loo Siew Poh, who used to head Haw Par, and Johnny Chin, chief executive of Intraco. In the reverse process former civil servants are asked to head government-linked enterprises. Sim Kee Boon, formerly at the Economic Development Board (EDB), is now chairman of Keppel Shipyards and Straits Steamship.

The local banking fraternity is a traditional Chinese preserve still dominated by the old-style *towkays* – Wee Cho Yaw and Richard Eu are good examples. Eu has also for many years presided over the Singapore Institute of Management.

Influential expatriates include Charles Letts, doyen of the British community who still serves on many of the republic's boards. Charles Tresyse, J.D. Neil, former managing director of Fraser & Neave, and Roderick Maclean who for many years directed the Singapore Chamber of Commerce, fall into a special category of expatriates who have "stayed on" and who still play an advisory role.

Some individuals in this small government-dominated society have a high visibility and a corresponding level of influence in business, especially where politics and business overlap. Dr Goh Keng Swee, former deputy prime minister and the architect of Singapore's economic advance, is now officially retired but much in demand in a very high level advisory capacity, including an economic consultancy role with China. Ong Teng Cheong, one of the two deputy prime ministers, also heads the National Trade Union Congress. Brigadier Lee, son of Prime

Minister Lee Kuan Yew and Minister of Trade and Industry, has supported his political rise on economic management of Singapore's affairs; he chaired the Economic Committee which collaborated with the private sector to tackle the recession. Academics in this determinedly cerebral administration wield influence beyond the campus. Professor Lim Pin is vice-chancellor of the National University. A former dean of the Law Faculty, Tommy Koh, is permanent representative to the UN. A former journalist, Wee Kim Wee, has become President of Singapore. The former president, Devan Nair, who has a strong trade union background, is now one of the most forthright and courageous critics of the government. Other *enfants terribles* who dare to question the establishment include Francis Seow, former solicitor general, and J.B. Jeyaretnam, the most effectual of the two opposition members of parliament until barred from the House in late 1986.

Labour unions

Minimum terms and conditions of employment are regulated by the Employment Act and additional terms and conditions of service are negotiated between unions and management and embodied in collective agreements certified by the Industrial Arbitration Court. Annual wage adjustments follow guidelines recommended by a tripartite National Wages Council, representing government, management and unions.

Central Provident Fund
Employers contribute to a compulsory Central Provident Fund (CPF) which provides an employee with his own fully-funded pension. To reduce operating costs, the employer's rate of contribution was reduced to 10% from 25% of a worker's pay in 1986. It is expected that the contribution will be increased – although not to 25% – as the economy improves.

The business framework

Singapore offers a straightforward business environment with minimum controls. A paternalistic government is determined that not a whiff of the corruption that seems endemic in some of the other Asian countries should be allowed to spoil the republic's squeaky clean image. They have largely been successful. This sets the pace for an unparalleled efficiency and honesty in the bureaucracy.

Registration

Persons wishing to carry on business in Singapore must seek registration under one or other of the two acts that regulate commercial activity: the Business Registration Act or the Companies Act, both administered by the Registrar of Companies and Businesses. The legal system is based on English law. For a fee of S$5 per request, members of the public can obtain the file of any company on microfilm from the Registry of Companies. An instant information service on businesses is available over the counter and through Telecoms' Telepac service.

Freedom of operation

There are few restrictions on the types of businesses that may be set up. Banks, finance companies, insurance and stockbroking firms require a licence from the Monetary Authority of Singapore (MAS), as do manufacturers of certain categories of goods, such as cigarettes and furniture, under the terms of Manufacturers' Act.

Foreign ownership There is no firm rule about local participation, nor even pressure for it; 100% foreign equity is the norm.

Forms of business

Business may be conducted through sole proprietorship, partnerships (up to 20 persons), or public or private limited companies. Most foreign firms decide to incorporate wholly owned subsidiaries. The alternative is to register a branch of the overseas parent. There seems little merit in this. Local corporate tax is the same for both (33%), but, in the home country, profits from a Singapore subsidiary are often not taxed unless remitted as dividends. If, moreover, the foreign firm seeks pioneer status or other investment incentives, then it is obliged to incorporate in Singapore. Joint ventures are of course another vehicle. And, because Singapore is the established regional centre, many firms choose it for their area representative office.

A limited company must have "Berhad" or "Limited" at the end of the name – "Sendirian Berhad" in the case of a private limited company. The formation of the company will incur legal fees and printing costs of about S$2,500. Additionally, a capital registration fee is payable, based on the company's authorized capital; the maximum fee is about S$35,000. The Stock Exchange of Singapore (SES) issues a listing manual for companies wishing to go public. They need a five-year earnings history and a minimum paid-up capital of S$3m. Every company must have at least two directors who are nationals. The company secretary must also be a national.

A branch is required to have two agents, both resident in Singapore and responsible for meeting all statutory requirements under the Companies Act.

A representative office must have approval from the Singapore Trade Development Board. It is permitted to promote the foreign company's trade with the republic, but is expressly prohibited from carrying on business with Singapore. It cannot invoice clients in Singapore.

A joint venture is most often a partnership formed for a specific operation. In general, the partners are subject to unlimited liability in respect of debts.

A sole proprietor, if a foreigner, must appoint a national or a permanent resident as his manager.

Incentives

Singapore offers an impressive array of incentives (many of which have been consolidated into the Economic Incentives Act) to encourage firms to locate in the city state. Firms targeted by the Economic Development Board (EDB) are made offers they find hard to refuse. Investment incentives are used to shape the pace and direction of Singapore's industrial development, providing new investments in priority areas. The government is careful at the same time not to overlook existing companies, propelling them where possible towards automation.

Tax incentives The EDB administers the award of tax incentives. The main one is the 5–10 year tax holiday granted to pioneer industries approved by the Ministry of Finance. Longer periods of pioneer status go to companies with an R&D component to their operations. Existing companies can qualify for a parallel tax holiday under an expansion incentive scheme: S$10m spent on new production equipment and machinery for manufacturing merits up to five years' relief. Other concessions are made for new fixed investment, establishing or improving warehouse facilities, providing technical and engineering services or international consultancy. In addition, relief is given on interest on foreign loans for the purchase of production equipment, and on approved royalties and other fees to nonresidents abroad. To encourage pioneer companies to continue their operations in Singapore, corporate tax as low as 10% is levied in the post-pioneer phase for up to five years.

Operational headquarters
Multinationals that set up operational headquarters in Singapore will be taxed at a concessionary rate of 10% for up to 10 years on domestic income; this may be extended, in approved cases, to foreign-source income. A 10-year exemption or pass-through provision also applies to dividend income. In order to qualify, total business spending must not be less than S$2m annually and firms must demonstrate – among other things – effective management control from Singapore. The government is not disposed to accept mailbox type operations.

R&D activities attract a double deduction of expenditure for an initial five years maximum. Companies may also set aside 20% of taxable income as an R&D reserve; this must be spent within three years.

Offshore services Export incentives under the Economic Expansion Incentives Act, previously applicable only to manufacturing, have been extended to services such as consultancy management, construction, technical and engineering services if undertaken for offshore projects.

Export expansion schemes are administered by the Trade Development Board. Companies which produce a minimum of S$10m worth per year of qualifying manufactured goods or Singapore domestic produce for export may be designated an approved "international trading company" with entitlements to tax concessions.

Various other schemes are aimed at promoting exports – for example, double tax deduction for trade fairs and trade missions, overseas trade offices and promotional publications.

Market development assistance This is a scheme to match dollar for dollar eligible expenditure up to S$10,000 per company per year.

Counter trade is encouraged. Approved pioneer companies enjoy full tax exemption on profits from this type of activity.

Key industries In a bid to establish

more high-technology initiatives, key industries have been singled out for investment promotion in such areas as advanced electronics and wafer fabrication.

Expatriate employment
The authorities adopt a very liberal attitude to expatriate employment at managerial levels. There is normally little difficulty in obtaining employment passes for senior executives of large foreign or multinational organizations, well-qualified specialists, regional representatives or personnel needed to start up new ventures. Passes issued by the Immigration Department are normally for one to three years, renewable. Professional-visit passes are issued to those permitted to work in Singapore on specific assignments.

Taxation
The principal tax in Singapore is income tax. There is no capital gains tax, gift tax or wealth tax.
Nonresidents An individual present or employed in Singapore for 183 days or more in a calendar year is treated as a resident for income-tax purposes. Income derived from sources outside Singapore is taxable only if received in Singapore. Income accrued or derived in Singapore is taxable whether or not the individual is resident.
Personal income tax is charged on a sliding scale from 3.5% to a maximum of 33%.
Corporate tax Companies are currently taxed at a flat rate of 33% on income after deductible expenses, depreciation allowances, trading losses, and donations to approved charities.
Property tax A flat 23% tax is levied on property computed on annual rental value. A 50% rebate is given on property tax for industrial and commercial properties. There is exemption for land under development.
Double taxation Singapore has tax treaties with most of the OECD countries and is negotiating the same with the USA.
Repatriation of funds There is free repatriation of profits and dividends. Indeed, no exchange control approval is needed for any payment, remittance or capital transfer in any currency.

Market entry
Singapore has a very small domestic market. It should be viewed therefore as a sophisticated industrial base and a services centre for the region. The republic, while sceptical of the ASEAN common market concept, acknowledges that its own growth is linked to the development of its neighbours and therefore encourages trade with them. Foreign firms will find most areas of business open to them; the exceptions are certain retail activities, thoroughly sewn up by the Chinese, and public utilities.

Importing and exporting
Most imports are duty free. There are some 2,200 items in the trading classification of which fewer than 200 attract import duty. These include liquor, tobacco and petroleum products; consumer products such as clothing, cars, electrical appliances and non-essential foodstuffs. A preferential rate of duty applies to goods consigned direct from ASEAN countries.
Import licensing Most goods are free of quota restrictions and can be imported without a licence. Import licences are required for goods originating or consigned from Albania, East Germany, Vietnam, Laos and Mongolia. They are also needed for certain products from

Japan, such as textiles, or to import rice and refined sugar. Imports from South Africa are prohibited.

Export controls There are no export duties on goods from Singapore. Quantitative restrictions are imposed on textiles and garments exported to Canada, Austria, Finland, the EC, Norway, Sweden and the USA. Other items, such as used vehicles, rubber, timber, are subject to export controls. Export licences are required for granite and sand.

Documentation Imports and exports require only two documents per consignment and they are usually cleared within two hours. Even this can be reduced for urgent shipments. Customs documentation and formalities are straightforward. Goods in transit require neither licences nor customs clearance and leave port within a day of discharge.

Free trade zones Singapore has six free trade zones, five for seaborne cargo and one for air cargo. These provide facilities for the storage and re-export of dutiable and controlled goods: free 72 hours storage for import/export of conventional cargo and containerized import cargo; 28-day storage for transshipment/re-export cargo; and seven-day storage for containerized export cargo.

Setting up

It is simple and easy to set up shop in Singapore. The government and its officers are pragmatic in their dealings, efficient and honest, and they recognize the need for flexibility. There are few formalities and few restrictions – no price controls, no local content requirement. Facilitating payments and other inducements are not required to smooth the way, as elsewhere. There is a wide selection of modern office accommodation in Singapore and a comprehensive range of factory buildings at the Jurong Industrial Estates and other industrial parks. There are no restrictions on foreign ownership of industrial or commercial property.

Distribution

It is probably better to use local people for sales and marketing, and there are many distributors who will provide coverage of Indonesia and Malaysia as well. The traditional enterprises fall into two distinct categories, both with regional connections – the European trading firms, such as Boustead and Sime Darby, whose commercial territory spreads beyond Singapore, and the Chinese merchants plugged into the overseas Chinese network region-wide. They are mainly small businesses, often still the original family concern.

For international firms trading in the region, Singapore is the natural distribution centre for machinery and capital goods. There are convenient feeder services to Indonesia, Malyasia and other destinations. With the rising costs of holding stocks in different places and as materials need to become more sophisticated, Singapore is becoming the warehouse of the region – a useful buffer stock, service and spare-parts centre.

Port facilities Singapore is one of the busiest seaports in the world. Working around the clock seven days a week, its cargo-handling services can cope with all types of vessel and cargo. The Port of Singapore Authority (PSA) houses the largest warehousing complex in the region with a fully computerized facility for high-value cargo and bulk space for general cargo. As the world's third largest oil-refining and distribution centre, it is a natural bunkering station.

Air transport Singapore has also become a major air hub, promoting direct trade and travel lines around the globe. Changi Airport's present freight handling capacity is around 480,000 tonnes/529,200 US tons.

Cargo is cleared with minimal customs and other formalities. It is usually delivered to consignees within a day. Urgent shipments can be cleared within four hours. Sea-air cargo for high-value, time-sensitive exports is a new area of specialization.

Road transport Most of
Singapore's roads are asphalted. Five
expressways criss-cross the island.

Rapid transport Construction of
the S$5bn Mass Rapid Transport
system, the largest single project
undertaken in Singapore, began in
1983. Phase One, covering 28km/18
miles, opened for passenger travel in
late 1987, and the entire network of
66km/41 miles and comprising 41
stations should be running in the
early 1990s.

Commercial transport, especially
trucking, is in the hands of the
Chinese who provide a cheap, reliable
service, available at all hours.

Advertising and PR

The creative world is the most
sophisticated in the region. Leading
agencies such as Ogilvy & Mather
and McCann Erickson have offices in
the republic, headed nowadays by
smart Singaporeans. There are few
restrictions except a total ban on
cigarette advertising. An inherent
puritanism stemming from the
leadership tends to restrain the more
explicit sex themes that appear in the
West. The result can be advertising
that is earnest but dull. The populace
is bilingual, even trilingual, so most
advertisements are carried in Chinese
(Mandarin), Malay and English.

Public relations is a growth
profession. Agencies tend to be
smaller, but many have international
back-up provided by firms such as
Burson-Marsteller and Hill and
Knowlton. Other names well-known
only in the Singapore context include
Richard Gibson and Eric Jennings.

Dealing with the Chinese

The Chinese dominate retail and
distribution trades, the small business
sector and much of the support
structure such as the supply of
construction workers. They have
their own, usually traditional ways –
the Pak Choy system, for example,
dictating the use of gangs of workers
on contract, paid by a very Chinese
version of profit sharing. There are
complex networks of contractors, and
sub-contractors. Nepotism is rife.

The language of commerce at this
grassroots level is invariably the
Chinese dialects. It is a sector
foreigners find difficult to penetrate.
The Chinese are expert bargainers
and you have to be tough to get the
better of them. Once a deal is struck
the Chinese contractor will be true to
his word; he will work hard and,
usually, will deliver on time. Most
local enterprises are shoestring
operations, under-capitalized and
short term, but they manage to
succeed on a formula of hard work
and thrift.

Patents, trademarks and copyrights

There is no provision for the original
granting of patents in Singapore.
Only those registered in the UK are
safeguarded. Once sealed there,
application can be made to the
Singapore Registry of Trademarks
and Patents for registration within
three years. Registered patents are
valid for 16 years.

Trademarks are protected under
the Trademarks Act. Those already
registered in the UK enjoy priority.
Initial registration is for seven years,
and this can be renewed for a further
fourteen.

The Merchandise Marks Act
makes provision against the false
application of trademarks and the
false use of trade descriptions.

Copyrights After considerable
pressure from the USA and other
countries, Singapore implemented a
comprehensive Copyright Act in
1987. This provides owners with a
mechanism to protect their interests
with adequate remedies in law, but it
is still up to them to police the
situation. Owners can seek out an
injunction to stop infringement or
can ask the Trade Development
Board to place restrictions on the
importation of the infringing
articles.

The financial scene

Singapore has long aimed at becoming an international financial centre. It first signalled these ambitions in 1968 by making the tax concessions that permitted the Asian dollar market to be established in the island-state. Once envisaged as the region's equivalent of London's Eurodollar sector, the size and structure of this market have changed over time, restricting Singapore's role in it. The republic has nonetheless continued to be an innovator, especially in the areas of financial futures and the broking of foreign stocks.

Central banking

The operations of all Singapore's banking institutions are very closely monitored by the Monetary Authority of Singapore (MAS), which fulfils most of the classic functions of a central bank except that of bank note issuance (which is handled by the Board of the Commissioners of the Currency). The MAS takes the task of maintaining monetary stability seriously and has acted over the years to prevent the internationalization of the country's currency. It uses sparingly its powers to change the reserve and liquidity ratios required of banks and in 1986 gained increasing flexibility in the use of open-market operations in government debt to control money supply, when it began large-scale auctions of such paper for the first time.

Domestic banking

Singapore has 13 local banks but the Big Four – DBS Bank, United Overseas Bank, Oversea-Chinese Banking Corporation and Overseas Union Bank – account for most of the business. Formerly known as the Development Bank of Singapore, DBS Bank is majority state-owned but listed in the Stock Exchange of Singapore. So are the rest of the Big Four, each of which has a significant stake in one or more of the remaining smaller institutions. The total local assets of indigenous institutions amount to only around half those of the 24 overseas banks with full branch licences.

Savings A very active player in the savings market is the Post Office Savings Bank of Singapore. The government decided in 1985 not to license the POSB as a commercial bank.

The Central Provident Fund is a compulsory savings scheme similar to a pension fund. It has a massive volume of funds under its control.

Foreign banking

By far the biggest of the foreigners in asset terms are Citibank, Bank of America and Bank of Tokyo, while Malayan Banking, Standard Chartered Bank and Hongkong and Shanghai Banking Corporation have the largest branch networks.

Restricted branch licences are held by 14 institutions headquartered abroad. They are permitted only one outlet each and may not take time deposits of less than S$150,000 or any savings deposits.

Offshore branches The business of the 80-plus foreign banks with offshore branches is based on the activities of their Asian Currency Units (ACU) but they are permitted to do a small amount of onshore lending. Leaders in this category are Fuji Bank, Dai-Ichi Kangyo Bank and Sanwa Bank.

Merchant banks The 70 or so foreign-owned merchant banks, which are required to be Singapore-incorporated subsidiaries rather than branch operations, engage in activities such as domestic corporate advisory work and mergers and acquisitions. Half of them also have ACUs.

Offshore banking

Institutions in all four categories of bank – full, restricted, offshore and merchant – which Singapore licenses to do business in the city can participate in the offshore Asian dollar market by keeping ACUs. It is in such separate accounts that foreign currency deposits taken from overseas are collected before being re-lent offshore.

The bulk of the work in arranging such loans is, however, typically done in Hong Kong. The number of Asia-Pacific customers looking for loans has shrunk over the years as many borrowers have established sufficiently good credit records to allow them to issue notes, bonds or other paper instead. In the past, there was a dearth of investors in Asia prepared to buy these instruments and consequently they came to be first offered for sale from London. That this picture is changing is shown by the growing volume of secondary market trading in the paper done in Singapore and Hong Kong.

Stock market

Of the 317 companies listed on the Stock Exchange of Singapore, 183 are Malaysian incorporated entities which make up just over 50% of the market's total capitalization.

The twin listing of Singaporean and Malaysian entities on each other's exchanges dates back to the 1930s when the two British colonies operated a joint exchange. That arrangement came to an end in 1973 but the problems and varying ambitions of one can still spill over onto the other.

In 1985, for example, the collapse of the Singapore-incorporated Pan-Electric Industries listed on both exchanges pushed Kuala Lumpur to follow Singapore's example and impose an unprecedented three-day cessation in trading. In late 1986 another cloud appeared on the horizon when the MAS described the Exchange system of fixed brokerage commissions as "anachronistic" and called instead for the negotiated fees more befitting an international financial centre. With government appointees outnumbering brokers on the committee which runs the Singapore Stock Exchange, the proposal seems likely to be implemented eventually. Many Malaysian brokers, however, are against adopting such arrangements and failure to obtain their compliance would mean the delisting of Malaysian stocks on the Singapore Stock Exchange.

Meanwhile, February 1987 saw the hesitant start of the Stock Exchange of Singapore Dealing and Automated Quotation (SESDAQ) which is geared to be a second-tier market handling the shares of small and medium-sized companies. SESDAQ is working toward a link-up with NASDAQ (National Association of Securities Dealers Automated Quotations), the huge US securities exchange.

As a start, the closing prices of dozens of NASDAQ stocks will be transmitted to Singapore, where local brokers will make a market in them.

Commodities market

A Singapore-USA link is already operating in other financial commodities with the Singapore International Monetary Exchange's (SIMEX) tie-up with the Chicago Mercantile Exchange. Under this arrangement investors can use either exchange to offset positions on the other in deutschmark, yen, pound sterling, Eurodollar, US treasury bonds and gold futures contracts, or to open new positions. The USA-Singapore link-up is not very successful, partly because Singapore is too cautious, too regulated and lacks market expertise. In addition, SIMEX offers Nikkei index futures (the major indicator of the Tokyo stock market's performance) and intends to move towards areas such as options futures.

Who can help

Lawyers

There is no end of reputable local law firms in Singapore. Many still bear the name of their European founders, but may be staffed entirely by Singaporeans. The judiciary under Chief Justice Wee Chang Jin has the highest reputation for integrity. The legal system is based on the English model, but the profession is not divided as in England between barristers and solicitors.

Major law firms include

Allen & Gledhill 36 Robinson Rd 18–01, City House, 0104 ☎ 2251611

Donaldson & Burkinshaw 24 Raffles Place 15–00, Clifford Centre, 0104 ☎ 5339422

Drew & Napier 24 Raffles Place 23–01, Clifford Centre, 0104 ☎ 5350733

Lee & Lee Advocates & Solicitors 5 Shenton Way Level 19, UIC Bldg, 0106 ☎ 2200666; Lee Kuan Yew's family firm

Arthur Loke & Partners 21 Collyer Quay 16–00, Hongkong Bank Bldg, 0104 ☎ 2247166

Rodyk & Davidson 6 Battery Rd 38–01, Standard Chartered Bank Bldg, 0104 ☎ 2252626

Murphy & Dunbar 583 North Bridge Rd 10–03, Blanco Court, 0718 ☎ 2969996

Tan, Rajah & Cheah 9 Battery Rd 15–04, Straits Trading Bldg, 0104 ☎ 5322271

Foreign law firms There are many well-known foreign law firms in Singapore. Their practices are restricted to international legal matters and finance and they do not enjoy the right of appearance in Singapore courts.

Accountants and consultants

There are many accountants in Singapore experienced in advising potential investors on the establishment of a business organization in the republic. Many are subsidiaries of the Big Eight or other international firms. Accountancy firms will give investment advice, assist with tax submissions, and also enter into executive recruitment.

Consultants Singapore has a large diversified consultancy base with many firms of international origin and repute. Investors can probably be serviced by the consultancy groups they use worldwide.

Other sources of help

The Economic Development Board operates a one-stop service giving help and advice to the foreign investor. 24 Fl Raffles City Tower ☎ 3362288.

The Department of Statistics in the Fullerton Building is a source of reliable, prompt and up-to-date data.

Embassies Foreign embassies and in particular their commercial sections have smartened up their efforts to provide practical assistance and support to their compatriots. The Ministry of Foreign Affairs in Singapore publishes a Diplomatic and Consular List which may be obtained from the National Printers.

Singapore International Chamber of Commerce Founded in 1837, the chamber is the longest established private sector representative body. Its credibility over the years gives it ready access to key areas of government and its members sit on numerous government advisory committees and statutory boards. The Chamber maintains a large secretariat and provides an information service which is expatriate oriented.

Media The *Business Times* is probably the best newspaper for the foreign executive, but the local press is far from representative of the sophistication Singaporeans have achieved in other areas. Business people therefore look more to regional publications such as the *Far Eastern Economic Review, Business Asia* and *The Asian Wall Street Journal*. Foreign correspondents rarely last long in politically sensitive Singapore.

Business and cultural awareness

Singapore is a model to the world for its ordered quality of life. It has been dominated by a handful of men who have charted its course without interruption for three decades. This is a comfortable, safe environment – predictable, and rather dull. It is also the most regulated society this side of the Iron Curtain.

A multiracial society

The tiny republic of Singapore sees itself as a multiracial society but in fact is overwhelmingly Chinese (76.3%). Malays (15%) are the poorer section of the population; Indians (6.4%) are the other chief minority. Government, however, is very conscious of a lack of homogeneity and cohesion. Since the race riots of the 1960s, even the mention of racial tension is barely tolerated. At the same time Singapore does not wish to be perceived as the third China. It has made a very deliberate effort to cultivate a modern, unified state with its own Singaporean identity.

Origins Singapore's population is almost entirely of immigrant stock. Hokkiens and Cantonese, largely from the artisan and labouring classes, form the majority. Teochews come next, with some Hakka, and a small number of Babas – Straits-born Chinese from across the Causeway. There is a generation gap in Singapore society. Some of the older generation cherish migrant memories that go back to the pre-Communist era in China, and may still hanker after their ancestral village. They are trapped in their dialect group, whereas the younger generation are united by the common bond of English and to a growing extent the Mandarin of Beijing. After the Communist victory of 1949 links with China were broken and loyalty to the clan and to the motherland weakened considerably. The modern Singaporean of ethnic Chinese origin is curious about China, but no more than that, sharing a common cultural past and a common interest in food. It is in these "uprooted Chinese," as

Lee Kuan Yew has described them, that a Singapore identity has been forged.

The Tamil population consists mainly of workers and shopkeepers from southern India and Sri Lanka. The Gujaratis, Sindhis and Sikhs from northern India were traders attracted to the great emporium of the East. The Malays are mostly from the peninsula and because of their shared identity in Islam relate easily to the Arabs and Indian Muslim settlers.

Here too there is a generation gap: young and old tend to be divided on the issue of Malaysia. Half of the original cabinet in Singapore hailed from the other side of the Causeway. It is the younger group, products of nationalist propaganda, who are the true Singaporeans.

Values

Modern Singapore is still basically a Confucian and Oriental community, obedient to authority and group association, but onto this have been grafted Western notions of individual achievement. Once more, the generation gap parallels the East/West split. Confucianism wins in the devotion to family. Filial piety is an unquestioned virtue. The government has even institutionalized the Confucian ethic in the three-generation concept – a return to the extended family system (modifed to three generations under one roof) as a means of taking care of the aged within the bosom of the family. Younger Singaporeans tend to favour the nuclear family of the Western pattern. All groups, however, are somewhat aghast at what they regard as the callousness of the West towards the elderly, left alone or consigned to nursing homes.

Commercial instincts Although the old-style entrepreneurs are today being replaced by technocrats, something of the gambler's instinct and pragmatism has been passed on. Singapore is still an opportunist, consumer-oriented society and it is becoming increasingly materialistic – despite the government's self-conscious effort to legislate for cultural and spiritual values.

The work ethic At separation, Singapore with no natural resources was expected to be the ailing twin to sturdy Malaysia, but, through hard work, diligence and discipline, it achieved a national transformation to reach a prosperity unequalled anywhere in the region.

The success ethic Even more than the work ethic the Chinese of Singapore subscribe to the success ethic. It is this probably more than any other factor that has made them undeviatingly loyal to Lee Kuan Yew's regime and made them capable of the most staggering obedience – simply because the government has always delivered.

Meritocracy The republic has an overwhelming fixation with paper qualifications. The cabinet is extremely cerebral and it runs Singapore as a Mandarin elite. All the top talent is pre-empted for the civil service while generous scholarships maintain the intellectual feedstock. Commerce in the republic has an almost frenzied air of competition and high pressure salesmanship.

Hubris Success has bred a degree of overconfidence which, allied to the feeling of racial superiority in the Chinese, can easily turn to arrogance. The original inhabitants of the Yellow River civilization looked upon their neighbours as barbarians. Today's Singaporeans often appear to look down on neighbouring inefficiencies or old-world Western decadence.

Puritanism The contemporary set

of under-25's may go for casual chic or the designer labels of the West, but Singapore society is as a whole more inclined to a spartan puritanism. *Playboy* is not available in the bookstores. The government tends to be somewhat straitlaced.

Corrruption Singapore's leaders have scrupulously eschewed personal enrichment from public office to a degree that distinguishes them totally from surrounding regimes. That same integrity permeates the civil service, which – like the government – is well-paid to forestall temptation. Not a whiff of corruption is tolerated. The rare offender is severely, and publicly, punished.

Authoritarianism

Singapore remains faithful to Confucianism in its acceptance of, and preference for, a strongly authoritarian regime.

Dissent is not tolerated A government too powerful to challenge has bred a degree of political apathy. Debate and dissent tend to be stifled at birth. Government can be very heavy-handed, using its full weight to crush the slightest and always exceptional opposition. The unions, once a hotbed of communism, have been tamed. Local newspapers are docile. The Printing and Press Act takes care of foreign publications by allowing the government to restrict circulation, without appeal. In the workplace Singaporeans suffer from excessive deference, agreeing automatically with the most senior person present. Singapore is on Amnesty International's list of governments that detain political opponents without trial. This lack of intellectual freedom is totally accepted by native Singaporeans.

Regimentation and regulation The size of the island makes it eminently manageable. Lines of communication are short, the party line being handed down through the press and TV to an uncomplaining public. The government legislates for hygiene – exhorting new habits of teethbrushing and practically eliminating the Chinese habit of spitting. It legislates politeness, in taxi drivers or air hostesses, begetting a new form of mechanical and synthetic courtesy. It legislates where you live, who your neighbours are, the amount of noise you can make, how you spend you retirement benefits, how many children you can have and – almost, from its publicity campaigns – the type of person you should marry.

A speed limit of 50 mph is strictly enforced on all motorists. One youth was jailed for a day and fined S$3,000 for evading a 60 cent bus fare. Drivers are fined not just for parking without a ticket but for displaying the ticket untidily. So-called "killer litter" thrown from government apartment blocks, even if the culprit is only a child, can result in repossession of the apartment. An innocent picnic requires a permit. Cigarette advertising is banned. Drug smugglers are put to death. Breakdancing was quickly outlawed. Rollerskating is banished to restricted areas. Voting is compulsory.

Singaporeans are comfortable with this level of restraint. Westerners have to learn to curb their irritation. The pay-off for the island's population is an orderly and well-protected existence. The government has all but eradicated secret societies, gang warfare, opium smoking, trade union strikes, and all forms of political turmoil. Singapore is comparatively free from violence, vandalism, and high crime rates.

Social engineering The quiescent nature of this society is nowhere better demonstrated than in the government's policy of social engineering. Singapore has one of the highest rates of national savings in the world. It is compulsory to save. Workers save because 23% of their wages are docked as contribution to the Central Provident Fund (CPF). The employers used to contribute a similar amount. Retirement benefits

are drawn at 55, but until attaining the age of 60 the pensioner is compelled to invest a minimum of S$30,000 in a bank deposit, property or annuity plan – in order to prevent the gambling away of savings. The CPF is used by the government to achieve a fully funded welfare system and create a property-owning middle class. Following the recession, however, employers were relieved of part of their CPF contributions. The employee lost 12% of his benefits and accepted this loss without any murmur. At the same time, a two-year wage freeze was imposed. There were no openly disgruntled workers.

Genetic engineering Even more controversial are the government attempts at genetic management. The first was in the area of birth control. From a high of 4% in the 1950s, the birth rate has been slowed to 1.1%. Abortion and sterilization were legalized and today 36% of all pregnancies are terminated. The two-child norm was ruthlessly encouraged; the right to maternity leave insurance was withdrawn in the case of the third or subsequent child. Such unwanted offspring were disadvantaged when it came, to school places and so on. Now, however, the policy is reversed in favour of selective breeding. Two-fifths of female graduates it was discovered are unlikely to marry. Male graduates who made a habit of marrying down the intellectual scale are accused of creating a low performance society. Even a "love boat" strategy was adopted; the Social Development Unit pays for graduates to meet on cruises and at beach resorts, and claims to have married off 250 of these potentially superior parents. The manoeuvre on the whole met with unaccustomed resistance.

Overprogramming The more serious downside is that conditioning the population to habits of uncritical obedience will in the end stifle creativity and deny to Singapore's planners the innovation they seek in industry and commerce.

Living standards

Standards of living are the highest in the region. The majority of today's Singaporeans belong to the middle class and are showing a growing taste for imported luxury items. More than four-fifths of Singapore's population are now housed in Housing Development Board apartments. Three-quarters own their own HDB homes. Malays are dispersed among the Chinese to obviate racial ghettos. Cars are prohibitively expensive in a deliberate attempt to keep the city centre reasonably free from traffic.

Education

The overall literacy rate is 86%, one of the highest in Asia. Illiteracy is largely a legacy of the past and confined to the older migrant population. Education in the English language is provided at pre-school, primary, secondary and tertiary stages to a high standard. The English examination system is adopted. English is used for higher education, government, finance and commerce. Pupils are offered their mother tongue as a second language. Mandarin is also encouraged for unifying purposes and dialects are discouraged. Cantonese films, for example, are now banned on TV. The Chinese university and Chinese language schools have gone. Singaporeans are becoming a bilingual if not trilingual society.

Women

A growing number of Singaporean women are educated and go out to work – 80% in the 20–24 age group and 50% in the 30–34 age bracket; 2.6% are university graduates. Professional women do best in government-linked firms and many of them are government scholars. But they still play a subordinate role to men in both politics and in business. Women are better represented in the foreign business sector. Female expatriates are found mainly in banking, law, and consultancy, where they are accepted for their specialized abilities and do not suffer the cultural constraints that apply to Asian women. The latter are often relegated to the role of secretary.

The business method

Business hours are 9–5 but most people work longer hours. Lunch hour is 1–2; Friday is a long lunch hour (2hrs) for Muslims. The government works a six-day week; the private sector usually takes Saturday morning off. Singapore has a large number of public holidays. The two main ones are Chinese New Year and Christmas. Foreign visitors should avoid business trips to the republic just before and for about two weeks after these holidays. Singapore works hard the rest of the year. Printers, clerical staff, supplies staff will operate round the clock if necessary. The financial sector enjoys an advantageous time zone position and can conduct business with Europe, USA, and Japan within an eight-hour working day.

Meetings with government officials are brisk and businesslike. Little socializing is required – in fact, public servants shun this. Government servants are equally conscious of the need to preserve objectivity. Decisions go by logic. If your case is well presented it may need only one meeting. Singapore's officials are strongly business oriented and pragmatic. But they are meticulous about correct procedure. A secretary is usually present and will take down verbatim notes of the discussion to avoid any future dispute. Bureaucrats are wedded to minutes and written memos. The system makes them ultra cautious and anxious to protect their reputation for honesty. Negotiations can be tough. Public servants represent the cream of the crop and make very worthy opponents. Success has also bred a degree of arrogance and aggressiveness.

Private sector dealings The contemporary entrepreneur is very polite and extremely forceful. The older style *towkay* (who still dominates the family business as the patriarch) cares little for appearances but expects deference to his standing. His sons will prefer plush offices, prestigious restaurants and will seek to impress. The foreign businessman conversely will be tacitly judged on the class of hotel he uses, the cut of his suit and the car he runs. The modern Singaporean, far from distrusting foreign business people, values them for their international connections. He will likewise be at pains to demonstrate a worldly approach. Foreign joint venture partners, foreign linkages and overseas associates enhance his status with his peers, as does an overseas assignment. He is an indefatigable attender of conferences. Because of a prevailing academic approach in both the public and the private sector Singaporeans rely on rational economic analysis, rather than the old intuitive flair of the entrepreneur. It is the computerized approach to business – it prizes the expert but is no longer so inclined to take risks. Business visitors should bring to the negotiating table as much statistical support as they can, preferably in chart or graph form. Technical expositions are often best presented on video.

Courtesy plays a particularly important part in negotiations with the older towkays. They are rarely comfortable with an outright "no," tending to postpone a harsh decision or to refer you to a colleague. Old habits die hard. The Chinese traditionally conducted business through relationships and still find it important to establish good will first before sealing a business deal. Visitors who take the trouble to inquire after a man's family will be well received.

Face Whatever the overlay of sophistication "face" remains supremely important. However educated and reasoning, no Singaporean cares to be beaten in argument. Any reflection on his

capabilities will reveal unsuspected sensitivities hidden beneath a tough exterior. He will be equally conscious of the "face" of others. Both sides must win.

Status Singapore is a very status-conscious society, but status is defined in terms of an academic elite and by personal achievement, not social class. At the same time, wealth also continues to command respect. Like all else status is codified – by job, by job title, by qualifications and professional standing, by the standing of your organization. Traditional deference informs both business and social encounters. The most senior person present is given due respect, and in negotiations is the one given the most say.

Business cards enable you to calibrate with some degree of accuracy where someone stands. Visitors' cards should give details of rank, academic qualifications and so on. They should be printed in English and, if possible, Chinese, the latter usually on the back. The exchange of cards is a serious ritual – the card being held with both hands (at the corners).

Dress Singapore's business scene is fairly informal. Government servants are often very casually dressed and, for men, a shirt and tie is usually sufficient for the office or most business meetings. The banking community tends to wear full business suits.

Hospitality is an essential tool of business. Lavish entertainment will precede, even accompany negotiations and celebrate their conclusion. Visitors can be overwhelmed by a surfeit of social engagements. It is important to return hospitality, which is best done at prestigious hotel restaurants.

SINGAPORE

Most people who know Singapore are deeply partisan about the island republic. Its detractors say the city is antiseptic, the government high-handed and the people over-regimented; that compared with Hong Kong it lacks drive and vigour. Its defenders would say that of the two, Singapore comes out ahead: it is a clean and beautiful city, complete with parks and greenery and litter-free streets; it is orderly, with little poverty or serious crime; and if the government does tend to intervene in the life of its citizens, at least this has resulted in a stable and harmonious society.

Singapore was founded in modern times by Sir Stamford Raffles, an official of the British East India Company who was made lieutenant governor of Java at the age of 30. He recognized the advantage to Britain of a port midway between China and India and landed in Singapore on January 29 1819. It was then an island of thick jungles and swamp, inhabited by a handful of fishermen and their families, and with the advantage of a deep, well-sheltered natural harbour. The seeds of modern Singapore were sown even at that early stage: the city was to be a free port and detailed plans for controlled development were drawn up, with each racial group allotted sites for their settlements.

Under Lee Kuan Yew, the city has developed its strikingly modern appearance. Indeed one criticism of the government is of its insensitivity to the past; much of the city's former charm has been obliterated in favour of a high-tech avalanche of glass, steel, marble and concrete. Greater care is belatedly being lavished on the surviving shophouses of Little India and Chinatown, and on the fine European churches and administrative buildings. Enough colour and history remain to attract 3m tourists a year, more than the entire population of Singapore.

Arriving

Singapore is easy to reach by air from all key points in Asia, Australia, Europe and North America. There is a good road link from Malaysia but it is always congested at the weekend. The train journey from Bangkok via Kuala Lumpur is comfortable but slow.

Changi International Airport

Changi opened in 1981 and is one of the world's most comfortable and efficient airports. Allow 25min to clear the airport, less if travelling first class with priority baggage clearance. There is a S$12 departure tax (S$5 to Brunei and Malaysia).
Facilities are excellent and include licensed money-changers, banks, hotel reservations desks, a business centre, upmarket restaurants serving Continental, Japanese and Chinese food, plus a café, buffet and ice-cream parlour, VIP lounges, a free 30min audiovisual introduction to Singapore, mail and tele-communications desks, day rooms with showers, hairdressers, medical facilities and a good shopping arcade. Facilities are open from 7am to 11pm or later. Everything is well signposted in English, with comprehensive information on computerized screens. The opening of a second terminal in 1990 will make Changi the largest airport in the region. Flight information ☎ 542 4422 (arrivals and departures within the next hour) and 542 4433 (3 hours ahead). Other

inquiries ☎ 542 1234. Air cargo inquiries ☎ 542 3518 (import), ☎ 542 3642 (export).

City link Taxis are the easiest way to get into the centre of Singapore. The journey time to most hotels is generally less than 30min.

Hotel transport Hotels will meet arriving guests by arrangement. The cost is around S$40 but several hotels now provide the service free. Check at the meeting service desk in the first-floor arrivals hall that your car has arrived, and then take the travelator to the basement level for the Passenger Crescent car pick-up area.

Taxi The rank is immediately outside the terminal on the same level as the arrivals hall. Taxis are plentiful and the ride to most hotels costs S$13–15.

Car rental Avis, Hertz and Sinat desks are in the arrivals hall, but passengers arriving after 6pm without a reservation may find them closed.

Getting around

The central area of Singapore is compact and taxis are the usual way of getting about, though the Singapore Mass Rapid Transport System (MRT) subway system (opened in 1987) provides a clean, fast and inexpensive service covering the centre and suburbs.

Hotel transport The top hotels all have chauffeur-driven limousines (usually Mercedes) from S$85 an hour.

Taxi Cabs are plentiful at most times of the day or night although at peak hours (8–9 and 5–6 Mon–Fri, and lunch time Sat) you may have to wait at the central district pick-up points. Taxis may be hailed anywhere; in addition, each street has a specially designated rank. Most vehicles are comfortable, clean and air-conditioned. The major cab companies all have their own distinctive liveries and all have a taxi roof sign, but no "for hire" indicator. Most trips within the central tourist and commercial belt

cost around S$4, but there are a number of extra charges, in particular the S$2 surcharge for all cars carrying fewer than four passengers entering the Central Business District (CBD) between 7.30am and 10.15am Mon–Sat, and the S$1 surcharge for vehicles leaving the CBD between 4pm and 7pm Mon–Fri, and noon to 3pm Sat. There are also surcharges for the use of radio cabs and for journeys after midnight. Taxi firms in the CBD include *Comfort Taxi Service* ☎ 452 5555, *Singapore Commuters* ☎ 474 7707, and *SABS Radio Taxi* ☎ 250 0700. Most drivers speak adequate English but their knowledge of Singaporean street names leaves much to be desired.

Driving Motorists are courteous and the traffic laws are strictly enforced with on-the-spot fines. Traffic drives on the left. Travel to Malaysia across the Johor Causeway is relatively easy during the week, but long lines build up on Friday evening leaving Singapore and Sunday evening coming back.

There are numerous self-drive car and limousine rental firms. International firms include *Hertz* ☎ 734 4646 and *Avis* ☎ 737 1668. *Sintat* ☎ 235 5855 is a reliable local firm with lower rates.

Walking is practical for short distances, but you are liable to get uncomfortably hot after more than a couple of blocks. You can be fined on the spot for jay walking, so use pedestrian crossings on roads marked with double yellow lines.

Buses are useful for sightseeing. Good value one-day or three-day Singapore Explorer Bus tickets are available at hotels together with a colour-coded map.

Train The station on Keppel Road is the southern terminus of the service linking Singapore to Bangkok via Kuala Lumpur, Butterworth and Haadyai. The total journey time is 41hr, though the twice daily air-conditioned express to Kuala Lumpur takes only 7hr. Reservations

SINGAPORE

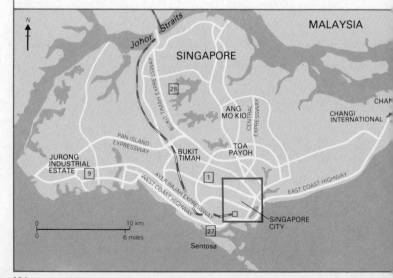

● HOTELS

1 Goodwood Park
2 Hilton
3 Hyatt Regency
4 Marina Mandarin
5 Oriental
6 Pan Pacific
7 Shangri-La
8 Sheraton Towers
9 Westin Stamford and Plaza
10 Mandarin
11 Marco Polo
12 **Regent**
13 Raffles

■ RESTAURANTS

Domus (hotel 8)
Fourchettes (hotel 5)
Frisco (building 6)
Gordon Grill (hotel 1)
Harbour Grill (hotel 2)
Inn of Happiness (hotel 2)
Latour (hotel 7)
Li Bai (hotel 8)
Maxim's de Paris (hotel 12)
Mövenpick (building 23)
1 New Orleans
Palm Grill (hotel 9)
Pine Court (hotel 10)
2 Le Restaurant de France
3 Restaurant 1819
4 Suntory
5 Shashlik
6 Casablanca

☐ BUILDINGS AND SIGHTS

1 Botanical Gardens
2 Cavanagh Bridge
3 City Hall
4 Galeries Lafayette Department Store
5 Government Publications Department
6 Hong Kong Bank Building
7 Isetan Department Store
8 Istana (President's palace)
9 Jurong Bird Park
10 Lucky Plaza
11 Marina Complex
12 Merlion Statue
13 Metro Department Store
14 Orchard Point Post Office
15 Parliament House
16 People's Park Complex
17 Printemps Department Store
18 Robinsons Department Store
19 St Andrew's Cathedral
20 Singapore Conference Hall
21 Singapore Handicrafts Centre
22 Singapore International Chamber of Commerce
23 Standard Chartered Bank Building
24 Sultan Mosque
25 Supreme Court Building
26 Victoria Memorial Hall and Theatre
27 World Trade Centre
28 Zoological Gardens

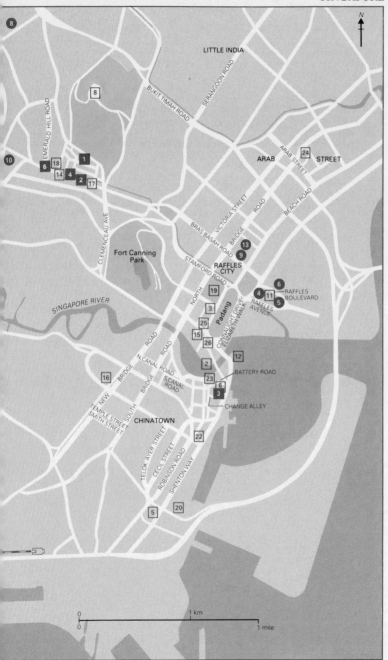

should be made at least a week in advance, through the hotel travel desk or at the station ☎ 222 5165.

Area by area

Singapore lies off the southern tip of the Malaysian Peninsula, separated from it by the narrow Johor Straits, 137km/60 miles north of the equator. The republic consists of the diamond-shaped island of Singapore, and 57 others, of which fewer than half are inhabited. The total land area is 618 sq km/225 sq miles but is constantly being extended by land reclamation. Most of the island is less than 15 metres above sea level, with Tin Hill (Bukit Timah) as the highest point at 177 metres. You can drive from one end of the island to the other in 30min. The Central Business District lies either side of the Singapore River at the southern tip of the island. Industry is mainly confined to the southwestern district of Jurong. The centre of the island is largely residential with several attractive parks and reservoirs. Areas to the north and east are still surprisingly rural with fish farms, vegetable gardens, small villages (*kampongs*) and, on the coast north of Changi airport, fishermen's huts built out over the water on stilts.

Central Business District (CBD) The focal point of the city is still the spot on the northern bank of the Singapore River where Sir Stamford Raffles landed to claim Singapore for the British. The river separates the financial district on the south side from the tourist and shopping district on the north. Battery Road, Shenton Way (the Wall Street of Singapore), Robinson Road and Cecil Street are the financial heart of Singapore, crowded with (mostly characterless) metal and marble-clad skyscrapers. The first foreign institutions in Singapore still occupy the prime positions. The Hongkong and Shanghai Banking Corporation and the Standard Chartered Bank buildings hug the riverside while numerous shipping, banking, trading

and insurance buildings rise up behind. On the western fringes of the financial district stand shuttered and crumbling prewar shophouses; to the south the once busy waterfront has been turned into a shaded walkway, dominated by the statue of the Merlion – a mythological creature half lion and half fish which has been adopted as the symbol of Singapore. Opposite the waterfront is the island of Sentosa, the British forces wartime base and now a crowded weekend leisure resort.

Colonial Singapore An elegant collection of early 19thC public buildings, the seat of government, lies north across the river from the financial district along Connaught Drive. The buildings include the original East India Company court house, the Victoria Theatre, Victoria Memorial Hall, Parliament House and the domed Supreme Court Building – formerly the Europa hotel where Joseph Conrad used to eavesdrop on customers in the crowded sailors' bar. In the adjacent City Hall, Lord Louis Mountbatten accepted the formal Japanese surrender on September 12 1945. Set back a little way is the Anglican St Andrew's Cathedral, completed in 1861.

All these buildings enclose the east side of the green expanse known as the Padang. The spirit of old-time colonialism lives on in two expatriate haunts, the Cricket Club and, to a lesser degree, the Tanglin Club.

Orchard Road This area was transformed in the 1970s when the first high-rise hotels and shopping malls were built. Some green plots still remain undeveloped but for the most part this is now the tourist mecca of Singapore. Emerald Hill Road, one third of the way up Orchard Road, survived wholesale demolition and its original richly decorated façades of the Nonya (Straits Chinese) shophouses have been painted emerald and white and now form an arcaded pedestrian precinct with outdoor cafés and craft shops lit at night by gas lamps.

Chinatown Because of its proximity to the financial district, Chinatown has suffered continual erosion from high-rise development, but the Smith Street, Temple Street and New Bridge Road districts still have their characteristic tenements with weathered shutters and baroque ornamentation. The Thian Hock Keng Temple on Telok Ayer Street, dedicated to the Queen of Heaven and protector of sailors, marks the original Singapore waterfront. Some streets are still dominated by specialist trades: mask-makers in Ann Siang Hill, funeral requisites in Sago Street.

Little India has Serangoon Road as its main thoroughfare, while Buffalo Road commemorates the sacred animals of the Hindu. The fragrance of incense hangs over the area and the streets are full of sacks, bundles and boxes from which merchants sell spice, brassware and brightly coloured textiles.

The Arab Street district houses the distinctive Sultan Mosque on North Bridge Road, which was built in the 1820s as part of the price paid to the Sultan of Johor by the East India Company for sovereignty over Singapore.

The suburbs Some 81% of Singapore's population is housed in government-built apartment blocks spread across the central belt of the island. The rich prefer the leafy Bukit Timah district. The East Coast district is rapidly becoming popular with the newly affluent.

Hotels

Singapore's hotels are among the best in Asia. Most are in the Orchard Road area but several of the city's newest hotels and its oldest, Raffles, are in the colonial district much closer to the financial district. Five of these hotels are in two large complexes: the Raffles City, opened in 1986, and the Marina Square complex, opened in 1987.

All rooms in hotels given full entries have air conditioning, 24hr room service, TV, radio, minibar and IDD telephone. All hotels have a travel desk and a business centre providing photocopying, typing, telex and fax. Quoted rates may be subject to 10% service and 3% tax. Always ask about discounts.

Goodwood Park $$$
22 Scotts Rd, 0922 ☎ *737 7411*
TX *24377 Fax 732 8558* • *AE DC MC V*
• *123 rooms, 108 suites, 4 restaurants, 1 bar*
Goodwood Park is a small luxurious hotel which retains a feeling of prewar grandeur. It was originally built as a club by German expatriates in 1900 in imitation of a Rhineland castle, and stands in extensive tropical gardens, a brief walk from the Orchard Road shopping area. In the 1930s the rich and grand such as the Duke of Windsor preferred the Goodwood to Raffles. It was fully modernized and restored by the prominent Singaporean businessman Khoo Teck Puat in 1978, and the original building is now flanked by two modern wings. A cloister-like garden courtyard contains two pools and is full of delightful corners and verandas. The atmosphere is elegant without being aloof, and guests – mainly European business people – receive a warm welcome from the friendly staff. The rooms are big and airy; many have a circular dining table as well as writing desk. The Gordon Grill (see *Restaurants*) is much used for entertaining, and good Chinese and Japanese restaurants are also on offer. Business is often discussed over tea in L'Expresso coffee shop. Shops, hairdresser • 2 pools • business centre, 5 meeting rooms (capacity up to 350).

Hilton $$
581 Orchard Rd, 0923 ☎ *737 2233*
🆇 *21491 Fax 732 2917* • *AE DC MC V*
• *406 rooms, 29 suites, 5 restaurants,*
3 bars
The Hilton has recently been lavishly
refurbished. The spacious rooms are
decorated in bold colours and have
writing desks and several telephone
points. There are two nonsmoking
floors, and the top-floor suites,
designed by Givenchy, include
extravagances like whirlpool baths
and steam showers and large
furnished balconies. The convention
trade is important to the hotel, and
the business centre has a large staff.
Shops, hairdresser, florist • pool,
gym, sauna, nearby clubs for tennis,
squash, golf • 8 meeting rooms
(capacity up to 150), ballroom
with audiovisual facilities
(capacity 700).

Hyatt Regency $$
10–12 Scotts Rd, 0922 ☎ *733 1188*
🆇 *24415 Fax 732 1696* • *AE DC*
MC V • *1,015 rooms, 73 suites,*
5 restaurants, 2 bars
This 22-floor twin-tower complex is
in the Orchard Road area. In the
newly built Regency Terrace wing,
set apart from the main tower and
built around the landscaped pools,
rooms have an "instant tropics" feel
with wicker furniture, louvred doors
and abundant greenery. Some rooms
have balconies and large bathrooms
with separate showers and dressing
rooms. Shops, florist, hairdresser,
beauty salon, disco • 2 pools, tennis,
squash, gym, sauna, jacuzzi, massage
• reference library, 3 meeting rooms
(capacity up to 2,000) with
simultaneous translation and
audiovisual facilities.

Marina Mandarin $$
Marina Sq, 6 Raffles Bvd, 0103
☎ *338 3388* 🆇 *22299 Fax 339 4977* •
AE DC MC V • *557 rooms, 48 suites,*
3 restaurants, 3 bars
One of the three independently
managed hotels in the Marina Square
complex. Rooms are spacious and

opulent with particularly well-
appointed bathrooms, though only
the suites have large desks. The decor
is Chinese-inspired. Various
restaurants serve Italian, Chinese and
international cuisine, and the
English-style Cricketer bar shows live
satellite coverage of sporting events
such as the Wimbledon tennis
championships. Shops, florist,
hairdresser, disco • pool, jogging
track, tennis, squash, gym • 10
meeting rooms (capacity up to 700)
with audiovisual facilities and
simultaneous translation.

Oriental $$
Marina Sq, 6 Raffles Bvd, 0103
☎ *338 0066* 🆇 *29117 Fax 339 9537* •
AE DC MC V • *Mandarin Oriental* •
457 rooms, 61 suites, 4 restaurants,
4 bars
Shut off by soundproof glass
partitions from the Marina Square
shopping mall, the Oriental aims for
the sophisticated atmosphere and
very high standards of service that
mark the group as a whole. Guest
rooms are variously decorated; only
the executive rooms offer generous
workspace. Shops, hairdresser, florist
• pool, gym, jogging track, squash,
tennis • computer rental, 8 meeting
rooms (capacity up to 700).

Pan Pacific $$
Marina Sq, 7 Raffles Bvd, 0103
☎ *336 8111* 🆇 *38821 Fax 339 1861* •
AE DC MC V • *800 rooms and suites,*
7 restaurants, 3 bars
The biggest of the three Marina
Square hotels with 47 floors, the Pan
Pacific seeks to put itself ahead with
high-tech business services, including
access to Infomagic, a Canadian-
based business and economic news
information service with world share
price coverage. The business centre is
open 24hr. Bedrooms are reasonably
spacious with balconies; those on the
Kingfisher floor have executive desks.
Shops, hairdresser, florist, disco •
pool, gym, sauna, tennis, solarium •
8 meeting rooms (capacity up to
1,200).

Shangri-La $$
22 Orange Grove Rd, 1025
☎ *737 3644* ⓉⓍ *21505 Fax 733 7220* •
AE DC MC V • *750 rooms, 60 suites,*
5 restaurants, 2 bars
Many people rate the Shangri-La
Singapore's best hotel. Part of the
appeal is the splendid gardens, now
lush and mature. All rooms in the
Garden Wing have bougainvillea-
clad balconies, and those facing
inwards look over carp-filled
ponds and tree-fringed pools.
Rooms in the Valley Wing are among
the most spacious in Singapore, with
bay windows and country-house
furnishings: chaises longues, sofas,
occasional tables and large desks.
Guests may opt for Chinese, Japanese
or French cooking (see *Restaurants*).
The poolside Waterfall Café offers
snacks and full meals. The business
centre is open 24hr. Shops, florist,
hairdresser, disco • 2 pools, gym,
jacuzzi, massage, tennis, squash,
mini-golf • 12 meeting rooms
(capacity up to 1,400) with
audiovisual and simultaneous
translation facilities.

Sheraton Towers $$$
39 Scotts Rd, 0922 ☎ *737 6888*
ⓉⓍ *37750 Fax 737 1072* • *AE DC MC V*
• *412 rooms and suites, 3 restaurants,*
1 bar
This hotel is making unstinted efforts
to attract a loyal clientele. Smiling
staff greet guests at the airport,
clothes are pressed on arrival, and
afternoon tea and breakfast are served
by a butler. Both the Domus
(Western cuisine) and the Li Bai
(Cantonese) are as distinctive in their
decor as in their menus (see
Restaurants). Guest rooms are more
lacklustre, but each has multiple
telephone sockets and a large desk.
Shops, hairdresser, disco • pool,
gym, sauna, massage • 7 meeting
rooms (capacity up to 500) with
audiovisual facilities.

Westin Stamford and Plaza $$
2 Stamford Rd, 0617 ☎ *338 8585*
ⓉⓍ *22206 Fax 338 2862* • *AE DC MC V*

• *2,049 rooms, 120 suites, 13*
restaurants, 4 bars
These two linked hotels cater largely
for business travellers and, despite
their size, offer service that is
civilized and personal. From the top
of the 73-floor Westin Stamford you
can see into Malaysia and Indonesia,
though the rooms are not as spacious
or luxurious as those in the smaller
Westin Plaza. The restaurants offer
Chinese, French, Italian and
Japanese cuisine, and include a
superior Palm Grill (see *Restaurants*).
The business centre is open 24hr.
Shops, hairdresser, florist, disco •
2 pools, gym, jacuzzi, massage,
whirlpool bath • tennis, squash • 42
meeting rooms (capacity up to 6,000)
with simultaneous translation and
audiovisual facilities.

OTHER HOTELS
Carlton ($$) *76 Bras Basah Rd,*
0718 ☎ *338 8333* ⓉⓍ *42076*
Fax 339 6866 • *AE DC MC V*. Opened
in 1988 at the crossroads of the
financial and shopping districts. 26
storeys with a 3 storey atrium
featuring a fountain and greenery. All
rooms have large bay windows. Pool,
fitness centre and full business
services. Meeting rooms.
Mandarin ($$) *333 Orchard Rd,*
0923 ☎ *737 4411* ⓉⓍ *21528 Fax 732*
2361 • *AE DC MC V*. Dominated by
tour groups but near the centre with
business services, pool, gym,
tennis and squash.
Melia ($$) *45 Scotts Rd, 0922*
☎ *732 5885* ⓉⓍ *36811 Fax 732 1332* •
AE DC MC V. Small but well equipped
hotel opened in 1988. Some distance
from the Central Business District
but next to Newton MRT station. Its
241 rooms and suites are comfortable
and culinary options include a
speciality seafood restaurant. Business
centre, pool and health centre.
Omni Marco Polo ($$) *247 Tanglin*
Rd, 1024 ☎ *474 7141* ⓉⓍ *21476*
Fax 471 0521 • *AE DC MC V*. Despite
dated, toffee-coloured decor and old-
fashioned furnishings, the Marco
Polo has retained a loyal clientele and

equally loyal staff. The new wing is smarter, as are the poolside terrace rooms with private patio. Excellent restaurants.

The Regent ($$) *1 Cuscaden Rd, 1024* ☎ *733 8888* ⊤⊠ *37248 Fax 732 8838* • *AE DC MC V*. Formerly the Pavilion Inter-Continental. Glitzy, somewhat impersonal but with full business services, pool and gym.

Raffles ($$$$) *1–3 Beach Rd, 0718* ☎ *337 8041* ⊤⊠ *21586 Fax 339 7650 AE DC MC V*. Established in 1886 Raffles is one of Singapore's historic sights. When it reopens in 1990 following extensive renovations it aims to be once again one of the city's best hotels, despite its smaller size. Exclusive suite-only accommodation, a location near the financial district and a special atmosphere should prove attractive to business people.

Clubs

Singapore expatriates often entertain in their clubs. Some, like the *American Club*, 21 Scotts Rd ☎ 737 3411, and the *Republic of Singapore Yacht Club*, 249 Jalan Buroh, Jurong ☎ 265 0931, offer temporary membership to members of affiliated clubs in other parts of the world, as does the commercially run *World Trade Centre Club*, 13-01 World Trade Centre ☎ 273 2066. Other prestigious clubs include the *Singapore Cricket Club*, Connaught Drive ☎ 338 9271, the *Tanglin Club*, 5 Stevens Rd ☎ 737 6011, the *British Club*, 73 Bt Tinggi Rd ☎ 467 4311, and the *Singapore Town Club*, 11–01 Straits Trading Bldg ☎ 532 2189.

Restaurants

For a city of such international importance Singapore has few sophisticated restaurants geared to top-flight entertainment. The majority cater for tourists and locals in search of inexpensive ethnic cuisine and make little attempt at creating smart surroundings and atmosphere. Most of the best restaurants are in hotels but even they heavily promote fixed-price buffets. Most restaurants charge 10% service and 3% tax on top of the stated prices.

Domus $$$
Sheraton Towers Hotel ☎ *737 6888* • *D only* • *AE DC MC V*
Domus is a good choice for high-powered business occasions, as it is one of the few restaurants in Singapore to combine elegance with imaginative cooking. Large mirrors framed by polished wood panels make the dining room seem larger than it is; however, there is plenty of space between the tables, set with silver, glass and china specially designed by Pierre Cardin. The seven-course set dinner menu changes daily. The short *à la carte* menu offers grilled seafood, US and Scotch beef, duck, venison, veal and lamb. The waiters are knowledgeable and the wine list is well balanced.

Fourchettes $$$
Oriental Hotel ☎ *338 0066* • *AE DC MC V*
The Oriental hotel's flagship restaurant is ideal for high-level business entertaining: service is polished, and the dining room's panelled walls are hung with fine old portraits. Guests may choose from a lavish display of meat and fish, served grilled or *flambé* with a choice of sauces. Long wine list.

Frisco $$
Hong Kong Bank Bldg, B1 02, 21 Collyer Quay ☎ *220 3777* • *AE DC MC V*
A popular lunch-time spot for those working in the financial district. Mostly steaks and seafood. Efficient service.

Gordon Grill $$$
Goodwood Park Hotel ☎ *737 7411* •
AE DC MC V
Many expatriates are regular
customers here. The atmosphere is
convivial and the decor is elegant
with green drapes and cream marble.
Steaks, fish and fresh oysters are the
standard fare, but the menu also
features haggis. Extensive wine list
and selection of single malts.

Harbour Grill $$$
Hilton Hotel ☎ *737 2233* • *closed Sat,
Sun L* • *AE DC MC V*
Chefs at the Hilton's Harbour Grill
have attracted a loyal clientele
among gourmets and business people
for their *cuisine en évolution*. Dishes
combine local ingredients with a
strong French influence. The five-
course Surprise Gourmet Dinner
changes daily. The dining room is
decorated with murals of Singapore's
early history. Fine wines at top
prices.

Inn of Happiness $$
Hilton Hotel ☎ *737 2233* • *AE DC
MC V*
Enjoying fine views from the top of
the Hilton, and elaborately decorated
in Chinese-style with red lanterns,
green roof tiles and a pond, the Inn
of Happiness is popular with Chinese
business people for its Cantonese
dishes. Useful for business meals
during the week, but often very
crowded at weekends, when special
promotions take place.

Latour $$$
Shangri-La Hotel ☎ *737 3644* •
AE DC MC V
Authentic French cuisine in elegant
surroundings has won the Latour a
solid following. A failsafe choice for
entertaining in the evening or for a
working lunch, when a good value
fixed-price menu is available.

Li Bai $$$
Sheraton Towers Hotel ☎ *737 6888* •
AE DC MC V
The usual Chinese clutter is absent
from this distinctly upmarket
restaurant; just a hint of the Orient
remains in the black lattice screens.
Tables are crisply laid out with
eggshell porcelain and silver.
Standard Chinese dishes are given a
boost by judicious use of additional
ingredients: shark's fin soup is
flavoured with Xinhua ham, and
fried lobster with a tangy black bean
sauce.

Maxim's de Paris $$$
Regent Hotel ☎ *733 8888* • *AE DC
MC V*
The Pierre Cardin chain has
spawned a clone in Singapore,
lavishly decorated in the Tiffany
style of the Paris original. The menu
is traditionally Parisian and the
cheeseboard is excellent. Wide range
of vintage wines.

Mövenpick $$
*B1-01, Standard Chartered Bank
Bldg, 6 Battery Rd* ☎ *221 0340* •
closed Sun • *AE DC MC V*
A branch of the Swiss chain
(another branch is at B1-01 Scotts
Shopping Centre, 6 Scotts Rd
☎ 235 8700), strategically placed to
capture the business lunch trade.
Customers from nearby offices come
in for seasonal dishes, an
exceptionally good salad bar, daily
specials and a *menu dégustation*. Steak
tartare, raclette and numerous veal
dishes are the staples. Nonsmoking areas. Relatively inexpensive
French, German and Swiss
wines.

New Orleans $$$
*Holiday Inn Park View, 11 Cavenagh
Rd* ☎ *733 8333* • *AE DC MC V*
This restaurant offers a complete
change of style with Creole and
Cajun food, possibly too robust for
some, but with a good range of fish
dishes. The jazz band attracts a
crowd in the evening but lunch is
more suitable for business
entertaining, at widely spaced tables
beneath a high ceiling.

Palm Grill $$$
Westin Plaza Hotel ☎ *338 8585* •
closed Sun • *AE DC MC V*
An established venue for business
entertaining. Though vast, service is
good and diners feel well looked after.
Standard grill room fare is leavened
by *nouvelle cuisine*. Reasonably priced
wines.

Pine Court $$
Mandarin Hotel ☎ *737 4411* • *AE DC
MC V*
Popular with Chinese businessmen,
the Pine Court specializes in the
grander dishes of the northern
Chinese cuisine such as Beijing duck.

Le Restaurant de France $$$
Hotel Meridien, 100 Orchard Rd
☎ *733 8855* • *closed Sat, Sun, L* •
AE DC MC V
Frequent return visits to France by
chef Patrick Lannes ensure that the
menu always contains some genuine
innovations. The use of fresh herbs,
wild ingredients (mushrooms,
truffles and asparagus) and melting
sauces are particular features.
Knowledgeable regulars, who include
top business figures, ask for their
own off-menu favourites, or order
the special dishes in advance.

Restaurant 1819 $$$
*Tuan Sing Towers, B1, 30 Robinson
Rd* ☎ *223 4031* • *AE DC MC V*
A safe choice for business
entertaining under the chandeliers of
one of Singapore's oldest Continental
restaurants, located in the financial
district. The service is polished, the
surroundings Victorian with heavy
panelling and deep upholstery, and
the menu offers competently
prepared seafood and imported prime
meats. Extensive wine list.

Shang Palace $$$
Shangri-La Hotel ☎ *7373644* • *AE DC
MC V*
Excellent Cantonese cuisine in an
extravagant setting. The dining room
is modelled on a Shang dynasty
courtyard with carved screens, wood

paneling and enormous Chinese
lanterns. Seafood is a speciality and
dim sum is served at lunchtime.

Suntory $$$
06-01, Delfi Orchard, 402 Orchard Rd
☎ *732 5111* • *AE DC MC V*
One of an international chain run by
the Japanese whisky firm, Suntory is
arguably the best Japanese restaurant
in Singapore and attracts a smart
cosmopolitan clientele. It offers a
wide choice: individual rooms
specializing in *sushi, teppanyaki,
tempura* and *shabu shabu*; there is an
extensive range of set menus and *à la
carte* in the main dining room.
Regulars praise the Kobe beef,
prepared in four styles.

Good but casual
As well as a galaxy of restaurants
providing every sort of Eastern food,
a modest establishment popular with
the locals is *Shashlik*, 06-19 Far East
Shopping Centre, 545 Orchard Rd
☎ 732 6401. Run by the chefs of the
former highly regarded Troika, it
serves East European dishes such as
borscht with sour cream, blinis, and
stroganoff. Russian specialities are
served at the *Balalaika Room* at the
York Hotel, 21 Mount Elizabeth
☎ 737 0511. Also highly rated is
Casablanca, 7 Emerald Hill Rd,
Peranakan Place ☎ 235 9328, a
white-walled former warehouse
serving unpretentious French dishes
and a wide range of wines by the
bottle or glass.
Eating outdoors Most informal of
all are the food markets, often serving
delicious food at a fraction of the cost
of a restaurant. These "nightclubs
for the poor" exist all over Asia, but
only in Singapore are the standards
of hygiene sufficiently regulated to
ensure that an evening's dining
under the stars will not be regretted
the following day. You settle at a
table and then select dishes from the
surrounding hawker stalls. Each stall
charges separately and credit cards
are not accepted. Some food markets
specialize in a particular dish: the

Satay Club, Elizabeth Walk, serves barbecued chicken, mutton or beef on skewers; the exclusively Singaporean *Rasa Singapura*, Singapore Handicraft Centre, Tanglin Rd, is known for excellent oyster omelettes. The *Whitley Road Hawker Centre* is mainly Cantonese with barbecued meats and grilled prawns. *Scotts Picnic Food Court*, Scotts Shopping Centre, 6–8 Scotts Rd, covered and air-conditioned, is for the less adventurous. Stalls serve seafood, tandoori, vegetarian snacks and much else. The *Seafood Centre*, East Coast Parkway, is a conglomeration of seafood restaurants all serving similar dishes; some accept credit cards.

Bars

So many bars offer some form of musical entertainment that it is almost impossible to find anywhere for a quiet conversation. Some bars attract a business clientele simply by being close to the financial district. Among these are the *Stamford Arms*, Straits Trading Bldg B1-09, Battery Rd, which has good bar food and piped music. *Wall Street*, at the Amara Hotel, 165 Tanjong Pagar Rd, serves good open sandwiches and shows recent sports videos. Slightly more upmarket are the Westin Stamford's *Compass Rose Bar* and the Westin Plaza's *Somerset Bar*, where an American jazz group performs daily.

The Raffles Hotel is bound to have lost some of its old colonial atmosphere by the time it reopens after refurbishment in 1990, but the chance to drink a gin sling in the place of its birth may make it worth a visit.

Moving up into the main hotel district, *Saxophone* at 23 Cuppage Rd (off Orchard Rd) is a lively bar-cum-restaurant in a row of restored prewar Chinese houses. Customers sit either at tables in the street, in a high-ceilinged bar on the ground floor or in the bistro upstairs (where there is an accomplished jazz band).

Two quieter but friendly bars are in the Centrepoint Bldg, 176 Orchard Rd: *Bier Keller* (01-57) and *Bulls and Bears* (03-45), both with a wide range of imported beers. Less central, but worth seeking out, are the *Palms Wine Bar*, 261 Holland Rd, with occasional live entertainment and a wide selection of wines; *Casablanca* (see *Restaurants*); *The Green*, Ground Fl, Unit 19/21 Goldhill Podium Block, which has a golf-club atmosphere and country and western music; and *The Yard*, 294 River Valley Rd, an English-style pub.

Entertainment

The best guide to the arts is the monthly *Arts Diary*, free in hotels. Otherwise check local newspapers and the SBC Videotext service.

Theatre, dance, music Drama depends largely on the efforts of local expatriates, but *The Stage Club* ☎ 251-1380 sometimes puts on top-class theatre at various venues. Contemporary dance is popular in Singapore with regular performances by touring professional companies. The Singapore Symphony Orchestra, founded in 1979, is worth hearing, and soloists and small groups of musicians give regular lunchtime concerts. The central box office for all performances is at *Victoria Concert Hall* ☎ 338 1230. There are regular performances of Singaporean, Malay, Thai, Chinese and Indian music and dance at the Hyatt Regency and Mandarin hotels. Evening performances are usually accompanied by a buffet supper of regional dishes.

Cinema Singapore gets the big blockbuster movies as soon as any other country in the world and has a keen cinema-going audience, but films with explicit sex are either censored or not shown. Most cinemas are clean, comfortable and air-conditioned. Top cinemas showing undubbed English films include *Capitol*, North Bridge Rd ☎ 337 9759, *Jade* ☎ 293 2581 and

Prince ☎ 298 4905 (both at Shaw Towers, Beach Rd), *Lido*, Orchard Rd ☎ 737 3414, and *Orchard*, Grange Rd ☎ 737 6588. For "art" films, see *Arts Diary* for details of the Singapore Film Society which meets at the *Goethe Institut*.

Discos *Thank God It's Friday*, Far East Plaza 04–44, Scotts Rd ☎ 235 6181, and *Celebrities*, B1-47 Orchard Towers, Orchard Rd ☎ 734 5221, are both disco/bistro combinations with live bands interspersed with recorded sounds. Lively hotel discos include the Century Park Sheraton's *Ridley's*, the Shangri-La's *Xanadu* and the space-age *Scandals* at the Westin Plaza. Discos with a big local following are the huge, converted riverside *Wharehouse*, 332 Havelock Rd ☎ 732 9922, and *Rumours*, Forum Galleria, Orchard Rd ☎ 732 8181. Well-heeled trendies go to the *Rainbow*, Ming Arcade, Cuscaden Rd ☎ 733 3779, for its imported Australian and US bands, and *Peppermint Park*, Parkway Parade, Marine Park Rd ☎ 344 5888, where the special effects are spectacular.

Nightclubs *Tropicana Theatre and Restaurant*, Scotts Rd ☎ 737 6433, and the *Neptune*, Oversea-Union House, Collyer Quay ☎ 224 3922, are both popular with Chinese business people. Lavish Chinese food is served and international cabaret and dance bands provide the entertainment. For clubs with hostesses *Oasis*, Kallang Park ☎ 344 9702, and *Maxim*, Supreme House, Penang Rd ☎ 338 6555, are regarded as the smartest.

Shopping

There is little to choose between prices in Singapore and Hong Kong. Both are duty-free ports and Singapore has all the latest electronic gadgetry and the finest in arts, crafts and jewellery from every corner of Asia. Here too are designer-label clothes from Japan and the West and the traditional Oriental silks and batiks. You can be confident of

paying the lowest world prices for cameras, hi-fi, personal computers and watches and relatively little for gold, silver, jade, ivory, pewter, pearls, crocodile-skin shoes and bags, and rattan furniture.

When buying from small stores and street markets, you are expected to bargain, but the eventual price may not be lower than in the major department stores, which accept credit cards and will arrange shipping; *Robinson*'s in particular prides itself on keen prices. Singapore has enough pirates and fakers to make it necessary to beware of exceptionally large discounts. Be sure to obtain a receipt for every purchase, and to check that the goods you buy have all their accessories, are compatible with electrical standards at home and have the manufacturer's worldwide (not just local) warranty. Most shops open daily 10–10.

Singapore divides into several shopping areas: Orchard Road is the smartest, mixing specialist shops with department stores which sell a huge range of goods: *Metro, Printemps, Robinsons, Tangs* and *Galeries Lafayette* are the best for quality. Midway down Orchard Road is *Lucky Plaza*, a shopping complex with the best bargains in cameras and electronic goods. Farther up, beyond the junction with Scotts Road, are the more upmarket galleria and department stores. In the Wisma Atria you will find the Japanese *Isetan* store, which sells smart designer wear and accessories, and the boutiques of leading European perfumiers and couturiers. Next door, the *Hilton Hotel Arcade* continues the quality theme with fine jewelry and antique stores.

The Tanglin Road area, at the top of Orchard Road, is a good place to start for antiques and gifts. The *Singapore Handicrafts Centre* on Tanglin Road, is a covered mall displaying the crafts of some 16 Asian countries. It is an excellent place for souvenirs. Highlights include sculpture and woodcarving from

Indonesia and Malaysia, metalware and lacquerware from India and pewterware from Singapore. Prices are reasonable and some shops feature craftsmen displaying their skills. Open daily 10.30am-6pm.

Other shopping districts may offer little that cannot be found on Orchard Road, but each has its own distinctive flavour. Chinatown has lost its street stalls but still retains a hint of its old colour. South Bridge Road and the *People's Park* complex are in the centre of the jewellery trade, with shops specializing in gold, silver, jade and pearls. Orchid motifs, overlaid with enamel, gold or platinum, and made into necklaces and earrings, are a particular feature of Singapore. Off Collyer Quay in the financial district Change Alley, a narrow lane crowded with money-changers and traders, still attracts the curious but most antique dealers have moved to Orchard Road. Safer and more reliable are Serangoon Road in Little India, a busy market for gold embroidered saris and cheesecloth blouses, brassware and Indian carvings; or Arab Street for wicker baskets, rattan furniture and colourful hand-printed textiles.

Sightseeing

Singapore is primarily a city of parks and gardens plus picturesque, but small and disappearing ethnic quarters. All of these can be explored easily and without a guide.

Peranakan Place Emerald Hill Road, off Orchard Road, is one of the few surviving complete streets of houses built by early Chinese settlers. The Straits Chinese, or Peranakans – you will also hear the terms Nonya or Baba used for Peranakan women, costume and cuisine – created a distinctive lifestyle and language, adopting Malay, Portuguese and Indian elements. The delicate architecture of their buildings, a style dubbed Chinese Baroque or Chinese Palladian, can be seen at its best in this district. One building has been turned into a living museum full of beautiful and intricately carved furniture with a restaurant serving Nonya food. *Open 11-6.*

Botanic Gardens A public park and research centre founded in 1860 by experts from London's Kew Gardens. Several of the original wrought-iron planthouses and the director's house still survive. Here in 1877 "Mad" Henry Ridley first propagated the Brazilian rubber plants from which grew the vast rubber industry of Malaysia. Highlights include a remnant of the rain forest which once covered Singapore, the black swans on the main lake, the lotus pond studded with pink flowers and water lilies, the colourful orchid enclosure and the waterfall garden, plus countless lizards, birds and butterflies. *Open Mon–Fri, 5–11; weekends 5–midnight.*

Mandai Orchid Gardens Many varieties of the national flower bloom on the hillside of this large commercial orchid farm. *Mandai Lake Rd. Open 9–5.30.*

Singapore Zoological Gardens This is an "open" zoo in which the 1,600 animals roam freely in enclosures resembling their natural habitats. The zoo is also an important breeding centre for endangered Asian species, including the cheetah, Siberian tiger and cloud leopard. *Mandai Lake Rd. Open 8.30–6.30.*

Guided tours

The standard half-day city bus tour is a good way to get an idea of the city. *American Lloyd* (Shangri-La Hotel ☎ 737 6445; Westin Plaza hotel ☎ 339 6912) is one of the best for group tours by car. The *Registered Tourist Guides Association of Singapore* ☎ 338 3441 can fix you up with a personal guide for around S$20 an hour. The Singapore Tourist Promotion Board also publishes an excellent free booklet in several languages entitled *Singapore – Tour It Yourself.*

Harbour cruise Tours of the harbour and some of Singapore's southern islands are organized by the *Port of Singapore Authority* (by motor launch), *Eastwind* ☎ 533 3432, and by *Watertours* ☎ 533 9811 (in diesel-powered Chinese junks). Reservations can be made at all hotel travel desks or at Clifford Pier, Collyer Quay, in the financial district.

Out of town
Sentosa The resort island of Sentosa, opposite the financial district, is very crowded at weekends. Attractions are the fine views of the main island, a waxworks museum, a museum of local insect and butterfly life, and a nightly spectacular musical fountain show. The Rasa Sentosa hawker stalls provide inexpensive local snacks. Ferries leave the World Trade Centre pier every 15min from 7.30am till late, and a cable car operates from the PSA Tower, next to the World Trade Centre, 10–7.

Malaysia Organized day-trips to Kukup on the west coast of Malaysia, 100km/63 miles from Singapore, are offered by most hotels. They provide an opportunity to visit rubber, oil, palm, cocoa and coffee plantations. Kukup itself is a picturesque coastal village where most houses are built over the water on stilts. See *Kuala Lumpur* for other trips.

Spectator sports
Most games of any significance take place at the National Stadium in Kallang. The *Singapore Sports Council* ☎ 345 7111, ext 399, provides details and handles reservations.

Cricket Matches take place in an appropriately colonial setting on the Padang, Sat and Sun, Mar–Sep ☎ 338 9271.

Horse-racing This is both a social event and an outlet for the Chinese mania for gambling. Races begin at 2.15 every Saturday afternoon during the season at the *Singapore Turf Club*, Bukit Timah Rd ☎ 469 3611.

Polo Matches are played Tue, Thu and weekends, Feb–Oct, at the *Singapore Polo Club*, Thomson Rd ☎ 253 5548.

Rugby is played on the Padang every Sat, Sep–Mar.

Keeping fit
Apart from the comprehensive sports facilities at Marina Complex and the Hyatt Regency, Westin and Shangri-La hotels, there are many sports centres.

Badminton *Singapore Badminton Hall*, Guillemard Rd ☎ 345 7554, open 7am–11pm daily; reserve between 10am and noon.

Boardsailing *East Coast Sailing Centre*, 1210 East Coast Parkway ☎ 449 5118.

Golf Singapore has more golf courses than any other city in South-East Asia; the *Golf in Singapore* leaflet from the Singapore Tourist Promotion Board gives full details of charges. Most clubs also have pools and squash and tennis courts. *Singapore Island Country Club*, Upper Thomson Rd ☎ 459 2222, is the premier course, but the *Keppel Club*, Bukit Chermin ☎ 273 5522, is nearest to the city. Other courses include *Sentosa* ☎ 472272; *Tanah Merah*, Changi Coast Rd ☎ 542 3040; *Jurong*, Science Centre Rd ☎ 560 5655 and *Changi*, Netheravon Rd ☎ 545 1298.

Jogging Many jog in the Botanic Gardens (see *Sightseeing*).

Riding Contact the Saddle Club, at the *Singapore Turf Club*, Bukit Timah Rd ☎ 469 3611, ext 295, and *Singapore Polo Club*, Thomson Rd ☎ 256 4530.

Sailing Members of overseas yacht clubs are generally welcome at the *Republic of Singapore Yacht Club*, 249 Jalan Buroh, Jurong ☎ 265 0931 and *Changi Sailing Club*, Netheravon Rd, Changi ☎ 545 2876.

Squash *National Stadium* ☎ 440 8622.

Tennis *Singapore Tennis Centre*, East Coast Parkway ☎ 442 5966.

Water-skiing *Ponggol Boatel*, Ponggol Point ☎ 481 0031.

Local resources

Business services

Your hotel should be able to help you with whatever support services you need. Singapore has a burgeoning service sector and no shortage of firms offering every kind of business facility round the clock. One central agency, *Worldwide Business Centres*, 111 North Bridge Rd 11–04 ☎ 336 6577, has fully serviced office accommodation with secretarial staff, telex and fax.

Photocopying and printing There are photocopy shops almost everywhere, of which some also undertake small printing jobs with free pick-up and delivery. These include *ABBA Enterprises* ☎ 732 1103; *Columbia Plan Printing and Copy Centre* ☎ 223 1133; *Greenland Copier Services* ☎ 468 1398 and *Lam Ann Photocopy Services* ☎ 468 8631. Quick and reliable printing firms include *Inco* ☎ 534 1032; and *Easiprint* ☎ 336 2420.

Secretarial Joan Tooke's *Secretarial and Employment Agency* ☎ 222 2644 and *Temporary Services* ☎ 732 6933 have bilingual staff.

Translation Interlingua ☎ 222 3755 and *Worldwide Translation Services* ☎ 737 7672.

Communications

Local delivery Cougar ☎ 225 3225; *Pronto* ☎ 747 9011; *Steiner Services* ☎ 337 4214.

Long distance delivery DHL ☎ 344 8955. *TNT Skypak* ☎ 745 3122; *Federal Express* ☎ 742 9000.

Post office The *General Post Office* is in the Fullerton Building on Fullerton Rd ☎ 532 3753. It is open 24 hours a day for limited services. The *Orchard Point Post Office*, 160 Orchard Rd, B1-16/17 is open 8.30–8 daily.

Otherwise normal post office hours are 8.30–5, Sun 8.30–1. There are post offices in most main streets; all sell cartons for parcel mail.

Telephones The telephone service is extremely efficient and local calls made from business or private phones are free. Calls from public pay phones cost 10 cents. IDD calls can be made from most hotel phones, but there is a surcharge of up to 20%. International calls cannot be made from public phones but can be made from a number of post offices. For collect calls or the international operator ☎ 162.

Telex and fax Many post offices offer these services; call the Post Office Inquiry Service ☎ 181.

Conference/exhibition centres

Singapore is one of the best equipped cities in Asia for conventions. The *World Trade Centre*, Maritime Sq ☎ 274 7111 is the main venue for trade exhibitions and the *Singapore Conference Hall*, Shenton Way ☎ 222 9711, is the main convention centre. Several hotels have purpose-built convention centres with simultaneous translation and audiovisual facilities. For planning assistance and information, contact the *Singapore Convention Bureau*, Raffles City Tower 37-00, 250 North Bridge Rd ☎ 339 6622.

Emergencies

Hospitals Singapore's medical and dental facilities are among the best in the world. Many doctors are trained overseas. Most hotels have their own doctor on 24hr call. For 24hr emergency rooms: *American Hospital* ☎ 345 1516; *Gleneagles Hospital* ☎ 473 7222; *National University Hospital* ☎ 772 5000. For emergency dental treatment, *American Hospital* ☎ 344 7588; *National University Hospital* ☎ 772 4922; *Angmo Kio Dental Centre* ☎ 452 2884.

Pharmacies Registered pharmacies are numerous and generally open from 9am–10pm.

Police Singapore is one of the safest cities in Asia. In an emergency ☎ 999 or the Central Police Station ☎ 535 2725.

Embassies and consulates

Australia 25 Napier Rd ☎ 737 9311

Austria 1 Scotts Rd, 22-04 Shaw Centre ☎ 235 4088
Belgium International Plaza, 10 Anson Rd 09-24 ☎ 220 7677
Canada 14-15th Fl, IBM Tower, 80 Anson Rd ☎ 225 6363
Denmark 101 Thomson Rd, 12-01 Goldhill Sq ☎ 250 3383
Finland 101 Thomson Rd, 21-02/03, Goldhill Sq ☎ 254 4042
France 5 Gallop Rd ☎ 466 4866
Greece 51 Anson Rd, 11-51 Anson Centre ☎ 220 8622
Indonesia 7 Chatsworth Rd ☎ 737 7422
Ireland 541 Orchard Rd, 08-02 Liat Towers ☎ 732 3430
Italy 101 Thomson Rd Int, 27-02-03, Goldhill Sq ☎ 250 6022
Japan 16 Nassim Rd ☎ 235 8855
Malaysia 301 Jervois Rd ☎ 235 0111
Netherlands 541 Orchard Rd, 13-01 Liat Towers ☎ 737 1155
New Zealand 13 Nassim Rd ☎ 235 9966
Norway 16 Raffles Quay, 17-01 Hong Leong Bldg ☎ 220 7122
Philippines 20B Nassim Rd ☎ 737 3977
South Korea 101 Thomson Rd, 10-03 Goldhill Sq ☎ 256 1188
Spain 79 Robinson Rd, 27-00 CPF Building ☎ 220 4222
Sweden 111 Somerset Rd, 05-08 PUB Bldg, Devonshire Wing ☎ 734 2771
Switzerland 1 Swiss Club Link ☎ 468 5788
Thailand 370 Orchard Rd ☎ 737 2644
UK Tanglin Rd ☎ 473 9333
USA 30 Hill St ☎ 338 0251
West Germany 545 Orchard Rd, 14-01 Far East Shopping Centre ☎ 737 1355

Government offices

The *Trade Development Board* ☎ 271 9388 is mainly involved in the promotion of Singapore's exports. The *Economic Development Board* ☎ 336 2288 offers a one-stop service to foreign investors. The *Ministry of Foreign Affairs* ☎ 330 5728 has directorates variously responsible for trade and diplomatic relations with different countries. The *Ministry of Communications and Information* ☎ 270 7988 deals with official information on government policy and activities, while the *Government Publications Department* ☎ 223 0834 is a source of reliable statistics. *Immigration Department* ☎ 532 2877; *Customs and Excise Department* ☎ 222 3511.

Information sources

Local media The two local morning English language newspapers are the *Straits Times* for general news and business coverage and the *Business Times* for in-depth trade, commercial and economic news. Both cover the major regional markets – Kuala Lumpur, Jakarta and Hong Kong – as well as Singapore. Financial news is also carried on the hotels' teletext service 6am–midnight.

Tourist information The main office of the *Singapore Tourist Promotion Board*, 36-04 Raffles City Tower, 250 North Bridge Rd ☎ 339 6622, has helpful and knowledgeable staff who can answer just about any inquiry. The *Tourist Information Centre* in the Singapore Handicraft Centre, 163 Tanglin Rd ☎ 235 5433, is less useful but has a comprehensive stock of maps and literature. Most hotels provide access to the SBC Text Information Service on Channel 5; this gives general information on Singapore plus weather, travel and currency rate details.

Thank-yous

Singapore has scores of gift shops selling flowers, gift hampers of food, wine, chocolates and fruit. Two of the best are *Princess Flower Shop* ☎ 737 6821 and *Christanio de Florist* ☎ 286 0085. Both are open daily till late. The *Marco Polo Hotel Cake Shop* (open 9–6) specializes in chocolates. The *Wine Corner* at the Hyatt hotel offers a comprehensive selection of fine wines (open noon–2.30 and 7–11.30).

Planning and reference
Entry details
Documentation Every visitor must have a passport or an internationally recognized travel document.

Visas are not required for visitors staying up to 14 days with the exception of nationals of communist countries and India who require a visa for entry. Anyone expecting to stay beyond the visa-free period should normally apply for a visa in advance from a Singapore embassy or representative office in their own country, although British and British Commonwealth, American, EC and ASEAN citizens may easily obtain an extension for up to three months' stay at the Immigration Department in Singapore ☎ 532 2877.

Driving licence Drivers must be over 23 and have held a driving licence for at least one year. An international driving licence is not required.

Health precautions Anyone arriving from a yellow fever zone within the previous 6 days must have a valid vaccination certificate. Inoculation against cholera, typhoid and polio is advisable.

Customs regulations Singapore is virtually a duty-free port. Items which still attract duty are tobacco and alcohol, clothes and furniture (except for personal use), and motor vehicles. A licence is required to import gold, platinum and precious stones (except personal jewellery), vaccines, meat, animals, plants, seeds, pre-recorded video and audio tapes, telecommunications equipment, arms, ammunition and explosives (medicines for personal use should be clearly labelled and accompanied by a doctor's note explaining what they are and why they are required). Drug trafficking attracts severe penalties, including death. Duty-free allowances are 1 litre/45 fl oz of spirits or wine; 200 cigarettes or 50 cigars or 250gm/9oz of tobacco. Duty-free allowances are not available to those people travelling between Singapore and Malaysia.

Climate
Singapore is only 1° north of the equator, so the climate is much the same – hot and wet – all the year round. The temperature is generally around 30°C/87°F at noon and 24°C/75°F at night with only minor seasonal variations. Humidity is usually high at 85–90%. It rains all year but most often in the early morning. November to March, when Singapore is affected by the northeast monsoon, is the wettest period. July is the driest month.

In such hot and humid conditions, it is best to wear lightweight clothes and avoid synthetic materials. White shirt, tie and smart trousers, or skirt and blouse, are the standard business dress. A jacket is needed only if the air conditioning feels chilly, although one or two exclusive restaurants and nightclubs still insist on a sober jacket and tie for men and a dress or skirt for women.

Holidays
Christian, Muslim and Chinese holidays vary from year to year according to their respective and differing calendars. The following are the only public holidays.
Jan 1 New Year's Day
Late Jan/early Feb Chinese New Year (two days)
Late Mar/early Apr Good Friday
May 1 Labour Day
Mid-May Vesak Day
Late May Hari Raya Puasa
Mid-Jun Dragon Boat Festival
Early Aug Hari Raya Haji
Aug 9 National Day
Late Oct/early Nov Deepavali
Dec 25 Christmas Day

Money
Local currency Singapore's currency is denominated in dollars and cents. Notes are available in denominations of S$10,000, 1,000, 500, 100, 50, 25, 10, 5 and 1, and coins in denominations of 50, 20, 10 and 5 cents. S$50 notes are the highest value generally acceptable in shops, and taxi drivers may protest at

giving change for even this amount. Brunei and Malay dollars no longer circulate freely, but major foreign currencies, particularly US dollars, can be used to pay for large purchases in department stores. There are no exchange control limits.

Changing money Banks and licensed money dealers give the best rates. Hotels are invariably 5% below the bank rate. Beware of unlicensed dealers or anyone whose rates and charges are not clearly displayed. Traveller's cheques in all freely negotiable currencies are easily exchanged, although passports must be produced; banks usually charge a S$2 handling fee, whatever the amount cashed. If you use traveller's cheques to pay for goods, you are expected to hold out for a good rate as part of the bargaining process. Just about every international bank has an office in Singapore, and all the local banks handle foreign exchange. Most banks open Mon–Fri, 10–3, Sat, 9.30–11.30am. Exceptions are the five branches of the Development Bank of Singapore which open until 3pm on Sat. The banks at the airport are open 7am–11pm; hotel exchange desks generally provide a service for guests 7–10pm and many licensed money-dealers dotted around the Orchard Road area are open until 10pm.

Credit cards are widely accepted, but shops in which bargaining is the norm will not give their best prices for credit card transactions. Some places charge a commission of 2–5%, much against the wishes of the card companies.

Tipping is strongly discouraged by the government and by employers. Consequently no one expects it.

South Korea

The Republic of Korea occupies the southern part of the peninsula it shares uneasily with communist North Korea. South Korea hurtled through the process of industrialization in a quarter of a century, and by 1987 stood on the verge of developed-country status, with the prospect of further growth at more than 5% a year in the medium term. Political development, however, has lagged behind economic success.

The ancient kingdom of Korea was a Japanese colony from 1910 to 1945. Japanese rule was brutal and exploitative, involving a process of assimilation tantamount to cultural genocide. In 1945 Japanese troops north of the 38th parallel were ordered to surrender to the Russians, those south of it to the Americans, and the parallel became the border between two Korean states set up under the auspices of the respective victors. In 1950, North Korea invaded and almost overran South Korea. A US-led UN expeditionary force not only repelled the invader but had in turn almost overrun North Korea when Chinese troops intervened. The border today is the ceasefire line where fighting stopped in 1953. North Korea's leader Kim Il-sung has never renounced reunification by force as a possible last resort, and this threat still influences politics in the South.

Since 1948, two short interludes of instability have punctuated three long periods of authoritarian rule under Presidents Rhee (1948–60), Park (1961–79) and Chun (1980–87). President Rhee was forced out by student riots, and Park's military coup a year later cut short a democratic experiment. Park was assassinated in 1979, and again a military strongman moved in.

South Korea's social and economic conditions are capable of sustaining the truly representative institutions it has lacked. The country is cohesive in race and language. Land reform consolidated under President Rhee has reduced inequality, while the expansion of schooling he started has left Korean men and women well educated.

In 1962 President Park launched a war-torn, aid-dependent economy, virtually without exports or domestic savings, into headlong pursuit of industrialization through export of manufactures, so successfully that growth has averaged 8.7% for some 25 years and per capita income rose from US$90 in 1961 to US$2,296 in 1986. Unemployment is low, inflation low, real pay has risen strongly, the current account is in surplus, and foreign debt, though very large, is manageable and falling.

The key to South Korea's politics is the perceived threat from its northern neighbour. North Korea's armed forces outnumber the South's and are deployed for lightning attack. Kim Il-sung's dream of reunification is held in check by the US presence – 42,000 US troops support the South's own army – and the influence of the USSR and China, which fear being dragged into world war.

The political scene

The main political issues since 1981 have been the legitimacy of the government and the mechanism for choosing a successor to take over the presidency in February 1988. The desire to stage the 1988 Olympic Games successfully in Seoul was universal, given the psychological as well as economic importance of the event. Following student and labour unrest and middle-class resentment during 1987, the government conceded opposition demands for a free presidential election and the release of political prisoners.

Government legitimacy

Although the government of President Chun Doo-hwan had the appearance of constitutional normality, its origins were violent. Blood was spilt when Chun seized control of the army in December 1979, following the assassination of President Park. More was shed during student demonstrations in May 1980, and protesters against the ensuing political clampdown were massacred in Kwangju.

Questionable constitution The 1980 constitution under which Chun ruled was approved by plebiscite, but under martial law with most opponents locked up. Chun's election in 1981 was held under the indirect system this constitution stipulated, which was open to manipulation.

The opposition

Until 1985, Chun faced only token opposition, and his technocrats could concentrate with brilliant success on the second leg of the economic miracle. Gradual political relaxation, however, encouraged the opposition to form the New Korea Democratic Party (NKDP)just in time to contest the parliamentary election of February 1985 and win 29% of the vote, outpolling the official Democratic Justice Party (DJP) in the major cities.

Time to talk

To lower a temperature raised by an increasingly violent student campaign for direct elections, talks started between government and opposition parties in mid-1986 to discuss constitutional change. The ruling party's offer of a prime ministerial system split the NKDP, a minority being willing to consider it if other freedoms were conceded, the majority sticking to their demand for direct presidential elections. The majority group, led by Kim Young-sam and Kim Dae-jung, formed a new party, the Reunification Democratic Party (RDP).

The 1987 climb-down In June, the DJP nominated Chun's military crony Roh Tae-woo as its candidate. Students erupted into protest, this time with clear support from their middle-class elders. As police battled to control street rallies, the reintroduction of martial law looked possible. In late June Roh endorsed all the opposition's main political demands and President Chun agreed to implement them. Roh was transformed overnight from Chun's ally into people's friend, presumably with Chun's blessing.

Poised for freedom

A referendum in October 1987 approved a new constitution which provided for direct presidential elections in December, the first in 16 years. Neither Kim Young-sam nor Kim Dae-jung was prepared to step down as candidate. This split in the opposition opened the way for Roh to win the election, claiming 36% of the vote. The two Kims together polled 54%. In elections in April 1988 the DJP lost its majority in the National Assembly.

The economic scene

South Korea became a US$100bn economy in 1987, with merchandise exports worth almost US$45bn. Continuing industrial growth makes it an important market for capital goods, and it seems set to sustain its current account surplus which will permit rapid reduction of its $36bn foreign debt.

Human resources

Human rather than natural resources are South Korea's key endowment. Its 41m population, packed 410 per square km/1,062 per square mile, is increasing by 1.5% a year, a rate halved by birth control over the past 25 years. There is little migration in or out, and no division of race or language – although provincial loyalties are strong. The urban population is 63% of the total.

Education Korea has long given high priority to education, with secondary school enrolment at 90% and university enrolment at 22–23 students per 1,000 people (see *Business and cultural awareness*). Local R&D is starting to yield "firsts" in high-tech areas.

Labour force Self-employed and family workers accounted for 46% of total employment in 1986, against 59% in 1976. In 1986, for the first time, the manufacturing sector's share of total employment (25%) exceeded agriculture's (24%).

Natural resources

Korea's export successes have relied on sweat and skill: it has nothing else to sell. Output of anthracite covers less than 18% of energy needs. Offshore drilling has found no commercial quantities of oil or gas. A little tungsten is exported, but lead and zinc output falls short of domestic needs, while copper and iron deposits are negligible. The mountainous terrain makes paddy land scarce, and Korea has to produce yields near the world's best to achieve self-sufficiency in rice.

Agriculture

Korean agriculture is based on owner-occupation of smallholdings, with little tenancy or hired labour. The "green revolution," based on improved seed, fertilizers and credit, found ideal conditions among Korea's well-educated rice farmers. Yields soared, making Korea in normal years only a marginal importer of rice. Affluence is increasing the demand for meat and dairy products and in response, livestock numbers have been greatly increased.

Leaving the land The farm population fell by 30% between 1974 and 1984. As the young leave for the towns, machinery helps an ageing farm population to cope. Power tillers numbered only hundreds 25 years ago; now there are about 600,000.

Infrastructure boom

Huge expansion has matched the physical infrastructure to the needs of a boom economy. In the 20 years up to 1984, the paved road network grew 16-fold to 24,000km/15,000 miles (including 1,400km/870 miles of motorways); the merchant fleet grew from 167,000grt to over 6.3mgrt, with maritime freight volume tripling in ten years; the number of telephone subscribers grew by 18% a year, giving every other home a set; power generating capacity rose by 16% a year; and there was a sixfold rise in the number of hospital beds. Even the railway system expanded. Only housing supply fails to match the needs of a swelling urban labour force, and that is improving.

External trade

In 1962, when Korea committed itself to exporting manufactured goods, exports were worth US$55m, mostly primary products. In 1987, they were more than US$47bn, mostly manufactures. Export volume has risen by about 24% a year, three times as fast as world trade in manufactures. The USA accounted for 40% of Korea's total exports in 1986, Japan and the EC for 27%. Korea's worst fear is US protectionism and it is also a major target of US pressure for trade reform. During 1987 it made an effort to open its markets to American goods in order to cut its trade surplus with the USA (US$7.2bn in 1986). The deficit with Japan was US$5.4bn in 1986. *Quality counts* Initially, cheap labour sold cotton textiles and simple assemblies. Now, 256k memory chips, cars and consumer electronics feature prominently. Clothing sells more on quality and fashion as others undercut Korean labour costs. *Imports* are dominated by machinery, fuel and raw materials; licensing or high tariffs keep out consumer goods and food imports are minor. Technical and equity links help to make Japan the major source of machinery. It supplied 35% of total imports in 1986, the USA 21% and the EC 10%.

Balance of payments

At its worst, in 1980, the current account deficit was US$5.3bn; this reflected increasing interest rates on a rising foreign debt and a US$6.2bn oil bill. By 1986, it had turned into a US$4.7bn surplus, thanks to an all-round fall in oil prices, interest rates and the exchange rate. Exports at US$33.9bn exceeded imports by US$4.3bn. The invisible trade deficit was only US$600m, despite a US$4bn outflow of investment income (mostly interest payments). Net income from tourism surged to US$900m, while shrinking remittances from overseas construction companies still came to US$635m.

The 1986 current account surplus was matched by a rise in reserves and a US$2.5bn capital outflow, mostly repayment of foreign debt. Relatively small direct investment inflows are beginning to be offset by Korean investments abroad. Gross reserves of US$8bn at the end of 1986 gave more than three months' import cover.

External debt

In the mid-1980's South Korea was the fourth largest Third World debtor, after Mexico, Brazil and Argentina, although its debt service ratio was lower than theirs and it has never rescheduled.

Between 1979 and 1985, total external debt rose from US$20.3bn to US$46.7bn, mainly to finance current account deficits. Debt servicing on medium- and long-term debt cost, at worst, 21.5% of export earnings. In 1986, total debt was cut to US$44.5bn and by the end of 1987 it was about $36bn. With exports up by 27%, the debt service ratio fell sharply. Never a problem debtor, South Korea should see a steady decline in its external debt.

Currency

Korean exports have proved extremely sensitive to exchange rate movements, their growth faltering only when the Korean won has been temporarily overvalued and bouncing back quickly after devaluation. In 1975, for instance, after an 18% devaluation against the dollar in December 1974, export volume jumped by 23% despite world recession. A similar pattern recurred in 1980.

Exchange rate management (now in relation to a currency basket) has been made harder by huge recent fluctuations in the rate between yen and dollar, the currencies of Korea's major supplier and major market. The aim has been to stay competitive in the US market, but devaluing only just enough to achieve this against the rising dollar of the early 1980s meant becoming extremely uncompetitive in relation to Japanese, Taiwanese and European producers.

Trade implications Between February and October 1985, therefore, the won was pushed down further against a now weakening dollar. Competitiveness was greatly restored in Europe and Japan, while Korean goods became unbeatable on price in the USA. In the 18 months from October 1985, the won was pushed up very gently by 6% against the dollar, and then under increasing US pressure by 21% in 1987-8. This still did little to blunt Korea's edge in US markets but meant further depreciation against the yen. Now it is Japan that finds it hard to beat Korean prices in third markets.

Budget
A major success of President Chun's government has been to reduce both central government and public sector deficits to about 1% of GDP. The government sees taxation as a proportion of GDP rising from 17.6% in 1986 to nearly 20% in 1991, to pay for an 8.3% a year real rise in spending.

Revenue Value-added tax provided 24% of tax revenue in 1986, customs duties 14%, income tax 13% and corporation tax 9%. A further 14% comes from a surcharge on internal, customs and local taxes, earmarked for defence.

Spending Defence took 27% of central government spending in 1986. Education takes 17–18%, health, housing and social security about 12%.

Size and growth of the economy
In 1961, on the eve of the dash for export growth, GNP per head was US$90 – just 5.6% of Japan's. In 1986, it was US$2,296, about 14% of Japan's. South Korea's US$100bn-economy status was reached in 1987 after real GNP growth of 8.7% a year between 1962 and 1986. More impressive yet, given the troubled international background, GDP growth averaged 8.3% a year measured from the trough of the 1980 recession.

The role of industry
In 1962, manufacturing accounted for only 9% of GNP; in 1986, it accounted for 33%, and about 90% of exports. Korean industry is dominated by a few giant conglomerates (*chaebol*), of which Hyundai, Daewoo, Samsung and Lucky-Goldstar are probably the best known.

Imported raw materials Apart from food processing, industry depends almost wholly on imported raw materials and fuel. It still incorporates many imported parts in export goods and it relies heavily on imported machinery and technology, despite progress in capital goods production and local R&D. This import dependence of an export-oriented industry explains why exports and imports of goods and services both account for around 40% of GDP.

Export-led industrialization began with the labour-intensive conversion of imported raw materials. Cotton went out again as clothing, leather and rubber as footwear, timber as plywood, rubber as tyres. Radios made an early appearance in the export list, joined by TV sets in the 1970s.

Heavy industry The 1970s also saw a government drive to develop heavy industry. In some cases, such as the steel sector, the effort paid off, but in others the second oil crisis destroyed potential markets (shipbuilding) or raised costs (petrochemicals), leaving surplus capacity, while the expansion of the heavy machinery industry was simply over-ambitious.

Main products South Korean industry now offers world markets small cars, white goods, microwave ovens, VCRs, colour TV sets and many other consumer electronics and computer-related products. Korea still sells a great deal of clothing and footwear but, recognizing that it cannot compete on labour costs with China or Indonesia, it is moving up-market, selling quality goods under its own brand names.

The business climate

By the late 1980s, South Korea's economy was moving into a more mature phase. Earlier striving for the greatest possible growth was being tempered by expenditure on research and promotion of higher value-added products, while government plans included the restructuring of industry to rationalize uncompetitive businesses and widen the economic base away from reliance on a handful of big conglomerates.

Government attitudes to business

The sixth five-year development plan, adopted in 1987, emphasized economic efficiency and stability. The government redefined its role as that of a promoter rather than a regulator, while retaining the option of intervention in an industry or particular firm to defend wider economic interests.

Small business boost The new policy was to tone down or remove measures that encouraged the growth of giant business groups at the expense of flexibility, as well as other laws which promoted and protected particular industries. Small and medium-sized businesses were earmarked for encouragement, with an expected crackdown on restrictive business practices which effectively shut out the smaller operator and a streamlining of procedures to set up new firms or expand existing ones. Small enterprises have already benefited from government and private initiatives to increase the number of agencies serving their needs.

Financial initiatives The government has actively promoted venture capital firms in order to build up the country's future technology base. Carrot and stick policies have pushed more companies towards a listing on the Korea Stock Exchange, while central bank control over banking and credit looked set for gradual relaxation.

The public sector

The Korea Monopoly Corporation, Korea Electric Power Corporation and the Korea Telecommunication Authority are three of the 100% government-owned enterprises. The state also controls the railways, procurement and grain management. In addition, in the middle of 1987 there were about 30 companies in which the government had a substantial stake and more than 70 in which it had an interest.

Privatization plans During the mid-1980s the government announced plans for the gradual privatization of some of its holdings. Three significant names were Pohang Iron and Steel Corporation (POSCO), the Korean Electric Power Corporation and the Korea Exchange Bank.

Efficiency drive The reorganization of the Office of Monopoly into the Korea Monopoly Corporation in April 1987 reflected the government's recognition that its businesses must become efficient, responsive and market-oriented. In 1986 revenue from monopoly business had contributed 8.7% of the national budget.

Government influence Outside the public sector government exerts influence through guidelines rather than regulations. Ex-government officials often move into top positions in private sector firms, and this can provide an indirect channel for government influence.

Foreign investment

The government's efforts to attract foreign capital to Korea in the 1980s resulted in total foreign investment of US$1.4bn for 1982–85, compared with US$1.2bn for the whole of 1962–81. The bulk of foreign investment since the early 1960s has come from the USA and Japan. This reliance on the same two countries both for investment and as main trading partners has led the government to try to attract other investment sources, particularly from Europe.

Chemicals, electronics and machinery figure prominently as chosen areas, but the list of projects open to foreign investment is constantly being reviewed.

The government finds foreign investment – which is non-debt-carrying and often technology-intensive – very attractive. However, the stringency of the terms and conditions which it imposes, the negative list of prohibited and restricted projects and the thoroughness with which an application to invest is examined, are indicative of its desire to retain a large degree of control over precisely how and where foreigners do business in Korea.

Notable foreign investors Lotte Shoji International's (Japan) stakes in the Hotel Lotte and Pusan Hotel Lotte add up to more than US$600m, making it the single largest foreign investor. Others of significance are General Motors' 50:50 joint venture with Daewoo Motor, Ford's stake in Kia Motor and Caltex's in Honam Refinery. In the foods sector Nestlé and General Foods are tied up with Hanseo and Dongsuh Foods respectively.

Power in business

The chaebol Despite moves to broaden the base of the economy, it is likely that the big conglomerates (*chaebol*) will remain a dominant force. In the rapid industrialization and growth of the 1970s these giants, aided by preferential government policies, encompassed a wide range of businesses under one umbrella. To limit their power the *chaebol* have been forbidden to enter certain areas and industries, and in certain cases instructed to dispose of some of their holdings. However, the fact that they account for a large proportion of Korea's exports, ensures their

continuing position of influence.

The *chaebol* were originally family concerns, and although the power may now have transferred outside the family their structures remain autocratic. The tendency for senior civil servants to move into industry means the position of chairman or president is often largely ceremonial. Nonetheless the following people are very influential: Koo Cha-kyung, chairman of Lucky-Goldstar and chairman of the Federation of Korean Industries; Chung Ju-yung, honorary chairman (and founder) of Hyundai and former chairman of the Federation of Korean Industries; Chung Se-jung, chairman of Hyundai; Lee Byung-chull, chairman of Samsung; Kim Woo-choong, chairman of Daewoo, and Kim Suck-won, chairman of Ssangyong.

Old school tie At national level the key positions are the president's economic adviser, the head of the Economic Planning Board, and the heads of the ministries. As with many chains of influence in Korea, the links may have as much to do with being alumni of the same high school or university, or having family connections, as with rank.

Unions

In late 1987, following a wave of more than 3,600 strikes and double-digit wage increases, changes in the labour-laws gave the hitherto much-controlled unions significant new rights to organize, bargain collectively and strike. In 1988 industrial unrest eased but wage settlements still ran at 14%.

Employers

The main employers' forum is the Federation of Korean Industries, a private non-profit organization established in 1961. It has a wide spectrum of members covering most aspects of the economy, and sponsors research and policy-making initiatives (see *Who can help*).

The business framework

The fast-moving nature of South Korea's economy calls for a thorough investigation of available structures and regulations for any prospective business venture, especially as changes are often made without warning.

Company structures

There are four types of company in South Korea: a stock company (*chusik hoesa*), a limited liability company (*yuhan hoesa*), a partnership (*hapmyung hoesa*) and a limited partnership (*hapcha hoesa*). The majority of Korean companies are stock companies and this is the vehicle normally chosen by the foreign investor. Some foreign investors prefer the limited liability company; this has between two and fifty members, is simpler to set up than a stock company, and restrictions can be put on share transfer. A foreign company may not become involved in partnerships.

Company boards must elect one or two representative directors, who have the power to bind the company to agreements. It must be specified whether they can act independently or only jointly. In a joint venture it is usual to elect one Korean and one foreigner as representative directors, acting jointly.

The minimum capital needed to form a company is 50m won. There are no "paper companies."

Foreign ownership

The minimum level of foreign investment is US$100,000. This is reduced to US$50,000 if the foreign investor introduces technology and receives permission to participate in a small to medium-sized joint venture. The government prefers certain projects to have a Korean majority ownership, and instances where foreign ownership is less than 50% may receive swifter approval if other conditions are met. This applies in particular to projects designated for small and medium-sized enterprises, as well as specific projects covered by Mining Law, Fisheries Law, Petroleum Business Law, Marine Transportation Act and Ship Safety Act.

Rules and regulations

Foreign business people need to be aware of a number of rules and regulations. A weather-eye should be kept open for sudden changes, but useful background can be gleaned from English-language summaries put out by the Ministry of Finance's Foreign Investment Promotion Division, also available from chambers of commerce and major law firms. The following are key pieces of legislation.

The Foreign Capital Inducement Act covers procedures and regulations for foreign investment, loans, and technology transfers. Doing business under the terms of this act may speed up approval and make tax exemptions and other incentives available. A "negative list system" sets out prohibited and restricted areas for foreign investment, rather than stating areas in which investments may be made. Amendments passed in 1987 sought to simplify procedures, expand automatic approval, delegate approval authority from the Ministry of Finance to the Bank of Korea and rationalize tax incentives for foreign-invested companies.

The Foreign Exchange Control Act regulates movement of foreign currencies in and out of the country. In practice, bringing funds into the country is easier than sending them out. Both transactions are subject to approval. The act regulates many areas including possession and transfer of foreign currency funds, establishment of service contracts, securities transactions, and capital transactions and remittances not covered by the Foreign Capital Inducement Act.

Remittances from a project not already approved by the government must be separately authorized. It is thus wise to get the project and transfers from it approved in advance, in which case remittances will be automatically approved. The Ministry of Trade and Industry issues import and export licences, sometimes through delegated authority, according to "banned," "restricted" and "automatic approval" lists.

Corporation and income tax laws are relevant even to investors planning to set up only liaison or exploratory operations in South Korea. If a foreign company is deemed to have a permanent presence in the country, it may be liable to tax on all income it earns from its Korean business, whether generated by its local operation or not. An office is deemed permanent if it is considered to be producing income, even if it is ostensibly an agency or liaison office. Care must therefore be taken that an operation is not seen as income-producing if that is not the intention. If tax is payable, the Office of National Tax Administration has the power to assess it on deemed rather than declared income.

Automatic approval Projects will be approved, in theory, within ten days, and need not be reviewed by the Foreign Capital Project Review Committee, if the project is not on the negative list, if the foreign ownership is less than 50% (it may be greater than 50% in certain types of export and import projects), if the amount of foreign investment is less than US$3m, and if the foreign investor does not apply for tax exemptions or reductions.

Incentives

Tax exemptions Projects are eligible for tax privileges if they fall into any of the following categories: projects improving the balance of payments by meeting the obligatory export quota; projects accompanied by large amounts of capital or advanced technology; projects in the manufacturing sector with investment by non-resident Korean nationals; projects in a free export zone in accordance with the Free Export Zone Establishment Law; other designated projects, such as those fostering small and medium-sized industries where the foreign ownership is less than 50%.

Eligible projects may receive five years' exemption from the following taxes: income and corporation tax on a foreign-invested enterprise in proportion to the foreign ownership; acquisition and property taxes in proportion to the foreign ownership; tax on dividends paid to foreign investors; tax on royalties in accordance with a technology inducement contract, and income tax for foreign staff seconded under a joint venture agreement.

Depreciation Instead of taking the five-year exemption from corporation and income tax, a foreign-invested enterprise may instead choose "accelerated depreciation" at a rate calculated by multiplying the normal depreciation rate for a given capital asset by the "foreign investment ratio" (foreign investment divided by local equity).

Retroactive tax collection If conditions under which the tax exemptions have been granted are not complied with, there is provision for the retroactive collection of taxes.

Official enterprise zones Two free export zones are open to joint ventures and wholly foreign-owned concerns planning to export their products. Mason Free Export Zone is on the south coast and Iri Free Export Zone on the west coast. They offer simplified approval procedures and tax privileges. Other industrial sites offer advantages for those wishing to sell into the domestic market.

Repatriation of funds For approved foreign investments, the government guarantees unlimited remittance of profits and dividends, principal, interest and commissions related to foreign loans, and royalties for imported technology in accordance with contract terms agreed at the start of the project.

Setting up
Premises Office accommodation is cheaper than in Hong Kong and Tokyo, but there are relatively few buildings offering high-class premises. It pays to negotiate and to contact other tenants to find out their terms and conditions. Rent is generally paid in the form of a large up-front returnable sum (key money) and a monthly rental. There may be a maintenance fee to cover utilities. Air conditioning and heating may be subject to government control and not be available 24 hours a day, despite promises. Some buildings have designated contractors.
Staff The international hotel business centres often have lists of secretarial staff looking for work in foreign companies.

Insurance Local insurers have tie-ups with foreign insurance companies, and many have overseas staff in their branches.
Bank accounts To receive operating funds from abroad an account at a foreign exchange bank is required. Cheque books are not in common use and payments are normally made in cash, by bank draft or direct debit.
Chops and seals A company chop or seal is not essential, but may be requested in certain circumstances. Care must be taken with its use; if registered, it carries the same weight as an authorized signature.

Expatriate employment
The application procedure for a working visa is relatively simple, but can take time. Normally a long-term visa should be obtained while the applicant is out of the country. A company considering employing a foreigner already in Korea must make sure that his or her visas, permits and so on are in order.

Market entry
South Korea still has a relatively small and open foreign community, and the best, most up-to-date and pertinent advice on potential problems can usually be obtained from foreigners who have already established a presence.

Import and export
General and special trading licences must usually be obtained for those wishing to import and export goods. There are numerous regulations depending on the types of products involved. In most instances an authorized foreign exchange bank may issue an export or import permit. This authorization is needed even if the goods are on the automatic approval list. Import or export of restricted items needs endorsement from the relevant ministry or other body. Exports under a deferred payment scheme require an export licence from the Ministry of Trade and Industry.

The Office of Customs Administration provides information on restricted goods and duties payable.
Import controls All imports, other than those paid for with foreign aid funds, are divided into three categories: automatically approved, restricted and prohibited. Permits are automatically approved for most raw materials and capital and consumer goods not produced domestically. There is a special list of restricted items whose import the government wants to limit. Luxury items and certain domestically produced goods are among those on the prohibited list.

Technology licensing agreements are usually referred to as technology assistance agreements (TAAs). Once the relevant ministry has approved the agreement, it will be examined by the Fair Trade Commission to ensure compliance with the Fair Trade Law. TAAs will not be approved in certain circumstances, notably if the main purpose is to sell raw materials, parts or accessories; if the technology is low-level, outdated, or encroaches on a domestically-protected industry; and if the agreement contains unfair conditions or would contravene other Korean laws and provisions. The length of the agreement and level of royalties depend on negotiation with the relevant ministry. Royalties tend not to exceed 5% but the level may be improved if the technology can be shown to be essentially new to Korea and necessary to the economy. Royalties under the Foreign Capital Inducement Act are generally exempt from Korean tax for the first five years. In general a technology licence may mean a technology transfer, because the TAA may not require the licensee to stop using unregistered technology at the end of the agreement, except where this would infringe registered property rights.

Intellectual property

Pressure from Korea's trading partners has led to amendments of existing copyright, patent and trademark legislation, as well as the formulation of a "Computer Programme Protection Act." In the main these changes have been substantive as well as procedural. In late 1986 South Korea granted the USA special protection of intellectual property rights, allowing retroactive protection for 10 years in the case of printed material and five years for software. EC countries were anxious to secure equal treatment but talks on the issue in November 1987 failed to achieve total agreement.

Copyright The new legislation is intended to replace the old copyright law which had not been amended since 1957. In particular the new law tightens up the circumstances where there may be "fair use" of copyrights. Misunderstanding and disputes will be settled by a copyright deliberation committee, and licensed copyright intermediary agents will be available to help with negotiations. Civil and criminal actions are available to deal with copyright infringements.

Computer law Although the provisions and protection of computer programmes are similar to those in the copyright law, specific legislation is to be enacted.

Patents There has been domestic pressure to delay tighter patent legislation, especially from the pharmaceutical and chemical industries where process rather than product patents existed. However, the government has formulated new legislation which among other things extends the patent term from 12 to 15 years.

Trademarks Since 1986, trademark licence applications have not needed any accompanying technology. The Unfair Competition Law has been amended to extend counterfeit protection to nationals of Paris Convention member countries. Further amendments will allow exclusive as well as non-exclusive trademark licences.

Establishing a presence

Through an agent This is the simplest and cheapest route. The agent is not allowed to make money for his principal and therefore obviates the complications of foreign remittances and exchange control. However, the scope of business an agent may conduct is strictly limited to liaison activities such as arranging third party purchases of goods or conducting market research. Using an agent involves no legal presence in Korea; business cards, telexes and so on are in the name of the agent. It may be wise to choose an established agent with several clients, making it easier to prove he is not an employee. Korea Export Buying Offices Association and the Association of Foreign Trading Agents of Korea can give advice and provide potential contacts. See also the organizations listed in *Who can help*.

Through a representative office
For tax purposes this type of office must not be income-producing, but it has the advantage that the staff are employees of the parent company. It is fairly simple to set up, provided the scope of the business does not fall into the restricted or prohibited category. As the parent company has no legal presence in Korea, most office assets will be in the representative's name.

Through a distributor This often provides the simplest vehicle for product sales. The distributor normally deals with the Korean authorities, which can be an added advantage. Appointment of a distributor needs government approval. In the approval process the government will seek to protect the distributor, which can mean contractual points agreed by both parties being overturned.

Opening a branch entails a legal presence in Korea, which makes the parent company liable to tax on all income generated in the country, not just that produced by the branch office. A business plan must be presented before approval is given to open a branch. Any change in the type of business conducted may mean reapplying for approval. If income is to be remitted out of Korea, permission must be obtained before the branch is established, and remittances will be possible only for the types of business approved. It is also essential to comply exactly with procedures for bringing in operating funds, or it may be difficult to get the money out should the operation fold.

Outlets
Retail outlets in Korea are still, generally, small and numerous. Wholesalers also tend to be small,

very competitive and to suffer from cash flow problems. Apart from the electronic goods outlets of major trading companies like Lucky-Goldstar and Samsung, most sophisticated consumer products are sold through department stores.

Freight
Sea Pusan and Inchon are the main ports. Pusan is in the southeast corner of the peninsula and Inchon about one hour's drive west of Seoul.
Road Expressways and main roads connect industrial sites and the major cities. South Korea's road system is not well developed, but all points on the peninsula are accessible within a day.
Rail Trains carry 50% of domestic freight, and are subsidized by the government.
Air Kimpo International airport is served by a number of international carriers and there are direct services to and from Hong Kong and Japan, the region's two major hubs.

Advertising and market research
The advertising market is regulated and has grown up only in the past 20 years. The leading agencies are affiliated or otherwise linked with overseas agencies, although separate offices are likely to be allowed in the future. The main agencies and their affiliations are: Korea First Advertising (Ted Bates, Hakuhodo), Oricom (McCann-Erickson), Dae Hong (S&SC), LG Ad (BBDO), Union (Grey), Korad (Ogilvy & Mather), Dong Bang (Leo Burnett), Samhee (Lintas) and Nara (J.W. Thompson).

Greater competition in consumer goods has led to the growth of market research agencies, though lack of experience means their emphasis is often on data-gathering rather than conclusion-drawing. Some of the major firms are: A.C. Neilson, Frank Small & Associates, Hankook Research Co, IMS Korea, Korea Consulting Group Ltd and Korea Survey (Gallup) Polls Ltd.

The financial scene

South Korea's banking system was established only in 1950, and all the commercial banks were effectively government organs until 1982, selectively financing industrial expansion with cheap credit. This, plus a low level of savings deposits and tight monetary policy, led to credit shortages and the growth of a "kerb market" – trading outside the recognized institutions. Many of the commercial banks had major problems in 1985 because of the large number of bad debts and had to be bailed out by the central bank. Recent moves towards liberalization and the growth of secondary institutions are now making for a healthier financial climate.

Central banking

The Bank of Korea (BoK), under the Ministry of Finance, is the central bank with overall responsibility for banking supervision and control of the money supply and credit, according to policies set by its Monetary Board. It issues the local currency, acts as banker to the government, handles business related to the National Investment Fund, holds the national foreign exchange reserves, determines interest rates on foreign exchange loans and deposits, and approves foreign exchange payments. Stated policy is gradually to relax government control, instead influencing credit via open-market operations, control of rediscount rates and the commercial banks' reserve/asset ratios and abolition of the "kerb market."

The Monetary Board is the part of the BoK responsible for formulating and regulating banking and monetary policy, eg via control over interest rates.

Commercial banking

The big seven The Hanil Bank, Bank of Seoul & Trust Co, Korea First Bank, Choheung Bank, Commercial Bank of Korea, Shinhan Bank and KorAm Bank operate nationwide and have many branches overseas. The government had sold its controlling interest in the first five by 1982, while the last two were established only in 1982–83.

Local banks There are also ten local banks: Daegu Bank, Pusan Bank, Chungchong Bank, Kwangju Bank, Cheju Bank, Kyunggi Bank, Chonbuk Bank, Kangwon Bank, Kyongnam Bank and Chungbuk Bank. They are not permitted to have branches nationwide, but have a few offices overseas. Most lending is on short terms, stretched via rollovers or renewals where necessary, and relying on the Bank of Korea to act as lender of last resort when banks are unable to raise funds in the market.

Special banks

These conduct specialist loan and deposit business, competing with the commercial banks for deposits. The government-owned Korea Development Bank and Korea Exchange Bank both tap the international credit markets, the former for major projects which may also use international aid funds and in which it often holds an equity stake on behalf of the government, and the latter monopolizing most of South Korea's international commercial banking business.

The Export-Import Bank of Korea extends specialist trade finance and supplier credits to foreign buyers of Korean exports. The Korea Long-Term Credit Bank provides investment funds to companies with government holdings of under 50%.

Other specialist institutions include: the Small and Medium Industry Bank (provides financial services to smaller companies); the Citizen's National Bank (gives short-term credit to small enterprises and individuals); and the Korea Housing Bank.

Merchant banks

Six merchant banks on the UK model were established in 1975, mostly with foreign partners. Although designed to help develop capital markets, investment banking (such as loan syndications, corporate bond issues and underwriting securities) and advisory services for inward investors, restrictions have led these banks to pursue other business such as short and medium-term finance and leasing. Since 1984 they have been allowed to handle cash-management accounts.

Foreign banks

Some 50 branches and 20 representative offices of foreign banks conduct business similar to that of the commercial banks, subject to Foreign Exchange Control Act regulations. Foreign banks are empowered to operate special credit funds for foreign companies and joint ventures. Until recently, they did well out of bringing loans into the country under the "swap system," whereby funds are imported in foreign currency, and onlent in won, but restrictions have recently been placed on this business as the need for foreign funds has declined.

Non-banking financial institutions

Investment and finance companies grew up to fill the vacuum in unsecured short-term loans. Now numbering more than 30, they are second only to the commercial banks in size and are highly competitive.

Venture capital is a recent phenomenon, the main participants being the Korea Technology Development Corporation, the Korea Development Investment Corporation (a Korean-foreign joint venture) and the Korea Technology Finance Corporation (under the Korea Development Bank).

Other financial intermediaries include the mutual savings and finance companies and credit unions, the life and non-life insurance companies, the National Investment Fund (which channels money into infrastructure and basic industries), the National Housing Fund, the Korea Credit Guarantee Fund and the Credit Insurance Fund. There are five leasing companies, mostly Korean-foreign joint ventures.

The securities market

The main securities-trading forum is the Korean Stock Exchange (KSE), established in 1956 and regulated by a US-style Securities & Exchange Commission and a Securities Supervisory Board. By the end of 1986, it had 355 listed companies. Limited equity markets, low returns from equity investment and a reluctance to dilute ownership have handicapped the KSE's development, but tight credit and government policies are pushing more companies towards a listing. The government has directly encouraged the holding of equities by placing some of its holding in Pohang Iron and Steel Corporation (POSCO) with the institutions. Once listed, companies are allowed to issue bonds, subject to approval from the Ministry of Finance.

About 30 member companies of the Korea Security Dealers Association trade as brokers or on their own account, arrange issues, act as underwriters, etc. The Korea Securities Finance Corporation specializes in providing finance to such companies. There are also a few securities investment trust companies, whose business is shared by the merchant banks.

Direct foreign investment in South Korean companies is not possible at present. Joint ventures can be listed on the KSE, but few are. The stock market is open to foreign investors through specialized funds such as the Seoul Trust.

Who can help

Lawyers

The intricacies of Korean law require the use of a local lawyer. Senior partners of the major firms often speak excellent English and many also employ foreign, usually American, lawyers. Foreign law firms are not permitted to practise.

Kim & Chang, Seyang Bldg, 233 Naija-dong, Chongro-ku, Seoul ☎ 737 4455.

Kim, Chang & Lee, International Insurance Bldg, 120 5-ka Namdaemun-ro, Chung-ku, Seoul ☎ 777 9061/5.

Kim, Shin & Yu, Leema Bldg, 146-1 Susong-dong, Chongro-ku, Seoul ☎ 735 5822/4.

Shin & Kim Kyunghee Bldg, 1-122 2-ka Shinmun-ro, Chongro-ku, Seoul ☎ 732 6336.

Kim & Kim, Kyobo Bldg, 1 1-ka Chong-ro, Chongro-ku, Seoul ☎ 735 2980.

Accountants

The following are the leading accountants linked with foreign firms. They provide services in accounting, auditing, taxation and management consultancy.

An Am & Co (affiliated with Arthur Andersen) Kyobo Bldg, 1, 1-ka Chong-ro Chongro-ku, Seoul ☎ 739 9000.

Ahn Kwon & Company (member of Deloitte Haskins & Sells International) International Insurance Bldg, 120 5-ka Namdaemun-ro, Chung-ku, Seoul ☎ 753 0215/9.

Dongsuh Accounting Corporation (Ernst & Whinney), Miwon Bldg, 43 Youido-dong, Yongdungpo-ku, Seoul ☎ 784 6901.

Saedong & Co (affililated with Touche Ross International), DLI 63 Bldg, Youido-dong, Yongdungpo-ku, Seoul ☎ 784 5268.

Samil Accounting Corporation (member of Coopers & Lybrand International), Kukje Center Bldg, 191 2-ka Hangang-ro, Yongsan-ku, Seoul ☎ 739 3191.

San Tong & Co (member of Klynveld Peat, Marwick, Goerdeler) Koreana Bldg, 61-1 1-ka Taepyong-ro, Chung-ku, Seoul ☎ 733 2345.

Seihwa Accounting Corporation (associated with Price Waterhouse), Royal Bldg, 5 Danju-dong, Chongro-ku, Seoul ☎ 736 7801.

Yong Hwa Accounting Corporation (member of Arthur Young International) Daeyu Bldg, 25-15 Youido-dong, Yongdungpo-ku, Seoul ☎ 783 5261.

Other help

The following organizations can provide information on investment procedures. The Ministry of Finance's Foreign Investment Promotion Division and One-stop Service Office cover the relevant ministries and agencies, including the Ministry of Justice and the Office of National Tax Administration.

Foreign Investment Information Service, Ministry of Finance, 171-11 Chungang-dong, Kwachon, Kyong-do, Seoul ☎ 503 9258/9.

Federation of Korean Industries, 28-1 Youido-dong, Yongdungpo-ku, Seoul ☎ 783 0821/6.

Association of Foreign Trading Agents of Korea, Danguk Bldg, 45-14 Youido-dong, Yongdungpo-ku, Seoul ☎ 782 2205/9, maintains comprehensive data on trading agents in Korea.

Small & Medium Industry Promotion Corporation, Center for Foreign Investment Services, 27-2 Youido-dong, Yongdungpo-ku, Seoul ☎ 783 9611/8.

Korean Trade Promotion Corporation, 10-1 2-ka Hoehyon-dong, Chung-ku, Seoul ☎ 753 4181/9, has branches in many cities abroad.

Korean Chamber of Commerce and Industry, 45 4-ka Namdaemun-ro, Chung-ku, Seoul ☎ 757 0757, is a useful downtown source of Ministry of Finance publications.

Local business magazines include *Business Korea* ☎ 784 4010; *Korea Business World* ☎ 783 5430/2; *Korea-Europe Economic Report* ☎ 718 0145/6.

Business and cultural awareness

If there is a secret to business success in Korea, it lies in establishing a good relationship with your local counterparts. This will bring an understanding of the difference between business theory and practice, new business techniques and introductions to the right contacts. But the process of establishing a good personal relationship – like the Korean process of decision-making – is substantially slower than in the West. Taking enough time will prove well worth the trouble: in Korea personal loyalty brings dividends.

Type of society

South Korea today is a product of 5,000 years of history – a combination of Confucianism, Buddhism, Taoism, Japanese imperialism and 30 years of the economic miracle. The last may have had a great impact on the outward appearance of Korea and its population but behaviour and attitudes are still rooted in the values and standards of the past. In the Chosun Kingdom (1392–1910), Korea's avoidance of foreign ties and contacts earned it the sobriquet "the hermit kingdom." A foreigner doing business in Korea today must recognize that he or she is working in a Korean context and not, as yet, an international one.

Religion

Buddhism, Christianity and Confucianism are the most important faiths. Traditional animist practices have been absorbed into these religions, and it is common to find individuals who amalgamate two or more beliefs.

Buddhism arrived in Korea about AD372 and spread rapidly, becoming the state religion by the end of the 7th century. Buddhism gained in status, political power and artistic influence until abuse of its power led to a separation of religion and state from the late 14th century and official disapproval and oppression prevailed. Since 1945 reforms and stricter standards have have led to a revival of interest in Buddhism.

Christianity Evangelizing missions have had a great influence on the development of modern Korea, especially in education and welfare programmes. The first Roman Catholic priest arrived in 1785, and the religion spread gradually throughout the 19th century. Intolerance of foreigners and foreign ideas led to persecution, and many Catholic martyrs have been canonized. Treaties with foreign powers in the late 19th century protected missionaries, and Protestant missions began to be established in 1884.

Estimates put the total number of Christians in South Korea at 8 million, with Catholics accounting for about 20%. Korean Christians are characterized by their doctrinaire beliefs – the question "Do you smoke?" may bring the reply "No, I'm a Christian" – but this does not generally affect business practice.

Confucianism has no organized structure, but a number of associations observe Confucian rituals, and most Koreans observe at least some of its precepts in their daily lives. The emphasis on filial piety, reverence for ancestors and elders and the importance of ceremony can be traced to Confucian teachings, though growing internationalism is weakening the strength of some of these ideals.

Education

At the basic level the literacy rate is high (95–98%). A taxi driver, for example, has no problem reading Korean directions. Physical training plays a very important role at all levels of education.

Primary schools Free primary education for children aged six to eleven has been compulsory since 1953.

Middle school is for ages 12–14. Entrance exams have been abolished in order to equalize schools and opportunity, and places in a district are allocated on a lottery basis. Both middle and high-schools are fee-paying but the government intends to make middle-school education free and compulsory by 1991.

High school, for ages 15–17, can be vocational or academic. To enter, students must pass a state exam.

Higher education A large number of students, proportionately similar to that in the USA, go on to university or college. Lifelong and crucial relationships are formed at this stage. Most institutions are private, but scholarships and other schemes enable less wealthy students to attend. Entrance exams are stiff and admission to the most prestigious institutions is highly competitive. Four of the best known are Seoul National, Korea, Yonsei and Hankuk universities.

A combination of respect for learning and a competitive graduate job market leads many students into higher degree courses. Some study abroad, which the government encourages with various sponsorship schemes.

Language skills English is widely taught in schools and understood by the younger generation, though written skills tend to surpass spoken language ability. People over 45 or 50 are more likely to speak Japanese as a second language, as that is the language in which they did their schooling.

Attitude to foreigners

As very few Koreans, especially outside Seoul, have travelled, their experience of foreigners is limited. It is not expected or desired that the foreigner should behave like a Korean. If he or she shows respect and understanding for Korean feelings, such sensitivity will generally be reciprocated.

With a large US military presence, Korean attitudes towards Americans are often ambivalent – a mixture of gratitude and misunderstanding of the Americans' easy familiarity and exuberant approach.

The Japanese occupation (1910–45) and suppression of many things Korean created enormous domestic resentment. However, the 1965 normalization treaty, the high levels of Japanese investment and Korea's own increased wealth have, at least superficially, eased relations with Japan.

Friendly greetings Many Koreans will tell you that they are uncomfortable with Westerners who speak good Korean or who try to assimilate into their society. However, a few words of greeting are greatly appreciated.

Business practices

Koreans tend to work long hours, and socializing often revolves around the office and colleagues, involving drinks after work and company picnics.

Office hours are usually from 9am to 6pm, although it is common to work later. Junior staff stay until their bosses leave. Most offices are open on Saturdays from 9 to 3. The lunch-hour is usually 12 to 1.

Telephone contact All communication should be through the office. It is unwise to phone your contact's home unless specifically requested to do so. Business discussions over the phone are not recommended, even if you know the other party well. Face-to-face meetings are preferable and limit the possibility of language misunderstandings.

Business attitudes

Status and age The traditional respect for age rather than position will mean that a young (or young-looking) executive may encounter problems in meeting senior Korean personnel, convincing the Korean side that his/her company is taking the project seriously, convincing them that he or she has decision-making authority, and in negotiating a deal. The situation will be helped by a senior title and an introduction.

Women Korean women in positions of authority are rare and, despite educational opportunities, the prospects for advancement are slim. This is gradually changing, but some companies still have a policy of employing women only until they are 30 or married, whichever is the sooner. A foreign female executive may well find herself treated as an honorary man. In general, Korean men have less trouble dealing with a foreign woman than a Korean (or Korean-looking) female executive. In certain industries, such as textiles, Korean men are more accustomed to encountering women in authority.

Meetings

How to set them up "Cold-calling" is not very effective in Korea. A Korean would be very reluctant to contact someone he did not know, and is therefore uncomfortable being contacted in this way. You should be introduced, preferably by a Korean. If this is not possible, communication by telex or letter – setting out the nature of your company, your position and the purpose of your call – will increase the likelihood of being granted a meeting.

Appointments made a long time in advance should be confirmed. It is not always possible to finalize an itinerary far in advance, and Korea's more flexible attitude to time-keeping means that schedules should not be packed too tightly.

Whom to meet? Foreign business people often make the mistake of wishing to deal only with very senior management. It is more important to discover the level, or person, at which projects are assessed and recommendations made. Because of various factors, including language

skills and technical expertise, this will tend to be at middle management level. Once recommendations have been made, these are unlikely to be overturned on technical grounds. Personal loyalties may come into play, and it is therefore better to save the often limited access to senior management for situations when goodwill can be established and a deal can be cemented.

Conducting meetings All meetings begin with pleasantries, and the length of these will tend to increase with the seniority of the participants. At a first meeting it is especially important not to rush things; the Korean side will, eventually, move faster if they are comfortable with you. Discussions take time, and the hierarchical nature of companies means that decisions can rarely be made then and there. Whether discussions are carried out in English or through an interpreter, it may be necessary to go over something several times to make sure both sides have the same understanding. Sensitive subjects are sometimes better covered through an intermediary, such as a lawyer.

Get it in writing Koreans view an agreement as being open to negotiation until it is signed. It is therefore advisable, though not foolproof, to have written records of what has been discussed and decided.

Ask around Do not rely on only one opinion when faced with a practical or bureaucratic problem. There is often more than one way of interpreting a regulation.

Etiquette

Dress A jacket and tie are essential, and a business suit is required for formal situations or in the financial community. Older offices may not be air-conditioned in the summer. Women should dress conservatively.

Deference to seniority Senior executives should sit nearer the head of the table, whether at a meeting or a social occasion. In a car the right-hand rear seat is the senior position.

Greetings The handshake is becoming more widespread, and is often used to show how cosmopolitan someone is. Unless you are very knowledgeable it is wise to avoid bowing; inclining the head is safer.

Gifts are not expected, but if given should be presented at the end of a meeting. They should be given and received using both hands, and opened in private.

Names and titles

Korean names usually consist of three syllables, with the first being the family name and the following two the given names (for example Kim Hee Sun). These are sometimes reversed in English (Hee Sun Kim, or H.S. Kim). To make matters clearer many Koreans hyphenate their given names and/or put a comma after their family name (Kim, Hee-Sun). The conventions are formal, given names are rarely used, "Call me Jack" is only likely to produce embarrassment, and it is advisable to wait for a Korean to initiate a more familiar mode of address. The use of someone's title alone ("Director") or as an adjunct to his name ("Director Kim") is respectful. Given the predominance of a handful of surnames, individuals are usually referred to in conversation and correspondence by their full names.

Business cards

Names are often indistinct to a Westerner on introduction because of the Korean habit of self-effacement, as well as the unfamiliar sounds. Exchanging cards limits the need for repetition and reduces embarrassment on both sides. As Korea has a phonetic alphabet, Hangul, most Western names can be rendered easily into Korean, and business travellers would be well-advised to have English on one side and Korean on the other.

Cards are exchanged whenever you meet someone new. They should be presented right way up, using both hands. Normally this is done after the handshake, although, with older people in particular, this is sometimes reversed.

Entertainment

This may be at a Korean or a Western restaurant. Whereas a Korean may take you to either, a foreigner is expected to use a Western or possibly Japanese restaurant. In either situation the refusal of an alcoholic drink, especially in the evening, may cause offence.

General rules Shoes must be removed when entering a Korean-style dining area, where seating is usually on the floor. It is normally a mistake to pour your own drink or to pour one for your host until he has poured one for you. When pouring a drink or holding a glass to receive one, it is polite to use both hands. You should not raise business matters unless your host does.

Kisaeng parties These are all-male Korean-style meals with hostesses in attendance. They are characterized by copious quantities of alcohol and singing. To refuse to sing is impolite, however bad your voice. Your hosts may use these occasions to raise issues they would not discuss at a formal meeting. These should be noted but not referred to afterwards unless raised by the Korean side. Regardless of your reaction to Kisaeng parties, they are attempts to further personal relations and should be understood as such.

Hostess bars A variation on the Kisaeng party is the hostess bar. In general your host will take great pleasure in explaining the conventions and rules of these types of entertainment. Although in some cases the girls may be available for "further entertainment," this is by no means universal or compulsory.

Golf The golf course is another place where you can improve relations with your Korean contacts. An invitation to play should be accepted whenever possible.

SEOUL

Area code ☎ 02

Seoul, capital of South Korea, has been the centre of the country's trade, education and politics since the foundation of the Yi Dynasty in 1392. Some of the palaces and gates of the early city remain, but for the most part Seoul was pounded to rubble during the Korean war of 1950–53. When that war ended, the boundary between North Korea and South Korea, protected by a permanent garrison of some 40,000 servicemen of the US Eighth Army, was drawn at the 38th parallel. Seoul lies just 56km/35 miles south of this line and the air raid drill, which is supposed to halt all activity in the city for half an hour every fifteenth day of the month, is only the most obvious indication of the continuing tension between the two parts of the divided country.

Since the ending of the war, the city has been redeveloped in a determined effort to create a metropolis which reflects the aspirations of this modern, independent and industrially successful nation. Seoul's selection as the site for the 1988 Olympics was a great source of national pride and added impetus to the round-the-clock construction programme under way. Thirty-floor office towers now dwarf the 14thC city gates, once part of the old city wall. The skyscrapers are symbols of progress and modernity but would win no architectural awards. Beyond the city centre, concrete apartment blocks and factories sprawl in every direction.

Although positively ugly, Seoul has much to recommend it. The streets are kept impeccably clean. Multi-lane highways cut through the heart of the city ensuring that there is less of the congestion and incessant horn-blowing which characterizes other cities in Asia. A recently opened subway, one of the most extensive in the world with 108 stations, carries 5m commuters a day. The city is always full of flowers; azaleas grow like weeds, building entrances all have colourful displays and all the sidewalks are lined with gingko trees.

Seoul's population is now 10m, almost a quarter of South Korea's 42m total and still growing at 5% per annum. It has doubled in the past ten years alone, and some 60% of Seoul's inhabitants were born post-1950, with no direct experience of the traumas of the Korean War or Japanese occupation. Nevertheless, they are waging their own struggle. The students that fill the city's 40 universities and the young people who make up a large part of the factory workforce have repeatedly taken to the streets to demonstrate against the government and demand the right of free elections.

The prevailing view among Seoul-ites is that "democracy is something we have got to achieve to prove our maturity as a nation," a sentiment that sums up the progressive and determined outlook which characterizes Seoul and its people.

Arriving

Most people fly to Seoul, but it is impossible to get directly from North to South Korea. There are also no flights from China, Eastern Europe or the Soviet Union.

Kimpo International Airport

Kimpo receives some 200 flights a day and is always busy. Immigration procedures can be slow and customs inspectors tend to check all baggage; allow 60min to clear the airport. Departing passengers have to pay a W5,000 airport tax.

Facilities. Staff at the hotel reservations desk are helpful and there is good, free literature on events in Seoul. On arrival it is best to change money at the desks beyond customs rather than at those in the crowded arrivals hall. The restaurants, bars and buffets are adequate rather than comfortable, but several airlines have VIP lounges with complimentary refreshments for first-class and business-class passengers. The duty-free shops offer much the same wide range of goods as the one at the Hotel Lotte downtown at identical prices. The Cultural Property Preservation Bureau, which will certify antiques and reproductions for export, has an airport office ☎ 662 0106. Airport inquiries ☎ 663 0041.

City link The airport is 25km/15 miles west of Seoul. The journey into the centre takes 30–40min.

Hotel transport is the most efficient way to get into town and must be arranged in advance. Drivers wait in the arrivals hall holding placards.

Taxi There is a licensed rank to the far right of the terminal exit doors, and there is sometimes a 20min wait. A prominent board by the rank gives typical fares to the principal hotels – around W3,500 to those in central Seoul. Ignore offers from unlicensed touts; they charge many times the official rate.

Car rental Hertz Korean has an office at the airport which can be contacted via the Airport Information Desk ☎ 664 7684 or 585 0801. Limousine service is also available if reserved in advance.

Bus There are two routes via the main hotels; one ends at Sheraton Walker Hill, the other runs south to the sports complex. Buses leave every 10min from outside the terminal exit and routes are clearly signposted; they do not always stop directly in front of the hotel and you may find yourself struggling with baggage through long pedestrian tunnels and across hair-raising highways. Services operate from 5.30am to 9.30pm; the flat-rate fare is W500.

City Air Terminal Situated in the Korea World Trade Centre this new terminal provides transport to and from Kimpo Airport and easy access to downtown Seoul. Its facilities include duty-free shopping, money exchange and a post office. ☎ 556 0039.

Getting around

An efficient subway and a plentiful supply of inexpensive taxis make Seoul an easy place to get around.

Hotel transport Many hotels run their own fleet of taxis which are air-conditioned, but may not have meters. The fare should be agreed in advance using the hotel rep in order to avoid misunderstandings.

Taxis are usually plentiful at all times of the day and night. They can be hailed in the street and many streets have a rank with a yellow shelter. Drivers speak little English and are remarkably dim about the city's geography; always get someone to provide you with a business card or, even better, written directions in Korean.

At busy times of day, taxi drivers often pick up several passengers going the same way. A short journey typically costs W2,000. Tipping is not necessary but drivers will not proffer change if the amount is small.

Radio taxis are beige and charge double the regular fare ☎ 414 0150.

Driving Travelling by car in Seoul can be an exciting and frightening experience. *Hertz* ☎ 585 0801 has self-drive cars and limousines. Traffic drives on the right.

Walking For short distances of up to five blocks, it is best to walk. The grid network of downtown Seoul is easily navigated and walking is normally quite safe at all times. Jay walking is a serious offence. Walkers must cross at designated crossings and obey the lights. At major junctions there are pedestrian tunnels which double as shopping plazas, so it is easy to lose all sense of direction and emerge at the wrong exit.

Bus The airport bus (see *Arriving*) is a useful way of getting around once you know which hotels it serves. City buses are an ambitious undertaking for the first-time visitor.

Subway Seoul's excellent subway reaches out far into the industrial and residential suburbs. Line 1 is the most likely to be used by visitors; it runs through the heart of the city and connects two railway stations. Maps are everywhere. Entrances are not signposted but are easily found at main road intersections. Maps in the ticket hall show the fare. Some ticket offices close at 6pm, so you must have W100 coins for the machines after that time.

Outside Seoul

Air *Korean Air Lines* (KAL) is the exclusive carrier for all domestic routes. Flight times to all the major cities are under 60min. Tickets from all travel agents or direct from KAL ☎ 756 2000.

Driving is feasible if you are prepared to risk getting lost once off the main routes. Highway toll charges add to the costs but gasoline is not expensive, and filling stations are frequent. *Hertz* ☎ 585 0801 and *Sungsan* ☎ 552 1566 have car rental offices nationwide.

Train The *Korean National Railroad* operates an extensive and reliable network. The service used by visitors is the *Saemaul Ho* or Super Express Service. The trains are comfortable and air-conditioned, with a dining car. Tickets guarantee a numbered seat and are bought from hotel travel desks or from the rail office at 168 Pongnae-dong 2-ka, Chung-ku ☎ 392 0078. Reservations are advised.

Area by area

Seoul– the word means "capital" – grew up between two hills encircled by a 16km/10-mile wall. Its modern commercial heart is built on top of the ancient city; five gates which have survived from the original nine divide central Seoul from the sprawling suburbs. Each of the city's 13 administrative wards has a name ending in -*ku* (or -*gu*). Each *ku* is further sub-divided into "villages" called -*dong*. Main roads, ending in -*ro* (or -*lo*) and -*no*, are segmented into stretches called -*ka* (or -*ga*) numbered sequentially from west to east, or north to south. This may sound confusing intially but visitors quickly get used to the system and find it an accurate guide to pinpointing destinations.

The centre Most of the major hotels, office blocks and government offices are in the ward of Chung-ku, known locally as "downtown," sandwiched between Pugaksan (North Mountain) and Namsan (South Mountain). The latter is a low hill topped by a television tower which acts as a prominent landmark; the hill is easily ascended by cable car and provides the best panoramic view of Seoul. City Hall Plaza is considered to be the centre of the city, though visitors who expect a good sweep of civic buildings will be disappointed. It is the busy intersection of five main roads; the most prominent building is the Seoul Plaza Hotel.

Leading off the Plaza, due east, is Ulchi-ro, with more of the city's premier hotels and an abundance of shopping arcades. These are not immediately visible from the street because they are all either underground or several floors up in the characterless skyscrapers which line both sides of the road.

Due south of the Plaza, the eye is drawn to the impressive 14thC Namdaemun Gate, stranded amid a sea of traffic. New buildings line the route, including the Samsung Building, home of one of Korea's

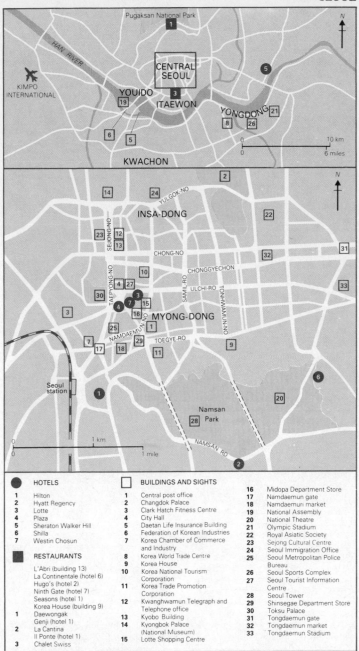

SEOUL

	HOTELS		BUILDINGS AND SIGHTS

HOTELS

1 Hilton
2 Hyatt Regency
3 Lotte
4 Plaza
5 Sheraton Walker Hill
6 Shilla
7 Westin Chosun

RESTAURANTS

L'Abri (building 13)
La Continentale (hotel 6)
Hugo's (hotel 2)
Ninth Gate (hotel 7)
Seasons (hotel 1)
Korea House (building 9)
1 Daewongak
  Genji (hotel 1)
2 La Cantina
  Il Ponte (hotel 1)
3 Chalet Swiss

BUILDINGS AND SIGHTS

1 Central post office
2 Changdok Palace
3 Clark Hatch Fitness Centre
4 City Hall
5 Daetan Life Insurance Building
6 Federation of Korean Industries
7 Korea Chamber of Commerce and Industry
8 Korea World Trade Centre
9 Korea House
10 Korea National Tourism Corporation
11 Korea Trade Promotion Corporation
12 Kwanghwamun Telegraph and Telephone office
13 Kyobo Building
14 Kyongbok Palace (National Museum)
15 Lotte Shopping Centre
16 Midopa Department Store
17 Namdaemun gate
18 Namdaemuri market
19 National Assembly
20 National Theatre
21 Olympic Stadium
22 Royal Asiatic Society
23 Sejong Cultural Centre
24 Seoul Immigration Office
25 Seoul Metropolitan Police Bureau
26 Seoul Sports Complex
27 Seoul Tourist Information Centre
28 Seoul Tower
29 Shinsegae Department Store
30 Toksu Palace
31 Tongdaemun gate
32 Tongdaemun market
33 Tongdaemun Stadium

233

most successful conglomerates, as well as many foreign banks, investment firms and gold brokerages. Behind, in the district of Myong-dong, is a maze of alleys crowded with shops, bars, restaurants and street stalls. Seoul station lies to the southwest of Namdaemun; it is a major architectural monument of the Japanese occupation.

The cultural centre of Seoul begins just north of City Hall Plaza, up Taepyong-no. First, on the left, is the Toksu Palace, a 19thC Renaissance-style building designed by a British architect. Just visible to the north is the red-brick Anglican cathedral, a beautiful Romanesque-style building erected in 1926; behind it is the former British Embassy, built in 1890, and a cluster of buildings now housing schools and places of worship.

A short walk north is another busy intersection, Kwanghwamun, dominated by the statue of Admiral Yi Sun-shin, celebrated for his naval victories over the Japanese in the 16th century. Beyond, on the right, is the Kyobo Building, one of Seoul's most prestigious business addresses, housing many foreign companies. Next door is the American Embassy and, opposite, the Sejong Cultural Centre, the main venue for concerts and international conferences. At the northern head of the avenue is the Kwanghwamun Gate, once the main entrance to the Kyongbok Palace, formerly the seat of government under the Yi Dynasty emperors who ruled Korea from 1392 until Japanese annexation in 1910. The palace is now entered from the gate in its eastern wall. Directly between Kwanghwamun and the palace is the old Capitol Building, built by the Japanese as their headquarters, and now housing the Korean National Museum.

Songbuk-dong North of the centre, through the Samchong tunnel which pierces Mount Pugaksan, is a green area of large houses, where many of Seoul's foreign residents live.

Namsan Park Mount Namsan, and the park which surrounds it, form a natural barrier to the southern spread of downtown Seoul. Even so, several hotels and high-rise apartment blocks have been built on the lower slopes to benefit from the green surroundings and views. The rest of the mountain is a park enclosing a botanical garden, theatres, libraries and the Seoul Tower, which stands 236-metre/775ft tall.

Itaewon Mount Namsan is pierced by three road tunnels which lead into the Americanized Itaewon district. The principal US Army base is immediately to the east, and the main street, Itaewon-no, is lined with fast-food restaurants, cafés and bars blaring out disco music and country and western hits, and hundreds of stores catering to foreigners. It is one of the few areas of Seoul where English is widely spoken and where US dollars are as acceptable as local currency.

Youido is an island in the Han river southwest of the city centre, notable because it is home to the National Assembly, the governing body of Korea, huge corporate office buildings, the Korea Stock Exchange and the Daehan Life Insurance Building (currently the tallest building in Asia).

Yongdong is the vast area south of the Han river which has been the subject of a comprehensive US$832m redevelopment, begun in 1982, to prepare for the Olympic games. As part of the enhancement programme, the river has been dredged and treated for pollution, and the concrete banks are once again lined with anglers. Recreational facilities, parks, new hotels and shopping precincts have all been built in the area and the massive Korea World Trade Centre opened next to the Olympic Stadium in 1988.

Kwachon is a southern suburb of Seoul where about half the government ministries are based. Eventually all the ministries will be relocated to this area.

Hotels

Seoul's hotels are among the dullest in the region. Even the newer hotels are beginning to seem tired and out of date. Public areas are just that; "popular price" restaurants and busy shopping malls within hotel lobbies attract large crowds, and the propensity of hotels to hang banners, flags and posters announcing special food promotions can make the coffee lounges and bars sometimes seem more like supermarkets. Staff are willing, but the language barrier is a problem; Japanese is often spoken. Hotel rooms are small, so to make sure of an adequate working space, it is best to ask for one on the executive floor, or a "superior room."

The city's best hotels are the Hilton and the Lotte; otherwise the choice is between hotels close to City Plaza or those which, like the Hilton, are in considerably less central but much more attractive locations. Advance reservations are advisable but rarely necessary and it is always worthwhile negotiating a discount or an upgrade.

All the hotels listed have 24hr room service, air conditioning, TV, radio, minibar and IDD. Standard business facilities include photocopying, typing, fax and translation. A service charge of 10% is additional to quoted rates.

Hilton $$$$$
395 Namdaemun-ro 5-ka, Chung-ku
☎ *753 7788* ☎ *26695 Fax 754 2510*
• *AE DC MC V* • *646 rooms, 66 suites, 6 restaurants, 2 bars*
The Hilton is near Namdaemun, the Great South Gate of ancient Seoul, on the lower slopes of Mount Namsan; thus it is only 5min from the city centre, but far enough away to seem remote from the noise and throng. The stark and shining 22-floor building won a top prize for architecture when completed in 1985 and the hotel has been rated one of the ten best in Asia. Most of the restaurants and services are around the atrium lobby with a fountain, plants and large Henry Moore bronze of a reclining woman. The Seasons (see *Restaurants*) is one of Seoul's top venues for business entertaining and the Genji, (Japanese) and Il Ponte (Italian) are popular with expatriates. All the rooms have picture windows, with Korean-style oak wood and paper lattice screens, large desks, armchairs and reproduction antique chests. The executive rooms are on the top two floors with a separate check-in and private lounge. The business centre is the best in Seoul. Shopping arcade, hairdresser, florist, disco • pool, sauna, jacuzzi, massage, gym • personal computer rental, library, 8 meeting rooms with audiovisual facilities (capacity up to 1,000), conference centre with 8-channel simultaneous translation and large screen video projection (capacity 3,000).

Hyatt Regency $$$$
747-7 Hannam-dong, Yongsan-ku
☎ *797 1234* ☎ *24136 Fax 798 6953*
• *AE DC MC V* • *567 rooms, 37 suites, 6 restaurants, 2 bars*
The Hyatt is set in extensive gardens high up on the south side of Namsan Park, some 20min from City Plaza, but only a short stroll from the Itaewon shopping district. The walls are of bare concrete, relieved by American oak partitions and many tropical plants. It is a big hotel, but quiet and relaxing. All the rooms are spacious and have views, the best being to the south. Two floors are given over to higher-standard executive rooms. Hugo's (see

Restaurants) is good for entertaining. The health facilities are Seoul's most comprehensive. Shops, florist, hairdresser, disco • pools, sauna, gym, jacuzzi, massage, tennis, squash • personal computer and typewriter rental, 6 meeting rooms (capacity up to 1,500).

Lotte $$$$$
1 Sokong-dong, Chung-ku ☎ *771 10* ⊤⊠ *23533 Fax 752 3758* • *AE DC MC V* • *888 rooms, 66 suites, 20 restaurants, 2 bars*
The Lotte is a vast hotel in the same building as a prestigious department store and labyrinthine shopping arcade. It is difficult to detect where the stores stop and the hotel begins, and several of the bars and restaurants are not in the hotel proper. The rooms are decorated in different styles, though without any particular flair; tartans predominate, except in the baroque suites where every item of furniture is heavily gilded in a mock-Venetian splendour. Standard rooms have limited working space; those in the newly-built east wing or the executive floors are better for those with much paper work to do. Shops, hairdresser, florist, disco • pool, gym, sauna, golf driving-range • 13 meeting rooms.

Plaza $$$$
23 Taepyong-no 2-ka, Chung-ku ☎ *771 22* ⊤⊠ *26215 Fax 756 3610* • *AE DC MC V* • *526 rooms, 14 suites, 8 restaurants, 2 bars*
This hotel is the most prominent building in City Hall Plaza. From most of its rooms it is possible to look down upon all the main landmarks of central Seoul, and for this reason it is popular with journalists who get a bird's-eye view of demonstrations. Most of the guests are American tourists, but a number of rooms are set aside as executive class, and there is a business centre. Shops, hairdresser, florist, disco • 8 meeting rooms with audiovisual and translation facilities (capacity up to 500).

Sheraton Walker Hill $$$$
San 21, Kwangjang-dong, Sungdong-ku ☎ *453 0121* ⊤⊠ *28517 Fax 452 6867* • *AE DC MC V* • *692 rooms, 78 suites, 8 restaurants, 2 bars*
Almost a 30min drive from City Plaza, the Sheraton is one of the last buildings east of Seoul before the countryside begins. It has a large theatre and convention centre which is one reason why people stay there. Another is its proximity to the Olympic Stadium and Korea Exhibition Centre on the opposite side of the river. It also appeals to golfers: two courses are only 20min away at the Sansung and Namsangdae Country Clubs. The hotel has a 24hr casino and a theatre restaurant staging twice-nightly Las Vegas-style shows to which Japanese business people and tourists flock. The rooms are adequate and the southerly views can be spectacular at dawn. Shops, hairdresser, florist, disco, casino • pool, sauna, jacuzzi, massage, gym, golf driving-range, jogging tracks, tennis • 16 meeting rooms (capacity up to 300), ballroom with projection facilities and simultaneous translation (capacity 1,480).

Shilla $$$$$
202 Jangchung-dong 2-ka, Chung-ku ☎ *233 3131* ⊤⊠ *24160 Fax 233 5073* • *Nikko Hotels* • *AE DC MC V* • *636 rooms, 74 suites, 7 restaurants, 3 bars*
Although shunned by many business travellers who regard it as remote, the likeable Shilla is only 20min from City Plaza. Its French restaurant, La Continentale (see *Restaurants*), compares favourably with the Hilton's Seasons and the service is considerate and attentive. There are views from every room over the 9ha/23-acre gardens either north over the city or south to the river. Sports and health facilities are good and the business centre opens longer hours than most (7am–10pm). Shopping arcade, florist, hairdresser, disco • pools, sauna, jacuzzi, massage, gym, jogging track, tennis, squash •

personal computer and typewriter rental, library, news teleprinter, 14 meeting rooms (capacity up to 200), convention hall with audiovisual facilities and simultaneous translation (capacity 2,500), Korean-style banquet hall.

Westin Chosun $$$$$
87 Sokong-dong, Chung-ku ☎ *771 05* ⓉⓍ *24256 Fax 752-1443 • AE DC MC V • 455 rooms, 22 suites, 5 restaurants, 2 bars*

For many years the Chosun, just off City Plaza, was the only Western-style hotel in Seoul and thus has the kind of reputation that pioneering hotels acquire in the folklore of old Asian hands: an oasis of civilization, the best watering-hole in town, the place with the classiest ladies of the night. So much is legendary; the hotel today is colourless and shabby.

The small lobby throngs with Japanese, American and Korean executives, meeting for breakfast, lunch or dinner, or arriving for seminars and presentations in the conference rooms. The lower floors serve as offices for airlines, shipping, air freight, insurance and general trading companies. The rooms are adequate, not spacious, with free-standing desks and Korean decor – lattice windows, paintings by local artists and fabrics patterned with traditional flower and bird themes. Restaurants include the Continental Ninth Gate for business entertaining (see *Restaurants*), the Japanese Sushi-Cho and the informal Yesterday serving tacos, pasta and pizza. Shops, hairdresser, florist, nightclub • pool, sauna, gym • library, office equipment rental, 6 meeting rooms.

Restaurants

Despite an abundance of restaurants lining every street and alleyway in Seoul, the best advice for a Western visitor is to stick to the hotels. There is enough to come to terms with in Seoul that is alien and strange, without adding to the difficulty by eating in restaurants where nobody speaks English and the dishes are unfamiliar; and it would be a serious mistake to entertain local business people in Korean restaurants even if you are familiar with the rituals that accompany the meal. Imported wines and spirits are expensive and smart dress is essential in hotel restaurants. Koreans tend to dine early, a legacy of the midnight curfew which lasted nearly 30 years and was finally lifted in 1982.

L'Abri $$$
Kyobo Bldg (also known as Daehan Kyoyuk Insurance Bldg) 147 Sejong-no, Chongno-ku ☎ *771 85 • AE DC V*

The Kyobo Building houses the greatest concentration of foreign firms in Seoul, so this charming restaurant run by M. Boudet-Ferouillet from Nice is always full of Western business people entertaining Korean clients. The dining room is light and airy, panelled in light oak and otherwise unadorned apart from fixed glass and oak lattice screens which divide tables from each other and ensure privacy without obscuring the view of other diners. The short

but varied menu mixes *nouvelle* and classic French cuisine. There is no cheese board, but there is a good choice of pastries. Some fine but expensive Bordeaux wines.

La Continentale $$$$
Hotel Shilla ☎ *233 3131 ext. 417 • AE DC MC V*

A welcoming restaurant with Korean staff who trained in France and are fluent in English, La Continentale is patronized almost exclusively by senior business people. The decor is in a classical style, with flowery chintz and reproduction antiques everywhere, and widely spaced tables.

There are three even more florid private dining rooms. Many of chef André Sertron's dishes are rich, though grilled meat and fish are also on the menu. Every dish is decorated with flowers. The long, mainly French, wine list includes wines intended to impress your guests by their price and readily recognizable name.

Hugo's $$$
Hyatt Regency Hotel ☎ *798 0061* •
AE DC MC V
The combination of expertly prepared cuisine and a view over the hotel gardens has won Hugo's a business clientele that is warm in its praise. The decor is minimal (black lattice screens) creating a spacious feeling. The menu is mainly straightforward grills – beef, venison, lamb, sole and trout – but includes a few more inventive dishes. In season, brightly coloured tiger prawns, lobster and crabs are available.

Ninth Gate $$$
Westin Chosun Hotel ☎ *771 05* •
AE DC MC V
The Ninth Gate was Korea's first French restaurant and has been a smart and favoured venue for business entertaining since it opened. The cuisine is classical in style – salmon, caviar, *foie gras*, scallops and grilled meat – and the atmosphere is relaxed. Ask for a window table looking out onto the small, pagoda-like Temple of Heaven in the hotel garden, once part of the Ninth Gate complex in the 14thC city wall.

The Seasons $$$
Hilton Hotel ☎ *753 7788* • *AE DC MC V*
The Seasons gets the top vote of local expatriates because its menu changes monthly and, for those who have to entertain a lot and are health conscious, it always has a "light and lean cuisine" option. The decor is a relaxing light grey with Art Deco etched-glass screens. Standard items which are always available include roast beef, soufflé of lobster, fondue and a selection of fresh fish. Besides the long wine list, there is usually a wine-of-the-week promotion featuring adequate wines at well below normal prices.

Good but casual
Asian All hotels have Korean dining rooms with menus in English, but for a change try the fixed-price buffet at *Korea House*, 80-2 Pil-dong 2-ka, Chung-ku ☎ 266 9101, which was originally established as a centre for staging Korean cultural dance, music and craft exhibitions; the staff are very helpful in explaining the various styles of the local cuisine. Also popular with resident foreigners is *Daewongak*, 323 Songbuk-dong, Songbuk-ku ☎ 762 2818, about 20min drive from downtown Seoul. The restaurant consists of a number of thatched pavilions shaded by trees. It specializes in barbecued ribs cooked at your table. Sweet and sour dishes predominate at Seoul's not very authentic Chinese restaurants but there are numerous excellent Japanese restaurants. The *Genji* at the Hilton is one of the best.
Western *La Cantina*, in the Samsung Building opposite the Hotel Lotte ☎ 777 2579, serves Italian and seafood dishes in a cheerful atmosphere: terracotta tiles and bare brick walls, statues of the Venus de Milo and inevitable chianti bottles. Smarter, and serving its own homemade pasta and deep-dish pizza is *Il Ponte* at the Hilton. *Chalet Swiss*, 104-4 Itaewon-dong, Yongsan-ku ☎ 797 9664 is another enjoyable eating house where the clients are mostly European and American; it serves sausages, steaks and fondue.

All of these restaurants fit into the $$ price category and accept credit cards.

Bars
Koreans hardly ever meet after work for a drink, except as a prelude to dinner. Resident expatriates rarely drink out either, because of the high

tax on imported liquor, preferring to entertain at home or have a beer in the office. Of course, few will decline an invitation and the preferred rendezvous are the *Ninth Gate Lounge* at the Westin Chosun hotel, *Bobby London* in the Hotel Lotte basement, a kitsch but comfortable mock-British pub, the *Oak Room* at the Hilton, and, for cocktails with a view, the *Skylark* at the Plaza hotel. Happy hours, between 6 and 8pm, usually mean free canapés rather than cheap drinks. Most hotel bars also offer imaginative fruit cocktails and the local OB (Oriental Brewery) beer is excellent.

Hostess bars are ubiquitous and extremely expensive. Few hostesses speak more than a few words of English. A relatively respectable one to try is the *Tiger Bar*, opposite the Westin Chosun hotel.

Entertainment

Seoul has a surprisingly varied entertainment scene. Events are listed in *This Week in Seoul*, a free *Korea Herald* newspaper supplement available in hotels or the tourist office, and the TV *Guide Korea*. Itaewon is the main district for bars, discos, blues, jazz, soul and reggae music. Much is aimed at US army servicemen.

Theatre, dance, music The *National Theatre* ☎ 274 1151 is home to six companies performing Western ballet and opera and modern English language plays. The *Sejong Cultural Centre* ☎ 736 2720 is the usual venue for visiting artists and frequently hosts top-class music and dance productions. The resident *Seoul Philharmonic Orchestra* and *Seoul Metropolitan Opera* perform regularly. Both have produced world-class singers and soloists including the violin virtuoso, Kyung Wa Chung. Watch out, too, for visiting opera and Broadway singers at the Hilton hotel's convention centre.

For traditional Korean music and dance there is the *Seoul Nori Madang Open Air Theatre* 47 Bunji, Samsil-

dong, Kangnam-ku ☎ 414 1985 near the Seoul Sports Complex, the *Korea House Theatre* at 80-2 Pil-dong 2-ka, Chung-ku ☎ 266 910 and the *Po Suk Jung* theatre restaurant at the Hotel Lotte. The *Kayagum* at the Sheraton Walker Hill puts on Las Vegas and traditional-style shows every evening at 5 and 7.30, with the option of dinner-and-show or show-only tickets.

Cinema Imported films, mainly from the USA, are shown with Korean subtitles at the *Piccadilly* ☎ 765 2245 and *Dansongsa* ☎ 764 3745.

Nightlife The Sheraton Walker Hill has a 24hr casino. All the major hotels have discos which attract a young Korean and Western clientele, with the latest sound and lighting effects and British disc jockeys. *Rainforest* at the Hilton is the most elegant and respectable, followed by *Xanadu* at the Westin Chosun. *Annabelle's*, at the Lotte, is popular with tourists and has live entertainment nightly.

Shopping

Seoul is no exception to the Asian rule – it is always worth haggling. The best buys are antique or reproduction chests and occasional tables, and porcelain. Shopping hours are Mon–Fri, 10–7.30, Sat, 9.30–1.30; smaller shops are open until 10pm, and at weekends. Department stores open 10.30–7.30 six days a week. Korean cabinet makers are highly skilled and turn out fine solid elm chests, with silver and bronze catches, hinges and chasing. They are available in several sizes suitable for coffee tables, blanket boxes or cocktail cabinets. Even new furniture looks gracefully antique. The potters of the Inchon Valley, 39km/24 miles west of Seoul, make porcelain of great beauty, continuing the centuries-old traditions of green-blue Koryo Dynasty celadon, with inlaid designs, and white Yi Dynasty porcelain decorated with black iron-glaze bamboo patterns. Anyone who has admired a piece in the Korea National Museum will very likely find a reproduction. For reliable quality, go to hotel arcades or major department stores such as *Lotte*, 1 Sokong-dong, Chung-ku (closed Tue), *Midopa*, 123 Namdaemun-ro 2-ka, Chung-ku (closed Wed) and *Shinsegae*, 52 Chungmu-ro 2-ka, Chung-ku (closed Mon). All these will arrange shipping.

The *Insa-dong District* (also known as Mary's Alley) has the biggest concentration of shops dealing in arts, crafts, antiques and reproductions, including the *Korea Antique Centre*; be prepared to bargain and do not buy from any dealer who will not give you an official export certificate. This is required for antiques which are more than 50 years old, and the time it takes to apply for one on your own is not compatible with a crowded schedule. Similarly, the busy visitor should stick to hotels and major stores for Korea's other bargains: inexpensive amethyst and topaz jewellery, bamboo baskets and lampshades, rich brocades and watered silks, and eelskin leather goods. Those with more time will find them all for sale in Itaewon, the long, packed shopping street south of Namsan Park where, owing to the closeness of the US army base, prices are quoted in dollars and bargaining is conducted in fluent English.

Street markets For browsing and hard-to-beat prices try the giant market of Tongdaemun, by the East Gate, or Namdaemun, by the South Gate. These sell everything under the sun.

Tax refunds are available for individual purchases in excess of W50,000 at authorized department stores and hotel arcades. You must produce your passport and complete a Tax Refund Form, specifying the currency the refund should be paid in. You will be given two copies of the sales certificates, one of which the customs officer will retain on departure, the other you keep. The refund (minus a service and handling charge) is sent to your home address by mail, usually within 20 days of your departure.

Duty-free shops are heavily promoted. Prices are much lower than in Japan, but Western visitors will find few bargains.

Sightseeing

Seoul's two great attractions are the former palaces of the Yi Dynasty emperors. The main sights outside the city can only be visited by those with a day or two to spare.

Kyongbok Palace Built in 1392, the palace served as the seat of government until it was burnt down in 1592 by slaves. It was rebuilt in 1867 by Queen Min for her son Sunjong, the last king of Korea. Buildings include a ten-floor pagoda and several beautiful pavilion complexes, and the landscaped grounds are an attraction in all seasons. Within the grounds are two museums. The *National Museum* occupies the Capitol Building and contains a rich collection of celadon from the Koryo Dynasty (935–1260) as well as Yi Dynasty paintings, clay figures and bronzes. The *National Folklore Museum* illustrates country life and crafts. *Open 9–4 or 5.30 depending on season; National Museum closed Mon, Folklore Museum closed Tue.*

Changdok Palace Like the Kyongbok Palace, this was destroyed by fire in 1592, but it was the one that the Yi Dynasty kings chose to restore and to which they moved the seat of government in 1611. Since then it has been almost continuously occupied by the Korean royal family; several descendants still live in the Naksonjae complex in the palace grounds. Only the Tonhwamun entrance gate remains of the original early 15thC building, and it is mainly the Piwon or "Secret Garden" that visitors come to enjoy. This richly planted park full of trees, lakes, wandering paths and pavilions was so called because it was once exclusively

for the use of the royal family. Even now, visitors must join a guided tour to see it. Information ☎ *762 9513*.
Other museums include the *Museum of Modern Art*, which has works by Korean contemporary artists. *San 58-1, Makkye-dong, Kwachon, open 9–5.30; 9–4.30 Nov–Mar*. The *Suk Too-Sun Memorial Museum* at Dankook University has a display of traditional clothing. *Open Tue, Thu 10–4*. The *Kimchi Museum* is devoted to the history, ingredients and preparation of Korea's national dish. *28–27 Pil-dong 3-ka, Chung-ku; open 9–6*.

Guided tours
Seoul has scores of travel agents all offering the same standard packages. Two of the leading ones with outlets in all major hotels are *Korea Travel Bureau* (KTB) ☎ 585 1191 and *Global Tours* ☎ 323 0171. Both offer half-day tours of the city and will arrange flight and hotel packages for the more distant destinations.

Out of town
Suwon This walled city lies 40km/25 miles south of Seoul. Although it is rapidly industrializing and has a population of 500,000, the restored fortifications provide a quiet green promenade around the old city with good views. The total circuit is 5.5km/3½ miles and can easily be walked in under 3hr. The walls and fortified towers were originally built by King Chongjo the 22nd Yi monarch who reigned 1776–1800. Chongjo intended to move the Korean capital to Suwon, and the southern city gate certainly compares in grandeur to those of Seoul. The independent traveller can take one of the regular trains to Suwon from Seoul station ☎ 392 0078, or go by taxi, which gives the option of visiting the other nearby sights – the interesting Buddhist temple at Yongju, or the tourist-orientated Korean Folk Village. Either way the journey takes under an hour.
Panmunjom This barrack building

straddling the demarcation line between North and South Korea is where the armistice was signed in 1953, ending the three-year Korean war. Since then it has been the venue for talks between the two sides whenever a potential conflict develops. The journey from Seoul is 56km/35 miles and passes through once heavily-bunkered valleys that saw the fiercest of the fighting during the Korean war, ending at Taesong-dong on the south side of the demilitarized zone. Visitors are given a military escort courtesy of the United Nations Command to the Panmunjom talks site for a tour of the conference room. Other highlights are the ornate observation tower with panoramic views into North Korea, and a tunnel, discovered in 1978 which, it is said, was intended to allow a massive invasion of Seoul by Northern troops. Panmunjom can only be visited by joining an 8hr tour (daily except Sat and Sun) organized by the Korean Travel Bureau ☎ 585 1191 which has desks at most hotels.
Kyongju in the southeast has Korea's greatest concentration of historic monuments and is listed by UNESCO as one of the 12 most important historical districts in Asia. There are 60 Buddhist temples in the city, including the 8thC Pulguksa Temple, and hundreds more in the surrounding mountains. Over 200 members of the Shilla royal family, rulers of Korea from 660 to 935, are buried in a cluster of graceful tumuli in the city, and the splendid golden crowns, girdles and statues excavated from the tombs are displayed in the Kyongju National Museum. The flight from Seoul takes less than an hour and hotels include the Kolon ☎ (0561) 29001, the Chosun ☎ 29601 and the Tokyu ☎ 29901.
Cheju Island is 55min by air, off the southern tip of Korea. Apart from its lush mountain vegetation, its thatched houses, waterfalls and ancient volcanic rock sculptures, it has fine beaches and sports facilities.

Many foreigners stay at the Hyatt Regency ☎ (064) 33 1234.

Spectator sports

The 24th Olympic Games took place in Seoul in September 1988 and the Seoul Sports Complex in Chamsil ☎ 418 8800, specially built for the Games, is the most up-to-date in the region.

Baseball and soccer are the most popular spectator sports. Both are played at the *Tongdaemun Stadium* ☎ 265 2431.

Horse-racing has a regular following three days a week at the *Happy Park* track in southeast Seoul, across from Songsu Street Bridge ☎ 500 1114.

Taekwondo (literally "kicking and punching") is Korea's own national sport. It is a martial art which originated in China but which the Koreans have perfected over 13 centuries and exported to some 80 nations affiliated to the World Taekwondo Federation. Students learn the art at the *Kukki-won Gym* on the southern outskirts of Seoul, where demonstrations are regularly staged for tourists ☎ 567 1058.

Keeping fit

Many of the big hotels, especially those around Namsan Park, offer an extensive range of sporting and fitness facilities. You might also try the *Clark Hatch Fitness Centre* at 2–6 Sunhwa-dong, Chung-ku ☎ 752 5269.

Golf Korea has the finest golf courses in Asia although all of them are outside Seoul. They attract Japanese enthusiasts and are always busy. Most will allow guests on weekdays, if accompanied by members. Those closest to Seoul (all 30min by car from City Hall Plaza) are *Namsungdae* ☎ 403 0071, *Yuksa* ☎ 972 2111 and *Dong Seoul* ☎ 470 2141. The *Korea Golf Course Business Association* ☎ 783 8271 publishes a guide to all the country's 33 golf courses called *Golf Korea* and will assist with reservations.

Jogging There are several stretches along the Han river which have been landscaped as running tracks and sports parks. The most central is along Youido Island, south of the river. More picturesque are the two routes round Namsan Park, using the toll roads which carry very little traffic, especially early in the morning. The easiest route is 3km/2½ miles, mainly level, starting from the toll gate by the cable car station and ending at the National Theatre toll gate. The more strenuous route continues for about 4km/2½ miles, starting with a steep uphill jog to the Seoul Tower, followed by a gentle run down to the final toll gate by the Namsan Library.

Skiing Three resorts are within a 60min drive of Seoul: *Chonmasan* ☎ 744 6020, *Yongin* ☎ 744 2001, and *Bears Town* ☎ 546 7210. Hotel travel desks will assist with transport and accommodation.

Local resources

Business services

The major hotels can provide most of the services you are likely to need; the Hilton provides the best range of facilities.

Communications

Long-distance delivery DHL 12–1 Pukchang-dong, Chung-ku ☎ 716 0001. Most hotel business centres act as agents for DHL and charge a small handling fee.

Post offices handle all types of mail and will pack international parcels for you free of charge. The *Central Post Office* is at 21 Chungmu-ro 1-ka, Chung-ku ☎ 775 0014 and open daily 9–6.

Telephone Local calls can be made from red or green booths located in hotels, office buildings and subways throughout Seoul. Two W10 coins are needed to make a call. Long distance calls within Korea can be made from hotel phones or yellow telephone boxes in post offices and take W100 and W10 coins. All hotels have IDD. Collect and credit card calls

can be made from any phone ☎ 1035 (Australia, Canada, France, Germany, Hong Kong, Italy, Philippines, Singapore, Spain, Taiwan and USA) ☎ 1037 (other countries). Inquiries ☎ 1030.
Telex and fax The only public telex booth is at the *Kwanghwamun Telegraph and Telephone Office*, 80-2 Sejong-no ☎ 739 4839. Fax can be sent from here or from major post offices.

Conference/exhibition centres

The *Korea World Trade Centre* which opened in 1988 adjacent to the Olympic Stadium incorporates the *Korea Exhibition Centre* ☎ 550 1211 along with an airport terminal, a shopping centre and a hotel as well as the *Trade Tower* where conference facilities and business information services are available.

Embassies and consulates

Australia 58–1 Shinmun-ro 1-ka, Chungro-ku ☎ 730 6491
Austria Room 1913, Kyobo Bldg, 1-1 Chong-ro 1-ka, Chongro-ku ☎ 732 9071
Belgium 1-65 Tongbinggo-dong, Yongsan-ku ☎ 793 9611
Canada 10th Fl, Kolon Bldg, 45 Mugyo-dong, Chung-ku ☎ 753 2605
China 83 Myong-dong 2-ka, Chung-ku ☎ 776 2721
Denmark Suite 701, Namsong Bldg, 260-199 Itaewon-dong, Yongsan-ku ☎ 795 4187
Finland Suite 1602, 16th Fl, Kyobo Bldg 1 Chong-ro 1-ka, Chongro-ku ☎ 732 6223
France 30 Hap-dong, Sodaemun-ku ☎ 362 5547
Greece 55 Changyo-dong, Chung-ku ☎ 752 9662
Indonesia 1-887 Youido-dong, Yongdungpo-ku ☎ 782 5116
Ireland Hilton Hotel ☎ 753 7788
Italy 1-169 Shinmun-no 2-ka, Chongro-ku ☎ 730 4092
Japan 18-11 Chunghak-dong, Chongro-ku ☎ 733 5626
Malaysia 4-1 Hannam-dong, Yongsan-ku 795 9203

Netherlands 1-48 Tongbinggo-dong, Yongsan-ku ☎ 793 0651
New Zealand Korean Publisher's Bldg, 105–2 Sagan-dong, Chongro-ku ☎ 720 4255
Norway 124-12 Itaewon-dong, Yongsan-ku ☎ 795 6850
Philippines 559-510 Yoksam-dong, Kangnam-ku ☎ 568 9131
Spain 726-52 Hannam-dong, Yonsan-ku ☎ 794 3581
Sweden 8th Fl, Boyung Bldg, 108-2 Pyung-dong, Chongro-ku ☎ 720 4767
Switzerland 32-10 Songwol-dong, Chongro-ku 739 9511
Thailand 653-7 Hannam-dong, Yonsan-ku ☎ 795 3098
UK 4 Chung-dong, Chung-ku ☎ 725 7341
USA 82 Sejong-no, Chongro-ku ☎ 732 2601
West Germany 4th Fl, Daehan Fire and Marine Insurance Bldg, 51-1 Namchang-dong, Chung-ku ☎ 779 3271

Emergencies

Hospitals Most hotels have in-house nurses on call. Locals report that hospital services are not such that one would want to test them out except in emergency. The *Severance Hospital*, Shinchon-dong, Sodaemun-ku ☎ 392 0161 has a foreigners' clinic with Western staff; in extremity a doctor will come to the hotel. Charges are comparable to those anywhere in the Western world. American Express is generally accepted in payment. Dental services are good. Although there is no emergency service, *Dr Lee*, Hotel Lotte ☎ 779 2277 will take patients at short notice.
Pharmacies Hospitals dispense their own prescriptions. Pharmacies have prominent green cross signs and sell most Western non-prescription drugs (open 10–7; closed Sun).
Police Seoul is a safe city with a very low crime rate. There are police stations on every major street, and the police are courteous and ready to give directions. The main station is

the *Seoul Metropolitan Police Bureau*, 17 Namdaemun-no 4-ka, Chung-ku ☎ 755 4400. It should be contacted for lost property. In emergency ☎ 112.

Government offices

All government offices are listed in the front of the Seoul area telephone directory. *Office of Customs Administration* ☎ 562 7140; *Ministry of Commerce and Industry, International Trade Promotion Bureau* ☎ 720 4137.

Information sources

Local media The *Korea Herald* and *Korea Times* are English-language papers that both cover economic and business news frankly and in depth. The weekly *Business Korea* and *Korea Business World* carry in-depth reports on Korea's economy, trading relations and industrial segments, plus profiles of companies and business figures. The *TV Guide Korea* listings magazine is the best sports and entertainment guide.
Tourist information The Korea National Tourism Corporation publishes free maps and guides to Seoul and Korea generally. All can be obtained from the *Tourist Information Centre*, 10a Ta-dong, Chung-ku ☎ 757 0086 (open daily 9–6). There are also information kiosks in several of Seoul's main streets.

Thank-yous

Flowers and chocolates There is no advantage in looking beyond the hotel florist and delicatessen for flowers and chocolates. Florists will deliver, stores will not. Otherwise, the best selection is in the *Lotte Department Store Food Hall*, in the basement ☎ 771 25 (closed Tue).
Wines and spirits can be bought at any supermarket but imported alcohol is only available in "Foreigners concessionaries" (the best is in the *Hotel Shilla* arcade) or duty-free shops; the most central is in the *Lotte Shopping Centre* ☎ 776 3940 (closed Tue).

Planning and reference

Entry details

Documentation All visitors must possess a valid passport; those with confirmed outward bound tickets may stay up to 15 days without a visa. Anyone planning to stay longer must obtain a visa unless they are citizens of the countries which have negotiated visa exemptions. These include most countries in Western Europe. Extensions up to a maximum of 90 days can be obtained from Department of Immigration offices ☎ 776 8984 (head office) ☎ 664 7611 (airport). Beyond that, an entry permit must be obtained from the Ministry of Justice and this requires the support of your embassy.
Health requirements Inoculation against cholera, polio and typhoid is advised.
Driving licence Visitors who intend to drive must be over 21 and hold an international driving licence.
Customs regulations All baggage is inspected on arrival and departure, and visitors have to complete a written declaration of articles in excess of the duty-free allowances which are: 400 cigarettes or 50 cigars or 250gm/9oz of tobacco or a combination not exceeding 500gm/18oz; 2 bottles of wines or spirits not exceeding 1,520ml/1 quart; 50gm/2oz of perfume; gifts and samples up to the value of W100,000. In addition, gold, watches and valuables worth up to W100,000 in value and money in excess of US$5,000 must be declared. Duty will be levied on valuables you declared on arrival but cannot produce on departure. Subject to a satisfactory explanation, foreign currency in excess of what you brought into the country will be confiscated.

A maximum of 1.2kg/2lb of red ginseng may be exported, provided it is accompanied by a sales receipt. Pre-1910 antiques can only be exported with a licence from the Cultural Property Preservation

Bureau ☎ 737 3655. Usually, official tourist outlets provide a certificate of sale. Visitors who encounter difficulties at customs (reproductions have been mistaken for genuine articles) can call the airport office of the bureau ☎ 662 0106.

Climate

Korea has four distinct seasons. Winter (temperatures minus 9–8°C/ 15–46°F) when conditions in the mountains are perfect for skiing, and air streams from Siberia give several very cold days, followed by milder ones. Spring (5–22°C/41–72°F) can be unpleasant when dust-laden winds arrive from the Gobi Desert. Summer is hot (16–29°C/61–84°F) and brings occasional torrential downpours. Autumn (0–19°C/32–66°F) is dry and often cloudless.

Koreans dress smartly in the Japanese style for business and entertaining: lightweight, light-coloured suits for men and modest dresses for women. Off-duty dress is smart sports shirts or blouses, and slacks.

Holidays

There is no period when Korean businesses close for an extended period. National holidays last a day and then everyone gets back to work. Some are variable, dependent on the lunar calendar.

Jan 1   New Year's Day
Mar 1   Independence Day
Apr 5   Arbor Day
Late Apr/early May   Buddha's birthday
May 5   Children's Day
Jun 6   Memorial Day
Jul 17   Constitution Day
Aug 15   Liberation Day
Late Sep/Oct   Thanksgiving Day
Oct 1   Armed Forces Day
Oct 3   National Foundation Day
Oct 9   Hangul Day
Dec 25   Christmas Day

Money

Local currency The unit of Korean currency is the Won (W). Bank notes are issued in W500, 1,000, 5,000 and 10,000 denominations, and coins in W1, 5, 10, 50, 100 and 500.

Changing money Korean currency is virtually impossible to obtain outside the country but there are numerous exchange counters at the airport, at banks, hotels and department stores. The latter two give the lowest rates, often 5% below that given by banks, which vary little from one to another, using the official rate set by the Bank of Korea. The US$ and the Japanese Yen are the most readily negotiable currencies, but all freely traded currencies and traveller's cheques can be exchanged at banks. Only hotel currency exchange desks are open late and on Sunday; standard hours 7am–10pm. Bank opening hours are Mon–Fri, 9.30–4.30; Sat, 9.30–1.30. The *Korea Exchange Bank* and the *Bank of Korea* have the largest networks, but all banks handle foreign exchange and credit card cash advances. All the leading international banks have representative offices in Seoul. Keep all exchange certificates because they may be asked for when converting Korean currency back to foreign currency at the airport exchange desks.

Credit and charge cards are accepted virtually everywhere in Seoul, sometimes even in the cheapest restaurants. Outside Seoul, credit cards are accepted everywhere that a tourist or business traveller is likely to visit, but only in outlets setting out to attract foreigners' patronage. To be safe, visitors should carry US$ traveller's cheques or currency as well.

Tipping Hotels and restaurants charge 10% service. Additional tipping is discouraged with prominent notices but many staff expect to be given at least the small change, if not a full 10% of the bill. Taxi drivers will not return change if the amount is small. Bar hostesses expect a minimum of 10%.

Taiwan

Taiwan is one of the great economic success stories of the postwar era. But this success has been achieved in the bizarre political context of an authoritarian right-wing regime which harbours the belief that it is still the legitimate ruler of all China. Taiwan's sovereignty extends over 86 islands, but the vast bulk of its 19.5m population live on Taiwan island itself. Much of Taiwan, which is divided virtually in two by the Tropic of Cancer, is mountainous and only about a quarter of the land is arable. Nevertheless the country is more or less self-sufficient in food, despite its very high population density.

There is a politically important divide between "native Taiwanese" and "mainlanders." The latter are the 1.5m or so who came over with Generalissimo Chiang Kai-shek in 1949 as he lost the civil war with the Communists which followed the end of World War II. But most inhabitants of Taiwan today are descendants of various vintages of Chinese immigration from the mainland.

From 1895 to 1945, the island was under Japanese occupation. In its rush for growth and prosperity, Taiwan benefited from the relatively good infrastructural base left behind by the Japanese and from the strong political, economic and military assistance of the USA. Taiwan hardly needs that help now, having successfully transformed its economy from one based on agriculture to one dominated by manufacturing and service industries with phenomenal export sales. The country is now facing the threat of a backlash. It is one of the prime targets of the protectionist trend in US politics and its tariff barriers are now tumbling down in nervous anticipation of US retaliation.

The major challenge for Taiwan now is that of further economic transformation away from its dependence on manufacturing exports in order to maintain the high levels of growth it has seen in the past four decades. This challenge concerns both domestic political opposition and Beijing. There is, of course, a wide gap between Taiwan's claim to be the legitimate government of all China and Beijing's claim to be the legitimate government of Taiwan. But the fact that even modest movements between the two communities are taking place reflects more fundamental political factors which may be working towards long-term reconciliation. One of these factors is the agreed recovery by China of Hong Kong in 1997. At present, Hong Kong is a convenient entrepôt through which Taiwan and China can channel mutually beneficial commercial and cultural contacts which both would be embarrassed to acknowledge. After 1997, China and Taiwan will either have to conduct business openly, route it some other way, or halt it altogether.

International pressure for a reduction of its trade surplus will inevitably make Taiwan a market of growing importance for exporters, especially those in the USA. In turn, its own remarkable exporting success will continue to attract investment from overseas.

The political scene

The relationship with mainland China is still the central issue in Taiwanese politics, dictating the structure of government and the framework in which all debate is conducted. Government under the ruling Nationalist Party (the Kuomintang, or KMT) is premised on the fiction that it is the legitimate successor to the government of the Republic of China, founded in 1911.

Wheelchair politics

The head of state is the president, who is elected to a six-year term by the National Assembly. This includes about 1,000 life members elected in 1947 and about 150 members elected in 1980. The president governs through a 300-member Legislative Yuan and appoints a prime minister to head the Executive Yuan, subject to the consent of the Legislative Yuan. The 77-member Provincial Assembly and its administrative body control domestic affairs. The Legislative Yuan is remarkable for its age: 70% of its members are over 70 years old. Many attend only with difficulty and even then seem to have trouble following the proceedings. Most of them notionally represent the mainland constituencies for which they were elected in 1947 in the last truly national elections.

President and undisputed strongman of the KMT until his death in early 1988 was Chiang Ching-kuo, the son of Generalissimo Chiang Kai-shek. Vice-President Lee Teng-Hui, a native Taiwanese, was sworn in as his successor. Then in May 1989 the conservative premier Yu Kuo-hua was replaced by the reformist KMT Secretary General Lee Huan.

An old man in a hurry? In 1986 and 1987 Chiang had sponsored a dramatic liberalization of the political scene in Taiwan and a rejuvenation of the KMT hierachy. In 1986, a theoretically illegal party, the Democratic Progressive Party (DPP), was allowed to contest the December elections and took about a quarter of the votes. Its platform was vague, but it provided a focus for Taiwanese nationalists' resentment of the mainlanders' political dominance. It called for "self-determination," a hair-split away from the still seditious call for independence from mainland China. In 1987, the martial law under which Taiwan has been governed for four decades was replaced by a new national security law, embodying some widening of political freedoms.

Foreign relations

Neither Taipei nor Beijing will allow its diplomatic partners to adopt a "two Chinas" policy. Every country has to choose between the two regimes and only 23 countries now recognize Taiwan, notably South Africa and most of Central America, although more than 100 have trade with it.

No, no, no Taiwan's China policy is summed up by the three no's: no contact, no negotiation and no compromise. China's current softly-softly approach is to promote the "one country-two systems" line promised for Hong Kong and Macao. There is little sign of any sympathy for this in any sector of Taiwan opinion, but China has never renounced the use of force if peaceful reunification takes too long. Despite official rhetoric to the contrary, there have been links with China, via trade, shipping and postal communications through Hong Kong. And in 1987 the Taiwan government began to relax its total ban on *unofficial* contact with China. Nevertheless, Taiwan spends over a third of its national budget on defence and keeps almost 500,000 men and women under arms.

The economic scene

Taiwan has moved in less than 40 years from what was little more than a plantation economy to one of the fastest growing new members of the industrial world. The government estimated per capita GNP for 1987 at US$5,900 - on a par with, say, Spain or Greece and higher than South Korea - and few outsiders believed this was over-optimistic. Over the 30 years to 1985, Taiwan's GNP grew at a real annual average of 8.6%. By the end of 1986, market price GNP stood at an estimated US$78bn.

Human resources

The population of just under 20m is well educated, young and healthy. Nine years of schooling are compulsory and over 90% of the population are literate. Almost a third are under 30; life expectancy is at developed-country levels - 70 years for men, 75 for women. The birth rate has fallen steadily, and is now at less than 20 per thousand. There is a continuing trend away from the land to industry: in 1952, 52% of the labour force were in agriculture; by 1986 this had fallen to 16%. The unemployment level is below 2%.

Natural resources

Apart from its ability to feed itself, Taiwan does not have natural resources to thank for its economic triumphs. It has some coal, some oil and some natural gas, but has to import almost 90% of its energy requirements. There has been limited success in off-shore oil exploration, but the pattern of energy imports will be radically altered in the foreseeable future only by Taiwan's nuclear-power programme. Similarly, there are reserves of copper, gold, manganese and other minerals, but none is of great significance.

Agriculture

Taiwan was a sugar plantation colony during the Japanese occupation. Now, however, less than 2% of exports are primary agriculture products, and agricultural production is declining. The past decade has seen slight drops in output of sugar cane, rice and sweet potatoes, the major crops. Taiwan is still, just, a net food

exporter, with surpluses in rice, fish, fruit and vegetables, but has to import some non-rice grains and most of its beef requirements. Agriculture was the basis of Taiwan's economic take-off into the economic big league, following a remarkably effective land reform in the early 1950s when the old estates and plantations were phased out and tenant farmers and labourers bought their own land on government credit.

Infrastructure

In the 1970s Taiwan's infrastructural shortcomings caused one of the major bottlenecks to development. Although communications networks were relatively advanced even then, they failed to keep pace with the headlong rush to industrialize and export. An increasingly self-confident government has since then - encouraged in recent years by the need to placate the USA by finding something American on which to spend its trade surplus - devoted large chunks of public finance to a series of highly ambitious infrastructural schemes. Plans for the late 1980s include a subway system for Taipei, a new freeway in the north, and double-tracking more of the railway network.

Airports Chiang Kai-shek International Airport is at Taoyuan, some 40km/25 miles from Taipei, and has all modern facilities. Kaohsiung International is at the southern end of the island. Most of the main cities are connected by domestic air services.

Roads The road network covers

more than 19,000km/12,000 miles, most of it surfaced. A good highway links the main centres between Keelung and Kaohsiung.

The railway extends the whole length of Taiwan, mainly along the west coast, the main, electrified route serving Taipei-Kaohsiung.

Ferry services ply the waters between Kaohsiung and the Pescadores islands, and from Taitung to the Lanyu islands. A car ferry service links Keelung and Hualien.

External trade

Taiwan relies more on its trade than most countries. Exports account for about 55% of GDP.

Exports Manufactures accounted for virtually all exports in 1986, and in early 1987 the USA was taking about 46% of Taiwan's exports. The most important items in 1986 were electronics (19%), clothing (8%), footwear (9%), fibres and fabrics (7%) and toys (5%).

Imports Main imports are electrical machinery, machinery and tools, basic metals, chemicals, transport equipment, logs and timber, and raw cotton. Electronics imports were up to about 15% of total purchases by early 1987. Oil, because of lower prices, had fallen to only 8% of the import bill, from the towering position it had occupied in the 1970s. As in so many countries in the region, imports from Japan far exceed those from of any other country. In 1986, 34% of imports were of Japanese origin, as against 22% from the USA. West Germany accounted for 5% and Saudi Arabia for 4%. There was also clearly a growing amount of illicit trade – mostly through Hong Kong – with the mainland, encouraged by Beijing as part of its "three-links" policy (trade, shipping and mail) but frowned on and occasionally threatened by the ruling KMT.

US anger Benefiting in part from the slide of the US dollar against the yen and deutschmark, Taiwan built up a huge trade surplus of US$15.6bn in 1986, of which the USA accounted for almost 90%. This has made Taiwan one of the *bêtes noires* of US protectionists, especially as it has itself been a heavily protected market. Taiwan's barrier of import duties is now being taken down at what appears to be breakneck speed. The alternative seems to be US legislative retaliation, or an even more dramatic appreciation of the New Taiwan dollar. As it is, Taiwan currency crept up by some 15% against the US dollar in the 18 months following the G5 Plaza accord of September 1985; but, like South Korea and Hong Kong, Taiwan faced US pressure for a further revaluation. Perhaps even more fundamental for the long-term resilience of Taiwan's exports is the effort to move into higher technology, as Taiwan loses its comparative advantage as a low-cost producer.

Curb on shoe exports An example of Taiwan's response to protectionist sentiments in the USA is the shoe exporting industry's decision in 1987 to limit its sales abroad to the same level as 1986: 841m pairs. The only exceptions were the UK, Canada and France, with whom Taiwan's shoemakers have for several years had "gentlemen's agreements" on export levels. The Taiwan Footwear Manufacturers' Association, of which most of 1,000-plus shoe factories on the island are members, voted overwhelmingly to impose the restraints.

Drastic tariff cuts on more than 860 items in early 1987 represented the seriousness with which US anger had been taken. In 1988 further cuts were made on some 3,500 items as part of the government's policy to phase out its protection of home industries within a year. The target is to cut tariffs to a maximum of 5% on basic materials, to no more than 10% on intermediates, and to around 20% for downstream products. "In future we'll foster industries using education, research and development, information – including better planning – and financial tools such as are used worldwide, instead of protectionism,'' according to George Young, director of Taiwan's Industrial Development Bureau.

Balance of payments

Its hefty trade surpluses in merchandise exports have allowed Taiwan to register current account surpluses that have increased each year since 1980. But this glowing balance of payments performance is not an unqualified boon. One of the walls which Taiwan's siege mentality has built around the country was a rigid set of foreign exchange regulations. The effect of this was that until July 1987 exporters had to surrender their foreign exchange on receipt for local currency at the Central Bank of China.

Foreign exchange reserves In other words, the trade surplus was translated almost immediately into the country's foreign exchange reserves. By the time these topped US$50bn in March 1987 – second in the world only to Japan's – few even in Taiwan saw them as a wholly welcome provision against the proverbial rainy day. Rather, they have created pressures both on the money supply and for the relentless appreciation of the local currency. Alongside the dismantling of tariff barriers, the unravelling of exchange controls was the next major step in Taiwan's financial modernization.

Currency and prices

The currency is the New Taiwanese dollar (NT$). In the past it was officially pegged to the US dollar but, since 1979, the link between the two has been fairly loose. The fall in the US dollar and the corresponding rise in the NT dollar have led to repeated calls from the USA for the Taiwan government to revalue the currency.

Controls In July 1987 the government ended almost four decades of stringent currency controls and allowed companies and individuals to invest abroad freely. The decision by the cabinet came after an embarrassing increase in foreign currency reserves as a result of Taiwan's large trade surplus and speculative inflows of capital on the expectation of a revaluation of the local currency. Under the new rules, individuals and companies are each year allowed to remit abroad up to US$5m or its equivalent in other curencies.

Inflation has since 1983 been minimal or negative, though some rise for the late 1980s is likely as money supply and labour and raw material costs exert upward pressure.

Capital inflows

After substantial US aid in the 1950s and 1960s, Taiwan now receives no aid or concessionary finance. External debt is modest, and devoted almost entirely to public enterprise development projects. Taiwan is keen to attract foreign investment, particularly in the higher technology industries.

Government finances

The government of Taiwan knows it cannot rely forever on its traditional exports to maintain the momentum of economic growth achieved since the early 1950s. Policy is thus directed at upgrading the technological capacity of industry and stimulating domestic demand.

Deficit spending Budgets in the second half of the 1980s have therefore become exercises in deficit spending which would have appalled the fiscal conservatives who managed Taiwan's budget until then. In 1987 an expansionary budget aimed to put domestic demand in place of exports as the chief engine of growth, and a 10% pay rise was given to all government employees, including the armed forces.

Expenditure Defence and foreign affairs are still the largest single area of government expenditure, budgeted at 37% of total outlay for the fiscal year 1987.

Revenues Tax income is the government's most important source of revenue, at 55% of the total. This will be hit by the reduced tariff earnings which the government is having to countenance to placate its irate US partners. Although Taiwan's tax base is thus revealed to be somewhat narrow, there is no indication that in the foreseeable future the government is going to have the slightest difficulty in financing its planned budget shortfalls.

Domestic investment

One of the worrying features of Taiwan's economy in recent years has been the low rate of domestic investment. Fixed capital formation has actually been falling as a percentage of GDP, to 18% in 1986, although there were signs of an upswing in 1987. This disinclination to invest is in spite of the very high national savings rate, and has its origins in an inefficient and underdeveloped capital market in Taiwan, as well perhaps as in a more intangible nervousness about the country's long-term relations with China. The government, anxious for evidence that Taiwan's manufacturers are investing for the future and not just cashing in on the boom while it lasts, has been easing investment guidelines for both domestic and overseas entrepreneurs.

Investment overseas

Taiwan enlisted Dr An Wang, chairman of Wang Laboratories of the USA, as part of its drive to promote Taiwanese investment abroad. Dr Wang announced the formation of a US$500m multipurpose fund, called the Golden Gate Development and Investment Fund, in which Taipei took a 30% share and Wang Laboratories 10%. The government and Dr Wang then tried to persuade Taiwan's private sector to put up the remaining

US$300m. The fund is aimed at helping Taiwanese companies invest in overseas ventures, especially in the USA, thus enabling them to develop new products, expand their market shares abroad and help in the transfer of new technology. It will also help foreign suppliers to sell and distribute their products and services in East Asia.

Political focus The fund has a political focus, too, in that Taiwan sees the fund as confirming its commitment to investment in, and its continued economic cooperation with, the USA, its major trading partner. Ties between the two nations became increasingly strained as Taiwan's trade surplus with the USA continued to climb. Two significant trade disputes erupted in 1986–87. The fund received the support of US Treasury Secretary James Baker and Trade Representative Clayton Yeutter.

Industry

Manufacturing industry is the cornerstone of the economy, accounting for 39% of net domestic product in 1986. The most important items produced are textiles, footwear and clothing, electrical machinery and appliances, and plastic products.

Private control This industrial base is largely in private hands, and is concentrated in small and medium-scale enterprises. About 84% of all industrial production, and 88% of manufacturing output, comes from the private sector. These proportions are in fact increasing, as a gradual sell-off of all state-owned assets proceeds.

Costs are rising Taiwan is no longer a low-cost producer, in comparison with the less developed countries. But so far productivity improvements have offset living-cost increases, and it has kept its competitive position. The challenge now is to maintain that position with a more realistically valued currency, and a less protected domestic market.

The business climate

The government of Taiwan has combined an enthusiasm for capitalism and private enterprise as the fountainheads of prosperity with an acute awareness of its national self-interest. Hence a business climate of considerable attraction to Taiwan's indigenous entrepreneurs has been at times less appealing to the overseas business community. Not only have Taiwan's own nascent industries developed their muscle under a protective cordon of tariffs, but foreign investment has been welcomed only in certain limited spheres. All that is supposed to be changing now, but Taiwan is still a market of more allure to the buyer from abroad than the seller, and to the investor in those areas in which Taiwan seeks to promote higher technology.

Private sector dominant

From the early days of postwar reconstruction, when the Taiwan government – funded in large measure by US aid – controlled the lion's share of industrial production, the role of the private sector has steadily grown. In 1952, the private sector accounted for 43% of industrial production; in 1985, for 84%. However, these figures conceal a growing proportion of the mining and extractive industries in government ownership. The state has reduced its share of manufacturing to 12%, but this has been mainly in the heavy, "smokestack" industries of China Steel Corporation and the petrochemicals and other downstream production of the state-owned China Petroleum Corporation (CPC). Nevertheless, the trend to decreasing public sector involvement in the ownership of industry is likely to continue; in 1987 CPC began the privatization of its distribution network.

Reluctant private investors The reluctance of the private sector in the mid-1980s to invest in either capital formation or in research and development for the sunrise industries has led to a new surge of government intervention and support for industry – at precisely the time when Taiwan is telling the world that its industries are going to stand on their own two feet without government protection.

Foreign investment

After a slump in the early 1980s, foreign investment in Taiwan picked up in 1984 and by 1987 was running at about US$1bn a year. Even this is not a huge amount for an economy the size of Taiwan's.

The deterrents Investors have been deterred by the political uncertainty over the future relationship with China, by the cumbersome and bureaucratic red tape that still entwines some of Taiwan's approval procedures, and by the difficulties sometimes encountered in repatriating profit and capital because of the years of stringent foreign exchange control. With uncertainty over the long-term future of Hong Kong also now diverting some funds to Taiwan, and with the relaxation of some of the constraints of "economic martial law," Taiwan is enjoying a mini-boom in foreign investment.

Japan is main source In 1986, about 8% of foreign investment was classified as coming from "overseas Chinese," including about 2% from Hong Kong. Of investment that even Taiwan concedes as foreign, much the largest source is Japan, with 33% in 1986, followed by the USA with 18%. European countries combined provided 24% of foreign investment.

Japanese business investment in Taiwan has played a major role in the latter's strong economic growth. Japanese trading companies handle as much as a quarter of Taiwan's exports, and joint ventures and technical cooperation, together with Japanese components and sub-assemblies, have meant more high-value exports. This involvement has been going on for more than 20 years, but Japanese investment boomed in Taiwan in 1986 and is set to continue for the foreseeable future. During 1986 the Taiwan government approved US$253.6m-worth of Japanese investment applications. This was 75% up on the previous year and constituted the largest single contribution to the US$770.4m total. Potential investors visited the island in large numbers as the yen appreciated against the dollar and the Taiwan government began a series of liberalizations.

Sectors for investment The government has been engaged in a major effort to attract foreign investment in the information technology and computer industries. Taiwan's comparative advantage in the 1970s as a home of cheap, well-disciplined and highly productive labour for the less capital-intensive industries is now somewhat eroded; in the textile, footwear and clothing industries Taiwan's own manufacturers are looking overseas for cheaper production outlets.

Power in business

Small is beautiful One of the more remarkable features of Taiwan's industrial success has been the broad base of small and medium-size companies on which it is founded. In 1985, private enterprises with operating capital or business revenue of under US$1m accounted for all but 2% of all enterprises and 55% of GDP. However, there are a number of significant corporations. These include the government-owned energy and heavy industry operations, as well as private sector conglomerates.

Major private corporations The list of the ten leading private sector exporters in 1986 shows the new-found dominance of the consumer electrics business in Taiwan's trade. The list is somewhat misleading, however, in the light of the enormous importance of small firms in the textile and garment industries. It is also an indication of how many of the world's leading electronics manufacturers have joint ventures or subsidiaries in Taiwan. Not included in those listed in the box on this page are Wang, Matsushita, Atari, Digital Equipment and Philips, all of which also have production capacity in Taiwan.

Leading export firms
Tatung Co Monitor screens, fans, refrigerators, televisions, audio systems, motors
RCA Taiwan Ltd Televisions, television components, remote tuner systems
Nan Ya Plastics Corporation PVC sheets, plastics, polyester fibres and filament
Far Eastern Textile Ltd Yarn, piece goods, printed and dyed cloth, knitwear, woven apparel, polyester fibre and filament
Ching Shing Textile Co Ltd Yarn, polyester fibre, fabrics and garments

Texas Instruments Taiwan Ltd Transistors, diodes, regulators, semiconductors, calculators
General Instrument of Taiwan Ltd Mercury relays, super-rectifiers, monitor yokes
Colins Co Ltd Garments
Atari Taiwan Manufacturing Corporation Video and home computer systems
Formosa Chemicals and Fibre Corporation Rayon staple fibre, detergent, blended yarns, nylon filament, knitting fabrics.

Employment

Taiwan has a large and well-educated workforce. At the end of 1986, just under 8m workers were employed, representing almost 98% of the labour force, and unemployment frequently hovers near zero. A third of those working were employed in manufacturing.

Wages are no longer low by international standards, especially in the profitable, export-oriented manufacturing sector. In manufacturing as a whole, the unit labour-cost index had reached 106 by 1986 from a base of 100 in 1981. This included a leap to 184 in the textile labour-cost index and, according to Taiwan's official figures, an actual decline in labour costs in the electronics industries to 89 on the index. However, over the same period, productivity had climbed to an index of 138 for manufacturing industry as a whole, with a rise to 172 in the electronics sector, and a decline to 83 in textiles. In terms of hard cash, this meant, by the final quarter of 1986, that average manufacturing earnings in Taiwan had risen to NT\$13,960 a month.

Union controls eased Labour unions in Taiwan have traditionally been the docile tools of government policy. Union leaders have generally progressed through the ranks of the ruling Kuomintang party. There are stringent restrictions on the right to strike, and those who work for private sector operators of public utilities are not allowed to strike at all. Strikes are effectively outlawed for other workers by Article 36 of the law which governs the handling of labour disputes, which was first promulgated in 1928, and last amended in 1943. Article 36 bans stoppages of business during times of national emergency. Although Taiwan's 40-year emergency came to an official end in July 1987, strikes were still severely limited because of the provision debarring workers from striking while a dispute was in the course of mediation or arbitration. There have been increasingly frequent reports of labour disruption in Taiwan since strikes were formally legalized in 1988.

Labour standards How long this state of legalized industrial discipline can last is open to question. The huge US labour organization, the AFL-CIO, had an impact in hastening the introduction of a revision of the 1984 Labor Standards Law in 1987. This is a compendium of provisions governing the basic minimum terms employers can offer their staff, as well as health, safety and welfare provisions. Some of the basic features of the law deal with hours worked, annual leave, minimum age of workers, minimum wages, maternity leave and pensions.

Other labour reforms promised by President Chiang in December 1986 moved at an unusually quick pace through the government bureaucracy. The pace was stimulated by the poor showing of KMT union candidates in the December 1986 elections and the suggestion by the AFL-CIO that Taiwan be excluded from the list of countries eligible for GSP preferences because of its failure to grant full rights to workers. The reforms aimed to unify under one bureau many of the labour safety and supervisory functions that used to be dispersed among a number of different government organizations. This caused a major bureaucratic tussle between various spheres of influence which stood to lose kudos and power when the new body was established in July 1987.

Labour insurance There is a mandatory national insurance scheme to cover workers for maternity, sickness, disability, unemployment and death benefits. In addition, companies are required to set up employee welfare funds. The minimum contribution is 1% of registered capital at the time of establishment, plus 0.05% of revenues. Few firms find this onerous.

The business framework

Foreigners are allowed to set up shop in Taiwan either with wholly owned subsidiaries or through joint ventures with local or other foreign partners. They may also establish branch or representative offices. All foreign involvement in business in Taiwan has to be approved by the Ministry of Economic Affairs (MOEA).

Types of company

The legal concept of company in Taiwan embraces four classifications. These are:

• unlimited company

• limited company, a company with between 5 and 21 shareholders, with liability limited to the contribution of share capital

• unlimited company with limited liability shareholders – some shareholders have unlimited joint and several liability for the company's obligations, while others have liability limited to their equity contribution

• company limited by shares. This requires at least seven shareholders, all of whose liability is restricted to the amount of their equity contribution. It corresponds closely to the US corporation, and is the most popular vehicle for the overseas investor.

Joint ventures The term joint venture has no legal status in Taiwan, so in practice most joint ventures form companies to carry out their business. There is a requirement for a minimum capital of NT$1m.

MOEA Whether you are establishing a joint venture or a subsidiary, the first port of call is the MOEA, which will require a detailed proposal, including an investment plan. The MOEA's Investment Commission is a fast worker, as these bureaucracies go, and undertakes to come up with a decision within two months of the date of application.

Other business entities

Partnership The law provides for both general and limited partnerships, but even in so-called limited partnerships there has to be one or more general partners, with unlimited liability.

Branches Subject to meeting capital adequacy and registration requirements, foreign corporations are allowed to establish branches in Taiwan. Working capital has to be provided by the head office and may not be repatriated; nor may profits. To establish a branch, recognition from the MOEA's Commerce Department is needed. When MOEA approval is granted, the branch then has to register with the local authorities. A branch may carry out almost any form of business, except manufacturing. As under most jurisdictions, the home company will be regarded by the Taiwanese authorities as responsible for all the branch's obligations. The head office will have to nominate a branch manager to be responsible for business in Taiwan, and a representative of its interests. The manager and the representative do not have to be different people.

Liaison and representative offices are not allowed to generate operating income in Taiwan, but the representative may negotiate and sign contracts on behalf of his or her company. The functions of a liaison office are the more restricted of the two, though not clearly defined.

Foreign ownership rules

The body governing foreign investment in Taiwan is the Investment Commission of the Ministry of Economic Affairs (MOEA). The key step in legal terms in investing in Taiwan is to gain Foreign Investment Approved (FIA) status from the MOEA. Strictly speaking, this is not an absolute legal requirement, since foreigners are technically able to invest in domestic enterprises. However, only FIA investors can remit their profits and repatriate capital overseas. The MOEA offers its own advisory service to would-be investors via the Industrial Development and Investment Centre.

Approved sectors The MOEA lists six categories of investment application that it can consider. The investment must be in enterprises engaged in scientific and technical research; enterprises manufacturing goods needed in Taiwan; service enterprises needed domestically; enterprises with an export market; or projects which complement important industrial, mining or communications enterprises. There is also a catch-all provision covering any investment "conducive to the economic and social development of the Republic of China."

In practice, Taiwan's quite extensive and professional sales pitch to potential investors has been concentrated on export markets, and in recent years, within that, on high-technology and information industry investors.

Restrictions There is no restriction on the percentage of foreign ownership of enterprises in Taiwan. However, restrictions do apply to the following sorts of investment. In a limited company, foreign ownership must be kept to below 50% of total equity capital, and the number of foreign shareholders to less than one-half of the total number of shareholders. In investment trusts, foreign ownership must be less than 40% of registered capital, or less than 49% in the case of an international investment trust company.

Closed sectors One important feature of Taiwanese protectionism has been the closure of sectors of its domestic markets to foreign investors. Some of these barriers are under attack, notably the insurance market, where in 1987 the government raised the quota of US

insurance companies allowed to open branches (but not to incorporate locally). However, the protected inland transport market remained closed to foreigners. In addition, certain industrial sectors deemed strategic are barred to private enterprise, whether domestic or foreign. These are tobacco and liquor, armaments, public utilities, and petroleum and upstream refining operations.

Forms of investment The laws covering foreign investment are the Statute for Investment by Foreign Nationals and its twin, the Statute for Investment by Overseas Chinese. According to Article 3, foreign investors may pay in their capital in one of four ways:

• in cash – which has to be in foreign exchange remitted from overseas

• in fixed assets, raw material, equipment or commodities for sale to raise working capital; in all these types of investment, the foreign investor must himself provide the foreign exchange to pay for import into Taiwan of the asset to be capitalized

• by providing technical know-how, or patent rights, up to a maximum of 20% of the investment in the case of patent rights, and 25% in the case of know-how

• in NT dollars, if principal, profit, loan interest or any other income from an investment in Taiwan is approved for the settlement of the foreign exchange transaction needed to invest.

Incentives

Besides the benefits of 100% ownership, and the right to repatriate profit and capital, investors are also given a 20-year "non-expropriation" guarantee. Views as to the value of this differ, of course, since the political risk of investment in Taiwan is one that is to a certain extent out of the hands of the government anyway, namely the long-term intentions of the government in Beijing. In addition, a wide range of tax concessions are available to new investments (both domestic and foreign). These include:

- a five-year income-tax holiday
- accelerated depreciation allowances; these are available not just for new investments, but for expansions, new fixed asset purchases, and so on. Naturally, the acceleration is normally offered as an alternative, not in addition, to the tax holiday. The choice is, by and large, the research and development investor's
- expenditure against tax
- import duty waivers for productive machinery or parts; these are selectively available
- a refund of some of the duty paid on raw materials used for export products
- a maximum income tax of 22% for "key capital-intensive and technology-intensive" enterprises
- a further tax rebate, of 15% of income tax payable, for companies who go for a public listing of their shares on the Taipei Stock Exchange.

Science Park Taiwan has been trying very hard to attract investment in its Science Park at Hsinchu, about 72km/44 miles south of Taipei. This is devoted to electronics, precision instruments, energy sciences, biochemical engineering and to software houses. In addition to the normal range of perks, low-interest finance is available to Hsinchu investors, along with help in finding the capital, either from local private-sector sources or from the government-owned Bank of Communications or China Development Fund.

Expatriate employment

Although foreign investors are encouraged to train local personnel to take on senior technical and managerial functions, FIA companies do not normally have too much trouble in putting expatriates into Taiwan. A personal guarantor is usually required for long-term residents. "Alien resident" status is available for expatriates. This status is evidenced by a certificate issued by the police, which may be renewed annually for an indefinite period. Holders of this certificate need exit permits for travel outside Taiwan.

Taxation

Taiwan's tax system is in flux. For years the government has relied for much of its revenue on the high and almost all-embracing tariffs on imports. As these tariffs are reduced or done away with, the tax base begins to look a bit thin.

Income tax For corporations, this is known as "profit-seeking enterprise income tax." It is charged on a sliding scale with a maximum of 30%. For individuals it is known as "consolidated (personal) income tax," and is on a sliding scale peaking at 60%.

Commodity tax This is an excise tax levied on a number of specific goods, whether domestically produced or imported. It ranges from 2% up to a maximum of 120% on cigarettes and liquor. Also subject to the tax are cosmetics, white goods, and cars, trucks and motor-cycles.

Business tax This is a composite tax introduced in 1986 to try and harmonize the complex systems of the value-added tax that applied to most sellers of goods, and the Gross Business Receipt Tax System which covered the service sector, such as banks, insurance companies and even restaurants. The initial rate of business tax was set at 5%, with a few exceptions, such as reinsurance premium income and "special" restaurants and nightclubs.

Land tax is levied at a rate of 1.5% per annum on the assessed value of industrial land.

Building tax This is levied annually on assessed values, with slightly higher rates for business buildings (3–5%) than for non-business or residential property (1.38% for residential property used by the ratepayer himself).

Remittance of funds

The overseas investor has the choice of denominating his capital in foreign currency or in NT dollars. In either case, repatriation of the capital is limited to the amount of foreign exchange invested, and this has to be bought at the exchange rate prevailing when the remittance is made.

Restrictions No repatriation of capital may be made until 12 months after the enterprise has completed one successful year of operation. Normally, capital may not be repatriated at a rate of more than 15% per year, though application may be made for 100% repatriation after two years of operation. Dividends may be paid only out of profits; subject to this restriction, they may be remitted at any time. Loan capital may be remitted only in line with the amortization schedule approved with the original investment application. Similarly, where technology or know-how has been capitalized, royalty payments may be made only as agreed in the MOEA investment approval.

Market entry

Traditionally, the Taiwanese market has been a very hard one to crack because of the protectionist policies that the authorities have pursued. These are now being reformed, but difficulties remain. As in so many countries, a good agent is essential.

Importing and exporting

In addition to the market constraints on imports into Taiwan – tariffs have priced many of them out of the reach of all but the conspicuous consumer – Taiwan has other legal barriers. Imports are classified into three categories.

Prohibited imports include narcotics, a few luxury items, and goods from the mainland, which nevertheless find their way in either through the clandestine direct trade conducted by intrepid fishermen or, in far greater quantities, via Hong Kong.

Controlled imports This category covers military supplies, poisonous chemicals, explosives, and so on. It also covers goods sold by government monopolies – petroleum and some of its products, for example. Tobacco and wine and beer (but not hard liquor) are now off this list, however. Also included in the list are some items for which there are import substitutes, or which relate to an emerging industry. By and large, items on the controlled list may be imported only by government departments or trading companies.

Permissible imports The list of permissible imports covers about 26,000 items, which may be imported by any registered trader. About 14,500 items, however, still require an import licence, issued by the Board of Foreign Trade of MOEA.

Customs duties Almost everything is taxable when it goes into Taiwan. Under tremendous US pressure, these tariffs are coming down fast, and Taiwan is fond of producing elaborate statistics to show that its average import duty rates are lower than those of some of its fiercest critics. But many remain sceptical. In 1986, the first round of tariff cuts was invalidated by the practice of the Taiwanese authorities of charging the tariffs on the basis of their own inflated valuation tables, rather than ad valorem.

Harbour construction fee This is charged at a rate of between zero and 4% on the dutiable value of goods that come in by sea.

Special enterprise zones There are three export processing zones (EPZs): at the port of Kaohsiung, at Nantze and at Taichung. As the name suggests, they are available only for export industries. The advantages which these EPZs offer over normal FIA investments include certain tax concessions, greatly simplified procedures and exemption from customs duties.

Agents

There is no legal constraint on most Taiwanese enterprises contracting directly with overseas companies. But, as in so many other parts of the world, business is a question not just of price and product, but of contract and commission. Ideas as to how to go about finding an agent are obtainable from organizations such as the Anglo-Taiwan Trade Committee (in London) and the Economic Co-ordination Council of North American Affairs (with offices in Washington, Chicago, Los Angeles, Houston, New York and Toronto). These organizations are experienced in advising individuals or companies about conducting business in Taiwan.

Distribution

Taiwan has good internal communications, large and efficient ports, and quite advanced telecommunications facilities. The bottlenecks that hampered the rapid growth of the 1960s and early 1970s are hardly a factor now. Internal communications are a source of annoyance to many foreign business people because the rates charged seem to reflect the closed and protected nature of the market.

Insurance, advertising and PR

The service industries for business are still relatively primitive, both in terms of PR and advertising support and in the restricted insurance market that is only just being thrown open to the rigours of competition. Private-sector contracts are normally on a cif basis, but because of the restrictions on public-sector placement of insurance, government bodies have tended to contract on a c&f basis.

Patents, trademarks and copyrights

One of the areas where Taiwan has consistently received a bad press is that of intellectual property protection. The law requires foreign nationals and companies to register patents and trademarks with the National Bureau of Standards of the MOEA and their copyright with the Ministry of the Interior. Patents for inventions are given 15 years' protection, and for improvements the legal life is 10 years. Copyright lasts for the author's life plus 30 years. *Leader in piracy* Despite the copyright and patent laws, Taiwan is one of the world's leaders in tape, video, publishing and computer-software piracy, and for the manufacture of low-cost parodies of others' products and designs. As with so many other contentious issues, Taiwan has little option but to take action now on piracy, so fierce is the pressure from trading partners.

The financial scene

The government has traditionally maintained fairly strict control over financial institutions and foreign exchange. However, in July 1987 martial law was lifted after 38 years and foreign exchange controls have been eased. Leading local banks are able to determine a narrow range of interest rates over prime. In a market generally characterized as underdeveloped, the Ministry of Finance has wide powers over policy in the banking, monetary and fiscal areas.

The banks

Central Bank of China The CBC is both the government's bank and an agency under the Executive Yuan. It issues the local currency; it controls the money supply, credit and public debt via its control over interest rates and local banks' reserve/asset ratios; and it acts as the government's fiscal agent and oversees all foreign exchange operations.

The CBC controls the money market via open market operations, the main instruments being treasury bills, negotiable certificates of time deposit (CDs), bankers' and commercial acceptances, and commercial paper. Other participants in the money market include the commercial banks, the bill-financing companies, corporations and individuals.

The commercial banks number 25, in 16 of which the government has a majority stockholding. Given the underdeveloped capital market, these banks are an important source of funds for industry. They provide short and medium-term credit to local enterprises and foreign investors, underwriting of securities and other normal banking operations. Under "appointment" by the CBC they can engage in foreign exchange business. Some have branches overseas. The leading domestic bank is the Bank of Taiwan.

Development banks provide specialist medium and long-term credit, and some venture capital to their respective sectors. The main development banks are the Bank of Communications, the Farmers Bank of China, the Export-Import Bank of China and the China Development Corporation.

Foreign banks, mainly US banks, have 32 branches and 14 representative offices in Taiwan. These banks perform similar functions to local commercial banks except that they are subject to restrictions on the types of deposit held, limits on private credit and restrictions on the handling of commercial paper. Exchange controls restrict their operations further, and their major role is the funding of foreign companies' local operations.

An offshore banking centre was established in May 1984, enabling both local and foreign banks to engage in lending and deposit business for overseas clients free from exchange control regulations and with a range of tax exemptions on their offshore earnings. In 1987, there were 14 local and foreign banks which had OBU licences.

Other financial institutions
Investment and trust companies number eight in all. They are not allowed to accept public deposits, but provide a wide range of agency and fiduciary services, particularly the acceptance of trust funds. They also provide medium and long-term loans similar to those of the development banks.

Other institutions include eight business banks, supplying credit to small and medium-sized firms, about 75 credit cooperative associations, a handful of bill-financing companies offering short-term funds, over 20 leasing companies and a postal savings system. There is also a substantial high-interest rate grey market, which – according to some estimates – provides as much as 30% of all private sector financing.

The securities market
The Taipei Stock Exchange (TSE) has hitherto not been a major source of capital, but amendments to the securities and exchange law allowed new stockbrokerages to be set up and the development of integrated stockbroking and market making. Opened to indirect foreign investment in 1984, there are various vehicles available for this, including the Taiwan-Overseas International Investment Trust Co and a few specialized funds of which Taiwan (ROC) Fund is the biggest. Most trading on the stock exchange is in local companies' shares, not bonds. Direct portfolio investment on the TSE was possible for foreigners only through one of the four mutual funds until June 1989 when it was announced that three foreign brokers would be allowed seats on the TSE.

Who can help
Trade centres and trading houses
Those whose countries do not have diplomatic relations with Taiwan will find the commercial functions normally undertaken by an embassy are handled by a curious mixture of "trade centres" and trading houses. (See *Taipei.*)

Lawyers
Many of the big London and New York law firms cover Taiwan out of Hong Kong, from where they hope to service their clients' needs in Hong Kong itself, in mainland China, and in Taiwan. Many thus retain links with local companies. Three of the biggest Taipei firms are *Lee & Li*, 201 Tunhua North Rd ☎ 715 3300 ☒ 11651; *Tsar & Tsai Law Offices*, GF Wan Chen Trade Bldg, 477 Tunhua South Rd ☎ 781 4111 ☒ 22732; and *Wenping & Co*, 8th Fl-5, 695 Tunhua South Rd, ☎ 511 8160 ☒ 11962.

Accountants
Many of the world's leading accounting firms have offices in Taipei through arrangements with local partnerships, for example: *Andrew Chang and Associates*, (Peat, Marwick, Mitchell and Co), 742 Mingshen East Rd ☎ 713 8001 ☒ 23184

Chen, Chu & Co (Price Waterhouse and Co), 142 Chunghsiao East Rd, Section 4 ☎ 721 6686 ☒ 24241
Chiang Lai, Lin and Co CPAS (Touche Ross), 131 Nanking East Rd, Section 3 ☎ 712 1717 ☒ 10648
T.N. Soong & Co (Arthur Andersen, Coopers & Lybrand, Ernst & Whinney, Deloittes), 53 Nanking East Rd, Section 2 ☎ 551 7272 ☒ 11442

Consultants
The following Taipei-based firms specialize in helping foreign firms: *China Management Consultants Inc*, 57 Fushing North Rd, Section 2 ☎ 331 2862

Columbia Associates Ltd, 285 Nanking East Rd, Section 3 ☎ 713 2731 ☒ 10451
International Consulting Inc, 66 Minsheng East Rd ☎ 541 4484
Investec (Taiwan) Ltd, Suite 1403, 147 Chienkuo North Rd, Section 2 ☎ 531 6226 ☒ 28514
SGV-Soong & Co, 53 Nanking East Rd, Section 2 ☎ 521 7761 ☒ 11442
Taiwan Investment and Business Consultants, 624 Mingchuan East Rd ☎ 713 3222 ☒ 27591

Useful government contacts
National Tax Administration of Taipei, Ministry of Finance, Tax Service Center, Foreign Affairs Office, 547 Chunghsiao East Rd, Section 4 ☎ 763 1010
Commerce Department, Ministry of Economic Affairs, 15 Foochow St ☎ 351 7271
Industrial Development Bureau, MOEA 109 Hankow St, Section 1 ☎ 331 7531
Industrial Development and Investment Centre, 10th Fl, Yumin Bldg, 7 Roosevelt Rd, Section 1 ☎ 394 7213
Board of Foreign Trade, MOEA Head office, 1 Hukou St ☎ 351 0286
China Productivity Center, 340 Tunhua North Rd ☎ 713 7731

Local publications
Statistical sources include *Industry of Free China* produced by the cabinet office. It comes out monthly, like the budget bureau's *Monthly Statistics of the Republic of China*, and the Central Bank's *Financial Statistics Monthly*. If you need to know more, there is a *Statistical Data Yearbook* and a handy pocket-sized version, *The Taiwan Statistical Data Yearbook*. **Media** There is an English-language press in Taiwan, but it is only just emerging from 40 years of enforced patriotism. Both the weekly *Free China Journal* and *Economic News* are unabashedly pro-government. For more dispassionate comment and news, one is forced to the Hong Kong regional press.

Business and cultural awareness

Taiwanese will sometimes compare their position in the world to that of the European Jews at times of widespread antisemitism. They feel unliked, shunned, that their business partners are rather shamefaced about dealing with them – but go on dealing with them just the same because Taiwan can deliver the right goods at the right price and has carved for itself a unique niche in the world market. This attitude gives rise to a cynicism and arrogance that, in fact, many Westerners find rather appealing.

Taiwan society

It is no longer so important for the visitor to shy away from talking about politics. But you should still avoid phrases which suggest that the Kuomintang is not the rightful government of all China. There are other things to remember: Taiwan is not Taiwan but the Republic of China; the people who live there are "Chinese," not "Taiwanese" (which has other connotations, being the term used to distinguish pre-1949ers from the mainland families who fled then); Beijing is Peiping (pronounced Beiping) and is under the temporary control of "the Communists," not any sort of government; and so on. But apart from high-level government officials, nobody is really going to mind if you make a *faux pas*. The colour of your money far outshines the colour of your politics. One should not, however, underestimate the emotional importance for the older generation of the issue of Chinese reunification. If you have been to China ("the mainland") there is no reason to hide the fact; on the contrary, you will find a very interested audience for your impressions, which will probably confirm your listeners' belief that they are better off where they are.

A Chinese society Politically there is an important divide between the mainlanders and the native Taiwanese. Culturally, the gap is almost imperceptible to the outsider. Taiwan is an authentic – some would argue the most authentic – Chinese culture. Not just since 1949, but for centuries, Taiwan has been a safe haven for Chinese culture at times of internal upheaval or external threat. The National Palace Museum outside Taipei houses perhaps the finest collection in the world of Chinese art.

Religion As in other Chinese cultures, religion is a hotch-potch of Confucianism, Buddhism, Taoism, Christianity, ancestor worship and just plain superstition. As, strictly speaking, Confucianism is not a religion at all, but an ethical system in which the family plays the paramount role, there is no conflict between the Confucian tradition and upholding a variety of spiritual beliefs. In traditional China, it was said that a man should follow Confucius in his career, Buddha in the temple, and the Taoist sage Lao Tse in his garden. Religious observance is inseparable from loyalty to family traditions. The pull of the home village is an emotional and spiritual expression of a religious belief. Many Chinese exiles want to go home to die, or to invest something in the site of their ancestors' graves – that they themselves may have never seen. Temple attendance is not something that can be slotted into a weekly routine. It features rather at annual festivals, such as "hungry ghosts" when fake money is burnt to appease restless wanderers in the afterlife, or Chinese New Year when every Chinese family tries to reunite. Religious observance has its pragmatic side. Supplication to the deity can produce results, usually at a price.

With gods on their side The extent of superstition in Chinese life often defies belief. *Feng-shui* or "the winds and waters" is still a fundamental principle of both architecture and interior design. Its methods are obscure, requiring the expensive advice of a professional "*feng-shui* man" or geomancer. They seem to be based on the idea of keeping bad spirits out, but leaving them some form of escape if you are unfortunate enough to share office space with them. Even young, foreign-educated Taiwanese will point out to you, when a business collapses, that its headquarters were notorious for their dodgy *feng-shui*.

Gambling is not so much a pastime as an incurable disease. Chinese New Year is celebrated in many offices with a game of poker which may last twelve hours and may cost the loser not just his thirteenth month's bonus but a good chunk of his regular salary, too. In 1987 an idiotic game known as *Ta Chia Le* (Everybody Happy) – a kind of primitive secondary market in the winning numbers in the official state lottery – became epidemic. Factories stopped work, phone lines were jammed, and the number of nervous breakdowns soared.

Sex Taipei and Kaohsiung have their sleazy areas, with hostess bars which are really rather stylish clip-joints. More downmarket and characteristically Taiwanese are the barber-shops which sometimes offer haircuts, but may have a back room for more intimate services. As in most cultures, however, there is a double standard about sexual behaviour, and Chinese life is decorous, not to say prudish. Public displays of affection, especially kissing, but also cuddling are looked on as rather unseemly.

Face The old sociological cliché is that Western society is characterized by guilt cultures, while Oriental cultures are run on "shame" principles. To the extent this covers the ubiquitous concept of "face," it is an apt description of Taiwan. This has practical implications. If you are meeting with a colleague who has little to contribute and is there to carry bags and take notes, you should nevertheless give him or her face by, for example, seeking his or her opinion at some point. Humiliation is in the eye of the beholder. If you go out for a meal with local colleagues, and intend to split the bill, wait until you are back in the privacy of your own office. If you want to bawl somebody out, do not do it in public.

The business method

It is taken for granted in Taiwan that business matters more than everything – apart from the most acute family crisis. People have little compunction about calling you at home at ungodly hours and expect little mercy in return, whatever your business relationship. Taiwan thrives on the adrenalin of deadlines, doing deals and beating the competition. Strangely, this may not be apparent to the visitor on a prospecting, market-sounding trip. "Courtesy calls" are just that – wrapped in more formality of polite verbiage than you find almost anywhere. Quite often photographs are taken to commemorate what may seem to be a most banal and fruitless meeting.

Business hours are usually 9–5.30. In setting up appointments you should keep within these times. A first afternoon meeting would be at 2: business lunches are at 12 or 12.30 with the expectation of being back at the desk by then.

Business meetings If you are setting up meetings yourself, it is worth telexing in advance, and asking the hotel business centre to call round and confirm the meetings on arrival. Keep courtesy calls and cold marketing visits short and to the point. Although, when you have established a business relationship, you will be expected to sacrifice your personal life to making the deal work, a rigid separation between home and office applies at the early stages of contact. At meetings, observe the ritual-exchange courtesies, drink the tea and coffee you are offered when your host bids you, and only then explain why you have come.

Business cards are essential. It is best to have one side of your card printed in Chinese characters. Most of the Taiwanese business community carry two different sets of cards – an English and a Chinese version. It is tactless but not disastrous to use the same cards as on the mainland. Chinese characters have been simplified by the Beijing government in a way that makes it obvious if cards have been printed for a trip to the mainland.

Prejudices There are real and significant prejudices against women, blacks and the young. There is also a prejudice against whites, but this is of a somewhat different type. These prejudices are, however, not that hard to overcome: the business ethic is so dominant that prejudice will soon evaporate in the face of a person's ability to deliver the goods.

Dress Men will be expected to wear a jacket and tie for any meeting of significance, even in the most humid summer weather (all buildings have air conditioning). Women should wear dresses or suits. Casual wear for men is slacks, open neck shirt or designer T-shirt. Women are rarely casual in their dress.

Language
The national language is Mandarin Chinese, although most residents also speak a local Taiwanese dialect, which is very close to Fukienese. English is the lingua franca of international business and many of the younger generation speak excellent and idiomatic English. Taxi-drivers and even hotel staff, however, are not likely to have more than the most rudimentary grasp of English. It is worthwhile, therefore, having the addresses you will be visiting most often written down in Chinese, and trying to memorize at least the Chinese version of your

hotel's name. As in most countries, you earn respect for trying to grapple with the local language.

Forms of address Chinese names, like Chiang Ching-kuo, are made up of the family or surname (Chiang) which comes first, a name usually given to all siblings of the same sex (Ching) and a distinctive third syllable (kuo). So, in Western terms Ching-kuo is the given name. Business partners should be addressed by their family name. Because there are a lot of Lis and Wangs and Chiangs and Kuos, many people use their initials, placed in front of the surname in the Western fashion – "Mr C.K. Chiang," for example. It is important to remember the initials, especially when, as you often will, you find yourself dealing with a family firm and confronted by large numbers of senior people all with the same surname. The Western-influenced young often take foreign given names as well ("George Wang Kuo-ching").

Hospitality
You will rarely be invited into a Chinese home. This is not necessarily out of either a lack of friendliness or embarrassment at living conditions. Those who do give dinner or drinks parties tend to be the most Western-influenced. The normal form of hospitality is to give a large dinner at a Chinese restaurant. In reciprocating, it is probably safer to take your guests to a Western restaurant. In a Chinese restaurant, the menu is for foreigners: the Chinese rarely deign to peruse it. Ordering is carried out by the host who knows what the restaurant does best. The Taiwanese will drink tea and perhaps a soft drink, and occasionally beer. Few can drink very much without flushing embarrassingly. The Hong Kong taste for the most expensive brandies is, however, spreading into Taiwan, where, because of high import duties, cognac has become even more of a status symbol.

TAIPEI

Area code ☎ 02

As the capital of one of Asia's most prosperous nations, Taipei is working hard to improve its ugly appearance, and the resulting real-estate boom has created a new affluent middle class. Because of strict exchange controls (which have now been eased), the citizens of Taipei have had no outlet for their wealth than ploughing it back into business or spending it on luxury goods. Indicative of this are the expensive foreign cars that clog the roads and create appalling pollution.

Investment in industry has contributed to the city's broad manufacturing base; textiles still dominate but electronics and plastics are increasingly important. These are the big foreign exchange earners, but the city produces a huge range of products from toys to luxury yachts. Taipei has become a bargain basement for buyers and wholesalers from all over the world and the resulting demand has spawned thousands of companies and hundreds of general merchants and middlemen.

All this helps give Taipei a fast, go-ahead feel, but most companies are still family concerns and rarely employ more than 100 staff. There is an overwhelming sense of pride in the achievements of the nation since 1949. Many pay lip sevice to the idea that the government of Taiwan is still the true government of mainland China in exile. Taipei is always referred to as the "provisional" capital.

Arriving

Most visitors to Taipei stop over between visits to Tokyo and Hong Kong, arriving at Chiang Kai-shek (CKS) International airport. There are also direct flights from Hong Kong and Japan to Kaohsiung, in the south, the centre of Taiwan's ship-building industry. For flights to other Taiwanese cities it is necessary to transfer from CKS to the domestic airport in central Taipei.

Chiang Kai-shek Airport

Opened in 1979, CKS is one of the most efficient and technologically advanced airports in Asia. Travelators carry passengers from the arrival gate to the vast immigration hall where procedures are handled swiftly. Those carrying dutiable goods can either leave them in bond or pay the duty; offices for both purposes are just beyond the customs lines. It usually takes no more than 20min to clear the airport.

Facilities There is a tourist information and hotel reservations desk and a bureau de change. Unused Taiwan currency can be changed at the Bank of Taiwan office in the departure lounge. The duty-free shop carries a wide stock of top-quality whiskies and cognacs but limited selections of other goods. The CKS tourist service centre will deal with airport inquiries ☎ 03-3834631. There is an airport departure tax of NT$300.

City link The airport is 50km/32 miles southwest of Taipei. Hotel shuttle buses offer the best compromise between expensive taxis and the slower airport bus service. Allow 45min by taxi or hotel transport and 60min or more by bus.

Hotel transport Most visitors travel to Taipei by a hotel shuttle bus. This should be requested in advance but can be ordered through the tourist information desk in the airport. The fare is about NT$250. Most hotels provide a limousine service, if reserved in advance, costing around

NT$1,500 one way.

Taxi The rank is to the left of the terminal exit. Cabs into Taipei charge 50% on top of the metered fare (though not on the trip from Taipei to the airport). The total usually comes to more than NT$600. At night, the charge is higher.

Car rental Hertz (Formosa Rent-a-Car) will arrange a self-drive car to meet you at the airport, or a limousine ☎ (080) 211 3333 (toll-free).

Bus The no. 2 bus calls at the major hotels along the Chungshan North Road, Taipei Railway Station, and the Hilton and Lai Lai Sheraton hotels before terminating at the Chunglun Bus terminal on Pateh Road. Buses leave every 15min. Tickets, costing NT$72, are sold at the "Limousine Coach" desk in the airport foyer.

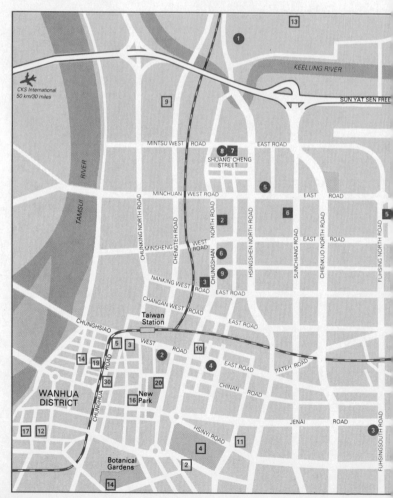

Getting around

Taxis are best for short distances across town. For business calls, the host company will usually send a car to meet you but if not, it is best to travel by limousine.

Hotel transport The main hotels rent out limousines starting at NT$250 per hour. Some have a minimum 4hr hire period and charge extra per kilometre after the first 200.

Taxis are abundant in Taipei and range from old wrecks to brand-new Mercedes. The fare is the same for both — about NT$50 for a short journey. Apart from the names of the leading hotels, most drivers do not understand English and you will get nowhere without an address written in Chinese characters. Use business cards and the hotel taxi dispatch service for this. Once the driver has the address he can be relied upon not to get lost.

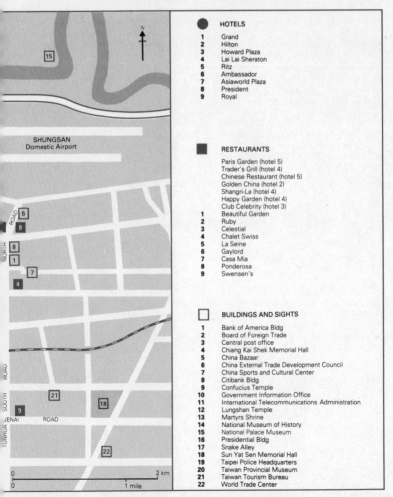

● **HOTELS**

1 Grand
2 Hilton
3 Howard Plaza
4 Lai Lai Sheraton
5 Ritz
6 Ambassador
7 Asiaworld Plaza
8 President
9 Royal

SHUNGSAN
Domestic Airport

■ **RESTAURANTS**

Paris Garden (hotel 5)
Trader's Grill (hotel 4)
Chinese Restaurant (hotel 5)
Golden China (hotel 2)
Shangri-La (hotel 4)
Happy Garden (hotel 4)
Club Celebrity (hotel 3)
1 Beautiful Garden
2 Ruby
3 Celestial
4 Chalet Swiss
5 La Seine
6 Gaylord
7 Casa Mia
8 Ponderosa
9 Swensen's

□ **BUILDINGS AND SIGHTS**

1 Bank of America Bldg
2 Board of Foreign Trade
3 Central post office
4 Chiang Kai Shek Memorial Hall
5 China Bazaar
6 China External Trade Development Council
7 China Sports and Cultural Center
8 Citibank Bldg
9 Confucius Temple
10 Government Information Office
11 International Telecommunications Administration
12 Lungshan Temple
13 Martyrs Shrine
14 National Museum of History
15 National Palace Museum
16 Presidential Bldg
17 Snake Alley
18 Sun Yat Sen Memorial Hall
19 Taipei Police Headquarters
20 Taiwan Provincial Museum
21 Taiwan Tourism Bureau
22 World Trade Center

267

Allow plenty of time for journeys – even a few blocks will take 20min.
Driving Hertz ☎ (080) 211 333 (toll free) and *Central Auto Service* ☎ 881 9545 will provide self-drive cars and limousines. Driving in Taipei is very demanding and stressful.
Walking Humidity and thick traffic fumes make walking extremely unpleasant. Take special care when crossing roads.
Public transport Only dirty and crowded buses as yet. Tunnelling is in progress for a new subway.

Outside Taipei
Air The domestic airline system is the fastest way of reaching other cities and is inexpensive: the one-way fare Taipei to Kaohsiung is around NT$1,000. *China Airlines* (CAL) ☎ 715 1212 and *Far Eastern Air Transport* (FAT) ☎ 361 5431 are the two main carriers. Reservations can be made from hotel travel desks or at airline offices. Taipei's domestic airport (Shungsan) is less than a 30min drive north of the city centre. Its facilities are limited.
Driving The North/South Expressway runs down the west side of Taiwan. All the road numbers and exits are clearly marked but there are no English-language signs off the expressway. Driving standards are very erratic. The two leading car rental firms are *Hertz*, which has outlets in all cities, and *Central Auto Service* ☎ 881 9545 which also has 9-seater mini-buses. Both supply good maps and can provide drivers.
Bus De luxe express buses travel between Taipei and Kaohsiung faster than the train, taking 4hr. Services depart frequently from the terminal next to Taipei Railway Station. One-way tickets cost NT$420. For reservations contact your hotel or the bus depot ☎ 311 9466.
Train The Taiwan Railway Administration operates the east-coast line which links Taipei and Taitung, and the west-coast line linking Taipei to Kaohsiung via

Taichung. There are hourly departures in each direction and a reserved seat on a comfortable, clean, air-conditioned and punctual *Tzuchiang* (TC) express service costs about 50% of the equivalent air fare. Free tea is served on the journey and there are dining cars on all services, plus sleeping cars on night trains. Tickets from hotel travel desks or Taipei Railway Station ☎ 311 0121.

Area by area
Taipei lies in a basin surrounded by mountains, which unfortunately trap both moisture and industrial smog. Large areas remain undeveloped but changes are planned.
The city centre lies on the eastern bank of the wide Tamsui river which flows into the Taiwan Straits some 20km/12 miles to the northwest. At its heart is the Presidential Plaza which fills with festive crowds for the annual "Double Ten" day pageant celebrating the Nationalist Party's declaration of the Republic of China in Beijing on October 10 1911. One of the massive gates of the city's 19thC defensive walls still remains in the plaza, facing the Presidential Building where the main executive branches of government have their headquarters. Nearby are the city's major parks and memorials, including the massive Chiang Kai-shek Memorial Hall completed in 1980.

Chungshan Road, which begins at the imposing Ming-style marble gates to the Chiang Kai-shek Memorial, is Taipei's main street. It runs north to the spaghetti-like freeway interchange in front of the Grand hotel. On both sides of its length are cinemas, shops, hotels, office blocks and department stores, and all the main east/west roads cross it, divided into numbered sections.
Southern Taipei Chungshan Road was already densely built up when building regulations were relaxed in 1978 and developers have found it easier to acquire large plots of land further south. As a result, businesses

are moving to Fuhsing and Tunhua roads, which now have the most modern office blocks and upmarket shopping plazas; prestige-conscious companies have all relocated there.

Old Taipei is in the Wanhua district between Chunghua Road and the river. It is crowded with alleys and noisy markets. At night the area around Huahsi Street comes alive with foodstalls, hawkers and vendors of snake soup, venom, bile and blood, all sold for medicinal purposes. At the centre of this "snake alley" market is the Buddhist Lung Shan Temple built in the early 18th century, hit by an incendiary bomb in 1945, and rebuilt in 1957.

Other areas Beyond the centre the city has spread in every direction. The economic boom in Taiwan has attracted large numbers of country people to the capital, increasing its population to 2.5m.

Yangmingshan (Grass Mountain) to the north of Taipei is the nearest point to the city where it is possible to experience the unspoiled natural beauty of the island, despite the large number of new villas belonging to wealthy Taiwanese and expatriates.

The modern port is now at Keelung, 40km/25 miles to the northeast, from where container trucks shuttle down the freeway to Taipei.

Hotels

Few could fail to be charmed by the Ritz or impressed by the Grand, but most of Taipei's many hotels do not warrant great enthusiasm. One practice peculiar to Taipei is the selling of guest lists by hotel staff to publishers who circulate them daily to business subscribers. Visitors to Taipei can expect to be showered with business cards, invitations and even telephone calls from voracious salesmen. The better hotels are now trying to stamp this out.

The hotels given full descriptions all have a shuttle bus and/or limousine service to and from the airport. They also have minibars, 24hr room service, English-speaking staff, a travel desk and standard business facilities which include photocopying, typing, telex and fax; not all hotels have IDD telephones yet. Room rates are quoted exclusive of service (10%) and local tax (5%). Taipei is promoted heavily as a convention centre but during the hot summer months of July and August reservations are not essential.

Grand $$$
1 Chungshan North Rd, Section 4
☏ *596 5565* ▣ *11646 Fax 594 8243*
• *AE DC MC V* • *447 rooms, 83 suites, 6 restaurants, 1 bar*
The Grand is a vast red and gold structure modelled on the Imperial Palaces of the Forbidden City in Beijing. The rooms, furnished in Chinese style, are also huge; all have balconies overlooking the city, and bathrooms the size of a typical hotel room. There are two cavernous dining rooms serving Chinese and Western cuisine, plus a 24hr coffee shop. In the evening the hillside

gardens are a peaceful and attractive place for a stroll in the cooler hillside air. However, the hotel is flawed by slow and offhand service. Shops, hairdresser • massage, use of elite Yuan Shan Recreation Club with pool, tennis, bowling alley • 15 meeting rooms (capacity up to 500), convention hall (capacity 1,500) with simultaneous translation.

Hilton $$$$
38 Chunghsiao West Rd, Section 1,
☏ *311 5151* ▣ *22513 Fax 331 9944*
• *AE DC MC V* • *477 rooms, 23 suites, 6 restaurants, 1 bar*

A prime central site was chosen for the Hilton, the city's first high-rise building and first prestige hotel. The hotel is much used for business functions and working lunches. It is known as the "Trader's Hotel" because of the large number of buyers who use it, and the 36 rooms on the two executive floors are large enough to accommodate meetings of six or more quite comfortably. All have IDD telephones. The popular Trader's Grill (see *Restaurants*) has won several international food awards and the Golden China Restaurant is in·demand for banquets. Shops, hairdresser, disco • gym, sauna, jacuzzi, massage • 6 meeting rooms (capacity up to 460) with audiovisual equipment.

Howard Plaza $$$$$
160 Jenai Rd ☎ 700 2323 ⊤⊠ 10720 Fax 700 0729 • AE DC MC V • 471 rooms, 135 suites, 6 restaurants, 3 bars
A modern but somewhat soulless new hotel, offering excellent amenities and service. It has three floors of luxury boutiques and a vast central atrium the height of the building, scaled by glass-fronted elevators. Half the rooms overlook the atrium and the other half have views over the city. The single rooms are small but the twin rooms are spacious. All rooms have armchairs, sofas and desks. The restaurants offer French, Chinese and Japanese menus. Shops, hairdresser, florist • outdoor pool, gym, sauna • 10 meeting rooms (capacity up to 100), conference hall (capacity 800).

Lai Lai Sheraton $$$$$
12 Chunghsiao East Rd, Section 1 ☎ 321 5511 ⊤⊠ 23939 Fax 394 4240 • AE DC MC V • 657 rooms, 48 suites, 10 restaurants, 3 bars
Taipei's biggest hotel teeters on the borderline between flashiness and grandeur. Elegant marble floors, panelled walls and well-chosen paintings jar with the atrium's fairground atmosphere, gaudy painted lions and light-bulb

encrusted glass elevators. Apart from several suites furnished in Arabian style, most of the rooms have classical furnishings, modern amenities and are very large, easily transformed into an office during the day. The business centre will help make local business contacts. Shops, hairdresser, florist, disco • pool, sauna, massage, jogging track, gym, tennis, squash • 12 meeting rooms (capacity up to 80) convention hall (capacity 2,000) with simultaneous translation.

Ritz $$$$$
155 Minchuan East Rd ☎ 597 1234 ⊤⊠ 27345 Fax 596 9223 • AE DC MC V • Leading Hotels of the World • 138 rooms, 82 suites, 3 restaurants, 1 bar
The Ritz is small and intimate, decorated throughout in Art Deco style. Guests are greeted by the manager and shown to their rooms as if arriving for a country house weekend. Rooms are opulent with closed-circuit television showing the latest English-language movies. The Paris 1930 is Taipei's top business entertaining venue (see *Restaurants*), and the library-like Matisse Lounge has a business service desk. Shops, hairdresser • gym, sauna, jacuzzi, massage • 5 meeting rooms (capacity up to 600).

OTHER HOTELS
Ambassador ($$$) *63 Chungshan North Rd, ☎ 551 1111 ⊤⊠ 11255 Fax 561 7883 • AE DC MC V.* Excellent restaurants, good views from rooms, pool, nightclub popular with Japanese businessmen.
Asiaworld Plaza ($$$$) *100 Tunhua North Rd ☎ 715 0077 ⊤⊠ 26299 Fax 713 4148 • AE DC MC V.* New, efficient but impersonal.
President ($$$$) *9 Teh Hwei St ☎ 595 1251 ⊤⊠ 11269 Fax 591 3677 • AE DC MC V.* Popular with Western business visitors who like a lively atmosphere.
Royal ($$$$) *37 Chunghsiao North Rd ☎ 542 3266 ⊤⊠ 23915 Fax 543 4897 • Nikko Hotels • AE DC MC V.* Small, elegant and central.

Clubs

The *Banker's Club*, Worldwide House, 685 Minsheng East Rd ☏ 715 2135 is male-orientated and restrained. The *American Club in China*, 47 Pei An Rd ☏ 594 8260 has more family members and is popular with expatriates. Both clubs have pleasant bars and dining rooms and are used by expatriates to entertain visitors.

Restaurants

The top two restaurants in Taipei for business entertaining are Paris 1930 at the Ritz and the Hilton's Trader's Grill, both serving French influenced cuisine. Elsewhere you will not go wrong by asking local business people for their recommendations. Taipei's restaurants are remarkably inexpensive by Western standards, but drinks can add heavily to the total cost of a meal. At a normal business lunch most guests will drink the excellent local beer or fruit juice, but for a celebration or banquet the host is expected to buy brandy or whisky by the bottle and heavy drinking is part of the ritual of cementing a relationship. Remember that most Taiwanese consider business matters too confidential to discuss in restaurants.

Dinner usually begins at 7 and rarely finishes later than 9. Reservations are always advisable.

Paris 1930 $$$
Ritz Hotel ☏ *597 1234* • *AE DC MC V* • *jacket and tie required*
The Art Deco style of the Ritz is carried through into its restaurant. Tables are placed too closely together for private conversation in the central dining area but there are several secluded glass-screened banquettes along the walls. The menu changes every two weeks but can always be relied upon to provide a choice between French provincial and classic cuisine. The Paris 1930 is *the* failsafe choice to impress important clients.

Trader's Grill $$$
Hilton Hotel ☏ *311 5151* • *AE DC MC V* • *jacket and tie required*
Another excellent choice for business entertaining though not in the same class as the Paris 1930. In an otherwise plain interior, brass bowls filled with bread, fruit and flowers hang on chains from the ceiling to give an appropriate "market place" feel. The cooking is fresh, well prepared and served in generous portions.

Chinese restaurants
Although Taipei business people will be most impressed by an invitation to dine at one of the top-class hotel restaurants serving international cuisine, they are, at heart, just as happy to be entertained at a Chinese restaurant. Those in the main hotels are the safest choice. All have descriptive English-language menus and staff who will give trustworthy advice on dishes and seating arrangements. The *Chinese Restaurant* at the Ritz, regarded as the best in town, serves Hunan-style cuisine; the *Golden China* at the Hilton offers Cantonese food; and the *Shangri-La* at the Lai Lai Sheraton specializes in Sichuan cooking.

Taiwanese food differs somewhat from mainland Chinese cuisine and has been influenced by Japan. Fresh seafood predominates and the choice includes deep-fried shrimp, grilled clams or eel, poached squid and turtle soup. These can be tried at the *Happy Garden* at the Lai Lai Sheraton, or the *Club Celebrity* at the Howard Plaza.

Chinese restaurants not in hotels are more informal and privacy cannot be counted upon. One of the best and most popular is the *Beautiful Garden*, 230 Tunhua North Rd ☏ 715 3921. It offers an eclectic range of regional Chinese dishes including pigeon and melon soup and steamed crab claws. The *Ruby*, 135 Chungshan North Rd, Section 2 ☏ 571 1157, serves excellent Cantonese dishes and has several private dining rooms. *The Celestial*, 3rd Fl, 1 Nanking West Rd ☏ 563 2380, is the newest and most sophisticated restaurant for Beijing (Peiping in Taiwan) duck and other northern Chinese dishes.

All these restaurants are in the $ or $$ price ranges and will accept credit cards but those outside hotels are likely to prefer cash.

Western and Indian cuisine
Chalet Swiss, 47 Nanking East Rd, Section 4 ☏ 715 2702 serves Swiss and Continental food and fondue; the excellent *La Seine*, 14 Lane 550, Minchuan East Rd, serves French cuisine; *Gaylord*, 328 Sungkiang Rd ☏ 543 4003, specializes in northern Indian food and its lunch buffet at weekends is very popular. The lively *Casa Mia*, 628 Linshen North Rd ☏ 591 7478, serves authentic Italian food but abandon all hopes of a quiet meal on evenings when the restaurant shows videotapes of recent soccer matches. Two chains offer good American food: *Ponderosa* at 303 Tunhua North Rd ☏ 716 8223 and 18 Nanking East Rd, Section 1 ☏ 581 4037, serves big steaks and salads; *Swensen's* at 109 Jenai Rd, Section 4 ☏ 752 4076, is known for fine ice cream and also has a huge variety of salads.

All these restaurants are in the $ or $$ price ranges, but check in advance if you want to pay by credit card.

Bars

The Lai Lai Sheraton has three bars and its central position makes it a favourite rendezvous for after-work

or pre-dinner drinks. For off-duty drinks, visitors can relax in the English-style "pubs" which have recently sprung up. In the alleyways south of the President hotel a cluster of bars serve over 100 imported beers, as well as inexpensive Western meals and snacks. Regular live jazz, folk music or cabaret entertainment are offered at *Ploughman Pub*, 9 Lane 25, Shuang Cheng St; *Waltzing Matilda*, a few doors down and an offshoot of the Hong Kong bar of the same name; the *Hope and Anchor*, 16 Shuang Cheng St; and *Sam's Place*, 2 Lane 32, Shuang Cheng St.

Entertainment

For general information on the arts scene in Taipei the monthly English-language magazine *Bang* carries listings and reviews and is available from hotel newsstands. Major events are also listed in *This Month in Taiwan* and the two daily English newspapers, *China News* and *China Post*.

Music, drama, opera English-language drama in Taipei is rare, but several theatres put on weekly concerts by visiting artists and local Taiwanese groups. The *New Aspect Theatre*, 503 Tunhua South Rd ☏ 709 1966, has the best visiting orchestras and soloists and organizes an international arts festival every February to April. The *China Sports and Cultural Centre* 55 Nanking East Rd, Section 4 ☏ 715 1337, hosts a mixture of events, including talent contests sponsored by local TV stations and performances of Western classical music by the Taipei City Symphony Orchestra. The *Social Education Hall*, 25 Pateh Rd, Section 3 ☏ 731 5931, has free Chinese classical and contemporary music performances.

Cinema Rambo is tame stuff to Taipei cinema audiences who prefer bloody Kung-fu movies in Chinese. The best venue for international films, in their original language with subtitles, is the *German Cultural Centre*, 24 Hsinhyi Rd, Section 1

☎ 394 7294. The *Taipei Fine Arts Museum*, 181 Chungshan North Rd, Section 3 ☎ 595 7656, is the best place for "art" movies.

Discos and nightclubs *Tiffany's* at the Hilton is Taipei's liveliest disco. The *Disco Nightclub* at the Lai Lai Sheraton is a less overpowering alternative, and the *Arc de Triomphe* at the Asiaworld Plaza Hotel is where the sophisticated Westernized young crowd go. Nightclubs with hostesses are tame compared with those that flourished during the Korean and Vietnam wars, but still offer spicy distractions for those who want them. The *Charlie Brown Club*, 21 Shuang Cheng St ☎ 591 3686, is the safest for the unaccompanied visitor since taking a "private room" is not obligatory and it is possible merely to listen to the music or dance with hostesses.

Shopping

The best buys in Taipei are jade and coral jewellery, snakeskin leather goods, brassware and sports equipment. The island also abounds in marble (veinstone) from which bowls, vases and suchlike are carved. Apart from these genuine local products Taiwan is notorious for pirated books, records and tapes, as well as fake designer watches. The government has started a clean-up campaign, but visitors determined to buy a fake Rolex can still do so with the help of a knowledgeable local guide.

Department stores Open daily 10–9.30, these are good places for one-stop shopping and all accept credit cards. The leading stores are *Asiaworld*, 337 Nanking East Rd, Section 3; *Evergreen*, 6 Nanking East Rd, Section 2; *Far Eastern*, 32 Paoching Road; *Lai Lai Shopping Mall*, 77 Wuchang St, Section 2; and *Today's* at 14 Nanking West Rd or 41 Chunghua Rd, Section 1.

Craft shops Inexpensive government-run craft shops are excellent for reproduction antiques and lacquer ware, wood and jade carving, fans, embroidery and porcelain. The *Taiwan Crafts Centre*, 110 Yenping South Rd (open Tue–Sun, 10–6) and the *Chinese Handicraft Mart*, 1 Hsuchou Rd (open daily 9–5.30) are good for inexpensive gifts. For more expensive but very high quality reproductions the shop at the National Palace Museum (open daily 9–5) cannot be bettered.

Markets and smaller stores give you a chance to bargain but payment must be in cash. Aim to knock 30–50% off the price originally quoted, but expect to pay outrageous amounts for "antiques." Remember too that most old objects, other than coins and poor-quality porcelain, cannot be exported. Good areas for browsing are the junk shops of Chunghua Rd, popularly known as Hagglers' Alley, and the stores surrounding the Ambassador Hotel in Chungshan North Rd, Section 2. Other street markets, which mostly come alive after dark, are the *China Bazaar*, Chunghua Rd, and *Snake Alley*, Hwahsi St.

Shipping The major department stores all handle shipping and insurance. The Central Post Office has a packing section where you can have parcels safely packed, checked by customs and sent by air or sea.

Sightseeing

The only sight you should not miss is the National Palace Museum.

National Palace Museum In the suburb of Waishuanghsi (Shihlin), about 20min by taxi from the Grand hotel, is a huge selection of treasures – bronzes, paintings, porcelain, jade, calligraphy and rare books – amassed by successive Chinese emperors over 1,000 years. Some 10,000 of the 60,000 items are exhibited at any one time. *Open 9–5; 1hr guided tours in English at 10 and 3.*

Botanical Gardens A colourful and peaceful spot in summer with 2,000 species of Taiwanese flora. Within the gardens is the *National Museum of History* containing treasures largely excavated from tombs in mainland China. *Nanhai Rd. Open 9–5.*

Taiwan Provincial Museum
Covers geology, wildlife and the life and culture of Taiwan's aboriginal tribes. *2 Hsiangyiang Rd. Open 9–5.*

Guided tours

Travel companies offer group or individual tours of the city and to places outside Taipei. Either use the agent based in your hotel or one of the following members of the Taiwan Visitors' Association which all have English-speaking guides: *Associated Tours* ☎ 771 7284, *Gloria Travel Service* ☎ 563 5313, *Supreme Travel Service* ☎ 521 3133 and *Taiwan Coach Tours* ☎ 595 5321.

Out of town

Peitou This attractive hot springs resort in the Yangminshan National Park is less than an hour's drive north of Taipei. Blind masseuses knead tired limbs before or after a soak in hot sulphur spring water. A short walk from the town centre is Hell's Valley, where hawkers boil eggs in the bubbling sulphurous pits and sell them for their supposed medicinal value.

North coast The drive around Taiwan's northern coastline makes a rewarding trip. *Tamsui* is the first destination, 20km/12 miles northwest of Taipei on the estuary of the Tamsui river and the Taiwan Strait. It was occupied by the Spanish in the 17th century and the pink-walled Fort San Domingo with its rusting cannons is the island's most important colonial monument. It was once Taiwan's major port but is now a sleepy fishing village with numerous seafood restaurants. The north coast road continues to the beautiful *Yehliu National Park*, a series of coral beaches eroded by wind and sea into fantastic formations. From here there is a choice of routes: the short circuit back to Taipei by the mountain road from Chinsan winding through

terraced rice fields and farming villages, or you can continue along the main highway to *Keelung*, a natural deepwater port second in size to Kaohsiung. Its main attraction is the towering statue of Kuan Yin, the goddess of mercy worshipped by the seafaring Fukkienese who settled in Taiwan. Beyond Keelung lies the *Northeast Coastal Scenic Area*, a lovely region of tranquil villages and unspoiled beaches surrounded by evergreen hills.

South of Taipei Not far south of Taipei is the popular picnic and boating resort of *Pitan* or Green Lake. From here a 30min drive along the course of the Hsientien River brings you to the aboriginal village of *Wulai* where the local Atayal tribe now grow prosperous on proceeds from handicrafts, song and dance shows and tips from photographers. There are fine waterfalls at Wulai but those at *Toucheng* and *Chiaoachi* are less spoiled. To reach them take Route 9 which winds through Taiwan's central mountain range to the east coast, some 50km/30 miles from Taipei. From Toucheng a road leads inland to *New Peak Falls (Hsin Feng)*. There are swimming pools by the parking area but it is more enjoyable to follow the path to the canyon where there is a natural pool at the foot of a 50-metre cascade. In the hills behind Chiaochi are the 60-metre *Wu Feng Falls* with a viewing platform.

Taroko Gorge Day trips to Taiwan's most spectacular natural sight involve a short flight to Hualien Airport followed by a guided bus tour. This takes you along the 20km/12 mile Cross Island Highway, cut through the sheer marble cliffs of the gorge. There are viewing platforms, temples and bridges at regular intervals. At *Wen Shan* you can swim in the hot spring pools or the rushing cold river just a few steps away. Trips usually include a visit to a marble factory and a performance by members of the Ami aboriginal tribe.

Spectator sports

Taiwan competes at international level in baseball, basketball and soccer. Contests take place at the *Taipei Municipal Baseball Course*, 2 Nanking East Rd, Section 4 ☎ 771 2913 and the *Municipal Stadium*, 5 Tunhua North Rd ☎ 771 1202.

Keeping fit

The Grand hotel has the best sports facilities, followed by the Lai Lai Sheraton and Howard Plaza. Or try the *Clark Hatch Fitness Centre* in the Bank of America Bldg, 205 Tunhua North Rd ☎ 713 7842.

Golf There are many fine golf courses within a 60min drive of Taipei. Most can be used by nonmembers during the week but at weekends they are strictly limited to members and their guests. The *Peitou Kuo Hua Country Club* ☎ 621 2882 is regarded as the best. Otherwise there are courses at Tamsui, the coastal village 20km/12 miles northwest of Taipei: the *New Tamsui* ☎ 621 2466, the *Ta Tun Golf and Country Club* ☎ 621 3271 and the *Taiwan Golf and Country Club* ☎ 621 2211.

Jogging Those staying at the Grand can run in the grounds. Otherwise New Park is the most popular green space.

Tennis The Mandarin hotel's *Royal Sports Club*, 166 Tunhua North Rd ☎ 712 1201 has C.R. Wu, one of Taiwan's best professional tennis players, as coach; reasonably proficient players can arrange individual and group tuition.

Local resources
Business services

Hotels will usually be able to provide whatever business support services you require. Freelance secretaries and translators can be found through classified ads in the *China News* and *China Post*. Many consultancy firms and trading companies provide secretarial support, guides, translators and photocopying services as part of a package including airport pick-up, hotel reservation, meetings

with suppliers and shipment supervision. Such is the competition for custom that these services are often provided free, but with a strong moral obligation ultimately to place an order. One of the most reliable all-round consultancy firms is *Overseas Buyers Service Center*, 9th Fl, Union Commercial Bldg, 137 Nanking East Rd, Section 2 ☎ 551 5295.

Communications

Long-distance delivery DHL (head office) 82 Chienkuo North Rd, Section 2 ☎ 503 6858 (inquiries) or 503 8378 (documents). Open Mon–Sat, 8.30am–10pm.

Post offices Stamps may be bought at any hotel. Taipei's *Central Post Office* is on the North Gate intersection, on Chunghsiao West Rd, just west of Taipei Railway Station. Open Mon–Fri, 8–6, Sat 8–1.

Telephone Public pay phones cost NT$1 for three minutes. Overseas calls from phones without IDD can be made by dialling 100; international operators speak English. English-language inquiries ☎ 311 6796.

Telex and fax At the *International Telecommunications Administration* (ITA) main office, corner of Hangchow South Rd and Hsinyi Rd (open daily 24hr).

Conference/exhibition centres

Currently the main venues are the *Taipei World Trade Center*, 5 Hsinyi Rd Section 5 ☎ 725 1111 and the *Taipei International Convention Centre*, an ambitious new venue next door on Hsinyi Rd. Many of Taipei's better hotels also have extensive convention facilities. (See also *Hotels*.)

Embassies and consulates

Few governments have had embassies in Taiwan since the major Western nations recognized the People's Republic of China in 1978 and severed diplomatic relations with Taiwan the following year. However, most maintain cultural and trade missions, and most also provide consular services.

Australian Commerce and Industry Office, 4th Fl, 148 Sungkiang Rd ☎ 542 7950.

Austrian Trade Delegation, Suite 806, Bank Tower, 205 Tunhua North Rd ☎ 715 5221.

Belgian Trade Association, Suite 901, Worldwide House, 685 Minsheng East Rd ☎ 715 1215.

Canadian Trade Office, Suite 707, Bank Tower, 205 Tunhua North Rd ☎ 713 7268.

China Chinese/Japanese Interchange Association, 43 Chinan Rd, Section 2 ☎ 351 7251.

Danish Trade Organization, 4th Fl, 12 Lane 21, Anho Rd ☎ 721 3386.

France Asia Trade Promotion Association, 8th Fl, Chia Hsiu Bldg II, 96 Chungshan North Rd ☎ 713 8216.

Greece Hellenic Organization for the Promotion of Exports in Taiwan, 6th Fl, 125 Roosevelt Rd, Section 3 ☎ 391 0597.

Indonesian Chamber of Commerce, Room 802, Khang Ning Bldg, 289 Sungkiang Rd ☎ 502 5131.

Japan (see China)

Malaysia Friendship and Trade Exchange Center 1-2 Fl, 102 Tunhua North Rd ☎ 713 2626.

Netherlands Council for Trade Promotion, 5th Fl B, 687 Mingsheng East Rd ☎ 713 5760.

Philippines Asian Exchange Center, Room 902, 112 Chunghsiao East Rd, Section 1 ☎ 341 3125.

Singapore Trade Representative Office, 9th Fl, TFIT Tower, 85 Jenai Rd, Section 4 ☎ 721 0664.

South Korean Embassy, 345 Chunghsiao East Rd, Section 4 ☎ 761 9360.

Spanish Chamber of Commerce, 5th Fl, 122-4 Chunghsiao East Rd, Section 4 ☎ 711 2402.

Swedish Industries Trade Representative Office, Room 1503-A, 15th Fl, Chia Hsin Bldg, 96 Chungshan North Rd, Section 2 ☎ 562 7601.

Switzerland Trade Office of Swiss Industries, 12th Fl, 50 Hsinsheng South Rd, Section 1 ☎ 393 1610.

UK Anglo-Taiwan Trade Committee, 11th Fl, 36 Nanking East Rd, Section 2 ☎ 521 4116.

USA American Institute in Taiwan (consular services) 7 Lane 134, Hsinyi Rd, Section 3 ☎ 709 2000; American Trade Center, 600 Minchuan East Rd ☎ 713 2571.

West German Trade Office, 15th Fl, 87 Sungkiang Rd ☎ 571 9028.

Emergencies

Hospitals The hotels have doctors on 24hr call. Expatriates in Taipei use the *Adventist Hospital*, 424 Pateh Rd, Section 2 ☎ 771 8151 for dental treatment and medical emergencies. The staff speak English and most of the doctors trained in British or US hospitals. Patients must pay in advance in cash or by credit card. Charges are comparable with the cost of private treatment in the USA and Europe.

Pharmacies Usually open 9.30–6. Although pharmacists may know little English they will recognize the proprietary names of drugs when written down and all can be bought without prescription. Prices are about double those in the USA or Europe.

Police Foreigners in Taipei are rarely the victims of crime. Visitors are likely to deal with the police only in the event of a road accident, or if trying to trace lost possessions. The police are courteous but slow to take sides in a dispute, and often make no attempt to clear the roads of damaged vehicles until those involved have reached an agreement. In emergencies ☎ 110; otherwise English-speaking policemen can be contacted at police headquarters ☎ 311 9940.

Government offices

The *Government Information Office* ☎ 341 9211 disseminates official statistics and information about government policies. The *Ministry of Economic Affairs* ☎ 393 2131 supervises foreign investment. For customs information contact the *Inspectorate General of Customs*

☎ 741 3181 and for tax advice the *Foreign Affairs Office, National Tax Administration* ☎ 763 1313 ext. 241/5.

Information sources
Local media Taiwan has two English-language daily papers, the morning *China Post* and the evening *China News*. The latter has the best business and economic coverage.
Tourist information A very limited range of brochures and maps can be obtained from the *Taiwan Tourism Bureau* at CKS International Airport, and at its head office, 9th Fl, Continental Bldg, 290 Chunghsiao East Rd, Section 4 ☎ 721 8541. The Bureau has a tourist information hot line for emergency assistance, accidents, language problems, lost and found and travel information ☎ 717 3737. It also publishes two monthly official guides which are available in all hotels: *Travel in Taiwan* and *This Month in Taiwan*.

Thank-yous
Chocolates Asiaworld Plaza Department Store, 337 Nanking East Rd, Section 3 ☎ 715 3777 has the best selection.
Florist Top Gifts Company, 187 Sungkiang Rd ☎ 503 9847 will deliver flowers and baskets of fresh fruit anywhere in Taipei.
Wines and spirits The *Taiwan Tobacco and Wine Monopoly Bureau*, regulates the import and sale of all foreign alcoholic beverages in Taiwan and its shop at 83 Chungshan North Rd, Section 2 ☎ 563 4809 (open Mon–Fri 8.30–11.45 and 1.30–4.30) has the best selection. Supermarkets and hotel arcade stores have more limited and expensive stocks.

Planning and reference
Entry details
Documentation All visitors to Taiwan must have a valid passport and an entry visa. A "visitor" visa, good for both business and tourist travel, is valid for three months from the date of issue and for a stay of up to 60 days. This may be extended twice for a total stay of six months by applying to the *Foreigner Service Center* at the Police Headquarters, 89 Ninghsia Rd ☎ 537 3680. Visas are readily granted to all nationalities except those of Communist countries. Applicants for an extension need three identical photographs, a passport and an airline ticket out of the country. People whose passports show that they have visited China are no longer barred from entering Taiwan.
Driving licence An international driving licence is essential.
Health precautions Inoculation against cholera, typhoid and polio is advisable.
Customs regulations A written declaration is required from each passenger on entry and exit. Duty-free allowances are 200 cigarettes or 25 cigars or 450gm/1lb of tobacco and 1 litre/1 quart of wine or spirits. Medicines must be declared but are not liable for duty except in commercial quantities. Gold, including jewellery, must be declared and amounts in excess of 156gm/5oz can be imported only by special permit. Those who exceed the limit can leave the goods in bond at the airport until departure. Currency in excess of US$1,000 must be declared so that it may be taken out again; and no more than NT$8,000 can be imported. Personal possessions and other articles, including samples, can be imported duty free up to a maximum value of NT$10,000. Samples and trade goods must not exceed half this amount. In practice, only frequent visitors to Taiwan (those who make more than two trips in and out a month) are likely to face a stringent customs inspection.

Climate
The summer months (May to September) are hot, humid and stormy. Temperatures rarely fall below 28°C/83°F and the humidity is 80% plus. Typhoons may occur also

during this period; life can be brought to a standstill in the south, but Taipei rarely suffers more than heavy rains. There is a cooler, drier period between December and March when temperatures range between 5–20°C/40–69°F although Taipei is slightly colder and the mountains get a brief covering of snow. The most pleasant seasons are March to May and September to November when temperatures are 25°C/77°F plus but the skies are clear and sunny and the humidity bearable.

Business dress in Taiwan is shirt, tie and lightweight trousers or a light and modest blouse and skirt. Jackets are worn to important meetings and in the best hotels and restaurants where the air conditioning is turned up high.

Holidays
The two major holidays in Taiwan are the Chinese or Lunar New Year, usually falling during the first two weeks of February and lasting for ten days, and the week following Double Ten Day (October 10th), also known as Chinese Independence Day. This commemorates the abdication of the last Ching emperor in 1911 and the founding of the mainland Republic of China. During these periods businesses and restaurants close.
Public holidays are:
Jan 1–3 New Year
End Jan/early Feb Lunar New Year
Mar 29 Youth Day
Early Apr Ching Ming
May 1 Labor Day
Mid-Jun Dragon Boat Festival
Mid-Sep Mid-autumn Festival
Sep 28 Confucius's Birthday
Oct 10 Chinese Independence Day
Oct 25 Taiwan Retrocession Day
Oct 31 Chiang Kai-shek's Birthday
Nov 12 Dr Sun Yat-sen's Birthday
Dec 25 Constitution Day

Money
Local currency The unit of currency is the New Taiwan dollar; notes are issued in denominations of 1,000, 500, 100, 50 and 10, and coins in denominations of 10, 5, 1 and 0.5. Notes are the most used and obtaining change is no problem. NT$1 coins are useful for public pay phones and NT$10 coins for tipping.
Credit and charge cards are widely accepted in any outlet catering to foreigners in Taipei and Kaohsiung but are not welcomed for small transactions under NT$1,000.
Changing money There are no bureaux de change in Taiwan; the choice is either a bank or hotel. Banks all give the same rate and hotel rates are only slightly lower. All will change traveller's cheques in any major currency. Banks offering exchange facilities, and whose branches will be found in any central Taipei street, are the Bank of Taiwan, City Bank of Taipei and the First Commercial Bank of Taipei. Thirty leading US and European banks also have full service facilities in Taipei. Opening hours are Mon–Fri, 9–3.30; Sat, 9–noon.
Tipping Airport porters expect NT$20 per bag. Otherwise tipping is entirely at your discretion. Nobody gets upset if not tipped but taxi drivers and waiters show evident pleasure if they are. Tips need not be a full 10%; the small change is enough.

Thailand

Thailand in the 1980s has steadily gained recognition for its economic potential and, through membership of ASEAN, as a significant voice in regional affairs. This recognition is dispelling Thailand's image in the West as a nation which is both the "land of smiles" and a country of chronic instability, shaken by rapid changes of government at home and threatened by the Communist takeovers in 1975 in the neighbouring countries of Indochina.

The changing perception has been helped by the years of unbroken civilian government since 1980. Meanwhile the country's economic strengths have become more visible, ironically, during the region's recent economic downturn. Thailand's rate of growth, never so glittering as that of neighbours such as Singapore and Malaysia in more prosperous times, has proved more consistent in adverse circumstances. Thailand in the 1980s has built on its inherent economic strengths: rich natural resources, a pragmatic entrepreneurial class which has avoided industrial white elephants, and prudent fiscal management.

Westerners' unfamiliarity with Thailand is partly explained by the fact that, alone among the countries of South-East Asia, it was never colonized – a source of pride to Thais. Western ideas did play a key role in the modernization of Thailand, but they were imported, not imposed.

Trade with the West began in the 16th century, when the country was known as Siam, but it was not until the mid-19th century reign of the reform-minded King Mongkut that contacts were strengthened. The process of transforming Thailand into a modern state was greatly speeded up by his son, King Chulalongkorn, who introduced a European-style cabinet, established a standing army, laid the basis for the modern civil service and revised the legal code according to Western standards.

A coup in 1932 replaced absolute monarchy with a constitutional form of government. Monarchy as an institution was, and still is, revered, but power passed to a succession of military strongmen for much of the following 50 years. Civilians have been running the country since 1980, with the army's blessing.

Business confidence slumped in the early 1980s as depressed world prices for Thailand's major commodities cut growth. But helped by a shift from exports of primary products to processed foods and the fast rise of export-oriented industries, including textiles and the products of newer industries, such as artificial flowers, sports shoes and gems, the trade deficit in 1986 was reduced by more than half. Moreover, these exports look sustainable. Thailand's prosperity is set to continue and its business potential, not tied to a few vulnerable commodities, is becoming clearer to foreign investors, who by 1987 accounted for about 10% of the Thai market's turnover – three times as much as in 1985.

The political scene

Thailand is a constitutional monarchy with the trappings of parliamentary democracy. Government is conducted by an appointed prime minister and cabinet who exercise their authority with the consent of the army as well as that of the legislature. Political parties' efforts to play a greater part in government, and military resistance to those efforts, have been a perennial source of domestic tension. Since Thailand switched from absolute to constitutional monarchy in 1932, there have been 14 more coups or attempted coups but stability since 1980 has raised hopes that democracy is firmly rooted.

Not quite a democracy

Legislature Parliament is composed of a senate appointed by the king for six years and dominated by the military, and a 357-member house of representatives elected for a four-year term. The prime minister, nominated by the king, must have army support to function effectively.

Political parties rank well behind the army and civil service in the power structure but, as civilian government becomes more entrenched, are seeking to increase their leverage. Their main obstacles include the army's enduring image of itself as the true defender of national interests.

Party politics remain dominated by personalities and money, not issues – electoral platforms are shallow and almost indistinguishable. As a result, MPs have proved incapable of uniting in large, stable blocs and party loyalties are tenuous. Competition for a share of government is intense, less from any commitment to a set of policies than from a desire to gain access to the financial rewards of office and patronage opportunities. The biggest and best-established of some 15 parties are the liberal-leaning Democrat Party, the centrist Social Action Party and the Chart Thai Party, with strong links to big business and the army.

The military Although he has expressed support for the democratic process, the army commander-in-chief, General Chaovalit Yongchaiyudth, is adamant about the army's role in preserving stability in a parliamentary context riven by irreconcilable interests.

The monarchy As head of state, His Majesty King Bhumibol Adulyadej (Rama IX) transcends politics and is a focal point of national identity. As patron of all Thailand's religions, he has promoted social harmony in the strife-torn far south, where most of the citizens are Malay Muslims. Confidence in the ability of the Crown Prince to take over these duties is not high; he is known less for his sense of public service than for his playboy pursuits. There are those who believe Princess Mahachakri Sirindorn would be a far more able monarch than her brother but tradition would have to be set aside for a woman to ascend the throne.

Foreign relations

Thailand's chief foreign policy objective has been to end Vietnam's occupation of Kampuchea. Vietnamese attacks against Khmer resistance in Kampuchea have spilled across the Thai border and there have been clashes between Thai and Vietnamese forces. In addition, the proximity of about 140,000 Vietnamese soldiers has caused an influx into Thailand of some 150,000 Khmer refugees. Unlike his predecessors for whom the threat from Indochina was the chief foreign policy preoccupation, Prime Minister Chartchai Choonhavan, who took office in 1988 has resolved to turn Indochina from "a battleground into a market place".

The economic scene

The resilience of Thailand's economy was demonstrated in 1986 when exports surged by nearly a fifth and by almost as much again in the first half of 1987. The economy has traditionally been based on a wide range of natural and agricultural resources which have made Thailand a major food exporter and have enabled it to grow more consistently than some of its ASEAN neighbours in the face of fluctuations in world trade.

The economy has become more diversified with the growth of export-oriented light-manufacturing industries. At constant 1972 prices GNP reached US$13.9bn in 1986 and per capita income US$763. But the real annual growth rate of 7% in the 1970s fell sharply in the face of low world commodity prices in the first half of the 1980s. Export revival and rising investment have brought a recovery that has gathered pace and made Thailand a favoured South-East Asian location for investors.

Human resources

Thailand's population, estimated in mid-1986 to be 52.7m, is growing by 2.1% a year. As an overwhelmingly agricultural country, only a small proportion of the population live in cities, and the urban scene is dominated by the single great complex of Bangkok-Thonburi, whose population is officially put at 6.2m. Chiang-Mai, the second city, has only 204,000 inhabitants. The other main centres – Songkhla, Chon Buri, Nakhon Si Thammarat – have even fewer.

Educational standards are relatively high; the overall literacy rate is estimated at 70–80%. But jobs are hard to come by in a market of 6% unemployment and considerable underemployment.

Urban drift Even if the annual birth rate falls to 1.7% under the impact of recent family-planning schemes, there will still be 4m new job seekers entering the market every year. Hence, the government hopes that over the period of the sixth development plan (1987–91) projects will be implemented in the most impoverished rural areas to reduce the drift of people to the cities. The vast majority of the country's 500,000 female prostitutes are young women from the countryside who have failed to find any other way to support themselves.

Natural resources

Thailand's main natural resources lie in its agricultural potential, in particular in the capacity of the central plain to produce a substantial surplus of rice, of which it is the world's largest exporter. Large areas of upland have also been opened up for the cultivation of maize (Thailand is the world's fourth largest exporter), cassava (tapioca), kenaf, cotton and pineapple.

Rubber and scarcer timber On the more humid and equatorial coastal plains of the southern peninsula rubber production has increased. But, as a result of the expansion of agricultural production (and illegal logging), the country's timber resources have shrunk to less than 20% of the total area, and in 1988, after flooding caused by deforestation in the south, the government banned logging.

Minerals Thailand is well endowed with minerals, the southern tin deposits being the most important. Mining for tin has now extended offshore into the Andaman Sea. Other minerals being worked include tungsten, lead, fluorite and lignite. There are also deposits of sapphires and rubies, and massive rock-salt and potash deposits are known to underlie the Khorat Plateau. There is significant demand in the region for potash – at present met mainly by

Canada – and Thailand's Ministry of Industry sees the mining of potash as a viable ASEAN project.

Fisheries are an important source of export revenue, but over-fishing has reduced the marine catch and future opportunities appear to be concentrated in aquaculture.

Energy deficit reduced Since the discovery of natural gas in the Gulf of Thailand, the country has been reducing its serious deficit of energy supplies, and the gas finds onshore in the Nam Phong area of Khon Kaen province are promising. Small amounts of petroleum have also been identified in the north-central plain province of Kampaengphet.

Agriculture

Although its share of GDP fell to 17.4% in 1986, agriculture remains the backbone of the economy. It supports some 70% of the population, accounts for a third of export earnings, and provides the raw materials for a significant share of manufacturing exports.

Smallholders Thai farmers, who mainly work small plots, have proved highly adaptable to new crops in response to market conditions. But much of the rise in output has resulted from expansion of the cultivated area, which has almost doubled since 1950.

Boosting and broadening output The government now hopes to reduce the area under rice by a quarter by 1991 and concentrate instead on increasing yields. Spurred by the declining world price for rice and for some of its other established exports such as maize and tin, it is also encouraging other crops such as coffee, tobacco, soya beans and cotton, as well as boosting livestock and dairy farming.

Infrastructure

A well-developed transport infrastructure includes over 12,800km/8,000 miles of primary all-weather roads, backed up by a substantial network of secondary and feeder roads. There are also more than 3,840km/2,400 miles of railways, almost entirely single-track. The railways have lost heavily to competition from road transport, but play an important part in moving bulk commodities.

Cargo problems The biggest port, Bangkok's Klong Toey, has reached the limits of its capacity and congestion is a perennial problem. It handled 5m tonnes/4.5m US tons of containerized cargo in 1986, plus conventional and bulk cargoes.

A new port After prolonged debate, plans are moving ahead to build a new deep-sea port on the eastern seaboard southeast of Bangkok at Laem Chabang. The intention is to have it operating in 1990. The Port Authority of Thailand has received the go-ahead also to develop facilities at Sattahip, but to keep them separate from the container freight station at Bang Sue.

Air fleet expanding The country's flag carrier, Thai Airways International, operates a fleet of 26 aircraft, expected to rise to 30 in 1988, and has plans for further rapid expansion. Thai Airways Company serves some 24 domestic destinations and also Hanoi, Vientiane and Penang. The two companies were planning to merge in 1988.

External trade

Demonstrating Thailand's economic resilience, exports grew by 19.6% to US$8.7bn in 1986, and by a further 18% in the first half of 1987 over the same period of 1986. Combined with a 3% drop in imports, the result largely of lower oil prices, the trade deficit was slashed from US$1.3bn in 1985 to US$306m in 1986. During 1987, rising imports, stimulated by higher domestic growth, were expected to push the deficit back up to US$1.2bn.

Wide range of exports This strong export performance partly reflects the sheer diversity of Thailand's export goods and the fact that a higher than usual proportion – more

than a third – goes to developing countries where demand tends to grow faster than in industrialized markets and where sales are less threatened by protectionist barriers.
Main exports are rice, tapioca, textile goods, rubber, maize, sugar, precious stones, integrated circuits, tin, and canned fish and fruit.
Protectionism denounced The US Farm Act, with its protectionist clauses, is a target for bitter Thai denunciation. Although the impact of US legislation has not been so great as feared, the Thai concern reflects the growing importance of the US market, which takes a fifth of exports, well ahead of Japan in second place. In imports, these positions are reversed, Japan supplying a quarter of the total.
Principal imports are crude oil, non-electrical machinery, chemicals, iron and steel, electrical machinery, and diesel fuel.
More imports from ASEAN In July 1987, Thailand offered preferential treatment to a wider range of imports from fellow members of ASEAN. The aim was to liberalize inter-ASEAN trade while counteracting the growing protectionism in industrialized countries. However, promises of this kind by ASEAN members frequently remain unfulfilled.

Balance of payments
The current account swung sharply from a US$1.62bn deficit in 1985 to a small surplus, the first for 20 years, of US$38.5m in 1986. The main factor was the dramatic saving on oil imports because of lower prices, but a 19% rise in exports also helped. Following the fall in oil prices, remittances from workers overseas, notably in the Middle East, have dwindled.
Tourism revenues are rising Tourism overtook rice in 1983 as the biggest single foreign exchange earner, and gross income reached US$1.5bn in 1986. Investment in

hotels and other facilities for foreign holidaymakers is continuing, and planners project annual revenue of US$2.5bn from tourism by 1991.
Tourism has contributed to the growth of prostitution – now a ubiquitous service industry in Thailand – and is likely to be affected in the future by greater awareness of the threat of AIDS.
Reserves have been rising since 1985 and by the end of March 1987 stood at nearly US$3.9bn (including gold).
Currency The baht was pegged to the US dollar until November 1984 when it was devalued by 14% against the US currency. Since then parity has been fixed against a basket of currencies.

External debt
Thai fiscal authorities have a well-established reputation for prudence, but a sharp rise in foreign borrowing lifted the total external debt from US$8.3bn in 1980 to US$18bn at the end of 1986, of which US$13bn was public debt. The debt-service ratio had risen to nearly 29% of export earnings by the end of 1986.
Ceiling imposed Since 1985, the government has placed a maximum of US$1bn a year on new external borrowing. It has also skilfully refinanced existing loans, taking advantage of Thailand's excellent credit rating to reduce the costs of borrowing and to space maturities.
Spread of the debt Of total public debt, some 34% is owed to multilateral aid agencies, notably the World Bank, 27% to bilateral donors, especially Japan, and 39% to private creditors, chiefly financial markets.

The budget
Current account improvements have allowed the government to relax its 1985 austerity drive. The budget for fiscal year 1987/88 proposed a 7% rise in spending to US$9.4bn, including US$1.5bn for investment.
Composition of revenue The proportion of revenue from direct taxes is about 39%. Customs and

excise duties provide about 48%.

Allocations Debt service eats up nearly a quarter of total spending. In 1987/88, defence was allocated 19.3% of the total, education 18.6%, administration 11.6% and agriculture 7.4%.

Serious deficit The country's improving economic performance is overshadowed by an apparently uncontrollable budget deficit. This rose in 1985 to US$2.15bn, nearly 5% of GDP, and was estimated to have remained close to that figure in 1986. Future growth may well be hindered unless the deficit is reduced.

Inflation has remained low throughout the 1980s and was expected to be around 2% in 1987.

Development plan

Priorities of the sixth economic development plan (1987–91) are elimination of fiscal imbalances, more equitable distribution of growth, easing of unemployment and reduction of rural poverty. The plan, a general guideline rather than a detailed blueprint, expects GDP to grow at 5% a year, including 2.9% for agriculture, 6.6% for industry and 6.4% for mining. Inflation over the plan period is forecast at 2.3% a year.

Shift to private sector

Achievement of plan targets depends on a sharp move from the public to the private sector, reversing the trend of recent years. Private investment, up by 0.2% in 1986 but still one of the lowest rates in Asia, is intended to rise by 8.1%.

The private sector is being systematically encouraged to become involved in development projects. The State Railways of Thailand have agreed to hand over development and management of the container freight station at Bang Sue port to private interests. The developers of Sattahip port will also be from the private sector, Kone Corporation of Finland being one of the interested parties. It was announced in December 1986 that such privatization would extend to Laem Chabang port and to the two southern regional ports at Phuket and Songkhla.

Housing development A US$21m World Bank loan is supporting Thailand's housing policies and strengthening the National Housing Authority's planning capabilities and policy development. The loan will finance construction of about 11,000 homes and serviced plots, as well as supporting infrastructure and community amenities in the Bangkok area and six other cities.

Industry

The share of manufacturing in GDP has hovered around the 20% mark for the past decade, but this does not reflect its growing weight as a source of export revenue and employment. While agricultural output fell marginally in 1986, manufacturing grew by 5%.

Import substitution Industrial development has focused on import-substitution industries producing construction materials, alcoholic beverages and consumer goods for the home market. Vehicles are assembled from imported kits.

Manufacturing for export There has been a growth in manufacturing industries for export since 1980, notably in textiles, footwear, food processing and canning. The 1986 appreciation of the yen saw a sudden spurt in investment in such industries from Japanese firms seeking a more competitive base for their imports and attracted by Thailand's low labour costs. Taiwan has also become an important investor in these sectors.

Little heavy industry Apart from oil refining, little heavy industry has emerged. A petrochemicals complex is being built on the eastern seaboard at Mab Tapud (the National Petrochemicals Corporation's various downstream facilities to the natural gas separation plant are complete). Plans for a major fertilizer complex have stalled, however, because of doubts about its commercial viability.

The business climate

The sudden influx of foreign capital reflects Thailand's emergence as one of the Asian countries most favoured by investors. The mixed economy has a dynamic private sector, with a track record of flexibility and quick response to market opportunities, which is the main engine of economic growth. The 1987-91 development plan emphasizes the need for the private sector to expand into activities that previously have been in the public preserve.

The public sector

The state sector is still a powerful element in the economy despite the government's intention to introduce privatization.

State-owned enterprises There are 68 enterprises in which the state has a majority stake, their combined annual investment of some US$1.3bn exceeding that of central government. They include public utilities, transport and communications, but also span key financial institutions such as Krung Thai Bank, organizations to promote and market agricultural products and some manufacturing capacity.

Programme of reform In 1985 the government acquired a 75% stake in 24 ailing financial institutions in a drive to reform and stabilize the financial system and raise its standards of management.

Trimming back Government policy, however, is to trim back the scope of state-enterprise activities. This is not because they constitute a major drain on the economy as in many other developing countries – overall revenues have been rising faster than expenditure. But the authorities have been concerned by a sharp rise in state-enterprise spending during the 1980s, and by the reliance on foreign and domestic borrowing. A small number of the biggest enterprises – especially the Bangkok Mass Transit Organization and the State Railways of Thailand – have made heavy losses.

Recruiting private expertise In a bid to raise efficiency and standards of service in state enterprises, the government intends to recruit some management from the private sector and to set stringent criteria for financial performance.

Reducing state holdings The government also plans to dispose of, or reduce, its holdings in most manufacturing enterprises.

The private sector

Thailand's private sector already generates some 65% of domestic investment and this seems set to rise. The sixth plan calls for an 8.1% annual increase in private investment, compared with a rise of 1% in public investment.

Contracting out Opportunities for the private sector are emerging from moves to contract out services in transport and communications, including ports, industrial estates, toll roads and expressways.

Incentive package Investment and savings levels fell in the early 1980s to among the lowest in the region; analysts worried that they were too low to sustain Thailand's above-average rates of growth. In December 1986, in an attempt to improve the investment climate, the government announced a package of incentives, including a reduction in business tax, to only 0.1% for export industries.

Steep rise in investment Following the introduction of the incentive package, investment rose dramatically in 1987, encouraged by the rapid improvement in the domestic economy and exports. A sudden increase of interest from foreign investors has been an important factor. The value of proposed new investment approved by the Board of Investment (BoI) in the first half of 1987 more than doubled to nearly US$1bn.

Foreign investment

Thailand encourages foreign investment and allows it access to most areas of the economy open to the private sector, subject to conditions on the extent of foreign participation.

Two funds for channelling foreign investment have been set up, both listed on the London stock exchange: the Bangkok Fund set up by Merrill Lynch in September 1985, and the Thailand Fund set up in 1986 and underwritten by the World Bank's International Finance Corporation and three private Western banks.

Japan dominates Japan is much the biggest source of foreign investment. Japanese companies seeking BoI privileges in the first half of 1987 proposed some US$650m worth of new investment, compared with US$23m in the same period of 1986.

USA and Taiwan follow The USA was the second biggest source of foreign investment in 1986, but in the first half of 1987 was overtaken by Taiwan, with some US$205m-worth of proposals compared with US$175m proposed by US firms. The UK ranked fourth.

Actual inflows As measured by investment inflows rather than registered capital, Hong Kong, Singapore and the Netherlands are also high up the table of foreign investors, trailed by West Germany.

The attractions Thailand's most positive attributes cited by investors include its political stability, a pattern of economic growth more consistent than that of many of its neighbours and a sizable domestic market. Export-oriented manufacturers are also particularly attracted by a low-cost labour force that is easily trained and loyal. Thais are also aware, in theory, of the need to protect patents, trademarks and other rights in order to attract new technology.

Power in business

The main actors on Thailand's economic stage are multinational corporations, local corporate interests, Thai families and Chinese entrepreneurs.

Multinationals A table of Thailand's biggest companies would feature foreign firms and their subsidiaries or joint ventures, including Shell Company of Thailand and Thai Shell Exploration and Production; Esso Standard Thailand; Unocal Thailand; the distribution companies Diethelm and Berli Jucker; Toyota Motor Thailand; Tri Petch Isuzu Sales; Siam Motors; and Mitsubishi Company.

Local corporate interests wielding much power in the economy include the Crown Property Bureau. This manages the Crown's extensive real estate as well as its financial operations, centred on the Siam Commercial Bank, and its industrial holdings, principally a 37% stake in the Siam Cement Group – Thailand's biggest company in terms of assets. The Metro Group is a leading exporter of tapioca and rice and is diversifying into agro-industrial products and textiles. The Central Department Store Group is active in retail, hotels (Hyatt Central Plaza) and garment manufacturing, and the Laem Thong company is involved in agro-industries, flour milling, jute bags and banking.

Thai families with significant business power include the Sophonpanich family. Its members control Bangkok Bank, South-East Asia's biggest local bank; they have wide interests in financial services, insurance and leasing, and minority holdings in shipping and textiles. The Lamsam family are major shareholders in Thai Farmers Bank and in textile operations and jute milling. The Wang Lee family control Nakornthon Bank and are active in insurance and in commodity exports. The Techapaibul family control Bangkok Metropolitan Bank and have interests in financial services and real estate.

Thai Chinese Industrial and financial power has traditionally revolved around Thai Chinese families exploiting a strong base in banking and finance to build a network of commercial interests. With the growing diversification and sophistication of the Thai economy and the continual assimilation of the Chinese into Thai culture, the influence of these families is, however, likely to diminish.

Labour unions Strikes have averaged only around 20 a year in recent years. Thailand has some 450 registered unions grouped in congresses of which the most important are the Labour Congress of Thailand and the Thai Trades Union Congress.

The business framework

The main forms of business under Thai law are sole proprietorships, unregistered or registered partnerships, limited companies, unincorporated joint ventures, branches of foreign companies and representative offices. Most foreign companies entering Thailand set up either as private limited companies or as branches.

Limited companies

Private limited companies require a minimum of seven promoters, or founders, of whom one must be a Thai national or a foreigner with Thai residency. There is no minimum capitalization, but the registrar of the Ministry of Commerce must be satisfied that the proposed amount is sufficient to accomplish the stated objectives of the company.

Nationality requirements The law does not restrict the number of directors or their nationality, but one of them must be a Thai citizen or resident. As a condition for granting promotional privileges, the Board of Investment (BoI) may stipulate the number of Thais on the board.

The minimum value of shares is B5 and may be allotted as paid-in cash, services or property. At least 25% must be paid-in and a bank guarantee for 25% presented for registration.

Public limited companies may offer shares to the public if they have capital in excess of B5m and the approval of over half the shareholders. Unlike private limited companies, they may also issue debenture and convertible preference shares.

Foreign ownership rules

The Alien Business Law of 1972 lays down rules about foreign participation, employment of expatriates and ownership of land. However, for companies receiving BoI privileges or operating under special treaties such as the Thai-US Treaty of Amity and Economic Relations, such controls may be amended or waived and tax concessions negotiated for.

Acquiring land Thailand does not allow foreigners to own land, but BoI-promoted projects may be allowed to acquire property subject to certain conditions. Special dispensations to buy land for industrial purposes may also be granted by the Council of Ministers.

Levels of ownership Limits to foreign equity participation vary according to sector, subject to exceptions negotiated with the BoI. Rice milling theoretically must be 100% Thai-owned. Maximum foreign involvement permissible in glass bottle manufacture is 25%; in tourist promotions 30%; and in livestock ventures, meat processing, production of animal feed and onshore mining it is 40%. Foreign ownership in industrial ventures selling mainly in Thailand is normally limited to 49%. But if production is mainly for export then majority foreign ownership is allowed, and if it is totally for export then 100% foreign ownership may be authorized.

Previously closed sectors are being opened to foreign companies as a way to boost employment opportunities for Thais, increase exports, develop areas of the country hitherto neglected and assist privatization.

Investment stipulations To obtain a five-year investment permit, companies must bring in B5m worth of capital, B2m of it within a year of receiving the permit. After a specified period which may vary from 10 to 25 years, majority ownership should pass to Thais.

Incentives

Thailand's Investment Promotion Act provides significant tax and other concessions to companies granted promotional privileges by the BoI. Sectors in which incentives are being provided are those that help Thailand's balance of payments, exploit local resources, conserve energy or develop alternative resources, transfer technology, or contribute in other distinctive ways to industrial development and generate employment. Such sectors include agriculture, animal husbandry, food processing, mining and mineral prospecting, manufacture of chemicals, petrochemicals and fertilizers and of garments for export, production or assembly of electronics, and services.

Range of incentives Tax holidays and exemption from duties on imports of machinery and raw materials for the project feature prominently in the incentives offered to foreign investors. Tariff protection is accorded against competing foreign products; capital and profits may be repatriated; and interest and principal on foreign loans may be remitted in the form of foreign currency. Further benefits are available to projects located in areas being promoted by the government to boost economic growth in the provinces.

Tax incentives include exemption from corporate income tax for three to eight years. Leases in this period may be carried forward and deducted as expenses for five years. Exemption is granted from up to 90% of import duties and business taxes on imported raw materials and components. There is exemption for up to five years from withholding tax payable on goodwill, royalties and fees, and exemption from tax on dividends during the income-tax holiday. Moreover, there is full exemption from, or a 50% reduction of, import duties and business taxes on imported machinery.

Special zones Additional incentives for firms locating in the special investment promotion zones include reduction of up to 90% of business tax on the sale of products for up to five years; 50% reduction of corporate income tax for five years after expiry of the tax holiday or from the start of earning income; permission to double income tax-deductible costs of water, electricity and transport; and permission to deduct from income tax 25% of investment costs of installing infrastructure for 10 years from the start of earning income.

Export-enterprise incentives include exemption from import duties and business tax on imports of raw materials and components and on re-exports; exemption from export duties and business tax; and permission to deduct from corporate income tax 5% of the increase in export earnings each year, excluding insurance and transport costs.

Establishing a presence

Starting a business in Thailand is becoming easier as the government grows more consistent in its approach to privatization and takes steps to attract foreign investors. English is becoming widely spoken in the business community and professional advice from accountants and lawyers is readily available.

Representative offices are permitted if their purpose is to engage in non-trading activities, search for Thai products for export to other parts of the company, or conduct market surveys. Representative offices of commercial banks are accepted in accordance with the Commercial Banking Act.

Foreign branches may be set up by obtaining a certificate of registration from the Ministry of Commerce's Department of Registration.

Expatriate employment

Work permits are issued to foreign business people by the Labour Department, normally for the duration of the applicant's visa, provided he or she is not employed in one of 39 occupations closed to expatriates. These include accounting, law, architecture, engineering and domestic brokerage. Business people should enter on a non-immigrant visa, not a tourist visa (which is not renewable).

Taxation

Companies registered in Thailand or incorporated abroad but doing business in Thailand are subject to corporate income tax and are likely to be liable to customs duties, business tax and municipal tax.

Corporate income tax is usually at 35%, reduced to 30% for companies listed on the stock exchange.

Business tax is levied on gross monthly receipts of certain categories of business. The rates vary from 1.5% to 40% for the sale of goods, 3–15% for banking, 2.5–3% for insurance, 3–10% for services. Municipal tax is 10% of business tax. Business tax is deductible from income tax and does not apply to exports.

Tax liability of branches In law branches are treated the same as head offices. Foreign companies may therefore find themselves in certain circumstances liable for taxes on transactions between the parent company and third-country clients, even without dealing through the Thai branch.

Taxable dividends The dividends of a Thai subsidiary remitted to a foreign parent are subject to a withholding tax of 20% of gross dividends. Currently, however, the tax is applied only to the net amount remitted, equivalent to 16.6% of the gross.

Withholding tax Payment of interest, fees and other monies to foreign shareholders is subject to a flat 25% withholding tax. Such payments by a branch to a head office may, however, be considered as a taxable remittance of profit.

Remittance of funds The Bank of Thailand (the central bank) normally permits remittance of profits, dividends, and interest and principal payments on foreign loans as well as fees, royalties and the proceeds of liquidation of a business. The Bank may, however, set a ceiling on such remittances.

Market entry

In a country where personal relationships can make the difference between the success or failure of a business deal, and where aspects of the market are still relatively undeveloped, a local partner or agent with local contacts and operating experience is essential.

Importing and exporting

Import of raw materials by companies operating in priority sectors has been facilitated recently, and firms producing for export

benefit because supply restrictions are waived.

Controls Import licences are required for 71 classes of controlled goods, which include specified food products, tobacco, minerals, crude oil, metals, paper products, plywood, textiles and garments.

Tariffs are set on about 2,000 items. Most duties are between 25% and 60% – but can reach 100% on luxury items. Business tax is also payable on a wide range of imports and exports.

Export tariffs apply only to rice, scrap iron, raw hide, rubber, wood, raw silk and powdered fish.

Tariff refunds The Customs Department undertakes to refund tariff payments on goods involved in production, mixing, assembly or packing for export. A production formula calculating refundable duties must be submitted for approval. Other duty and business tax concessions are also available for export-related transactions.

Distribution

Advice on trade and distribution is provided by many of the major shipping companies and agents. Distribution of goods is handled to a significant extent by major trading companies such as Diethelm, Berli Jucker, Borneo Company, and East Asiatic. Distribution agents who cover most of the country are located mainly in Bangkok, although supplies to southern, peninsular Thailand are also handled by agents based in Malaysia.

Freight and cargo Bangkok airport has been growing as a regional centre for air freight, helped by the completion in 1985 of a new cargo terminal which now services 47 airlines and freight-forwarders. Bangkok port is much the biggest terminal for containers and other cargoes, but suffers seriously from congestion. There is an extensive road network and almost 4,000km/2,500 miles of railways. Bulk commodities are usually moved by rail, but most other goods are now carried by road.

Agents and promotion

Advice on how to locate and choose an agent with local contacts and experience may be obtained in the first instance from embassies and chambers of commerce, but also from commercial banks, legal and accounting firms and a number of smaller business consultancy firms.

Advertising and PR There is a wide range of advertising companies in Bangkok, but no particular medium that offers a comprehensive exposure. Advice is recommended before engaging in any promotional activity.

Insurance

Thailand's insurance market is still small and relatively unsophisticated, but considered secure and with sufficient capacity to enable firms to place any insurance they require without difficulty. Insurance law in Thailand is fairly straightforward and most claims are settled promptly.

American International Assurance, Commercial Union, Guardian Assurance, Sun Alliance and New Zealand Insurance Company are the main Western companies, with Taisho Marine & Fire representing Japanese interests. Heath Hudig Langeveldt and AIG are brokers with international links.

Patents, trademarks, copyright

Some (perhaps reluctant) tightening of the laws protecting patents, trademarks and intellectual property rights has occurred in recent years, but infringements of trademarks and copyrights are widespread.

Protection for processes A 1979 Patents Act protects new investments, processes and designs, but excludes, among others, pharmaceutical products, farm machinery and computer programs.

Trademarks may be registered for 10 years, renewable for similar periods, and the first user enjoys exclusive use.

Copyrights Thailand's Copyright Act of 1978 and its 1986 amendment protect the foreign copyrights of countries that are party to the Berne Convention.

The financial scene

The expansion and modernization of agricultural and industrial enterprises in Thailand have been accompanied by an increasing sophistication of the country's financial system. However, there is still a large informal sector.

Banks and other financial institutions

The Bank of Thailand is the central bank, directly responsible for regulating other financial institutions within the limits set by, and under the close surveillance of, the government. It has been given increasing powers over recent years to intervene in other banks' management and forestall bad practices, especially corruption.

Commercial banks Thailand's 30 commercial banks handle around 65% of its loan business, three-quarters of which is, in turn, in the hands of the four leading institutions: the Bangkok Bank (the largest bank in ASEAN), Krung Thai Bank, Thai Farmers Bank and Siam Commercial Bank.

Foreign banks In 1987 there were 11 foreign banks with branches in Thailand. The largest of these are Chase Manhattan, Mitsui Bank, Bank of Tokyo, Bank of America and United Malayan Banking Corporation.

The Government Savings Bank operates as a non-profit organization under the control and guarantee of the government but with an autonomous management. It makes loans to enterprises and individuals, sells domestic traveller's cheques and runs a small life-assurance business.

Finance companies There are more than 100 finance companies, which are forbidden to take deposits in the way that banks do and so they raise money by issuing promissory notes and other forms of IOU.

IFCT The Industrial Finance Corporation of Thailand functions as a development finance company, specializing in financing fixed assets through medium and long-term loans to industry.

SIFO The Small Industries Finance Office provides financial assistance to small industrial enterprises at relatively low rates of interest, and gives them technical assistance.

BAAC The purpose of the Bank for Agriculture and Agricultural Co-operatives, 99% owned by the Ministry of Finance, is to provide credit for rural undertakings.

The informal sector

The bulk of rural lending is derived from the informal sector.

Middlemen At the forefront are the middlemen who operate in the rice sector. They typically have outstanding loans of about the same level as the commercial banking sector – but charge 10 times more interest.

Credit societies Roughly equal in size to the formal sector's finance companies and the Government Savings Bank combined, are the *pia-huay* or revolving credit societies, which hold about one-third of all Thai household savings. Some of these societies have become so-called chit-funds, a primitive version of investment trusts.

The markets

The Securities Exchange of Thailand (SET) was created in 1975 but has only recently become active. The SET lists nearly 100 companies, which at the end of 1986 had a market capitalization of US$2,878m. The exchange is primarily responsible for regulating the market and is, in turn, supervised by the Ministry of Finance.

The fledgling corporate bond market disappeared in 1977 when a new Public Company Act rendered only very specifically defined entities eligible to make issues in it.

Who can help
Law firms

Major law companies provide a wide range of services covering corporate affairs, tax, joint ventures, and patents, trademarks and copyright. Leading law firms include:
Baker and McKenzie, 12th Fl, Srivikorn Bldg, 18/8 Soi Asoke, Sukhumvit Rd ☏ 258 0364.
Chandler & Thon-ek Law Offices, 10th Fl, Southeast Insurance Bldg, 315 Silom Rd ☏ 234 8475.
International Legal Counsellors (*affiliate of Kaplin Russi & Vecci*), 18th Fl, Bangkok Bank Bldg, 333 Silom Rd ☏ 235 0780.
Marut Bunnag International Law Office, Room 501, 5th Fl, 302 Silom Rd ☏ 233 0518.
Price Sanond Prabhas Wynne and Suprawat, Vithayu Place, 89/17 Wireless Rd ☏ 252 9944.
Tilleke & Gibbins, 4th Fl, Wang Lee Bldg, 297 Surawongse Rd ☏ 234 5173.
Vickery Prapone Pramuan and Suthee, 9th Fl, Central Plaza Office Bldg, 1693 Paholyothin Rd ☏ 541 1235.

Accountants

Major accountancy firms similarly undertake – in addition to auditing services – management consultancy, executive recruitment, tax consultancy and assistance in the search for joint-venture partners.
International affiliates Firms locally incorporated in Thailand but affiliated with major international companies include:
Coopers & Lybrand Associates, 90/14-6 North Sathorn Rd ☏ 235 2871.
Ernst & Whinney, Sinthorn Bldg, Wireless Rd ☏ 250 0233.
Peat Marwick Mitchell & Co, 4th Fl, Boonmitr Bldg, 138 Silom Rd ☏ 236 7877.
Price Waterhouse, 56 Surawongse Rd ☏ 233 1470.
SGV-Na Thalang & Co, 514/1 Larnluang Rd ☏ 280 0900.
Touche Ross International Jaiyos & Co, 298 Silom Rd ☏ 235 7008.

Other sources of help

An early point of contact for many business people in addition to their respective embassies may be the *Thai Chamber of Commerce* ☏ 221 6532, or one of the foreign chambers of commerce in Bangkok. These include:
The American Chamber, 3rd Fl, Kian Gwan Bldg, 140 Wireless Rd ☏ 251 1605.
British Chamber, 6th Fl, Bangkok Insurance Bldg, 302 Silom Rd ☏ 234 1140.
Franco-Thai, 9th Fl, Kian Gwan Bldg, 140 Wireless Rd ☏ 251 9385.
German-Thai, 4th Fl, Kongboonma Bldg, 699 Silom Rd ☏ 236 2396.
Main agency for investors The main government agency for potential investors is the *Board of Investment*, 16th–17th Fl, Thai Farmers Bank Bldg, 400 Paholyothin Rd ☏ 270 1400. Details of its services may be obtained from its overseas branches at: Five Worlds Trade Center, Suite 3443, New York, NY 10048 ☏ (718) 466 1745; Bethman Strasse 58, 6000 Frankfurt am Main ☏ (069) 281 091; 12th Fl, Royal Exchange Bldg, 56 Pitt St, Sydney NSW 2000 ☏ 278905; 3rd Fl, Akasaka Brighton Bldg, 1-5-2 Akasaka, Minato-ku, Tokyo 107 ☏ (03) 582 1806.
The media The principal sources of published information on the Thai economy include Bangkok's two English-language daily newspapers, the *Bangkok Post* and the *Nation Review*.
English-language business journals include *Thailand Business*, published by the Industrial Financial Corporation of Thailand; *Business in Thailand*; *Business Review*.
Reference publications include *The Siam Directory: The Book of Facts and Figures*; *The Thai Chamber of Commerce Business Directory*; and *Thailand Industrial Buyer's Guide*.

Business and cultural awareness

Among Asian countries, Thailand ranks as one of the most open and hospitable, but also as one of the most culturally elusive and perplexing. Visitors are easily charmed by Thais' gracious manners and beguiling smiles, but appearances can be deceptive. The Thai smile can both convey pleasure and conceal anger.

Thai society

Thais have a strong sense of their identity and history. Visitors will often be reminded that Thailand has never been subjugated by a foreign power, that the word *thai* means free. As a result, their relations with foreigners, unburdened by any post-colonial hang-ups, are in a sense easier than in many other Asian countries. But foreigners are welcomed only on Thai terms. Thais generally consider themselves fortunate to have been born in their own country, and are protective of its attributes. Although not uncritical of their country themselves, they resent outsiders who disparage it or who are patronizing towards it.

Freewheeling pragmatists

Thailand is a country of freewheeling pragmatists bound by strong social and cultural traditions. Its religion, Buddhism, and its monarchy provide the essential underpinning of political unity and social harmony. Together with nationhood, they are the symbols most strongly projected in established public life.

Hierarchy and status Something of Thailand's past as a nation of rice cultivators in which government was the preserve of a small educated elite still survives in its hierarchical and highly structured society. Economic development is altering the social equilibrium and broadening the distribution of power and wealth, but society is still permeated by patron-client relationships.

Reciprocal obligations Status, whether based on social rank, political position or wealth, confers reciprocal obligations on superiors and subordinates. There is a Thai adage that applies in business as in politics: "If you follow a senior man, the dog will not bite." Subordinates promote the interests of their superior in return for the advancement they achieve in his service.

The monarchy stands at the apex of society and retains considerable influence in national affairs. The coup d'état in 1932 that converted Thailand from absolute to constitutional monarchy removed the king's direct political authority, but not the status that places him closer to divinity than ordinary mortals. As the focal point of public loyalty, the monarch is a key force for national unity.

The prestige of the monarchy has increased under the present incumbent, King Bhumibol, ninth and longest-reigning member of the Chakri dynasty. Royal sanction for political leaders is no mere constitutional nicety but, as a source of legitimacy, an important political asset. Concern about the king's successor is widespread, however.

Members of the royal family and their images are an object of reverence. *Lèse-majesté* is a serious offence.

Religion More than 80% of Thais subscribe to Buddhism; a minority, about 1m, in southern provinces bordering Malaysia are Muslims. There are also about 270,000 Christians, mainly in Bangkok and in the north. Most of the immigrant Chinese adhere to Confucianism. The king defends the Buddhist faith and is in turn supported by the Sangha, the Buddhist clergy. Monks enjoy a special status outside the main framework of social hierarchy, and are thus second to none.

Modern trends are changing interpretations of Buddhist doctrine, but popular notions of the faith, fused with animism, remain firmly rooted in daily life. The *wat*, or temple, continues to be an important institution for social and educational, as well as religious, purposes.

Thais venerate images of the Buddha. Disrespectful treatment of such images in private homes would be offensive and in public could prompt action by the law.

Education for the great majority of Thais is through government schools, augmented, mainly in Bangkok, by private schools offering higher standards at high cost.

Considerable public investment has gone into the schools systems since the 1960s and 1970s. The result is that Thailand claims 80% of the population over the age of 11 have had some schooling.

Geographical imbalances There are, however, major imbalances. Quality and availability of education vary considerably according to the province. Many children do not progress much beyond primary school. A disproportionately high percentage of secondary school pupils are concentrated in Bangkok. Enrolment in the country's 14 universities has grown much faster than in other parts of the educational system, but job opportunities have not expanded to match higher expectations.

For those who can afford it, education overseas is much sought after and carries prestige.

The sexes The role and status of women are somewhat ambivalent and influenced to a great extent by the individual's social and educational background. Women are subordinate, generally speaking: they are "the hind legs of the elephant" to Thais, powerful but still behind. Men monopolize positions of power in public affairs, while women's role, in the popular view, is to support and please them – the gentle moon to the man's sun. Yet many women fill top company jobs and senior bureaucratic positions. Few foreign women executives work in Thailand, but there is no inhibiting social barrier of the sort encountered in many Muslim countries.

Rules of sexual decorum
Thailand's reputation as a sexual playground is justified by its extensive prostitution industry, but visitors should not be deluded into drawing broader conclusions about the virtue of women outside it. Strict rules of propriety govern public contact between men and women. Society frowns on physical contact between the sexes in public and even more so on displays of affection. Visitors do well to observe scrupulously the rules of decorum.

The business method

Visitors will find different approaches to business, depending on whether they are dealing with older government officials or younger technocrats, businessmen from Thai families or those with Thai Chinese backgrounds. There are no firm rules, only experience, to guide the approach to these groups. Remember that government service carries prestige in Thai society and that meetings with officials tend to follow formal and well-established rituals.

Office hours Hours of business are 8am–5pm Monday to Friday, with lunch from 12–1. Some private businesses work half a day on Saturday. Offices, particularly in government, close promptly and appointments cannot be expected outside these hours except for social purposes.

Face-to-face transactions Phone calls on business matters should be made within office hours, though Thai Chinese businessmen are more flexible on this point. As a rule, business is not transacted on the telephone, but face to face.

Appointments in advance
Executives visiting Thailand should seek to have appointments arranged directly by their head office or their hotel, or by consultants or agents in

Bangkok. They should avoid putting themselves in the position of having to negotiate for appointments with the secretaries of those they wish to meet.

Business meetings Thai society is as status-conscious as it is hierarchical. Conversational preliminaries are a means to establish respective status as determined either by organization and rank or by family and social connections.

Business cards are exchanged at virtually every first meeting and should be carried in abundance. There are no Japanese-style rituals for presenting cards. Business people intending to reside in Thailand may find it advantageous to have them printed in English and Thai.

Demeanour Avoidance of conflict is the governing principle of every aspect of life, including business negotiations. Thais shun confrontation, which leaves little room for the openness, candour, argument and criticism that is part and parcel of business and politics in the West. Instead, Thais subscribe to the concept of *krengjai*, the meaning of which spans "deference" and "consideration" and usually applies to the attitude of subordinate to superior.

Acquiescent subordinates As a result, foreign business people are often frustrated by the tendency of subordinates simply to accept, at least outwardly, the view of a superior rather than express a differing opinion. Even more frustrating may be the differences between what is apparently agreed, for example on price and timing, and what is actually done. It may be more profitable to inquire of business associates what may be feasible in such matters than bluntly to state what is wanted and ask if it can be achieved.

Avoiding confrontation It is far preferable to settle disagreements through negotiation, informal discussion and behind-the-scenes manoeuvrings, than through confrontation. Flattery is often the best prelude to criticism.

Time-keeping Thais do not regard time with the same deference as Westerners, and have a rather flexible approach to appointments and time-keeping. Foreign business people may also find their Thai counterparts have limited planning horizons. However, these habits are rapidly changing among younger people and those who have studied or worked abroad.

Dress Visitors should remember that dress, for Thais, is one measure of status. It is better to overdress than underdress. At business meetings men should wear suits and women should err on the side of formality and sobriety. Note the conservative dress of Thai female office personnel. Revealing or figure-hugging clothes should be avoided. Black is worn only for funerals.

Hospitality

Personal, not institutional or corporate relationships, are the decisive factor in most matters. Invitations to lunch or dinner are standard procedure for promoting contacts with business associates. Visitors should not be surprised if an invitation issued to a Thai and his wife brings only the former. Nor should they be surprised by the comparative rarity of invitations to the homes of Thais. Many Thais are shy of bringing *farangis* (foreigners) to homes they feel may not match living standards in the West. It is normal for women to accept invitations to dinner on their own and to entertain. The level of social sophistication that applies in Bangkok, however, is not the rule upcountry, where women are advised to proceed more conservatively.

Senior person pays Whoever issues the invitation normally pays. Bills are not shared. At impromptu gatherings, the senior person pays.

Language

English is now widely spoken in Bangkok government and

commercial circles. Nonetheless, those intending to stay any length of time in Thailand should learn the language at least to the level where they can handle elementary conversation. Thais appreciate the effort as a gesture of interest in their country, and foreigners will also find social contacts with Thais more entertaining in almost direct proportion to their ability to understand and express themselves in the language.

There is an important proviso: Thai is a tonal language. The meaning of words which, in phonetic script, may have exactly the same sequence of letters, varies according to which of five tones they carry. A perfectly innocent word spoken in one tone can be impolite in another.

Even when a foreigner begins to acquire a measure of confidence in chatting with teacher, friends or taxi drivers, it is prudent to tread carefully before attempting to show off at formal social occasions or business meetings. The mistakes that can be passed off as amusing in informal circumstances merely look foolish in formal surroundings and can give offence.

Etiquette

Thais use two names, the personal preceding the family name. The latter came into use only in the 1920s and in conversation it is the first name, preceded by *Khun* (equivalent to Mr, Mrs or Miss) or the appropriate title that is used. Letters also address Thais by their first names: Dear Khun (or title) then name.

The order of introductions

Address the lower-ranking individual first, which allows him to greet the superior first, who may then respond.

Handshakes are widely used between Thais and foreigners in official and business circles, but note that the Thai form of greeting, the *wai*, avoids physical contact. Such avoidance is often preferable when male visitors are greeting Thai female officials, executives or staff.

The wai is achieved by bringing the hands together, fingers upwards, and is governed by a number of conventions. Suffice it to say that the more the head is bowed and the hands are brought level with the face, the greater the respect conveyed.

When greeted by a *wai*, the visitor does well to respond accordingly, except where there is a substantial gap in rank or social position. Do not, for example, return the *wai* of the office messenger, waiters or waitresses, maids or children. Always *wai* monks, however. It is improper to touch them – absolutely so in the case of women.

Do's and don'ts Do not show anger or irritation or offer blunt criticism. Anger not only breaks all the rules about avoidance of conflict, it also causes considerable, possibly irreparable, loss of face to whoever displays it. Criticism similarly smacks of confrontation. Such discourtesy may be met by studied politeness, but this only disguises the cost.

Stay calm in the face of frustration and difficulty. Thais applaud the quality of *jai yen*, which literally means "cool heart." Coolness coupled with respect and politeness does not betoken weakness – it is appropriate behaviour.

Body language Never touch a Thai person's head and do not point your feet at him or her. The sense of hierarchy has a physical dimension: the head is the most important and respected part of the body, the feet the most lowly and despised. To sit with the legs crossed in the presence of a monk or a member of the royal family or in a court of law is a sign of disrespect that invites reproof. Keep both feet firmly on the ground.

BANGKOK

Area code ☎ 02

The popular image of Bangkok as a city of waterways, temples and massage parlours is only partially accurate. Many canals have been filled in and, apart from the commercialized Floating Market, it is necessary to travel a long way up the Chao Phraya river valley to see traditional Thai waterside life. The city's 300 temples (or *wat*) are concentrated to the north of the commercial centre. However, the highly visible trade in sex continues and provides an income for thousands of prostitutes and hundreds of VD clinics.

Bangkok has been called a great pancake, as it spreads for miles across a flat plain. For the most part, buildings in Bangkok are low constructions, a dull backdrop to the frantic traffic, the pungent smells of spicy Thai food, the bright colours of fruit and vegetables, and the richly patterned Thai silks. At night the neon lights go on and everybody in the city comes out to shop, eat and play.

Tourism is Bangkok's number one industry and accounts for the relative prosperity of its citizens by comparison with those in the rural areas.

Bangkok expects an increase in the number of business visitors. Those who come will not, if they are wise, rush away without spending a day or two purely for pleasure. Difficult as the city is to negotiate, and overly-romanticized, it is still one of the most rewarding cities in Asia to visit.

Arriving

Nearly 40 international airlines and several charter operators fly to Bangkok and there are frequent flights between Bangkok and the other Asian capital cities. The rail system which links Singapore to Bangkok via Kuala Lumpur is popular with tourists, but too time-consuming for most business travellers; it takes 34hr from Kuala Lumpur, and 41hr from Singapore.

Bangkok International Airport

BIA, sometimes still referred to by its former name, Don Muang Airport, has been expanded and modernized to cope with the 8m passengers that use it every year. As a result efficiency has increased and it should not take more than 30 minutes to clear the airport. Departing passengers have to pay an airport tax of B20 on domestic and B200 on international flights.
Facilities Arriving passengers face a barrage of official and unofficial persons offering to find them a taxi or a hotel, or to carry their bags. The set fee for porters is B5 per bag. There is a tourist office but the service is lacklustre. Staff at the hotel desk are even less helpful and particularly reluctant to tell you about discount rates. They will, however, phone through and make a reservation on payment of a deposit (B200–600, depending on the room rate).

The duty-free and other shops are open 7am–midnight and offer a range of goods including silk, jewellery, tobacco, alcohol, confectionery and gifts. The restaurant on the 4th floor is open 6am–midnight, the self-service cafeteria 24hr. In addition, there are various airline VIP lounges, banks, left baggage, lost and found, mail, telex and medical services. For air cargo and inquiries ☎ 523 6201.
City link BIA is only 25km/16 miles from the centre of Bangkok but it is a slow journey into town along congested roads. Allow at least

60min. It is best to take a Thai Airways sedan or arrange to be met by hotel transport.

Hotel transport Air-conditioned cars for about B300 and luxury limousines from B800 must be arranged in advance with the hotel.

Taxi Cabs are available but travelling by taxi is not without its problems. There is a sign at the rank showing recommended fares to hotels and other destinations, but the actual fare has to be negotiated. Drivers regard the recommended fare (about B150–200) as the minimum. Use only licensed taxis, which have a yellow licence plate and a rooftop taxi sign; unlicensed taxis may not be insured. Male travellers should expect all taxi drivers to spend most of the long journey into town trying to fix them up with massage or other "services."

Car rental Avis ☎ 233 0397 and Hertz ☎ 253 6251 can provide limousines and self-drive cars at the airport.

Bus Thai Airways has a "limousine service" counter in the middle of the arrival concourse where you can buy a ticket for transfer to your hotel. The limousine is an air-conditioned eight-seater minibus. The fare is B100 and the journey can take up to 90min as the route depends on the destinations of the passengers. You can ask for an air-conditioned sedan which takes up to four passengers, costs B300 and goes direct to your hotel. The drivers of both services often hard-sell Thai Airways city tours throughout the journey.

Getting around

Bangkok is the one city in Asia where it is better to avoid public taxis. Business travellers should use hotel transport which is more convenient, and is inexpensive and reliable. Most visitors regard a ride in a three-wheeled *tuk-tuk* as part of the Bangkok experience, but few have the patience to attempt using Bangkok's confusing public transport. Allow plenty of time for journeys; roads are always congested

and the one-way system is complex.

Hotel transport Major hotels run fleets of private taxis. A typical short journey costs B50. Try to provide the address and phone number for out-of-the-way destinations so that drivers can phone and ask for directions. Most drivers speak passable English and many will try hard to persuade you to go on shopping or nightclub tours. Better hotels also provide a luxury limousine service with less pushy drivers at B500–800 per hour.

Taxi No taxis in Bangkok have meters; bargaining is the rule and this is not easy, as few drivers speak English and all start by quoting outrageous rates. For short journeys – from one end of Ploenchit Road to another, for example – the fare should be about B30. For longer ones – the Oriental hotel to the offices on Ploenchit Road, for example – it should be about B60. Most drivers know the major hotels, buildings and tourist sights, but their knowledge of other destinations is very patchy. Try to provide the address in Thai script.

Driving Even long-stay expatriates do not drive themselves in Bangkok. Self-drive cars and limousines are available from *Avis* ☎ 233 0397 and *Hertz* ☎ 253 6251. Traffic drives on the left.

Walking Foreigners on foot attract the attention of hawkers and touts, and an accurate map of Bangkok's myriad of streets has yet to be produced. Only consider walking to places within 10min of your hotel or between nearby appointments. When it is hot you won't even want to do that.

Outside Bangkok

Air Thai Airways operates services to all major towns and cities in Thailand. Most flights depart in the morning or early afternoon, and are most heavily used during the Oct–May tourist season. Information and reservations ☎ 280 0070.

Driving Thailand's main roads are good but drivers are fast and careless,

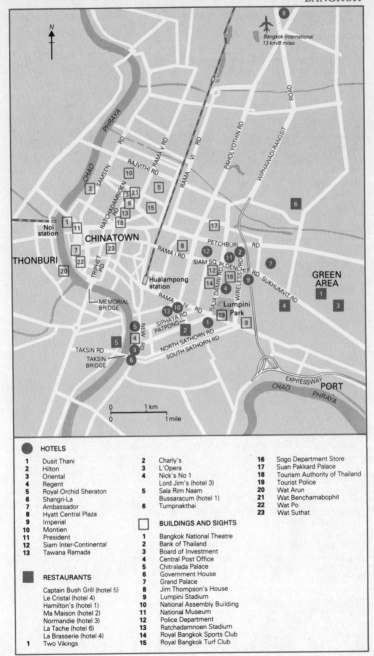

HOTELS

1 Dusit Thani
2 Hilton
3 Oriental
4 Regent
5 Royal Orchid Sheraton
6 Shangri-La
7 Ambassador
8 Hyatt Central Plaza
9 Imperial
10 Montien
11 President
12 Siam Inter-Continental
13 Tawana Ramada

RESTAURANTS

Captain Bush Grill (hotel 5)
Le Cristal (hotel 4)
Hamilton's (hotel 1)
Ma Maison (hotel 2)
Normandie (hotel 3)
La Tache (hotel 6)
La Brasserie (hotel 4)
1 Two Vikings

2 Charly's
3 L'Opera
4 Nick's No 1
Lord Jim's (hotel 3)
5 Sala Rim Naam
Bussaracum (hotel 1)
6 Tumpnakthai

BUILDINGS AND SIGHTS

1 Bangkok National Theatre
2 Bank of Thailand
3 Board of Investment
4 Central Post Office
5 Chitralada Palace
6 Government House
7 Grand Palace
8 Jim Thompson's House
9 Lumpini Stadium
10 National Assembly Building
11 National Museum
12 Police Department
13 Ratchadamnoen Stadium
14 Royal Bangkok Sports Club
15 Royal Bangkok Turf Club

16 Sogo Department Store
17 Suan Pakkard Palace
18 Tourism Authority of Thailand
19 Tourist Police
20 Wat Arun
21 Wat Benchamabophit
22 Wat Po
23 Wat Suthat

and English-language signs are difficult (if not impossible) to read at speed. If you want to travel by road, do so by limousine. *Avis* and *Hertz* are the most reliable limousine companies but there are many cheaper local firms.

Train There are four main express routes, north to Chiang Mai, northeast to Nong Khai, east to Ubon Ratchathani and south to Haad Yai (for Singapore). Daily services cover all these routes. Journeys are long; seats and couchettes in air-conditioned coaches can be reserved. Dining cars serve Thai food and Western snacks. Some trains depart from the main station (Hualampong), others from Noi Station on the west bank of the river. Hualampong sells tickets for both; ticket office open 8.30–6 weekdays, 8.30–noon weekends and hols. Information ☏ 223 7010.

Area by area

Bangkok has no clearly defined downtown area, just one giant sprawl in which housing, shops and industry are mixed in a bewildering amalgam. One way to begin to come to terms with the city is to understand its history. When Ayuthaya, the former capital of Thailand was destroyed by the Burmese in 1767, General Taksin retreated to the small trading post of Bangkok (80km/50 miles downstream) and established the new capital on the opposite side of the river to the modern city. This is now the suburb of Thonburi, whose most prominent landmark is Wat Arun, the richly decorated Temple of Dawn. It has remained relatively undeveloped and is the only area of central Bangkok which has retained an extensive network of canals.

Chinatown The Chinese traders who previously inhabited the site were shifted to the district between Yawarat Road and New Road on the east bank of the river, which has remained Bangkok's Chinatown to this day.

Grand Palace vicinity This was the first area east of the river to be developed by the Thais; almost all of Bangkok's most regal and ancient temples are here, within the sweep of the outermost canal. Three defensive canals forming concentric arcs to the east of the Grand Palace indicate the progressive spread of the city up to the mid-19th century.

The foreign quarter and New Road Beyond the perimeter of the canal, the buildings and the institutions they house reflect the introduction of Western ideas during the reign of King Mongkut, Rama IV. He permitted the first foreign settlement, constructed New Road, and donated a former palace for use as a traders' hostelry. The latter was the original Oriental hotel (now the Authors' Wing of the hotel), soon to be followed by docks, warehouses, banks, residences and embassies, many of which remain. They include the French embassy, the former Customs House, the Assumption Cathedral, the offices of the East Asiatic Company of Denmark (the most prestigious of the old trading companies) and the run-down Trocadero hotel.

The administrative district The constitutional reforms of King Chulalongkorn, Rama V, led to the development of the northern area of the city, where most government departments are to be found, along with the National Assembly building. Chitralada Palace, now the official royal residence, is also here.

East of the old centre After World War II the city developed rapidly and chaotically, and population has increased from 1m to well over 5m. Even so, some distinctive districts can be discerned. Rama IV Road has the main concentration of foreign service companies – notably banks, airlines and trading companies. Rama I Road and Ploenchit Road constitute the principal shopping district, where there are some striking buildings, including Sogo Department Store on Ploenchit Road.

Wireless Road and Sukhumvit Road house most of the foreign embassies in Bangkok. Many affluent Thais and expatriates live in houses in the *soi*, or lanes, which run north of Sukhumvit Road; known as the Green Area, this district also has a growing number of chic restaurants, designer boutiques and smart bars.

The airport road The Central Plaza complex on the airport road is becoming increasingly important as a shopping district. Much of the city's light industry is concentrated along this same road, and companies such as IBM, Ciba Geigy, 3M and the Thai Military Bank have all recently relocated to the northern suburbs. This will be the fastest growing sector of the city, with industrial estates zoned for the high-tech investment Bangkok hopes to attract, particularly from Japan.

The port The sprawling port area, an important part of Bangkok's economy, is in the southeast of the city below the junction of Rama IV Road and Sukhumvit Road.

Hotels

Bangkok's Oriental is one of the world's finest hotels. But there are attractive and efficient alternatives for which reservations do not need to be made so far in advance. The Regent will suit those who like a hotel to be calm and graceful. The Sheraton and Shangri-La both share prime riverside positions with the Oriental, and consequently attract large numbers of tourists. These, with the Hilton and the Dusit Thani, represent the best in Bangkok, but the second tier, listed under "other hotels" are of a high standard and can often be persuaded to discount rooms by up to 50%, particularly during the June–September low season.

All rooms in the hotels listed have air conditioning, 24hr room service, TV, radio and minibar; most have IDD phones. Standard business facilities include photocopying, typing, telex, fax and translation. A 10% service charge and 11% tax are additional to quoted rates.

Dusit Thani **$$$**
Rama IV Rd, 10500 ☎ *236 0450*
TX *81170 Fax 236 6400* • *AE DC MC V*
• *Nikko Hotels* • *488 rooms, 37 suites, 7 restaurants, 3 bars*
Most visitors who stay at the Dusit Thani choose it because it is central to the Rama IV Road business district. It is also within walking distance of Patpong nightlife. Its big "Landmark" executive rooms have full-size writing desks, large beds, sofas, wardrobes and bathrooms. Some are smartly panelled, others are decorated in pastels and overlook the fountain courtyard around which the hotel is built. There are several restaurants with French and Asian cuisine (see *Restaurants*). Shopping arcade, hairdresser, florist, disco
• pool, sauna, tennis, squash, gym
• personal computer rental,
8 meeting rooms (capacity 50–500) and ballroom (1,200) with simultaneous translation, film and video projection.

Hilton **$$$**
2 Wireless Rd, 10500 ☎ *253 0123*
TX *72206 Fax 253 6509* • *AE DC MC V*
• *350 rooms, 37 suites, 4 restaurants, 2 bars*
The Hilton is situated on Bangkok's tranquil "embassy row." The central lobby is almost part of the extensive garden; mature trees, some of which provide fruit for the hotel's restaurants, press right up against the glass walls providing a natural filter for the strong sunlight. All the rooms have large furnished balconies, the best being those facing inwards to the

pool and park. The executive floor rooms are very spacious; standard rooms are comfortable but nothing very special. Shops, hairdresser, florist, disco • pool, sauna, jacuzzi, massage, gym, tennis, squash • typewriter rental, 6 meeting rooms (capacity up to 280), ballroom (720) with audiovisual facilities.

Oriental **$$$$**
48 Oriental Ave, 10500 ☎ *236 0400*
☒ *82997 Fax 236 1939* • *AE DC MC V*
• *Mandarin Oriental Group* • *368 rooms, 30 suites, 5 restaurants, 1 bar*
The Oriental is Bangkok's most famous hotel, recipient of countless awards for its style and service and the standards it sets. It has saved the Chao Phraya riverfront and the alleyways which lead down to it from decay. All the best antique and craft shops in Bangkok are to be found around the hotel, and the Oriental Pier is the starting point for most excursions to riverside attractions. The hotel has found favour with senior bankers, and even monarchs and prime ministers, yet it is far from aloof from tourists. The staff are as forthcoming with help and advice on how to have fun in Bangkok as they are efficient in laying on an elegant private lunch or meeting deadlines for typing an important report. Guests are given every encouragement to relax and enjoy their visit while the staff – in a ratio of four staff per room – take the strain supervised by the ever-accessible Kurt Wachtveitl, the hotel's General Manager. The original hotel – now the Author's Residence with its superbly furnished suites – has been extended by the addition of the Tower Wing, built in 1958 and the new River Wing. All the rooms have river views and sumptuous furnishings. The riverside restaurants include The Normandie, Lord Jim's and Sala Rim Naam (see *Restaurants*) and there is a nightly barbecue in the exotic gardens. Shopping arcade, hairdresser, florist, night club • pool, jogging track,

gym, tennis, squash, golf driving-range and use of nearby golf course • 10 meeting rooms (capacity up to 800).

Regent **$$$**
155 Rajadamri Rd, 10500 ☎ *251 6127*
☒ *20004 Fax 253 9195* • *AE DC MC V*
• *368 rooms, 32 suites, 5 restaurants, 1 bar*
This calm and graceful hotel, although not on the river, is in a quiet and green corner of the city, close to the central business district and surrounded by the trees and park of the Royal Bangkok Sports Club. It is also next door to the city's up-market Peninsula shopping mall. A causeway flanked by lotus ponds and hand-carved sandstone elephants leads to a lobby of pillared elegance. Either side of the lobby are the guest rooms built around tree-filled courtyards, with views over the Sports Club or gardens of the diplomatic residences. The rooms are large, with full-sized desks, well-decorated and stylish. The main restaurant, Le Cristal, is one of Bangkok's best (see *Restaurants*). Staff are efficient, quiet and reserved in the Thai manner. The business centre is open daily. Shops, hairdresser, florist, delicatessen • large pool, sauna, gym, tennis, squash • 12 meeting rooms (capacity up to 150).

Royal Orchid Sheraton **$$$**
2 Captain Bush Lane, Siphya Rd, 10500 ☎ *234 5599* ☒ *84491*
Fax 236 8320 • *AE DC MC V* • *702 rooms, 74 suites, 5 restaurants, 2 bars*
Just along the river bank from the Oriental, the Royal Orchid is Y-shaped to make the most of the river view. Most rooms are designed to meet the relatively undemanding needs of tourists; if you want a desk and plenty of space, ask for an executive room in the Tower. The hotel is light and airy, with glass walls giving onto the swimming pool, and terraces which are built out on stilts over the river. Clean and simple, white marble floors and walls,

fountains and a mass of orchids fill the large lobby which has plenty of comfortable areas in which to talk business over coffee or cocktails. Shops, hairdresser, florist • pool • 10 meeting rooms (capacity up to 190), ballroom (1,500) with audiovisual facilities.

Shangri-La $$$$
89 Soi Wat Suan Plu, off New Rd, 10500 ☎ 236 7777 ⊠ 84265 Fax 236 8579 • AE DC MC V • 650 rooms, 47 suites, 5 restaurants, 2 bars
The river view is the chief attraction of the Shangri-La and some of the Club Class rooms are situated in the corners of the tower, with floor-to-ceiling windows on two sides and a large free-standing desk. It is not an especially attractive section of the river, but the dawn view can be magnificent. From the main lobby, several restaurants including La Tache (see *Restaurants*) and lounge areas lead down to glass walls overlooking the central swimming pool complex. Fans, pot palms and lowered shutters create a neo-colonial atmosphere, and the marble walls are hung with some fine Thai woodcarvings. Service is friendly and easy-going, and the business centre staff are a good source of information on local firms, government ministries and contacts. Shops, hairdresser, florist • gym, sauna, hydropool, massage, tennis, squash • office equipment rental, 6 meeting rooms (capacity up to 200), ballroom (2,000) with simultaneous translation and audiovisual facilities.

OTHER HOTELS
Ambassador ($$) *171 Sukhumvit Rd, 10110 ☎ 254 0444 ⊠ 82910 Fax 253 4123 • AE DC MC V.* Tower complex with big shopping arcade; business and sports centres, wide choice of bars and restaurants; often used for sales conventions.
Central Plaza ($$$) *1695 Paholyothin Rd ☎ 541 1234 ⊠ 20173 Fax 541 1087 • AE DC MC V.* On the same site as the Bangkok Convention Centre and International Expo Centre, in a district to which several major corporations have relocated, but a 20–30min drive from central Bangkok. Excellent service, particularly in the business centre.
Imperial ($$$) *6 Wireless Rd, 10500 ☎ 254 0023 ⊠ 82301 Fax 253 3190 • AE DC MC V.* Small and friendly, close to embassies.
Montien ($$) *54 Surawongse Rd, 10500 ☎ 234 8060 ⊠ 81160 Fax 236 5291 • AE DC MC V.* One of Bangkok's older hotels (established 1966) but being upgraded. Central.
President ($$) *135–26 Gaysorn Rd 10500 ☎ 253 0444 ⊠ 81194 Fax 253 7565 • AE DC MC V.* Recently revamped Meridien group hotel.
Siam Inter-Continental ($$$) *Rama I Rd, 10500 ☎ 253 0355 ⊠ 81155 Fax 253 2275 • AE DC MC V.* Built round an attractive lake, with theatre which hosts visiting and local performers. Attractive rooms in low-built terraces around gardens.
Tawana Ramada ($$) *80 Surawongse Rd, 10500 ☎ 236 0361 ⊠ 81167 Fax 236 3738 • AE DC MC V.* Formerly the Sheraton, central, and opposite Patpong nightlife.

Clubs
The *Royal Bangkok Sports Club* is one of Asia's oldest and most distinguished, with enviable recreation facilities and a fine dining room. Membership is very exclusive and almost totally Thai. It has a wholly owned subsidiary, the *Polo Club* ☎ 253 8941 to which many Bangkok expatriates belong, which allows limited use of the parent club's facilities. The *British Club*, 189 Surawongse Rd ☎ 234 2592 is an expatriate and gentlemanly sanctum.

The hotel price symbols reflect the price at the time of going to press for one person occupying a standard room. For what they mean see *Using the guide.*

Restaurants

It is always safest to err on the side of formality when entertaining and opt for one of the top hotel restaurants; this is in tune with the Thai's preference for calm conversation and reserved behaviour. For top-level entertainment, particularly if your guests include Thai ministers or important business figures, it is best to take a private dining room at the Oriental hotel. Wine in all restaurants is prodigiously expensive. Many Thais drink fruit juice or spirits in preference. Smart dress is essential in all restaurants given full entries, and reservations are always advisable.

Captain Bush Grill $$$
Royal Orchid Sheraton Hotel
☎ *234 5599* • *AE DC MC V* • *closed Sat and Sun L*
This fresh, white-pillared dining room with river views is popular with younger Thai businessmen. The cuisine is Continental, unpretentious and dependable. Short list of mostly vintage wines.

Le Cristal $$$
Regent Hotel ☎ *251 6127* • *AE DC MC V* • *closed Sat and Sun L*
Le Cristal is very simple, uncluttered and elegant; a few Thai paintings, a cluster of antique cut-glass ceiling lamps and an arrangement of orchids provide a minimum of decorative colour. It sets out to be Bangkok's top business restaurant, and attracts a status-conscious clientele. The cuisine is French, combining classical and *nouvelle*, and the fixed price lunch menu changes daily.

Hamilton's $$$
Dusit Thani Hotel ☎ *236 0450* • *AE DC MC V*
Popular for business entertaining because it is central rather than for any out of the ordinary ambience or culinary spark, this smart grill-room offers prime cuts and lobster, along with a short list of very expensive premier *grands crus* wines.

Ma Maison $$$
Hilton Hotel ☎ *253 0123* • *AE DC MC V*
Admired for its superb all-teak interior, modelled after the Thai palace style, Ma Maison has a good value fixed-price luncheon and is well-used by the offices and embassies in the neighbourhood. In the evening, when a range of grilled meat and seafood is served, the atmosphere becomes more subdued and suitable for formal entertaining.

Normandie $$$$
Oriental Hotel ☎ *236 0400* • *AE DC MC V* • *D only*
Formal and elegant, with discreet and attentive service, the Normandie is the first choice of top business people of all nationalities. The restaurant has been designed to make the best of the river views. Chef Jean Bardet's innovative country-style cooking leaves a lasting impression.

La Tache $$$
Shangri-La Hotel ☎ *236 7777* • *AE DC MC V* • *closed Sun*
La Tache is a medley of Art Deco stained glass and Charles Rennie Mackintosh standard lamps. The reasonably priced four-course lunch makes it popular for informal working lunches. The evening sees a change to more formal dining.

Good but casual
La Brasserie, Regent Hotel ☎ 251 6127, serves European bistro style cuisine. Local expatriates use it for entertaining one another, overseas colleagues and younger, more westernized Thais. The same spectrum of clientele celebrate special occasions at the atmospheric *Two Vikings*, 2 Soi 35, Sukhumvit Rd ☎ 258 8843 (closed Sun). It is named after the nationality of the owners

rather than the cuisine, which is generally regarded as the best Continental food in Bangkok, served in the six antique decorated rooms of a 19thC mansion. *Charly's*, 66 North Sathorn Rd ☎ 234 9035, is also set in a restored villa within extensive grounds but has retained fewer of the building's original features. More popular with expatriates than Thais, it specializes in steak and fondue. *L'Opera*, 55 Soi 39, Sukhumvit Rd ☎ 258 5605, is unanimously regarded as the best for authentic Italian food and conviviality. *Nick's No. 1*, 17 Soi 16, Sukhumvit ☎ 259 0315 established in 1952 and serves Hungarian food, and Kobe Steak *à la Nick*.

All three hotels on the Chao Phraya river – the *Oriental* ☎ 236 0400, the *Royal Orchid Sheraton* ☎ 234 5599 and the *Shangri-La* ☎ 236 7777 serve barbecues by the riverside every evening from 7pm; in the opinion of many locals, the poolside barbecue at the *Hilton* ☎ 253 0123 is best of all for the choice of food and the romance of the illuminated gardens.

The abundance of local seafood varieties, some rarely found outside Thailand, is best at *Lord Jim's*, Oriental Hotel ☎ 236 0400. At lunch the restaurant serves a large and impressive buffet, and there is an extensive evening menu. The Oriental's *Sala Rim Naam* off Charoen Nakorn Rd ☎ 437 6211 is a good way of discovering Thai food without a native guide. The menu is a selection of the less traumatically hot Thai dishes as a concession to foreign taste, beautifully presented on banana leaves and bronze platters. Members of the Fine Arts Department of Thailand perform courtly dances from 8.30pm onwards. If you prefer Thai food without the performance, try the *Bussaracum*, Dusit Thani Hotel ☎ 236 0450.

There are several huge restaurants on the outskirts of Bangkok of which the original and most famous is *Tumpnakthai*, 131 Ratchadapisek Rd ☎ 277 8855. The restaurant consists of 63 traditional wooden pavilions around a lake regularly treated to control the mosquitoes, connected by duckboard walkways and capable of seating 3,000. It is so popular that reservation is essential. Dishes range from *sashimi*, through Chinese, to regional Thai. If there is a fault, it is that the waiters do not allow sufficient time to absorb the menu and can be a little officious with the indecisive.

All these restaurants fit into the $$ or $$$ categories and take credit cards.

Bars

Almost any of the hotel bars and cocktail lounges around the city centre are pleasant for informal conversation, although there is no doubt that for business entertaining the *Bamboo Bar* at the Oriental hotel is the most charming and deservedly popular. *Library 1918* at the Dusit Thani hotel is a good central alternative.

Imported spirits in hotel bars are expensive; fortunately the local Kloster beer is excellent, and most bars serve a range of fruit cocktails.

The bars in the Patpong district are often much tamer than their notoriety would suggest. There are around 75 altogether, packed into two lanes which link Surawongse Road and Silom Road. Bars like the *Kangaroo Pub*, with its Australian atmosphere, cold beer and sports videos, *Bobby's Arms* and *Trattoria da Roberto* are pleasant places to enjoy a drink or light meal. Others, including *King's Castle*, *Limelight*, *Pink Panther* and *Superstar* are bars plus disco and dancing partners, but it is up to you whether you want company or not; you will not be pestered. The many go-go bars provide free entertainment in the form of tame and often amateurish dancing by bikini-clad Thai girls.

Entertainment

Theatre, dance, opera The *Bangkok National Theatre* presents

Thai drama, concerts by the Bangkok Symphony Orchestra and occasional performances by visiting artists. Keep an eye on the entertainment page of the *Bangkok Post* for details, and also for Thai dance and music evenings at the *Thai Cultural Centre*, Ratchadapisek Rd ☎ 245 7711. Occasional performances are also given in the major hotels. The Siam Intercontinental stages contemporary dance and comedy theatre at its *Playhouse* ☎ 253 0355; the Hilton and Oriental have irregular shows, and the Dusit Thani sometimes provides an evening of opera highlights in its *Library 1918* cocktail lounge.

Cinema Most of Bangkok's better cinemas are in and around Siam Square. The *Bangkok Post* gives details of screenings. Foreign films are rarely shown. Local films are mostly kung fu, slapstick or simple love stories.

Discos *Bubbles* at the Dusit Thani hotel and *Diana's* at the Oriental are both first-class discos with bright lights and professional DJs.

Nightclubs Jazz lovers will find a huge range of clubs offering good live bands. Best for progressive jazz are the *Graham-Paige Jazz Club* in the Gaysorn Shopping Arcade, 135-2 Gaysorn Rd ☎ 253 7607 or *Brown Sugar*, 231-20 Sarasin Rd ☎ 250 0103. For trad jazz the best are the *Napoleon Lounge*, 76 Patpong I ☎ 236 4999 and *Bobby's Arms*, Patpong II ☎ 233 6828 (Sun). *Tiara*, at the Dusit Thani hotel, is considered the city's best nightclub; this penthouse restaurant offers fine night views and international cabaret stars. Las Vegas style floor shows are the attraction at *Gigi*, Supakarn Shopping Centre (on the opposite side of the river from the Shangri-La hotel) ☎ 437 9601.

Shopping

Thai textiles are particularly appealing to Western tastes. Buying at source is obviously cheaper than in the department stores of the West, though shipping charges for bulky items may add significantly to the cost. Many of the shops listed in the *Tourist Authority of Thailand Shopping Guide*, and most hotels, provide this service. Most shops open Mon–Sat 8.30am–9pm, and increasingly on Sunday. Many department stores open Mon–Sat, 10–7.

Thai silk is famous for its fine quality and is available in an infinite number of colours and patterns. The *Jim Thompson Thai Silk Company*, 9 Surawongse Rd (open daily 9–6), was revived single-handedly after World War II and is still regarded as the most original and stylish. Almost as good are *Design Thai*, 304 Silom Rd, and *Star of Siam* at the Oriental hotel. There are literally hundreds of other outlets in the streets surrounding the major hotels; all sell ready-made garments and will make suits, blouses and dresses in 24hr. Many of these shops sell equally striking Thai cotton by length or made up into bedspreads and cushion covers.

Handicrafts Most tourist shops and stores carry a wide range of sculptures – human figures, animals, birds and fish, in bronze, painted wood or old teak. These shops will often stock a range of stoneware pots, bronze ornaments and cutlery, baskets, carved wooden boxes and genuine and reproduction antiques; the stock varies little from shop to shop. For shopping in air-conditioned comfort, go to the *Oriental Plaza*, by the Oriental hotel (the shop next door, sponsored by the Thai royal family, called *Chitralada* is especially good for northern Thai crafts), the *Peninsula Plaza* next to the Regent hotel and the *Siam Centre* in Siam Square. The *River City Shopping Complex*, next to the Royal Orchid Sheraton, has a particularly good range of antiques. However it is almost impossible to export antique religious images, and even religious reproductions must be licensed. Export licences are granted by the *National Museums Department* *of Fine Arts* ☎ 221 4817. The process takes at least a week, often much longer, so most visitors have to rely on the dealer to do the paperwork and handle shipping; only use a shop recommended by the Tourist Authority of Thailand, which will give assistance in case of any difficulties. Many of the shops in New Rd and Silom Rd sell silver utensils and fine jewellery made by the northern hill tribes; by law the silver must be at least 92.5% pure. Thai potters produce grey-green celadon glazed pottery in shapes and and designs virtually indistinguishable from ancient Chinese wares. For the best selection go to *Celadon House*, 278 Silom Rd.

Sightseeing

Bangkok has many rewarding sights and it is worth allocating at least a day to see them. Their distance from the business areas prohibits a quick visit between meetings.

Floating market Bangkok's floating market now exists almost solely for the benefit of tourists and consequently has lost any feeling of vitality and genuine commerce. Consequently some tour operators now take visitors to the provincial market at Damnoen Saduak, 80km/50 miles from the city. In either case, you must rise early. The market closes at noon, but peak activity is between 7 and 8am. Trips to the city market usually stop at the *Wat Arun* and at the sheds where the magnificent royal barges, used on religious and ceremonial occasions, are moored.

Grand Palace Until recently the Grand Palace had served as the home of the Thai royal family from its foundation in the late 18th century. The oldest building on the site is the *Wat Phra Keo*, the Temple of the Emerald Buddha. It serves as a "chapel" to the Royal Palace and contains one of the most venerated Buddha images in the world. The interior of the temple is covered in murals depicting the earthly life of the Lord Buddha and the surrounding wall shows scenes from the Hindu Ramayana epic. The rest of the Palace complex is composed of many elaborately decorated buildings with the multi-tiered roofs and golden spires typical of classic Thai architecture. Shorts and sleeveless shirts are not permitted and photography is only allowed within the grounds, not inside the buildings. *Open 8.30–11.30 and 1–3.30; exterior area only, Sat and Sun.*

National Museum Located in a former palace, built 1782, is one of the best presented museums in South-East Asia, housing religious sculpture, objects from the Grand Palace, tribal artifacts and much else. *Open 9–noon and 1–4; closed Mon, Fri and public hols.*

Suan Pakkard Palace A private museum whose attractions include the traditional buildings and well-kept gardens of the palace complex, plus a rich collection of bronze and stone art, furniture and ceramics. *Sri Ayutthaya Rd. Open Mon–Sat 9–4.*

Jim Thompson's house An enchanting building created from six old teak houses built by the side of a canal and surrounded by lush gardens. It houses the antique collection of the legendary American who came to Bangkok as a serviceman towards the end of World War II, stayed to rescue the Oriental hotel from decay and went on to revitalize the Thai silk industry, meanwhile building up a fine collection of stone and bronze sculpture, porcelain, paintings and woodcarving from all over South-East Asia. *Soi Kasemsan I, off Rama I Rd. Open Mon–Fri 9–4.*

Temples Bangkok has hundreds of *wat*, of which four are particularly rewarding and are all within a short distance of the Grand Palace. *Wat Po* (also known as *Wat Jetabon*) is famous for the huge reclining Buddha, one of the largest in the world. The feet of the image are inlaid with mother-of-pearl depicting scenes from his life. The large temple complex is crammed with pavilions and the cloisters contain 394 gilded images. *Wat Suthat* is visited for its richly carved and gilded doors and remarkable murals. *Wat Benchamabophit* was completed in 1911 and faced with Carrara marble from Italy, hence its popular name, the Marble Temple. It is considered the most beautiful of all the city's temples. *Wat Arun*, however, remains for most visitors the most striking of the city's landmarks; its style is influenced by the Khmer religious architecture of neighbouring Cambodia. The temple with its five tall *prang* (spires), of which the central one is 80 metres/250ft tall, predates the founding of the city and served as the royal chapel for the few years that the capital was located on this side of the river. It is on the west bank of the Chao Phraya, and can be reached by ferry from the Tha Tien landing stage by Wat Po. *All the temples open 8–5.*

Guided tours

There is no shortage of tour operators in Bangkok, indeed visitors have to become adept at fending them off. *Thai Airways* ☎ 513 0121 specializes in small group tours by chauffeur-driven car or minibus, but the hotel-based tour companies are just as reliable. Ignore all approaches from unofficial "cowboy" guides. As a general rule, tour operators are best for out-of-town trips, but it is easy enough to tour the sights of the city without help.

Boat trips Afternoon trips by converted rice barge along the Chao Phraya river and what is left of the city's canals, provide the opportunity to photograph the Grand Palace and riverside temples as well as watch the busy river life. *Chao Phraya Chartered Co* ☎ 233 0581 is one of the leading operators, and the *Oriental hotel* has dinner cruises every Wednesday starting at 7.30pm. If you have a Thai speaker in your party, you can charter a barge for up to

8 people for B200 per hour and explore the lesser known Klongs of Thonburi, at the Tha Rachini landing stage by Phraphuthayotfar (Memorial) Bridge.

Out of town

Ayuthaya (80km/50 miles north) The best day-trip from Bangkok is to visit the ruins of the city which served as the capital from 1350 until its destruction by warring Burmese in 1767. It can be reached by road, but better by far is to cruise up-river on one of the Oriental hotel's river cruises and return by coach (or vice versa). Alternatively, you can charter one of the hotel's boats which can take 100 seated or 180 standing passengers, for the day or evening; for details ☎ 236 0400. The principal sights include the ruins of the former royal palace and government buildings whose remaining pillars and walls convey an idea of the city's former size and grandeur, and several restored temples and monasteries. A tour usually includes a visit to the Royal Summer Palace at Bang Pa-In, an eclectic but charming mixture of Greek, Chinese, Thai, Renaissance and Gothic buildings demonstrating King Chulalongkorn's taste for Western architecture.
Chiang Mai (600km/375 miles north) is the principal city of northern Thailand with many imposing temples dating from the 13th century. From the city you can join hotel-organized tours to hill-tribe villages, or trek in the mountains. The city is an important centre for native crafts. Thai Airways has several flights between Bangkok and Chiang Mai daily (1hr, B2,550 return).

Spectator sports

Horse-racing takes place every Sun starting at 12.15pm and alternates between the *Royal Bangkok Sports Club*, Henri Dunant Rd, and the *Royal Bangkok Turf Club* on Phitsanulok Rd.
Thai boxing (Muay Thai), boxing

with the hands, feet, knees and elbows, attracts huge and exuberant crowds and can be seen any night in Bangkok. Bouts take place at the *Rachadamnoen Stadium*, Rachadamnoen Rd, and the *Lumpini Stadium*, Rama IV Rd.

Keeping fit

Bangkok's hotels generally have good sports facilities which, in the case of the Regent and the Hilton, are in particularly attractive settings.
Golf There are challenging courses and reasonable green fees that attract many visitors, especially Japanese. The most popular is the *Navatanee Golf Course* ☎ 374 6127, designed for the 1975 World Cup Tournament. It is necessary to reserve well in advance, especially for weekend play. The *Railway Training Centre* course ☎ 271 0130 staged the Thailand Open in 1987. The Oriental hotel arranges round trips to the *Ekachai Golf and Country Club* ☎ 314 0392 which is easily reached in 30min by car. Other clubs within a short distance of the city centre are the *Royal Thai Army* ☎ 521 1584 and the *Royal Thai Navy* ☎ 393 1652; both open to the public.
Jogging The Hilton's spacious grounds are ideal. Otherwise, since road-running in Bangkok is hazardous, go to Lumpini Park.

Local resources
Business services

Most Thais have a limited command of English and dealing with firms that offer business services in Bangkok is rarely easy. In most cases, it is least frustrating to use hotel business centre services.
Photocopying and printing *Arcadia* ☎ 258 7274 or *Tana Press* ☎ 236 4358 for rapid small jobs. *Graphic Art* ☎ 233 0304, *New United* ☎ 284 0466 or *Sriboon* ☎ 286 1153 for big and colour jobs.
Secretarial *Datasource* ☎ 234 7751 and *Lynn* ☎ 589 6382 both handle word processing from manuscript or audio tape.

Translation and interpreters ECC *Translation Service* ☎ 245 3404; *International Translations* ☎ 233 7714; and *Japanese English and Thai Translations* (*JETT*) ☎ 233 4097 are the companies most often used by business and embassies, with a good knowledge of commercial and legal documents.

Communications
Local delivery Most hotels will arrange this service which is otherwise not generally available.
Long-distance delivery Major companies include *DHL* ☎ 286 8618, *TNT Skypak* ☎ 259 0253.
Post office The *Central Post Office* is on New Road just beyond the junction with Surawongse Road. Open weekdays 8.30–5, Sat 8.30–noon.
Telephone Local calls from public boxes cost 1 baht, and only 1 baht coins are accepted. Callers sometimes experience some delay in getting through, since the system (currently being updated) lacks sufficient lines to cope with demand. Long-distance domestic calls can be made direct from hotel telephones, or through the operator (☎ 101) on older telephones. Most hotels also have IDD phones but charge 20% or more for the service. Otherwise, call the international operator ☎ 100. There is an international telephone office at the *Central Post Office*, open 24hr every day.
Telex and fax Telexes can be sent from the *Central Post Office*. Fax is not widely available outside hotels.

Conference/exhibition centres
All the major hotels have these facilities but the *Central Plaza* ☎ 541 1234 has the most commanding position in this market. Within the hotel complex is the Bangkok Convention Centre (capable of seating up to 3,800), the *Bangkok International Exposition Centre*, a ballroom (capacity 1,800) and six smaller function rooms (80–130).

Embassies

Australia 37 South Sathorn Rd
☎ 287 2680
Austria 14 Soi Nandha, Soi
Altkarnprasit, off South Sathorn Rd
☎ 286 3011
Belgium 44 Soi Pipat, off Silom Rd
☎ 233 0840
Canada 11th Fl, Boonmitr Bldg, 138
Silom Rd ☎ 234 1561
Denmark 10 Soi Attakara Prasit,
South Sathorn Rd ☎ 286 3930
Finland Amarin Plaza, 16th Fl, 500
Ploenchit Rd ☎ 256 9306
France 35 Custom House Lane, off
New Rd ☎ 234 0950
Greece Royal Orchid Sheraton Hotel
☎ 234 5599
Indonesia 600–2 Petchburi Rd
☎ 252 3135
Ireland United Flourmill Bldg, 205
Rajawongse Rd ☎ 223 0876
Italy 399 Nang Linchee Rd
☎ 286 4844
Japan 1674 New Petchburi Rd
☎ 252 6151
Malaysia 35 South Sathorn Rd
☎ 286 1390
Netherlands 106 Wireless Rd
☎ 252 6103
New Zealand 93 Wireless Rd
☎ 251 8165
Norway 690 Sukhumvit Rd
☎ 258 0531
Philippines 760 Sukhumvit Rd
☎ 259 0139
Portugal 26 Bush Lane, off New Rd
☎ 234 0372
Singapore 129 South Sathorn Rd
☎ 286 2111
South Korea 12th Fl, Sathorn Thani
Bldg, 90–45 North Sathorn Rd
☎ 234 0723
Spain 104 Wireless Rd ☎ 252 6112
Sweden 11th Fl, Boonmitr Bldg, 138
Silom Rd ☎ 234 3891
Switzerland 35 Wireless Rd
☎ 253 0156
UK Wireless Rd ☎ 253 0191
USA 95 Wireless Rd ☎ 252 5040
West Germany 9 South Sathorn Rd
☎ 286 4229

Emergencies
Hospitals All major hotels have

doctors on call. Several privately run
hospitals provide 24hr service, have
European doctors and will accept
credit cards in payment for services.
Costs are similar to private medicine
in the West. They include the
Bangkok Nursing Home ☎ 233 2610,
the *Bangkok Christian Hospital*
☎ 233 6981, the *Camillian Hospital*
☎ 391 0136, and the *Bangkok
Adventist Hospital* ☎ 281 1422. A
medical practice favoured by
expatriates is that of *J.P. Dickson &
Partners*, the British Dispensary, 109
Sukhumvit Rd ☎ 252 8056. For
dental treatment they use the *Siam
Square Clinic* ☎ 252 8921 which is
open 8.30–-6 exc Sun.
Pharmacies usually carry a green
cross illuminated sign and are found
in every shopping centre, generally
open 8.30am–9pm. The *British
Dispensary* 1, Oriental Avenue (close
to the Oriental hotel) is well-stocked.
Hotel newsstands also have a wide
range of non-prescription drugs, and
all hospitals have dispensaries.
Police Do not flaunt large amounts
of money or jewellery in Bangkok or
be careless with handbags. Thieves
who slash handbag straps and bags
are rife in crowded places,
particularly on buses. Bagsnatchers
on motorcycles tour alleyways at
night, and mugging is on the increase
– though nowhere near as common
yet as in the West. Avoid offers from
touts or even friendly strangers. One
profitable ploy involves taking
visitors for a river cruise – often the
person concerned will pay all the
costs and seem genuinely hospitable
until he and the boat owner threaten
to dump you in the middle of the
wide river unless you part with your
valuables. Among other con tricks is
the offer of a drink which is drugged;
the victim may wake days later to
find all his posessions gone. Never
leave valuables in your hotel room;
put them in the hotel safe. In
emergency, call the police mobile
service ☎ 123. Special tourist police
help visitors out of difficulties and
provide information ☎ 281 5051.

Government offices

Immigration Office ☎ 286 9176,
Revenue Department ☎ 281 5777,
Board of Trade ☎ 221 9350,
Industrial Estate Authority
☎ 253 3218, *Bank of Thailand
(central bank)* ☎ 282 3322, *Customs*
☎ 249 0431.

Information sources

Local media The *Bangkok Post* and
the *Nation* both have business
supplements which carry useful
information. There is also an evening
paper, the *Bangkok World*.
Tourist information There is the
office of the *Tourism Authority of
Thailand*, Ratchadamnoen Rd
☎ 282 1143, but the *Tourist
Assistance Centre* ☎ 281 5051 and
hotel desks have the same
information. A free publication
Bangkok This Week is available in
most hotels, lists cultural events and
hotel restaurant special promotions;
it also has advertisements for shops,
restaurants and go-go bars.

Thank-yous

The *Hilton* hotel ☎ 253 0123 has an
excellent florist, and its delicatessen
Hilton Gourmandise is the best in
Bangkok for handmade chocolates,
vintage wines, and food hampers
(open 8am–9pm) although *The
Regent Shop* and *Oriental Flowers*
(both in the Regent hotel
☎ 251 6127) also have a good
selection of gifts (open 7am–8pm).
Otherwise, all hotels have florists
which will arrange deliveries, and
there are many liquor stores on the
main streets of Bangkok carrying
most spirits brands but rarely much
of a choice of wines.

Planning and reference
Entry details

Documentation All visitors must
have a valid passport. Nationals of 55
countries, including all of non-
Communist Europe, Canada, the
USA, Australia, New Zealand and
ASEAN member states can stay in
Thailand for 15 days without a visa,
but no extensions are granted.
Officially a confirmed onward travel
ticket is needed, but checks are rarely
made. Anyone who wants to stay
more than 15 days must apply for a
visa in advance. Tourist visas issued
overseas allow a stay of 60 days, and
are valid 90 days from the date of
issue. Again, extensions are rarely
granted: when they are, the
Immigration Department asks for a
cash deposit or bank guarantee equal
to the cost of an onward travel ticket.
"Non-immigration" visas are valid
for 90 days. Anyone who stays longer
must obtain a tax clearance
certificate, regardless of whether or
not they have earned income in
Thailand, before they are allowed to
leave. Visa extensions are issued by
the Immigration Division, Soi Suan
Phlu, South Sathorn Rd, Bangkok
☎ 286 9176. For a tax clearance
certificate, apply to the Revenue
Department, Chakkaphong Rd,
Bangkok ☎ 281 5777. Both are open
Mon–Fri 8.30–noon, 1–4.30.
Driving licence Visitors intending
to drive must hold an international
driving licence.
Health requirements Travellers
who have been in a yellow fever-
infected area within six days prior to
arrival in Thailand must have a
relevant certificate of inoculation.
Cholera, typhoid and polio
vaccinations, plus both maloprim and
nivaquine (anti-malaria pills) are
advisable.
Customs regulations Customs
clearance forms are usually issued by
airlines during the flight to Bangkok.
Currency (but not traveller's
cheques) in excess of US$10,000
must be declared as well as video
players, televisions, cassette
recorders, radios and gold. Import of
more than B2,000 in Thai currency,
pornography, narcotics or firearms is
prohibited. No duty is charged on
reasonable personal effects, but all
forms of merchandise are heavily
taxed. Duty-free allowances are 200
cigarettes or 250gm of cigars or
tobacco, and 1 litre of wine or spirits.

Visitors may not take out more than B500 in Thai currency and US$10,000 in foreign currency (or the amount declared to customs on arrival if higher). A licence is required from the Bangkok National Museum ☏ 224 1370 for exporting reproductions of Bodhisattva or Buddha images (or fragments thereof). It takes at least five days for the Museum to issue a licence, but reputable dealers will handle the application and shipment for you. Genuine antique images are rarely allowed out except for temporary study, or for worship by practising Buddhists.

Climate

Bangkok is hot and humid for most of the year, with temperatures of 30–34°C/86–93°F during the day, falling to 24°C/75°F at night. Mar–May is the hottest season, when temperatures of 38°C/100°F are not uncommon and the humidity rarely falls below 80%. Jun–Oct is the rainy season, with most rain falling around dusk, and causing frequent flooding even in the capital. During Nov–Feb – the main tourist season – it remains hot but the sky is clear and it is less humid.

A jacket is only necessary for the most formal meetings and first-class restaurants. Otherwise short-sleeved shirt and tie or safari suit are acceptable business dress; women should dress modestly. Freer styles can be adopted for weekends and sightseeing, but shorts are frowned upon in better hotels and restaurants.

Holidays

As usual in Asia many public holidays vary from year to year because they are calculated according to the lunar calendar.

Dec 31 and Jan 1	New Year's Eve and Day
Mid Feb	Magha Puja
Apr 6	Chakri Day
Apr 13	Songkran Day (Thai New Year)
Early May	Ploughing Ceremony
May 5	Coronation Day
May/Jun	Visakha Bucha
Jul	Asalaha Bucha
Aug 12	Queen Sirikit's Birthday
Oct 23	Chulalongkorn Day
Dec 5	King Bhumibol's Birthday
Dec 10	Constitution Day
Dec 25	Christmas Day

Money

Local currency The Thai monetary unit is the baht, divided into 100 stang (or satang). Notes are issued in denominations of 500, 100, 20 and 10, along with 5 and 1 baht, and 50 and 25 stang coins. Older coins do not carry their denomination in Arabic numerals. A supply of 20 and 10 notes is useful for paying taxi drivers who cannot be counted on to give change for larger notes. Otherwise getting change is not a problem.

Changing money All major international currencies are exchangeable, but US dollars are the most widely used. Banks often ask to see the original purchase agreement before cashing a traveller's cheque. Banks give the best rate of exchange. Authorized money changers which operate in major stores and hotels usually offer a rate not far below the bank rate while hotels are generally 5% below. Banks open Mon–Fri, 8.30–3.30 and most offer exchange services. The major banks, with central branches, are the Bangkok Bank, Bank of Ayudhya, Bangkok Metropolitan, Siam Commercial, Thai Danu, Thai Military and Union Bank of Bangkok. About twenty international banks have offices in the city. Hotels, airlines, larger shops and better restaurants accept major credit cards.

Tipping

In most hotels and restaurants, where service charge is added, tipping is not necessary. Never tip taxi drivers. B20 is appropriate for hairdressers and masseuses, B10 per bag for porters except at the airport where the fee is fixed at B5 per bag.

International dialling codes

Before dialling the country's code, dial 010 (from Hong Kong), 000 (Indonesia), 00 (Malaysia), 00 (Philippines), 005 (Singapore), 001 (South Korea), 010 (Taiwan). Omit the initial 0 from the city code. The figures in brackets indicate how many hours the country is ahead or behind Hong Kong, Malaysia, Philippines, Singapore and Taiwan.

Australia	61	(0–+2hr)
Austria	43	(−7hr)
Belgium	32	(−7hr)
Canada	1	(−11hr 30min–16hr)
China	86	
Denmark	45	(−7hr)
France	33	(−7hr)
Greece	30	(−6hr)
Hong Kong	852	
India	91	(−2hr 30min)
Indonesia	62	(−1–+1hr)
Ireland	353	(−8hr)
Israel	972	(−6hr)
Italy	39	(−7hr)
Japan	81	(+1hr)
Malaysia	60	
Netherlands	31	(−7hr)
New Zealand	64	(+4hr)
Norway	47	(−7hr)
Pakistan	92	(−3hr)
Philippines	63	
Portugal	351	(−8hr)
Singapore	65	
South Korea	82	(+1hr; +2hr May–Oct)
Spain	34	(−7hr)
Sweden	46	(−7hr)
Switzerland	41	(−7hr)
Taiwan	886	
Thailand	66	(−1hr)
UK	44	(−8hr)
USA	1	(−13–18hr)
W. Germany	49	(−7hr)

Conversion charts

Length

centimetres (cm)	cm or in	inches (in)
2.54	= in 1 cm =	0.394
5.08	2	0.787
7.62	3	1.181
10.16	4	1.575
12.70	5	1.969
15.24	6	2.362
17.70	7	2.756
20.32	8	3.150
22.86	9	3.543
25.40	10	3.937
50.80	20	7.874
76.20	30	11.811
101.60	40	15.748
127.00	50	19.685

Mass (weight)

kilograms (kg)	kg or lb	pounds (lb)
0.454	= lb 1 kg =	2.205
0.907	2	4.409
1.361	3	6.614
1.814	4	8.819
2.268	5	11.023
2.722	6	13.228
3.175	7	15.432
3.629	8	17.637
4.082	9	19.842
4.536	10	22.046
9.072	20	44.092
13.608	30	66.139
18.144	40	88.185
22.680	50	110.231

Distance

kilometres (km)	km or miles	miles (mi)
1.609	= mi 1 km =	0.621
3.219	2	1.243
4.828	3	1.864
6.437	4	2.485
8.047	5	3.107
9.656	6	3.728
11.265	7	4.350
12.875	8	4.971
14.484	9	5.592
16.093	10	6.214
32.187	20	12.427
48.280	30	18.641
64.374	40	24.855
80.467	50	31.069

Volume

litres (l)	litres or UK galls	UK galls
4.546	= l 1 gall =	0.220
9.092	2	0.440
13.638	3	0.660
18.184	4	0.880
22.730	5	1.100
27.276	6	1.320
31.822	7	1.540
36.368	8	1.760
40.914	9	1.980
45.460	10	2.200
90.919	20	4.399
136.379	30	6.599
181.839	40	8.799
227.298	50	10.998

Temperature

°F	32	40	50	60	70	75	85	95	105	140	175	212
°C	0	5	10	15	20	25	30	35	40	60	80	100

313

Index

advertising: Hong Kong 33; Indonesia 74; Malaysia 111; Philippines 146; Singapore 183; South Korea 222; Taiwan 259; Thailand 290

agents: Hong Kong 33; Indonesia 72; South Korea 221–2; Taiwan 259; Thailand 289, 290

agriculture: Hong Kong 22; Indonesia 65; Malaysia 101; Philippines 138; South Korea 213; Taiwan 248; Thailand 282

Ahmad Yahaya, Tunku 105

aid: Hong Kong 24; Indonesia 66; Malaysia 103; Taiwan 250

AIDS 283

Alien Business Law (1972), Thailand 287

Allied Bank, Philippines 142

American Business Council, Malaysia 113

ancestor worship, Taiwan 262

Anglo-Taiwan Trade Committee 259

animism: Malaysia 115; Philippines 149; South Korea 226

anti-British directive, Malaysia 102, 106

anti-communism, Indonesia 62

Aquino, Benigno 136

Aquino, Corazon "Cory" 135, 136, 141

Arab Malay Bank 105

ASEAN 10, 12, 63, 99, 110, 171, 175, 279, 283

Asian Currency Units (ACUs) 184, 185

Asian Development Bank 21, 103, 147

Association of Foreign Trading Agents of Korea 222

Ayala, Chito 141

Ayala, Jaime Zobel de 142

Bahasa Malay 116

baht 283

Baker, James 251

Bakrie, Achmad 70

Bakrie, Nirwan 70

Bali 8, 64

Bambang Trihatmodjo 70

Bangkok 297–312

Bangkok Bank 286, 291

Bangkok Fund 286

Bangkok Mass Transit Organization 285

Bangkok Metropolitan Bank 286

Bank for Agriculture and Agricultural Cooperatives (BAAC), Thailand 291

Bank of America 35, 147, 148, 184, 291

Bank Bumi Daya 75

Bank Bumiputra Malaysia 105, 112

Bank Central Asia 70

Bank of China (BOC) group 28, 29, 35, 36

Bank of Communications 257, 260

Bank Dagang Negara 75

Bank of East Asia 34

Bank Ekspor and Impor Indonesia 75

Bank Indonesia 71, 75

Bank of Korea (BoK) 218, 223

Bank Negara Indonesia 75

Bank Negara Malaysia 103, 112

Bank of the Philippine Islands 142, 147

Bank Rakyat Indonesia 75

Bank of Seoul & Trust Co 223

Bank of Taiwan 260

Bank of Thailand 289, 291

Bank of Tokyo 184, 291

banks: Hong Kong 38, 40; Indonesia 75; Malaysia 104, 112; Philippines 147, 150; South Korea 223; Taiwan 259–60; Thailand 291

Barclays 35

Barisan Nasional 99

Barlow, Henry 113

Basic Law Drafting Committee, Chinese for Hong Kong 21

Beijing government, China 19, 20, 21, 246, 247, 249, 262

Berne Convention 290

Bhumibol Adulyadej, King (Rama IX) 280, 293

birth control: Singapore 189; South Korea 213; Thailand 281

Bond, Alan 28

Borneo 98, 99

branch offices: Malaysia 107; South Korea 222; Taiwan 255; Thailand 289

British Malay Trade Association (BMTA) 113

Buddhism 8: Malaysia 115; South Korea 226; Taiwan 262; Thailand 8, 293–4; Theravada 8

Bumiputra (ethnic Malays) 98, 99, 104, 105–6

Bumiputra status companies 108

bureaucracy, Malaysia 107

Campos, José Yao 142

Capital Issues Committee (CIC), Malaysia 107, 112

cards, business: Hong Kong 40; Indonesia 79; Malaysia 117–18; Philippines 150; Singapore 191; South Korea 229; Taiwan 264; Thailand 295

Central Bank of China 250, 259–60

Central Bank of the Philippines 144, 145, 147

Central Provident Fund (CPF), Singapore 178, 184, 189

chaebol (South Korean conglomerates) 215, 217

Chakri dynasty 293

changing money: Hong Kong 61; Indonesia 97; Malaysia 134; Philippines 169; Singapore 210; South Korea 245; Taiwan 278; Thailand 312

Chartchai Choonhavan 280

Chart Thai Party 280

Chase Manhattan Bank 291

chemicals, Singapore 174

Chiang Ching-kuo (CCK) 247

Chiang Kai-shek 246, 247, 254

Chicago Mercantile Exchange 185

Chin, Johnny 178

China, "open door" policy 10–11, 16

China, relations with: Hong Kong 18, 21, 28, 29; Indonesia 66; South Korea 211; Taiwan 246, 247

China Banking 142

China Development Corporation 260

China Development Fund 257

China International Trust and Investment Corporation (CITIC) 29, 36

Chinese: in Hong Kong 18, 39–40; in Indonesia 64, 69–70, 77; in Malaysia 98, 99, 105, 106, 110–11, 115; in Taiwan 262; *peranakan* 77; in Philippines 135, 142; in Singapore 170, 177, 187; *totok* 77

Chinese Gold and Silver Exchange Society 37

Chinese language 111

Chinese New Year 262, 263

Ching, Alfred 142

Ching Tan 142

Chiyu Banking Corporation 36

Choheung Bank 223

Chosun kingdom (1392–1910) 226

Christianity 8: Indonesia 78; Malaysia 115; Philippines 149; South Korea 8, 226; Taiwan 262

Chulalongkorn, King 279
Chun Doo-hwan, President 211, 212, 215
Chung, Sir Sze-yuen 20
Chung Ju-yung 217
Chung Khiaw Bank, Singapore 112
Chung Se-jung 217
chusik hoesa (stock company) 218
Citibank 35, 139, 140, 147, 148, 184
Citizen's National Bank, Korea 223–4
civil service: Hong Kong 19; Indonesia 63; Singapore 171
climate: Hong Kong 61; Indonesia 96–7; Malaysia 134; Philippines 168; Singapore 209; South Korea 245; Taiwan 277–8; Thailand 312
clothing industry: Hong Kong 25; Singapore 174
coal, Indonesia 65
Cojuangco, Eduardo 141
Cojuangco, José 136, 141
colonialism 8, 18, 19, 98
COMECON 63, 66
Commercial Bank of Korea 223
commercial law, Hong Kong 26
commercial paper, Philippines 147
commodities market: Hong Kong 37; Indonesia 75; Malaysia 112; Singapore 185
Communism 10, 18, 21; Philippines 135, 136, 142; Singapore 171; Taiwan 262; Thailand 279
Communist coup (1965), Indonesia 62
Communist "emergency" (1948–60), Malaysia 98
company law: Hong Kong 30–1; Malaysia 107–8; South Korea 218–21
company structure: Hong Kong 30–1; Malaysia 107; South Korea 218; Taiwan 255
computer law, South Korea 221
Concepcion, José 141
Confucianism 8, 18: Singapore 187–8; South Korea 226; Taiwan 262
conglomerates, South Korea (*chaebol*) 215
Congress, Philippines 136
consensus: Indonesia 77–8; (*pakikisama*), Philippines 152
Constitution: Indonesia (1945) 62; Philippines (1987) 136, 143; South Korea 212

consumer products, Singapore 174
contracting, Indonesia 72
copyright 12; Hong Kong 33; Indonesia 74; Singapore 183; South Korea 221; Taiwan 259; Thailand 290
corruption, Indonesia 62
"Council of Trent" 136
credit and charge cards: Hong Kong 61; Indonesia 97; Malaysia 134; Philippines 169; Singapore 210; South Korea 245; Taiwan 278; Thailand 312
Credit Insurance Fund, Korea 224
credit societies, Thailand 291
Crown Property Bureau, Thailand 286
currency: Hong Kong 24, 61; Indonesia 66, 97; Malaysia 103, 134; Philippines 138, 169; Singapore 173, 209–10; South Korea 214–15, 245; Taiwan 250, 278; Thailand 283, 312
customs allowances, *see* duty free allowances

Dai-Ichi Kangyo Bank 184
DBS Bank 184
debt, external: Indonesia 66–7; Malaysia 103; Philippines 139; South Korea 214; Thailand 283
Dee, Peter 142
defence: Singapore 171; Taiwan 247
Democrat Party, Thailand 280
Democratic Justice Party (DJP), South Korea 212
Democratic Progressive Party (DPP), Taiwan 247
development plans: Indonesia 67; Philippines (1987–92) 137, 139, 140; South Korea (1987–92) 216; Thailand (1987–91) 281, 284, 285
distribution: Indonesia 74; Malaysia 110–11; Philippines 146; Singapore 182–3; South Korea 222; Taiwan 259; Thailand 290
dress: Hong Kong 40, 61; Indonesia 96–7; Malaysia 117, 134; Philippines 150, 168; Singapore 191, 209; South Korea 228, 245; Taiwan 264, 277–8; Thailand 295, 312
driving licence requirement: Hong Kong 60; Indonesia 96; Malaysia 133; Philippines 168; Singapore 209; South Korea 244; Taiwan 277; Thailand 311

Dunn, Lydia 20, 40
Dutch, in Indonesia 62
Dutch language, Indonesia 78
duty-free allowances: Hong Kong 60–1; Indonesia 96; Malaysia 134; Philippines 168; Singapore 209; South Korea 244–5; Taiwan 277–8; Thailand 311–2

Economic Coordination Council of North American Affairs 259
economy: Hong Kong 21–5; Indonesia 64–7; Malaysia 100–3; Philippines 137–9; Singapore 172–4; South Korea 213–15; Taiwan 248–51; Thailand 281–4
education: Hong Kong 22, 39; Indonesia 78; Malaysia 100, 116; Philippines 137, 150; Singapore 172, 190; South Korea 213, 226–7; Taiwan 248; Thailand 281, 294
electronics: Hong Kong 25; Singapore 174
embassies: Malaysia 113; Singapore 186
Employers' Confederation of the Philippines 142
employment: Hong Kong 29–30; Taiwan 254; expatriate: Indonesia 72; Malaysia 109; Philippines 145; Singapore 181; South Korea 220; Taiwan 257; Thailand 289
energy: Indonesia 64–5; Malaysia 101; Philippines 137; Thailand 282
Enrile, Juan Ponce 136
ethnic groups: Indonesia 64, 77; Malaysia 114–15; Singapore 187
etiquette: Hong Kong 40; Indonesia 79; Malaysia 114–16; Philippines 151; Singapore 191; South Korea 228–9; Taiwan 263–4; Thailand 295–6
Eu, Richard 178
Executive Council (EXCO), Hong Kong 19
Export Credits Insurance Corporation, Hong Kong 27, 33
Export-Import Bank of China 260
Export-Import Bank of Korea 223
exporting: Hong Kong 32–3; Indonesia 73; Malaysia 110; Philippines 145–6; Singapore 181–2; South Korea 220–1; Taiwan 258–9; Thailand 289–90

exports: Hong Kong 22–3;
Malaysia 102; Philippines
138; SE Asia 12; Singapore
173; South Korea 213–14;
Taiwan 249; Thailand 282–3

"face": Indonesia 77; Malaysia
116; Philippines 149;
Singapore 191; Taiwan 263
Fam, Michael 178
Far East Bank 141, 147
Farmers Bank of China 260
Federation of Hong Kong
Industries 38
Federation of Korean
Industries 217
Federation of Malaysia, see
Malaysia
Fernandez, José 141
finance companies: Malaysia
112; Philippines 147; South
Korea 224; Thailand 291
financial scene: Hong Kong
34–7; Indonesia 75; Malaysia
112; Philippines 147;
Singapore 184–5; South
Korea 223–4; Taiwan 260;
Thailand 291
Five-Power Defence
Arrangement 171
Ford, David 19
foreign banks: Hong Kong 33;
Indonesia 75; Philippines
147; Singapore 184; South
Korea 224; Taiwan 260;
Thailand 291
Foreign Capital Inducement
Act, South Korea 218–19,
221
foreign companies, Hong
Kong 26
foreign exchange controls:
South Korea 218–19, 224;
Taiwan 259
foreign exchange market,
Hong Kong 35–6
foreign investment, see
investment, foreign
foreign ownership rules:
Indonesia 71–2; Malaysia
107–8; Philippines 143–5;
South Korea 218; Taiwan
255–6; Thailand 287–9
foreign relations: Malaysia 99;
Singapore 171; Taiwan 247;
Thailand 280
Fuji Bank 184
funds, repatriation of:
Malaysia 109; Philippines
145; Singapore 181; South
Korea 219–20; Taiwan 258

G5 Plaza accord 249
garments, see clothing
industry
gas: Indonesia 65, 66;
Malaysia 101; Thailand 282

GATT (General Agreement on
Tariffs and Trade) 20
GDP: Hong Kong 21, 22, 24;
Indonesia 64; Malaysia 100;
Singapore 170, 173; South
Korea 215; Thailand 281
Geh Ik Cheong 106
geothermal power, Indonesia
65
Germany, West 249, 286
GNP: Philippines 137; South
Korea 215; Taiwan 248;
Thailand 281
Goh Chok Tong 171
Goh Keng Swee 170, 178
Gokongwei, John 142
gold, Philippines 137
gold, trading, Hong Kong 37
Golden Gate Development
and Investment Fund 251
government, Hong Kong 18,
19, 20, 38
government finance: Hong
Kong 24; Malaysia 103;
Singapore 173–4; Taiwan
250–1
government intervention:
Singapore 172, 188–9;
Taiwan 252
Government Savings Bank,
Thailand 291
government spending: Hong
Kong 24, 27; South Korea
215

halal food 110
Hang Seng Bank 34
Hang Seng Index 29, 37
Hasan, Bob 70
headhunters, Malaysia 113
health precautions: Hong
Kong 60; Indonesia 96;
Malaysia 133; Philippines
168; Singapore 209; South
Korea 244; Taiwan 277;
Thailand 311
Heavy Industries Commission
(HICOM), Malaysia 103, 104
Hibernia Bank of California 70
high technology: 12; Malaysia
108; Singapore 176
Hinduism 8: Indonesia 78;
Malaysia 8, 115; Singapore 8
holidays: Hong Kong 61;
Indonesia 97; Malaysia 134;
Philippines 168–9; Singapore
209; South Korea 245;
Taiwan 278; Thailand 312
Hong Kong 11, 18–61, 246,
286
Hong Kong, Special
Administrative Region of
China (1984) 10–11, 18, 20
Hong Kong Association of
Banks (HKAB) 34
Hong Kong Banking
Commission 36

Hong Kong city 41–61
Hong Kong Code on
Takeovers and Mergers 31
Hong Kong Commodities
Exchange Ltd 37
Hong Kong dollar 24
Hong Kong Federation of
Trade Unions 30
Hong Kong General Chamber
of Commerce 38
Hong Kong Index 37
Hong Kong and Kowloon
Trade Union Council 30
Hong Kong Society of
Accountants 31
Hong Kong Stock Exchange
Ltd 37
Hong Kong Trade
Development Council 27, 38
Hongkong Land 28
Hongkong and Shanghai
Banking Corporation (HSBC)
24, 28, 34, 38, 112, 147, 148,
177, 184
honour, debt of, Philippines
152
hospitality: Hong Kong 40;
Indonesia 79–80; Malaysia
118; Philippines 151–2;
Singapore 191; Taiwan 264;
Thailand 295
hostess bars, South Korea 229
hours, working: Hong Kong
40; Indonesia 79; Malaysia
117; Philippines 150;
Singapore 190; South Korea
227; Taiwan 263; Thailand
294
House of Representatives:
Philippines 136; Thailand
280
housing: South Korea 213;
Thailand 284
Housing Development Board,
Singapore 190
Hu, Richard 178
Hua Chiao Commercial Bank
36
Hua Chiao Commercial Bank
36
Hukbalahap rebellion (1948–
53) 135
Human Settlements
Regulatory Commission 144
Hutama "Tommy" Mandala
Putra 70
hydroelectricity, Indonesia 65

IMF (International Monetary
Fund) 139, 145
immigration, Hong Kong 22
import-substitution: Indonesia
67; Thailand 284
importing: Hong Kong 32–3;
Indonesia 73; Malaysia 110;
Philippines 145; Singapore
181–2; South Korea 220–1;
Taiwan 258–9; Thailand
289–90

imports: Hong Kong 21, 23, 25; Indonesia 66; Malaysia 102; Philippines 138; Singapore 173; South Korea 12, 214, 215; Taiwan 12, 249, 258; Thailand 283
incentives: Malaysia 108; Philippines 144–5; Singapore 174, 180; South Korea 219; Taiwan 256–7; Thailand 288
Independent Commission Against Corruption (ICAC), Hong Kong 19
Indians: Indonesia 64; Malaysia 8, 98, 99, 115; Singapore 8, 171, 187
Indochina 279
Indonesia 8, 11, 62–97; independence (1949) 62
Indonesian Democratic Party (PDI) 63
Indonesian language 78
Industrial Arbitration Court, Singapore 178
Industrial Coordination Act (ICA), Malaysia 107
Industrial Development Bureau, Taiwan 250
Industrial Finance Corporation of Thailand (IFCT) 291
Industrial Master Plan, Malaysia 103
industrial training, Hong Kong 27, 30
industry: Hong Kong 25; Indonesia 67; Malaysia 103; Philippines 139; Singapore 174; South Korea 215; Taiwan 246, 251; Thailand 284
Industry Department, Hong Kong 38
inflation: Hong Kong 24; Indonesia 67; Philippines 137; Taiwan 250; Thailand 284
infrastructure: Hong Kong 22; Indonesia 65; Malaysia 102, 111; Philippines 137; Singapore 172; South Korea 213; Taiwan 248–9; Thailand 282
insurance: Hong Kong 33; Malaysia 111; Philippines 146; Taiwan 256, 259; Thailand 290
Inter-Governmental Group on Indonesia (IGGI) 66
International Tin Council (ITC) 101
investment, foreign: Hong Kong 28; Indonesia 69; Malaysia 104; Philippines 140–1, 143–5; Singapore 176–7; South Korea 216–17, 218, 224; Taiwan 252–3; Thailand 279, 286

investment: Hong Kong 24, 26; Indonesia 67, 71; Philippines 135, 139; Singapore 176, 180; South Korea 224; Taiwan 251, 256, 260; Thailand 284, 285–6, 288, 292
Islam 8: in Indonesia 62; in Malaysia 99, 110, 111, 115–16
Islamic Conference Organization 99

Israel 109
Jacobs, Piers 19
Jakarta 81–97
Jakarta Stock Exchange 75
Japan 139, 141, 286
Japan, relations with: Hong Kong 23, 28; South Korea 211, 214, 216; Taiwan 249, 252–3
Japanese 69, 150
Japanese companies, Singapore 175, 177
Japanese occupation, Taiwan 246
Javanese culture 62
Jayme, Vincente 136, 141
Jenkins, Peter 113
Jerone, Don 113
Jeyaretnam, J.B. 178
Joint Declaration, Sino-British (1984) on Hong Kong 20, 26
Joint Liaison Group, Hong Kong 20–1
Jurong 170, 175–6

Ka Wah Bank 36
Ka-shing, Li 20
Kadoorie, Lord 20
Kampuchea 280
Khmer 280
Kilusang Mayo Uno (KMU) 142
Kim Dae-jung 212
Kim Il-sung 211
Kim Suck-won 217
Kim Woo-choong 217
Kim Young-sam 212
Kisaeng parties 229
Koh, Tommy 178
Koo Cha-kyung 217
KorAm Bank 223
Korea: see North Korea; South Korea
Korea, reunification 211
Korea Credit Guarantee Fund 224
Korea Development Bank 223
Korea Development Investment Corporation 224
Korea Exchange Bank 216, 223
Korea Export Buying Offices Association 222
Korea First Bank 223

Korea Housing Bank 224
Korea Long-Term Credit Bank 223
Korea Monopoly Corporation 216
Korea Securities Finance Corporation 224
Korea Security Dealers Association 224
Korea Stock Exchange (KSE) 216, 224
Korea Technology Development Corporation 224
Korea Technology Finance Corporation 224
Korean Chamber of Commerce and Industry 225
Krung Thai Bank 285, 291
Kuala Lumpur 99, 119–34
Kuala Lumpur Commodity Exchange 112
Kuala Lumpur Stock Exchange (KLSE) 107, 112
Kuomintang (KMT) 247, 254, 262
Kwok, Robert 106

Labour Congress of Thailand 287
Labour Department, Hong Kong 30
labour force: Hong Kong 22, 25, 26, 29; Philippines 137; Singapore 172; South Korea 213
Lamsam family 286
land: Hong Kong 31; Thailand 287
land ownership, Indonesia 72
land reform: South Korea 211; Taiwan 248
language: Indonesia 78; Malaysia 116; Philippines 149, 150; South Korea 227; Taiwan 264; Thailand 295–6
languages, SE Asia 12
Lao Tse 262
Lapas family 142
Lau, Joseph 29
law firms: Hong Kong 38; Indonesia 76; Malaysia 113; Philippines 148; Singapore 186; South Korea 225; Taiwan 261; Thailand 292
Lee, Domingo 142
Lee Byung-chull 217
Lee Hsien Loong, Brigadier-General 171, 178
Lee Kuan Yew 10, 170, 171, 175, 178, 187, 188
Lee Teng-hui 247
Legislative Council (LEGCO), Hong Kong 19
Letts, Charles 178
Liberal party, Philippines 136

liberalization 10: South Korea 223; Taiwan 247
Liem Sioe Liong 69, 70
Lim, Patricia 142
Lim Goh Tong 105
Lim Pin 178
literacy: Malaysia 100; Philippines 137; Singapore 172, 190; South Korea 226; Thailand 281
living standards, Singapore 190
Locsin, Teodoro 136
Loo Siew Poh 178
Lopez family 141
Luym, Lu Do 142

Maclean, Roderick 178
Mahachakri Sirindorn, Princess 280
Mahathir Mohamad, Datuk Seri, Dr 99, 100, 102
Majapahit 62
Makati Stock Exchange 147
Malayan Banking 105, 112, 184
Malays 114–15; see also Bumiputra
Malaysia 11, 98–136
Malaysia Mining Corporation (MMC) 101, 105
Malaysia Plan, fifth (1986–90) 104; third 102
Malaysian British Friendship Association 113
Malaysian Chinese Association (MCA) 99
Malaysian Companies Act 107
Malaysian Indian Congress 99
Malaysian Industrial Development Authority (MIDA) 108, 109, 112, 113
Malaysian Institute of Economic Research 103
Malaysian Institute of Management (MIM) 113
Malaysian International Chamber of Commerce and Industry (MICCI) 113
Maltri riots (1974), Indonesia 69
Mandarin Chinese 190, 264
Manila 139, 153–69
Manila Stock Exchange 147
manufacturing: Hong Kong 18, 25; Malaysia 98, 102, 103, 107; Philippines 144; Thailand 284
Marcos, Ferdinand 135, 136, 141
market entry: Hong Kong 32–3; Indonesia 73–4; Malaysia 110–11; Philippines 145–6; Singapore 181–3; South Korea 220–2; Taiwan 258–9; Thailand 289–90

markets: Hong Kong 35–7; Indonesia 75; Malaysia 112; Philippines 147; South Korea 224; Taiwan 260; Thailand 291
martial law, Taiwan 247, 259
Mason Free Export Zone 219
Matthews, Jeremy 19
media: Hong Kong 38; Malaysia 113; Philippines 148; Singapore 186; Taiwan 261; Thailand 292
Melanesians, in Indonesia 64
Merchandise Marks Act, Singapore 183
Metro Bank 142
Metropolitan Bank and Trust 147
MIDA, see Malaysian Industrial Development Authority
minerals: Indonesia 64; Malaysia 101; Philippines 137; Thailand 281–2
Ministry of Economic Affairs (MOEA), Taiwan 255, 258, 259, 261
Ministry of Finance: South Korea 218, 225; Taiwan 259
Ministry of Justice, South Korea 225
Ministry of Trade and Industry, South Korea 219
Mitsui Bank 291
Mochtar Riady 70
Mohar, Raja Tan Sri 106
monarchy, constitutional: Malaysia 99; Thailand 279, 280, 293
Monetary Authority of Singapore (MAS) 177, 184, 185
Mongkut, King 279
Multi-Fibre Agreement 20, 32
multinationals: Malaysia 105; Philippines 145; Singapore 175, 177, 180; Thailand 286
Murdani, Benny 78
Muslims: Indonesia 77, 78; Philippines 149; Thailand 293

Nacionalista Party, Philippines 136
Nair, Devan 178
Nakornthon Bank 286
Nanyang Commercial Bank 36
Naquiddin, Tunku 105
National Agriculture Policy, Malaysia 101
National Electricity Board, Malaysia 104
National Energy Coordinating Board (Bakoren), Indonesia 64–5
National Housing Authority, Thailand 284

National Housing Fund, Korea 224
National Investment Fund, Korea 224
National Joint Chambers of Commerce, Malaysia 113
National Pollution Control Commission, Philippines 144
national security law, Taiwan 247
National Tax Administration of Taipei 261
National Trade Union Congress, Singapore 178
National Wages Council, Singapore 178
Nationalist Party, Taiwan 247
Netherlands 141, 286
Netherlands East Indies 62
New China News Agency (Xinhua) 21, 29
New Economic policy (NEP), Malaysia 98, 100, 104, 114
New Korea Democratic Party (NKDP) 212
New People's Army, Philippines 136
New Society Movement (KBL) 136
North Korea 211

OECD 11
offshore banks: Philippines 147; Singapore 185; Taiwan 260
oil: Indonesia 62, 64, 65, 66; Malaysia 101; Philippines 137; Singapore 174, 177
Olympic Games (1988), Seoul 212
Ong Teng Cheong 178
Ongpin, Jaime 136
OPEC 65
Ople, Blas 136
Overseas Chinese Banking Corporation (OCBC) 112, 177, 184
Overseas Economic Cooperation Fund, Japan 103
Overseas Union Bank 184

Pak Choy system 183
Palanca, Carlos 142
Palmerston, Lord 18
Pancasila 62, 77
Pao, Sir Y.K. 20, 29
Paris Convention 33, 221
Park, President 211, 212
Parti Islam Sa-Malaysia (PAS) 99
patents 12: Hong Kong 33; Indonesia 74; Malaysia 111; Philippines 146; Singapore 183; South Korea 221; Taiwan 259; Thailand 286, 290

PDP-Laban party, Philippines 136
People's Action Party (PAP), Singapore 171
People's Consultative Assembly (MPR), Indonesia 63
Permodalan Nasional Berhad (PNB) 104, 105, 112
Philippine National Bank 141, 147
Philippine Nationalist Party 136
Philippine Trade and Industry Center 148
Philippines 11, 135–69
Philippines Development Bank 147
Philtrust Bank 142
Pillai, J.Y. 177
Pimentel, Aquilino 136
PMA (joint ventures), Indonesia 71
Po Sang Bank 36
population: Hong Kong 21–2; Indonesia 64; Malaysia 98, 100; Philippines 137; Singapore 172, 187; South Korea 213; Taiwan 246, 248; Thailand 281
Port of Singapore Authority (PSA) 175, 176, 183
ports: Hong Kong 22, 26; Malaysia 111; Singapore 182; South Korea 222; Thailand 282, 290
Post Office Savings Bank of Singapore 184
printing, Singapore 174, 177
Printing and Press Act, Singapore 188
private sector: Indonesia 68–9, 71; Malaysia 98, 104; Philippines 139, 140; Singapore 176; Taiwan 252, 253; Thailand 284, 285–6
Private Sector Divestment Committee, Singapore 176
privatization: Hong Kong 27; Indonesia 69; Malaysia 104; Philippines 140; Singapore 176; South Korea 216; Thailand 288
Productivity Council, Hong Kong 25, 27 38
property, foreign, Hong Kong 28
property rights, Thailand 286
prostitution, Thailand 281, 283, 294
protectionism: Indonesia 67; Taiwan 256
public sector: Hong Kong 27; Indonesia 68; Malaysia 104, 107; Philippines 140; Singapore 175–6; South Korea 216; Thailand 285, 291

race riots (1969), Malaysia 98, 100, 114
racial diversity 8–10; see also ethnic groups
Raffles, Sir Stamford 170
railways: Hong Kong 22; Indonesia 65; Malaysia 102; Philippines 137; South Korea 213, 222; Taiwan 249; Thailand 290
Rama IX, King (Bhumibol Adulyadej) 280
Razaleigh Hamzah, Tengku 99
Regional Council, Hong Kong 19, 20
Registered Designs Act, UK (1979) 33
religion 8: Hong Kong 39; Indonesia 78; Malaysia 115–16; Philippines 149; South Korea 226; Taiwan 262–3; Thailand 293–4, 296
Republic of Korea, see South Korea
resources, human: Hong Kong 21–2; Indonesia 64; Malaysia 100; Philippines 137; Singapore 172; South Korea 213; Taiwan 248; Thailand 281
resources, natural: Hong Kong 22; Indonesia 64–5; Malaysia 98, 100–1; Philippines 137; Singapore 172; South Korea 213; Taiwan 248; Thailand 281–2
Reunification Democratic Party (RDP), South Korea 212
Rhee, President 211
ringgit 103
Rizal Commercial Development Bank 142
roads: Indonesia 65; Malaysia 102; Philippines 137; Singapore 183; South Korea 213, 222; Taiwan 248–9; Thailand 282, 290
Roces, Ramon 142
Roh Tae-woo 212
Rosario, Ramon del 141
Royal Bank of Canada 35
rubber: Malaysia 98, 100, 101; Thailand 281
rupiah, Indonesian 66

Saguisag, Rene 136
salaries, see wages
Salonga 136
Sangha 293
Santos, Dante 141
Sanwa Bank 184
seaports: Indonesia 65, 74; Malaysia 102; Singapore 172
Securities and Exchange Commission (SEC) 37, 143, 144, 147

Securities Exchange of Thailand (SET) 291
Senate: Philippines 136; Thailand 280
Seoul 230–45
Seoul Trust 224
Seow, Francis 178
services sector: Hong Kong 18, 26; Malaysia 104
Shao-shung, Yao 142
Shing, Li Ka 29
Shinhan Bank 223
shipping companies: Indonesia 74; Thailand 290
shipping register, Hong Kong 21
shoes: Malaysia 118; South Korea 229; Taiwan 249
Siam Commercial Bank 286, 291
Sigit Harjojudanto 70
Sikhism, in Malaysia 115
Sim Kee Boon 178
SIMEX 185
Singapore 11, 98, 170–210, 286;
Singapore Stock Exchange 185
Singapore Technology Corporation 176
Siy, Ramon 142
Small Industries Finance Office (SIFO), Thailand 291
Small and Medium Industry Bank, Korea 223
Social Action Party, Thailand 280
Sophonpanich family 286
Sorianos 142
South Africa 109
South Korea 11, 211–45
Spanish influence, in Philippines 135, 150
Standard Chartered Bank 24, 28, 34, 36, 112, 147, 148, 177, 184
State Economic Development Corporations, Malaysia 104
status: Indonesia 80; Singapore 191; South Korea 227–8; Thailand 293
stock company: Hong Kong 18; Indonesia 75; Malaysia 112; South Korea (chusik hoesa) 218
stock markets, Philippines 140, 147; Singapore 185
strikes: Indonesia 70; Philippines 142; Singapore 172; South Korea 217; Taiwan 254
Suharto, President 62, 63, 68–9, 70
Suharto family 68, 70
Sukarno 62, 63
Sutrisno, General Try 63

Sy, Henry 142
Sy, Ramon 142
Sycip, Washington 142, 148

Taipan families, in Hong Kong 28
Taipei 265–78
Taipei Stock Exchange (TSE) 260
Taiwan 11, 246–78, 284, 286
Taiwan Footwear Manufacturers' Association 249
Taiwan (ROC) Fund 260
Taiwan-Overseas International Investment Trust Co. 260
Taiwanese 246, 262
Tam, Maria 40
Tan Sri, Tan Seng Kee 105
Tan Sri Abdullah Salleh 106
Taoism 226, 262
tax, revenues: Hong Kong 24; Malaysia 103; Philippines 139; South Korea 215; Taiwan 251; Thailand 283–4
taxation: Hong Kong 31–2; Indonesia 72–3; Malaysia 108, 109; Philippines 144; Singapore 180, 181; South Korea 219; Taiwan 257; Thailand 288, 289
Techapaibul family 286
technology assistance agreements (TAAs), South Korea 220–1
technology transfer, Indonesia 69
Technology Transfer Board, Philippines 145
telecommunications: Malaysia 104, 111; Philippines 137; Singapore 175; Taiwan 259
television: Indonesia 74; Philippines 146
textiles, Hong Kong 25
Thai Chinese 287, 294
Thai Farmers Bank 286, 291
Thai Trades Union Congress 287
Thai-US Treaty of Amity and Economic Relations 287
Thailand 11, 279–312
Thailand Fund 286

tipping: Hong Kong 61; Indonesia 97; Malaysia 134; Philippines 169; Singapore 210; South Korea 245; Taiwan 278; Thailand 312
titles: Indonesia 80; Philippines 152; South Korea 229
tobacco industry, Singapore 174
tourism: Indonesia 66; Singapore 174; Thailand 283
towkays 106, 111, 118, 177, 191
trade: Hong Kong 2–3, 18; Indonesia 66; Malaysia 102; Philippines 138; Singapore 172–3; South Korea 213–14; Taiwan 249–50; Thailand 282–3
trade centres, Taiwan 261
Trade Department, Hong Kong 38
trademarks: Hong Kong 33; Philippines 146; Singapore 183; South Korea 221; Taiwan 259; Thailand 286, 290
transmigration policy, Indonesia 64
transport: Indonesia 74; Singapore 172, 174, 183
Tresyse, Charles 178
Tun Ismail Ali 105
Ty, Wellington 142

unemployment: Taiwan 254; Malaysia 100; Singapore 172; Thailand 281
Unido party, Philippines 136
Union Bank 36
unions: Hong Kong 25, 30; Indonesia 70, 72; Malaysia 106; Philippines 142; Singapore 178, 188; South Korea 217; Taiwan 254; Thailand 287
United Development Party (PPP), Indonesia 63
United Malayan Banking Corporation 112, 291
United Malays National Organization (UMNO) 99
United Overseas Bank 184
universities: Hong Kong 39; Indonesia 78; South Korea 227

US Farm Act 283
USA: in Hong Kong 27–8; relations with Thailand 286; protectionism 12; relations with Indonesia 69; relations with Philippines 135, 136, 138, 140–1, 150; relations with South Korea 211, 214, 216–17, 227; relations with Taiwan 246, 249
USAID 66;
USSR, relations with South Korea 211

Vietnam 280
Vietnamese, in Hong Kong 22
visas: Hong Kong 60; Indonesia 96; Malaysia 133; Philippines 168; Singapore 209; Taiwan 277; Thailand 311

wages: Hong Kong 18, 25, 30; Philippines 137; Singapore 172; South Korea 211; Taiwan 254
Wang, An 251
Wang Lee family 286
warehousing: Hong Kong 33; Indonesia 73–4
Wee Chang Jin 186
Wee Cho Yaw 178
Wee Kim Wee 178
Wilson, Sir David 19
women: Hong Kong 40; Indonesia 79; Malaysia 118; Philippines 151; Singapore 190; South Korea 228; Taiwan 264; Thailand 294
work permits: Indonesia 72; Malaysia 109, 114; Thailand 289
World Bank 24, 103, 139, 283, 284, 286
Wu, Gordon 29

Yang di-Pertuan Agong 99
Yap, Emilio 142
Yeutter, Clayton 251
Yong Poh Kong 105
Yong Pung How 177
Yongchaiyudth, Chaovalit 280
Young, George 250
Yuchengco, Alfonso 142

Zobel family 142